T0328128

Bank Risk Management
in Developing Economies

Bank Risk Management in Developing Economies

Addressing the Unique Challenges of Domestic Banks through Risk Management

Leonard Onyiriuba

ELSEVIER

AMSTERDAM • BOSTON • HEIDELBERG • LONDON
NEW YORK • OXFORD • PARIS • SAN DIEGO
SAN FRANCISCO • SINGAPORE • SYDNEY • TOKYO

Academic Press is an imprint of Elsevier

Academic Press is an imprint of Elsevier
125 London Wall, London EC2Y 5AS, United Kingdom
525 B Street, Suite 1800, San Diego, CA 92101-4495, United States
50 Hampshire Street, 5th Floor, Cambridge, MA 02139, United States
The Boulevard, Langford Lane, Kidlington, Oxford OX5 1GB, United Kingdom

Library of Congress Cataloging-in-Publication Data
A catalog record for this book is available from the Library of Congress

British Library Cataloguing-in-Publication Data
A catalogue record for this book is available from the British Library

ISBN: 978-0-12-805479-6

For information on all Academic Press publications
visit our website at https://www.elsevier.com/

  Working together
to grow libraries in
ELSEVIER **Book Aid** developing countries
International

www.elsevier.com • www.bookaid.org

Publisher: Nikki Levy
Acquisition Editor: Scott Bentley
Editorial Project Manager: Susan Ikeda
Production Project Manager: Debbie Clark
Designer: Matthew Limbert

Typeset by Thomson Digital

I dedicate this book, with love, to my mother – Cyrina Chijiago Onyiriuba – and children – Tobe, Ezzy, Chub, Som, Ama and Chi

Contents

PART II   PARADIGM SHIFT, CONCERNS, AND INSIGHTS

3.   Banking Revolution, Paradigm Shift, and Risk Management in Developing Economies

4.   Enterprise Risk Management—A Paradigm Shift and Applications in Banking

Section A
Public Concern and Outcry

7. Risk, Safety, and the Future of Deposit Money Banks in Developing Economies

8. Money Laundering Links with Bank Risks and Management in Developing Economies

Section B
New Insights and Concerns

11. Country Risk of Banking in Fledgling Economies Mired in Slippery Political Terrain

12. Public Sector Banking Analysis and Risks Management in Developing Economies

14. **Bank Governance Pitfalls, Failings, and Risk Management in Developing Economies**

PART III REINVENTING RISK MANAGEMENT

Section A
Credit Risk

15. **Bank Credit Risk Issues and Management Requirements in Developing Economies**

16. Bank Assets Portfolio Structure and Risk Management in Developing Economies

17. Sensitizing Bankers in Developing Economies to Securitization Risks and Management

Section B
Liquidity Risk

20. Bank Liabilities Portfolio and Liquidity Risk Management in Developing Economies

21. Bank Liquidity Crisis and Funding Risk Management in Developing Economies

Section C
Market Risk

23. Market Risk, Interest Rates and Bank Intermediary Role in Developing Economies

24. Foreign Exchange Markets and Triggers for Bank Risk in Developing Economies

25.　Money Market Workings, Instruments, and Bank Risk in Developing Economies

Section D
Operational Risk

27. Bank Operational Risk Dynamics and Management in Developing Economies

28. Bank Work, Employees, and Operational Risk Management in Developing Economies

Preface

One of my intentions for this book is to address specific concerns of banking stakeholders in developing economies. This is without prejudice to looking at issues which underlie the cause of the book with a critical eye. Domestic and foreign subsidiary banks in developing economies take on and manage risks differently. The latter seem immune to financial crisis that often rock banks in developing countries—ostensibly with support from their parent banks. Never in the checkered history of Nigeria's banking, for example, has the industry had a foreign subsidiary bank that became distressed or failed. The implication is that foreign subsidiary and domestic banks in developing economies are worlds apart on risk management.

The domestic banks aspire to cater to the financial services needs of all sectors—including the highly risky informal economy—apparently pitching in with national economic development policies. Foreign banks subsidiaries, in contrast to domestic banks, shun risky sectors. They adopt preconceived target markets definitions, risk acceptance criteria, and standardized risk models targeted at structured and riskless sectors with which their well-honed exotic risk models fit in. Thus their financial services are usually keyed to the vibrant sectors—apparently in response to dictates of safety and the bottom line. This explains why a foreign bank subsidiary in a large country, such as Nigeria would perhaps have less than 10 branches when its domestic counterpart of comparable asset size would have over 500.

I address, in this book, these departures and specific risk concerns at issue that apply to developing countries worldwide and affect the banks cross the board in this book.

BACKGROUND

Banking around the world is ever in a state of flux. Bank managements try, but all to no avail, to be on top of risks in a rapidly changing world of modern banking. The problem is deepening, if anything. The increasing sophistication of contemporary banking doesn't help matters. Nowadays a host of change–driven risks—most of which are novel in nature—threaten the survival of banks as going concerns. This is the troubling dimension which risks in modern banking have assumed.

Banks in developing economies are particularly vulnerable. There is now—more than ever before—snowballing concern with worsening risks in developing economy banking. Banks in developed economies seem to be making progress on the control of novel risks, which the great march of revolution in banking occasions. But the same cannot be said of their counterparts in developing economies. Of course banking in developing economies is still relatively in embryo. As the industry matures, its future development and performance will depend on how well risk is managed. Two main reasons justify this view. First, risk impinges on the capacity of banks to do business. Second, developing economies are nowadays unusually volatile.

Thus banks in developing economies must work with a painstaking prognosis of the future of their business. Method in the way risk is managed—and uncertainty is anticipated—should inform the prognosis. The starting point is for the stakeholders to be fully apprised of the making of risk and uncertainty. Needless to say, risk and uncertainty underlie the central dynamic of success in banking. Thus learning deeply about risk and uncertainty and their implications for bank management is pertinent. As bank managements, staff and other stakeholders deepen their knowledge of risks and uncertainties, they will want to hone their risk management abilities. That puts them right on top of their work and investment in banking. This is the road map to managing banking risks in developing economies, which this book furnishes.

Unfortunately the risk managers in developing economies seem to be deficient in experience for managing novel risks. Their experience hardly provides a clue about the dynamic, let alone control, of such risks. Yet they must get to grips with the tide of novel risks in the wake of continued revolution in banking. This will have significant positive implication for banking. Ironically banking in developing economies seems to be booming—ostensibly debunking concerns about possible threat of risk and uncertainty. Strange though this may seem, the reality is that this fluke is usually truncated by either neglect of the unusual risks and uncertainties or failure to anticipate them.

OVERVIEW AND TARGET AUDIENCE

This book is a practical text that furnishes a holistic approach to learning about the creation and control of bank risks in developing economies. It is enriched with tales and scenes of risk and uncertainty—as well as empirical examples and illustrations—that have practical ramifications for banking in developing economies.

The book situates bank management in the context of risk, uncertainty, and revolution in banking—differently from the classical method. Doing so, it sheds light on the creation, dynamics, and control demands of risks that have been the bane of the industry. It posits—as its main thrust—that banking crisis in developing economies is rooted in the interplay of, and failings in managing, composite risks. It analyzes the paradigm shift which this approach informs. In doing so, it defines risk management best practice in banking. It discusses best practice inner workings. Then it pinpoints how risk management best practice should power the success of banking in developing economies.

With this book, its target audience is equipped with an in-depth knowledge of contemporary risks in developing economy banking, with implications for bank management and the future of the industry. The book leans toward academic need of students and faculty. Yet practitioners and analysts will find it quite insightful and useful. I have deliberately included topics and chapters that help fulfill this expectation. For example, while giving students and faculty insights into the practical demands of risk control in banking operations, Chapters 27–30—covered in Part III that deals with *Reinventing Risk Management*—are tailored more to the needs of practitioners.

This approach optimizes the appeal of the book without compromising its strong orientation to student academic need. That orientation is evident in the grammatical constructions of the chapter topics and is mirrored in a more academic style of writing—typical of a college textbook. I adopted particular features of this approach that usually stand out in academic textbooks. Each chapter starts with *Learning Focus and Objectives*, followed by *Expected Learning Outcomes*. There are end of chapter *Summary*, *Questions for Discussion and Review*, *References*, and books for *Further Reading*.

STRUCTURE AND ORIENTATION OF THE BOOK

Banking is bedeviled by a myriad of risks. However, four of the risks—credit risk, operational risk, liquidity risk, and market risk—stand out. In terms of attention and emphasis, credit risk tends to get the lion's share, underscoring its complication and wider significance for banking all over the globe. In this book, I adopted a holistic theme and approach. First, I subsume emerging markets under developing economies. Then I posit that banking crisis in developing economies is rooted in the interplay of, and failings in managing, composite risks.

This approach brings out clearly the commonality of risk types, characteristics, and patterns of incidence in developing economies. It does not obliterate emerging markets, but rather informs their standing as yet a part—but the topmost tier—of developing economies. I analyze the paradigm shift which this approach informs. In doing so, I defined risk management best practice in banking. I discussed best practice inner workings. Then I pinpoint how risk management best practice should power the success of banking in developing economies. Underlying this approach is my conviction that every successful business has its game plan all worked out—the things it does differently, or in unique ways, through which it adds value, overcomes threats, optimizes opportunities, and beats competition.

The approach I adopted for this book represents a departure from the classical literature, which the competing books symbolize. The competing books deal with the subject from the traditional perspective of assets, liabilities, and balance sheet management under which banks in developing economies—like their counterparts elsewhere—have not fared well. Ironically, the authors of the competing books not only gravitated toward the classical literature, they were oriented to the highly advanced financial economies of the developed nations— ostensibly to solve some complex financial issues. The modeling of financial functions to explain some banking behavior is typical. Incidentally, these issues and the authors' method are alien to practical banking in the developing World.

BENEFITS TO TARGET AUDIENCE

The book empowers its audience with new insights and competences necessary for managing novel risks in banking. Specifically it solves the following five main problems for its target audience:

- Lack of—and inability to apply—competence in a wide range of contemporary risk management skills.
- Frustration of wealth creation for stakeholders of developing economy banks due to inefficient or flawed risk management.
- Crisis in developing economy banking apparently caused by method in classical risk management literature.
- Dearth of practical texts on and guide to novel, peculiar, and change-driven risks in developing economy banking.
- A craving for a simple structure, devoid of complex models, for dealing with risks in developing economy banking.

UNIQUE SELLING POINTS

Deals practically with all known, felt, and anticipated developing economy banking risks in one unparalleled volume

This book does not—unlike the competing books—compartmentalize or deal with, or view banking risks in "silos" or in isolation from uncertainty. It adopts a holistic theme and approach that meet target audience needs.

A simplified text, easy to understand, and use

The target audience needs a noncomplex text devoid of the technicalities of the exotic literature on developed economy banking that are of no immediate relevance now and in the foreseeable future for managing risks in developing economy banking.

Devoted solely to the cause and course of managing risks peculiar to banking in developing and emerging economies

None of the competing books addresses novel and evolving risk issues specific to banking in developing and emerging economies. The books, on the contrary, deal with technical issues in highly developed financial markets.

Consistency in fulfilling curriculum-based learning programs and needs

The book comprehensively covers materials included in core academic and professional basic, intermediate, and advanced practice of banking, bank management, and risk management in banking courses.

Topical theme and appealing chapter subjects targeted at a buoyant audience

This feature ensures that the book has a long effective shelf life. The book will enjoy this advantage for as long as lending institutions exist; universities offer courses in banking, finance, and investment; and banking remains a fundamental business fraught with risks.

Propitious for evolving thinking on risk management best practice and good corporate governance in developing economy banking

The book addresses banking stakeholders' concerns bordering on neglect of best practice and flawed corporate governance—both of which have been fingered as culprits for crises in developing economy banking.

Tunes in to a paradigm shift that fits well with the Basel Accords—the widely acclaimed international point of reference for risk management in banking

This book represents a departure from the classical literature which focuses on assets, liabilities, and balance sheet management by which developing economy banks—like their counterparts elsewhere—have not fared well.

Leo Onyiriuba
Lagos
June 2016

Part I

Background and Overview

Chapter 1

Risk, Uncertainty, and Banking Dynamics in Developing Economies

Chapter Outline

LEARNING FOCUS AND OBJECTIVES

It is not always that risk-taking in banking is informed by a sense of responsibility to protect the bank against financial loss. On occasion, some bank employees may take on risk, careless of its consequences for the bank. Careless risk-taking results in loss of income to the bank or exposure of its asset to harm. So bank employees should be very knowledgeable about risk, and always take only calculated risks. That way, risk consciousness is institutionalized and helps the employees to stick with the bank's risk acceptance criteria for all functions, transactions, and deals. My objectives for this chapter are based on these views, intended to teach the reader:

- Definitions and applications of meaning of risk and uncertainty at different levels of learning and conceptual development.
- Pioneering thoughts, evolving thinking, and contemporary perspectives on risk and uncertainty.
- How risk situates in uncertainty—in theory and practice—and influences the fate of banking in developing economies?
- The reality of risk to banks in developing economies, and risk contrasts between domestic and foreign subsidiary banks.

EXPECTED LEARNING OUTCOMES

Bankers in developing economies—like their counterparts in the developed world—need to be well versed in the dynamics of risk and uncertainty. This is a critical success factor in a rapidly changing age of technological innovation in banking. Thus, my intention for this chapter is to facilitate learning about the phenomena of risk and uncertainty—in conceptual and practical ways. I also want to regenerate interest in the effective management of risk as the foundation of success in banking, especially in developing economies. The reader will—after studying this chapter and doing the exercises in it—have learnt and been better informed about:

- Why there exists a divergence in definitions and constructs of risk and uncertainty found in the literature?
- Pioneering thoughts, evolving thinking, and contemporary perspectives on risk and its relationship to uncertainty.
- How risk can be defined from the perspectives of two opposing outcomes—opportunities and threats—with implications for banking?
- Characteristics of risk and uncertainty and how they should inform business choices of banks in developing economies.
- Insights into reasons domestic banks in developing economies—compared with their foreign subsidiary counterparts—face peculiar risks.

OVERVIEW OF THE SUBJECT MATTER

Every successful business has its game plan all worked out—the things it does differently, or in unique ways, through which it mitigates risk, adds value, overcomes threats, optimizes opportunities, and beats competition. It would seem that this business strategy is either lacking or is the main challenge of banks in developing economies. The problem, though, is more evident in domestic than foreign subsidiary banks. Bankers in developing economies tend to be overwhelmed by the magnitude of risks they face in their everyday work. This is understandable given that banking in developing economies is still in embryo. It is neither fully mature nor in the mold of banking in advanced financial markets. However, as the industry matures and consolidates, its future development will depend on how well risk is managed.

Bankers should have a clear picture of the cause and outcome of risk taking in mind. They should work with confidence and sense of purpose to actualize business objectives. These pragmatic attributes should then power their risk-taking appetite. Domestic banks in developing economies, in contrast to their foreign subsidiary counterparts, tend to take on risk sometimes to satisfy irrational business motive. Lift the veil of their risk-taking and you would be shocked at how they take risk to excess. Reckless risk-taking is a recipe for banking crisis and bank managements must shun it. The path to success is for banks to follow best practice founded on logic, calculation, and due process. Unfortunately, the risk appetites of the banks tend to be unfounded due to inordinate pursuit of budget goals mainly.

Yet risk should be effectively managed if banks in developing economies are eyeing to attain world class standards of operations and financial performance. That is also why and how the banks may serve the needs of the public and return appreciable wealth to the shareholders. Bankers must work with effective risk management strategy. It is the desideratum for confident and successful banking in developing economies. Two main reasons justify this view. First, risk impinges on the capacity of banks to do business. Second, developing economies tend to be volatile and unusually in flux. Thus bankers in developing economies must work with a painstaking prognosis of the future of their business. They should do so in the context to influence of risk and uncertainty on their performance outcomes.

The starting point is for the bankers, indeed all stakeholders in banking, as well as analysts, academics, and students to be fully apprised of banking risk and uncertainty events—their creation, dynamics, and impacts on business outcomes for the banks. Needless to say, risk and uncertainty underlie the central dynamic of success in banking. Thus learning deeply about risk and uncertainty and their ramifications for banking is pertinent. As the stakeholders in banks deepen their knowledge of risks and uncertainties, they will want to hone their risk management abilities that puts them right on top of their work. This is the primary road map to effective management of bank risk in the developing economies.

DISTINGUISHING DOMESTIC BANKS FROM FOREIGN BANKS SUBSIDIARIES

I should at the outset clarify the contexts in which I used "domestic banks" and "foreign subsidiary banks" in this book. It is necessary that I do so since readers may otherwise interpret their meanings in different ways—right or wrong— from individual perspectives or be lost. There are only very subtle differences between this book's contextual and normal usages, though. Yet I feel obliged to apprise the readers of the subtle nuances of their meanings from the perspective of this book.

Let me first situate domestic banks in the context of this book. Then I put foreign subsidiary banks into perspective. Throughout this book, I have used domestic bank to denote first and foremost a bank that is wholly indigenous to the country of its incorporation, operation, and domicile. Second, and in sync with this meaning, a domestic bank must necessarily be incorporated, operating, and domiciled in a developing country. Thus, "developing country" should be understood as the primary connotation of this definition. The implication is that while developed countries do have domestic banks, I am concerned strictly with only domestic banks in developing countries. I also restrict my interest—in the case of foreign bank subsidiaries—to developing countries, in much the same vein.

Similarly, I have in the entire book interchanged uses of foreign subsidiary bank and foreign bank subsidiary. I used either of them to refer to a bank that is incorporated, operating, and domiciled in a developing country and has another bank as its parent, holding, company that is incorporated, operating, and domiciled in a developed country. But for a change it would introduce in the context that I intend for this book, it would have sufficed to refer to foreign bank subsidiary simply as a bank that is incorporated, operating, and domiciled in a country different from that in which its parent, holding, bank is incorporated, operating, and domiciled. This second meaning omits "developing country" and "developed country" included in the first. Retaining the omissions will significantly change the context in which I used foreign bank subsidiary in this book. Sticking with the unique perspective of the book, I uphold the first meaning. The watchword, doing so, is "developing" vis-à-vis "developed" applicable to "subsidiary" and "parent" bank, respectively.

The two sets of banks—domestic and foreign subsidiaries—do not always face the same risk situations. They are also not equally exposed to operational hazards due to differences in the business orientations. This exerts a great influence over attitudes of the banks toward risk. Differences in the risk-taking behavior of the banks can also be explained in terms of internal and external influences to which the banks are subject. The business orientation and most of the influences on risk-taking practices of foreign subsidiary banks originate from their parent banks. The parent banks arm their subsidiaries worldwide with proven but standard international operating guidelines. Thus, there is a strong risk culture to which every employee is subject. That culture becomes the central dynamic of their successful banking. It is a sort of rallying point for unifying all work roles toward risk-based best practice, with implication for the bottom line. In view of this, foreign subsidiary banks are more likely to be obliged to adopt best practice across-the-board and therefore better positioned to manage risk well than their domestic bank counterparts.

The business orientation and risk-taking tendencies of the domestic banks are rooted in local conditions and happenings of which they are susceptible. However, the main challenge of domestic banks is really a crisis of identity. In some banking situations, they try to copy risk models of the foreign subsidiary banks and in others, they will want to assert their individuality rather than copying. This is the foundation of risk management albatross for domestic banks in the developing economies. They may at one time emphasize best practice and at another turn a blind eye to its neglect. They adopt this operational attitude either as an escape from reality or as unusual exigencies of banking in the developing economies dictate. But it leaves the employees confused about the direction of the bank's risk management policy. In this sense, multiple or irregular operational standards, characteristic of the management of domestic banks, does not augur well for risk management, let alone institutionalize a risk culture.

Some banking risks defy exotic influences, though. Such risks tend to take a heavy toll on both domestic and foreign subsidiary banks—either in equal or disproportionate measures. I highlight risks of this nature as I discuss topics related to them in this book. Most important, I discuss risk management similarities and departures between domestic and foreign subsidiary banks in all the chapters or applicable topics.

REALISTICALLY DISTINGUISHING DOMESTIC FROM FOREIGN SUBSIDIARY BANKS

There are subtle nuances of meanings of domestic and foreign subsidiary banks that are capable of clouding the real distinctions between the two categories of banks. I expatiate on this view and give an example right away to buttress it. Those who are familiar with banking in Nigeria may be surprised that I excluded Ecobank and Stanbic IBTC Bank from the category of foreign subsidiary banks in Table 1.1 and elsewhere in this book. Let me at once clarify the reasons why the two banks do not make the list of foreign subsidiary banks in Nigeria from the perspective of this book. The meanings I ascribed to domestic banks and foreign banks subsidiaries in distinguishing between them in the preceding section are yet applicable and pertinent to the explanation I now proffer.

TABLE 1.1 Domestic and Foreign Subsidiary Commercial Banks in Nigeria[a]

Domestic banks	Foreign subsidiary banks	Quasi-foreign subsidiary banks
Access	Citibank Nigeria	Ecobank Nigeria
Diamond	Standard Chartered	Stanbic IBTC Bank
Fidelity		
FBN		
FCMB		
GTBank		
Heritage		
Keystone		
Skye		
Sterling		
UBN		
UBA		
Unity		
Wema		
Zenith		

[a]The number of listed commercial banks is 19, down from 21 after acquisition of Mainstreet Bank Limited by Skye Bank PLC, and the merger between Heritage Banking Company Limited and Enterprise Bank Limited to form Heritage Bank Limited.

I reiterate that foreign banks subsidiaries must necessarily have their parent, holding, banks in developed countries. The inevitable corollary, as well as the implication, of this condition is that foreign banks subsidiaries must be incorporated, operating, and based in some developing countries. These are altogether the overriding considerations in designating particular banks foreign subsidiaries. Thus, in the context of this book, the parent banks must, of necessity, base themselves in developed economies while their foreign subsidiaries, in contrast, must be based in developing economies. These clarifications bear on the underlying import of the distinction between the two sets of banks. They also help shed light on why and how exotic banking practices dictate differences in operations and financial performance of the domestic and foreign subsidiary banks in the developing economies.

With the clarifications in mind, I now proceed to explain the reasons I limited foreign banks subsidiaries in Nigeria to just two—Citibank Nigeria Limited and Standard Chartered Bank Limited. I mean reasons why I treated Ecobank and Stanbic IBTC Bank as quasi- and not real foreign banks subsidiaries.

Notwithstanding that Ecobank is a subsidiary of Ecobank Transnational Incorporated (ETI), with headquarters in Togo, I do not consider it as a foreign bank subsidiary in Nigeria. The reason is that ETI is domiciled in and has all of its 36 subsidiaries in Africa—one of the developing regions of the world. As in the case of Ecobank, I also do not consider Stanbic IBTC Bank as a foreign subsidiary bank in Nigeria. This is notwithstanding that Standard Bank—renamed Stanbic Bank in 1992—was once a subsidiary of Standard Chartered Bank with headquarters in Britain. Neither is the fact that South Africa is one of the top-rated emerging economies designated as BRICS that are making steady progress toward development pertinent. The overriding consideration is that its parent, Stanbic Bank, is incorporated, operating and headquartered in South Africa and has all of its 11 subsidiaries in yet one of the developing regions of the world—Africa. The distinctions and the related explanations focusing on Nigeria are a proxy for other countries in the developing world.

CASE STUDY 1.1 The Fate of Domestic Banks in Developing Economies—the Case of Nigeria

Banking in Nigeria—as in other developing nations—has had its own ups and downs. Interestingly, events of the late 1980s and, especially, early 1990s when I started a career in banking epitomize the ups and banking spirit of the time. Those events stick in my mind and continue to inspire my writing. You could feel the heady atmosphere of banking—ostensibly a reflection of the welcome deregulation of the industry in 1986. Most bankers had very bubbly personalities and did their jobs with missionary zeal. More than a quarter of a century on, I reminisce the banking euphoria of that epoch still. That era represented a watershed in Nigeria's banking development. Ironically, it also underlay an impending doom.

Complacency in dealing with risk was the order of the day. Profligate banking was a commonplace. As it turned out, sadly, the fun was short-lived. The bankers got carried away, apparently oblivious to the crunch that was already well underway. The situation was largely the same—and apparently the setting for risks in banking—in other developing economies.

Ted's chat over lunch with his colleagues at Bank Connect Limited on some of the causes of risk in banking is quite instructive (Onyiriuba, 2013). Risk contrast between domestic and foreign subsidiary banks in developing economies is mirrored in their chat about the state of banking in Nigeria. Now, here they go, Ted starts with the startling findings from his postgraduate study of banking in Nigeria. The study investigated bank liquidity crisis that had become a source of constant worry not only to the public but the shareholders and regulatory authorities. There was widespread distrust in the banking system, caused by perceived risk of deposits in the banks. Besides, lack of confidence in the banking system also derived from past experiences of bank distress and failure in the country. Unlike him—who had just started a career in banking—his colleagues at Bank Connect Limited were worried by the state of the industry. One afternoon, they discussed the situation dispassionately over lunch.

"During the 1930s," one of them recalled, "only one domestic bank survived the banking system distress which the country experienced." He regretted that "distress was yet to set in again in the early 1950s after the banking boom of the late 1940s." Ted was held spellbound as he listened to things he didn't know about the industry in which he worked so hard to start a career. "As in the 1930s experience," another of his colleagues corroborated sadly, "the domestic banks were severely hit by the banking crisis of the 1950s—only four domestic banks survived the scourge."

Ted now had something to contribute to their discussion. "I thought that the problems which caused domestic banks failure in the past were fixed before the deregulation of the industry in 1986," he wondered. "My thinking was that the explosion in the number of banks after the deregulation evidenced return of stability to the industry," he said naively.

"You are wrong," interposed the most senior among them. "The boom had given way to distress and failure by mid-1990s. In late 1995, out of the 120 banks in Nigeria, at least 60 were considered distressed—up from the 1994 figure of 47 and only 8 in 1991. In December 1995, the problem had worsened with the liquidation of 5 banks, while 5 others were placed under interim management boards, and 17 taken over by the Central Bank of Nigeria. As at March 31, 1998, 15 commercial and 16 merchant banks had been liquidated by the regulatory authorities. None of the foreign subsidiary banks was affected in all these distress, failures, and regulatory interventions," he explained.

They continued analyzing the problems critically to settle their curiosity about the happenings in the industry. "It is ironic that banks, which ordinarily should be a haven for savers, investors, and businesses, are now regarded with skepticism by the public," Ted regretted. "The recurring bank distress, occasional need of the banks for bailout funds, and the unpredicted outright failure of some banks exacerbated the problem," corroborated his colleague.

Not infrequently, the incidents created crises which caused untold hardships and miseries to people, businesses, and the society. Unlike Ted, some of his colleagues had seen heart-stricken problem of the industry, which sometimes threatened the foundation of society, in the incidence of bank failure. At the root of the problem, in most cases, was failed management of the lending portfolio (credit risk) and funding (liquidity risk) of the banks, among other causes.

One of the bankers now narrated his personal experience about which Ted hitherto did not know. "I had personal experience in working for two failed banks and in a third that became distressed, managed to survive, but was ultimately acquired by another bank," he informed. "In all cases," he argued, "poor risk management accentuated liquidity crisis of the banks, which caused distress." He told them how—as a manager—he had tried to check inefficient banking practices. He had, according to him, "seen the agonies of bank failures firsthand—some of which could have been averted with sound banking policies, regulation, and supervision."

Ted and his other colleagues were speechless as they listened to some of the untold stories of contemporary banking crisis in Nigeria—a typical developing economy. Finally, he dropped the bombshell as his colleagues remained bewildered. "The banks that were worst hit by liquidity crunch, distress, and failure were the so-called new generation banks which did not have the resilience of the old generation banks. The former were touted as "cowboy banks" which were doing "voodoo banking" and were staffed by some of the so-called "bad guys and gals of banking," he revealed.

"I'm surprised at what you're saying," Ted managed to say disappointedly. "While I remain a banker," he hinted, "I will want to see a significant improvement in the conduct of banking business." He then said his vision for the industry, one that lay at the root of his ambition as a banker. "I understand that poor ethics rubbished the image of the industry in the past as most of the banks wallowed in infringement of regulatory policies and guidelines. I'm sad that bankers were associated with such a negative image. I think I should make a change, set a good example, and prove that banks could be reliable." He resolved to work hard toward making it to the apex of a bank and shun all forms of unethical practices.

Exercise for class or group discussion

1. To what extent would you agree or disagree that poor risk management is the bane of banking in developing economies?
2. Why would or wouldn't you think that the statistics of bank distress and failure in Nigeria—highlighted in Ted's chat with his colleagues—are a proxy for the situation in developing economies worldwide?
3. Would it be right or wrong—in your opinion—to conclude that the chat evidences threat to banking in the developing countries?
4. What reasons would you suggest underlay the bankers' dispassionate appraisal of the banking situation in Nigeria?
5. How would you have reacted to the startling revelations about banking in Nigeria or elsewhere—were you a banker or aspiring to be?

Tips for solving the exercise
Ted's chat over lunch with his colleagues at Bank Connect captures the salient points of the need for domestic banks in developing economies to manage risk well. Of course that summarizes the whole essence of this book. Often bankers are caught napping and risk-induced crisis festers, causing distress—and, on occasion, outright failure—of the business. Frequently, this happens largely because the bankers fail to anticipate risk and uncertainty. This book is really about how to reverse the trend and set banks in developing economies on a proven path of success—a proof founded on the effective management of composite risks. In order to achieve this goal, bankers must have the right attitude to risk, curtail, or tame risk appetite, and match hope for budget goal to a sense of realism. If they follow Ted's convictions, they can't go wrong. They should commit themselves—like Ted did—to working toward "a significant improvement in the conduct of banking business." Bankers should, above all else, individually resolve to "make a change, set a good example, and prove that banks could really be reliable." This is the overriding lesson for bankers in developing economies and elsewhere (Onyiriuba, 2013).

The use of Nigeria as the setting for this chat is purely for illustration purposes and to demonstrate how certain thorny banking issues play themselves out in the developing economies. While the dates and statistics of bank distress and failure are real, the names used for the bank and individual are imaginary and do not relate to any known or unknown real bank or person in Nigeria or elsewhere.

CONCEPTUALIZING AND DEFINING RISK AND UNCERTAINTY

The knowledge we have today about risk and uncertainty builds on the pioneering works of famous writers on the subject—including Knight (1921), Hardy (1924), Willett (1951), Markowitz (1952), Pfeiffer (1956), and Houston (1968) (See also Appendix 1 for detailed analyses of pioneering thoughts and evolving thinking on risk and uncertainty that can help you figure out their implications for banking in developing economies). The works of these pioneers establish association between risk and uncertainty. The nature of the relationship underscores the significance of uncertainty in causing and defining risk. Uncertainty is subjective—technically forming the basis of risk or upon which risk is defined. Hardy (1924) corroborates this view, opining that risk exists where chances of cost, loss, and damage are uncertain (p. 1). This establishes one view of the links between risk and uncertainty in financial analysis.

Owing to uncertainty, bank managements—like their counterparts in other businesses—are incapable of seeing beyond the realm of the present when they make critical decisions that could lead to a financial loss. This fact underlies the bane of banking—as in other businesses. Knight (1921) makes this point more forcefully. Statistical tabulation, according to him, is irrelevant to business decision as it neither adds value nor provides guidance. The reason is that events that characterize business decisions do not lend themselves to statistical tabulation. Such events are in general unique and therefore lack attributes for statistical application (p. 231). To put it simply, business decision is shrouded in uncertainty—thus rendering application of statistical tabulation a futile endeavor. Knight's contention raises statistical question of analysis, possible for the quantification of risk but impossible in the case of uncertainty. The impossibility to create a group of actual or possible occurrences of a particular event to determine uncertainty renders any attempt at statistical analysis irrelevant. In the case of risk, on the other hand, it is possible to employ probability distribution as a statistical tool for analysis.

Risk is omnipresent. It is endemic in every facet of life. As Field (1987) observes, living with risk is a reality of human condition (p. 4). Irukwu (1974) holds a similar view in arguing that risk has been part and the bane of human existence since time immemorial (p. 4). Like the pioneers, he associates risk with uncertainty. This relationship establishes the foundation of insurance. Without uncertainty—as really the only certain element of human life and endeavors— there wouldn't be a need for insurance. Thus the objective in insurance is to mitigate uncertainty, with its concomitant risks. This goal is attained—for all intents and purposes—when insurance substitutes certainty for uncertainty (p. 5). These views also denote omnipresence of uncertainty—not a definition of risk nonetheless.

The World Bank (2013) posits leading—and somewhat summary of—contemporary perspectives on risk and uncertainty. It defines risk simply as "the possibility of loss," (p. 5) *which* "can be imposed from outside or taken on voluntarily in the pursuit of opportunities" (p. 61). It categorizes risk into two broad types—systemic and idiosyncratic risks. While the former "is common to most members of an entire system," the latter "is specific to some members of a system" (p. 61). The Bank notes that "risk is not all bad, however, because taking risks is necessary to pursue opportunity." Opportunity is defined as "the possibility of gain" that represents "the upside of risk" (p. 11). It notes that "confronting risk, as the possibility of loss, is a burden—but it is also necessary to the pursuit of opportunity." This is because "risk and opportunity go hand in hand in most decisions and actions taken by countries, enterprises, and families as they seek to improve their fate" (p. 5). Clearly, the World Bank's views advance pioneering thoughts and evolving thinking on risk. I sift out the two main planks of contemporary perspectives on risk—and their relationship to uncertainty—from the Bank's definitions.

Pioneering thoughts and evolving thinking hinge on defining risk as a function of uncertainty—the inability to foresee the future correctly. The World Bank defines uncertainty in this context as "the situation of not knowing what the outcome will be" (p. 61). This ordinary meaning, according to the Bank, contrasts with "deep uncertainty," which it defines as "a situation in which parties to a decision do not know or cannot agree on the key forces that shape the future, the probability distributions of the main variables and parameters in their models, or the value of alternative outcomes." (p.81) The Bank talks about "the repercussions of extreme instances of lack of information and knowledge—so-called *deep* uncertainty" (p. 16). The repercussions refer to exposure to some danger or chance of an adverse consequence. I mean the possibility of loss.

Let me now sift out the two main planks of contemporary perspectives on risk and uncertainty. Nowadays risk is seen as an uncertain event whose possible outcome could be positive or negative and affects some objective accordingly. This implies that risk has two components. The one is a *threat* and the other an *opportunity*. As a risk, threat has a negative effect on objective while opportunity has a positive effect. Thus, risk is embodied in uncertain event that could have adverse or beneficial effect on the ability to achieve objective. The event is often fallout of pursuit of objective or derives from an external occurrence. This underscores the creation of risk in chances of future occurrences. Uncertainty connotes or is linked with risk because it has a negative or positive effect on possible outcome of choice or decision for the future.

Definite characterization of risk in terms of *uncertainty* and *loss* is the high point of the interplay of thoughts and perspectives on the subject. This twofold characteristic of risk—uncertainty and loss—is critical to a proper understanding of the real issues in any attempt to effectively manage risk. The risk manager must appreciate that risk borders on probability of occurrence—implying that the adverse or positive event may or may not happen. That defines the uncertainty part. In the other aspect—loss—risk materializes, leaving someone or business exposed to unexpected loss, usually financial or other adverse consequences. The lesson here is that individuals and businesses should ever be conscious of risk, and effectively manage it—one way or another. In order to mitigate or manage risk, uncertain future happenings should be anticipated—as much as possible. It becomes possible, in this way, to make informed choice or decision in dealing with risk and uncertainty that informs it (See also Appendix 1 for detailed analyses of pioneering thoughts and evolving thinking on risk and uncertainty that can help you figure out their implications for banking in developing economies).

APPENDIX 1 Conceptualizing and Defining Risk and Uncertainty

Pioneering thoughts

Knight (1921) elucidates his profound thoughts on the inner meaning of risk and uncertainty, one that contributes significantly to deep understanding of the terms. He distinguishes between risk and uncertainty in terms of ability and inability to measure their occurrence. He depicts risk as uncertainty that could be measured. Logically it follows, as he argues, that uncertainty is not measurable. Knight uses the terms "measurable uncertainty" and "unmeasurable uncertainty" in defining risk and uncertainty, respectively (p. 233). This construction approximates to, but contrasts with, contemporary application of probability in comparing risk with uncertainty. Thus, risk and uncertainty are assumed to exist depending on whether or not particular events lend themselves to statistical probability measures. While risk could be measured objectively using statistical probability and distribution functions, uncertainty cannot because it is subjective. In this context, risk and uncertainty are reconstructed to show how they relate to "objective probability" and "subjective probability"—constructs that are widely applied nowadays in defining risk and uncertainty. Yet the nomenclatural differences between "measurable uncertainty" and "objective probability"—depicting risk—on the one hand, and "unmeasurable uncertainty" and "subjective probability"—depicting uncertainty—on the other, do not blur understanding of the subject matter of distinction between risk and uncertainty with regard to measurability.

Willett (1951) establishes a correlation between risk and uncertainty in terms of "objective" and "subjective" events, in much the same vein as the foregoing. He attaches "risk" to objective events and "uncertainty" to subjective occurrences—and shows how they correlate (p. 6). Houston (1968) analyzes Willet's definition of risk, noting that it comprises two major aspects. The first aspect relates to the usual objective-subjective distinction according to which risk is seen as a real world event, empirically measurable and statistically quantifiable. The second aspect equates risk with a variation concept which cannot be identified in terms of the degree of probability (p. 152). Similarly, Mowbray (1930), Huebner (1935), Manes (1935), and Beard (1957) were among the pioneers whose thoughts shed light on the meaning of, and relationship between, risk and uncertainty.

In his famous portfolio theory, Markowitz (1952) explains the concept of risk in a very subtle way. He proffers a rule that could be likened to a veiled definition of risk where he argues that expected return on an investment is desirable while variability of return is undesirable (p. 77). He clarifies how the terms "expected return" and "variance of return" that he uses in the theory compares with "yield" and "risk" that are rather in common use by other authors. He defends his deviation from the norm, arguing that "expected return" could substitute for "yield," on the one hand, and "variance of return" for "risk," on the other, without change in meaning (p. 89). What may be sifted from this explanation is that Markowitz's concept of "variance of expected return" is simply a proxy for "risk." Or as Holton (2004) observes, the clarification Markowitz provides implies that the use of "risk" by other authors approximates with his notion of "variance of return" (p. 21). Markowitz's groundbreaking theory has real life applications, especially in the investment field from which banking greatly benefits. It is given—based on his portfolio theory—that variability of expected returns underlies the risk of investment decisions. The variability in question is underlain by uncertainty of future events and outcomes. Thus, the risk associated with a project or investment is the chance that its future returns might vary from expectation. An investment will be more or less risky depending on the degree of variability of its expected returns. For two investments, the one with greater variability of expected returns relative to expectation would be riskier than the other.

On his part, Pfeiffer (1956) underscores the view that risk relates to real world events and is measured by probability while uncertainty relates to feelings and is therefore not amenable to statistical measurement. Thus measuring uncertainty relies on intuition—or as Pfeiffer puts it—on "a degree of belief" (p. 42).

Houston (1968) appraises Pfeiffer's definitions, noting the emphasis on the objective-subjective characterization of risk and uncertainty. He also distinguishes between Pfeiffer's and Willett's thoughts. In contrast to Willett, according to him, Pfeiffer posits that a single probability value should measure risk and uncertainty. It does not matter whether that value is calculated in objective or subjective terms—provided it measures the chance of an adverse event occurring (p. 154).

Evolving thinking

Holton (2004) holds a similar view with regard to Knight (1921) definition of risk. He praises and describes Knight's definition as famous for relating risk to objective probabilities, on the one hand, and uncertainty to subjective probabilities, on the other. The flip side of the praise is quite instructive. Holton takes a hard look at the definition he praises and identifies a flaw in it. Knight's definition, according to him, is not a true definition of risk after all. The flaw he identifies is that Knight fails to address the "exposure" component of risk in his definition. Expatiating on this criticism, he argues that risk should be defined not only in terms of uncertainty but outcomes or exposure—which he equates with "possible consequences" (p. 20).

Rose (1987) relates the phenomena of risk and uncertainty to banking practice during the 1980s. She points out that emphasis on bank management in the 1950s focused on devising effective strategy for managing bank assets. Bank management's concern in the 1960s and 1970s, according to her, centered on liability management—ostensibly how to ensure that banks operated at adequate liquidity level. Then she concludes that the situation changed in the 1980s to concern about risk. The new concern bordered on how to measure and control risk in ways that optimize benefits to stakeholders in the banking industry (p. 54). This contention, which underpins the cause of risk management in banking, holds true still—and would remain relevant in the foreseeable future.

The World Bank (2013) posits a view on risk and uncertainty which corroborates that of Rose (1987). The Bank stresses the need to stay on top of risk and uncertainty. It notes that "the world is constantly changing, and with change comes uncertainty. Amid this uncertainty, people must consider different options for how to prepare for risks they may face" (p. 60). Lee Iacocca (1987), renowned as an insurance pundit, gives an all-time forceful advice on the right attitude toward risk. He cautions that risk should not be taken on as a life or death affair. Otherwise there's nothing wrong, according to him, about taking on some risk. He notes that risk taking is important for individuals and businesses to be able to compete, but advises against taking a deadly risk (Insurance Information Institute, 1987). The import of Iacocca's advice is that individuals and businesses should not just blindly take on risk. That is the bottom line.

Unfortunately, there is no consensus on the definition of risk. What appears rather as a common understanding is that an authoritative, universally accepted definition of risk is elusive. I briefly review some of the criticized definitions. There is a common view that "risk is an objective doubt about a possible outcome." This view is lacking in precision. It is wrong to think of all doubtful outcomes as constituting a risk without reference to the cause of the doubt. For instance, there could be doubt as to whether a pregnant woman would put to bed a baby boy or girl. There could also be doubt as to whether she would survive the childbirth or die in the process. Can these two situations of objective doubt equally lead to a conclusion that pregnancy is a risk? The former state of doubt does not qualify for the existence of risk, unless an additional baby boy or girl to the family is unwanted because of some circumstances of the family. In such a situation, those circumstances define what is at stake. The latter state of doubt is a clear example of a risk. It presents two possibilities (outcomes), one of which is attractive and results in a gain (surviving childbirth and having a baby); the other is horrible and causes an irreparable loss (dying in the process of childbirth).

Risk is often defined as "the uncertainty of loss." Proponents of this definition claim that it is meritorious based on its brevity and avoidance of situations where the occurrence of a particular event is certain (Amaonwu, 1989). Unfortunately, the premise of this thinking is erroneous. It leaves room for criticism, exemplified in the question which Mordi and Obi (1988) asks: "How about the uncertainty of gain or even uncertainty of no-loss-no-gain or break-even, which are also possible?" As Mordi points out, if gain or break-even is uncertain, loss may occur and result in a risk. Where gain or break-even is certain, according to him, loss would not be uncertain, there would be no loss, and the question of risk would not arise. Therefore, there cannot be uncertainty of loss where gain or break-even is certain. This argument introduces a somewhat controversial dimension to the views on risk.

The "uncertainty of loss" definition of risk may be accepted if it implies the likelihood of loss because of inability to correctly predict expected outcomes on account of uncertainty of future events. Gain, loss, and break-even are all possibilities in a given situation. The uncertainty of one renders the others uncertain. Thus, the definition of risk as the uncertainty of loss cannot be accepted as given. Another flaw in this definition is that it is vague and therefore likely to cause confusion of risk with uncertainty. While uncertainty creates risk, the two terms connote different meanings and are never regarded as synonymous. It would also be wrong to define risk solely in terms of uncertainty. This is evident in Holton (2004) that picks holes in Knight's (1921) definition of risk.

SUMMARY

Pioneering works of famous writers such as Knight (1921), Hardy (1924), Willett (1951), Markowitz (1952), Pfeiffer (1956), and Houston (1968) establish association between risk and uncertainty. The nature of the relationship underscores the significance of uncertainty in causing and defining risk. Evolving thinking, like the pioneering thoughts, hinges on defining risk as a function of uncertainty—the inability to foresee the future correctly.

Some of the notable contributions to evolving thinking on risk and uncertainty include Irukwu (1974), Field (1987), Rose (1987), Mordi and Obi (1988), Amaonwu (1989), Holton (2004), and World Bank (2013)—with The World Bank (2014) also positing leading contemporary perspectives. Unfortunately there is no consensus on the definition of risk. What appears rather as a common understanding is that an authoritative, universally accepted definition of risk is elusive. Nowadays risk, in general, is seen as an uncertain event whose possible outcome could be positive or negative and affects business or other objective.

Thus risk has two components—*threat* and *opportunity*. Threat has a negative effect on objective while opportunity has a positive effect. The two main characteristics of risk are *uncertainty* and *loss*. Understanding of this twofold nature of risk is critical to managing risk. Future development of the banking industry in developing economies depends on how well uncertainty is anticipated and risk managed. The reason is that risk and uncertainty underlie the central dynamic of success in banking. Thus learning deeply about risk and uncertainty and their ramifications for banking is pertinent.

There tends to be differences in the way domestic and foreign subsidiary banks in developing economies manage risk. Yet the two sets of banks emphasize risk management more or less depending on their unique circumstances.

QUESTIONS FOR DISCUSSION AND REVIEW

1. In what respects do pioneering thoughts, evolving thinking, and contemporary perspectives on risk and uncertainty compare?
2. Do you consider the view that there is no consensus on the definition of risk an overstatement? Why or why not?
3. Why—in your opinion—has an authoritative, universally accepted definition of risk remained elusive?
4. How will understanding of risk components and characteristics help banks in developing economies to succeed?
5. What are the possible causes of differences in the way domestic and foreign subsidiary banks manage risk?

REFERENCES

Amaonwu, O.E., 1989. Risk quantification. International Conference on Risk Management, Enugu, Nigeria, 19–23 March, 1–16.
Field, M.H., 1987. Risk and expectation. J. Inst. Actuar. 114 (1), 1–14.
Hardy, C.O., 1924. Readings in Risk and Risk Bearing. University of Chicago Press, Chicago.
Holton, G.A., 2004. Defining risk. Financ. Anal. J. 60 (6), 19–25.
Houston, D.B., 1968. Risk, insurance and sampling. In: Hammond, J.D. (Ed.), Essays in the Theory of Risk and Insurance. Scott, Foresman and Company, Illinois.
Insurance Information Institute, 1987. Insur. Rev. XLVIII (3), 34 & (10), 37.
Irukwu, J.O., 1974. Accident and Motor Insurance in West Africa. The Caxton Press, Ibadan.
Knight, F.H., 1921. Risk, Uncertainty and Profit. Houghton Mifflin, Boston.
Lee, I., 1987. Quoted in Insurance Information Institute. Ins. Rev. XLVIII (3), 34 & (10), 37.
Markowitz, H.M., 1952. Portfolio selection. J. Fin. 7 (1), 77–91.
Mordi, Obi, 1988. Statistics for agricultural insurance scheme in Nigeria. Twelfth Annual Conference of the Nigeria Statistical Association, Ogun State Hotel, Nigeria, 25–28 October, 1–11.
Onyiriuba, L., 2013. On the Road to Self-Actualization. NFS Data Bureau Limited, Lagos.

Pfeiffer, I., 1956. Insurance and Economic Theory. Richard D. Irwin, Inc., Illinois.

Rose, Peter S., 1987. Quoted in Nwankwo, G.O., 1991. Bank Management: Principles and Practice. Lagos: Malthouse Press Limited, p. 138.

Willett, A.H., 1951. The Economic Theory of Risk and Insurance. University of Pennsylvania Press, Philadelphia.

World Bank, 2013. World Development Report 2014 Risk and Opportunity—Managing Risk for Development. World Bank, Washington, DC. http://dx.doi.org/10.1596/978-0-8213-9903e3. License: Creative Commons Attribution CC BY 3.0.

FURTHER READINGS

Beard, R.E., 1957. "Analytic expressions of the risks involved in general insurance." Transaction of XVth International Congress of Actuaries. New York, vol. II, p. 232.

Huebner, 1935. Life Insurance, fourth ed. D. Appleton-Century Co, New York, p. 3.

Manes, A., 1935. Insurance, principles and history. Encyclopedia of the social sciences, vol. 8. New York: Macmillan Co., p. 95.

Mowbray, A.H., 1930. Insurance: Its Theory and Practice in the United States, first ed. McGraw-Hill Book Co., Inc, New York, pp. 4–5.

Chapter 2

Perspectives on Predisposition of Banking to Risk in Developing Economies

Chapter Outline

LEARNING FOCUS AND OBJECTIVES

Risk is inherent in the nature of banking. It determines financial performance, perhaps, more in banking than most businesses. The proneness of banking to risk is linked to certain internal factors of operations and external, mainly, social forces. Apparently, bank managements tend to be helpless with everyday challenges of dealing more decisively with risk. I should apprise readers of the factors that create risks to which banks are prone, especially in developing economies. Five objectives—founded on the need to fulfill this, ostensibly, reader expectation—underlie the essence of this chapter. Thus, my intention is to:

- Explore why risk is inherent in banking, doing so, investigate reasons banking is more prone to risk than most businesses.
- Identify and discuss events that create risks in banking and factors contributing to the predisposition of banking toward risk.

- Assess the commonality and variations of intensity of proneness to risk between domestic and foreign subsidiary banks in developing economies.
- Analyze the implications of variations and high intensity of proneness to risk for domestic banks in developing economies.
- Provide tips as well as guides to mitigating the proneness of domestic banks to risk in developing economies.

EXPECTED LEARNING OUTCOMES

The challenges of doing business and managing risks associated with it are intricately intertwined and daunting. This aptly captures the lot of banking in developing economies. Managing risk in banking is particularly a daunting task, to say the least. Risk management hardly becomes second nature in banking. One reason is that risk events in banking are mostly unforeseeable. They are ever in a state of flux, if anything. The natural proneness of banking to risk is another reason. In view of these facts, I place emphasis in this chapter on learning about the predisposition of banking—more than other businesses—toward risk, especially in the developing economies. The reader will—after studying this chapter and doing the exercises in it—have learnt and been better informed about:

- Reasons risk is inherent, the causes of risk, and risk-predisposing factors in banking, especially in developing economies.
- Internal and external factors that create risks in banking and contribute to the predisposition of banking toward risk.
- Commonality—as well as variations of intensity—of proneness of domestic and foreign subsidiary banks to risk in developing economies.
- Possible implications of variations and high intensity of proneness of domestic banks to risk in developing economies.
- Tips and guides to anticipate and check predisposition of domestic banks toward risk in developing economies.

OVERVIEW OF THE SUBJECT MATTER

There are several reasons why banking is more prone to risk than most businesses. The main risk factors derive from the nature of banking itself. The role of banks as a depository for money is the foremost factor. This is one of the basic functions of banks. It serves some operational need for the bank, but it is also a service banks render to their customers. Thus banks take money as deposits from customers for safekeeping. Unfortunately, this service is not rendered without some risk to the bank. Often the main risk is operational in nature.

Cash as bank inventory also portends risk. Banks need and maintain cash balances to satisfy statutory regulation for required reserves kept with the Central Bank. With cash balances, banks meet customer deposits withdrawal in three different forms. Some cash is compulsorily kept in reserve to meet general operating expenses or working capital needs. Cash balances of banks are held in the Central Bank. Of course, there is the vault cash—that is, cash kept in bank strong rooms at branches and the head office. Cash also exists in form of so-called "due from other banks." This represents one bank's deposits with other, sometimes local or correspondent, banks. Cash handling—for all intents and purposes—involves risk with which banks must contend in everyday operations.

The tendency of banks to overtrade is perhaps the most subtle cause of exposure of banks to risk in developing economies. Often banks fall foul of regulatory capital requirements—a situation that results from overtrading. In banking, the term "overtrading" is used in assessing capitalization of a bank vis-à-vis risks the bank takes. For instance, when a bank exceeds its permissible lending portfolio based on limits imposed by its regulatory capital, it is said to be "over lent." Such over lending situation smacks of overtrading and has liquidity crisis and risk implications, especially for the money deposit banks.

On occasion some bank employees in positions of trust may compromise on certain banking principles—thus predisposing the bank to risk. This happens especially with respect to maneuvering of internal operating policies of the banks. Often willful flouting of banking rules in this way is a direct consequence of employee infidelity. Whether seen from the perspective of infidelity or abuse, possible insider compromises are a real problem for banks. It is problematic because it has profound implications for the creation of risk in banking. A related risk factor is frauds in banking. Fraud has become a commonplace. Fraudsters beat internal control systems of banks, one way or the other. Thus frauds remain a major cause of recurrent huge financial losses to banks.

Banks financial dealings involve the use of other people's money in rendering services to customers and third parties. This role equally carries risks to the banks due to the nature, functions, and possible abuse of money. Most of the risks are underlain by chances that people sometimes have irrational desire or inordinate quest for money. A typical risk in the use of other people's money for banking—one that deepens risks facing banking—is when banks assume the risks of counterparties, willy-nilly, through lending. Needless to say, lack of or tainted best practice exacerbates risk in banking.

Incidentally, risks in banking tend to fester in societies where wealth is glorified without regard to enterprise, endeavor, or source of the wealth in general. Such social glorification of wealth encourages financial vices such as fraud and money laundering. In the final analysis, bankers must live with risks peculiar to their business. I have throughout this chapter and the entire book—where applicable—highlighted the risks and provided tips as well as guides to mitigating them.

COMMON, BUT VARYING INTENSITY OF, PRONENESS OF BANKING TO RISK

I think it is pertinent at this point that I assess the proneness of domestic and foreign subsidiary banks in developing economies to risk. I am guided by a gut feeling that proneness is common to the banks but with varying intensities.

The predisposition of banking toward risk cuts across all banks—domestic and foreign subsidiaries alike—in both developing and developed economies. Quite unusually for businesses, banking is heavily prone to risk. Incidentally, this establishes one of the risk features of banking common to domestic and foreign subsidiary banks in developing economies. However, the intensity of predisposition of banking toward risk varies—first, within banks of the same category, then between banks of differing categories and, indeed, across all banks in developing and developed economies. What do I mean by these seemingly generalizations? Are they really defensible? There could be more rhetorical questions. Yes, the questions are apt and pertinent if one should appreciate similarities between risk features of domestic and foreign subsidiary banks, as well as from where and how the risk features of the two sets of banks depart.

Domestic banks are an example of banks grouped into the same category. Foreign subsidiary banks are another example. Suffice it to say that domestic banks form a category quite distinct from foreign banks subsidiaries. Variation of intensity of predisposition toward risk "within banks of the same category" could then be read as "among domestic banks" or "among foreign banks subsidiaries" without a change in meaning. I should also clarify the notion of "between banks of different categories." It implies, in the context of this book, the division between domestic and foreign subsidiary banks. Thus, it could be read as "between domestic and foreign subsidiary banks as distinct categories" without a change in meaning or understanding. It follows that "across all banks" denotes all banks are considered as a single category of business organizations. These categorizations are necessary for accurately pinpointing similarities and differences between domestic and foreign subsidiary banks in developing economies—in terms of sensitivity and predisposition to risk.

The features of banking which underlie its risk sensitivity and predisposition seemingly cut across all categorizations of banks. All banks operate on the basis of being a depository for money. In doing so, their inventory is cash. These features aside, there is not to my knowledge of any banks category that does not take on the risk of borrowers, one way or the other, in funding them or their operations. There is yet the question of dealing of banks in money. This impels the banks to be constantly staking other people's money. Furthermore, probability of insider infidelity ranks high in banking right across the board. The same goes for incidence of frauds and a tendency to overtrading. Rules of best practice are equally either neglected or flawed with gaps in most banking situations. In some societies, mostly in developing economies, people tend to glorify wealth wrongly. This exacerbates operational risks in banking.

The foregoing is some of the features of banking that inform risk sensitivity and predisposition of banks in developing economies—whether domestic or foreign subsidiaries. The banks face these common challenges in varying degrees, though. However, differences in operational and internal control systems of domestic and foreign subsidiary banks dictate observed variations in the intensity of their risk sensitivity and predisposition.

CASE STUDY 2.1 Mirroring Risk of Domestic Banks in a Tale about a Banker's Career

Janet unexpectedly started having issues with her banking career (Onyiriuba, 2013). She wasn't comfortable with banking maneuverings, stress-laden work, and intrigues with which bankers came to grips. Of particular concern to her, one upon which the public often frowns, was about frauds in banking. She observed that both bankers and their customers had to contend with fraud—easily the canker of risk in banking. Insider abuse, especially in lending—generally seen as a hotbed of reckless banking—took its toll on shareholders' funds. She was especially disgusted that banks and customers could deliberately create loopholes to manipulate transactions. Banks employees who compromise themselves had become a commonplace—a situation that was not only disgusting but negated the ethics of their noble profession. Janet could not have imagined—while she worked as a lecturer at Anta University—that such problems existed in banking. The image of banking that she had hitherto was that of an industry that employed the cream of workforce, where professionalism and integrity held sway.

Soon she realized that she was utterly wrong—a fact that dawned on her only when one bank after another, including Frontline Bank where she was working at the time, started experiencing liquidity crisis. Unfortunately, the bankers failed to capitalize on regulatory intervention to turn over a new leaf. Management initiatives to tackle the problem, such as downsizing and reengineering, failed and some of the banks degenerated from distress to outright failure. It became obvious to Janet, after putting in more than fifteen years in the banking industry, that she would not realize her ambition as a banker. The regulatory authorities had classified Frontline Bank where she was working, as "terminally distressed" and was enforcing specific "holding actions" applicable to it. Depositors were unable to withdraw their deposits, approvals for credit facilities were arbitrarily rescinded, while salaries of employees were outstanding, slashed, or not paid regularly. The bank had technically failed. Fear had gripped the directors of the bank because they were likely to be prosecuted under the Failed Banks (Recovery of Debts) and Financial Malpractices in Banks Law. A number of bank executives had been jailed under this law at the time. Things got to a head when employees started avoiding customers because the bank had either reneged on their transactions, or lacked liquidity to meet customers' cash withdrawal requests.

At that point Janet decided to resign her appointment. She wanted to switch to another, reputable bank—one that was liquid and had a track record of good management. Two of the banks to which she applied for job invited her for interview. She honored the invitations but was unsuccessful. One of the banks offered her the post of an officer—a position she attained five years earlier. The best she could get from the other bank was an offer of assistant manager. She rejected both offers. She didn't understand why she should step down from her position of manager. Out of frustration, she resigned her appointment with Frontline Bank—without an alternative job!

A couple of months later, unemployment pangs descended upon her. She started facing the realities of her rash decision. She incorporated a company and started doing sundry purchase order contracts for companies. That kept her going for nearly a year before it dawned on her that she couldn't go far with it. At that point, she considered going back to banking and accepting any job she could lay her hands on. But her ego was the stumbling block—she couldn't handle it. "How on earth can I return to bank job and the industry I so much criticized?" She regretted. Her attitude reflected the biblical aphorism, "the soul is willing but the body is weak." She realized that she would be fulfilling William Shakespeare who had metaphorically stated that "pride goeth forth on a horseback grand and gay but cometh back on foot and begs its way." He felt ashamed at the possibility of returning to banking, perhaps to accept a post she had rejected several months before. Ultimately, she bowed to reason. She reverted to bank job as an assistant manager—two levels below the position she held at the time she quit!

Getting her bits and pieces together, Janet started forging ahead again in her checkered banking career. Once again, she started working her way up the corporate ladder. Soon she became impatient to make it to the top. In the midst of lingering banking industry crisis, she continued to switch jobs, from one bank to another. Then she was promoted Vice President at the age of 40. But, alas, two years later, she again quit banking! She had yet again become fed up with worsening banking crisis—a situation that kept bankers perpetually on their toes. Ostensibly, she was going through midlife crisis. What with a career into which she had put so much coming to an abrupt end yet again. It wasn't as if she was sacked, but she was just tired and fazed by the whole banking stress that never seemed to end soon or be ebbing. Thus, her resignation as Vice President was the culmination of her frustration in banking which started midway through her career. She had tried to cope but found it extremely difficult to come to terms with the peculiarities of banking in a developing economy. So she wanted to do something different. Yet even the "something different" was not certain.

Exercise for class or group discussion
1. Can Janet's checkered banking career be realistically explained from the perspective of risks to the domestic banks in developing economies?
2. Do you think—from your understanding of this case study—that personal ambition and midlife crisis contributed significantly to Janet's fate?
3. In your opinion, why would downsizing workforce or reengineering processes not be effective in dealing with full-blown bank distress?
4. How can banks in developing countries effectively invent or reinvent enterprise in the face of prolonged financial crisis?
5. In what ways do factors—identified in this case study—that breed risk also cause dissatisfaction with career in banking?
6. What factors do you think are responsible for the negative attitude of bankers toward regulatory interventions?

Tips for solving the exercise
Janet's experience of banking is really the epitome of the sad scenes of the repercussions of banking risks in developing economies. It touches the cause and crux of this book—the need and how to tame risk-taking excess in banking. The instrument for attaining this goal is a methodical approach to managing novel, change-drive composite risks—differently from the classical method. Pointers to rampant

crisis of banking in developing economies run through the whole tale, underscoring the seriousness of the problem. The main issues that came to the fore, besides bank managements' failings, include peculiarities of banking in the developing economies, lingering banking industry crisis, failure of bankers to capitalize on regulatory interventions to turn over a new leaf, and degeneration of some of the banks from distress to outright failure. The foregoing can be distilled into two main lessons. First, domestic bank managements should seek to invent or reinvent enterprise in the face of crisis rather than downsize workforce or reengineer processes as was the case in the tale. Second, as worsening banking crisis keeps bankers perpetually on their toes, their careers tend to be checkered. It is ironic—to say the least—that the same bankers yet find it difficult to turn over a new leaf under the auspices of regulatory interventions (Onyiriuba, 2013).

The setting for this real life case study is veiled to keep identity of the banks and banker in the tale confidential. The case study serves essentially only illustration purposes, in order to demonstrate how the tale plays itself out in banks in developing economies. The names used for the banks and individual in the tale are imaginary and do not relate to any known or unknown real banks or person anywhere in the world.

FACTORS OF GENERAL PREDISPOSITION OF BANKING TO RISK

Many will agree that banking is unusually prone to risk. Stakeholders in banking—nay, the public—appreciate this fact from personal experience. The stakes are really high in banking. The spate of banks crisis, distress, and failure around the world attests to the impacts of risks peculiar to banking. The nature of banking itself does not help matters. Certain factors are behind the creation of risks peculiar to banking. I mean features and tendencies of banking that predispose it to risk more than other businesses. Unfortunately, bankers must live with risks peculiar to their business. I have throughout this book—where applicable—highlighted the risks and provided tips as well as guides to mitigating them. Let me now identify and discuss the most troubling questions about risk creation in banking.

Bank as Depository for Money

Banks—first and foremost—are a depository mainly for money. This is one of the basic functions of banks. It serves some operational need for the bank, but it is also a service banks render to their customers. Thus banks take money as deposits from customers for safekeeping. Unfortunately, this service is not without risk. Often the main risk is operational in nature.

Fraud—a typical operational risk—somewhat has to do with the banking role of being a depository for money. Bank robberies exacerbate operational risk of banking, especially in developing economies. Even minor operational risk of vault cash shortage can be very debilitating sometimes—especially for officers who are tasked with balancing vault cash. Risk of deposits into bank accounts can be high or low depending on the uses to which banks put the deposits. For instance, risk tends to be high when deposits are applied in creating risk assets, that is, money loaned to borrowers.

The same goes for using deposits rather than shareholders' funds to finance fixed assets. Popular use of deposits is in money market dealings—especially in interbank trading. In doing so, banks are yet exposed to market risk that results from possible fluctuation in interest rates. In all cases, banks face three different but somewhat related constant realities, irrespective of what it does with or the uses to which it puts deposits. First, deposit is a liability and is represented on a bank's balance sheet accordingly. Second, the act of taking deposit itself imparts contractual obligation to a bank. Third, the bank will pay back deposit according to some agreement with the depositor.

Incidentally—and notwithstanding risks—money in the form of deposits is the main ingredient of banking. Thus banks will, are ideally expected to, and do often keep a large stock of money to meet day-to-day operational needs.

Cash as Bank Inventory

Banks need and maintain cash balances to satisfy statutory regulation for required reserves kept with the Central Bank. With cash, banks meet customer deposits withdrawal and general operating expenses or working capital needs. Cash balances of banks are held in three different forms, for safekeeping. Some cash is compulsorily kept in reserve with the Central Bank. Of course, there is the vault cash—that is, cash kept in bank strong rooms at branches and the head office. Cash also exists in form of so-called "due from other banks." This represents one bank's deposits with other, sometimes local or correspondent, banks.

Cash is not only part and parcel but the main component of money in a bank's depository at any point in time. Bank inventory also consists mainly of cash. Thus cash is the main trading asset of a bank. Notwithstanding its asset quality, cash—comprising currency notes and coins—does not in itself earn income for the bank. It is sterile. These facts have risk implications for the bank. Risk derives from the nature of cash as the most liquid asset. There are three aspects of risk implied in this unique nature of cash. First, cash and cash transactions can be easily manipulated to defraud a bank. Second, diversion or laundering of cash for illegal purposes is common. Third, cash is particularly tempting, especially for people on a low income. For these reasons, banks become more vulnerable to risk in a large-scale cash handling operations.

The domestic banks are particularly vulnerable to risk relating to cash as a liquid asset. They generate more cash than their foreign subsidiary banks counterparts due mainly to their extensive branch network. In most cases, branch banking strategy is informed by a need to boost financial intermediation of the banks through mass mobilization of deposits. Domestic banks target the local populace, small enterprises, and operators in the informal economy for mobilization of mass and cheap deposits. Cost of funds reduces drastically with cheap deposits. However, the pursuit of this liability-driven goal is fraught with challenges. There lies potent risks albatross for the domestic banks. First, as a business strategy, it requires a large workforce. Second, it demands opening of numerous retail branches in rural and sometimes remote communities. Third, it easily becomes unwieldy in terms of effective coordination of the branches. Of course, it exacerbates the risk of frauds.

The foreign subsidiary banks do not face these challenges. These target markets for cheap deposits—save for the public sector—do not appeal their liability generation strategy in the first place. Besides, they lack operational facility in terms of extensive branch network to handle mass banking and deposit mobilization challenges. Thus, they stick with their high street banking orientation. This banking orientation fits well with a cashless policy which is alien to most developing economies. But it skews how foreign subsidiary banks compare with domestic banks in real terms. Despite setbacks, cash remains the lifeblood of a bank—domestic and foreign subsidiaries alike.

Insider Infidelity and Abuse

On occasion some bank employees in positions of trust compromise on banking principles—thus predisposing the bank to risks. This happens especially with respect to the bank's internal operating policies. Often willful flouting of banking rules in this way is a direct consequence of employee infidelity. Whether seen from the perspective of infidelity or abuse, possible insider compromises are a real problem for banks. It is problematic because it has profound implications for creation of risk in banking.

Risk festers in banks where insider infidelity prevails. A typical risk is the probability that some employees would collude with customers or other outsiders to perpetrate fraud or other financial crime. In most cases, such criminal acts result in loss of money or income to the bank. Another form of insider-related risk is employee maneuvering of policy guidelines to satisfy some personal or other interests. Insider infidelity is yet also seen in thwarting of internal control in some or any way. In bank lending, for instance, insider abuse tends to be an intractable problem for banks management.

Banks should deal with the risk of employees and insider infidelity right from the cradle. One effective way to do so is to reinvent employee recruitment process. Subsequently, a rigorous employee appraisal process should follow suit. That consolidates gains from reinvented recruitment process. In this way, the bank maintains ongoing procedure for identifying and weeding out disgruntled and frustrated employees. This category of employees tends to be easily candidates for insider infidelity. Addressing their grievances or weeding them out—if doing so becomes inevitable—will significantly mitigate the risk of insider abuse.

Money Dealing—Staking Other People's Money

Bank financial dealings involve the use of other people's money in rendering financial services to customers and third parties. This role portends all sorts of risk to the bank due to the nature, functions, and possible abuse of money. Most of the risks are underlain by chances that people sometimes have irrational desire or inordinate quest for money. A lot of people crave money and would go to any lengths to have it. Most people engage in business, transactions, or work not only for self-actualization but money. Money is yet centerstage in most personal, corporate, and governmental calculations. In other words, money does wonders—to say the least. Thus the risk that banks face in financial services and dealings lies in the possibility of abuse and misuse of or wrongful and inordinate quest for money prevalent in society.

This trend demands that bankers should devise effective means to deal with unusual and wanton need for money which customers and third parties may exhibit and bring to bear on them. There should not be a choice of whether or not to do this since such need may be inimical to the business of the bank as a going concern. How well or badly the bank copes with or handles the contending need determines the level of risk it assumes in money dealing. The know your customer (KYC) rules can come in handy. Risk is checked, in this instance, through proper knowledge of the customer and motivation for their transactions. Banks should treat KYC as inviolable. Chances that a bank will mitigate risk increases when the bank uses KYC concurrently with standard operating procedures (SOP) as a fallback.

The foreign banks subsidiaries do have an edge over the domestic banks in investing, staking, and working with other peoples' money. They constantly keep an eye on risk. They adopt exotic risk and control models fashioned by international banking experiences of their parent, holding, banks. Their risk and control models are essentially tailored to meeting the unique needs of banking in developing economies. Usually, they are equipped with a road map to successful banking right from the outset. The domestic banks spend years learning the ropes in some critical banking areas. They make mistakes, learn from the mistakes, and forge ahead in pragmatic ways, ostensibly not scared of taking risks. This approach hardly pays off and should be shunned if domestic banks need to make progress.

Tendency to Overtrading

Often banks fall foul of regulatory capital requirements—a situation that results in overtrading. Let me briefly explain what "overtrading" means from the perspective of banking. Thereafter I proceed with discussing its risk implications. In the context of banking, the term "overtrading" is used in assessing capitalization of a bank vis-à-vis risks the bank takes. For instance, when a bank exceeds its permissible lending portfolio based on limits imposed by its regulatory capital, it is said to be "over lent." Such over lending situation smacks of overtrading and has liquidity crisis and risk implications for the bank.

Usually a bank that overtrades will experience liquidity pressure. In most cases, the pressure will be due to inability of the bank to meet its funding requirement at current level of operations. Thus "overtrading" refers to a situation in which a bank is having liquidity pressure and financial crisis because it is unable to meet funding requirement at current level of its operations. Naturally, the question that comes to mind is, why would a bank find itself in this nasty situation? The answer to this question is far from straightforward, but I will try to simplify it. I point out its complications first. Then I provide a simplification.

Most of the problems—and therefore risks—of banking that lead to distress or failure in some cases border on overtrading. The problem at issue is failure to manage or harmonize the relationship of bank capital to liquidity and capacity to take on risk. This is one of the major causes of risks peculiar to banking, especially in developing economies. Analysis of the three-pronged nature of the problem—capital, liquidity, and risk—is certainly beyond the scope of this discussion. However, it is amply discussed throughout this book in the relevant chapters. You can now see why it is difficult to give a straightforward answer to the question.

On the flip side, I now present the simple answer. Banks tend to undertake more business than their paid-up capital, unimpaired by loses, can support. They do so in pursuit of budget goal—usually the bottom line. In doing so, most bankers may unwittingly fail to observe significant rules for financial prudence and thus take on risk to excess. This problem is especially endemic in developing economies where banking regulation is still in its rudimentary form. Banking becomes ineffective under the circumstances.

In response to risks attendant on this banking tendency, the Basel Committee on Banking Supervision (1988) enacted the Basel Capital Accord, ostensibly to solve the problem. The Accord specifies "framework for measuring capital adequacy and the minimum standard to be achieved" by internationally active banks. It recommends "a weighted risk ratio" as a measure of capital adequacy. The ratio weights and relates the riskiness of a bank's assets and off-balance sheet exposure to its capital. The Capital Accord, as amended, and the other Basel Accords can solve the problem of overtrading in banking if well harnessed and properly implemented.

Banks in developed economies and their subsidiaries in developing economies have imbibed the main tenets of the Basel Accords. Accordingly, they are able to moderate their risk-taking. On the contrary, risk to domestic banks in developing economies is relatively higher. The domestic banks find it difficult or lack the skills and other resources to fully implement the Basel Accords. Their main problem tends to be with the risk weighting system and its application in determining appropriate regulatory capital. A common regulatory practice, while the banking system is developing at its pace, is to arbitrarily fix bank lower capitalization limit.

Taking on Financing and the Risks of Borrowers

Banks invest huge amount of funds in risk assets. Often risk assets strategy of the banks is anchored on a desire to build financial strength around the balance sheet, meet competition, and attain budget goal. This pursuit tends to be the driving force behind—as well as the justification for—risk that banks take in lending. Appreciating how and the fact that banks trade with depositors' funds in the financial markets add a wider perspective. Trading more on depositors' funds rather than equity exacerbates risk to the banks through increasing gearing. The bank's debt/equity ratio soars. In such a situation, the bank is using more borrowed than shareholders' funds for business. It is therefore desirable for a bank to trade more on equity than purchased funds. That way the bank faces less volatile operations and risk. Notwithstanding risk, unfortunately, a bank must create, build up, and maintain loan portfolios. To put it simply, risk-taking, in this case credit risk, is inherent and inevitable in bank lending.

It does matter though about the basis and quality of lending decisions and risk that banks assume in lending, especially to large business borrowers. Credit risk crystallizes default either through deliberate default by borrowers or through no fault of theirs as in the case of so-called force majeure. The bank has to absorb the loss of a credit facility, one way or another. There are two possible options open to the bank, though, under the circumstances. It can embark on loan workout in the first instance. In most cases, failure of loan workout leads to outright recovery actions. Usually banks opt for loan recovery as the last resort. The second option is to make full provision on and ultimately chargeoff the delinquent loan. Such chargeoffs diminish the bank's net worth. This is because loan losses are chargedoff on earnings. Loans chargeoff does have negative impact on bank reserves through diminution of shareholders' funds.

Loans—the main product of lending in banking—are both earning and risk assets. Pause for a moment and reflect on the connotation of "risk assets"—a term commonly found in banking, credit, and financial literature. Obviously, it denotes loans granted by banks or other lending institutions to borrowers, usually their customers. Loans are certainly assets and are reported in a bank's balance sheet accordingly. Now the real question is, what is the import of "risk" qualifying "assets" in describing loans as "risk assets" rather than simply "assets?" It means that loans, on the one hand, are assets and, on the other, a risk to the bank—all at the same time. Risk in question—the probability of default by the borrower and loss of the loan—tends to exacerbate with negative borrower characteristics. There is an unusual aspect of risk that a bank takes on when it lends money to borrowers, especially those in the business category.

The usual exposure of a bank to a borrower is termed credit risk. Strictly speaking, this implies that there is a probability that the borrower may default on repayment of the loan. The bank loses asset in the loan—that is to say, funds it committed to the loan are lost—when default occurs. But there is an unusual aspect of exposure of banks in lending to borrowers that is often overlooked. Banks, maybe inadvertently, also take the risks of the borrowers they finance. In accessing credit facilities, businesses and other borrowers indirectly transfer their risks to the banks. This may sound a bit far-fetched, but banks technically assume the risks of their borrowing customers. One reason is that loan repayment depends on the success of everyday business, undertaking, or endeavor of the borrower. A related factor is ability of the borrower to utilize the loan effectively and strictly for the purpose it was granted in the first place.

Thus, in lending money to a borrower, a bank assumes that the business of the borrower will succeed and that the borrower will utilize the loan properly and promptly repays it on its due date. In reality, these assumptions sometimes fall through. Often the rigor of so-called credit analysis—with all the hallmarks of risk mitigation that informs it—appears irrelevant under the circumstances. This is one of the realities of lending that imparts risk to banking the world over.

Incidence and Complexities of Banking Frauds

Fraud is perhaps the most embarrassing factor of risk for bank managements around the world. It is also one of the major causes of income loss to banks in both developed and developing economies. In developing economies, domestic and foreign subsidiary banks alike are exposed—though in varying degrees—to risk and huge financial losses attendant on fraud. It is noteworthy that the dynamic of fraud and related financial losses may vary from one bank to another. On occasion, fraud is perpetrated by insiders—either deliberately or inadvertently. Fraud committed deliberately is more common. It is a clear criminal act in which some bank employee engages to achieve some purpose. The objective may be to fulfill some selfish personal objective. It could also be intended to settle some old scores. The reason behind it could be anything, but deliberate acts of fraud are a real source of difficult risk in banking.

Unfortunately, bank employees do sometimes inadvertently get involved in fraud. Let me give an example to illustrate one of the ways that such a situation may arise. Often competition in banking, especially in developing economies, drives bank managements into using phrases such as "We can!" "If you dream it, you can achieve it!" "Go for it!" and so on as battle cry to inspire line managers and workers lower down the rung. On the face of it, this motivational strategy makes sense. But its flip side is also instructive. It very often skews employees' judgment. As the battle cry is imbibed, the employees tend to be carried away and misapply it. The employees easily become overzealous and unknowingly commit themselves to irrational and fraudulent transactions—usually in pursuit of unrealistic business goals. This is the side effect of battle cry and a prod to get employees achieve budget goals. In most cases, inexperienced marketing employees are the main victims of overzealous adoption of battle cry in banking. They tend to be more eager to prove their competence and mettle than their more experienced colleagues.

Mastermind of bank fraud could also be an outsider. A variant of insider fraud is seen in collusion of bank employee with an outsider. So a bank faces and contends with all sorts of fraud-related risks at any point in time. This situation heightens anxiety about risk in banking. Comparatively speaking, the lion's share of fraud is observed among domestic banks in developing economies. Sadly, for the moment there is no solution to banking fraud and its incidence. Bank managements and stakeholders in banking appear to have settled, willy-nilly, to live with it. The virtual world of Internet banking complicates matters further. With Internet and related technologies, banking fraud assumes more troubling dimensions as it becomes more sophisticated with increasing incidence. Incidentally, banking fraud is nowadays perpetrated more in the booming virtual world—thus compounding its risk to banks.

I use the issue of frauds in banking as an example to illustrate where risk strategy of foreign bank subsidiaries departs from the traditional approach. The question of fraud continues to feature in discussions, as well as theoretical and practical analyses critical of banking in both developed and developing economies. The problem has become intolerable. Regulatory authorities are unrelenting, ever seeking a solution to this banking hydra that seems to have reached an all-time high. Foreign subsidiary banks are less prone to frauds than their domestic counterparts. The reason for this has to do with difference in operational structure of the two types of banks. Domestic banks, on the one hand, operate with numerous retail branches spread across every nook and cranny. Foreign subsidiary banks, on the other hand, have relatively very few branches—most of which are located in the high street. Some would rather categorize foreign banks subsidiaries as simply high street banks. Table 2.1 brings out this structural difference more clearly and is instructive.

The difference has implication for incidence of frauds in domestic and foreign subsidiary banks. Extensive branch networks fit well with mass retail banking while few branches are suitable for elitist banking strategy. Mostly, branches of banks—whether domestic or foreign subsidiaries—are the worst hit by frauds in developing economies. Usually, head offices of the banks report less frauds than branches, largely because most of a bank's fraud-prone transactions and processing either originate from or are done at the branches. Thus, the more branches a bank opens the more the predisposition of the bank toward risk, especially frauds. That explains why domestic banks tend to be more prone to the risk of frauds than their foreign subsidiary counterparts. I have so far given a cursory overview of the incidence and complexities of bank frauds.

The domestic banks in developing economies should invest in understanding the psychology of banking fraud which, for all intents and purposes, is really intriguing. That sheds light on the reasons most bank frauds succeed despite measures to check them. In most cases, psychological influences on bank fraud supervene. Domestic banks should equally invest in understanding the dynamic and character of perpetrators of bank fraud. That will complement the usual and new direct attack on the scourge of bank fraud.

TABLE 2.1 Branch Network of Selected Domestic and Foreign Subsidiary Banks in Nigeria[a]

Name of bank	Number of branches
Access	304
Citibank[b]	12
Diamond	249
Ecobank	180
Fidelity	220
First Bank	750
FCMB	283
GTBank	217
Heritage	200
Keystone	200
Skye	220
Stanbic	174
Standard Chartered[b]	42
Sterling	175

[a]*Figures are culled from Internet websites of the banks. Numbers may change as staff recruitment program of the banks is ongoing.*
[b]*Commercial banks that I recognize—for purposes of this discussion, chapter and, indeed, the entire book—as foreign subsidiary banks incorporated, operating, and domiciled in Nigeria.*

Gaps in Adoption of Rules of Best Practice

The rules of best practice have evolved with the ever-changing business and operating environments. Increasing sophistication and complexities of risk-taking in business has impacted evolution of realistic best practice, in much the same vein. World class businesses, organizations, and institutions have keyed performance to best practice as part of defining strategy for effective operations.

Multinational global banks—most of which are found in developed nations—make the statistic of businesses with sound and proven orientation to best practice. Their subsidiaries in developing economies adopt this orientation and are doing well in contrast to their domestic counterparts. This means that the rules of best practice are not of uniform applications among banks in developing economies. In essence, there are gaps in adoption of rules of best practice that creates loopholes for risks in banking.

Yet every bank should submit to best practice. There are obvious gains for the bank that subscribes to the rules of best practice. Institutionalizing best practice is effective in mitigating risk overall. One reason is that banking operations and services will be tuned in to international standards of efficiency, professionalism, and transparency. Another reason is that insider infidelity and abuse can be more effectively checked. Ultimately, best practice shores up public confidence in banking. It usually creates a win-win situation for the bank and employees, on the one hand, and the bank and other stakeholders in banking, on the other. For this reason, bank managements can do anything but neglect best practice in their business and strategy calculations.

Best practice implies that bank managements and staffs should defend, rather than abuse, internal banking policy and process. That way, bank members are able to imbibe professional conduct and exude confidence in dealing with all functions. Another import of best practice is that it acts as a check on bank managements and employees that may be bereft of scruples. Doing so, it builds high moral standing which bank managements need to discipline employees with moral issues. If this category of employees is not isolated and weeded—if need be to do so—it may be the exception rather than the rule to stick to banking policy, let alone fulfill risk mitigation rules and criteria.

Social Glorification of Wealth

In some contemporary societies, wealth is glorified without regard to enterprise or endeavor. Many of such societies are found among countries in the developing world. Individuals, businesses, and organizations are oriented toward how to amass money with less or no regard to source. This social malaise rubs off on public attitude toward banking—especially, and as seen, in corrupt societies that are often a haven for people that commit financial crimes. Such people use banks as a conduit for all sorts of illicit financial transactions and crimes. Often social glorification of wealth is the root cause of the crimes. It encourages financial vices such as money laundering and capital flight more in developing than developed economies. In this way, banks are exposed to numerous operational risks. Banks contend with unusual challenges in day-to-day operations on account of this "I must make it" mentality that symbolizes the wanton glorification of wealth. The risks deepen with increasing emphasis on, attention to, and pursuit of wealth without regard to source.

MITIGATING THE INTENSITY OF THE RISK-PRONENESS OF DOMESTIC BANKS

How can one then realistically reconcile the risk features of domestic and foreign subsidiary banks? Foreign banks subsidiaries target mainly wholesale, institutional, and investment banking customers. In doing so, they maintain a cursory inclination toward strictly retail banking while emphasizing corporate, commercial, and consumer banking in strategic sectors. Domestic banks, on the other hand, chase after customers in all sectors—almost with equal commitment but mean success.

In order to solve their risk-proneness challenges, domestic banks should—first and foremost—adopt a cautious branch expansion policy. Table 2.1 shows that while First Bank has 750 branches, Citibank has just 12, and Standard Chartered Bank 42. This structure imparts high risk-proneness to the domestic banks.

Although domestic banks work with appropriate standard operating procedures and process manuals, there is a need for them to reinvent risk attitude at all levels of employments and functions. Domestic banks managements should lead this cause, setting the right example for the employees to follow right across-the-board. A change in this direction is bound to ginger interest in institutionalizing a risk culture that permeates all functions and activities.

SUMMARY

Many factors account for the reasons why banking may be more prone to risk than most businesses. Risk-proneness is a common feature of all banks, whether domestic or foreign subsidiaries. However, the intensity of the banks to risk varies, with domestic banks being more prone to risk than their foreign subsidiary counterparts.

The main factors that impart risk-proneness to banks derive from the nature of banking itself. Banks are a depository for money. They take money as deposits from customers for safekeeping. Unfortunately, this service embodies operational risk. Cash as bank inventory also portends risk. Cash handling—for all intents and purposes—involves risk with which banks must contend in everyday operations. The tendency of banks to overtrade in the normal course of business is perhaps the most subtle cause of exposure of banks to risk in developing economies.

Often banks fall foul of regulatory capital requirements—a situation that results from overtrading. Overtrading definitely has liquidity crisis and risk implications for money deposit banks. On occasion some bank employees in positions of trust may compromise on banking principles—thus predisposing the bank to risk. This happens especially with respect to infringement of the bank's internal operating policies. In most cases, willful flouting of banking rules in this way is a direct consequence of employee infidelity. Whether seen from the perspective of infidelity or abuse, possible insider compromises are a real problem for banks.

Bank financial dealings involve the use of other people's money in rendering financial services to customers and third parties. This role portends all sorts of risk to the bank due to the nature, functions, and possible abuse of money. Risk of banking tends to fester in societies where wealth is glorified without regard to enterprise, endeavor, or source in general. Such social glorification of wealth encourages financial vices such as money laundering in developing economies.

QUESTIONS FOR DISCUSSION AND REVIEW

1. What are the reasons behind the lot of emphasis placed on managing risk in banking, especially in developing countries?
2. What factors inform and reinforce the thinking that banking is prone to risk more than most other businesses?
3. What, in your opinion, does the phrase "factors of risk" connote with regard to banking in developing economies?
4. How—based on empirical evidence at your disposal—does the nature of banking predispose it to unusual risks?
5. Do you think that banks really assume the risks of the counterparties once the banks grant them credit facilities?
6. Do you agree that domestic banks are more prone to risk than their foreign banks subsidiary counterparts? Give reasons for your answer.
7. What are the implications of proneness of banks to risk for banking practice and development in developing economies?
8. What do you consider to be the most important reason why risk is inherent in the nature of banking all over the world?

REFERENCES

Basel Committee on Banking Supervision, 1988. International Convergence of Capital Measurement and Capital Standards, as Amended. Bank for International Settlements, Basel.

Onyiriuba, L., 2013. On the Road to Self–Actualization. NFS Data Bureau Limited, Lagos.

Part II

Paradigm Shift, Concerns, and Insights

Chapter 3

Banking Revolution, Paradigm Shift, and Risk Management in Developing Economies

Chapter Outline

LEARNING FOCUS AND OBJECTIVES

Five objectives stand out in defining my focus in this chapter. The focus itself hinges on the dramatic transformation of the banking industry which came to the fore in developing countries in the early 1920s. In this chapter, I investigate influences on—and the significance of—this change. The objectives, doing so, are to:

- Identify the role of technology and innovation in powering global transformation of and revolution in banking.
- Assess the response of banks in developing economies to technological innovations in the age of change.

- Pinpoint risk management demands of revolution in banking on bank managements in developing economies.
- Evaluate the effectiveness of bank managements in developing economies from the perspective of risk control.
- Discuss lessons and implications of revolution in banking for bank risk management in developing economies.

EXPECTED LEARNING OUTCOMES

The transformation of banking in the wake of revolution that swept the industry worldwide has far-reaching effects on bank risk creation and management across all functions. This change is intriguing and has profound implications for the future of banking, especially in developing economies. The reader will—after studying this chapter and doing the exercises in it—have learnt and better informed about:

- the nature of innovative operations methods that characterize modern banking;
- how Internet technologies inform the foundation of the scientific revolution in the banking industry;
- revolution and transformation of contemporary financial services delivery systems;
- the forces that triggered and are sustaining the revolution in global banking business;
- the dynamic of the buildup of the great march of scientific revolution in banking;
- conceptual, research, and empirical evidence and risks of revolution in the banking industry;
- nature and mitigation of risk in Internet-aided banking revolutionary technologies.

OVERVIEW OF THE SUBJECT MATTER

Banking practice around the world is ever in a state of flux. This situation portends risk for operators and other stakeholders in the banking industry. Bank managements try, but all to no avail, to be on top of risk in a rapidly changing world of modern banking. The problem is deepening, if anything. The increasing sophistication of contemporary banking business doesn't help matters. Nowadays a myriad of change-driven risks threatens the survival of many banks as going concerns. Where threat to survival of the banks is not the issue or is in check, banking business and performance tend to be jeopardized. This dimension of risk in banking is really disturbing.

Banks in developed economies—and their subsidiaries in developing economies—seem to be making progress on control of novel risks which the great march of revolution in banking occasions. But the same cannot be said of their domestic counterparts in developing and emerging economies. Unfortunately, risk managers of the domestic banks are deficient in experience for managing novel risks. Their experience does not provide a clue about the dynamic, let alone control, of such risks. Yet they must get to grip with the tide of novel risks in the wake of revolution in banking. That way they would be able to identify, analyze, and effectively mitigate risk and prevent financial losses for their banks. This will certainly have significant positive ramifications for banking development and performance in developing economies.

Ironically, banking in developing economies may be booming, ostensibly debunking concerns about possible threat of risk and uncertainty to the banks and their business. Strange though this may seem, the reality is that banking in developing economies goes through a recurring cycle of boom to bust. Yet, in many developing economies, banking crisis in recent time originated from either the neglect of the unusual risks and uncertainties or failure to anticipate and manage risks and uncertainties well. On occasion, the attendant crisis leads to bank distress and failure. The repercussions of bank failure for the industry and society cannot be overemphasized. Thus, effective risk management remains one of the proven ways to check distress, failing, or failed banks in developing and emerging economies.

The application of technologies in banking heightens concerns about risk. In many profound ways, technology-driven methods of operation are both improving and creating risks in financial services delivery at the same time. The change leaves room for novel risks to supervene and cause unanticipated financial losses. This happens as new methods supplant the traditional approach to banking in a wave of strong march of revolution and innovation. The Internet underscores scientific revolution in modern banking. With its debut in late 20th century, theoretical constructs underlying methodological framework of banking became untenable and irrelevant.

The immediate implication of revolution and innovation in banking has been the transformation of financial services across the board. For example, banks nowadays meet most of the financial services needs of customers in real time. Also, notwithstanding risks, customers can now conduct banking transactions from anywhere in the world. This furnishes confidence which banks in developing economies need to embrace innovation and change—and ultimately globalize.

ANTICIPATION, BUILDUP, AND DYNAMIC OF REVOLUTION IN BANKING

Domestic and foreign subsidiary banks anticipated buildup and central dynamic of revolution that swept the banking industry across developing economies from the early 2000s differently. Foreign subsidiary banks had an edge over the domestic banks in terms of anticipation of the revolution, ostensibly riding on grounding by their parent banks. Incidentally, many domestic banks were barely emergent while the revolution was well underway. Nonetheless, they grappled with its demands based on a faulty anticipation of its associated risks. The background to this experience is quite instructive.

The traditional brick and mortar theory of banking became moribund and ultimately supplanted as a mode of banking operations following innovations which the Internet technology occasioned. That was the lot of a theoretical construct which required customers to physically visit branches of banks where they opened and operated accounts in order to conduct their banking transactions. Implicit in the traditional theoretical framework was a construct which held that savings, deposits, and other banking transactions were best secured when customers physically related with officials of their bank branches.

In those heady days of armchair banking, banks cared less about true customer satisfaction. They operated without depositor discipline in what might be termed the sellers' market. Banks kept manual ledgers and records of day-to-day transactions of their customers. The authenticity of funds transfer requests was corroborated with manually devised and administered test keys. In few cases, telex messages fulfilled that function for the banks. During that retrogressive era of banking, transaction turnaround time was anything but efficient or satisfactory. Customers waited for several minutes and sometimes hours in banking halls before they were served, a situation that engendered dissatisfaction and frustration for the customers.

The scientific revolution in banking, from market perspective, was painfully belated. The cause for a revolutionary change became manifest in the urgency to efficiently meet the banking needs of customers in rapidly changing societies that were becoming increasingly sophisticated. The market was ready and held unmistaken expectation for that change at the time it happened. Its rapid diffusion and adoption was in fact taken for granted, as a logical fulfillment, of a felt market need. The factors that aided the diffusion and adoption of the new scientific framework were rooted in the failure of the supplanted scientific constructs to meet the ever changing service needs of bank customers. It was thought that banking could not be conducted in real time without loss, or an unusual loss, of security of the underlying transactions. In fact, banking in real time was simply unimaginable. But the change was bound to happen.

With the Internet, ancillary banking products such as credit cards, debit cards, ATMs, and other innovative self-service banking facilities complemented product profiles of the banks. Thus, banking became efficient, fast, and convenient for both the banks and customers. Banking operations ceased to be drudgery. The facility of email, which the Internet facilitates, remains an irresistible technological breakthrough for everyone and all businesses. The globalization of the financial system by which the world is now seen as a global village couldn't have been possible without the Internet. The gain in efficient communications networks, under the auspices of the Internet, further consolidated factors that favored worldwide acceptance of the new scientific revolution in banking. In time, the efficiency of banking, engendered by the Internet, started telling positively in the bottom line of the banks.

The scientific revolution, which trumped up Internet banking, undoubtedly enjoyed worldwide sweeping acceptance. However, its acceptance was not achieved without misgivings about security of customer transactions. Thus, its acceptance was initially slow, especially in developing and emerging markets. It offered a curious welcome relief from drudgery of tardy and cumbersome banking operations for the professionals—the bankers. In the midst of its acceptance, the professionals and customers never hid their apprehension about possibility of increasing rate of bank fraud. From the perspective of instinct of self-preservation, the concern expressed by the bankers was understandable. One reason is that investigation of fraud might lead to indictment of innocent bank officials. Another reason is that annual loss of depositors' funds to bank fraud often accounts for whopping sums of money.

CASE STUDY 3.1 Unraveling the Mysteries of Card Fraud—Where does the Buck Stop?

Sally is a nonborrowing, high net worth, customer of Shanghai branch of Future Dawn Bank (The use of Shanghai as the setting for this tale, as well as the use of MasterCard, is purely for illustration purposes only and to demonstrate the risk of banking revolution in developing economies. While the incident is real, the names used for the bank and individuals are imaginary and do not relate to any known or unknown real bank or persons in Shanghai or elsewhere in the world. Similarly, MasterCard remains an exceptionally secure and reliable means of online payments. Its use in this case study does not in any call these attributes into question). She maintains personal current and savings accounts with the branch. She operates the two accounts satisfactorily—and has done so for more than five consecutive years. She reserves the savings account for building future financial security—the so-called saving for the rainy day. Thus she very rarely withdraws money from the savings account. On the contrary, the current account serves to conduct her everyday banking transactions. Thus, the current account is very active, with appreciable credit and debit turnover.

Then some marketing officer of the bank tries to sell an idea of Internet banking to her. She refuses to discuss, let alone subscribe to, the proposal as she makes her excuses. As the officer's persistence intensifies, she cites Internet fraud as the reason why she is reluctant to adopt e-banking. Yet the marketer will not give up—ostensibly, eager to win an account with great potential for online banking. Ultimately, Sally bows to marketing pressure. She reluctantly subscribes to Internet banking selfservice. Soon afterwards she realizes she is no more untutored or scared about Internet banking.

She approaches customer service with a request for Yuan MasterCard—an ATM debit card she can use only in China. With this Card, she can conduct limited selfservice banking online. She relishes the service and regularly connects to the bank's Internet banking platform to conduct one online transaction or the other. In each case of banking online, she uses her laptop on which she installs strong Internet security software. She is able to transfer money online from the current to the savings account. Paying bills regularly, checking account balance, and such like are prompt and not time-wasting anymore. On occasion she uses her ATM card to draw money from her current account—usually to meet immediate personal cash need.

Sally decides to travel to London during summer of 2015 to spend her annual vacation. She applies to her bank for—and is granted five thousand dollars—personal travel allowance (PTA). The bank debits her current account with the value of the PTA in Yuan equivalent. She takes her MasterCard with her to London for security reasons but leaves her GSM phone behind and switched off. She gets a phone she uses while in London from her friend who is a resident. In London, she goes sightseeing and relaxes. She is really having fun. Three weeks on, she is still having fun and not looking forward to her inevitable return to Shanghai the following week.

Then she returns home to resume work after the four week pleasurable vacation. Once she switches on her phone, she receives banking alerts and several other SMS messages. She reads and deletes the messages, one after another. Soon she sees one concerning a withdrawal of 250,000 Yuan from her current account. She feels strange as this startles her. She did not draw money from her account while on vacation. She grabs her laptop and quickly turns it on. She clicks on the Internet banking platform right away and checks if the debit is real. As she confirms the suspicious withdrawal, her jaw drops. She grows nervous, even as she manages to navigate the Internet banking platform—now searching for details of the drawing.

She finds a narration she considers pertinent. Someone withdraws the money on the Internet about two weeks after she leaves Shanghai for London. She heads to the bank to report and protest the fraud. She could not hide her fury as she confronts the branch manager. "Bill!" She calls him, shaking with rage. "There's fraud in my account." Bill is taken aback and doesn't think it's true. "What happened, Madam?" He asks in confusion. "I don't know exactly, but 250,000 Yuan is missing from my account," Sally answers—fuming still about the fraud. "How is that possible?" Bill queries her, apparently helpless with regret.

Sally is now becoming a bit impatient. She stands and sits intermittently as Bill tries to unravel the mystery drawing from her account. "Just a moment, Madam," he pleads with her, "I'm already screening withdrawals from the account." Suddenly Bill turns and says his finding to her. "Madam, your MasterCard was used for the drawing—to make a purchase online or so it seems," he explains. "Never—I mean, never!" Sally roars. "I wasn't in the country when the money was withdrawn. How could I have drawn money with Yuan MasterCard in London?" She queries. "I got my PTA from here, isn't it? Here you are—my Passport with my travel Visa." She flourishes the document from her bag and hands it to Bill. "Check it and be convinced that I was out of the country."

This evidence rattles Bill. "Someone must have used your MasterCard to draw the money," Bill opines. "Does anyone—spouse, your child, or other relative—know your PIN?" he queries. "No! Not at all! Not to my knowledge!" Sally answers in quick succession. "I'm sorry Madam, but this drawing couldn't be possible if your PIN is not compromised," said Bill point blank. Sally was upset and became irate. "That's nonsense!" She fumed as she berates Bill. She didn't hide her disappointment that Bill could imagine that she could let out her MasterCard PIN to anyone. "I don't want to take issue with you, Bill. Needless to waste my breath anymore," said she in anger. "Tell me, when will the bank credit my account with the 250,000 Yuan?" She asks, flaying the bank.

In response, Bill said simply "the bank is not liable for this fraud. I'm sorry Madam, but that is the truth." Sally storms out of his office—without uttering a word. She comes back, almost immediately, and vehemently says to Bill, "I'll get my money back—I assure you" she with all the more storms.

Exercise for class or group discussion
1. Do you think that the factors which influenced Sally to ultimately request for Yuan MasterCard were cogent enough?
2. Why do you think a bank will want to issue local currency ATM debit card in MasterCard or Visa Card brand?
3. What factors—other than Internet fraud cited by Sally in this case study—give cause for concern about e-banking?
4. Who do you think perpetrated the fraud? Which of the mechanisms of fraud might have been adopted for this crime?
5. In what way did Bill insinuate that Sally aided fraud on her account? Would you say his judgment was or wasn't fair?
6. Why would or wouldn't the bank be able to wriggle out of responsibility for the fraud in Sally's account?

Tips for solving the exercise
The fraud vindicated Sally's reluctance to adopt Internet banking. Ostensibly, she had a premonition that Internet banking would expose her account to some risk. Ideally, Internet banking is safe. But it is not foolproof. Thus, there is need for strict adherence to proven security measures. Personalized PIN and password—kept confidential at all times—are always a given for secured Internet banking. Three things are intriguing about this case study. First, Sally vehemently denied letting out her PIN or password. Unfortunately, this cannot be proven. She was in a dilemma about this situation. Bill capitalized on her dilemma and claimed that she compromised her password. Second, the bank may not wriggle out of the responsibility for the fraud. The fact remains that Sally forcefully absolved herself of responsibility for the fraud. As shown in the case, she did so amply based on verifiable facts. Third, the fraud was real and either Sally or the bank should bear the financial loss associated with it. It's really fluid to say who bears the loss, but regulatory inclination is to side with the customer. The issues at stake are straightforward and border on three questions. Did Sally really compromise her PIN or password? Can Sally convincingly plead that her password or identity was hacked? Was her laptop, someone else's laptop, or cybercafé used for the fraud? These questions, for all intents and purposes, are pertinent.

WELCOME, SKEPTICISM, AND CONCERN ABOUT BANKING REVOLUTION IN DEVELOPING ECONOMIES

Great enthusiasm heralded the revolution of banking in developing economies. The academia was eager to corroborate the new scientific revolution with pertinent empirical surveys. Some researchers (Chang, 2009; Sukkar and Hasan, 2005) investigated the utility in the technology acceptance model (TAM), developed by Davis (1989), in a bid to explain factors in acceptance of the innovation in Internet (online-real-time) banking. There have been other TAM-based scholarly studies on aspects of market acceptance of Internet-aided technologies (Davis et al., 1989; Davis and Venkatesh, 2000). Other researchers defined different research constructs to study aspects of electronic banking services powered by the Internet (Chang, 2007; Kivijärvi et al., 2007; Isern, 2008). A large and growing body of scholarly research (Chang, 2007; Chang, 2009; Kivijärvi et al., 2007; Sukkar and Hasan, 2005) has explored how customers of banks perceived and reacted to change occasioned by technology-driven innovations in serving their banking needs. The observed change was about how introduction of Internet banking positively transformed the quality and mode of service delivery to customers. Some of the resourceful researches investigated customers' expectations from the change (Chang, 2007), factors that influenced customer acceptance or rejection of the change (Chang, 2009), and the cause and level of customer trust or distrust in the change (Kivijärvi et al., 2007). Sukkar and Hasan (2005) developed a model to explain market acceptance of Internet banking in developing countries.

The studies point to the need to appreciate the premise of the emergent change in terms of its goal to improve the quality and mode of service delivery in the banking industry. The change also has positive implication for efficient transactions processing in banking. Chang (2007), for instance, corroborated significant attributes of service quality that were hitherto overlooked in marketing calculations of the banks. In some cases, as in Chang's (2009) study, factors such as perceived privacy protection, perceived security, and consumer innovativeness correlated positively with customers' intention to accept change. Kivijärvi et al. (2007) made a similar finding in their investigation of influence of consumer trust on acceptance of electronic banking service. They found that trust in Internet banking was more among Finish than Portuguese customers. The Portuguese Internet banking users, on the other hand, exhibited more trust in the information, measured in terms of "the accuracy of the information" and "the completeness and relevance of the information" (p. 57). However, there was no indication of differences in respondents' overall trust in Internet banking, a result that also supported the researchers' related finding of partial corroboration that observed cross-cultural differences affected trust in online Internet services.

The efficacy of the application, as well as the need and acceptance of the Internet in e-commerce transactions processing has remained a growing field of research for faculty and other scholars. The Sukkar and Hasan (2005) study contributes to the literature on the subject and its budding body of knowledge.

Like Chang (2009), the researchers offered a critical review of the usual TAM and adapted it to propose an expanded TAM. Doing so, however, their objective differed from Chang's. While Chang focused on behavior that informed adoption of online financial services, Sukkar and Hasan were concerned with operationalizing a TAM that would be appropriate for the study of e-commerce in developing countries. Their study can be credited with pioneering scholarly efforts to understand market response to the Internet revolution in banking from the perspective of developing countries.

A related study, Isern (2008), was premised on the innovation in electronic banking and financial services delivery caused by groundbreaking advances in information and communications technology. Tracing some of the resultant significant positive changes, she observed that electronic banking was thriving in countries across the globe "as clients click their mouse, press telephone keys, and slide cards to conduct their banking" (p. 1). As the driving force behind the observed changes permeated the banking industry, its influence manifested itself mainly in shifts in competition strategies. The thinking of the researcher, in view of the radical innovations, was that the global financial services industry was changed bound under the influence of electronic banking and financial infrastructure—typical of the Schumpeterian competition (pp. 1–2). This implied positive paradigm shift underscored the primary cause of the study which sought to establish cross-country relationships between technology-driven innovations and competition in the financial services industry. Perhaps the usefulness of this study is best seen in its improvement on competition theory by introducing breakthroughs in the information and communications technologies applicable to banking. The value of the study is also underscored by its broad scope. That made it possible for the researcher to tap experiences in countries from different regions of the world, including industrialized and less developed countries.

At the level of organizations, Gallo (2008) explored how resources possessed by strategic industries impacted their responses to changes in their business environments. Using the banking industry as setting, she researched the correlation between resources and response of organizations to external factors that impelled changes in business practices. For her, the banking industry presented a good choice in view of its experience of significant regulatory or deregulatory changes and maneuverings over the years. Besides, the industry has a good rating on amenability to empirical studies. Also, her research measures affected, albeit in varying degrees, all the banks subsumed under her study object. Gallo had assumed, at the outset, that the nature and quality of response to shocks caused by changes in the external business environment was a function of an organization's resource profile. Findings departed from her hypothesis in terms of predictability or similarity of patterns among firms. In relating firms to their resources, the study nonetheless proved the former to be preeminent (p. vii). There was an indication that some intrinsic factors could have a more decisive impact on how organizations responded to exogenous changes that affect their operations. (ibid)

CREATION, NATURE, AND DYNAMICS OF NOVEL RISKS IN BANKING REVOLUTION

Banking revolution in developing economies was much-heralded. Eventually, it dawned with increasing incidence of risks. Most of the risks were novel in their creation and dynamics. The revolution was a no mean feat—no doubt about it. But it's also much-vaunted in a sense. Apparently risk attendant on it dilutes the feat. Thus the revolution should be put into perspective. It left a trail of novel and difficult risks in its wake. Stakeholders in banking now contend with a myriad of risks in the wake of the revolution. The risks are rooted in advancing technologies, especially in the information and communications spheres.

Two critical resources—the Internet and chip technology—constitute the foundation and pillars of the revolution in banking. The so-called age of armchair, brick, and mortar, banking had run out of favor—and, building on the Internet technology, the age of silicon chip supervened. The need of stakeholders in banking ran to banking in real time under the circumstances. A new era of prestige banking dawned as innovative financial products and services took center stage. Unfortunately, fraudsters responded by honing their skills and methods. This reaction and situation created novel risks in banking—some of which I discuss in this chapter. It also set the stage for new and enduring challenges of risk control for bank managements in developing economies.

The result is that while bank managements are ever devising risk control measures, the fraudsters are equally unrelenting. Sometimes, particular risk controls are aborted at conceptual stages. This happens when it is realized that the fraudsters have answers to the intended controls. The implication is that fraudsters really anticipate—and sometimes—successfully preempt and counter bank risk control measures. Interestingly, they do so relying on the same technological innovation that underlies the revolution in banking in the first place. Strange though this may sound, it pictures the complication of novel risks in banking revolution.

Let me now discuss some of the typical examples of risks which revolution in banking occasioned and is sustaining. Critical risks are associated with Internet fraud, cybercrime, and cards fraud.

Internet Fraud (General)

The Internet—together with its associated and underlying technologies—is the chief agent of the revolution in banking. It has had profound impact on the conduct of business and personal activities. We all talk about the globalization phenomenon. I mean the radical engagement of technologies to transform the world into a so-called global village. It is to the credit of the Internet that hope for this change—anticipation of a time when all humanity would live in one global but virtual village—is now a reality.

The flipside of the Internet is that fraudsters manipulate it in equally profound but criminal ways. A typical manipulation that is a major side effect of the Internet is its use to defraud banks and their customers. This manner of fraud is as novel as it remains a worrisome albatross for the stakeholders in banking. It is one setback that taints the Internet as a revolutionary technological breakthrough.

Ideally, PINs and passwords are used in e-banking to authenticate electronic transactions and documents. That is why they are prime targets of financial crimes and the fraudsters. Thus, just as the Internet has great benefits for mankind, it has also dislocated the natural tendencies of most people and businesses. In these positive and negative ways, the Internet continues to impact all facets of human activities.

Phishing

Internet-aided email and SMS scams are nowadays a common mechanism of novel risk in banking. The Internet has made it possible for individuals to conduct certain banking transactions online via e-mails and GSM phones. The latter—more commonly referred to as telebanking—and the former are popular online banking services. The use of, and reliance on, banks' websites for Internet banking is also common. These Internet banking media are popular, especially among professionals, executives, and to less extent, the working class. Online banking particularly appeals to those who work to very tight schedules and therefore have less or no time for other banking platforms.

Banking online via websites, telephone or email tends to be fraught with risk—just as other forms of Internet banking. It affords customers facility to make inquiries, check account balances, pay bills, transfer money, and generally conduct simple self-service banking. Usually code, PIN, password, or token is required to authenticate the transactions. Unfortunately, fraudsters often manipulate these security features and defraud banks and accountholders. This happens especially where fraudsters set up fake websites of banks or send emails purported to be sent by the banks with the intention of getting PIN, password, or other banking information all by deception.

In the particular case of telebanking, certain software could be secretly used to install a code that diverts calls or messages to another phone. Thus the original phone owner will not receive call or SMS confirming updates to their bank account details. The message or call is rather diverted to the fraudulent phone. This will be real risk where the updates involve change of PIN or password. That way an accountholder could be swindled out of money.

Cybercrime

The banking economy around the world has been under a serious threat occasioned by climbing incidence of cybercrime. As usual, computer—and, of course, the Internet—facility is used for the crime. In a typical cybercrime or fraud, money is obtained by trick or deception from a bank account through the Internet. Some criminal illegally obtains the money by deceiving or tricking the accountholder or other targeted victim on the Internet. Suffice it to say that cybercrime is committed mostly on e-banking web platform.

The criminals use discreet schemes—all of which border on deception or trick—on their victims. That way they are able to elicit key banking security details which they now use to defraud the bank or accountholder. There is one real task for fraudsters in all cases of Internet-related financial crimes, especially cybercrimes that culminate in bank frauds. That task is how to know the PIN or password for particular bank accounts or customers. Cybercrime or other fraud committed on the Internet wouldn't be possible without knowing and using accountholder PIN or password.

Whether at a cybercafé, or a cyber in office or at home, some revolutionary technology makes it possible for criminals to access PINs and passwords for bank accounts. There may be several methods fraudsters adopt to achieve this goal. One likely method might be the use of keyboard reader. Once installed on a computer secretly—in this case, usually with criminal intention—keyboard reader records and stores user Internet or electronic banking and other information details. Nowadays cybercrime has become a criminal battleground, ostensibly a fast-growing industry of a so-called new economy.

Cards Fraud

Credit and debit cards frauds are perhaps the commonest examples to illustrate risk associated with technological revolution in banking. Fraud manifests itself mainly in criminal use of stolen cards to defraud banks and their customers. In addition to lost cards, fraud is perpetrated through forgery. A fraudster can hack into a bank's cards databases or a cardholder's computer and access critical banking information and details. Armed with the information, they can use a stolen or cloned card to draw money from a bank account. Sadly, while cards transactions and operations are booming in developing and emerging economies, answers have not yet been found to equally burgeoning cards frauds.

It may be possible for fraudsters to maneuver security of cards and swindle banks and cardholders out of money. Whenever card fraud occurs, it always presents a puzzle to unravel how security features of the card—such as chip, hologram, and so on—were manipulated to perpetrate the fraud in a cardholder's account. Yet, with the facility of advanced technology at the disposal of a fraudster, it might be possible to maneuver security features of chip-embedded cards.

MECHANISMS OF NOVEL RISKS IN BANKING REVOLUTION

The novel risks in banking revolution are somewhat interrelated and tend to share common mechanisms. Certain key words—Internet, computer, database, PIN, password, technology, e-banking, and so on—used in explaining the creation, nature, and dynamics of the risks underscore their interrelationships and commonality. Similarly, the mechanisms of the risks have much in common. In one way or another, the risks are rooted in hacking, cloning, deceit, and forgery—all of which constitute the Internet banking fraud mechanisms. For example, hackers use some technology to crack bank network computers, servers, or databases to either steal or change particular information, usually for fraudulent purposes.

There could be different settings but similar purpose for other mechanisms of fraud. Often the approach to fraud could be the use of convincing scams. Take deliberately misleading emails and SMSs in scams as example. The scams, usually persuasive, tend to be targeted at unsuspecting bank customers and accountholders. Victims are persuaded to read the emails or SMSs and carry out instructions contained in them, or to click on some "service" or other Internet site of a phantom bank. The idea tends to be "persuade the victims to believe that they could gain particular benefits if they follow the scams." For example, a scam may be in form of asking a bank accountholder to update some urgent information need on their Internet banking platform.

Those who follow the instruction lose security of their online banking PINs or passwords which the fraudsters use illegally to transfer money electronically from their accounts. In most cases, gullible bank customers are the victims of these scams. I should now briefly discuss some elements of the mechanisms of the novel risks to bring out their linkages more clearly. I focus on hacking, identity theft, cloning, email and SMS scams, and the use of computers and GSM phones for crimes.

Hacking into Computers and Databases

Technological revolution in banking has been a fertile ground for hacks targeted at bank servers, network computers of banks, personal computers of bank customers, and central databases of banks. Hacking exposes a bank, its customers and their accounts to some financial loss.

Hackers, for example, take advantage of the Internet to access databases of banks and perpetrate fraud. Hacking cracks security features of bank databases, rendering them vulnerable to information leakage and stealing. Hackers operate in a discreet manner, ever secretly exploring ways of getting information from network computers or servers. Their intention could also be to manipulate or alter information on computer databases. The targets of hacking include security codes, PINs of bank customers, and passwords for bank accounts used for Internet and online transactions.

The mechanism of hack remains shrouded in absolute secrecy. It is believed that hackers use some technological but secret means—most likely software installed on their computers—to get into their victims' computers without their permission or approval. Their objective, doing so, is to get or change specific information on particular accounts or databases which is then used, in most cases, to defraud the bank or its customers. Hacking is easier where computers or Internet browsers record or store—and this is often the case—user details such as codes, PINs, passwords, and browsing history.

Cloning Smartcard Chips and Websites

This is yet another example of the mechanisms of fraud that exacerbate risks occasioned by banking revolution in developing economies. As a scheme to defraud a bank or its customer, cloning is both a novel and confounding cause of risk in banking, especially in developing economies. It somewhat operates in the manner of Internet and identity theft frauds. Like these, it uses sophisticated technologies to crack bank databases. Often it does so taking advantage of security loopholes on the databases. The sophistication of cloning is as amazing as it is puzzling. The fraud occurs mainly in electronic banking, and is particularly applicable to cards operations (i.e., credit and debit card banking transactions).

It would seem that fraudsters adopt a method comprising four main steps to perpetrate the crime of cloning in banking. In the first place, the PIN or password for a customer's bank account is criminally obtained. Second, the PIN or password—now at the disposal of the fraudster—is copied onto a new but counterfeit chip. At the third step, the PIN or password is then used on an account different from that from which it was copied. Usually, such account is opened with fake or doctored documents and therefore fraudulent. Curiously, this implies that the usual authentication of account opening documents is bypassed. Finally, withdrawals that are made from the fraudulent account are electronically passed to (i.e., debited from) the authentic account.

There is yet another common type of cloning the mechanism of which departs from the foregoing. It does not involve manipulation of the chip technology. Instead, a bank's website or specific product or service site is cloned and posted on the Internet. The real and cloned websites would have very subtle nuances of difference, though. However, it would take an inquisitive mind to discern and spot the differences. For example, the cloned website would usually offer the same banking platforms and facilities as the real one—including Internet and online banking. Without taking care to know the real website, bank customers could be easily swindled out of money. This happens more frequently when the customers unwittingly conduct Internet or online banking transactions on the fake website.

Technological revolution in banking facilitates this crime and risk attendant on it. Otherwise, it wouldn't have been possible for fraudsters to clone themselves (or create multiples of themselves) and perpetrate bank fraud.

Theft of Identities of Bank Customers

Fraud relating to identity theft in banking is common and really disturbing. In identity theft crime, fraudsters usually target particulars of bank customers and accounts held on a database. They adopt some criminal schemes to steal customer personal information pertinent to their object.

The use of misleading text messages from GSM phones—popularly referred to as SMS for short—is common and has been on the increase. On occasion, depending on the target of interest and the stakes, e-mail frauds and SMS deception would be complementary and effective. There could be other criminal schemes, but e-mail and SMS scams stand out. The usual prime targets are customer bank details such as account number, PIN, and password.

Fraudsters employ the schemes to elicit one or more of these critical account details from unsuspecting customers. In some cases, spurious SMS or e-mails are used to solicit key account information. Equipped with all or any of the security information, a fraudster can draw or transfer money with ease from a bank account. Usually electronic banking, more commonly referred to as e–banking, is the means used for such fraud.

MITIGATING RISKS OF REVOLUTION IN BANKING

On occasion, banks take exception to card frauds. They claim that accountholders would have compromised their passwords or PINs for the frauds to succeed. Insisting on this argument, they repudiate liability for the frauds. Of course the accountholders would want to debunk such claim as spurious and unfounded. Doing so, they accuse the banks or their employees of negligence, dereliction, and collusion. Accountholders must have incontrovertible evidence. Otherwise their accusation would not make sense.

In the ensuing accusations and recriminations, bank-customer relationship suffers. In the end, the banks would bow to reason and allow peace to prevail. They take the loss willy-nilly. Usually, the banks do so under the auspices of fraud preventive and control directives of the regulatory authorities. However, taking the loss is always a bitter pill to swallow. In most cases, an observer would find it difficult to take sides—whether the bank or accountholder is right—in the issue at stake. Bank employees could compromise on fraud overtures, or collude with fraudsters outright. Similarly, it is possible for bank accountholders to willfully compromise their passwords or PINs. Tough! You would imagine—or wouldn't you? Looking into the risks and possible solution from both bank and customer perspectives is pertinent. Now the question is where should this conflict go from here? Your guess is as good as mine. Indeed, what happens is anybody's guess under the circumstances.

Yet novel risks in banking revolution should be stemmed one way or another. Interestingly, the risks affect the banks and customers alike. Therefore, an effective approach to mitigating the risks should involve roles by the bank managements—as well as the bank customers. The two parties should have individual and joint responsibility to deal with the risks. In the following discussions, I explore the specific roles that bank managements and bank customers are expected to fulfill in mitigating novel risks occasioned by revolution in banking. The bulk of the responsibility for novel risks control lies with bank managements. Let me at once summarize the expected risk-mitigating roles of the customers. I proceed thereafter with discussions about those of bank managements.

There are simple, but often neglected, and yet effective precautions that bank customers should take to prevent novel risks concomitant with revolution in banking. It is essential, for example, for bank customers to install Internet security software on their computers. In addition to solving the dangers of virus attack, it mitigates risk of e-mail and SMS scams. The risk of cybercrime can also be mitigated, in much the same vein. In the absence of a personal computer, such as laptop or other notebook, it is always safer to use only reputable and credible cybercafés for Internet banking. However, the use of cybercafés of any sort in itself demands vigilance. This is necessary to prevent identity theft and other cybercrimes.

Users of cybercafés should also avail themselves of yet another precautionary and risk-mitigating measure. They should ensure that they clear browsing histories of the websites they visited—and, especially, on which they conducted Internet or online banking. This should be done before logging out on the computer or Internet browser. A similar risk control measure concerns care in choosing computer and phone service centers. There is need here again to patronize only reputable and credible service centers. Such service centers are available in the cities, and are mostly owned by IT operators. The original equipment manufacturers (OEM) also provide or endorse some service centers.

Bank Management's Roles in Novel Risks Control

I must say that bank managements have always been at the forefront of novel risks management. Of course, it is proper for them to take the lead in managing risks attendant on banking revolution. One reason is that the risks pose a real threat to banks as going concerns. There is need—talking about another reason—to sustain the confidence of the customers in banks. Thus bank managements should ever court customer trust and do anything but allow it to wane. There are specific ways in which bank managements can—and usually do—contribute effectively to mitigating novel risks occasioned by revolution in banking. I identify four of the ways—sustained education of bank customers on fraud mechanisms and prevention, security of bank websites, secure encryption of data and files, and adoption of unique banking codes. Of course, computer audit, and reconciliation of accounts are equally pertinent.

Customer Education

Banks perhaps spend enormous portion of money earmarked for novel risks control on customer education. Banking advertisements advising measures to ensure security of Internet and online banking platforms are a common sight on newspapers, radios, televisions, and social media networks. Banks also use emails and text messages to sensitize their customers to the risks associated with electronic banking. The messages are really about how to detect email and SMS scams. Often the messages, carefully worded, enjoin bank customers to ignore strange, often enticing, emails. The same applies to curious text messages.

Scams tend to work on the human psyche. A typical scam creates and puts fear of some phantom banking risk into the targets—usually particular bank customers. The targets are then advised to take particular action which, if they do—usually unwittingly, facilitates fraud on their bank accounts. Typical action demands on bank customers in scams include—but are not limited to—request or instruction to disclose, update, or change their PIN or password as a check on a phantom risk. Unfortunately, some customers follow the instruction and, doing so, fall prey to the scam.

In response, banks nowadays step up customer education on how to detect scams and related financial crimes. Banks execute customer education program in several ways, including:

- Warning about the dangers of disclosing PINs, passwords, or other banking codes to a third party—including spouses, children, and friends.
- Caution that the bank will never ask for a customer's PIN, password, or other banking code via email, text message, or other medium.
- Advice that on no account should a customer act on emails or text messages asking for security information on their bank account.
- Alerting customers to new and evolving fraud tendencies and mechanisms, as well as preventive and control measures.
- Informing customers about how to recognize authentic emails and text messages from the bank. The banks advise the criteria customers should adopt to identify genuine messages as follows:
  - Text messages must always be sent to the same telephone number the customer filled in when opening their account with the bank.
  - Emails must always be sent to same email address filled in by the customer in their account opening applications forms.
  - SMSs and emails from the bank must always originate from unmistakable online addresses of the bank with which the customers should be familiar—as in, trendbank@trendbank.com.cn; customerservice@freshbanknigerialimited.com; alerts@allseasonsbank.co.uk; and so on.

Security of Bank Websites

Banks tend to adequately secure their websites. They do so as a fraud preventive measure. More security is seen on Internet and online banking platforms. The appeal of this mode of websites security consists in the difficulty it poses to fraudsters. It is difficult—if not impossible—to crack such secure banking platforms and sites. Banks have relied on this method of fraud prevention without regrets over the years. However, it is necessary for bank managements to adopt proven security software administered by credible IT firms and computer experts. The services of expert IT firms usually come in handy. Certain security policies and software—such as Windows firewall, antivirus software, spam blocking, and electronic filters—complement foregoing website security measures. Secure websites remain a must for fraud prevention and control in an age of banking revolution.

Encryption of Data and Files

Banks have a duty at all times to secure customer and other information on their databases, as well as data fed into their network computers. This responsibility entails information protection using a special code. When this is done, it becomes difficult—if not impossible—for fraudsters or unauthorized persons to access—let alone criminally manipulate—the information. Banks fulfill this role through a process referred to as encryption. This may sound too technical to the learner. Let me simplify its meaning. Encryption is a scientific process of protecting information on a computer system from criminal or other manipulations. It involves shielding computer information held on databases or files from unauthorized access, use, or change. Protection is achieved when the relevant information is put into a special code, often electronically generated. The essence of the code is that only some people—usually the authorized persons—can access the information for specific approved uses. Thus securing encryption of information on databases, or storing computer files in encrypted form, is an effective way bank managements can check risks of revolution in banking.

Adoption of Unique Banking Codes

Some unique codes have been in use to beef up security features of bank accounts and transactions in the wake of novel risks occasioned by revolution in banking. The codes help to check fraud and strengthen the integrity of banking transactions. The effectiveness of the codes in fraud control derives from their uniqueness—making it difficult, if not impossible, for fraudsters to manipulate. The main codes and related security devices include:

Branch code: used to prepare cheques to be sent to the clearing house in an order that groups them according to banks on which they are drawn.
Sort codes: a series of numbers printed on cheques and other financial instruments to identify particular branches of a bank that should handle them.
SWIFT code: the abbreviation of *Society for Worldwide Interbank Financial Telecommunication*—an organization that provides means for electronic payment through which member banks transfer money to one another.
MICR: abbreviation used in banking operations, especially in processing checks or other financial instruments for clearing. It refers to *Magnetic Ink Character Recognition*. A MICR check is a check that has MICR compatible features, or one that can be encoded on a payment instrument (i.e., cheque, draft, and so on) in clearing of the instrument.

There are several other security elements, including hologram, unique account numbers, bank verification number (BVN), secure code for online transactions, and tokens for Internet banking.

SUMMARY

Revolution and technological innovation have created and heightened concerns about novel risks in banking. This situation now leaves room for the novel risks to supervene and cause unanticipated financial losses to banks. The Internet underscores the technological revolution in modern banking. With its debut in late 20th century, theoretical constructs underlying methodological framework of banking became untenable. The traditional brick and mortar theory of banking became moribund and supplanted. The academia was eager to research and corroborate the new scientific revolution.

Stakeholders in banking now contend with a myriad of risks in the wake of the revolution. Typical risks which revolution in banking occasioned include Internet fraud, email and SMS scams, cybercrime, and cards fraud. These novel risks are somewhat interrelated and tend to share common tendencies. The mechanisms of the risks also have much in common. The risks are rooted in hacking, cloning, identity theft, deceit, and forgery—and affect the banks and customers alike. Thus an effective approach to mitigating the risks should involve roles by bank managements and customers.

Customer education, security of bank websites, encryption of data and files, adoption of unique banking codes, computer audit, and reconciliation of accounts are some of the effective risk-mitigation measures at the disposal of bank managements. The customers should—on their part—install Internet security software on their personal computers, and patronize only credible cybercafés, and clear browsing history. Yet, the use of cybercafés demands vigilance to prevent identity theft. The customers should exercise care in choosing computer and phone service centers, in much the same vein.

QUESTIONS FOR DISCUSSION AND REVIEW

1. In what specific ways are change-driven risks threatening the survival of banks as going concerns in developing economies?
2. How true is the view that domestic banks in developing economies seem not to be making progress on control of novel risks?
3. In what sense may it be right or wrong to argue that banking in developing economies goes through a recurring cycle of boom to bust?
4. How does the Internet underlie the scientific revolution, and sustain innovation, in contemporary banking?
5. What do you understand by the term "novel risks?" Which of the risks in modern banking would you consider novel—and why?
6. Should an effective approach to mitigate novel risks in banking necessarily involve roles by bank managements and customers?

REFERENCES

Chang, C.H., 2007. Customer Expectations of the Taiwan Banking Industry. Doctoral dissertation, Nova Southeastern University, 2007.

Chang, C.C., 2009. Consumers' Adoption of Online Financial Services: The Case of Taiwan. Doctoral dissertation, Alliant International University, San Diego, 2009.

Davis, F.D., 1989. Perceived usefulness, perceived ease of use and user acceptance of information technology. MIS Quart. 13 (3), 319–340.

Davis, F.D., Venkatesh, V., 2000. A theoretical extension of the technology acceptance model: four longitudinal field studies. Manag. Sci. 46 (2), 186–204.

Davis, F.D., Bagozzi, R.P., Warshaw, P.R., 1989. User acceptance of computer technology: a comparison of two theoretical models. Manag. Sci. 55 (8), 982–1003.

Gallo, D.M., 2008. Organizational Response to Change: A Resource-Based View from the Commercial Banking Industry. Doctoral dissertation, University of Massachusetts, 2008.

Isern, J., 2008. A Cross-Country Analysis of the Effects of E-banking and Financial Infrastructure on Financial Sector Competition: A Schumpeterian shift? Doctoral dissertation, Florida, Nova Southeastern University, 2008.

Kivijärvi, M., Laukkanen, T., Cruz, P., 2007. Consumer trust in electronic service consumption: a cross-cultural comparison between Finland and Portugal. J. Euromark. 16 (3), 51–65.

Sukkar, A., Hasan, H., 2005. Toward a model for the acceptance of Internet banking in developing countries. Inf. Technol. Dev. 11 (4), 381–398.

Chapter 4

Enterprise Risk Management—A Paradigm Shift and Applications in Banking

LEARNING FOCUS AND OBJECTIVES

I set out in this chapter to discuss the need for a holistic approach to risk management, one that is adapted to banking in developing economies. That adds value to the method in classical "silo" view approach. This implied paradigm shift solves problems inherent in treating banking risks in compartments. I pursue this end using framework of banking-oriented enterprise risk management (ERM). In doing so, I make my objectives to:

- Discuss the general and proven steps in risk management process which the dynamic nature of risk underlies.
- Analyze evolving risk management paradigm shift from the perspective of best practice in banking.
- Review and compare the classical "silo" view of risk management with the holistic ERM-inspired framework.

- Demonstrate the main features and applications of ERM as a risk control framework of banking in developing economies.
- Identify and discuss the significance, implications, and benefits of ERM to banks in developing economies.
- Examine the life cycle stages of risk management and relate the stages to the practice of banking in developing economies.

EXPECTED LEARNING OUTCOMES

There is a need to adapt a holistic framework of risk management to banking in developing economies. Such a "portfolio" view of risk will fill gaps in the classical method of treating risks in "silos." The ERM framework—with which I am concerned in this chapter—furnishes a paradigm shift on which the welcome holistic approach is founded. The reader will—after studying this chapter and doing the exercises in it—have learnt and been better informed about:

- Why effective management of risk is crucial for the success of a bank, especially in developing economies?
- Elements and factors that define risk and limit performance and growth of banks in developing economies.
- Methodical steps in risk management which the dynamic nature of risk and business environment underlie.
- How the classical method that views risk in "silos" contrasts a paradigm shift founded on a holistic perspective?
- The main features and applications of ERM as a risk control framework for banking in developing economies.
- Risk management best practice in banking—its inner workings and how it should power success of banking in developing economies.
- Applications and implications of the life cycle stages of risk management for banking in developing economies.

OVERVIEW OF THE SUBJECT MATTER

Although banking is bedeviled by a myriad of risks, four of the risks—credit risk, operational risk, liquidity risk, and market risk—stand out. There is a tendency to treat these and other risks in banking in "silos"—ostensibly to underscore their individualities and wider significance for banking in their respective spheres. While this approach may serve some useful purpose, it gives only a bird's eye view of the subject matter. A holistic theme that integrates all the facets of risks in contemporary banking is required. This gap has lingered without solution for long. I posit a paradigm shift that fills the gap. That is the main thrust of discussions in this chapter.

This approach represents a departure from the classical literature. The classical perspective focuses on assets, liabilities, and balance sheet management on which developing economy banks—like their counterparts elsewhere—have not fared well. Ironically, the authors of the classical literature gravitate toward the highly advanced financial economies of the developed nations—ostensibly to solve some complex financial issues. There are several exotic finance and banking titles that shed light on the leanings of the classical authors. The modeling of financial functions to explain some banking behavior is yet another example that is in the mold of the foregoing. Incidentally, these issues and the authors' method are alien to practical banking in the developing World. The observed shortcomings of the classical literature, highlighted above, strengthen the case for a paradigm shift on which the crux of this chapter—indeed the entire book—hinges.

A methodical approach should underlie the holistic approach and encapsulate the paradigm shift. I start by clearly defining the concept, and elements, of ERM. Then I review classical approach to risk management—comparing it with the paradigm shift—and highlighting, in doing so, implications for banking in developing economies. One of the outcomes of ERM implementation in banking is particularly intriguing. That outcome is the reorganization of bank risk management responsibilities right across the board. Nowadays ERM is conspicuous in the way banks organize functions and interfaces to mitigate risk. A chief risk officer now takes charge of all risk issues bank wide. Following this paradigm shift, internal control remains complementary but subordinated to risk management.

In this chapter and the entire book, I subsume emerging markets under developing economies. I posit that developing economy banking crisis is rooted in the interplay of, and failings in managing, composite risks. This approach does not obliterate emerging markets, but rather informs their standing as yet a part—but the topmost tier—of developing economies. I analyze the paradigm shift which this approach informs. In doing so, I define risk management best practice in banking. I discuss best practice inner workings. Then I pinpoint how risk management best practice should power success in developing economy banking.

MANAGING RISKS IN DOMESTIC AND FOREIGN SUBSIDIARY BANKS

Dealing with banking risks in more effective ways has been topical of late. Concern over risks in banking remains a question on everyone's lips. Of no less a commonplace is the quest for a dependable risk management technique in banking. A technique for risk control in banking would be adjudged dependable if it is simple, reliable, and cost effective. A simple technique ensures that members of the bank understand and can apply it correctly—and are accountable for its success at their individual work levels. With a reliable technique, the bank can anticipate, predict, and is assured of risk mitigation at a high or appreciable level of success. A good technique of risk management should, of course, be amenable to cost control. Otherwise it will lose much of its appeal for the stakeholders in banking and other interested members of the public. It follows that three factors—simplicity, reliability, and cost effectiveness—form the foundation of a good technique of risk management. These factors make varied inputs to defining risk management.

I explore risk management in order to define it in the context of present-day realities and demands of domestic and foreign subsidiary banking. Thereafter I look at the significance of risk management and pinpoint reasons that impel bothering with risk management in banking. I had defined risk in Chapter 1 from the perspectives of two opposing outcomes—threat and opportunity. These risk outcomes correspond to the characterization of risk in terms of uncertainty and loss. In both threat and opportunity, risk is underlain by uncertainty—and therefore the probability of loss or gain. Thus risk has a definite effect on some banking objective. One reason is that banking objectives—like those of most profit-motivated organizations—revolve around loss and gain. Ideally banks strive to avoid or mitigate loss and maximize or optimize gain concurrently. The second reason follows from the first. Loss avoidance and the pursuit of gain are primary motives for committing a bank's resources to risk management.

How then may one define risk management to underscore its very essence in banking correctly? This is the real question. The essence in question lies in appreciating the motives behind risk taking and risk management in banking. The quest of banks for a reliable technique of risk management—for all intents and purposes—transcends mere motives and wishful thinking. There is need to always anticipate and be conscious of uncertain future happenings in order to effectively manage risk. It becomes possible—doing so—for the banks to make informed risk management choices and decisions. The foundation is in adopting a precise definition of risk management that fits well with the bank's purposes. I now proceed with defining risk management. I do so against a backdrop of risk control needs of a bank as a going concern.

Simply defined, the phrase "risk management" refers to the process a bank adopts to keep adverse events effectively in check while maximizing opportunities open to the bank. This straightforward definition implies that a bank should take specific actions to forestall adverse events happening to it or its business, on the one hand, and to maximize the potentialities of gain in its business or other activities, on the other. Let me expand on this view. Risk management is really all about how a bank secures or positions itself, its resources, and its operations against possible dangers and to take advantage of opportunities. In order to achieve this goal, the bank must devise and implement an effective technique for anticipating the probability of the adverse events and opportunities. The technique should represent—or approximate to—some methodological framework that guides the bank to mitigate the effects of adverse events that might derail its objectives and cause some loss to it, and to tap opportunities in its industry that could result in some and sustained financial gain.

Domestic and foreign subsidiary banks face and need effective techniques for managing composite risks. Though, risk profiles and tendencies of the two sets of banks differ significantly. Yet the effectiveness and success of risk management in both types of banks hinge on the integration of logical approach and systematic execution. Good methodology for effective risk management should be simple, logical, and systematic. Its objective should be to help identify, analyze, mitigate, and monitor risk and opportunities in every banking function, activity, or process. Risks are not equally important to the cause of the bank. Therefore, risks should be prioritized and management requirements for the risks should also be properly coordinated for effective execution. This approach optimizes positive outcomes of the bank's resources deployed for managing the risks.

CASE STUDY 4.1 Quitting Job for Pastures New—Lessons in Banking Best Practice vs. Budget Goal

Jose went the extra mile to land a bank job. (Extracted, with minor changes, from Onyiriuba, L. (2013). On the road to self-actualization. NFS Data Bureau Limited, Lagos, pp. 26–28 Although this is a real life story, the names of the bank and individual in the tale are imaginary and do not relate to any known or unknown real bank or person anywhere. The story is purely for illustration purposes only, in order to demonstrate how some challenges of banking play themselves out in developing economies.) While salary of 25,000 naira per annum that he earned in his former employment was a lot of money to him, it was a meager income in Lagos setting. He always struggled to make ends meet. But he couldn't continue like that for long lest he got weighed down by the attendant pressure on him. Unfortunately, the stress reached its crescendo sooner than he bargained. He was caught between showing fairness to his employer, on the one hand, and going for his ultimate dream of working in a bank, on the other. He had thought that resigning his employment less than three months after taking it up would smack of ingratitude. But he also reasoned that doing otherwise would be tantamount to losing sight of the big picture. He allowed reason—typical of a business sense—to prevail under the circumstances. He decided to look for a bank job, purely in response to an inner voice that had relentlessly urged him to do so. In yielding to this imaginary voice, he reckoned that he would be seen as an ingrate or not, depending on how he handled his resignation. In order to relieve himself of that burden, he frankly discussed his planned disengagement with his boss.

During his job hunt, Jose crisscrossed South Northern Nigeria where he was bred in quest of acquaintances that had contacts in banks. He foreclosed the unwieldy approach of sending out numerous unsolicited applications for job to different employers. Such applications only made the statistics of an avalanche of letters for the garbage can. He travelled at different times to different parts of Northern Nigeria. One of his ports of call was Unique Country University from where he graduated for his bachelor's degree. He met some of his former lecturers. They were happy to see him. Jose could feel their empathy as he discussed his mission with them. He got a note to the head of strategy at New Era Bank Limited. He also obtained a reference to a Lagos businessman who was a major shareholder of Frontline Bank Limited.

Back in Lagos, Jose met New Era Bank's head of strategy in his office. He acted on the note Jose bore to him. He seemed swayed by Jose's first class honors degree, and asked his secretary to invite him for an interview. Jose started rounds of interviews with some members of the bank's management, one after another, a week or so later. The interviews with those functional heads were rigorous, but exciting. In the end, he met the bank's chief executive officer. Jose's interview with him seemed a mere formality since they ended up chatting. Jose was hardly done with procedures at New Era Bank when he received an invitation for interview from Frontline Bank. He attended the interview. It consisted of a three-man panel of interviewers, including the bank's chairman. It was not a serious interview per se; it was rather more of a chat. However, he learnt one important lesson from the approach he adopted in looking for work in the bank. Job hunt ceases to be drudgery with good academic qualifications, experience, and social network. The experience and social network aspects were the missing link—one which underlay the frustration he faced—in his previous job searches.

A week later he received a letter from New Era Bank offering him employment as an officer on a salary of 36,000 naira per annum. The remuneration package was outlandish relative to his previous ones. He was elated when he read the offer which till date represented a watershed in his career endeavors. It was an occasion when he landed his dream job for the first time in his entire hunt for a job. He couldn't believe that at last he had got a bank job, would become a banker, and would soon start earning jumbo salaries and allowances. It sounded incredible, but it was real. The following day he accepted and returned acknowledgement of the offer letter to the bank. Then he started assembling documents the bank required, including two references. In time he fulfilled employment requirements of the bank and for his level. He commenced work in the bank in its head office in Lagos. On that same day, he was drafted to the bank's training school to join a class of about 35 other employees of the bank. The class comprised mainly the newly employed and a few handpicked existing staff. They went through intensive orientation and training program, which culminated in a written exam at the end of its 3 weeks duration. The results of the exam were communicated to each of the employees privately and copied to their files with the human resources office.

Exercise for class or group discussion

1. Define the phrase "big picture?" In what ways do you think banks in developing economies may or may not lose sight of "the big picture?"
2. What would you say is and isn't in reference when the term 'business sense' is used as in the context of this tale?
3. Do you think that bank managements in developing economies always allow reason to prevail in difficult business situations?
4. How, in your opinion, should bank managements respond to an 'inner voice' urging them to be expedient in dealing with regulation?
5. In what ways may banks in developing economies not sacrifice tact for a rigorous and exciting staff recruitment interviews?
6. Why should banks in developing economies always commit themselves to cost-effective training and manpower development?

Tips for solving the exercise

Banks in developing economies can avail themselves of three main lessons which Jose's experience implies. First, Jose's being "caught between showing fairness to his employer, on the one hand, and going for his ultimate dream of working in a bank, on the other" is pertinent—and instructive too. On occasion, banks in developing economies do have similar conflicts. Sticking to risk management best practice tends to be in conflict with budget goals. Often crises that banks in developing economies face are rooted in such conflicts. Second, that Jose's "job hunt ceases to be drudgery with good academic qualifications, experience, and social network" implies that banks could attain their desired financial performance without bending the rules, cutting corners, or fiddling the books. Third—and in much the same vein—it is instructive that Jose "was drafted to the bank's training school" the same day he commenced work. It would be uncritical of a bank to assign jobs to new recruits without adequate preparation. Training comes in pretty handy as an effective risk control technique for banks in developing economies.

LIFE CYCLE OF RISK MANAGEMENT PROCESS IN BANKING

There are some variations in risk management process ordering. However, there is a common understanding among writers on risk management. A general belief is that the process of risk management follows some steps—however different—in every business, organization, or industry. Certain steps are identifiable and satisfy the criteria of general acceptability as the life cycle stages of risk management. Three basic steps stand out irrespective of the risk events or setting. Risk is identified in the first step. The risk is analyzed, and mitigated, in the second and third steps.

One other view of the life cycle stages of risk management favors yet a three-pronged process made up of risk assessment, solution to the risk, and confirmation of solution to the risk. The assessment phase itself is broken down further into three steps—starting with risk identification, followed by risk analysis, and ending with planning for risk control. A third school of thought opines that risk should be managed in seven stages. Risk managers, according to this view, should—first and foremost—define the setting for the risk control task. The risks are thereafter specifically identified, analyzed, and assessed at the second, third, and fourth stages respectively. The remaining three stages—dealing with the risks, monitoring and review of actions toward solving, or mitigating the risks, and interaction with the stakeholders in risk control to get feedback— follow suit in this sequence. Obviously, there is no uniformity among the various stages of risk management life cycle.

I adopt a neutral stance on the contrasting stages since—to my mind—each of the approaches has its merits and demerits. This is notwithstanding that the three schools of thought share a common understanding. They are all agreed that some ordered steps and methodology underlie effective risk management. I adopt a synthesis of the approaches in discussing the purpose, process, and issues underlying the life cycle stages of risk management. Although the stages enjoy general applications, I focus on their fit with the demands of—and implications for—modern banking. With this purpose in mind, I propose and discuss a five-pronged life cycle of the risk management process.

Defining Risk Control Contexts

Risk management in banking does not take place in a vacuum. It takes place in rather identifiable contexts. The contexts in which banks execute risk management programs could really be intriguing, if anything. Ideally, bank risk management process makes sense only when it is situated in particular business and priority contexts. The factors that affect risk taking behavior and approaches to risk management often include a broad range of elements and issues in the bank's business environment. Thus, a bank should always clearly define its risk control contexts as a strategic measure. In most cases, the bank's business focus and plan—as well as its target markets definition, and risk acceptance criteria—will make the risk control context in some but, perhaps, not all situations. On occasion, it may be necessary to integrate the bank's risk culture (if it's well established and shared bank wide) with the risk control context. In doing so, it is essential that planned risk control strategies and actions fit with the basic thrusts of the risk culture and its underlying principles. It may be necessary— depending on the circumstances of the bank, to highlight the bank's business objectives, risk appetite, and risk tolerance in defining risk control context.

Identifying Potential Risks

The actual process of risk management really starts with the identification of proven and potential risks in the banking industry—focusing, in doing so, on specific risks the bank faces. Risk identification is all about discovering, listing, and knowing as much as possible about the risks. It is necessary to list as many of the existing and potential risks as can be conceivably identified if possible. This implies knowing the number, types, and characteristics of the risks—as well as their nature, structure, and incidence. How the risks may affect specific and general objectives of the bank should also be identified and documented. Record should be similarly kept of the probability, intensity, and severity of all the identified risks. This information comes in handy in prioritizing the risks as part of their identification process. Often a risk register serves the risk listing and characterizing purposes at the identification stage. The register documents available and anticipated information about all the risks the bank faces. Information that a risk register contains depends on the needs of the bank. There may be some variations between one bank and another. However, most risk registers would contain some information in common—such as title of the risk, probability of its occurrence, possible impact of the risk, staffs responsible for the risk, and suchlike.

Analyzing Risk Events and Issues

Risk analysis follows the conclusion of risk identification in the systematic process of managing risks in banking. At the analysis stage, the identified risks are evaluated for further documentation and action. This involves a two-step process. The approach of the first step is qualitative. It describes the nature, patterns, and incidence of the identified risks and, doing so, addresses the questions of probabilities and impacts of the risks. It is also necessary to show how the elements of the risks articulate with each other and affect the bank's business objectives. A quantitative approach is adopted for risk evaluation in the second step. It may not be possible to strictly quantify all risks in every situation. Yet it is essential to devise or derive some quantitative measure of risk—if possible. Some logical procedure, usually a statistical device, is needed in most cases to quantify the risks. Risk quantification could be really challenging. Often the challenge arises in finding and applying a valid technique in determining the magnitude, or estimating the value, of the risks. There may be yet challenge in interpreting the calculated value of risk, on the one hand, and relating it to the bank's or industry's standard risk acceptance criteria, on the other. A wide, small, or no variation is possible. What really matters is the extent of deviation of the calculated risk value from the standard criterion. That gives an insight into the magnitude of risk faced by the bank.

Mitigating Impacts of Risks

The whole essence of risk management in banking is to adopt and institutionalize a sensible approach to mitigating possible adverse effects of potential risks on the objectives of the bank as a going concern. Usually, risk mitigation is intended to minimize the adverse effects of risks, and maximize risk opportunities—and, doing so, optimize the bank's business objectives. The risk management process should ordinarily culminate with risk mitigation. This is because mitigation of risk is the end to which all the risk management processes are geared. In practice, however, risk management in banking extends to seeking, getting, and integrating feedback from the stakeholders. This terminal stage includes review of the fallout of the RM process. It includes monitoring of the process and communication about it at every stage of its execution. Risk mitigation, in concrete terms, focuses on suggestion of practical solutions to the risks. Risk is ultimately mitigated when measures designed to alleviate it is practicable. However, the main risk-mitigating measures at this stage are threefold. There is need to determine and appraise likely responses to the risks in the first place. Second, there should be careful evaluation of the risk-mitigation implications of choices open to the bank. Certain factors, such as the bank's risk appetite, risk tolerance, and cost-benefit analysis of the response options are always pertinent. Then the bank makes its choices of appropriate responses—those that fit well with its cause and need for effective risk management.

Monitoring and Feedback

The final stage of risk management—monitoring, review, and communication—build on feedback from the stakeholders in the bank. The feedback itself relates to all the risk management activities in the preceding stages. Essentially, the focus in this stage is to verify that applicable risk control measures are executed as planned at the prior stages. This focus involves a review of the risk control contexts, assumptions, objectives, and response outcomes. It is also necessary to review the bank's overall risk management policies and decisions which the policies underlie. The review is necessary to confirm that risk control outcomes are not skewed by possibly changing decision variables, such as banking regulation, operating environment, government policies, and so on. The foregoing is achieved against a backdrop of regularly monitored risk control activities and processes. Without monitoring, it would be difficult to assess the quality—and therefore effectiveness—of risk control assumptions, planning, and policy execution. It would not be easy, in that case, to vouch for the accuracy and validity of the overall risk management process. An integral part of the risk management process in the last stage is communication of information pertinent to execution at the stages to all the stakeholders in the bank. Communication reinforces risk management through information to, and feedback from, the stakeholders.

ERM CONCEPT—A PARADIGM SHIFT AND APPLICATIONS IN BANKING

ERM evolved out of the increasing need to devise a holistic process framework that would supplant and address the shortcomings of the traditional, "silo" view, approach to solving bank risk problems. The ERM framework departs from the traditional (classical) method in positing a "portfolio view" approach to managing risks in banking. Rather than take on risks in compartments or isolation, it centralizes and aggregates the risks in a way that ensures effective control planning, execution, and coordination.

The classical method of risk control—on the contrary—was rooted in the thinking that organizational risks should be treated in compartments in order to have good results. This thinking gave rise to the metaphorical use of the word "silo" to reflect the reasoning behind the compartmentalization view. Thus the metaphor applies to define and manage risks from the perspective of strict compartmentalization of organizational activities and functions. This represents and is the basis of so-called "silo" view of risks that characterizes the classical method. Risk management targets, outcomes, and responsibilities were defined and apportioned accordingly.

Method in classical risk control, with its adoption of a "silo" view of the risks, has implications in the context of risk management in banking. The implications derive from its shortcomings. First, it emphasizes management of the core banking functions and risks—mainly credit risk, liquidity risk, market risk, financial risk, business risk, and operational risk. Its emphasis was usually on mitigating physical hazards based on a strong insurance orientation. In most cases, it approaches risk management in an ad-hoc manner and usually geared to one-shot adverse events. Often the risks on target are foreseeable and within the execution planning time frame.

Taking a close look at Table 4.1, reflecting the risk control focus of the classical method, one notices a major setback. It neglects a whole gamut of risks,

TABLE 4.1 Depiction of the Classical Risk Management Process

	Credit risk	Liquidity risk	Market risk	Operational risk
Officer in charge	Chief credit officer	Treasurer	Chief financial officer	Chief of internal audit/operations control
Focuses on	• Management of counterparty credit risks based on some predetermined criteria. • Risk assets portfolio structure, measurement, and optimization • Reengineering of risk assets portfolio through loan securitization and creation of financial assets in derivative products	• Managing risks inherent in the dynamics of bank assets and liabilities to attain set liquidity targets • Trading in financial assets and instruments in interbank and other financial markets • Monitoring prevailing conditions to keep abreast of developments in the financial markets	• Mitigating interest and foreign exchange rates risks based on target investment limits • Management of portfolio returns on the bank's financial investments • Assessment of growth trends—expansion, limits, and implications	• Internal controls of everyday operational hazards associated with internal and external risk events affecting the bank • Inspection, audit, and review of banking operations and processing Controls • Provision of insurance against unforeseeable risks

most of which affect banking outcomes in profound ways. Strategic and reputational risks are typical. The same goes for country risk, especially in developing economies. Second, it focuses on assets, liabilities, and balance sheet management. It does this on the assumption that success in banking depends solely on balance sheet management. This thinking is erroneous for two main reasons. There are myriads of banking activities and functions that are also prone to risk—besides the balance sheet elements. Strictly focusing on balance sheet management lacks merit. It does not address influences on risks in the elements of the balance sheet, on the one hand, and interaction between risks and the influences in the outcomes of risk management, on the other.

The shortcomings of the classical method were now propitious for a paradigm shift. There are four main features of the paradigm shift. It debunked the "silo" view and tenets of the classical method in the first place. It posits a holistic and integrated approach to banking risks control. Its approach to risk management builds on investigation of influence of composite risks on banking outcomes. Then it underlay the emergence of ERM as a generic approach to effective risk control in organizations. The paradigm shift is seen in the invention of a new approach to composite risks control to supplant the classical method. In response to the new thinking, banks reengineered activities, operations, and processes. It also became necessary to reorganize risk management functions. Thus the notion of paradigm shift, strictly speaking, is founded on faulting the traditional "silo" view of banking risks. Soon the paradigm shift started taking root as banks embraced the change.

Ultimately the paradigm shift swept the business world as it recommends and defends a "portfolio" view of, and approach to managing, organizational risks. The word "portfolio" view may sound inappropriate in this context. It can be substituted with "full picture" of organizational risks without a change in understanding of its intent. Appreciating that risk management paradigm shift adopts a holistic view of composite risks is what really matters. This is unlike the classical method that emphasizes risk individualities and, doing so, treats risks in isolation from one another. In essence, the paradigm shift is the departure of the tenets of the "portfolio" view from those of the "silo" view. As Table 4.2 shows, the former—which ERM represents—posits a holistic approach to managing banking risks, many of which are composite in nature. This implies unification

TABLE 4.2 ERM Approach to Risk Management in Banking

Chief risk officer (CRO)				
Credit risk	Liquidity risk	Market risk	Operational risk	Hybrid risks
Chief credit officer	Treasurer	Financial controller	Chief inspector	Business, operations, and internal control managers

of all risk management approaches under a centralized control division headed by an executive-level director, designated as chief risk officer of the bank.

ERM HALLMARKS AND STRICT APPLICATIONS IN BANKING

Let me now briefly summarize the high points of the paradigm shift before proceeding with discussion of ERM functions and significance to banking in developing economies. The paradigm shift favors centralization of risk management, coordinated at the executive level. This forms the central dynamic of the mechanics of enterprise risk management in banking. Centralization makes it possible for the bank to adopt integrated and continuous treatment of all composite risks across all activities and functions bank wide. The paradigm shift not only marked an auspicious emergence of ERM, it created varied opportunities for risk understanding, diversification, and mitigation in banking. What then does the ERM concept mean, connote, and imply in banking? Words and phrases such as holistic framework, integrated approach, value-added process, and so on are often used to underscore the meaning and significance of ERM in banking. It is necessary to have an apt definition of ERM—beyond the insights which the regular words and phrases used to describe it furnish.

An integral part of the ERM's "portfolio" view of risks is its consideration of interrelationships between individual risks, on the one hand, and between the risks and influences on them, on the other. In all cases, the task of ERM is to apply and relate its "portfolio" view to the whole organization at three execution levels—business, operations, and organizational. COSO (2004), perhaps, offers the most authoritative definition of ERM—one that has gained wide international acclaim. COSO's definition of ERM lays emphasis on the involvement of the board of directors, top executives, and key employees in the risk management process. It demands full commitment of these personnel to ERM and helping achieve its cause. ERM tenets, according to COSO, should be applied in strategy formulation across all the enterprise activities. It suggests that ERM strategy should be informed by the same enterprise objectives it is intended to achieve, and for which it is designed in the first place. COSO expatiates on its definition further—pointing to other aspects of the ERM framework. ERM strategy should guide risk identification, evaluation, and mitigation—and, especially, assure attainment of the enterprise objectives.

The ERM philosophy and framework bear all the hallmarks of best practice expected in banking and to which banks in developing economies should aspire. ERM in banking should, first and foremost, be seen as a goal-directed process aimed at solving all risk problems that a bank faces now, or may face in the future. It guides effective risk management in specific ways. It defines elements of the risk management process, advises a unified approach to treating risks, and guides on how to effectively execute, review, communicate, and monitor bank wide process of risk management. It is possible to fulfill these demands because a common ERM language—however devised, but communicated—to which every bank employee is made to key is a forceful bonding factor. This is seen as not only strategic but a critical success factor for ERM in banking.

ERM FUNCTIONS AND SIGNIFICANCE IN BANKING

People from all walks of life believe that effective risk management is a key factor in surviving the stresses and hazards of everyday living. This fact is no less made manifest in banking. Indeed, there is no gainsaying the significance of effective risk management in banking. Without absolutely mitigating risks, a bank stands exposed to the danger of avoidable crisis that can lead to distress and failure. For this reason, bank managements can do anything but neglect to manage risk well. Of course they cannot afford to ignore potential risk events either. The reason is that an ignored risk portends more danger for the bank than a neglected risk. Yet neither neglect nor ignorance of risk is propitious for good bank management. Thus stakeholders in banking should—and indeed do—bother about risk and the effectiveness of risk management.

I examine the significance of risk management for banking from two main perspectives—the high stakes in risk taking and variability of expected risk-taking outcomes. Uncertainty about the probability of two possibilities—threat and opportunities—complicates and exacerbates concern about risk. Thus the cause and success of risk management in banking are rooted in solving risk-taking issues. However, it is the ability to temper business exposure, that is, perhaps, the greatest feat in managing risks in banking. The significance of risk management in banking that I now discuss derives from this thinking. Good risk management program and best practice, which ERM symbolizes, fulfills significant functions in banking. It—amongst other functions are as follows:

Builds and Broadens Risk Consciousness

Dealing with risks in banking will not be easy or possible if the employees across all cadres are not made aware of possible risks, as well as their incidence and probabilities of occurrence. In order to solve risk problems, it is necessary that a bank deliberately builds risk consciousness in the employees. This entails doing everything possible to increase risk awareness among the employees. Thus the employees can appreciate how risk taking may be beneficial—and also be detrimental—to the bank and its present and future business activities. Awareness of changing patterns and incidence of risk bank wide is strategic for the bank's survival. It is critical to effective risk management in the first place. The reason is that a bank cannot manage risks of which it is not aware. Inability or failure to manage risks well, on the other hand, impinges on the survival of the bank as a going concern.

Enhances Risk Sensitivities

It is important that banking activities—services, products, transactions, and so on—are made sensitive to risk. The whole of banking operations should be responsive to risk in order to guide risk-taking behavior and decisions bank wide. Increasing responsiveness to risk is pertinent in yet another way. It enhances proper understanding of how risk is created in the first place—as well as of the banking related events, activities, and so on that are prone to internal and systemic risks. One can look at this benefit of risk management from the perspective of risk-taking behavior in banking. A good risk management program informs and dictates risk-taking behavior, attitudes, and tendencies across all the banking activities and functions. In this way, a bank will be in a position to take only calculated or so-called "bankable" risks. It also makes it possible for bank managements to make informed risk decisions, as well as deal with risks in totality.

Institutionalizes Risk Culture

Getting a bank organized to fulfill its objectives is one of the significant benefits of a good risk management program. In this way a risk culture evolves and is institutionalized within the bank. Shared belief in risk management is now strong and transcends individual inclinations. Positive and functional attitudes toward risk follow suit and take center stage. The bank progresses when its objectives are keyed to positive and functional risk attitudes. Besides, institutionalization of risk culture bank wide fits well with the demands of best practice in banking. Thus effective risk management is germane to good bank management. These are some of the significant attributes of a risk culture that powers and sustains success in modern banking.

Maximizes Opportunities

A good risk management program makes it possible for a bank to maximize business opportunities. It does so in three main ways. It creates and enhances possibilities for anticipating adverse events, advancing financial services, and reducing operational costs. A bank should always seek to tap into risk management framework. Doing so, it can adequately secure itself against adverse events and unforeseeable contingencies. This is essential for the bank as it furnishes a pragmatic way to consolidates business plan, strategy, and operating results. In this way, a good risk management program closely aligns with the bank's objectives—and, especially, the bottom line—in the short, medium, and long run. This benefit is significant considering that risk, in the sense of a threat, can and do often derail or determine outcomes in banking.

Anticipates Risk Events

The effectiveness of risk management depends to a large extent on the ability to anticipate risk events. Principles underlying risk management and its alternative—crisis management—are mutually exclusive. Risk management, on the one hand, is guided by ordered principles and methodology while crisis management, on the other, operates in a fire fighting manner. Intervention timelines to solve risks also differ between the two approaches. Unlike risk management, crisis management does not anticipate and work out appropriate response to risk. It tends to be driven rather by unfounded anxiety over risk incidence and misguided thinking. Thus it does not deal with risk in real time—in contrast to risk management. Crisis management serves a postmortem need where the bank learns from an experience of risk—usually managed poorly—rather than from the solution to the risk. These contrasts are rooted in the fact that crisis management is reactive while risk management is proactive. Of course crisis management does not fare better in terms of cost control and timeline.

Optimizes Resources

A bank stands a much better chance of optimizing resources available for its operations when it manages risk well. This is a critical success factor in today's banking where banks are grappling with climbing operational costs and thinning margins. Intense competition in the industry complicates an already bad situation for the banks as it continues to take a heavy toll on market shares and earnings. Sticking with a proven risk management program remains a workable and sensible option to avoid financial crisis under the circumstances. Banks that follow this path easily optimize resources, build capacity for effective resource management, and are assured success in the long run. This is yet another cogent and fulfilling reason to adopt risk management.

SUMMARY

Risk management is the process a bank adopts to keep adverse events in check while maximizing opportunities open to the bank. It secures and positions a bank, its resources, and its operations against possible dangers and to take advantage of opportunities. Good risk management follows a simple, logical, and systematic process. Its objective is to help a bank identify, analyze, mitigate, and monitor risk and opportunities in every function, activity, or process. There is no uniformity among the various stages of risk management. However, five stages—synthesized from the various options—are satisfactory and relate to defining risk control contexts, identifying potential risks, analyzing risk events, mitigating impacts of risks, and monitoring and feedback.

ERM evolved out of the need to devise a holistic process framework that would supplant and address the shortcomings of the traditional, "silo" view, approach to solving bank risk problems. The ERM framework departs from the classical method by positing a "portfolio view" approach. Rather than treat risks in compartments or isolation, like the classical method, it centralizes and aggregates the risks in a way that ensures effective risk control planning, execution, and coordination. The shortcomings of the classical method were propitious for a paradigm shift. There are four main features of the paradigm shift. It debunked the "silo" view and tenets of the classical method in the first place. It posits a holistic and integrated approach to banking risks control. Its approach to risk management builds on investigation of influence of composite risks on banking outcomes. Then it underlay the emergence of ERM as a generic approach to effective risk control in organizations. The paradigm shift is seen in the invention of a new approach to composite risks control to supplant the classical method.

An integral part of the ERM's "portfolio" view of risks is its consideration of interrelationships between individual risks, on the one hand, and between the risks and influences on them, on the other. In all cases, the task of ERM is to apply and relate its "portfolio" view to the whole organization at three execution levels—business, operations, and organizational. The ERM philosophy and framework bear all the hallmarks of best practice expected in banking and to which banks in developing economies should aspire. ERM in banking should, first and foremost, be seen as a goal-directed process aimed at solving all risk problems that a bank faces now, or may face in the future. It guides effective risk management in specific ways. It defines elements of the risk management process, advises a unified approach to treating risks, and guides on how to effectively execute, review, communicate, and monitor bank wide process of risk management. It is possible to fulfill these demands because a common ERM language—however devised, but communicated—to which every bank employee is made to key is a forceful bonding factor. This is seen, for all intents and purposes, as not only strategic but a critical success factor for ERM in banking.

Good risk management program and best practice, which ERM symbolizes, fulfills significant functions in banking. It—amongst other functions—builds and broadens risk consciousness, enhances risk sensitivities, institutionalizes risk culture, maximizes opportunities, anticipates risk events, optimizes resources, and guides risk acceptance.

QUESTIONS FOR DISCUSSION AND REVIEW

1. Do you agree that the shortcomings of method in classical risk management were propitious for a paradigm shift that underlay ERM in banking?
2. How does the classical method of risk management compare with the ERM-inspired framework and process?
3. Is it possible to adapt the main features and applications of COSO's ERM definition to banking in developing economies?
4. What may be the banking challenges in applying the significance and implications of ERM in developing economies?
5. Why would risk management in banking follow some life cycle stages? Would the stages apply to banking in developing economies?
6. How may ERM evolve—informing risk control best practice—and power success of banking in developing economies?

REFERENCE

COSO, 2004. Enterprise Risk Management—Integrated Framework.

Chapter 5

Strategy, Paradigm Shift, and Positioning for Business and Risk Management in Banking

Chapter Outline

LEARNING FOCUS AND OBJECTIVES

Concern over risks in banking has been pushed to the forefront of developing economy analysis of late. Banks in developing economies are not only prone but vulnerable to risk. This weighs with risk models and tendencies of domestic and foreign subsidiary banks alike. However, some divergences are observed in their risk management techniques. The objectives of this chapter stem from risk control dichotomies between the two sets of banks—and are intended to:

- Assess the strategies and positioning of domestic and foreign subsidiary banks for risk control in developing economies.
- Investigate influence of risk factors in defining strategic intent and long-term objectives of the banks.
- Explore implications of the strategies and positioning of the banks for choice of target markets and risk acceptance.

- Discuss factors that domestic and foreign subsidiary banks in developing countries consider in formulating risk control strategies.
- Evaluate the process of evolving and implementing long-term risk control strategies and positioning of the banks.

EXPECTED LEARNING OUTCOMES

Domestic and foreign subsidiary banks in developing economies differ in their orientation and approach to the business. Foreign bank subsidiaries manifest unmistakable inclination toward risk-aversion. In comparison, domestic banks tend to take on and avoid risk with somewhat equal—often conflicting—minds. Thus domestic banks tend to be more vulnerable to risk. The reader will—after studying this chapter and doing the exercises in it—have learnt and been better informed about:

- Factors that domestic and foreign subsidiary banks in developing countries consider in formulating risk control strategies.
- How the banks in developing economies evolve, fine-tune, and implement strategies and position themselves for risk control.
- The central dynamic of strategic intent formulation and how it informs long-term objectives of the banks.
- How the banks define target markets—and identify, analyze, and manage risks inherent in their business sectors.
- The implications of risk control strategies and positioning of the banks for risk acceptance criteria.

OVERVIEW OF THE SUBJECT MATTER

Banks in developing economies should imbibe a culture of risk anticipation and management as critical success factors. One reason is that the dynamics of banking around the world is somewhat fluid. The reality is that banking around the world tends—and is subject—to globalization and is therefore prone to novel risks. This is the troubling dimension of contemporary banking with which banks in developing economies now contend. Another reason is that banks in developing economies are particularly vulnerable. There is now—more than ever before—snowballing concern with worsening risks of banking in developing economies. Presently, Citibank and Standard Chartered Bank are the only foreign subsidiary commercial banks in Nigeria. Two other banks in the country—Ecobank and Stanbic IBTC—may be regarded as quasi-foreign subsidiary banks. The remaining 15 banks (Table 4.1) make the list of domestic commercial banks in Nigeria.

Interestingly, the two sets of banks—domestic and foreign subsidiaries—take on and manage risks differently. Foreign subsidiary banks seem immune to financial crisis that often rock banks in developing countries—ostensibly with support from their parent banks. Take Nigeria, for example. Never in the checkered history of the country's banking has the industry had a foreign bank subsidiary become distressed or fail. The implication is that foreign subsidiary and domestic banks are worlds apart on risk management. Obviously, the risk models of foreign bank subsidiaries differ from those of domestic banks. The truth is that risk-taking tendencies of the two sets of banks also differ significantly.

Domestic banks aspire to cater to the financial services needs of virtually all sectors—including the highly risky informal economy—apparently pitching in with national economic development policies, goals, and aspirations. Foreign bank subsidiaries, on the contrary, deliberately shun risky sectors. They adopt preconceived target markets definitions, risk acceptance criteria, and standardized risk models targeted at the structured and riskless sectors with which their well-honed exotic risk models fit in. Thus their financial services are usually keyed to the vibrant sectors—apparently in response to dictates of safety, financial prudence, and the bottom line.

I present overview and subject matter of this chapter as a general case study of banks in Nigeria, with implications for banking in Africa and other developing economies. My main focus is on how domestic and foreign subsidiary banks tackle risks inherent in their target markets. A breakdown of this focus narrows down to risk issues and mitigation in the banking sectors. I deal with public sector banking risk model elsewhere in this book.

RETAIL BANKING FOCUS, RISKS, AND MECHANISMS OF CONTROL

The segregation of retail services as distinct banking functions evolved with the growth and increasing competition in the financial services industry. In most banks nowadays, this category of banking business has been elevated to a prominent position. This is informed by the need to cater adequately for the banking needs of small enterprises. In Nigeria, as elsewhere, small businesses—the categories of firms that are generally regarded as small, sometimes unincorporated, and, in most cases, informally managed—have made their mark.

In discussing significant elements, scope, and categories of retail banking, I underscore its operational success requirements. A bank that offers retail banking services must invest in particular operational infrastructure. Such infrastructure must be appropriate and fit with the underlying essence of retail banking. In general, that essence is the provision of efficient, low-cost transactions processing services to a large number of small businesses. In truth, however, the so-called low-cost service structure is implicit in a grand exploitative business strategy of the banks. Over the years, banks have exploited this market segment largely because it is relatively insensitive to pricing, charges, and maneuvering of transactions processing.

As I investigate aspects of this market segment, I discuss its banking potential, appeal, and risks. The informal nature of small businesses is reckoned to be a critical issue in lending to retail banking customers. One reason is that it impinges on their financial prudence. Another reason is that it exacerbates the risk of loans to them. I examine how banks could handle external financing needs of small businesses, which constitute the bulk of retail banking customers, to mitigate lending risks to them.

The drive in retail banking is about extending financial intermediation services to sole proprietors, clubs, churches, associations, and so on. In most cases, retail banking services are offered largely as over-the-counter transactions. In terms of transactional structure, it provides mainly facilities that a bank needs to offer pay-and-receive services to its customers. Another criterion of retail banking is that unit transaction volume is characteristically small. In some cases, retail banking services include financial intermediation in commodities distribution chains. On occasion banks render such services operators in industrial merchandising—provided that volume of transactions and amounts of money involved are small. Some categories of retail services are typically rendered as pay-and-receive transactions. There is yet a third situation in which retail services come in handy. It is in the provision of structure to offer collection services to large corporations such as blue chip companies. Retail banking extends, in some cases, to receiving various tax payments on behalf of government.

Banks that emphasize retail banking focus must have extensive network of cheap branches. However, certain advantages and disadvantages are associated with small and big branches, depending on a bank's business focus and strategy. A high street branch, on the one hand, should be big, conspicuous, and ambient. A market branch in a remote rural location, on the other hand, may be relatively small and inconspicuous. However, budget constraints and targets determine, to a large extent, the sizes and nature of branches. Yet, banks will not want to play down consideration for aggressive corporate image building and customer service. These factors do also influence choice of locations, sizes, and ambience for their branches.

As examples, GTBank and First Bank—which hitherto distanced themselves from market branches—are now serious contenders for retail transactions in marketplaces. This is not only intriguing but also instructive. Like them, Zenith, UBA, Access and some other banks have big, imposing, and strategically located branches, whether on high streets or elsewhere. The imposing logos, and uniquely designed buildings of the banks equally make unmistakable statements about their bullish marketing and customer service orientation and strategy.

Banks that implement retail banking strategy tend to develop core competences in particular low-end services. Unfilled banking needs of customers in rural communities drive this service orientation. However, in order to render the services well, the banks must have pertinent service structure. Their operations must be tailored to accommodate numerous small unit volumes of over-the-counter, and pay-and-receive transactions. Yet banks that maintain strong retail banking focus do so for some strategic reasons. Their aim may be to take

TABLE 5.1 Employee Strength of Some Domestic and Foreign Subsidiary Commercial Banks in Nigeria[a]

Name of bank	Number of employees
Citibank[b]	300+
Fidelity	4,000+
FBN	10,000+
Standard Chartered[b]	900+
Sterling	3,000+

[a]Figures are culled from Internet websites of the banks. Numbers may change as employee recruitment program of the banks is ongoing.
[b]Banks that I recognize—for purposes of this discussion, chapter and, indeed, the entire book—as foreign subsidiary banks incorporated, operating, and domiciled in Nigeria

exceptional advantage of a price insensitive market segment. Low level of competition in the retail market sector could also drive interest of the banks.

Particular operational setbacks tend to confront banks that offer retail services. Credit and operational risks are often high in retail banking. Cost of transactions processing is also high. This underlies a major challenge in dealing with multiplicity of small unit banking transactions in retail markets. Of course, as Table 5.1 shows domestic banks that maintain a heavy presence in the retail banking sector employ more workforce—with attendant operational risks—than their foreign subsidiary counterparts that focus more on corporate and investment banking.

BRANCH BANKING, COORDINATION, AND RISKS CONTROL

The foregoing explains why, as Table 1.1 shows, foreign bank subsidiaries in a large country like Nigeria would have far less number of branches than their domestic counterparts of comparable asset and liability portfolio sizes. Sifting through Table 2.2 (Chapter 2), the risk aversion of foreign subsidiary banks becomes more apparent. First Bank, for example, has over 750 branches nationwide compared to Citibank's paltry 12 in the same country. With just 42 branches, the other foreign subsidiary bank—Standard Chartered Bank—also manifests a similar deliberate risk aversion approach to the business in terms of network of branches. In banking, incidentally, risk incidence increases and exacerbates with increase in network of branches.

The banks are especially exposed to more operational risk at branch level. Fraud is a typical operational risk that bedevils branch banking in developing economies. The managements of domestic and foreign subsidiary banks certainly appreciate the risk of building up extensive network of branches. However, domestic banks appear helpless with risk—seemingly for reason of self-imposed obligation to operate numerous branches as outreach centers for low income populations. Most of the target beneficiaries are sole proprietors, majority of whom live in rural communities, engage in small economic activities, or operate in the informal economy. For foreign subsidiary banks, in direct contrast to domestic banks, the guiding principle seems to be "no passions" if banking needs are illogical, indefensible, risk-laden, or unprofitable. In this way, the foreign subsidiary banks wriggle out of some of their responsibilities to their host countries. They manifest this business sense in several ways. A typical example is seen in how they deftly cut their losses and wind unprofitable branches down. Then as required by the applicable banking laws, they make returns accordingly to the regulatory authorities.

Notwithstanding risk, domestic banks can still operate profitably with extensive network of branches. They can do this by anticipating and effectively managing risk in their markets. It may not be tenable or feasible to adopt a uniform risk management strategy for all branch locations or even target markets. There may be need for some flexibility to accommodate the peculiarities or unique attributes of each market. This may sound a bit far-fetched, but some of the domestic banks have successfully adopted it as a more pragmatic approach to manage risk of extensive branch banking. I give an example to illustrate how domestic banks can tap this risk management technique.

Domestic banks may open numerous branches outside the metropolises without taking undue risk. Branches can really be outreach centers for deposit mobilization. Naturally, liability generation in itself—especially in forms of savings, demand, and recurrent deposits—mitigates risk in banking. Thus branch development policy should be backed by target liability-driven lending, financial performance, and growth strategies. For example, the size of a branch's risk assets portfolio should be a function of its deposit liability base. Tying risk assets to deposit portfolio improves efficiency of lending, optimizes financial performance, and assures overall growth of the branch. However, these goals will be achieved only if gains in deposits are not offset by increasing lending. Otherwise, the benefit of increasing deposit liability would be a reduction in loan loss provisions and charge-offs. This has risk management implication. Deposit base should dictate risk assets portfolio in terms of permissible loan-to-deposit ratio. For branches outside the metropolises, commercial, and financial centers, loan-to-deposit ratio may not be more 30%. However, for lending to be efficient, bank-wide loan-to-deposit ratio could be as high as—but not more than—70%. In general, lending is said to be efficient when loan loss provisions and charge-offs related to it are minimal, and it does not jeopardize liquidity and financial performance.

This approach to managing branch banking risk adds a wider perspective. Domestic banks can help in channeling idle funds in the informal economy back into the formal sector for national economic planning and development. This is attained when the funds mopped up from rural communities and low income populations through branch outreach centers contribute—no matter how little—to reducing excess liquidity in the financial system. Although arguable without facts and figures, there are a lot of idle funds with these economic entities, especially in the informal economy. Branch banking can help unlock the potential of such funds for social change beyond their positive impact on risk management. Foreign subsidiary banks tend to be cautious—and understandably too—when it comes to these banking and risk-taking ideas. I discuss their risk management departures from domestic banks throughout and in every applicable chapter of this book. I take a look at specific risk concerns at issue that apply to and affect banks across the board in developing countries worldwide. Meanwhile I build the background on conceptual foundation of risk, its relationship to uncertainty, and its influence on banking in developing economies. That is what I do right away in Appendix 1 as I review pioneering thoughts, evolving thinking, and contemporary perspectives on risk, uncertainty, and banking.

CASE STUDY 5.1 Magnum Trust Bank PLC—Inventing Risk Control Focus in a Volatile Market

The need to review the focus of Magnum Trust Bank Plc and reconfirm its business thrust was identified last year (1998) when the new management assumed duty (Adapted from Onyiriuba, 1999. Magnum Trust Bank merged with four other banks—NAL Bank, NBM, Trust Bank of Africa, and Indo-Nigeria Merchant Bank (INMB)—in January 2006. Led by NAL Bank, the merged entities operated as a consolidated group with the name Sterling Bank PLC. In 2011, Sterling Bank assimilated the entire business interest of the erstwhile Equatorial Trust Bank under a merger arrangement. The use of Magnum Trust Bank PLC in this case study is purely for illustration purposes and to demonstrate how certain strategic banking challenges play themselves out in developing economies. The case study has no bearing whatsoever to the mergers in which Magnum Trust Bank PLC was involved or to Sterling Bank PLC in which Magnum Trust Bank PLC was assimilated through a merger deal.). At that time, if any strategy existed at all, it was hazy, incomprehensible, and fraught with misrepresentation. For instance, the focus on *retail banking* was easily misconstrued to mean total reliance on consumer and small business markets for banking relationships. Thus branches were located largely in marketplaces where small lot cash transactions, conducted largely at individual level, prevailed.

Underlying this approach was the urge to increase deposit liabilities while avoiding risk assets to a large extent possible. It was also intended to achieve cost efficiency in transactions processing. With experience, it is now common knowledge that market branches thrive with lending, some of which would go bad and be lost to the debtors because they are, in most cases, poorly structured. It soon became clear that the bank would not achieve its target growth, especially with the urgency engendered by the ever-increasing competition in the market, if the observed distortion of focus was not corrected. One reason is that growth will remain hampered if the bank is unable to attract large volume transactions, and sustain enduring relationships. However, the real task was how to immediately redefine, to the understanding and appreciation of staff, the concept of *retail banking* to avoid the unnecessary limitation of the bank's capabilities. In a practical sense, the actual lesson of experience here is that all segments of the total market require retail-banking services of sorts. However, there were several other unresolved strategic issues facing the bank at the time. What was the bank's vision? Strategic intent? Market focus? How should the bank be positioned to gain competitive advantage? Were the bank's internal processes efficiently organized? In other words, there was a need to evolve an enduring *strategic plan* for the bank.

In its wisdom, the executive management decided to involve as many staff as possible in the strategy development processes. Indeed, not less than 70 members of staff participated in the exercise that spanned 5 months, from April to August 1999. The objective was to avoid imposition of a plan by top management. In so doing, the plan becomes a popular long-term business blueprint for the bank. Working in various large and small groups, facilitated by ReStraL Consulting, management and staff brainstormed and agreed on every aspect of the final plan. It was indeed a rigorous but rewarding *drill* exercise to chart the course of future events for the bank.

Exercise for class or group discussion

1. Why did it become necessary to review the operational strategy of Magnum Trust Bank PLC in late 1990s?
2. Did the bank—in your opinion—correctly define its retail banking target markets, strategy, and positioning?
3. Do you think that the bank properly thought through its approach to inventing enterprise for risk control?
4. What factors, from this case study, may underlie the formulation of a bank's retail banking strategies and positioning?
5. What real risk control challenges are banks implementing retail banking strategies likely to face in their markets?

Tips for solving the exercise

Magnum Trust Bank was a small bank owned by a group of risk-averse investors. The bank was poorly capitalized and barely able to render normal universal banking services. Its low capitalization imparted risk to its business as a going concern. It also impacted its growth and financial performance. Intense competition and market volatility did not help matters. Harsh operating environment complicated the situation and problem of the bank. The foregoing were real threats to which the bank must respond appropriately if it were to remain a going concern. The fate of the bank thickened as it is apparently groping on a slippery business terrain. Eventually the anticipated response came in 1999 when the bank started tinkering with its business strategy and positioning. It was determined to reinvent enterprise and forge ahead. In the end, it decided in favor of a strong retail focus in all the market sectors.

WHOLESALE BANKING AND MECHANISMS OF RISK CONTROL

Wholesale banking also thrives in developing economies, with foreign bank subsidiaries often in the lead. Usually the targets are blue chips in all sectors—which could be multinationals, conglomerates, or ordinary corporates. Foreign bank subsidiaries flex muscle in this market segment and court the leading corporations. They tend to mitigate risk with a strong focus on corporate, institutional, and investment banking fields. Domestic banks are equally interested in this target market, though only a few of them may have the capacity to efficiently satisfy its banking needs. Most of the domestic banks lack some of the vital competencies required for effective wholesale banking. Yet they feebly chase after accounts in this target market due to skill gaps, wanting in best practice, liquidity pressure, and all. The few that do have the necessary capacity compete with foreign subsidiary banks. In all cases, domestic and foreign subsidiary banks rely on certain good features of the blue-chip companies as support for effective risk management. I examine the features of the blue chips that underlie a craving for their accounts by both domestic and foreign subsidiary banks.

Blue-Chip Companies

Generally acknowledged as well and professionally managed, blue chips have clear business strategies and unambiguous management succession plan. But a more apt description of a *blue chip* would be a company which has a triple "A" rating. The rating would be seen as credible if it is obtained from reputable independent rating agencies such as Moody's, Standard & Poor's, and so on. The blue chips maintain credible management accounts and audited financial statement and annual reports. In some cases, blue chips could be *multinational* corporations or *conglomerate* business organizations. It is rare to find other categories of companies that can truly be classified as blue chips. One reason is that they lack of the qualifying business and management finesse. I summarize the main distinguishing features of blue chips and multinationals as follows.

Private Sector Driven

Blue-chips are essentially large, private, and profit-motivated companies. Thus, the term *blue chip* may not be correctly applied to government-owned enterprises, parastatals, or agencies that are engaged in some business activities. It will also not be appropriate to describe *not-for-profit* outfits, especially nongovernmental organizations (NGOs), as blue chips even if they share the qualifying attributes. In developing countries, blue chip companies often exercise a great influence on government and business. Sometimes they dictate the direction of government–business relations and policy. The domineering influence of this category of companies is also evident in the huge human and material resources which it deploys to meet market expectations and competition.

Sales Turnover and Activities

Blue chips are usually successful large business corporations. Specific features differentiate them from regular constituents of the business community. They achieve remarkable annual sales turnover. This underpins the competition among banks for their banking transactions and relationships. Big and small banks alike pride themselves on having particular blue chip companies as customers. Key officers of banks are assigned special responsibilities in marketing and managing their banking relationships. Often bank managements are involved—on occasion leading the marketing drive.

Thus banks deliberately directed marketing drive at attracting and retaining banking relationships with the blue chips. This practice was defended as offering assurance of resilience for the banks in times of liquidity crisis. Blue chips assist banks with huge deposits, even at short notice, when liquidity pressure threatens their operations. This remains a major reason for the continuing relevance of the blue chips market.

Under the auspices of Pareto optimality principle, blue chips were once the hope of banks for attaining earnings goals with few accounts. For some banks such as Citibank, Standard Chartered, GTBank, and Stanbic, this business focus still holds sway. Yet there has been a radical departure from the craze for the accounts of blue chips. This is observed in how banks are redefining their target markets. Nowadays banks are increasing attention to retail, consumer, and commercial banking sectors. At the same, they are repositioning for a new sector—the middle-tier market.

Formal Organization Structure

We can yet distinguish blue chips by their formal organization structure. This implies that functions and activities are clearly defined and strictly observed by management and staff at all levels. Structured organization and method is a characteristic hallmark of blue chip companies. It establishes work roles and relationships among staff units, departments, and divisions.

Conceptualizing structure in this way delineates functional and line authorities—and responsibilities. This guides exercise of power and influence by members of the organization. It also reduces role conflicts. However, formal organization structure is not always or necessarily beneficial. Its success and benefits depends on the type of structure and functioning of its elements. A tendency to, and cost of, bureaucracy may negate the benefits of formal organization structure. Yet these attributes characterize some formal organization structure. The blue chips may share this characterization in some respects.

With formal organization structure, it becomes easy to fill vacant job positions. This could be achieved through external or internal advertisements, interviews, and recruitment from a short list of candidates. More importantly, it permits management succession plan. Without a succession plan, a company may be embroiled in controversy over who occupies a vacant management position. In most cases, tussle and scheming for key positions underlie the controversy.

Good and Focused Management

Blue chip companies do have good management teams. Often people who have requisite depth of experience, motivation, and commitment manage them. Good educational background and technical competence make the key characterizing attributes of members of management of blue chip companies. Merit is a common feature in the employment process of blue chip companies. Yet another best practice, one that gives out a feel of the professional conduct of the blue chips to the public, is the rigor of appraisal and monitoring of career paths of employees. Blue chip companies groom their hardworking employees to assume management positions. Most of their managers are graduates of various academic disciplines from some of the best universities around the world. Top management vacancies are rarely filled from external applicants. Retirement benefits are generous, but reflect the longevity and quality services the retirees rendered.

Realistic Business Strategy

Blue chips thrive with a focused and scrupulously evolved business strategy. In most cases, the orientation of business strategy is market driven. Strategy formulation is often rigorous. There is especially rigor in defining and determining the making of corporate vision. This involves formulation of the company's *core ideology* and *envisioned future*. Management and staff alike are then tasked to strictly adhere to the vision. But they can also be critical of the vision. This implies that there must be standard criteria for assessing the vision.

There are two main planks in a company's core ideology. It deals with the company's *core purpose* and its *core values*. The former defines the reason for the company's being or existence. In the latter, the distinctive morals, principles or ideals to which its employees are dedicated are catalogued. On the other hand, its envisioned future focuses on three main targets. It deals with the following aspects of the company's being:

- distinctive competences (i.e., typical business traits and skills)
- stretch goals (i.e., ideal but realistic business—especially, financial—targets)
- envisioned description (i.e., how the company wishes that its stakeholders and the public should perceive it and its activities)

Blue chips are always exponents of strategy development as a means of attaining success. Doing so, they bequeath a lifetime of orderliness and expectations to the business community. Working with strategy helps to dispel anxiety about future business upheavals or turbulence. It also positions a company well in its products markets. In this way the company can confidently face unforeseen contingencies.

Financial Accounts and Reporting

Blue chip companies are yet noted for a meticulous keeping of accounting data and records. As a result, they are usually equipped with reliable management information system. This is essential for business decision-making and success. The records also assist financial analysts and stakeholders of the companies—and, indeed, the public—in forming opinions about the financial performance of the companies. This is especially the case for quoted companies—those listed on the Nigerian Stock Exchange. Yet unquoted blue chip companies are no less meticulous with financial reporting. This is one of the features of the blue chips that bear the hallmark of best practice in business.

The accounting culture of blue chip companies emphasizes auditing of financial statement and up-to-date management accounts. Banks often require these two documents to make lending decisions on term loans and working capital or overdraft facilities. The accounts of blue chips are credible for two main reasons. Detailed illustrations and analysis enrich their financial statement and annual reports. Usually leading chartered accounting firms and consultants—in the same league as KPMG, Arthur Anderson, and so on—audit their accounts.

Banks have tried but all to no avail to stipulate and enforce this standard of practice on other categories of borrowing customers. This is one of the reasons it is easier to manage lending to the blue chips than other segments of the market. In terms of overall relationship management, blue chip companies prove more difficult than the other sectors on pricing of financial products and services.

CULTURAL ISSUES AND PROSPECTS IN BANK POSITIONING

Culture bind members of societies. In any society—and this is commonplace—people's behavior are patterned to conform to the cultural specifications of that society. As a *social heritage*, culture defines a people's norms, values, and mores as transmitted from one generation to another. From birth, children are trained to imbibe the custom of their people through the *socialization* process. The children internalize such teachings as unique characteristics that give meaning and expression to the culture of their people, and strive to uphold them. Since deviation from culture is either punished, or regarded with misgivings, members of a society strive to live according to their culture.

Consumers buy products, services, or ideas on the basis of what their culture approves of and this cultural influence relates to every aspect of life. However, this does not mean that every individual in the society would conform to the culture. It is not uncommon to find deviants within a group who might assert a counter culture. The culmination of the cultural diversity of most societies, therefore, is the difficulty which marketing practitioners encounter trying to identify, harmonize, and satisfy the consumers' needs. Many marketing efforts fall through because they appeal to a target audience that may not need the campaign, perhaps, on grounds of cultural prescription.

However, there is much that marketing can do to educate people on some cultural practices that have lost relevance with modernization of the societies. For instance, how can one justify a *cultural* practice, which discourages people from keeping their savings in the banks? In the past, that could be justified on grounds of ignorance, but it is intolerable today. Yet, the practice persists in some traditional societies. There is also a related cultural deficiency seen in the mutilation of currency notes as a result of poor handling. This practice is common among all cadres of people as seen in the *spraying of cash* during celebrations. The Central Bank of Nigeria once sponsored a number of radio jingles, newspaper and television advertisements to correct this flawed practice. However, more serious campaigns are needed against similar cultural practices that negate modern civilization orientations.

Evolving and Sustaining Banking Culture

Perhaps, one may admit that some partial transformation has been achieved in the sense that most of the people have embraced the banking culture, not without some misgivings, though. Many, mostly the illiterate, still keep a chunk of their monies at home for *safety*! This might sound absurd, but it happens. In situations like this, bank marketing could seek to change retrogressive cultural practices to the benefit of the society and mankind. In time, the weapon to achieve cultural reorientation of the type envisaged here is sustained education of the people. This is a task that should not be left for banks alone. Individuals, government, and private sector institutions have various roles to play. Yet, banks can integrate the required education into particular product and service offerings that demonstrate compelling benefits of keeping money within the banking system. The following illustrations demonstrate how banks can achieve this important goal.

- Banks could offer attractive interest rates on savings and fixed deposits to the customers and prospects. The banks should always consider interest they pay on savings and deposits as both obligatory and an incentive to retain and increase customer patronage.
- Gifts may also serve to predispose people to accepting a beneficial cause such as growing one's wealth through routine savings and investments in banking products. Thus, banks should offer irresistible gifts (sometimes in promotional contests) to customers and prospects.
- Children education incentives could be used as one of the tools for changing the cultural barrier to savings in the banking system. Such incentives could be offered to prospects categorized among the banking public that repudiate modern savings orientation.
- Product demonstrations could also be organized to communicate the benefits of savings in more effective manners. Banks could also sponsor home video plays that sensitize the people on the dangers of keeping large sums of money at home.

Some banks have tried to get savings deposits from their customers and prospects by packaging and offering products that have particular cultural appeals to the people. The Sterling Bank's *target* savings products for the *Christmas* and *Id—el-Kabir* religious festivals are good examples for reference. These products are designed to encourage people to save certain amounts of their annual incomes toward the celebration of these important *cultural* but religious events. Thus, banks can really translate certain cultural values into business opportunities, which they could exploit with particular marketing offerings. It is to the credit of the banks that they have fulfilled most of these suggestions with impressive results. There has been significant improvement in the banking culture of the people. This is now evident in the flourishing banking business in many developing countries and owes its cause to the combined campaigns of the stakeholders in banking against primitive savings practices.

Interest incentive to encourage *formal* savings habit demands a cultural reorientation of the people. For example, in the wake of the 1985 financial system deregulation policy of the Babangida administration in Nigeria, several finance houses emerged, paying high upfront interest rates on fixed deposits. Notwithstanding the spurious orientation of some of the finance houses, the people still patronized them because of the promise, and fulfillment, of upfront interest payment. While the normal banks should not do this, the fact remains that people need some incentives to renounce preference to keeping their savings outside the banking system. However, interest incentive may not be applicable to the Moslems since their religion does not encourage payment and receipt of interest for business transactions.

Role of Subcultural Values

Subcultures exert even a greater influence upon their members in terms of behavior than the dominant culture. They are easily carved out for market segmentation, and can be easily reached with specific marketing campaigns. Religious groups are a common subculture in society—one that has overwhelming influence on their followers. Every religion stipulates for its members what should be regarded as good or bad behavior in terms of what to eat, where to visit, what to wear and so forth. Through their teachings, some of the religions condition their members to accepting a lifestyle that anticipates gratification in the life to come at the expense of material gains in this world. As a result of such indoctrination, evaluation of certain goods and services by the members tend to be below par relative to what happens in the larger society. Religion is particularly powerful in shaping people's behavior in this way because religious beliefs are typically construed so as to make it impossible for people to demonstrate the truth or falsity of the beliefs they hold. Instead, the true believer finds in daily experience some confirmation of religious faith (Goode, 1971: 51).

Marketing officers in banks have really had to join some religious groups so as to attract deposits from them. Joining religious groups in this way may achieve the desired results. In doing so, for instance, the religious groups might have the impression that they are accepted even by the larger society. Yet, there could be more aggressive marketing strategies to tap into the overwhelming business opportunities that abound in sub–cultural groups and institutions in the societies. Consider the case of the defunct IBTC Ethical Fund in Nigeria which appeals to the devout religious practitioners. This is a capital market product that promises to pool funds from individuals, especially the religious adherents, for investment in quoted stocks of companies other than those that produce alcoholic drinks, cigarettes, and all such products. These are products the consumption of which certain religious beliefs prohibit. Perhaps the making of this product originated in the thinking of the bank's management that as many people dislike alcohol, smoking, and similar products, it would be appropriate and profitable to develop such a special product to serve their religious belief. In order to convert this thought into a profitable business opportunity, the bank introduced the Ethical Fund which is targeted mainly at those who by their religious inclinations dislike alcohol and cigarettes.

Supplanting the Unorthodox Banking Practices

A number of traditional *banking* systems exist in some developing countries. One of such native banking practices—one that remains an example of a cultural relic that borders on unacceptable savings practice—is the institution of the *esusu* thrift in Nigeria. It may go by different names in other developing economies. The term *esusu* denotes the cultural practice, mainly in the traditional societies of the south western Nigeria, by which certain persons routinely collect money *contributions* (i.e., deposits) from the artisans, petty traders, subsistence farmers, and other low-income individuals in the informal economy for safekeeping.

The *esusu* operators promise and pay the contributors, depositors, or owners of the monies interest on their deposits over an agreed period of savings, usually 30 days. From the pool of the money collected, the operators lend part of the *esusu* funds in their care to other persons that have various financial needs and charge fees that approximate *interest* cost. In another variant of *esusu*, with agreement of the *contributors*, the *collectors* (i.e., operators) also take a certain percentage of the money so contributed to cover their *operational costs*. The amount so *appropriated* is usually not more than 10% of each contributor's total deposits. It is from such appropriations and *interest* charges that the operators make their gains and could sustain their business. However, the major weaknesses of the *esusu* thrift include high risks of possible:

- denial of some, most, or all of the contributors' deposits by the operators because of lack of documentation of the *transactions*;
- loss of some, most, or all of the accumulated savings to theft from the collectors' home or elsewhere; and,
- misappropriation of the funds by the collectors to meet personal financial obligations.

From the foregoing, it is obvious that banks can capitalize on the damning disadvantages to dislodge the system and its operators. In so doing, they could effectively unlock the savings potential in the informal economy.

Most banks have simplified savings account documentation and substantially reduced, or even waived the requirement for initial deposit to open savings account. Many of the banks have also introduced appreciable operational flexibility and incentives for savings accounts. Some of the innovative improvements of savings accounts include:

- ability of account holders to deposit and withdraw from their accounts from any branch of the bank, made possible by WAN, which facilitates online-real-time banking transactions;
- issuance of check books (usually *not valid* for clearing) to the account holders. With the check books, the account holders could make regular withdrawals through third parties;
- reduction, or waiver of the ceiling on the number of withdrawals to be made from savings accounts; and,
- issuance of regular statements of accounts on savings accounts to the account holders.

Survival of the Unorthodox Banking Systems

However, notwithstanding these corrective and competitive measures, *esusu* thrift still survives and accounts for a chunk of money outside the orthodox banking system. Why and how does this practice survive the onslaught of the banks? Perhaps not many people realize that *esusu* thrift remains a flourishing business in the informal savings economy. The reasons for the enduring survival of the *esusu* thrift are not far-fetched. The system is relatively *more* simple, flexible, and convenient for the contributors and operators. It is particularly highly *informal*. With these advantages, people continue to patronize it in defiance to the promises of marketing and economic development theories. However, banks should not relent in campaigning against such unworthy competition. Yet, the ultimate solution is to open as many rural branches of banks as possible to cater for the banking needs of economic units that operate in the informal economy.

Perhaps a more difficult challenge for the banks is a variant of the *esusu* thrift, which exists not only in the traditional societies, but among the urban populations of the working class in some countries. It is a practice by which a number of people—usually work colleagues, friends, or associates—form an ad-hoc money *contribution and collection* group. The group makes regular financial contributions (savings) with understanding that participants (contributors) will, on rotatory basis, take turns to collect sum of the contributions of all the members on given dates or periods in particular months. Thus, the contributors form a group with the objective of meeting their personal financial needs from their regular contributions.

An illustration will help understanding of the practice. Let us assume that 10 work colleagues decide to form a *contribution and collection group*. They would make the following agreement (usually undocumented) from the outset:

- the members decide the date for the commencement of their contributions, say, March 31, 2016. Each member makes their initial contribution on this date or within agreed period;
- each of the members contribute equal amount of money on the particular date or period, corresponding to their starting date as agreed in (1) above, in the subsequent months;
- the number of months during which the members make contributions tally with the total number of participants in the group, that is, 10 months in our example;
- the participants decide the rotatory order which they will adopt in knowing the turns that each member may take to collect particular period's contributions; and,
- the sum of the contributions of all the members for a particular period is given to the member who has the right of turn to collect the contributions for that period.

Thus, according to their turns for collection, each of the 10 persons in this illustration will be entitled to the sum of all the members' contributions every 31st of the month, from March to December 2016. The members that have taken their collection turns continue to make the mandatory fixed contribution until the last person takes their turn. The program may or may not be rolled over after the termination of its tenure, depending on the financial needs of the members.

The practice engenders *forced savings* habit among the participants outside the orthodox banking system. In most cases, the saving is *target* driven, implying that the participants have particular financial obligations which they intend to solve in particular months. Thus, the members take turns that tally with the months in which they intend to solve their particular financial obligations. Besides, the arrangement offers *interest free loans* to the participants, without the rigors of documentation and collateral requirement. There might be exchange of postdated checks among the participants, which essentially provides only collateral *comfort*. This is why the group is effective and has been surviving. However, it is disadvantaged on grounds that often members who have taken their collection turns default in their obligation to continue making the contribution until the last member has equally taken their turn. Thus, the practice does not offer payment security to the participants. Unresolved defaults often lead to personal acrimonies among the members.

The savings need of the people that form the *contribution and collection groups* should ordinarily be met with savings products which the orthodox banks offer. However, normal savings account has not been quite attractive to most people because it lacks the *compulsion* to save, which such people need.

This is why the problem posed by the existence of *contribution* and *collection* groups remains real for the orthodox banks.

SUMMARY

Banks should always anticipate risk considering that their operations are subject to globalization and therefore prone to novel risks. This becomes troubling for banks in developing economies as they are particularly vulnerable. Domestic and foreign subsidiary banks take on and manage risks in different ways dictated by their circumstances. Some of the banks focus on retail financial services. Nowadays retail banking is a critical function. Operational success requirements for retail banking are seen in its elements, scope, and categories. Retail banking demands particular operational infrastructure that must be appropriate and fit with the objectives for the mass market.

Operational setbacks in form of credit and operational risks tend to be high in retail banking. Another major challenge is in dealing with multiplicity of small unit banking transactions in mass markets. Foreign bank subsidiaries operate with far less number of branches and workforce than their domestic counterparts. This is a deliberate risk aversion approach to the business. It is informed by the fact that incidence of risk exacerbates with increase in network of branches.

Banks face more operational risk at branch level. Fraud is a typical operational risk that bedevils branch banking in developing economies. Notwithstanding risk, domestic banks—in direct contrast to foreign subsidiaries—operate with numerous branches as outreach centers for low income populations. In this way domestic banks can mobilize cheap deposits—usually in form of savings, demand, and recurrent deposits—and thus mitigate financial risk. Doing so, domestic banks help channel idle funds in the informal economy back into the formal sector for national economic planning and development. On the contrary, foreign subsidiary banks tend to be cautious in tapping potential in retail banking.

Wholesale banking also thrives in developing economies, with foreign bank subsidiaries often in the lead. Most of the domestic banks lack some of the vital competencies required for effective wholesale banking. Usually the targets are blue chips—which could be multinationals, conglomerates, or ordinary corporates. The domestic banks feebly chase after these targets due to skill gaps, wanting in best practice, liquidity pressure, and all. Foreign bank subsidiaries flex muscle in this market segment and court the leading corporations.

QUESTIONS FOR DISCUSSION AND REVIEW

1. What do you understand by the terms "business strategy" and "market positioning" in the context of banking?
2. Why should banks in developing economies clearly define strategy and positioning for business and formulate appropriate policies?

3. How does domestic and foreign subsidiary banks' approach to strategy formulation compare in a named developing economy?
4. Define the term "retail banking" focus. What operational challenges do banks in developing economies likely to face in retail banking?
5. In what contexts would you say that wholesale banking is an appropriate business strategy for a bank in a developing economy?
6. Why do you, or do you not, think that branch banking should complement a strong retail operations focus in developing economies?

REFERENCES

Goode, W.J., 1971. Principles of Sociology. McGraw–Hill Book Company, New York.
Onyiriuba, L., 1999. Editorial: Evolving enduring target markets, Magnum Connect (in–house magazine of Magnum Trust Bank PLC, Lagos, Nigeria), Maiden edition.

Chapter 6

Bank Marketing Paradox and Risks Management in Developing Economies

Chapter Outline

LEARNING FOCUS AND OBJECTIVES

Risks in bank marketing are real. Managing the risks demands a radical approach, zero tolerance for deviation from—or compromise on—risk management rules, and proven integrity of marketing. In view of this, I set out writing this chapter with intentions to:

- Show how prebanking marketing initiatives can be applied to mitigate banking risks in developing economies.

- Relate relationship marketing to high stakes in banking and risk-mitigating strategy of banks in developing economies.
- Evaluate significance of internal and external information for mitigating bank marketing risks in developing economies.

EXPECTED LEARNING OUTCOMES

Bank marketing is ever challenging. Reward for successful bank marketing should not savor of risk. Ability to optimize gains from marketing at the least possible risk and cost to the bank is essential. In practice, risk mitigation starts with observing the know your customer (KYC) rules. The reader will—after studying this chapter and doing the exercises in it—have learnt and been better informed about:

- concept, nature and conduct of, and risk control justifications for, prebanking and relationship marketing initiatives;
- internal and external information needs, sources and significance for bank marketing risks control in developing economies;
- correlation between bank marketing risks control and the high stakes in banking in developing economies.

OVERVIEW OF THE SUBJECT MATTER

Marketing of banking products and services presents both challenges and opportunities to the banks and their customers. Banking itself is a highly respected profession—ideally associated with discipline, integrity, and sobriety. Not only is the industry highly specialized, the markets it serves are also distinctive. Service standard that customers expect is high. Customer tastes and preferences show marked sophistication in some ways. On occasion, high levels of human and material resources are required to effectively serve customer needs. Thus, marketing officers must possess particular attributes to be able to do their work well. In dealing with customers, they must be tolerant, and yet firm on policy issues and as a matter of principle.

Most banks clearly define their visions in ways that hinge success on certain core purposes and values to which everyone must adhere. Such banks tend to have zero tolerance for deviation from, or compromise on, the core purposes and values. Most of the attributes which marketing officers must possess derive largely from the bank's core values. Some of the values require to be professional, committed, and empathic in dealing with customers. Of course, integrity of the employees should not be called into question. In practice, though, there are no uniform values or attributes which employees in different banks must adopt for marketing or other activities.

Foregoing attributes are some of the cherished bank marketing success requirements. Success in this context is all about ability to optimize gains from target marketing at the least possible risk and cost to the bank. The usual starting point for risk mitigation in bank marketing is encapsulated in the famous KYC concept. As a banker, the belief in this concept is that you must truly know your customer to be able to deal with contemporary banking risks. In view of its key role in risk mitigation, I discussed the KYC philosophy extensively in Chapter 8 of this book. Presently, I focus on how to build and sustain success of risk management in bank marketing. That makes input into the hallowed KYC principles and is propitious for bank risk control in developing economies.

RISK CONTROL NEED FOR MARKETING IN BANKING

The financial services industry, like the real sector, needs marketing to build large customer base, grow the sector, and attain market-driven competitiveness. There is perhaps no economic activity that needs marketing to succeed more than the banking industry. The reasons are revealing. Customer satisfaction is at the top of the reasons. The questions of growth potential, nature of banking services, and budget pressure follow. Competition and cultivation of the market are no less important factors. In banking, influence of marketing tends to be more evident in maneuvering product development, pricing of services, and promotional strategies. These are the major elements of marketing mix that banks employ to achieve business objectives in their target markets. I quickly explain the justifications of marketing in banking.

Customer Satisfaction

The application of marketing in banking reflects a desire to continuously satisfy ever-changing taste, needs, and wants of customers. This fits well with marketing concept which remains the true and justifiable reason for being in business.

Growth Potential

Marketing is needed in banking to fulfill urge to tap into, and exploit, growth potential of the industry. New challenges of business arising from globalization of the financial system accentuate the need.

Nature of Services

The technical nature of most banking products and services often requires tasteful packaging and delivery to target markets. Marketing helps to position unique banking services to target markets.

Budget Pressure

Increasing pressure to meet budget goals—earnings, return on investment, and shareholders' expectations—are some of the reasons that marketing remains relevant in banking. With marketing, business goals are more aggressively pursued and realized.

Cultivation of Market

Banks need marketing to cultivate customers. In most developing economies, the depth of marketing is yet small. Thus, marketing is needed to open up markets, create awareness, and expand opportunities open to banks. In doing so, banking becomes more relevant to the widest segments of the mass market.

Competition

Most industries first realize the need for marketing when they face stiff competition. Soon competition begins to take a heavy toll on the business. The need for marketing in banking is even more acute. Cut-throat competition is intensifying and reducing transactions margins.

AVOIDING THE PITFALLS OF MARKETING CALLS

It is expected that the marketing officers, account officers, and relationship managers (as they are variously known) should make regular and organized calls to the existing and prospective customers assigned to them. This implies that the officers should as much as possible avoid casual calls because experience has shown that some customers often misrepresent the essence of informal visits. This happens more frequently when banking relationships turn sour and the affected customers are upset with the bank. In such a situation, when the customers become desperate, they tend to use whatever personal information they might have about the bank's officers against them.

CASE STUDY 6.1 Bank Marketing Call and Banking Relationship Gone Awry

A marketing officer, soon to be wedded, was making a call as account officer for a particular borrowing customer of a bank. In the course of discussions between the customer and calling officer, the latter mentioned his planned wedding arrangements, ceremonies, and associated expenses. With that information, the customer felt that financial assistance was being solicited toward the wedding ceremonies and gave a cash gift which the calling officer accepted.

In time, the credit facility that the customer had with the bank was classified as nonperforming and listed for remedial actions. The account officer tried, but to no avail, to resuscitate the account by identifying and stopping some of the pranks of the customer, including suspected diversion of cash inflows to other noncredit committed banks. When it became obvious that the customer's default on the loan was rather deliberate, the bank decided to call in the loan.

Besides expressing disappointment in the customer, the account officer played active role in the ensuing loan recovery actions taken by the bank. As the bank continued to pile up pressure to repay the loan, the customer remained evasive. The customer afterward threw the bombshell by saying that the account officer was in the habit of seeking personal financial gains on the account. The customer further alleged that the dilemma of the account arose from misrepresentation of its circumstances by the account officer.

In debunking the allegations, during one of the meetings between the customer and loan recovery team of the bank, the account officer insisted that the customer was adopting diversionary tactics and trying to buy time in order to continue with the loan default. Nonetheless, the account officer admitted that the customer once gave him a cash gift to assist in his wedding ceremonies and did not see how such freewill gift would be the reason for not paying back the loan.

Exercise for class or group discussion
1. As the line supervisor of the marketing officer, how would you handle this incident?
2. Does the incident allude to conflict of interest on the part of the marketing officer?
3. Did the account officer err by bringing up innocuous personal matter during an official marketing assignment?
4. How can bank marketing officers go about this important assignment to ensure success?
5. What are the tasks involved in, and the workable approaches for, executing bank marketing calls?
6. Why and how should bank managements always monitor activities of field marketing officers?

Tips for solving the exercise
If satisfactorily accomplished, marketing calls would serve to strengthen a bank's market offerings and enhance its ability to satisfy customer needs. It would also help to improve the bank's earnings and returns to shareholders. No matter how one tries to analyze this case, it is strongly advised that marketing officers should not discuss—let alone divulge—personal or confidential information about them, their colleagues, or the bank in the course of their marketing assignments and activities. They should, above all, not make demands for personal favor from customers. These are some of the circumstances that could put some otherwise diligent marketing officers in an awkward position. This happens especially when such act is the reason a banking relationship fails. Avoiding casual or informal calls is also pertinent. It saves marketing officers embarrassment for which they never bargained. As much as possible, marketing officers should always plan and formalize visits to existing and prospective customers.

INTEGRATING CUSTOMER NEEDS WITH MARKETING GOALS

In bank marketing, customer needs and goals of bank management must drive strategy, resource allocation, results expectation, and rewards for performance. The bank must devise effective and discreet methods for ascertaining customer needs. Once established, appropriate product and service offerings should be developed to satisfy the needs. It is imperative that banks always appreciate their customers—their individualities, preferences, and idiosyncrasies. Otherwise marketing efforts and strategies may not succeed. This success criterion is not and will, indeed, never be served by lavishing caring on only the customers that maintain big accounts, so-called prime customers. The bank's caring disposition should be extended to customers at the lower rung. Such customers really hope to grow in business with support from their banks and should be encouraged.

There are, at any one time, three main variables in the needs profile of customers that banks cannot afford to ignore. It is immaterial whether the customers make the prime status or not. The overriding customer needs which banks must satisfy as growth and survival strategies are:

- Assurance of *safety* of customer investment with the bank. Typical investments exist in forms of savings, fixed, and demand deposits.
- Provision of operational facility and personnel that work for and enhance overall *convenience* of transactions processing for customers.
- Offering of well researched services, and effective networks and delivery systems that add real, measurable, *value* to needs of the customers.

Once a bank recognizes, channels resources, and is tuned in to meeting these needs, it starts to gain a competitive advantage. Strengthening competitive capabilities of the bank would then translate into increasing earnings through growing market share. In general, customer loyalty drives increase in market share.

Often banks make the mistake of thinking that they could earn customer loyalty with good ambience, evidenced in locations, buildings, and office furnishings. This is especially the case with banks implementing branch expansion strategies, but nothing could be further from the truth. It is a tragedy that bank managements do not always appreciate the interplay between customer needs and marketing goals. Yet customer needs should always be in harmony with marketing goals. That's the bottom line.

MANAGING RISK THROUGH PREBANKING MARKETING RESEARCH INITIATIVE

Marketing serves, in varying degrees, the needs of the bank and customers. Potential customers might want to know available facility at the disposal of the bank to handle critical banking transactions. Perhaps it would also be imperative to ascertain whether in practice the bank strictly honors agreements, is customer friendly, is committed to customer service, and is oriented toward measurable real value in serving customer needs. In addition, customers might want to find out the bank's policy toward their kind of business. That will help them reassess their preference for banking relationship. Exploratory research can resolve these issues for the customers. With the benefit of hindsight, the customers could confidently relate with the bank.

Exploratory research—in the sense I have used it—is a preliminary investigation, which seeks to confirm the cause, establish aspects, or corroborate certain research variables. It is not a full-blown research, but the forerunner of it.

Customers may not have the time or patience to embark on elaborate exploratory research covering the three components. However, they should be able to study the experience of some others who have had dealings with the bank with which they intend to start banking relationship. They could also obtain useful information from newspapers, financial reports, and radio and television news. Yet a veritable source of authentic information for customers is other customers. Through personal interaction with current customers, prospective customers can find out useful information about the bank. Satisfied and happy customers would extol the bank and its offerings, in what is often termed word-of-mouth advertising. Dissatisfied and unhappy customers would most likely fully open up to inquiries about shortcomings of the bank's offerings, relationship management, customer care, and so on.

The bank, on its part, should engage marketing to establish, appreciate, and satisfy critical market needs. Need satisfaction remains the surest way to attract and retain customers. Mostly, a bank that adopts this marketing orientation will gain increasing market share over the long run. The greatest utility in prebanking marketing is the facility it offers a bank to preempt customer complaints. The bank attains this goal when it offers needs fulfilling services to the customers. Without such marketing effort, it would be difficult for the bank to have a large and increasing pool of satisfied customers.

In view of these illustrations, bank customers could engage in prebanking marketing just as banks do to optimize customer relationships. Marketing, from customer's perspective, would be necessary when the customer, either existing or potential, wants to:

- open a current, fixed deposit, savings, domiciliary or other type of account with the bank;
- apply for bank credit facility that may be available in any of the bank's lending products;
- present certain precious material possessions for safekeeping with the bank;
- make any serious business inquiries that could trigger banking relationships of sorts.

The customer would not go wrong with any marketing effort that they make to prepare for the eventual transaction. The customer would simply need to make such prebanking inquiries to ensure they make the right decisions. The customer should at least do an exploratory research to ascertain how best to package applicable proposals to the bank. Customers that follow this procedure succeed with their banking transactions. Such customers tend to integrate their banking needs—embodied in requests, proposals, or intended transactions—with the bank's marketing objectives.

Customers who enter into banking relationship without going through this rudimentary marketing practice may end up with regrets. For such customers, one cause of regret could be realizing that they had gone to the wrong bank in the first place. Often, customers feel disappointed when banks decline their requests, proposals, or transactions. Such customers tend to think that poor packaging is the culprit for their fate. This thinking is erroneous and borne out of inadequate knowledge of a bank's operating procedure or requirements. Yet another regrettable finding could be that an intended transaction does not satisfy a bank's risk acceptance criteria.

In all of the foregoing, the customers and bank would have wasted otherwise useful time before arriving at such a futile end for the declined requests, proposals, or transactions. This explains, in one sense, why and how marketing remains the key to business success—for the bank and customers.

CULTIVATING STAKEHOLDERS IN BANKING FOR MARKETING RISKS CONTROL

It is not just only bank customers—depositors, borrowers, and accountholders—that need relationship marketing. Investors, contractors, consultants, and banking regulatory authorities also need marketing to foster beneficial banking relationship. I ask questions that guide thinking on the relevance of marketing in fostering banking relationship.

- How would investors ensure that they realize and optimize expected returns from their investment in banks?
- In what ways should banks and shareholders maintain mutual understanding of the cause and basis of their relationship?
- How can banks and regulatory authorities foster cordial relationship through mutual understanding of each other's business, focus, and operations?
- What should contractors and consultants of banks do to remain top contenders for work or supply tenders?

In all of these questions, relationship marketing is aided when both parties— the bank and its stakeholders—make continuing deliberate effort to understand each other's needs. Some examples would serve to illustrate how this could be achieved.

Consider that bank managements might want the shareholders to approve particular policies regarding dividend payment, bonus shares, rights issue, or sale of equity stock. Without a clear understanding of the facts and assumptions underlying intended policies, there could be conflicts between managements and shareholders. The bank becomes the ultimate loser in possible misunderstanding that might ensue. With relationship marketing, the shareholders would try to find out why managements would want particular policies formulated. Bank managements, on their part, would try to establish and incorporate shareholder preferences in the intended policies. This is one of the ways to preempt relationship conflicts and controversies. Information that both parties need could be obtained during informal interaction between bank managements and major shareholders. It becomes easy for the former to get approval of the latter at board meeting to ratify intended policies. Thus, as in the marketing of physical products, neither of the parties is taken for granted.

The contractors and consultants of banks do not need aspects of relationship marketing described above any less than the shareholders. In general, banks relish aesthetics in office structure. In most cases, they insist on specific ambience. In addition, banks cherish distinctive office documents. Banks particularly do not compromise on the quality of jobs and, in most cases, are willing to pay compensating prices. Thus, contractors or consultants that intend to work for banks should first find out their needs and policies regarding contracts or jobs. In submitting their proposals to a bank, they should consider and be guided by findings from their marketing. Mode of payment for jobs, nature of the contractor's relationship with bank officers responsible for the jobs, and the bank's tenacity on contract agreements are some of the issues that require relationship marketing to be sustained at an optimum level.

Banks need to anticipate, appreciate, and adjust to regulatory policy thrusts and directions. With anticipatory and relationship marketing, the banks can forestall possible adverse effects of policy changes. Specifically, marketing would help the banks to maintain a cordial relationship with the regulatory authorities. For instance, the banks should devise ways of meeting deadlines on rendition of critical returns to the regulatory authorities. Perhaps the first step that a bank should take to demonstrate commitment to satisfy regulatory demands is to set up an effective compliance unit. With a chief compliance officer as the head, this unit should be strengthened with adequate level of employees and technology-driven work facility. This will help the bank to be on top of its relationship with the regulatory authorities. That mitigates risk of infraction of regulatory policies and guidelines and the attendant sanctions or penalties.

MITIGATING BANKING RISKS THROUGH RELATIONSHIP MARKETING

Banks and their customers have varied responsibilities in sustaining and optimizing beneficial relationships. The prebanking and prerelationship marketing described in the preceding sections should form the basis for consolidating mutual appreciation and satisfaction of each other's needs. I should mention some of the specific responsibilities of the parties right away.

Banks expect loyalty, and increasing volumes of transactions, and profitable dealings from customers. Needless to say, banks equally expect that its customers should bring only genuine transactions for processing or financing. Either at the beginning or during banking relationship, customers should fully disclose their personal and business identities to the bank. There should be no reservation of information for as long as KYC rules remain a regulatory risk control requirement. There is yet another critical issue that tends to weaken and introduce risk to banking relationships. It is how customers cope with decisions that banks make about their business requests, proposals, or transactions. Some customers may fault the fate of their requests, business proposals, or intended transactions after a bank takes decision on them. Banking relationship would be hurt under the circumstances when, in fact, that should not be the case. In the interest of relationship, customers should always be considerate when a bank declines their requests or transactions. Although banks rarely come out openly with reasons for their action, risk aversion is usually the factor at issue. In appreciating this fact, customers help sustain enduring risk-mitigating relationship with the bank.

The other parties with whom a bank has business dealings also have various roles to play in consolidating their banking relationships. The contractors and consultants of banks, for instance, could offer free postjob execution and related services. Such services should approximate to after sale service common in marketing industrial goods. In marketing parlance, this is alternatively referred to as postsale or after sale support service. Customers immensely treasure such free service. It may not be feasible or realistic to mention all that parties could do in all situations to strengthen relationship marketing in banking. Particular needs in each case should rather determine applicable or necessary actions to take.

INTERNAL RISK-MITIGATING INFORMATION FOR EFFECTIVE BANK MARKETING

Marketing employees should have a good understanding of their bank's market orientation, business focus, and goals in financial dealings. Banks tend to succeed more when understanding is the driving force behind target marketing. The success of marketing is also enhanced when the employees understand the dynamics, as well as mechanics, of the banking industry. It would be appalling to encounter marketing officers who have mere understanding of the vision, strategy, and market orientation of their bank. It would be particularly inexcusable that some marketing employees do not even have good—especially technical—knowledge of products and services their bank offers to the market. Such a situation increases bank marketing risks.

Marketing would equally be a perfunctory responsibility, fraught with risks, if the personnel engaged in it are not totally committed to the bank. However, employee commitment stems, first and foremost, from realizing that the bank holds the key to their personal employment goals. With this fact as a given, believing in—and knowing all there is to know about—the bank and its stakeholders becomes the drive for commitment and risk mitigation in bank marketing. In the first place, marketing employees should be conversant with the bank's ideology—comprising core purpose, core values, and the envisioned future of the bank. The employees should know and understand applicable market strategies and how the bank could meet, improve on, or beat the competition. This implies that the employees should at any one time know and harness the bank's strengths for business and growth, and deal with its weaknesses. But it also implies that the employees should be able to exploit opportunities open to the bank in the industry while monitoring and reporting on threats to its business, market share, or corporate existence.

Sound knowledge of these variables is a useful tool for developing effective risk-mitigating marketing plans. Let me now look more closely at specific risk-mitigation information needs for successful bank marketing in developing economies.

Bank-Related Marketing Information

There are numerous aspects of a bank and its functions about which marketing employees need adequate knowledge in order to mitigate risk and succeed. Critical areas of information need that relate to the bank itself include:

- Details about services which the bank offers to the market, especially distinctive features that set them apart from the competition.
- How development, quality, and uses of the bank's services reflect its commitment to superior benefits to customers?
- Value propositions that reduce cost of doing business with the bank—and how such cost reducing devices help the bank gain a competitive advantage.
- The bank's operational arrangements for efficient, fast and error-free transactions processing, especially in novel banking.
- Services and marketing strategies of other banks to which the marketing employees should find appropriate responses.
- The bank's channels structure for effective financial services delivery to the customers and prospects.
- Computer software or other IT processing capabilities with which the bank processes transactions, and how they support the bank's operations.
- Size, growth, and going concern potential of the bank, as reflected in its actual and projected balance sheets and operating results.
- Capital base and shareholders' fund (i.e., the bank's net worth) are always critical marketing variables—and a major measure of a bank's financial strength.

Marketing employees should have a working knowledge of, and be able to interpret, the bank's assets and liabilities portfolios. They also need to understand the composition and marketing implications of the balance sheet items. Bank marketers should always deliberately be seeking and acquiring particular and general knowledge about their bank. It cannot be overemphasized that they should be at least wellinformed about their bank. I should rather emphasize that such knowledge prepares them for marketing assignments—most of which are really challenging.

I discuss below particular risk-mitigating information for bank marketing. The information pertains to aspects of the bank with which marketing personnel should be conversant.

Background Information

Marketing personnel should be familiar with the founding, ownership, and evolution of the bank. Some banks may have passed through and survived challenging historical periods during which their contemporaries might have become distressed or failed. Historical antecedents of the successful banks can be a strong competitive edge. Marketing employees should exploit this strength. Strong experience spanning decades of successful banking practice is always an asset for bank marketing. Banks that enjoy this benefit abound in both developed and developing economies. This strength wins and sustains customer confidence in the face of cut-throat competition.

Financial Analysis and Standing

Credit and liquidity standing of a bank should never be in doubt. Some independent and reputable credit rating agencies should certify it. Required financial information bank marketing includes knowledge of positive changes in key balance sheet items over a period of at least 5 years. Comparative ratio analysis of the bank's financial performance over the same period also provides useful risk-mitigating marketing information. Marketing employees should especially keep abreast of changes in the bank's fortunes at any one time.

Branch Locations and Policies

Marketing personnel should know all the branch offices of their bank. Such knowledge should include information on hub and spokes arrangement the bank adopts to web its marketing loops. The most relevant information would be an understanding of where and why the bank locates branch offices in particular places, or parts of a country. Sustained growth in network of branches is an expansionist strategy. It appeals to the banks that want to build business strength in retail banking. Such banks also aim to rapidly grow deposit liability portfolio with a large pool of cheap deposits. Overall, knowledge of branch locations, policies, and coordination gives insight into peculiarities of banking needs and risks in different regions, as well as appropriate marketing responses.

International Offices and Affiliations

Many banks have international subsidiaries and offices. Some enter into foreign alliances and affiliations to facilitate international business and financial exchanges. This is usually done to advance customer service beyond countries of the banks' domicile. With such international offices, the banks could harness strength in diversifying products and services to the customers. It is therefore imperative for the marketing personnel to understand the thinking behind opening of such foreign offices, branches, or subsidiaries. Such information comes in handy in mitigating risks of international marketing. Country risk—often mirrored in political risk—is typical. Such risks should be considered in marketing international banking services and operations.

Operational Policies and Guidelines

Marketing officers should not be ignorant of operational standards of their bank. I mean guides such as standard operating procedure, credit policy manual, foreign exchange guidelines, and so on. These and similar working documents do not strictly apply to the marketing function. Yet it is important to appreciate their implications for effective bank marketing. Marketing officers will sometimes have to defend aspects of these policy documents in the course of their assignments. Of course, they need some of the information in the documents to sell or mitigate risks of particular banking services.

Goodwill and Reputation

Goodwill and reputation of a bank are critical intangible assets which marketing employees should leverage as the need arises. Few banks achieve good standing on goodwill. Such banks jealously guard against losing the feat. Information about a bank's goodwill is an important tool of, and strength in, bank marketing. Marketing employees should capitalize on such information to advance risk-mitigation cause of the bank in its target markets. In addition to mitigating risk, goodwill helps to beat or cope with the competition.

EXTERNAL RISK-MITIGATING INFORMATION FOR EFFECTIVE BANK MARKETING

There are many sources of external information relevant to risk-mitigation in bank marketing. Few of the sources are really invaluable. Marketing employees tap the main sources when they:

- Peruse available magazines, journals, and articles that relate to banking industry, services, and practices. From these information sources, they could gain or update their vocational knowledge.
- Read useful and related books, especially those that focus on banking industry, services, and practices.
- Read in-house magazine of the bank and publications of the Central Bank, Deposit Insurance Corporation, Stock Exchange, Securities and Exchange Commission, and so on. The marketing employees should, as much as possible, also read the in-house magazines and publications of competing banks.
- Get information from the press—including, in particular, newspapers, radios, televisions, and so on.
- Solicit and obtain relevant marketing information from prospects, especially those that currently have banking relationship with other banks.
- Visit and obtain information from relevant factories, marketplaces, warehouses, business offices, and so on.

Customers and prospects are an unusual source of pertinent risk-mitigating marketing information. Marketing employees should interact freely with them in a bid to not only understand their needs, but get useful marketing information. They should seek and get information from those with whom the bank has enduring business relationships. Useful information could be obtained from both satisfied and dissatisfied customers. This has proven to be one of the most veritable sources of risk-mitigating marketing information.

Bank marketing employees should appreciate the risk-mitigation significance of information pertinent to their assignments. It is essential that marketing employees are equipped with appropriate and relevant information. This is particularly important for field marketing officers. Whiting (1957: 9–14) identified certain reasons why salesmen need product knowledge. The reasons are applicable to personnel involved in marketing banking services. I have discussed the relevant information needs in the preceding sections. Now I should state why bank marketing employees need information. In addition to risk-mitigation, marketers need authentic information because—according to Whiting—knowledge builds enthusiasm, enhances courage, gives personal satisfaction, and bestows confidence. Without sound knowledge it would be difficult for marketers to answer objections, deal with competition, have self-assurance, and gain the confidence of prospects.

PROSPECTS FOR THE FUTURE

In the future, marketing is likely to be a tougher banking function. One of the major requirements for successful marketing in developing economies would be appetite for information and knowledge. Mostly, information search and utilization would target evolving markets in all sectors. In doing so, satisfaction of customer needs will continue to be given precedence. This goal should be pursued with sufficient knowledge of all that are at stake in banking. Thus, marketing officers should cultivate a habit of gathering, analyzing, and using information pertinent to their assignments. Success of marketing would depend even more on the extent to which information and knowledge positively impact banking outcomes in measurable terms.

SUMMARY

The usual starting point for risk mitigation in bank marketing is encapsulated in the famous KYC rules. Influence of bank marketing reflects in maneuvering, pricing, and promoting services. Marketing officers should make regular and organized calls to existing and prospective customers. However, they should avoid casual calls.

Customer needs and goals of bank management must drive strategy, resource allocation, results expectation, and rewards for performance. Banks should devise effective methods for ascertaining customer needs. Once established, appropriate services should be developed to fulfill the needs. Overriding customer needs include safety of deposit, convenience of transactions, and value-added offerings. Marketing serves, in varying degrees, the needs of banks and customers in prebanking marketing setting, with exploratory research support. Thus, banks and their customers, as well as stakeholders in banking have responsibilities in sustaining and optimizing beneficial relationships. Prebanking and prerelationship marketing should form the basis for consolidating mutual appreciation and satisfaction of each other's needs.

Marketing employees should have a good understanding of their bank's market orientation, business focus, and goals in financial dealings. Banks tend to succeed more when understanding is the driving force behind target marketing. The success of marketing is also enhanced when the employees understand the dynamics, as well as mechanics, of the banking industry. Marketing would be a perfunctory responsibility, fraught with risks, if the personnel engaged in it are not totally committed to the bank. However, employee commitment stems from realizing that the bank holds the key to their personal employment goals. With this fact as a given, believing in—and knowing all there is to know about—the bank becomes the drive for commitment and risk mitigation in bank marketing.

There are many sources of information relevant to risk-mitigation in bank marketing. Some of the sources are really invaluable and marketing employees should tap them. In doing so, they should appreciate the risk-mitigation significance of information pertinent to their assignments. In the future, marketing is likely to be a tougher banking function. Its success would depend on the extent to which information and knowledge positively impact banking outcomes in measurable terms.

QUESTIONS FOR DISCUSSION AND REVIEW

1. In what sense can risks in bank marketing be correctly or wrongly described as significant or inconsequential?
2. What are the implications of prebanking marketing and relationship marketing initiatives for risk management in banking?
3. Of what significance is information for mitigating bank marketing risks in developing economies?
4. How should bank managements ensure that gains from marketing are optimized at the least possible risk and cost to the bank?
5. Why does bank marketing risks control correlate with high stakes in banking in developing economies?

REFERENCE

Whiting, P.H., 1957. The Five Great Rules of Selling. McGraw–Hill Book Company, Inc, New York.

Section A

Public Concern and Outcry

Chapter 7

Risk, Safety, and the Future of Deposit Money Banks in Developing Economies

Chapter Outline

LEARNING FOCUS AND OBJECTIVES

Banking regulatory authorities adopt certain measures in evaluating the risk and safety of deposit money banks (DMBs). The Basel Committee on Banking Supervision (2006) recommends standardized approaches applicable to internationally active banks. I assess the common measures which the authorities use in developing economies. I identify a framework that approximates to a standard methodology for evaluating the safety of DMBs in developing economies. This underlies my focus in this chapter—which is geared to:

- Demonstrate the practical options for assessing the risk and safety of DMBs in developing economies.
- Investigate why and how DMBs in developing economies should be safe, efficient, and earn depositor confidence.
- Characterize the approach of regulatory authorities to measuring the risk and safety of DMBs in developing economies.
- Strengthen analytical framework for evaluating the risk and safety of DMBs in developing economies.

- Discuss how the trade-off between risk and return bear on the risk and safety of DMBs in developing economies.
- Investigate how the risk-return principle sheds light on the relationship between risk and safety of DMBs in developing economies.
- Identify the lessons to be learned from the myths and misguided thinking on the safety of DMBs in developing economies.

EXPECTED LEARNING OUTCOMES

It is essential that DMBs are safe at all times. That earns depositor confidence and ensures that banks operate strongly as going concerns. It is the responsibility of banking regulatory authorities to devise, invent, and reinvent measures of safety of banks. The common measures used for banks in developing economies build on some fundamental financial ratios—including cash reserve ratio, liquidity ratio, loan-to-deposit ratio, and so on. The reader will—after studying this chapter and doing the exercises in it—have learnt and been better informed about:

- Why and how DMBs in developing economies should be safe, efficient, and earn depositor confidence?
- The approach of banking regulatory authorities to measuring the safety of DMBs in developing economies.
- Practical options for managing risks of DMBs in developing economies.
- The approach of the regulatory authorities to measuring the risk and safety of DMBs in developing economies.
- How analytical framework for evaluating the risk and safety of DMBs in developing economies may be strengthened.
- The trade-off between risk and return and its bearing on the risk and safety of DMBs in developing economies.
- How the risk-return principle sheds light on the relationship between risk and safety of DMBs in developing economies.
- Lessons of the myths and misguided thinking on the safety of DMBs in developing economies.

OVERVIEW OF THE SUBJECT MATTER

A DMB should always and necessarily be run as a going concern, though this may sound a bit far-fetched in some cases. This implies that bank management can do anything but compromise the safety of the bank it runs. It is common knowledge that banks often cut corners, cook the books, and report bogus earnings. That is the reason reported earnings of banks are often seen as mere "paper profit." In many cases, this view presupposes that financial statement and accounts of banks are just window dressing. Of course not all banks are guilty of these charges. Good management dictates that bankers should be strictly committed to upholding the ethics of their profession. Doing so, they should strive to adhere to international best practices.

There is yet another misguided thinking on the safety of banks—one that has become commonplace—in foregoing erroneous sense. It is a view that upholds thinking that assurance of protection for customer deposits is a proxy for DMB safety. Often this view is stretched to imply and accommodate security of customer banking transactions and relationships in DMB safety calculations. These are pure suppositions and represent uninformed departures from methodology for DMB safety analysis and evaluation. Deposit insurance—often provided and funded with taxpayers' funds—may furnish some comfort and therefore a measure of protection to the banks and customers. But this is never dependable as a safety measure. It works on the basis of fulfilling some conditions precedent which the intended beneficiaries may not be in a position to fulfill at the time a bank becomes distressed or fails. In reality, indices of safety of DMBs differ significantly from measures of financial performance. Secured dynamics of transactions does not definitely make the index. Safety of a DMB should be understood in the context of a holistic mechanism which ensures continuation of operations of the DMB as a going concern.

I hold and build this perspective on the understanding that a lot of intricate issues underlie the business of banking. Such issues, considered significant, should be taken into account in determining the safety of DMBs in developing economies. Needless to say, this view is anchored in the banking evaluation system. Ideally, there should be a proven methodology to evaluate the safety of the DMBs in developing economies. What really happens in practice is that banking regulatory authorities adopt a set of financial measures, ostensibly to fill the gap. This has hardly been efficacious considering that DMBs in developing economies still become distressed and fail under largely avoidable circumstances.

SAFEGUARDING BANKS AGAINST INTERRELATED RISKS IN DEVELOPING ECONOMIES

Some financial pundits—the World Bank, Amaonwu (1989), Irukwu (1974), and Nwankwo (1991)—are all agreed that banks should be safeguarded, one way or the other, against potential risks. Effective risk management safeguards DMBs. It is also imperative for the success of a bank. Risk must be anticipated, measured, and planned for at any point in time. That is the reasoning behind the concept and applications of risk management in banking. Statistical probability is used to measure the likelihood that an event will occur.

The World Bank (2013) argues that risk management "is the process of confronting risks, preparing for them (exante risk management), and coping with their effects (ex-post risk management)" (pp. 12, 61). In its opinion, "the goal of risk management is to both decrease the losses and increase the benefits that people experience when they face and take on risk." It suggests that "risk management needs to combine the capacity to prepare for risk with the ability to cope afterward—taking into account how the upfront cost of preparation compares with its probable benefit." The Bank insists that for risk management to be strong, it should include "knowledge, protection, insurance, and coping." These components of risk management, according to the Bank, "interact with each other, potentially improving each other's quality" (p. 12).

Irukwu (1974: 4–5) identifies three methods for solving the risk problem as prevention of the loss, assumption of the risk, and insurance. Nwankwo (1991: 154–155) argues that banks stick with risk avoidance strategy in their day-to-day operations. That explains the preference of the banks for short-term, self-liquidating, risk assets. On the strategy of risk transfer, it is obvious that not all risks are transferable by means of insurance. In fact, most banking hazards would not satisfy the characteristics of insurable risks. This has implication for risk management in banking. Banks should constantly anticipate risk. For practical purposes, they should be able to identify, analyze, and mitigate risks in the course of their operations. In order to succeed, banks should work out and adopt an efficient strategy for risk management. The banking literature, fortunately, is replete with workable risk management principles, theories, and practices. Yet, controversy over appropriate risk management methodology, regrettably, lingers.

SITUATING RISK AND SAFETY OF DEPOSIT MONEY BANKS IN DEVELOPING ECONOMIES

In the investment field, risk is usually understood as the variability of expected returns. Rational investment decisions are based on the expectation of commensurate returns, or cash inflows. However, at the time of commitment of funds, it will not be certain if the expectation will be realized. One reason is that future events on which the expectation depends are uncertain, and can alter forecasts about future outcomes. Thus, risk results from the inability of investors to make forecasts of future cash flows or returns with certainty, or based on the current events or situation.

The situation is not different in the case of banking—especially in developing economies where markets tend to be volatile. One question immediately springs to mind. Why is a lot of emphasis placed on managing risk in banking, especially in developing countries? The straightforward answer that I give right away is quite instructive. Banking is unusually risky—indeed, riskier than most businesses. Does this answer hit the nail on the head? Perhaps, it doesn't and I qualify it accordingly. The great emphasis on risk and uncertainty in banking derives from the nature and functions of banks in the first place. Let me give a more plausible reason, one that is informed by the modified answer. Banking is inherently oriented to risk taking. No matter how it is analyzed, risk is endemic in banking—apparently more than it is in most businesses.

If it were true that banking is more prone to risk than most businesses are, it would equally have been true that some factors inform or reinforce that conclusion. What are the possible factors? Why are the factors certain to create risk in banking? Does the effect of the factors cut across banks in developing economies and elsewhere? In what ways may banks check the factors and mitigate risks attendant on them? I answered these questions in Part I of this book. I provided information that is essential if the reader is to have informed answers. Then I assessed implications of the answers, but a word of caution: three aspects of risk tolerance underlie the implications. Bank management may want to adopt one of the three possible attitudes toward risk. It may decide to be averse to risk, risk neutral, or seek risk. With this point in mind, I discussed that why banks are more prone to risk than most businesses, especially in developing economies.

I am concerned, presently, with relating risk taking in banking to the safety of DMBs in developing economies. A bank may want to take on or avoid particular risks for some reasons. Common reasons for taking on risk in banking include the need to meet budget goals, win particular accounts, increase market share, and so on. These risk-taking reasons make sense in situations where opportunities underlie the risks taken on. However, a bank should avoid risk taking, or be neutral to risk, where the risks are underlain by threats. Indeed, banks in developing economies should always be cautious about the risks they want to take on. They should especially, first and foremost, anticipate and plan for risk taking. That way they will be consolidating their safety. This is, perhaps, the reason banking reforms around the world—especially in developing economies—are often geared to curtailing appetite of the DMBs for risk taking. The objective, doing so, is to institutionalize a sound banking culture and system that ensures that the DMBs are safe at all times.

The need for safety of DMBs cannot be overemphasized. Neither should it be compromised without serious repercussions. DMBs should ever seek to manage risk well. That is the roadmap to success in the long run. There is a temptation here, though. On occasion, banks tend to be lured by profit motive into taking on risk to excess. This is not to say that banks should always be risk averse. Neither does it imply that banks should always have a risk preference disposition. Best practice demands that risk taking in banking should be informed by a sensible cause. In pursuit of that cause, banks should strive to strike the right balance between their appetite for risk and budget goals. A bank would be adjudged to have struck the right balance when it takes moderate risk and significantly tames overambitious budget goals. Usually, the risk-return principle is always instructive. Failure to follow or balance its tenets with the realities of banking in developing economies could be a recipe for financial crisis. The inverse relationship between risk and return which underlies the principle provides the guide that bank managements need. There is always a trade-off between the two possible business outcomes: a higher risk tends to result in more profit, while less risk is often achieved at the expense of more profit.

The trade-off between risk and return has a bearing on the risk and safety of DMBs in developing economies. The more liquidity a DMB achieves and retains for its operations, the less profit or returns it makes. Suffice it to say that there is opportunity cost to increasing and retaining liquidity in banking. The real cost of liquidity is the lost or foregone opportunity to invest idle funds or utilize them to boost banking services and operations at a profit. Thus, liquidity is a critical approximation to less risk and more safety for a bank. In this sense, a bank may want to sacrifice profit for liquidity. The reverse is also true. Liquidity stress approximates to more risk and less safety for a bank and is often the result of taking on risk to excess—usually in asset creation. Overtrading and inordinate chase after budget goal can also plunge a bank into liquidity stress. The reward for risk taking, though, is increased profit. This is the expected outcome in most cases. Thus a bank that deliberately chases after profit or other budget goal might be unwittingly sacrificing liquidity.

RISK-SAFETY DIVIDE ACROSS DOMESTIC AND FOREIGN SUBSIDIARY BANKS

In the preceding section, I focused on some of the tested principles on which banks in developing economies can rely to succeed in the long run. It should be noted that domestic and foreign subsidiary banks (FSBs) are not equally averse to risk. There is also variation in their predisposition to risk. The domestic banks (DBs) tend to manifest a predisposition to excessive risk taking behavior. The FSBs, in contrast, adopt risk aversion tendencies and behavior and are uncritical of this disposition. Differences in attitudes to and tolerance of risk between the two categories of banks are often dictated by anxiety to remain going concerns. Incidentally, the FSBs tend to manifest the anxiety more than their domestic counterparts. This is ironic, considering that the FSBs enjoy and build strategy around strong liquidity base and technically foolproof operations, both of which are critical for safety in banking. Cautiousness, perhaps, sheds light on their anxiety to be going concerns. On occasion, the anxiety would be unfounded after all, but the skepticism fuelling it sticks.

DBs appear to be less anxious about the going concern question, ostensibly due to some local conditions and influences that skew their orientation to business. The cultural context in which the banks operate would always be a major factor for consideration. It is a significant local factor in accounting for influences on domestic banking behavior, practices, and outcomes. Unlike the FSBs that draw cultural sensitivity and behavior from international banking experiences—especially their parent banks' countries of domicile—the DBs are largely bound to follow local cultural prescriptions and dictates. Thus DBs are more culture bound than FSBs in the same business environment and setting. Cultural influence is at times seen in admission of external interferences in the workings of DBs.

Take separation of ownership from control as example. There is concern about possible blurring of separation of ownership from management in the running of DBs. This situation has been a major cause of interference and, on occasion, maneuvering of internal banking policies and practices by the board of directors. A common manifestation of risk inherent in this situation is the vexed issue of insider abuse in banking. Some think that the buck stops with the shareholders that have controlling interest in the DBs. The blame may be rightly laid at the door of such shareholders, no doubt about it. Unfortunately, however, talks about the problem rather than solution to it dominate discussions in banking, financial, and regulatory circles. As would be expected under the circumstances, recriminations ensue. Usually, this outcome does not resolve the problem. It ends in passing the buck, to say the least.

FSBs may have this setback—but, unlike the DBs, certainly not in appreciable measure. The question of influence of individual shareholders with controlling interest may not arise in FSBs. Most FSBs are wholly owned and subject to control by their parent banks. The nature of the parent banks' influence on the FSBs does not distort the time–honored business principle of separation of management from ownership.

CASE STUDY 7.1 The Rat Race Syndrome—Implications for Bank Risk Management

Pete's relocation to Lagos was not a simple decision (Extracted, with minor changes, from Onyiriuba, 2013. On the Road to Self-Actualization. NFS Data Bureau Limited, Lagos, pp. 24–26. Although this is a real life story, the names of the bank and individual in the tale are imaginary and do not relate to any known or unknown real bank or person in Nigeria or elsewhere. The story is set in Lagos, Nigeria, purely for illustration purposes only, in order to demonstrate how implication of the tale plays itself out in bank risk management in developing economies). Friends, family, and relations sometimes marveled at his high risk appetite. For them it was a big gamble that he took in uprooting himself from AU Community to Lagos without assurance of where to stay in Lagos. Curiously, he had resigned his journalism appointment even as he had not made a good arrangement to relocate to Lagos. Of course he had taken a firm stand to accept the new job he got, so he must find a way to relocate. It was in that state that he set out to Lagos, apparently from certainty to uncertainty. But it would appear that he took the risk with his eyes open, largely because he was convinced that his cause was noble. Yet it was a leap in the dark in quest of greener pastures and self-actualization. He was driven by hope which informed the adventure and its bearing. That hope was rooted in envisioning his future as a fulfilled man.

Pete was barely settling to work for Mega Consulting when he realized that he had apparently not gained income in real terms from the change of job. While working in AU Community, he earned 5000 naira per annum. With that income, he was able to rent, furnish, and live in a comfortable three bedroom flat. Food was cheap. He regularly bought food items in large quantity. He cooked and ate what he relished. Life and living were ordinary, without great demands. Coming to Lagos reversed those gains. Everything dramatically changed. Although his income increased in nominal terms to 25,000 naira per annum when he started working for Mega Consulting, he was unable to meet the basic needs that he easily satisfied in AU Community. Cost of living was considerably higher in Lagos. He usually walked from his residence to his workplace in AU community, but in Lagos, the reverse was the case. Sometimes he went to work in a cab up to a point before transferring to a bus, and vice versa. Such mode of commuting, requiring multiple transfers, was common in cases where people lived far away from their workplaces. His plight worsened with knowing that landlords in Lagos demanded at least 2 years rent upfront on property from new tenants. It dawned on him that he would perhaps have to work for up to 2 years or more before he could save enough money to rent an apartment, let alone start furnishing it.

In several other ways, Pete's new Lagos experience was certainly a far cry from that of the AU community. Perhaps the most intriguing finding, one that never appealed to him, was the preoccupation of Lagos residents with the rat race. It had become a way of life of sort for the people, ingrained in their psyche. Statements such as "I must make it," "I didn't come to Lagos to look at overpasses," "It's a dog eat dog Lagos," and "This is Lagos," were rife and slangs you were likely to hear where you find two or more people discussing their work, careers, or ambitions. It was rare to find overly lazy fellows. Pete particularly noticed septuagenarian cab drivers stuck in traffic jam on very busy roads, apparently unruffled, as they patiently waited for the vehicles to start moving. Everybody he met on the street, in an office, or even in a marketplace showed marked urgency in the way they moved, or conducted their affairs, transactions and so on. They easily became impatient with distracting or trivial issues. People were always in a hurry. Hurrying to where? Pete asked himself. While the question was on his mind, it remained a puzzle in the first couple of weeks. He couldn't make out what was driving the observed behavior. He couldn't but start reflecting deeply on those realities which, to the uninitiated, would not make sense. Looking back, he marveled at the contrast to how people worked and lived in other parts of Nigeria where he had lived before coming to Lagos.

Pete started adjusting to survive in Lagos, gradually but steadily. It was easy to do so because it fitted well with his mood, the drive that spurred him to quit journalism and leave AU Community. In less than six months of living in Lagos, he had become a complete Lagosian, fraught with the rat race, and succeeding at his level. Unlike when he was living in AU Community, he never had breakfast largely because of the early morning rush to work. For the first 6 weeks or so that he worked for Mega Consulting, he regularly woke up at 4 o'clock to start preparing for work and go to the office about half past 7 o'clock. Although he closed for work at 5 o'clock in the evening, he never got home earlier than 8 o'clock in the night. That was not bad by Lagos standard.

Exercise for class and group discussion

1. How does Pete's risk-taking appetite as highlighted in this tale compare with that of banks in developing economies?

2. What does the phrase "bankable risk" connote in banking? In what situations can it be realistically said that a given risk taken by a bank is bankable?
3. Why would it be right or wrong to associate banking in developing economies with the rat race syndrome?
4. In what ways does jumping on risk-taking bandwagons exacerbate crisis of banking in developing economies?
5. Are there lessons bank managements in developing economies should learn from the experience of Pete in this tale?

Tips for solving the exercise

Bank managements should be ever prepared to confront risk. There should be a sensible and defensible cause and motive for taking on particular risks in banking. It doesn't just have to be that the underlying transaction is bankable. A bankable transaction, for all intents and purposes, could backfire—and, depending on the magnitude of the concomitant loss, trigger financial crisis. The ramification of this tale is that bank managements in developing economies should always devise and apply appropriate and functional strategies to mitigate risks. It's always tempting to want to get around a risk instead of confronting it. An ignored risk could assume a more troubling dimension. That is why it is always better to act decisively in dealing with risks.

MEASURES OF RISK AND SAFETY OF DEPOSIT MONEY BANKS IN DEVELOPING ECONOMIES

The banking regulatory authorities in developing economies adopt a set of financial indices in assessing the health of banks. Ideally, the indices should be reliable as measures of risk and safety of the banks are at any point in time. The main indices in common use are the famed liquidity, cash reserve, and loan-to-deposit ratios. These ratios, strictly speaking, deal with bank liquidity—and understandably too. Liquidity is widely acknowledged as the lifeblood of a well-managed bank. Ironically, banks rarely rely on, or comply with, the ratios—even their internally generated ratios. The obvious reason for the banks' attitude toward the ratios is not far-fetched.

The ratios tend to limit banking space. Bankers plead this limitation in an attempt to downplay the benefits of the ratios. Otherwise, the ratios can really be relied upon to predict, as well as check, risk, and threat to banks as going concerns. Yet rather than acknowledge and tap this benefit, banks see the limits imposed on business by strict adoption of the ratios as punitive. As long as banks remain going concerns, bankers strive to find ways around liquidity crunch. Indeed, this is a wrong approach to dealing with risk and safety of banks in developing economies. In reality, it is always better to limit growth and sustain liquidity than chase after some expedient business goal and expose a bank to risk or compromise its safety. Experienced bankers in developing economies would attest to the sense in this view.

It is very difficult to gainsay the veracity of financial ratios. Incidentally, the ratios—bordering on issues in bank liquidity, cash reserve, and loan-to-deposit relationship—have implications for the risk of both domestic and FSBs. The ratios remain the foundation on which to build meaningful measures of safety of DMBs as going concerns in developing economies. Two complementary—and equally important—ratios are also pertinent. The additional ratios, loans-to-shareholders' funds, and classified loans-to-net worth, add a wider perspective. Using ratios derived from the balance sheet of First Bank of Nigeria Limited, Onyiriuba (2015) examined possibilities for measuring the risk, as well as safety, of DMBs in developing economies.

As I demonstrate in this discussion, the risk and safety of DMBs can be assessed using one, a combination, or all of the ratios. However, more reliable risk and safety measurement outcome is achieved when the ratios are concurrent with each other. Though this rarely happens in practice, it is nevertheless not unattainable. The ratios of some of the well-managed banks—those found among or in the mold of FSBs—can and sometimes do make the concurrence. In absolute terms the ratios do not indicate the actual risk or health of a bank. The relevance of the ratios is rather optimized when they are compared with particular internal benchmarks set by the bank. The regulatory authorities also do prescribe and enforce certain measurement indices. In some cases, there would be industry standard risk acceptance criteria with which the ratios should be compared.

Onyiriuba (2015) discusses aspects of the ratios—focusing on two main issues. He identifies issues that militate against the efficacy of the ratios. I mean factors that give the ratios theoretical coloration and render them unattractive to banking analysts. Then he explores how to overcome the problems and, doing so, strengthen the intent of the ratios in practical terms. Two other measures of risk and safety of banks—stress test and value at risk—are exotic and largely alien to banking in developing economies. Yet they have a bearing on measurement of risks of banks of all types—whether in developed or developing economies.

SUMMARY

The essence of bank management is essentially to run a bank as a safely going concern at all times. Good financial performance does not always mirror safety of investment in a bank. Banks often cut corners, cook the books, and report bogus earnings. That is the reason reported earnings of banks are often seen as mere paper profit. Some also suspect that accounts of banks are just window dressing.

Assurance of protection for customer deposits should not be taken uncritically as a proxy for safety of money deposit banks. The same goes for security of banking transactions and relationships. Deposit insurance—often provided and funded with taxpayers' money—may furnish some comfort in terms of protecting banks and customers. But this is never dependable as insurance is predicated on some elusive conditions. Indices of safety of DMBs differ significantly from measures of financial performance. Neither is efficient management of deposit liabilities and portfolio a proxy for the indices. Secured dynamics of transactions doesn't definitely make the index. Safety of DMBs should be understood in the context of a holistic mechanism which ensures continuation of their operations as going concerns.

The trade-off between risk and return has a bearing on the risk and safety of DMBs in developing economies. The more liquidity a DMB achieves and retains for its operations, the less profit or returns it makes. This suffices it to say that there is opportunity cost to increasing and retaining liquidity in banking. The real cost of liquidity is the lost or foregone opportunity to invest idle funds or utilize them to boost banking services and operations at a profit. Thus, liquidity is a critical approximation to less risk and more safety for a bank.

The DBs tend to manifest a predisposition to excessive risk taking behavior. The FSBs, in sharp contrast, adopt risk aversion tendencies and behavior and are uncritical of this disposition. Differences in attitudes to and tolerance of risk between the two categories of banks are often dictated by anxiety to remain going concerns.

There is a set of financial indices that indicate how safe or unsafe a bank is at any point in time. In addition to liquidity, cash reserve, and loan-to-deposit ratios, it is necessary to also evaluate loans-to-shareholders' funds, and classified loans-to-net worth ratios. Unfortunately, the banks rarely rely on, or comply with, the ratios—even their internal ratios. The risk and safety of DMBs can be assessed using one, a combination, or all of the five measures. A more reliable risk and safety measurement outcome is achieved when the five ratios are concurrent with each other.

QUESTIONS FOR DISCUSSION AND REVIEW

1. Why and how should DMBs in developing economies be safe, efficient, and earn depositor confidence?
2. How would you characterize the approach of regulatory authorities to measuring the risk and safety of DMBs in developing economies?
3. In what ways may analytical framework for evaluating the risk and safety of DMBs in developing economies be strengthened?
4. Does trade-off between risk and return have an empirical bearing on the risk and safety of DMBs in developing economies?
5. How does risk-return principle shed light on the relationship between risk and safety of DMBs in developing economies?
6. What lessons would you learn from the myths and misguided thinking on the safety of DMBs in developing economies?

REFERENCES

Amaonwu, O.E., 1989. Risk Quantification. International Conference on Risk Management, Enugu, Nigeria, 19–23 March, 1–16.

Basel Committee on Banking Supervision, 2006. International Convergence of Capital Measurement and Capital Standards: A Revised Framework, As Amended. Bank for International Settlements, Basel.

Irukwu, J.O., 1974. Accident and Motor Insurance in West Africa. The Caxton Press, Ibadan, Nigeria.

Nwankwo, G.O. 1991. Bank Management: Principles and Practice. Malthouse Press Limited, Lagos, Nigeria.

Onyiriuba, L., 2013. On the Road to Self-Actualization. NFS Data Bureau Limited, Lagos, pp. 24–26.

Onyiriuba, L.O., 2015. Emerging Market Bank Lending and Credit Risk Control: Evolving Strategies to Mitigate credit Risk, Optimize Lending Portfolio, and Check Delinquent Loans. Academic Press, San Diego, USA.

World Bank, 2013. World Development Report 2014: Risk and Opportunity: Managing Risk for Development. World Bank, Washington, DC, http://dx.doi.org/10.1596/978-0-8213-9903e3. License: Creative Commons Attribution CC BY 3.0.

Chapter 8

Money Laundering Links with Bank Risks and Management in Developing Economies

Chapter Outline

LEARNING FOCUS AND OBJECTIVES

Financial system authorities all over the world are ever grappling with money laundering crimes. The drive in money laundering is to use loophole in the laws to hide or use illegal money in legal ways. This is achieved when money obtained illegally is successfully put into—and used through—legal businesses or bank accounts. Laundering money in countries different from that where the money was illegally obtained in the first place complicates the crime. But it also renders money laundering an intriguing financial crime. Often money laundering is linked with conducting unlawful banking and other financial transactions. The foregoing informs my objectives for this chapter—all of which are intended to:

- trace the foundation of money laundering—and, doing so, investigate its dynamics and mechanisms in developing economies,

- discuss legal frameworks, policies, and guidelines on money laundering control in developing economies,
- explore influence of economic and business demands on money laundering in developing economies,
- investigate the role of banks in developing economies as unwitting accomplices in money laundering,
- provide insights into the use of banks as a conduit for money laundering in developing economies,
- assess risk-based laws and financial system regulations on money laundering in developing economies.

EXPECTED LEARNING OUTCOMES

Money laundering has been a burgeoning financial crime around the world of late. It would seem developing economies are the worst hit by the money laundering scourge. The financial authorities try, but all to no avail, to keep it in check. Indeed, money laundering is a nightmare. The authorities fail to grapple with it. Money laundering has wider implications for a country's macroeconomic foundation. Curiously, money laundering manifests itself in different forms but with the same motive. The reader will—after studying this chapter and doing the exercises in it—have learnt and been better informed about:

- motives behind money laundering, especially motives underlain by corruption, fraud, terrorism, and suchlike;
- the dynamics of money laundering crime, with special focus on its impact on enterprise, productivity, and national income;
- process and mechanisms of money laundering, and measures to detect and check money laundering;
- influence of economic and business environment on money laundering in developing economies;
- domestic and international risk-based laws and regulations to check corruption and money laundering.

OVERVIEW OF THE SUBJECT MATTER

Money laundering is a fast growing social malaise, one that touches the fabric of society around the world. It features among contemporary issues in managing the financial system—in both developed and developing countries. The drive in money laundering is to use loophole in the laws to hide or use illegal money in legal ways. This is achieved when money obtained illegally is successfully put into—and used through—legal businesses or bank accounts. Many developing economies are nowadays major centers for money laundering and related crimes.

I define money laundering in the context of this book and, doing so, set the stage for discussions in this chapter. Certain questions are pertinent to understanding the chapter's main topic and its dimensions. What actually do we mean when we use the phrase money laundering? In what context does money laundering take place? Do banks play a role deliberately or inadvertently in money laundering? Or, how are banks connected with money laundering?

The answers to these questions may draw from varied perspectives. I gravitate toward a banking perspective, consistent with the theme of this book. However, I also do not neglect or downplay definition with a wider perspective and application. The function of money as a medium of exchange underlies the special focus on banking in this discussion. Money serves this purpose under the auspices of the banking system. Suffice it to say that banks facilitate financial transactions and exchanges—and often get embroiled in money laundering investigations and charges. This is also how, by implication and fate, some bankers who innocently handle accounts used for money laundering often get entangled in corruption charges, investigation, and prosecution in courts.

MEANING AND DOMESTIC-FOREIGN SUBSIDIARY BANKS LINKS

Now, I try defining money laundering. Money laundering exists in a situation where someone or organization obtains and uses illegal money in legal financial or other transaction. The money that is obtained illegally and the legal transaction for which it is used are made to not look illegal even as where the money came from is deliberately hidden or shrouded in secrecy. Money laundering could also mean the process of disguising and passing illegal money through a bank in order to legitimize it and avoid detection of its source. Money laundering may yet be defined in a somewhat broader context. A broadened meaning would be equating money laundering with a criminal act in which someone or organization puts money obtained illegally into legal businesses, transactions, or bank accounts—often in different countries—in ways that make it difficult to detect, trace or know the real source of the money.

Laundering money in countries different from that where the money was illegally obtained in the first place complicates the crime. But it also renders money laundering intriguing. Often money laundering is linked with conducting unlawful banking transactions. The tendency is to treat banks as accomplices in money laundering crimes. On occasion, the banks may unwittingly facilitate money laundering. Thus, as unwitting accomplices, the banks are all too often in the firing line. This is the unfortunate fate of banks in money laundering charges and investigation. This fate is fallout of the criminal use of the banking system as a conduit for money laundering. It is perhaps the most disturbing dimension of money laundering of late. This hints at a general answer to the defining questions on the connection of banking with money laundering. Nonetheless, I try to proffer comprehensive answers to the questions as I discuss the topics of this chapter in detail.

It should be noted that money laundering discourages enterprise, punishes hard work, and rewards unproductivity. Yet no country progresses without disciplined workforce, increasing productivity, and efficient reward system in both public and private sectors. These are a necessary, though not sufficient, conditions for sustainable economic growth and development. At the macro level, money laundering distorts and renders national income inconsistent with balance of payments accounting. These consequences of money laundering have wider implications for a country's macroeconomic foundation. Those implications—though worth exploring—are beyond the scope of this book. It would seem developing economies are the worst hit by the money laundering scourge. As a criminal act, money laundering curiously manifests itself in different forms but with the same motive behind it.

The banks used for money laundering cut across domestic and foreign subsidiaries. It all depends on which banks fit well with the purpose of the crime at any one time. Someone that has inclination toward money laundering will ordinarily want to open an account with a bank where they may find it easy to maneuver aspects of transactions processing rules. They are likely to look for a bank where KYC and processing rules are somewhat lax—or a bank where they are likely to get easy accomplice for processing of their money laundering transactions. These conditions may exist more or less in domestic or foreign subsidiary banks. To this extent, the two types of banks have sure had their share of money laundering risks.

CASE STUDY 8.1 Remaining Steadfast in Noble Ideals—Application in Tackling Money Laundering

It took Clemens 24 months to finish and graduate from the MBA program at Anta University, Sri Lanka (Extracted, with minor changes, from Onyiriuba, 2013). He had completed and passed all the course work for the program within 12 months, but had to spend another 8 months on research project. It was unusual to spend that length of time on research work for a full time Master's degree program. Some of his course mates who finished earlier than him attributed his late graduation to the disposition of his supervisor. They wondered why he did not apply for change of supervisor when he was registering for the program like many others who were assigned to the same supervisor as him. Unknown to him, his supervisor was seen as a difficult lecturer who took interest in failing students and making life uncomfortable for them. Some intimated that only few students ever successfully completed research projects under his supervision.

When these facts dawned on Clemens, he was philosophical about them. Otherwise, he could have yet applied for change of supervisor. He could do so by switching interest from his area of research supervision competence. That was what most of the other students who were privy to his supervisor's antics and frustrating disposition did through approved faculty channel. It was not until he was working on the proposal for his thesis that he realized that his supervisor had only him and one other student to supervise. On the contrary, each of the other professors had up to ten postgraduate students from Clemens's class to supervise. Yet Clemens opted to stick with his supervisor—believing, in doing so, that he possessed what it took to scale the heights in research work. He invoked the popular saying that "when the going gets tough, the tough gets going," to prop up his determination. Besides, he took a swipe at the critics of his supervisor. As a high school tutor, Clemens knew that students often tagged principled teachers as mean or sadists. He thought that his supervisor was a victim of that unfounded stereotype and hoped to disabuse his critics of that bias. However, while he made the case for fairness to him, he recognized the import of the age old saying that "the proof of the pudding is in the eating."

With persistence Clemens continued to make slow but steady progress toward completion of his research project. In time he started appreciating why his supervisor acted in a negative sense to most of the students. He was a highly principled lecturer who was easily pissed off with lazy students. He was opposed to taking a shortcut, the easy way out, on an academic task. Only sober, hardworking students worked well with him. He once told Clemens how he earned his doctorate degree through thick and thin and would not understand why students would want to shy away from rigorous academic work. Then Clemens made a great finding about him, one that was instrumental to his success in the Master's program. He usually insisted that postgraduate students should contribute something new to existing body of knowledge in their chosen research fields.

Once Clemens got that clue, he started thinking seriously of the contribution that he would make from his research. It was a bit difficult for him, largely because his research combined topics from finance and insurance. To which field should he aspire to make the contribution—finance or insurance? And what would be the nature of the contribution? He was confused and took it up with him. He passed the buck to Clemens, clarifying that it was the student's responsibility to make findings and report what was new for academic review. Clemens took the advice and started reviewing what he had on the drawing board critically. He reckoned that it had remained worrisome that private and government-owned insurers lacked a model for risk quantification and premium determination for purposes of agricultural insurance. So he decided to develop one that would suffice for his contribution to knowledge in the field of insurance. He christened the model "Analytical Framework for Risk Measurement and Premium Determination in agricultural insurance." He came up with the model after several weeks of failed attempts at devising something creative.

His supervisor commended his effort when he presented a sketch of the model to him. "I guess he did that with cautious optimism," Clemens told a fellow PG student after defending his sketch of the model. Nonetheless, he approved the model with minor corrections after Clemens fully developed it. He however set a new hurdle for Clemens. He held that the model would be of no use if it could not be put into practice. So he directed that Clemens should generate and use hypothetical data to test it to be sure that it was workable. Again Clemens went to work on the new challenge. Doing so, he conducted surveys, made some assumptions, and drew inferences from literature searches. Thus he was able to test the model with hypothetical data. At that point he started appreciating his supervisor as a crack academic, never minding his shortcomings. In fact, he felt that his supervisor's famed faults were indeed an asset for him. Clemens now became more confident about his thesis, proud of his accomplishment, and would want to flaunt it. With boldness reflecting that mood, he turned in his final thesis. His supervisor graded it, scored him an "A" grade. The external examiner reviewed and confirmed the grade.

Exercise for class or group discussion
1. In what ways are banking challenges of money laundering similar to the intricacies of Clemens Master's degree research?
2. How does Clemens' character and disposition shed light on attitudes of the authorities toward money laundering?
3. What lessons should banking regulatory authorities learn from Clemens' research and supervision convictions?
4. Why, in your opinion, should the authorities learn from Clemens in not giving up on money laundering perpetrators?
5. How does Clemens' reward compare with benefits of checking the use of banks as a conduit for money laundering?

Tips for solving the exercise
Money laundering may have defied solution in developing economies, but the authorities should not give up on its perpetrators. Developing countries do not lack antimoney laundering laws. What may be lacking is, perhaps, the political will to enforce the laws to the letter. It would seem that money laundering offenders have perfected ways around the laws. That way they could walk the streets with impunity. Some even get off scot-free. These and similar offender tendencies should be checked if antimoney laundering laws are to be fruitful. Winning the war against the crime requires persistence, constant review of strategy, and appreciation of the role of new economy methods. I should make the point clearly here that half-hearted attacks on money laundering would fail. Notwithstanding its intricacies, there should be a practical road map to solution. That way the authorities can crack the crime. Inventing appropriate political will to deal with the crime is a necessary, though not sufficient, step. The authorities should be relentless in tracking and prosecuting the offenders. The deterrent effective of these measures would act as a check on the crime (Extracted, with minor changes, from Onyiriuba, 2013).

The names of the university and individual used in this case study are imaginary and do not relate to any known or unknown real university or person anywhere in the world. The story is set in Nigeria, purely for illustration purposes only, in order to demonstrate how some money laundering challenges of banking play themselves out in developing economies.

MONEY LAUNDERING DYNAMICS AND LINKS WITH CORRUPTION

Money laundering is one of the criminal fallout of corruption in the society. It mirrors one of the mechanisms of corruption in yet another practical context. In reference here is a situation where citizens willfully seek, maneuver someone or the system, and obtain money illegally—usually by deception—which they then deposit in bank accounts or use for transactions in legal ways. This implies that laundered money must find its way into the banking system, failing which it has to be used for some legal transaction, or stashed away somewhere. The overriding challenge, in all cases, is how to disguise or hide the real source of the money while banking and utilizing it. In this way, money laundering makes a typical example and expression of corruption in society. There are basically two links that I seek to explore. One link is between money laundering and corruption—how the latter informs the former. The other link is how money laundering connects with banking. Presently, I focus on the first link. I deal with the second link throughout this chapter.

Money laundering is rampant in developing economies. The act is often seen in defrauding government, fellow citizens, and foreigners, and does not augur well for the economy. Corruption itself is associated with dishonest or illegal behavior by people in positions of authority. Some may think that only people in the government, so-called political office holders, and civil servants should be tagged as corrupt. The basis of this thinking is erroneous. Corruption is endemic in society. It exists in virtually all spheres of human endeavor. Captains of industry, corporate executives, entrepreneurs and, indeed, the public are not all always above board—in other words, no one may be. Corruption has become so widespread in society that no one, group, or institution may really be exempted from it. This may sound a bit far-fetched, or an overstatement—and understandably too. In that case, it should be heartbreaking that corruption is nowadays an indulgence for many—indeed, a boost to money laundering. Corruption thrives on possibilities of getting away scot-free which money laundering amply offers. If it were not for money laundering, there would be a lot more risk—for example—in looting public treasury. A lot of other corrupt practices would equally be unattractive. On the other hand, as long as possibilities exist for money laundering, including the use of banks—even if as unwitting accomplices—corruption will continue to fester. Nonetheless, the relationship between money laundering and corruption is a typical illustration of a chicken and egg problem. The corollary is that money laundering would not be flourishing in the absence of corruption. The two vices tend to be mutually reinforcing. I look at the two situations concurrently in this discussion.

The scale of corruption in developing countries has been high, growing to unacceptable proportions. It would seem corruption has become a way of life. Individuals are keen to jump on the corruption bandwagon. This abhorrent but regrettably overlooked lifestyle is prevalent in official and private economic dealings and depletes national wealth. Official corruption manifests itself in lack of accountability, misappropriation of public funds, settlement of opposition and strong interest groups, and frustration of the judiciary. In many countries, private wealth—earned through apparently unproductive activities—tends to exceed public sector wealth and finds expression in conspicuous consumption at the expense of the widening gap between the rich and the poor. Corruption exists in several ways. External aid or financing may be received for a project that would not be executed while the funds are diverted to some unspecified current expenditures. Individuals may collaborate with public officers to secure highly overvalued contracts from government. Contractors may receive payments for jobs that have not been—and may never be—executed. A large number of ghost workers may be retained in public sector pay-rolls. Justice may be perverted under the influence of gratification. There may be influx of imported goods on which official tariffs are evaded. The list is really endless.

Corruption and Money Laundering Tendencies

Corruption has bugged governments down in several countries—a situation that renders it a worldwide phenomenon. As the World Bank (1991) observed, "the problem is by no means confined to governments, or to the developing countries. In some countries, it has grown to alarming and destructive proportions." According to the Bank, "corruption was identified as a serious problem in ancient China and India, in England in the early 1800s. Every other year a scandal is a reminder that it continues in Europe, Japan, and the United States." Besides, it is easy to associate the failure of governments, especially in developing economies, with the official corruption of the leadership. And the Bank is categorical in its statement that "corruption has also contributed to the fate of many governments: it was a major justification for the military overthrow of the Ghanaian civilian government in 1981 and the Nigerian one in 1983; an important theme in the 1982 Mexican presidential campaign; a major reason for the fall of the government in the Philippines in 1986; and a problem the authorities consider of the utmost gravity in the USSR." There is no doubt that "corruption weakens a government's ability to carry out its functions efficiently." Indeed, "bribery, nepotism, and venality can cripple administration and dilute equity from the provision of government services—and thus also undermine social cohesiveness." These factors of market imperfection should be removed from the system as part of the overall strategy to achieve economic growth and development.

Most of the developed nations have considerably checked the vices in public places. In these countries, individual wealth is to a great extent retained within the domestic economy to boost aggregate investment, savings, and growth. The investments are secured by political stability, maximum returns to the investors, and government's commitment to the promotion of private enterprise. In many developing economies, on the contrary, private wealth amassed from the public funds is domiciled with foreign developed countries as hidden treasures. The developmental capacity of the economies is thus reduced to almost nil by such capital flight. This is the plight of most of the developing economies. Ironically, most of the countries are endowed with abundant natural and human resources even as their citizens remain impoverished as a result of corruption and mismanagement of the national wealth. Griffiths (1984) interprets this pitiable economic and political degeneration in a historical setting.

It is necessary to sanitize the polity with a view to getting rid of money laundering borne out of corruption. Unless this is achieved, the goal of economic growth and development would remain a mirage. But it would be difficult to solve corruption in society without first dealing with its causes. The World Bank (ibid) argues that "corruption can seldom be reduced unless its larger underlying causes are addressed." In expounding this view, the Bank opines that corruption "flourishes in situations where domestic and international competition is suppressed, rules and regulations are excessive and discretionary, civil servants are underpaid, or the organization they serve has unclear or conflicting objectives." Citing a typical example in Africa, it notes that "in Cameroon, obtaining all the authorizations and permits necessary to start a new business takes 2 years even for a well-connected businessman; the law requires 24 different steps involving 20 separate offices." The Bank sees the mixed outcomes of anticorruption laws in this light. In its opinion, "anticorruption campaigns are periodically undertaken, sometimes with success. But often the root causes remain: weak agencies fighting market forces with controls society considers excessive, discretionary, or illogical."

Mechanisms of Corruption and Money Laundering

Corruption is never accidental. It happens by design, if anything. For example, corrupt public servants may take millions of money in kickbacks. Business people could offer bribes to get critical permits. Law offenders may bribe the Police to escape justice. People on low rung of society may embrace corrupt practices while struggling to eke out a living. For such people corruption evolves and intensifies with changing demands of everyday existence. As a social vice, corruption takes on different shapes depending on the setting and stakes. The World Bank (1991) shares the view that "corruption manifests itself in a variety of ways" as it illustrates the pervasiveness of the problem. The Bank opines that "a common one is bribery of custom officials, who then allow in illegal imports, or legal imports at below-legal duties, or expedite clearance procedures." It argues that "this has been a serious problem in numerous countries: in the United States at the turn of the century, in Singapore in the 1960s, in Indonesia in the 1970s, and in Cameroon in the 1980s." It noted that "Police indulgence of extortion and other crimes in Hong Kong led to the creation of an anticorruption office in the 1970s." The Bank notes further that "in the late 1970s, an inquiry in Massachusetts revealed that 76% of a sample of public buildings had at least one "structural" defect that could not have occurred without inspectors' complacency." In much the same vein, the Bank found that "two-thirds of the names on the civil service roster in 1978 in Zaire were fictitious."

Most worrying, perhaps, is that actions of some heads of government fan the flames of corruption. This happens mainly where democracy has been jettisoned and personal rule enthroned and institutionalized. The whole system within the polity becomes tuned in to corruption and wastefulness. Gould (1980) cites this mark of decaying society in Mobutu Sese-Seko's 1977 speech to the legislative council. In Nigeria, the corruption of public officials remains a major social problem retarding growth and development. Corruption became so pervasive in Nigeria that Shonekan (1993)—then Head of the country's interim government—told the National Assembly that Government would "no longer ignore the issue of corruption which is now widely believed to be quite endemic in our country." Unfortunately, the regime was truncated in a wave of political upheavals. At this time it had become practically almost impossible to govern the country without first purging the economy of this social ill. Public institutions, functions, and services had turned overly wasteful, this being a significant factor in the country's economic downturn. In late 1970s, corruption had become widespread, endemic, and a worrying factor in the frustration of state progress. Government had been profligate with public expenditure, causing severe imbalances in both the domestic and external accounts. Successive government paid lip service to solving the problem. In 1990s, government institutions became almost crippled on account of corruption. The Chairman of the probe of a government corporation aptly dramatized the corruption scene in Nigeria. He noted that "God made man; Man made money; Money made man mad ..." The unwritten code in (*this corporation's*) style of management, therefore, would appear to be every one for himself and God for us all; make hay while the sun shines; and loot all lootables. This was the statement of the Chairman of the panel set up by Government to probe the operations of its parastatal that oversees the activities of the country's oil sector. It was made while the chairman was presenting their report to the Government.

ECONOMIC AND BUSINESS POLICIES VIS-À-VIS CHECK ON MONEY LAUNDERING

The practice of banking remains a highly regulated industry everywhere in the world. This is the reason stakeholders in banking must keep abreast of trends and developments in the industry. Some of the regulations that affect the industry operators seem immutable and have a long-standing history, while others are issued on an ad-hoc, quarterly, bi-annual, or annual basis to deal with emergent problems. For instance, the Acts establishing the regulatory bodies stand the taste of time, but credit, trade, and monetary policy circulars which Central Banks issue on an annual basis give direction to operators about possible economic targets that the government is pursuing. The most common policies of Central Banks are often geared to regulating, or controlling *liquidity* in the economy. The most critical regulatory indices with which bankers should keep abreast in order to function effectively include liquidity ratio, cash reserve ratio, and monetary policy—what they mean, how they affect banks and customers, and so on. It is especially important for the bankers to appreciate how these policies *positively* or *negatively* affect *wealth* and *capacity* to do business. The term *wealth* implies customers' investments in the banks as represented by term deposits and savings accounts. The *capacity to do business* may be positively or negatively affected by the bank's lending policies, which in turn largely derive from monetary policies.

Besides having working knowledge of the framework and mechanics of the applicable regulatory policies and guidelines, the bankers should keep abreast of changes in the economic policies of the government and the business environment. Bankers should not be concerned about the politics, or technical issues, of government economic policies. Their primary concern should be to know how the policies affect ordinary people that have particular banking needs. But they should as well be interested in how the policies affect the banking industry, the public, and the business communities.

Import restriction—or outright prohibition of goods prone to money laundering—can be an effective way to check money laundering. In that case, Customs service makes a list and descriptions of the banned goods, with warnings of penalties that await offenders. However, the usual negative effect of import restriction applies. Possible emergence of *black market* that encourages *smuggling* of the prohibited products is typical. Unfortunately, smuggling continues unabated, not-withstanding harsh penalties that are meted out to the offenders. Punishments range from prosecution in the law courts, to confiscation and auctioning or destruction of the contraband goods.

Hiking up tariffs has long been favored as an effective instrument to check dumping of cheap and inferior imported goods on a country. In developing countries, it is also defended with the *infant industry* argument—in which case, it is aimed at protecting local industries against foreign competition. Its main objective is to substitute locally made goods for the imported ones. This is the reasoning behind the so-called import-substitution industries. Proponents of free trade criticize and do not believe in these arguments—nevertheless, they tend to serve some economic need of developing countries. Exorbitant tariffs can be targeted at expensive, usually ostentatious, goods that are predisposed to money laundering. The heavy tax can discourage the crime by increasing its stakes.

Often government may prescribe new, or modify existing, documentation of international trade transactions. For instance, the Standards Organization of Nigeria introduced product testing, certification, and the SONCAP—ostensibly to check importation of substandard products into the country. Unfortunately, businesses slowed down in the wake of the introduction of the changes, prompting opposition from the business communities to the policies. However, government retains the changes on grounds of perceived benefits to the public and economy in the long run. This policy can really be adapted to check money laundering. In order to fulfill this purpose, the SONCAP criteria should include investigation of the products and the sources of the money for their procurement.

Preshipment or destination inspection of goods imported into a country can serve to check money laundering. Under the preshipment system, Government approves inspection agents that examine goods to be imported into the country for compliance with information contained in the relevant import documents—including the suppliers' invoices. The inspection is done abroad, often in the exporter's country before the goods are shipped to the importer's country. Based on findings, the inspection agents issue either clean report of inspection (CRI) on goods that pass the examination, or discrepancy reports of inspection (DRI) on those that fail. Destination inspection of goods permits examination of imported goods at the port of destination. As in the preshipment case, inspection of imported goods is also carried out by agents appointed by the Government. Under this arrangement, the inspection agents issue risk assessment report (RAR) which provides required information on the imported goods. In both cases, the authorities can require verified modes and sources of financing for the goods in inspection reports. With the support of banks, this process can mitigate money laundering.

Government may introduce new, or change aspects of current, fiscal policies—with implications for increasing or reducing tax burdens on the people and businesses. Taxation is a powerful, but sensitive, public policy issue all over the world. The maneuvering of taxation policies remains one of the critical factors in the assessment of the performance of government. For instance, one would like to know if the tax regime has reduced purchasing power of the citizens more than it has empowered them with social amenities and infrastructure. However, taxation can be applied in detecting and checking money laundering. This is possible if documentation of a taxpayer's details include verifiable information on exact sources of their incomes. In order to achieve this purpose, there should a reliable means of tracking particulars of reported incomes of individuals, businesses, and organizations. Unfortunately, this has not been the case in developing countries—a major reason money laundering is festering.

DETECTING AND FORESTALLING MONEY LAUNDERING IN BANK ACCOUNTS

Money laundering often takes the form of unusual large deposit, or suspicious transaction, in a bank account. In most cases, it manifests itself as inflow into a domestic bank account from a foreign customer, bank account, or transaction. Reporting suspicious deposits and transactions to the authorities can help stem the crime. Deposits are considered suspicious when they are either unusually large, out of tune with normal deposits into an account, or exceed regulatory amount stipulated in the money laundering laws. Suspicious transactions tend to be irregular, awkward, or inconsistent with normal rules of banking or business. Monitoring transactions in customer accounts come in handy in forestalling money laundering. The same goes for training of bank employees and strict implementation of the Know Your Customer (KYC) rules for banking. Let me briefly discuss aspects of the KYC rules. I do so considering that KYC is the main instrument that banks and the authorities apply to checking money laundering—and it is effective.

Know Your Customer Rules

The notion of KYC, otherwise known as KYC for short, is now a central plank of contemporary banking practice. Banking operations build and thrive on due diligence founded on KYC procedures. KYC demands that a bank must have sufficient information on all persons, businesses, or other entities that constitute its customers. It is now a universal banking practice for banks to have identification evidence not only on existing but also potential customers. This has become a condition precedent to opening bank account. Banks are also required to obtain identification evidence on customers along with other bank account records. Once seen as an evolving paradigm, KYC is now an institutionalized response to growing concerns about debilitating banking fraud, financial malpractices, and laundering of illicit money through the banking system. In response to these crimes, regulatory intervention sought to address the problem along the lines of, "KYC." In fulfilling KYC, banks should take specific risk-mitigating actions. I discuss the critical risk-mitigating actions as follows.

Obtain Identification Evidence

A bank should certify that potential customers are who they claim to be. This is a prerequisite for starting banking relationships. Without proven information about a customer or potential customer, a bank will be taking unmitigated risk if it carries out, or agrees to carry out, banking transaction for them or on their behalf. It will be uncritical for a bank to conduct business in that way. It is therefore imperative that a bank should diligently obtain identification evidence on all its customers. This implies that a bank must have and document proper knowledge of its customers. The whole idea of 'KYCs' is based on this fundamental principle. Adequate information about customers is always very handy. It helps banks to detect and correctly report financial crimes to the authorities. Lack of sufficient knowledge of its customers renders a bank vulnerable to avoidable risks. When customers are unidentified, or unverified, a bank easily becomes haven for fraudsters who might use the bank to launder proceeds of crime. While identifying all relevant parties to a banking relationship, a bank should ascertain the true nature of the business in which the parties are engaged or wants to engage. Doing so, the bank could track and check inconsistent transactions that might border on suspicion of money laundering. Thus, identification evidence serves four useful risk-mitigating purposes for a bank. It helps a bank to:

- detect financial crimes,
- recognize and report suspicious banking transactions and activities,
- avoid its use for illicit activities,
- have protection against fraud.

Ascertain Nature and Level of Business

A central plank of customer identification is finding out exact nature of the business of an existing or potential customer. In seeking sufficient information about the customer, the bank should acquaint itself with the business in which the customer or potential customer is engaged or intends to engage. The bank should, as much as possible, extend its information search and gathering on existing and new customers. It should envisage pattern of transactions in the customer's account and anticipate possible risks and how to mitigate the risks. Knowing the nature and level of a customer's business—in the course of, or prior to contracting, a banking relationship as in opening an account—serves four basic banking information needs. It puts the bank in a position to:

- understand the purpose and reason for opening an account or a customer's need for a banking relationship,
- envisage and anticipate nature and level of transactions to be conducted through the account,
- be apprised of probable sources and utilization of funds in the course of the banking relationship,
- know more about customers' calling, sources of their income, and the making of their wealth (if applicable),

Establish True Identity of Customers

A bank should endeavor to establish the true identity of its customers. The usual components of identity include names used to open account, date of birth or incorporation, and residential or office address where the customer can be located. These are features—a set of attributes—which uniquely identify a natural or legal person for banking purposes. In the case of use of international passport, evidence of identity may be established with records of the passport's number, date, country of issue, and such other relevant information. In accordance with KYC, the Central Bank of Nigeria (CBN) warns banks to do anything but establish a business relationship, open an account, or undertake a significant one-off transaction or series of linked transactions without first verifying the identity of the customer (See Central Bank of Nigeria, *KNOW YOUR CUSTOMER MANUAL for banks and other financial institutions in Nigeria*). Used in this sense, "transaction" includes advisory service but excludes "provision of information about the availability of products or services or first interview prior to establishing a relationship"(ibid). The responsible officer must obtain documentary evidence of proper identity, standing, residence, office, and permanent addresses of potential customers. The use of photo identity card and proof of address consolidate customer identification.

Adopt Proven Identification Process

The procedure for identifying customers will be effective if it generates sufficient evidence that a bank is, or will be, dealing with a real person or organization (natural, corporate or legal) (ibid). In all cases, the CBN requires banks to obtain satisfactory evidence that a person of that name lives at the address given and that the applicant is that person, or that the company has identifiable owners and that its representatives can be located at the address provided (ibid). Face-to-face identification, in the case of private individuals, is recommended.

But identification evidence obtained through a remote means is also acceptable. However, the bank should state which of these procedures it adopted to verify identity of the customer. An existing customer—especially a prime or respected customer who is personally known the bank's director or official—can introduce a prospective customer. Members of staff, particularly marketing officers, can also introduce customers. While foregoing mode of introduction offers risk management comfort, it should be employed with caution. The overriding need for effective risk management is to insist on documentary identification evidence. In general, a bank should keep record of who introduced a customer and who authorized the introduction in the customer's mandate file. Such record serves some KYC need in the identification evidence sphere.

Certify Identification Documents

Customer service officers (CSO) should as much as possible make face-to-face contact with potential customers. The contact offers a platform for the CSO to interview and form opinion about potential customers. The CSO also obtains documentary evidence of identification of the customer at this stage. But this is not an absolute procedure or requirement. On occasion it may not be easy or possible to meet a potential customer face-to-face. In that case, documentary need is satisfied when a lawyer, banker, accountant, senior public servant or their equivalent in the private sector, certifies copies of the customer's identification evidence. In furtherance of KYC, the bank must know and be able to contact the person who endorses the documents. The usual identification evidence required of foreign nationals includes international passport, national identity card or documentary evidence of address. Certification of copies of these documents is required—and any of the following can provide it:

- an embassy, consulate or high commission of the country of issue;
- a senior official within the account opening institution;
- a lawyer or attorney.

CSO should sight original documents, and date and sign certified copies of the documents as identification evidence of the customer. This requirement is satisfied when CSO endorses certified documents with the phrase "original seen." The CBN further requires financial institutions to "always ensure that a good reproduction of photographic evidence of identity is obtained and where this is not possible, a copy of the evidence certified as providing a good likeness of the applicant"(ibid).

RISK-BASED LAWS AND REGULATIONS AGAINST MONEY LAUNDERING

There is hardly any country that has not enacted antimoney laundering laws. The laws seek to investigate, prosecute, and punish convicted suspects of money laundering offences. In most cases, the laws provide for, and back, legal action to check disguising and passing of illegal money and transactions through the banking system. The laws may exist in different forms, but with the same purpose of curbing money laundering. Often the law touches related financial crimes.

In some cases, the same law is enacted to simultaneously check money laundering and corrupt practices. Take the case of Nigeria as an example. General Sanni Abacha, then Military Head of State of Nigeria, had in 1996 insisted that what was needed to find "lasting solutions to our socio-economic problems ... *was* break with the traditional approach of scratching the surface only for fear of upsetting powerful and entrenched interests." He did not leave anyone in doubt as to his determination "to cleanse our society and make life safe and more meaningful for our people." He clarified the most worrying aspect of the problem as he noted that "over the last 25 years, more than 53 billion naira was invested in government parastatals, but by the end of 1992 when their assets were privatized, they were worth only 900 million naira." In his opinion, apparently widely shared in the country, "the colossal wastage of public funds through mismanagement, fraud, embezzlement and other white-collar crimes have contributed in no small measure to the poor state of our economy and social service." Then he assured that "no administration worth its name can allow this unacceptable situation to continue." (Excerpt from an address by the Military Head of State of Nigeria, General Sanni Abacha, to the *National Workshop on Crime Prevention and Control in Nigeria* on 20 May, 1996).

Government promulgated *Public Enterprises Regulation Commission Decree* of 1997 to try and punish "all those who have contributed to the failure of our public institutions and parastatals through such monumental mismanagement of public funds ... to ensure that present and future executives of such institutions operate according to set rules and procedures." A similar law, *Failed Banks (Recovery of Debt) and Financial Malpractices in Banks Decree 1994*, had earlier been enacted to deal with distress in the banking sector caused by executive fraud and mismanagement of funds. Regrettably, the regime could not deal with corruption and money laundering when confronted with them. Although it had announced that the "monumental mismanagement" of public funds took place over a 25 year period to the end 1992, the corrective Decree would not affect crimes committed prior to November 1993 when the regime took over power.

Experiences with enactment, enforcement, and success or failure of antimoney laundering laws vary widely from one country to another. However, the constant fact if that every country is making some effort to deal with the crimes in decisive ways. Unfortunate for banks, risks attendant on these financial crimes remain a big albatross for them. Domestic and foreign subsidiary banks share fate on this issue.

SUMMARY

Money laundering is a contemporary issue in managing the financial system—in both developed and developing countries. It is a crime in which someone uses loophole in the laws to hide or use illegal money in legal ways—often through the banking system. As unwitting accomplices, banks are all too often in the firing line. Money laundering discourages enterprise, punishes hard work, and rewards unproductivity. At the macro level, it distorts and renders national income inconsistent with balance of payments accounting. Thus the consequences of money laundering have wider implications for a country's macroeconomic foundation. Money laundering curiously manifests itself in different forms but with the same motive.

Money laundering—for all intents and purposes—is one of the criminal fallout of corruption in the society. It mirrors one of the mechanisms of corruption in yet another practical context. In reference here is a situation where citizens willfully seek, maneuver someone or the system, and obtain money illegally—usually by deception—which they then deposit in bank accounts or use for transactions in legal ways. This implies that laundered money must find its way into the banking system, failing which it has to be used for some legal transaction, or stashed away somewhere. The overriding challenge, in all cases, is how to disguise or hide the real source of the money while banking and utilizing it. In this way, money laundering makes a typical example and expression of corruption in society.

Corruption is nowadays an indulgence for many—indeed, a boost to money laundering. Corruption thrives on possibilities of getting away scot-free which money laundering amply offers. If it were not for money laundering, there would be a lot more risk—for example—in looting public treasury. A lot of other corrupt practices would equally be unattractive. On the other hand, as long as possibilities exist for money laundering, including the use of banks—even if as unwitting accomplices—corruption will continue to fester. Nonetheless, the relationship between money laundering and corruption is a typical illustration of a chicken and egg problem. The corollary is that money laundering would not be flourishing in the absence of corruption. The two vices tend to be mutually reinforcing.

Money laundering often takes the form of unusual large deposit, or suspicious transaction, in a bank account. In most cases, it manifests itself as inflow into a domestic bank account from a foreign customer, bank account, or transaction. Reporting suspicious deposits and transactions to the authorities can help stem the crime. Monitoring transactions in customer accounts also come in handy. The same goes for training of bank employees and strict implementation of the KYC rules for banking. There is hardly any country that has not enacted antimoney laundering laws. The laws seek to investigate, prosecute, and punish convicted suspects of money laundering offences. In most cases, the laws provide for, and back, legal action to check disguising and passing of illegal money and transactions through the banking system.

QUESTIONS FOR DISCUSSION AND REVIEW

1. How does the foundation of money laundering inform its dynamics and mechanisms in developing economies?
2. In what ways should the authorities reinvent attacks on money laundering in developing economies?

3. Assess the role of banks in developing economies as unwitting accomplices in money laundering?
4. Do banks in developing economies really lend themselves to being used as a conduit for money laundering?
5. Why have risk-based laws and regulations on money laundering not been effective in developing economies?
6. What are the motives and mechanisms of money laundering in your country or other a named developing economy?
7. Would you say that current methods of detecting money laundering through banks accounts are effective and reliable?
8. How should the authorities improve effectiveness of current approach to checking money laundering?
9. In what ways money laundering and corruption—seen to be endemic in society—truncate a bank as a going concern?

REFERENCES

Gould, D.J., 1980. Patrons and clients: the role of the military in Zaire politics. In: Mowoe, I. (Ed.), The Performance of Soldiers as Governors. University Press of America, Washington, D.C., p. 485.

Griffiths, I., 1984. An Atlas of African Affairs. Methuen, London and New York, 1984.

Onyiriuba, L., 2013. On the Road to Self–actualization. NFS Data Bureau Limited, Lagos, pp. 26–28.

Shonekan, E., 1993. Address to the joint session of the Nigeria's National Assembly on the occasion of his presentation of the 1993 budget on 27 January 1993.

World Bank, World Development Report 1991 the challenge of development, New York: Oxford University Press, pp. 131–132. Unless otherwise acknowledged, the views in quotes are taken from this source.

Chapter 9

Bank Crisis, Distress Syndrome, and Failure Risk Management in Developing Economies

Chapter Outline

LEARNING FOCUS AND OBJECTIVES

Scenes of banking risks and uncertainties—evident in crisis, distress, and failure—manifest themselves mostly in developing economies. Corrective actions taken wrongly only plunge the bank into a deeper mess. In most cases, a bank that finds itself in this situation tries to regain liquidity for business operations. It starts running helter-skelter for some elusive solution. The usual promising solution—when everything else fails—lies in recapitalizing and reinventing the bank. Sadly, though, this last resort is always a bitter pill to swallow. The question then is why would a bank slip into crisis, become distressed, or fail-losing, in the process, its going concern goal? My purpose for this chapter is to:

- examine contemporary issues surrounding distressed, failing, and failed banks in developing economies;
- provide analytical framework that gives practical insights into bank crisis, distress, and failure in developing economies;

- put forth a framework that shed light on the creation of, and solution to, the problem of bank failure in developing economies;
- discuss a three-pronged methodology for analyzing bank crisis, distress, and failure in developing economies;
- highlight lessons and repercussions from historical and current evidence of the problem in developing economies.

EXPECTED LEARNING OUTCOMES

Bank failure has become a commonplace in developing economies the world over. The public will want to understand the causes of the problem, its syndrome, and possible solution. Domestic banks in developing economies tend to be more vulnerable than their foreign subsidiary counterparts. This compels a need to review current approach to managing the problem—with a view to reinventing it. It is also in tune with the urgent need now to stamp out the problem in developing economies. That way the industry would be strengthened to fulfill its intermediary and other financial roles. The reader will—after studying this chapter and doing the exercises in it—have learnt and been better informed about:

- causes and challenges of distressed, failing, and failed banks in developing economies;
- the need for analytical framework that gives practical insights into bank crisis, distress, and failure in developing economies;
- methodology for analyzing bank crisis, distress, and failure in developing economies;
- actions necessary to stem bank crisis, distress and failure in developing economies.

OVERVIEW OF THE SUBJECT MATTER

It is doubtful that the public appreciates the causes of bank crisis, distress, and failure—a problem that has become a commonplace in developing economies. The problem has evolved into a destabilizing phenomenon over time. Its syndrome continues to permeate all facets of the banking industry in developing economies. Even an informed public will want to understand the causes of the problem and its syndrome. The problem has persisted even as bankers in developing economies appear to thoroughly understand and be well-informed about it.

Banks in developing economies are vulnerable. Thus there is need to review current approach to failed resolution of the problem—with a view to reinventing it. Of utmost importance is the need now to check bank crisis, distress, and failure in developing economies. That way the banking industry would be strengthened to fulfill its role in developing economies. Unfortunately, the literature is deficient in critical information on the problem. Much of the literature scantily investigates and emphasizes the problem. Besides, the occasional inadvertent role of regulatory authorities in exacerbating—or their attempts at resolving—the problem is not sufficiently researched or published.

What really happens when a bank becomes distressed or is failing? Actions taken wrongly only plunges the bank into a deeper mess and crisis rather than solve the problem. In most cases, a bank that finds itself in this situation tries, but all to no avail, to regain liquidity for its business. Often it starts running helter-skelter for some elusive solution. Soon interbank borrowing takes center-stage. However, the resort to panic takings and borrowings in the money market has never been effective in solving a deep-seated liquidity crisis. It increases the cost of funds to an already loss-making business, if anything. Similarly, the crunch is never helped by liquidating risk assets portfolios. Typically a risk asset is a contractual obligation that should run its course. So bank managements cannot just start tinkering with the terms of ongoing or performing credit facilities—except where default is proven or apparent. Even in that case, some legal process—which, in most cases, takes long and is often fraught with un-necessary technicalities—must be followed to recover bad loans.

The foregoing are typical scenes that breed unethical practices and exacerbate risks of banking in developing economies. The usual promising solution—when everything else fails—lies in recapitalizing and reinventing the bank. Sadly, though, this last resort is always a bitter pill to swallow.

FRAMEWORK FOR SOLVING DOMESTIC BANKS CRISIS, DISTRESS, AND FAILURE

Bank crisis, distress, and failure are mostly peculiar to domestic banks in developing economies. Hardly do foreign banks subsidiaries experience these problems. The straightforward implication of this is that foreign subsidiary banks are better managed than their domestic banks counterparts. I make this point with respect to differences in risk management between the two sets of banks. Solving the crisis, distress, and failure risks challenges of domestic banks demands a four-pronged analytical framework. First, investigating how historical evidence sheds light on the problems is pertinent. Second, there is need to exactly define the problems. Then a review of discredited and criticized banking practices of the banks follows. The fourth element of the framework consists of anticipation of the problems.

Historical Evidence

As Table 9.1 shows, the total assets of distressed banks in Nigeria accounted for 7.7% of that of the industry in 1997, down from 11% and 19.8% in December 1996 and 1995, respectively (Nigeria Deposit Insurance Corporation, 1995). The observed decline could be as a result of loan recovery efforts, or sale of some fixed assets by the distressed banks. Similarly, the ratio of total deposits

TABLE 9.1 Indices of Distressed Banks in Nigeria as at December 1997

	Distressed banks	Potentially distressed	Total industry
Number of banks	47	2	115
	(₦'000)	(₦'000)	(₦'000)
Total assets	56,262,750	3,531,503	739,242,665
Total deposits	29,425,850	1,832,735	326,006,815
Total loans and advances[a]	47,450,743	2,196,015	290,393,015
Insider loans and advances[a]	4,718,364	25,113	8,410,737
Nonperforming loans[b]	38,871,276	905,819	74,951,422
Recapitalization[c]	42,428,740	39,389	22,428,740

[a]include leases.
[b]include advances and leases.
[c]represents recapitalization requirement.
Sources: CBN and NDIC annual reports 1997.

of the distressed banks to the total of the industry decreased from 19.1% and 14% in December 1995 and 1996, respectively, to 9% in December 1997. As at March 31, 1998, the following domestic commercial and merchant banks in Nigeria had been liquidated by the regulatory authorities:

Allied Bank of Nigeria PLC
Amicable Bank of Nigeria Limited
Commerce Bank Limited
Commercial Trust Bank Limited
Co-operative and Commerce Bank PLC
Credite Bank Limited
Highland Bank of Nigeria Limited
Mercantile Bank of Nigeria PLC
North–South Bank of Nigeria PLC
Pan–African Bank Limited
Lobi Bank of Nigeria Limited
Pinnacle Commercial Bank Limited
Progress Bank of Nigeria Limited
Republic Bank Limited
United Commercial Bank Limited

Abacus Merchant Bank Limited
ABC Merchant Bank Limited
Century Merchant Bank Limited
Continental Merchant Bank Ltd
Crown Merchant Bank Limited
Great Merchant Bank Limited
Group Merchant Bank Limited
ICON Ltd (Merchant Bankers)
Merchant Bank of Africa Limited
Nigeria Merchant Bank PLC
Prime Merchant Bank Limited
Royal Merchant Bank Limited
Victory Merchant Bank Limited
Alpha Merchant Bank Limited
Kapital Merchant Bank Limited
Financial Merchant Bank Limited

This clearly indicates the sustained run on the distressed banks as depositors lost confidence in the banking system. There was also a sharp decline in the size of loan portfolio of the distressed banks during this period. From 37.8% and 23.7% in December 1995 and 1996, respectively, the ratio of total loans of the distressed banks to that of the banking system decelerated to 21.2% in December

1997. It is noteworthy that part of the rescue measures for the distressed banks was to stop further lending, while pursuing aggressive loan recovery strategies. This explains the observed steady decline of their loan portfolio during the period under review. As would be expected—and this is perhaps the strongest indication of the distress symptom—the ratio of nonperforming loans of the distressed to the industry maintained an upward trend. The ratio was 67.4%, 79.8%, and 82.0% in December 1995, 1996, and 1997, respectively (All ratios in this section were derived from CBN and NDIC annual reports for 1995, 1996, and 1997).

Defining the Problem

What is the meaning of *distressed*, *failing*, and *failed* bank? What are the common causes of bank distress and failure? How can the symptoms or early warning signals of bank distress be detected?

Discredited Practices

Are there domestic banks practices which are generally regarded as unethical by the public, analysts, and the regulatory authorities? Do such practices, and to what extent do they—contribute to domestic banks crisis and distress? Can such practices be effectively curbed—how, by what means, and for what outcomes?

Anticipating Distress

Is it possible to correctly anticipate domestic banks crisis and distress? What roles can the stakeholders—owners, employees, customers, regulatory authorities, and the society in general—play in stemming domestic banks crisis and distress? How can domestic banks crisis or distress be effectively managed if, for any reason, it cannot be prevented?

Questions pertinent to the underlying challenges of the problems of bank crisis, distress, and failure guide analysis of the framework. Let me now discuss aspects of the problems implied in the analytical framework. I do so under three headings—anticipating and analyzing domestic banks' distress syndrome, Solving domestic banks crisis, distress, and failure risks, and detecting early warning signs of domestic banks' distress.

ANTICIPATING AND ANALYZING DOMESTIC BANKS' DISTRESS SYNDROME

If a bank is unable to raise funds quickly to meet its maturing, operating, and statutory financial obligations, and this has become a continuing or frequent occurrence, it can be said to be illiquid. Illiquidity reflects inadequacy of cash inflows over time relative to outflows. This implies that the bank is unable to easily, or can with a lot of difficulty, raise funds from the money market—even if at higher than normal average cost of funds. If the situation persists such that it becomes obvious that the funding capacity of the bank has been impaired, then we can say that distress exists, has set in or occurred.

I define the phrase bank distress or distressed bank from three pertinent and related perspectives. It depicts, first and foremost, a condition of persistent upset in a bank's normal business operations. Second, the upset results largely from insufficiency of funding or difficulty in attracting deposits from existing customers or prospects and the money market. Third, as a result of the inadequate funding, the bank is unable to meet customers' deposits withdrawal, requirements for statutory reserves, and day-to-day running of its operations. Thus, distress is characteristically associated with inability to meet maturing obligations as a result of cash inflows deficiency or illiquidity. A bank will be considered distressed if its total liabilities are not represented or accounted for, over time, by the net value of its assets portfolio.

The regulatory authorities in Nigeria caution that "distress in the banking industry occurs when a fairly reasonable proportion of banks in the system are unable to meet their obligations to their customers, as well as their owners and the economy." The authorities inform further that "such inability often results from weaknesses in their financial, operational, and managerial conditions, which would have rendered them either illiquid and/or insolvent (CBN/NDIC, 1995)." It is not always that distress leads to bank failure. However, a failed bank would have been distressed in the first place. A bank may be temporarily distressed or regain liquidity and solvency after a prolonged period of distress, but a failed bank is extinct. Thus, a *failed* bank is a "bank whose license has been revoked or which has been taken over by the CBN or the NDIC"—in the case of Nigeria, (see *Failed Banks (Recovery of Debts) and Financial Malpractices in Banks Decree 18 of 1994*, Lagos: Federal Republic of Nigeria). It follows that not all distressed are failed banks, while all failed banks must have been distressed in the first place.

However, a *failing* bank has characteristics analogous to a distressed bank. The Banks and Other Financial Institutions (BOFI) Act No. 25 of 1991 refers to a failing bank as one which "informs the CBN that it is likely to become unable to meet its obligations; it is about to suspend payment to any extent; and it is insolvent." A bank is also referred to as failing where, after a special examination or investigation of its books and affairs, the CBN is satisfied that the bank is in a grave situation. The basis for establishing "a grave situation" includes serious breaches of the law, such as finding that:

- the bank has been carrying on its business in a manner detrimental to the interest of its depositors and creditors,
- the bank has "insufficient" assets to cover its liabilities to the public,
- the bank has been contravening the provisions of the BOFI Act No. 25 of 1991 (see section 32 (1)).

Former Governor of the Central Bank of Nigeria, Sanusi (1997) gave a boost to evolving thinking on the meaning of bank distress. He argues that a bank would be said to be in distress "where evaluation by the supervisory authorities depicts the institution as deficient in the following performance criteria:

- *Gross under-capitalization*
  This is considered a problem of the banks relative to its level of operations. The bank in this situation is really overtrading. That is, the rate of growth of its assets (especially, loans and advances) far exceeds its liabilities (in terms of shareholders' funds, i.e., share capital plus all reserves).
- *High level of classified loans and advances*
  The Prudential Guidelines (1990) and the Statement of Accounting Standards (SAS 10) spelt out criteria to be employed by banks for classification of performing and nonperforming credit facilities, the minimum amount of provisions to be made for each category of such loans as well as conditions attached to interest recognition. In line with these documents, many of the banks in distress were found to be carrying large amounts of nonperforming loans and advances. Because these loans and advances were nonperforming, the net realizable value was too low to cover, meaningfully, the underlying liabilities.
- *Illiquidity*
  The problem of illiquidity *is* reflected in the inability of a bank to meet customers' cash withdrawals and repayment of its interbank indebtedness. Because most of the loans were nonperforming, the expected cash inflows were not coming in to meet maturing obligations. This created a situation of illiquidity, which is a major contributory factor to the banking industry distress.
- *Low earnings*
  A bank that is in distress is often characterized by low earnings caused by huge operational losses and/or high cost of operations.
- *Weak and inefficient management*
  This problem *is* reflected in poor credit quality, inadequate internal controls, high rate of frauds, and forgeries."

There is always a sustained depositors' run on distressed banks, which signifies customers' anxiety about the safety of their deposits. Once the run is underway, it is always difficult to assuage or altogether stop. It is, for all intents and purposes, better to avoid rather than manage distress because of the unavoidable erosion of goodwill and credibility of the bank when it occurs. This is particularly pertinent considering that, in most cases, distress leads to bank failure.

SOLVING DOMESTIC BANKS' CRISIS, DISTRESS, AND FAILURE RISKS

The major causes of domestic banks crisis, distress, and failure include—but are not limited to—bad management, fraudulent practices, and undue deterioration of assets quality. Other causes include poor capitalization and weak earnings capacity resulting from high levels of nonperforming risk assets and rising cost

TABLE 9.2 Licensed and Operating Banks in Nigeria, 1985–1994

	Total number	Branch network	Total deposits (₦ billion)	Total assets (₦ billion)
1985	40	1,323	19.4	37.0
1986	41	1,394	20.5	48.0
1987	50	1,454	26.5	62.1
1988	66	1,711	33.9	76.4
1989	81	1,904	31.0	80.8
1990	107	2,001	45.1	111.7
1991	119	2,171	59.5	155.7
1992	120	2,364	97.7	231.6
1993	120	2,397	145.0	333.0
1994	116	2,259	177.7	350.7

Source: Various publications of the Central Bank of Nigeria and Nigerian Deposit Insurance Corporation.

of funds. Often unanticipated adverse regulatory policy changes exacerbate the problems, especially policies that cause prolonged liquidity crisis in the system. Sometimes adverse economic conditions cause bank crisis, distress, and failure in some developing economies. In the case of Nigeria, the problems lie, perhaps, in the explosion of the number of licensed banks, especially after the deregulation of the Nigerian economy in 1986 following the country's adoption of structural adjustment program. Table 9.2 shows the phenomenal increase in the number of licensed domestic banks in Nigeria between 1985 and 1994—many of which later failed.

In the discussion of the causes of bank crisis, distress, and failure that follows, I drew information from not only the literature and applicable research on the subjects but opinions of the regulatory authorities. This approach makes for a balanced analysis of the problems at issue. I did not assign relative contributory weights to the underlying factors in the problem. The reason is that weighting of the factors would be futile as the weights depend on peculiar circumstances of the banks and countries.

In the following discussions, I isolated the more specific factors which frequently result in bank distress.

Management Problems

A bank, like many other high-risk businesses, requires good management to succeed. The alternative—poor management—is perhaps the surest way to bank distress and failure. However, the variables that constitute good management may not be easily identified and generalized for all banks in all situations. Bank management would be considered bad or poor if it fails to scan its environment to determine and respond to contingencies which impart instability to the bank's operations. In such a situation, bank management might adopt a wrong leadership style. The result, in most cases, is poor morale, unsustainable labor turnover and sabotage. In some extreme cases, the bank becomes insensitive to customers' needs and begins to lose market share, earnings, and profitability.

The ineptitude of bank managements, especially those who flout their banks' policies and perpetrate insider abuses has been a major cause of bank distress and failure. Banks that have such managements easily become afflicted with boardroom squabbles, frauds, and forgeries. These risk elements often threaten the business. Constant infraction of banking operating rules ruins the fortunes of a bank and may be a cause of the bank's distress or failure.

Where bank management is adjudged weak and inefficient, the bank usually has low risk assets quality, control of operational costs, and earnings capacity. Banks that are poorly managed tend to experience occasional liquidity problems as a result of mismatch of assets and liabilities. Often poor management reflects in speculative transactions, high risk-taking appetite, and disregard for internal policies and controls. It is the quality of management that is the most critical resource for effective operation of a bank.

Fraudulent Practices

Frauds are a major cause of bank distress and failure in many developing countries. There is hardly any bank that is spared of this vice which threatens the vibrancy and survival of the banking system in both developed and developing nations. Even where internal control system seems foolproof—and irrespective of punishments meted out to the culprits—fraud remains an overwhelming issue. This is evident in Table 9.3 which shows the case of Nigerian banks. Fraud becomes a most intricate problem when bank employees are involved through acts of omission or commission.

TABLE 9.3 Frauds and Forgeries in Nigerian Banks, 1991–1994

	1991	1992	1993	1994
Number of banks with fraud cases	96	108	122	170
Amount involved in the frauds (₦ million)	388.6	421.8	1,419.1	3,390.4
Actual loss to the frauds (₦ million)	26.7	73.1	246.4	950.7
Ratio of actual loss to amount involved (%)	6.9	17.3	17.36	28.0

Source: Nigerian Deposit Insurance Corporation (NDIC) report, 1991–1994.

Manu—Executive Director, Operations, Nigeria Deposit Insurance Corporation—demonstrates a typical illustration of such fraudulent act. Manu (1997) states that "not only are bank management being consistently tempted, some of them are usually preoccupied with thoughts of how to exploit same to their personal rather than corporate benefits." He notes that "as a result, the day-to-day responsibility for managing banks has been replaced by personal enrichment crusades with debilitating consequences on bank performance and the stability of the banking system." Often—as would be expected under the circumstances—when a bank fails or is distressed, fraud dominates the culprits.

Assets Deterioration

The most important earning assets of a bank comprise loans and advances, otherwise known as risk assets. When the risk assets are of a high quality, it implies that the expected earnings are being realized, and servicing and repayment of loans and advances are not in arrears. Banks that have quality risk assets portfolio adopt the prudential guidelines for monitoring performance of the assets. This enables the bank to detect nonperforming loans and advances and make appropriate provisions against their possible losses. Table 9.4 summarizes the asset quality of Nigerian banks.

Increasing level of deterioration in assets quality can cause distress and failure. It occurs frequently in situations where risk assets are largely unsecured or poorly monitored, and prudential provisioning on nonperforming loans ignored or flouted. Asset deterioration is indicated when the performance of a large proportion of the risk assets portfolio begins to weaken as a result of decreasing level of activity, delayed or nonservicing of loans, and increasing volume of provisions or write-off of interest and/or principal on classified accounts.

Poor Capitalization

A bank should be adequately capitalized from the outset of its formation. Otherwise, it will not effectively trade on equity. Poor capitalization will portend

TABLE 9.4 Quality of Risk Assets of Nigerian Banks, 1994–1997

	1994	1995	1996	1997
Total loans, advances, and leases (₦bn)	109.1	175.9	213.6	290.4
Classified loans and advances (₦bn)	46.9	57.8	72.4	75.0
Ratio of classified to total loans (%)	43.0	32.9	33.9	25.8

Source: Central Bank of Nigeria and Nigerian Deposit Insurance Corporation, 1997.

TABLE 9.5 Classified Assets and Shareholders' Funds of the Banking Industry

	1994	1995	1996	1997
Classified loans and advances (₦bn)	46.9	57.9	72.4	75.0
Shareholders' funds (₦bn)	8.3	11.7	17.3	29.6
Classified loans: share-holders' funds (%)	567.7	496.0	419.8	253.1

Source: Central Bank of Nigeria and Nigerian Deposit Insurance Corporation, 1997.

a greater risk for a bank if it relies unduly on purchased funds to finance long-term assets creation or growth strategy. Table 9.5 gives an insight into the underlying nature of this risk by relating shareholders' funds to classified risk assets portfolio of the banking system. Under such circumstances, the buffer expected from shareholders' funds or its networth might not be enough to cushion the vagaries of the market on the bank's operations.

The function of capital for a bank, according to Ebhodaghe (1997)—former managing director of Nigerian Deposit Insurance Corporation—consists in serving as a "means by which losses can be absolved." He reasons that "capital provides a cushion to withstand abnormal losses not covered by current earnings pattern." An adequately capitalized bank can confidently satisfy customers' borrowing and deposits withdrawal needs, while pursuing its planned growth strategy.

Some banks engage in large volume transactions with very low paid—up capital. Yet, in relation to the level of its operations, a bank should be adequately capitalized. Otherwise, it would be overtrading and face the risk of pressure on its liquidity position.

Weak Earnings Capacity

The significance of earnings for bank management derives from the fact that a bank may not sustain unprofitable operations for a long time. Earnings drive operations and often dictate direction for the bank. Good earnings relative to asset base tends to enhance the confidence of the public in the bank. This positive impact increases market share and patronage over time. The reverse would be the case when as a result of weak capacity for earnings a bank reports operational losses. A one-off loss situation may be tolerated, but definitely not when it becomes a recurring outcome. In most cases, a run on a bank following successive reports of business losses is a consequence, as well as cause, of weak earnings capacity. For distressed banks, losses occur mainly as a result of high operating costs, weak internal controls, and poor assets quality. Such banks generally do not earn good returns from asset investments. Unless earnings on assets are optimized, a bank will not achieve impressive returns to the shareholders.

Rising Cost of Funds

Cost of funds is a measure of the price of money in the money market. It imparts conflicting behavior patterns to depositors and borrowers of funds. The funds surplus units—the depositors—are motivated by high and rising *real* interest on savings, while the funds deficit units—those that borrow—wish to enjoy low or concessionary interest on loans. These contrasting objectives often pitch the parties on price maneuvering schemes which may after all not be beneficial to either of them. Consider, for example, a situation where as a result of rising cost of funds in the money market, banks hike up lending rates in kind for existing and new loans. As the existing borrowers might not have anticipated this change in price, they may default on loans repayment. This is invariably the net effect, in most cases, of an unbearable sudden hike up in lending rates, especially in a depressed economy, because of its huge cost implication for the borrowers. For this reason, a bank may experience a high default rate on its loans and consequently become illiquid. Of course, a prolonged crisis of illiquidity could result in distress and failure.

Adverse Policy Changes

The contributory effects of adverse regulatory maneuvers and macroeconomic instability on bank failures are particularly evident in the less developed countries. Nigerian banking system witnessed an unprecedented distress in the 1990s due to adverse policy changes and maneuvering. The following examples are typical:

- Introduction of *stabilization securities* by the Central Bank of Nigeria as a direct money market instrument. With this instrument, the Central Bank decided how much with which the accounts of commercial and merchant banks with it should be debited as a means of controlling excess liquidity in the economy.
- Reversal in 1989 of the practice whereby government, its agencies and parastatals could directly operate accounts with commercial and merchant banks. Consequently, all public sector funds deposited with the banks were withdrawn at short notice and transferred to the Central Bank, causing a money panic and liquidity crisis in the money market.
- Adoption in 1986 of *structural adjustment programs* (SAP) by the government as an economic management strategy, (a detailed account of the pros and cons of structural adjustment programs in Africa could be read in Onyiriuba (2000: op. cit., pp.159–185)). Subsequent to deregulation of the financial sector, there was a multiplicity of banks some of which were ill-equipped with qualified manpower and resources for effective operation. With unsustainable rising price levels caused by local currency devaluation

in the wake of the introduction of SAP, banks inevitably accumulated a large stock of nonperforming assets which were ultimately charged off earnings.

DETECTING EARLY WARNING SIGNS OF DOMESTIC BANKS' DISTRESS

How may one recognize a distressed or failing bank? Is it possible or practicable to isolate and generalize symptoms of distress? I ask these questions and seek to offer any answers for the fact that most of the public will want to know how to identify and shun a failing bank. Such knowledge will particularly be helpful to them in redirecting investment decisions and preempting possible losses, especially for portfolio managers. Yet, it may not be easy to isolate all the signs of bank distress from a study of one or a sample of cases. One reason is that the experience by customers, regulatory authorities, and other observers or stakeholders of symptoms of distress in different banks often show marked divergence. It should be noted that, for different persons, indications of distress could be subject to selective perception. Thus, one may see impending distress in the context of frequent frustrations with the bank in transacting normal banking business. For instance, a recurring incidence of inability to honor customers' withdrawals from savings and time deposit accounts, as well as failure to disburse or allow drawings on approved credit facility, may be construed to be a sign of hidden distress.

However, the factors often adduced as warning signs of distress reflect a gamut of issues of which bank managements should be wary. There is still a problem—notwithstanding knowledge of these factors. Will all the factors manifest in every case of bank distress? Are some of the factors more important than the others in proving distress? Are the problems all equally important for a case of distress to be established? Bank managements should appreciate issues underlying these questions.

The experience of bank distress in Nigeria and other developing economies shows that the factors do not necessarily have to manifest in all cases. Some "healthy" banks may be associated with high employee turnover, frequent top management changes, and ostentatious spending. Yet it is unlikely that culpable acts of falsification of statutory returns, late submission of returns to the regulatory authorities, and use of political influence, may not be observed among the successful banks. The importance of each factor in evidencing distress is relative to particular cases. However, in most known cases of bank distress in Nigeria, the constant indicator is usually liquidity problems.

SUMMARY

It is doubtful that the public appreciates the causes and effects of bank crisis, distress, and failure—a problem that has become a commonplace in developing economies. Its syndrome permeates all facets of the banking industry. There is need to review current approach to failed resolution of the problem—with a view to reinventing it. Actions taken wrongly only plunges a bank into a deeper mess and crisis rather than solve the problem.

Understanding and solving bank crisis and distress requires a four-pronged methodological framework—comprising appreciation of the historical evidence, problem definition, investigation of banking discredited practices, and exploring possibilities of distress prevention.

If a bank is unable to raise funds quickly to meet its maturing, operating, and statutory obligations, and this has become a continuing or frequent occurrence, it can be said to be illiquid. Illiquidity reflects inadequacy of cash inflows over time relative to outflows. This implies that the bank is unable to easily, or can with a lot of difficulty, raise funds from the money market—even if at higher than normal average cost of funds. If the situation persists such that it becomes obvious that the funding capacity of the bank has been impaired, then we can say that distress exists, has set in or occurred. Bank distress is associated with inability to meet maturing obligations as a result of cash inflows deficiency or illiquidity.

The major causes of bank distress include—but are not limited to—bad management, fraudulent practices, and undue deterioration of assets quality. Other factors include poor capitalization and weak earnings capacity resulting from high levels of nonperforming risk assets and rising cost of funds. Unanticipated adverse policy changes by the regulatory authorities may also cause distress, especially policies that cause prolonged liquidity crisis in the system. Adverse economic conditions are also a major cause of bank distress. It may not be easy to isolate all the signs of bank distress from a study of one or a sample of cases.

The experience of bank distress in Nigeria shows that signs of distress do not necessarily have to manifest in all cases. Some "healthy" banks may be associated with high employee turnover, frequent top management changes, and ostentatious spending. Yet, it is unlikely that culpable acts of falsification of statutory returns, late submission of returns to the regulatory authorities, and use of political influence, may not be observed among the successful banks. The importance of each factor in evidencing distress is relative to particular cases. However, the constant indicator of distress is liquidity problems.

QUESTIONS FOR DISCUSSION AND REVIEW

1. To what extent would it be right to argue that credit and liquidity risks impact on the ease with which banks become distressed or fail?
2. What is the role of bank failure in the problems of evolution of the banking system in a named developing country?
3. How would you justify the contention that bank distress and failure on occasion originate from insider abuse?
4. In what ways do reckless and excessive risk-taking trigger treasury crisis in possible build-up of bank distress and failure?
5. How does bank distress and failure in Nigeria in the nineties inform the role of credit and liquidity risks in the problem?

REFERENCES

CBN/NDIC, 1995. Distress in the Nigerian Financial Services Industry. Page Publishers, Lagos.

Ebhodaghe, J.U., 1997. Financial distress and failure resolution, in NDIC Quarterly 7(3/4), Lagos: Nigeria Deposit Insurance Corporation.

Manu, B., 1997. Redefining the role of banks in deregulated developing economy, in NDIC Quarterly 7(3/4), Lagos: Nigeria Deposit Insurance Corporation.

Nigeria Deposit Insurance Corporation, 1995. Annual Report and Accounts, Lagos, Nigeria.

Onyiriuba, L.O., 2000. Economic Policy and Economic Development in English-Speaking Africa. Malthouse Press Limited, Lagos.

Sanusi, J.O., 1997. Avoidance and control of distress in financial institutions in MCPE Seminar Papers, Institute of Chartered Accountants of Nigeria.

Chapter 10

Banking Quirks, Regulatory Responses, and Supervision in Developing Economies

Chapter Outline

LEARNING FOCUS AND OBJECTIVES

It is not accidental that banking is a highly regulated business the world over. One reason is that banking has unique elements that bear on, and have wider implications for, macroeconomic management. The other reason for strict regulation of banking relates to its possible use as a conduit for financial crimes. The crux of the issues in banking regulation in developing economies should be understood in order to appreciate the banking quirks that inform it. The guides my focus in this chapter and its related objectives to:

- identify and situate banking quirks in the albatross for banking supervision in developing economies;

- evaluate the focus of banking regulation and how it informs the cause of autonomy for Central Banks in developing economies;
- define the critical issues and challenges of banking regulation and supervision in developing economies;
- examine the departures of banking regulation and supervision in developing economies from the Basel Accords;
- assess the responses of the regulatory authorities to distressed, failing, and failed banks in developing economies.

EXPECTED LEARNING OUTCOMES

Banking serves some economic objectives in every nation. The banking system fulfills, especially, particular national goals under the auspices of the Central Banks in developing countries. Its developmental roles in such countries are typical. The public needs and benefits from banking services in the pursuit of their economic aspirations. Thus, the quirks of banking tend to be intolerable—and the regulatory authorities respond accordingly. The reader will—after studying this chapter and doing the exercises in it—have learnt and been better informed about:

- the vibes that the public has about banking quirks, regulation, and supervision in developing economies;
- the failings, problems, and prospects of banking regulation and supervision in developing economies;
- the critical issues in, and challenges of, banking regulation and supervision in developing economies;
- how banking quirks possibly inform the albatross for banking supervision in developing economies;
- the focus of banking regulation and its bearing on the cause of autonomy for Central Banks in developing economies;
- divergence of banking regulation and supervision in developing economies from the tenets of the Basel Accords;
- possible regulatory authorities responses to distressed, failing, and failed banks in developing economies.

OVERVIEW OF THE SUBJECT MATTER

The banking system holds most of the aces in social change to which the developing economies aspire. If this is true—and I believe it is—then there should be no excuse for failure of banking in developing economies. Indeed, it should be all hands on deck to get banking right. The banking regulatory authorities should be at the forefront of this task. This is a call to duty and service in recognition of their roles as the watchdog for the stakeholders in banking.

Now I ask the real question. Have banking regulators in developing economies fulfilled this prized expectation to the satisfaction of the industry's stakeholders? This question is pertinent considering that the public tends to have bad vibes about banking regulation in developing economies. Obviously the question cannot be answered in the affirmative. Apparently, banking regulation in developing economies is riddled with failings. As would be expected, bankers and other financial system operators exploit the situation. Thus infractions of the rules of banking are common and exacerbated under the circumstances.

Unfortunately, banking supervision has not fared better. Often the work of the supervisory arms of the regulatory authorities seems, or is really, frustrated by the bankers. On occasion bank examiners come up against a brick wall in their investigation of the conduct of banks managements. In most cases, this happens where there is culpable breach of sensitive banking rules. Thus bank examines come under immense pressure to sweep curious findings under the rug. The intensity of the pressure depends on the seriousness of the offense.

Usually banking regulatory and supervisory authorities face two choices. They could stick with the ethics of their profession and shun inducements, or compromise themselves, succumb to pressure, and bungle their roles as the stakeholders' watchdog. This reality presents an "either or" situation that introduces irrational tendencies in banking. Those tendencies crystallize the crux of the observed banking quirks and regulatory responses in developing economies.

The domestic banks are often the main casualty of regulatory interventions to stem the quirks. Unlike them—and to the contrary—the foreign banks subsidiaries are scarcely caught napping by regulatory actions. This is instructive and bears on solving the challenges of the domestic banks in developing economies.

BANKING REGULATORY AUTHORITIES IN DEVELOPING ECONOMIES

Banking is—or ideally should be—a highly regulated business all over the world. This may sound a bit far-fetched, but I shed light on why it is true. In the first place, banks are a depository for the hard-earned cash, savings, and valuables of individuals, organizations, and institutions. Second, states and the public sector depend on efficiently functioning banking system to fulfill economic and social services to the citizens. Third, private enterprise and sector tend to flourish in countries where sound banking culture is institutionalized and has taken root. Fourth, failed—or the maneuvering of—banking explains most of the issues often raised about the poor performance of developing economies.

The Central Bank is the main regulatory authority for banking in developing economies. It exercises direct influence on the regulation and supervision the banks. In some countries, it may have joint responsibilities on these matters with a deposit insurance institution. The Central Bank of Nigeria (CBN) and Nigerian Deposit Insurance Corporation (NDIC), for example, independently— and, sometimes, on banking examination matters, jointly—supervise the banks. Nonetheless, the CBN remains the sole and autonomous authority for banking regulation in the country. It has some dotted reporting lines to the Presidency on some key national monetary issues, though.

There are other important nonbanking regulatory institutions whose roles complement those of the Central Bank and deposit insurance corporation. The institutions include the Presidency, Securities and Exchange Commission (SEC), and the Stock Exchange. In the case of Nigeria, the CBN recognizes the relevance of these institutions and draws some of the members of its Financial Services Regulation Coordinating Committee (FSRCC) from them. The FS-RCC serves as an advisory body to the CBN on policy and regulatory matters.

These bodies that make inputs into the frameworks for banking regulation in developing economies—using Nigeria as a reference point—fulfill varying but complementary roles. I now discuss the roles of the Presidency, Central Bank of Nigeria, and Nigerian Deposit Insurance Corporation.

The Presidency—in Democratic Governments

The Nigerian President signs the operating licenses that the Central Bank of Nigeria (CBN) issues to new banks. This is a major regulatory requirement that underscores the seriousness of banking as a business. Thus banks come into existence in the first place on the authority of the President. Another demonstration of the significance of banking is that the President appoints the Governor of the Central Bank while the Senate ratifies the appointment by a two third majority votes. Once ratified, the President cannot remove the Governor from office without two third majority votes of the Senate. These checks and balances ensure that the Central Bank enjoys the autonomy it needs to fulfill its monetary management functions as foreseen by the Act establishing it.

Central Bank of Nigeria

The CBN—established in 1958—commenced operations the following year with the mandate to manage the country's monetary economy. It functions through a board of directors. Its membership comprises the governor, four deputy governors, five directors, and a representative of the Federal Ministry of Finance. The Act establishing the CBN empowers it to be the apex regulatory institution for the country's banking system. In the exercise of this mandate, the CBN:

- issues licenses to new banks to enable them legally start formal operations and services to the public;
- invokes holding action, assumption of control, and acquisition, revocation of license, or liquidation of terminally distressed banks;
- supervises operations and activities of the licensed deposit money and other types of banks in the Nigeria;
- acts as the Banker for the Federal and States Government—including their agencies, Ministries, and parastatals;

- is the bankers' bank. In this capacity, the CBN acts as the lender of last resort to the deposit money banks;
- monitors, reviews, and controls the monetary aggregates that bear on the liquidity of the financial system.

Nigerian Deposit Insurance Corporation

The NDIC came into existence through the enactment of the Nigerian Deposit Insurance Corporation (NDIC) Decree 22 of 1988. It is a major stakeholder in the banking system due mainly to its provision of coverage for the eligible bank deposits. It regularly examines the books of the insured banks to ensure their compliance with the relevant banking rules. The NDIC is required under the Decree establishing it to:

- insure all bank deposits that qualify for coverage. In Nigeria, payment on the coverage in the event of bank failure is limited to ₦250,000.00 irrespective of the amount of the deposit. Encumbered deposits, such as those the depositors used as collateral to secure bank loans are not qualified for the insurance coverage;
- determine solvency standard for the banks in Nigeria that meets international requirements;
- collaborate with the CBN in ensuring the full compliance of the deposit money banks with the prudential guidelines on risk assets creation, monitoring, classifications, and ratings;
- ensure that the managements of the banks are qualified, competent, and of high integrity;
- review the financial statements of the banks to ensure that their reported earnings are correct—not just window dressing.

CASE STUDY 10.1 Doomsday Scenario—Lessons to Banking Regulators in Developing Economies

Some campus incidents put many people off (Extracted, with minor changes, from Onyiriuba, 2013. This tale is set in academia and not identified with any particular country, college or university in the world. It is presented here for the purposes of illustration and to demonstrate how the lessons of the tale play themselves out in banking in developing economies. The names—Union of Universities Faculty (UUF), Minister of Learning and Youth Development, and Joan—used in the tale are imaginary and do not relate to any known or unknown real life academic Union, Minister, government Ministry, and person anywhere in the world). Nefarious activities of misguided student cults are typical. Sometimes, the students dabbled in the cults to perpetrate surreptitious criminal acts against lecturers and fellow students. There was a striking incident of the act in the attack of a Professor by a gang of unidentified youths suspected to be members of a cult. The Professor was returning to his residence at dusk after the day's work when the incident happened in front of the entrance gate to his compound. His assailants had hidden in the bush near the gate from where they shot him in the head and fled, thinking that he was dead as he slumped in the driver's seat. But he survived the attack. He was quickly rushed to the hospital and later taken abroad for further medical treatment. That the Prof didn't return to his lecturing work after his treatment was instructive. Rather he dumped teaching and took up a new appointment as Director of External Relations in one of the high ranking banks.

Blackmail for sundry reasons also taints campus life. The practice is often linked to leakage of exam questions, sexual harassment, and trading—a sort of bartering—of exam marks. While some lecturers who are bereft of scruples get entangled in such vices, many shun the acts. Many of the lecturers who revel in the acts are perceived to be on the take most of the time. But the problem sometimes results from actions of mainly weak students. A lecturer must have the guts—indeed a strong will—to resist such students, contain their threats, and continue with lectureship. Some of the lecturers who insisted on passing only students who demonstrated academic brilliance were branded as wicked, mean, or sadists. In fact, lecturers who allowed themselves to be identified as such by students took a chance. This is the sad experience of campus life where values and morals are at low ebb.

The drama that attended the celebrated strike called by Union of Universities Faculty (UUF) was a defining moment in Joan's dissatisfaction with academia. It was a popular strike, one for which a lot of people showed empathy in its build-up. She was excited about the strike because she felt it was high time the neglect of universities and their employees stopped. She eagerly followed the strike—listening to news about it, watching discussions of it on television, and critically analyzing the contending issues. Sadly, negotiations between government and UUF ended in a stalemate. Prior to the impasse, the parties had gone through weeks of flexing muscles on the matters at issue. It was usual for the leaders of UUF to visit campuses to sell ideas and strategies of strikes to its members. In the case of this strike, the national president of UUF had gone round sensitizing lecturers on the need to embark on and sustain the strike. Joan attended one of the briefings and felt its outcome was encouraging. The meeting dispassionately discussed the agony and problems facing the universities, faculty, and students. It was heartening to hear lecturers pledge unalloyed support and commitment to the cause of the strike. Their speeches reflected confidence and resolution laced with understandable bitterness. Joan looked forward to positive changes that the strike would engender.

There was no reason to think that the strike would be a fiasco. Unfortunately, it turned out to be so as the Minister of Learning and Youth Development called UUF's bluff. He had warned of dire consequences that awaited the lecturers if they embarked on the strike. But UUF remained adamant and poised for a duel with Government over the raging issues. Thus it made good its threat and staged the strike. In response, on the same day the strike started, the Minister issued an ultimatum that if UUF did not call off the strike within 48 h, the professors and other academic employees living in university quarters would be evicted.

Apparently the threat did not go down very well. To many, it smacked of intolerance, the arrogance that characterized most government actions. Others felt it was an uncharitable show of impunity by the Minister. Joan was pissed off with how the Minister issued the threat, ostensibly to cow UUF to submission and foil the strike. "I watched him issue the threat on television and I felt it was usual, expected, and only provided a good ground for a test of will between the rule of law and the impunity with which the Minister acted," recalled Joan. "I had hoped that the strike would settle the long-drawn struggle of UUF to free our educational system from neglect and decay. So I didn't expect the lecturers to budge despite the threat, especially as public opinion supported their cause. But they did, to the utter dismay of the public—and especially people sympathetic to their cause," she told her acquaintance cynically. "I was stunned when I went to the campus the next morning and saw how professors were returning to work in haste. I later learnt that the scene was the same in other universities in the country," he enthused.

It would seem that the lecturers found it difficult to stomach the Minister's threat. But Joan couldn't appreciate why intellectuals who apparently had a genuine and noble cause should be so cowed. Whatever was the reason for their submission simply did not make sense to her. All that mattered to her was that the strike shouldn't have failed. Unfortunately her feelings were inconsequential as the strike had failed woefully and the status quo defended! As UUF called off the strike and academic employees returned to work the next day, she couldn't help imagining that her future as a lecturer hung in the balance.

Exercise for class or group discussion
1. Do you think that banking regulatory authorities in developing countries can be ruthless in their oversight functions?
2. Why—in your opinion—would it seem that the regulatory authorities for banking in developing economies find it difficult to be decisive?
3. What possible lessons should bankers and banking regulatory authorities in developing economies learn from this case study?
4. How may the banking regulatory authorities take action equivalent to that of the Minister of Learning and Youth Development?
5. Would the bankers see the Central Banks as fair if they borrowed ideas from the action of the Minister of Learning and Youth Development?

Tips for solving the exercise
I relate this tale to banking from two perspectives. First, the vile campus acts of faculty and students can be likened to ethical questions of banking in developing economies. Second, the actions taken by UUF and the Minister of Learning and Youth Development give hints about the implication of the tale for banking in developing economies. I piece these perspectives together and reiterate a point I have always emphasized about the need for banking regulation to have teeth so that it doesn't end up as a routine exercise. I should now add that banking regulators—like the Minister of Learning and Youth Development in the tale—must be ruthless and always act decisively. That is the way forward for effective regulation of banking in developing economies. While carrot and stick approach which the regulators fancy may be effective in some situations, it should be discreet. It cannot yet be relied upon to deal with complicated issues of banking in developing economies. The truth is that carrot and stick is no better than famed but ineffectual moral suasion which the bankers see simply as common courtesy. The bankers, on the one hand, take advantage of a propitious "carrot" and, on the other, get around the "stick"—leaving the status quo unchanged.

LEGAL INSTRUMENTS AND CHALLENGES OF BANKING REGULATION AND SUPERVISION

The regulation of banking requires an effective legal framework founded on a set of relevant laws focusing on the financial system. The laws should empower the authorities to exercise their functions without obstruction. Specific pieces of legislation should be the basis for enforcing the regulation of the banks under the laws. With legitimacy conferred on them by legislation, the authorities can deal with issues bordering on development of a sound banking and financial systems.

The contents and contexts of the banking laws and regulations may vary from one country to another, but with a similar intent. The financial landscape of a country determines the intensity of the laws and their enforcement. Usually, two of the applicable laws tend to have a greater impact on banking regulation in most countries. The first of the laws is an Act of Parliament that establishes the Central Bank. This law may be variously christened without changing its theme. Second, there is the law governing the banking practice. In Nigeria, the Banking Decree 1969 as amended, and the Banks and Other Financial Institutions Act (BOFIA) 1919 as amended are typical examples of the laws governing the practice of banking.

There would be several other pieces of legislation that complement the two main banking laws dependent on the banking challenges of the countries. For example, Kenya took the initiative and established the first ever deposit insurance scheme in Africa. Nigeria followed suit with the enactment of the Nigerian Deposit Insurance Corporation 1988 as amended. However, the idea of deposit insurance is not yet popular in many developing countries. The countries that have embraced it did so, perhaps, to stem the spate of banks distress and failure. Lack of interest in deposit insurance may be an indication that a country has a strong banking industry under the auspices of a sound financial system.

Most of the complementary banking regulatory laws focus on curtailing economic and financial crimes. There also is emphasis on laws to check drug trafficking and its related crime of money laundering through the banking system. The laws establishing Nigeria Drug Law Enforcement Agency (NDLEA), and Economic and Financial Crimes Commission (EFCC) are good examples. Some countries enact ad hoc laws to tackle some urgent problems of the banking industry. Nigerian Government enacted the Failed Banks (Recovery of Debts) and Financial Malpractices in Banks Act, No. 18 of 1994, to regulate the mismanagement of banks.

There is yet another legislation that is common and influence banking practice in developing countries. This legislation enacts the laws governing corporate businesses. In Nigeria, it is christened Companies and Allied Matters Act (CAMA) 1990. Some rules of banking provide ancillary guidance on banking practice in developing economies. Typical examples include the bankers' tariff, the constitution of the Money Market Association of Nigeria (MMAN) and Nigeria Interbank Settlement System (NIBSS).

The Observed Challenges and Implications

The finding that banking regulation modes and practices in developing economies diverge from Basel Accords provokes concerns in financial circles. The divergences are observed mainly in regulation of capital base, measuring capital adequacy, regulating liquidity risk, and response to failing and failed banks. I investigate the factors at issue to establish the basis of the divergences and assess their implications for bank risk management. I define the crux of banking regulation in developing economies against a backdrop of Basel Accords prescriptions for bank capital regulation. That sheds light on factors constraining effective banking supervision in developing economies, as well as supervisory framework that banking regulators in developing economies adopt and how it relates to Basel Accords.

One unanswered question continues to agitate the minds of analysts and observers of happenings in the banking industry in developing economies. The question borders on regulatory aberration. Why, despite regulation and supervision, has the condition of some banks deteriorated to levels where failure becomes inevitable? This has been a puzzling question over the years. It is usually too late to save ailing banks by the time regulators eventually intervene! Doing too little too late in this way compounds the problem for banks. In most cases, banks become terminally distressed such that they lose merger or acquisition appeal.

Certainly something is wrong with the regulatory oversight of deposit money banks in developing economies. The public, especially banking experts and analysts, believes that the approach to banking regulation and supervision leaves a lot to be desired. Banking supervision and indeed regulatory authorities are tainted, once they are found wanting as the stakeholders' watchdog. There are more postmortem activities than anticipation and prognosis of the risks envisaged in the master contingency plans of banks. For example, in the aftermath of the 2007–09 financial meltdown, the Central Bank of Nigeria (CBN) sacked the boards of eight banks—Afribank, Bank PHB, Equitorial Trust Bank, FinBank, Intercontinental Bank, Oceanic Bank, Union Bank, and Spring Bank—and appointed an interim management board for each of them. The CBN accused executives of the banks of professional misconduct. The misconduct was evident in abuse of office and insider abuse, especially in granting credit facilities. A typical insider abuse was the granting of unsecured loans to directors of the banks and their cronies. The lending not only contravened the law but made nonsense of best practice and internal credit policies of banks.

Curiously, the same CBN had given all banks in the country a clean bill of health while the global financial crisis was well underway! Although banking supervision had earlier uncovered the rot in the banks, it was not until 2009 before the hammer fell on the affected distressed banks. Investigation of the banks revealed how their CEOs subverted banking policy and control—and especially the internal credit processes of the banks. Executives of the banks not only compromised themselves but also rendered banking supervision ineffectual.

That was how, against the foregoing backdrop, this critical oversight function of the CBN started losing significance. It took courage—which Sanusi Lamido Sanusi, then the new CBN Governor, had in abundance—to restore confidence in the country's banking supervision. In 2009, the Governor took decisive steps toward reforming the banking sector. One of the major planks of the reforms was the prosecution of indicted executives of failed banks in Nigeria. The pay-off was worth the trouble involved in carrying out the reforms.

Now the public has a significant measure of confidence in the banks that survived the onslaught of the difficult reforms. Besides, many see nationalization of failed banks, as opposed to liquidation of them—as was the practice in the past—as a welcome development. The immediate import of the creation of "bridge banks" (i.e., nationalized banks) is that customers of banks are assured of the safety of their deposits in the event that a bank fails or becomes distressed. The bridge banks—Enterprise Bank Limited, Keystone Bank Limited, and Main Street Bank Limited—represent the former Spring Bank PLC, Bank PHB PLC, and Afribank PLC, respectively.

DEFINING ISSUES IN BANKING QUIRKS AND REGULATION IN DEVELOPING ECONOMIES

Many banks in developing economies often take uncalculated risks in jumping on service propositions bandwagon. Some of the banks jump on the bandwagon with risk-prone financial products, ostensibly letting budget goal cloud their judgment. Risk in this context is the uncertainty of possible outcomes of actions or decisions that bank managements take uncritically on the financial or other side of the business. Often they are ill-prepared and don't have strong convictions about their fancied but highly risky service propositions. That is the reason they easily succumb to externally induced pressure and operational risks. Ideally, bank managements should always anticipate risk and uncertainty and take decisions with a critical disposition.

Incidentally, regulation of banking in developing economies remains an arduous task, no doubt about it. Unstructured regulatory frameworks and half-hearted enforcement informed by unnecessary bureaucracy compound the task. A feature of the approach to regulation seen in most developing economies is a significant divergence from the Basel Accords. Regulatory authorities acknowledge this fact when they admit their inability to strictly adopt or implement the Basel Accords. Authorities hold this view on aspects of Basel I (Basel Committee on Banking Supervision, 1988), Basel II (Basel Committee on Banking Supervision, 2006), and Basel III (Basel Committee on Banking Supervision, 2010). Yet regulators have to exercise their oversight of banking one way or the other.

There are four main findings that shed light on disturbing issues in the quirks and regulation of banking in developing economies. The findings relate to actions of banks managements in response to regulatory actions and maneuverings. While the authorities are ever evolving and enforcing policies largely on a pragmatic basis, banks managements respond in kind—ever exploring expedient means of getting around the rules. I summarize the four findings as follows:

- the simple regulatory expedient of issuing occasional monetary policy circulars to deposit money banks;
- Central Banks taking a more pragmatic approach to the regulation of banking practices that often diverge from Basel Accords;
- imposition of fines, sanctions, and penalties on erring banks to serve as deterrents to breaches of banking rules;
- banks managements falling back on banking expediencies to circumvent difficult regulations and policies.

The foregoing introduces conflict in the making and enforcement of banking regulations in developing economies. Often it results in flawed banking supervision and truncated enforcement of banking rules. Regulators and banks go on doing their own things in this unhealthy way—ostensibly not wanting to rock the boat, but apparently risking systemic crisis in the financial system. Occasional roundtable discussions of the underlying issues by regulators and chief executives of banks under the auspices of Bankers' Committee meetings end in horse-trading.

Yet in order to prevent the financial system crises in developing economies that are often caused by unchecked credit risk-taking, banking regulation, and supervision must have teeth. Giving these oversight functions teeth would require an overhaul of the current approaches and mechanisms adopted by the regulatory authorities. Ideally, supervision should anticipate and preempt criticized banking practices. One of the lessons of experience learned about banking regulation in developing economies is that the rubber-stamping of banking supervision reports is inimical to a sound banking system. Regulatory authorities have a responsibility to the public to be diligent in the exercise of their oversight functions. In this way, the major outcome of banking supervision would be a strengthened banking system. Strengthening the banking system will serve the interests of banking stakeholders and the public.

The factors that define issues in regulation demand attention at the same time. I discuss the two most critical issues now. First I examine the question of autonomy for banking regulatory authorities, mainly the Central Banks. Then I explore the albatross for banking supervision in developing economies. In doing so, I highlight implications for bank risk management in developing economies.

AUTONOMY FOR BANKING REGULATORY AUTHORITIES

It is widely believed that the banking regulatory institutions should be strengthened and empowered to be able to effectively deal with the problems of the industry. There is a need for Central Banks to have full autonomy so that they could deal decisively with any threat of financial distress in the system. This has been elusive in some developing economies owing to bureaucratic encumbrance. Government freely interferes and often meddles in banking regulatory policies. In most cases, the functioning of the banking industry—nay, the financial system—is distorted as a result.

A related problem to the lack of autonomy for Central Banks in developing economies is political interference in banking policy initiatives and implementation. Ordinarily, government should distance itself from banking regulation for the sake of efficiency of the industry and returns to the stakeholders. Friction often observed between governments and Central Banks in developing economies arises where the former meddles in the regulatory roles of the latter. Friction arises especially where governments and Central Banks pursue conflicting policies borne out of contrasting perspectives on the financial economy of the countries. In order to avoid national embarrassment bordering on recrimination, the two bodies should harmonize their perspectives on monetary and financial policy management. In most cases, recriminations follow failures to account for conflicting policies.

In Nigeria, some success was achieved in 1998 when the CBN was granted instrument autonomy. The partial autonomy granted the CBN, according to Sanusi (2001), "insulates it from undue political interference in its conduct of monetary and financial policies and, thereby enables it to act more proactively and promptly in its policy responses to changes in economic conditions." The CBN was yet further empowered by legislation in 2007 when the country's National Assembly passed the CBN (amendment) Act that grants it full autonomy. This fits with best practice, the hallmark of efficiently functioning banking systems around the world. Autonomy should go hand in hand with a competitively composed board of directors (mostly experts in economics, banking, and finance). With the governor as chairperson of the board, the independence and accountability of Central Banks in monetary and financial policy management would be better assured.

ALBATROSS FOR BANKING SUPERVISION IN DEVELOPING ECONOMIES

Often the way that banks in developing economies maneuver regulations completely confounds regulatory authorities and other banking stakeholders. Financial analysts are no less intrigued by the seeming inability of the authorities to tame bank managements. Without disillusioning the reader, there are cracks in banking regulation and supervision in developing economies. Ironically, supervised banks constitute an albatross for regulatory authorities. Banks discreetly cut corners, cook the books, and perfect counters to punitive regulatory policies. In most cases, the financial statements and accounts of banks are just window dressing.

Regulators tend to dish out monetary policies while seemingly oblivious to banking rot. Banks circumvent key banking rules in several ways, including:

1. Cutting back the size of the outstanding portfolio of nonperforming loans and advances, often in collaboration with obligors.
2. Rebooking nonperforming but not yet charged off credit facilities—usually with the cooperation of obligors.
3. Generally dressing up the loan book to avoid huge specific loan loss provision on classified risk assets.
4. Boosting deposit liability through the negotiated rollover of maturing fixed deposits and similar purchased funds.
5. Taking interbank funds to satisfy critical evaluation indices—mainly cash reserve, loan-to-deposit, and liquidity ratios.

The first three of the circumvention modes address issues on the assets side of the balance sheet, while the last two deal with liability concerns.

Overall, banks employ the five methods above to manipulate financial records in end-of-month returns to regulatory authorities. With any luck, banks are assured of lower risk-based charges to their regulatory capital on the asset side. Satisfying the regulatory liquidity ratios identified in (5) earlier addresses the liability concerns. There is no uniform approach that all banks in all developing economies adopt in pursuit of the foregoing. Differences in methods may be observed among banks and economies, depending on the states of development of the financial system and the regulatory framework. For this reason it will be futile to attempt here to discuss details of the applicable approaches. Rather it suffices to appreciate that banks in developing economies have ways of maneuvering regulations and supervision contrary to the spirit of the Basel Accords.

REGULATORY RESPONSES TO FAILING BANKS IN DEVELOPING ECONOMIES

It would be wishful thinking to believe that regulation is a panacea for bank failure. It is ordinary that banks, like other businesses—even in the developed economies—fail in the course of operations. This may be why the Central Bank of Nigeria (CBN) postures equal minds in allowing free entry as it enforces exit on distressed banks. The CBN Governor had on January 30, 2001 announced that in continuation of distress resolution efforts, three banks had their licenses revoked and were transferred to the Nigerian Deposit Insurance Corporation (NDIC) for eventual liquidation. He stressed that efforts would be sustained in 2001 to address any symptom of distress in the system in a timely and decisive manner. It was not strange that the CBN was bluntly sounding that warning, considering the country's recent experiences with large-scale banking distress and failures that had brought untold hardships to the people.

The CBN and NDIC have control over and management responsibilities for distressed and failing banks. Sections 33 (2) and 34 (36) of the Banks and Other Financial Institutions (BOFI) Act No. 25 of 1991, as amended, empower the CBN to deal with distressed and failing banks. Nowadays, the CBN adopts more liberal approaches for the resolution of bank distress. It allows the shareholders of the distressed banks to decide their preferred distress resolution option in the first instance. The usual options are restructuring, mergers, take-overs (i.e., acquisitions), sale of the bank, and outright liquidation (where failure is inevitable). In collaboration with the NDIC, the CBN has implemented all of these options with mean success in most cases.

I now discuss the various approaches often adopted by the regulatory authorities in developing economies to resolve bank distress. My objective is to assess the effectiveness of the various measures. The most common approaches include moral suasion, holding action, assumption of control, and acquisition, revocation of license, or liquidation.

Moral Suasion

Prior to and during distress, regulatory authorities adopt moral suasion as a means of sensitizing banks to the dangers of distress and how to avoid it. In most cases, moral suasion involves specific recommendations to, and counseling of, banks managements on the need to maintain prudent operations. The Central Banks specifically urge banks to observe appropriate and approved operating guidelines, render accurate statutory returns, and strive to achieve the required financial and performance ratios. The authorities hold regular interactive sessions with the chief executives of the banks to discuss matters affecting banks in particular and the financial system in general. Under the auspices of the Chartered Institutes of Bankers, the Bankers' Committee provides perhaps the most effective forum for such interactions. However, it does not seem that moral suasion has been effective in managing or preventing bank distress in developing economies. The problem has obviously defied such a persuasive measure.

Holding Actions

The more drastic measures, usually adopted whenever moral suasion fails, are prescribed—in the case of Nigeria—in the BOFI Act 1991. Section 33 (2) empowers the Governor of the CBN to make an order restricting the activities of a distressed or failing bank. In line with the Act, the Governor may, by order in writing:

- prohibit the bank from further extending any credit facility; and
- require the bank to take any steps or any action, or to do or not to do any act or thing whatsoever, in relation to the bank or its business or its directors or officers, that may be considered necessary.

Often the scope of such holding actions is sweeping and covers a broad spectrum of restrictions. For instance, a failing bank may not, without the consent of the CBN, continue to advertise for deposits, embark on new capital projects, or dispose of any fixed assets. Such a bank is expected to beef up internal controls, recapitalize the business, perfect loan security documentation, and emphasize debt recovery. There are numerous other miscellaneous requirements that failing banks must satisfy in their bids for an effective turnaround.

It is doubtful that holding actions are an effective means of resolving bank distress in developing economies. The Nigerian experience supports this view. Of over 50 banks on which the CBN has administered holding actions since the 1990s distress syndrome, less than a 5% success rate has been attained. The high failure rate of the actions derived mainly from the magnitude of the observed distress prior to intervention by regulatory authorities. For example, the holding actions were most often imposed after the paid-up capital of distressed banks had been completely wiped out, while their stock of unsecured or undocumented nonperforming loans had become rather excessive.

It becomes overwhelming, under the circumstances, for the owners and managements of the banks to attain any measure of turnaround success, especially in terms of recapitalization. Some may argue that the delay in imposing "holding actions" is justified; authorities should be convinced beyond all doubts that such interference in the affairs of the bank is really the next resort in the plans to save the bank. This implies that the management of a bank has completely failed in restructuring or reengineering the bank for normal banking business in line with regulatory prescriptions.

Assumption of Control

Once holding actions fail to yield fruit, a Central Bank can invoke the law to assume control of the bank. In Nigeria, the power to take over management of a failing bank is given in Sections 34 and 35 of the BOFI Act 1991. Meanwhile, Section 33 (2) (d) and (e) empower the CBN, as a prelude to assumption of full control of a distressed bank, to:

- remove from office any director of the bank;
- appoint any person or persons as a director or directors of the bank; and
- appoint any person to advise the bank in relation to the proper conduct of its business.

In the event that the foregoing measures fail to rescue the bank, that is to say, "the state of affairs of the bank does not improve significantly," the BOFI Act 1991 provides that the CBN may assume control of the whole of the property and affairs of the bank, carry on the whole of its business and affairs, or assume control of such part of its property, business, and affairs as it considers necessary, or appoint persons to do so on its behalf [Section 34 (1)].

The assumption of control of a distressed bank by the authorities may be temporary, if the action succeeds, or lead to stiffer action if it fails. Success is attained when, and assumption of control by the authorities remains in force until such time as:

- the CBN is satisfied that adequate provision has been made for the repayment of deposits; and
- in the opinion of the CBN, it is no longer necessary for it to remain in control of the business of the bank [Section 35 (1)].

The banking regulatory authorities in Nigeria became innovative in the exercise of the foregoing power when they nationalized three failed banks in 2010 and christened them "bridge banks"—without assuming direct control of the banks.

Acquisition, Revocation of License, or Liquidation

The last resort of the regulatory authorities in the process of distress management is to acquire, restructure, and sell the failing bank, or revoke the operating license of and wind up the bank. In the case of Nigeria, the power of the CBN to do this is given in Section 36 (a) (b) of the BOFI Act 1991, where it stipulates that if the paid-up capital of the distressed bank is lost or unrepresented by available assets, the CBN may:

- apply to the Federal High Court for an order for it or its nominee to purchase or acquire the bank for a nominal fee for the purpose of restructuring and subsequent sale; and
- make an order revoking the bank's license and requiring its business to be wound up.

In Nigeria, the need has been identified to fully empower the Central Bank and Nigerian Deposit Insurance Corporation (NDIC) to deal with any threat of bank distress. The application of such empowerment climaxes when authorities, to pave the way for liquidation, withdraw the operating license of a bank. Yet, for practical purposes:

- it does not make good business sense to resolve distress through the liquidation of affected banks;
- liquidation generally causes great financial pain to depositors, shareholders, and employees;
- revocation of banking license further erodes the fragile confidence that citizens may have in the banking system.

Even when bank liquidation is unavoidable, there are still problems. First, it could take up to 3 years before the NDIC begins paying depositors. Second, not only will depositors of a failed bank suffer such a prolonged delay, each of them gets no more than the insured portion of their deposits, irrespective of the amount of their deposit with the bank. For bank depositors, this practice negates the true essence of insurance. It is an aberration of the acknowledged principle of indemnity on which the business of insurance is founded.

If the monetary authorities really want to help build a long-term deposit banking culture and reinstill confidence in the banking system, the NDIC should pay appropriate compensation to depositors of failed banks. This will allay the fear of loss of deposits due to bank distress or failure, and help to attract movement of much of the huge amount of money in private vaults to banks. Over the long run, it would become less attractive to hold money outside the banking system. Also, projections of money stock in the system for regulatory purposes will be more accurate and reliable. The impact of monetary policies will to a large extent be predictable, while unintended monetary shocks will be minimized.

SUMMARY

Banking regulation modes and practices in developing economies tend to diverge from the Basel Accords. Divergence is observed mainly in regulation of capital base, measuring capital adequacy, regulating liquidity risk, and response to failing and failed banks. But it borders regulatory aberration—a situation that renders regulatory oversight of deposit money banks in developing economies ineffective. Unstructured regulatory framework and half-hearted enforcement informed by unnecessary bureaucracy compound the problem.

There are four main findings that shed light on disturbing issues in the regulation of banking in developing economies. The findings relate to actions of regulatory authorities and the responses of banks managements to those actions. While the authorities are ever evolving and enforcing policies largely on a pragmatic basis, banks managements respond in kind—ever exploring expedient means of getting around the rules. In order to prevent the financial system crises in developing economies that are often caused by excessive risk-taking, banking regulation, and supervision must have teeth. Giving these oversight functions teeth would require an overhaul of the current approaches and mechanisms adopted by regulatory authorities.

It is widely believed that banking regulatory institutions should be strengthened and empowered to be able to effectively deal with the problems of the industry. There is a need for Central Banks to have full autonomy so that they could deal decisively with any threat of financial distress in the system. This has been elusive in some developing economies owing to bureaucratic encumbrance. Government freely interferes and often meddles in banking regulatory policies.

Often the way that banks in developing economies maneuver regulations completely confounds regulatory authorities and other banking stakeholders. There are cracks in banking regulation and supervision in developing economies. Ironically, supervised banks constitute an albatross for regulatory authorities. Banks discreetly cut corners, cook the books, and perfect counters to punitive regulatory policies. In most cases, the financial statements and accounts of banks are just window dressing.

It would be wishful thinking to believe that regulation is a panacea for bank failure. It is ordinary that banks, like other enterprises, fail in the course of business.

The banking regulatory authorities in developing economies adopt various approaches to resolve bank distress. The most common approaches include moral suasion, holding action, assumption of control, and acquisition, revocation of license, or liquidation.

QUESTIONS FOR DISCUSSION AND REVIEW

1. How will adoption of the Basel Accords benefit supervision of deposit money banks in developing economies?
2. Why and how do modes of banking regulation in developing economies diverge from the Basel Accords tenets?
3. How, notwithstanding supervision, would the condition of a bank deteriorate to a level where failure becomes imminent?
4. What factors contribute to banking quirks in developing economies? How do the banks frustrate regulation responses?
5. Why and how is banking about the most regulated business and what are the implications of this for the financial system?
6. What are the challenges, failings, and prospects of banking regulation and supervision in developing economies?

REFERENCES

Basel Committee on Banking Supervision, 1988. International Convergence of Capital Measurement and Capital Standards. Bank for International Settlements, Basel.

Basel Committee on Banking Supervision, 2006. International Convergence of Capital Measurement and Capital Standards: a Revised Framework—Comprehensive Version. Bank for International Settlements, Basel.

Basel Committee on Banking Supervision, 2010. Basel III: International Framework for Liquidity Risk Measurement, Standards and Monitoring. Bank for International Settlements, Basel.

Onyiriuba, L., 2013. On the road to self-actualization. NFS Data Bureau Limited, Lagos, pp. 11–14.

Sanusi, J.O., 2001. Keynote Address (Delivered as Governor, Central Bank of Nigeria) at the National Workshop on Monetary and Financial Policies Management, Lagos.

Section B

New Insights and Concerns

Chapter 11

Country Risk of Banking in Fledgling Economies Mired in Slippery Political Terrain

LEARNING FOCUS AND OBJECTIVES

Socio-political and economic decay are a common sight in developing economies. This and similar causes of country risk pose a threat to business. Militancy, terrorism, guerrilla and civil wars are typical signs that all is not well with governance and the polity. One cannot but wonder what could have gone wrong with peoples of the developing world. This is really thought-provoking and guides my objectives to:

- Analyze perspectives on, and historical antecedents to, country risk with implications for banking in developing countries.
- Investigate the creation and aspects of political risk that banks face and should mitigate in developing economies.
- Explore socio-political and economic realities in defining country risks that militate against the success of banks in developing economies.
- Evaluate the role of political maneuvering and ethnic politicking in festering country risk with which banks contend in developing economies.
- Demonstrate the risks and implications of dictatorship, personal rule, and politicization of the civil service for banking.
- Situate militancy, terrorism, guerrilla, and civil wars in the context of country risk for banking in developing economies.

EXPECTED LEARNING OUTCOMES

Country risk is a systemic phenomenon all over the world. It is, however, more endemic in developing economies. It reflects adverse conditions or the probability that some unforeseeable events would happen and cause loss to someone, business, or organization in a country. Thus a bank—like other businesses in the country—might cease to be a going concern, or fail. This is a real risk facing banking in developing economies. The reader will—after studying this chapter and doing the exercises in it—have learnt and been better informed about:

- Current thinking and perspectives on country risk, with implications for banking in developing countries.
- Aspects and the mechanics of political risk that banks face and should mitigate in developing economies.
- Socio-political and economic realities that inform country risks that militate against the success of banks in developing economies.
- Issues in political maneuvering and ethnic politicking that fester country risk with which banks contend in developing economies.
- How dictatorship, personal rule, and politicization of the civil service count in country risk, with implications for banking in developing economies.
- Risks that militancy, terrorism, guerrilla and civil wars pose to banking in developing economies.

OVERVIEW OF THE SUBJECT MATTER

Country risk is a pervasive feature of developing economies. It affects everyone—neither does it spare businesses. Government, organizations, and institutions also contend with it. Risk, in foregoing sense, implies adverse conditions in a country at any point in time that can cause loss to someone, business or organization. In relation to banking, it is the probability that some unforeseeable event in a country might cause a bank to incur loss, not be able to operate as a going concern, or fail outright. Risk of this nature underlies the main concern for banking in developing economies. Numerous factors impart risk to developing economies. The local populace may be disillusioned with politics, foment rebellion against the social order, or become militant in demanding some reforms. This exacerbates risk in countries that are unable to exercise effective control over their economic and political affairs. Apparently, political realities rub off on the economy and business outcomes.

Military intervention in politics remains a key factor of risk in developing countries. Usually, dictatorship and personal rule are the aftermath of military incursion into politics. Soon the polity heats up and begins to take a heavy toll on the populace. This may also happen when politicians fail to play by the rules, be accountable to the electorate, and manage state wealth well. Fragile political systems of the countries, adapted from Western democratic models, compound the problem. Today many developing countries are grappling with coups d'état, tainted democratic institutions, and leadership flux—all of which are political fallout of country risk. Some of the countries contend with terrorism, and guerrilla and civil wars—most of which are serious causes of risk in a country. Historical perspective on country risk in developing economies is quite instructive. Politics evolved along ethnic lines in some countries due to failure of colonialism to institutionalize racial integration within the polities. The imperialists recast precolonial political societies to form modern states. This action sharpened ethnic consciousness and rivalries by lumping heterogeneous peoples together in common territories. Thus ethnicity in politics of the countries is linked with colonial-induced disruption of organic equilibrium of otherwise politically stable traditional societies.

Many developing countries are drifting and experiencing debilitating sociopolitical and economic decay. It will be interesting to know what could have gone wrong with peoples of a common race who once had workable political culture built on indigenous democratic values and agricultural economies. This raises a number of thought-provoking questions: What factors are responsible for the political and economic decay in developing countries? What are the historical antecedents to the problems of the countries? How have postcolonial developing countries grappled with the challenge of governance? In what respect has political instability affected economic development in the countries? What measures may be useful in resolving the countries' crisis? Though pertinent, these questions are beyond the scope of this book. But they hold important lessons for bank managements which I investigate throughout this chapter.

CASE STUDY 11.1 Scene of Civil War Fallout—Implications for Banking in Developing Economies

The village square was filled to capacity in response to the town crier's invitation. All the people present appeared haggard, melancholic, and apprehensive. Discussions were in groups and in low tones. Most children who showed up at the gathering were suffering from one form of disease or the other. So were some adults. Others who seemed healthy showed conspicuous signs of malnutrition. Occasionally, they gave wan smiles.

Then, a roaring voice released an announcement which set the agenda for the gathering.

"It's my pleasure to ask all of you to please come this way," said the respected septuagenarian village head, to his kith and kin—beckoning them.

"We are here for a serious issue. Let all group discussions stop immediately," he ordered.

"You know that nobody can relax in the face of a menacing situation. The sound of gunfire is too close for comfort. We have come to the point where we can no more pretend about this war. Our lives, more than ever before, are now in dire danger. It's obvious that the enemy is determined to crush us at the slightest opportunity."

It would have been possible to hear a pin drop at the meeting ground as everybody kept sullen silence. Nobody could find their voice. Apparently, fear had engulfed them.

Many had given up hope of being alive to see the next day. There was a story of a man who sold all his inherited land in order to buy food for his only surviving son and himself. He hinged his action on the fact that they would not survive the war. In the ensuing silence, the village head continued in his baritone voice.

"Aerial and artillery bombardments in our neighboring towns and villages have intensified since this week and I consider it critical for us to come together and discuss our concern."

He sneezed heavily and cleaned his nose with his left hand. He didn't want to waste their time again on rhetoric and so he went straight to the main issue.

"Shall we desert this village in the face of the approaching enemy?" He asked point blank.

As he was talking, he noticed that he was addressing a group of downcast folks whose thoughts were very far from what he was telling them. Then a voice of dissent thundered from the crowd.

"You don't listen to radio," Elle sneered. "The GOC of the Military Base on the frontier that oversees our Wanda town and its environs has escaped to America. He has abandoned us. The International Broadcasting Corporation broke the news this morning. All of you who have been leaking out my hideout to the Biafra soldiers should bury your heads in shame. I will not be forced to go to war I didn't cause," he judged.

There was silence still. In the midst of the quiet, Elle was busy mimicking the village head—in a way that suggested that he was wasting their time as the enemy had overrun all their neighboring villages and towns.

"Go home and eat your last meal. We have no choice than to wait for the end. It's unfortunate that the doomsday scenario will play out," Elle advised.

The apprehension which had engulfed the people peaked with the revelation made by Elle at the gathering. The news that the GOC had fled to America did not also help matters. It was the worst news the people heard at the time—and it was very disturbing to them indeed. They had hitherto been assured that the GOC would use his invisible power to scatter the enemy and secure victory for them in the war. It therefore became very worrisome to hear that a GOC with such "magical" power had escaped to America for his dear life without informing the people entrusted to his care. In fact, the people had no positive hope without him in the saddle. The hope of the people was dashed at that.

Anger flared up in the gathering as a result of the discomforting report about the GOC's escape. But the report was founded on a malicious rumor, indeed. Thus, one of the elders in the audience—an ardent believer in the GOC—who couldn't control his emotions warned sternly about spreading false rumors about their idol, GOC extraordinaire.

"You must show respect to our great GOC—he's the leader we see and know here in Oku village and in the whole of Wanda community. Even if he has escaped to the moon, he's still our respected leader. I don't see anything pejorative about an accomplished soldier of his standing making a tactical retreat from a war zone—if ever he's done that. After all, we are all familiar with the popular saying that "he who fights and runs lives to fight another day. Please go on with your address," the man "ordered' the village head.

Later the village head continued with his address.

"If our answer is yes, where shall we head to and when shall we start the journey? I will prefer we stay here for the enemy to do with us what pleases them. I learned last night that they had started to bombard Umoko which is the most probable town to run to."

He blew his nose heavily again and one of the elders close to him responded with wishing him "long life"—the traditional prayer for someone who sneezed in that way.

Referring to the village head as a "man of honor," the elder made a short general remark.

"We will not die in this war," he prayed.

"Amen," chorused everybody.

The village head resumed his address to the gathering.

"If you look around, our number consists of the aged and children. Our great heroes have been killed in the field of battle. We starve every day, while fear dominates our lives. What life are we saving?"

Uneasy silence rained the gathering as the venerable elder took his seat after such a heart-rending address. No one found his voice again, even Elle who had proved stubborn at the beginning of the meeting. The elder had hit the nail on the head and nobody needed to be reminded that the matter at issue was serious. Certainly the words of the elders are words of wisdom. His words were food for thought. It left many people swallowed by despair and sorrow.

Suddenly, there was a stampede. Everybody in the gathering took to their heels, disappeared into a nearby bush and prostrated. Scampering women and children also made for the bush. A bomber from the enemy's side had mysteriously appeared, hovering menacingly around but without dropping bombs. As the sound of the engine of the bomber died in the silence that followed the stampede, the villagers started coming out from their hiding places and made for home. Thus, the meeting ended abruptly and no decision was reached.

Exercise for class or group discussion

1. What would have been your response to the fate of the village gathering if you were manager of a branch of a domestic bank in Wanda town?
2. How would you have reacted to the civil war assuming you were the managing director of a foreign subsidiary bank in the country at the time?
3. Would you have taken different decisions—or taken decisions differently—to mitigate risk if you had foreseen the civil war?
4. Do you think that normal approach to mitigating risk in banking would be feasible in the case of full-blown civil war?
5. What risk management advice can you give to bankers working in civil war-prone developing countries?

Tips for solving the exercise

The implication of this tale borders on country risk of banking in developing economies.

Many developing countries are facing adverse political conditions at any point in time. This affects banking performance as country risks manifest themselves in intractable forms. Thus banks contend with the probability that some unforeseeable event in a country their essence as going concerns. This risk is not only real but an albatross—a sort of nightmare—for bank managements in developing economies. Country risk informed by political realities easily rubs off on bank management—often in a way that portends a bleak future for banking. It behooves bank managements to always be on top of developments in the political landscape.

They should do so in pragmatic ways and as a risk control measure. They should anticipate country risk and situate it in the context of the bank's risk management contingency master plan. Of course, the need to constantly reinvent and adapt risk management process to evolving risk trends cannot be overemphasized (Extracted, with minor changes, from Onyiriuba, 2013. Although this is a real life story, the names of the towns, military titles, and individuals in the tale are imaginary and do not relate to any known or unknown real towns, military titles, or persons anywhere in the world. The story serves purely illustration purposes only, in order to demonstrate how banking risks implied in the tale play themselves out in developing economies).

LOCAL POPULACE DISILLUSIONED WITH POLITICS

The local populace easily becomes disillusioned with politics. Often disenchantment with government follows as a country falls into anarchy. The hardline elements in the local populace may want to foment rebellion against the social order or demand some reforms. These possible incidents typify realities in developing economies that create political risk for banking. There are historical antecedents, though, to the creation of this type of risk. Take the influence of colonialism on some of the developing countries as an example. The anticolonial campaign had the objective of securing self-rule for the people. Colonial freedom was seen as simply substitution of indigenous for foreign rule, without reflection on the real burden of self-rule. Political activists were united by a common cause of wresting power from the imperialists. Their nationalism rested on crisis of confidence in the economy. Ironically, the crisis deepened after the ouster of colonial administration. The resultant political conflicts threatened survival of the newly independent states. Apparently, politicians lacked proper understanding of democratic demands of the hard-won independence.

The populace hoped that their beleaguered democracies would be reinvented and usher in an era of economic prosperity. This hope slipped through the net as political maneuvering blurred the real vision of independence. While the politicians looked to self-rule to fulfill their ambitions, the citizenry dreamt of the good life. Ideally, self-rule should institutionalize peaceful, progressive, and stable governance built on indigenous economic base. This might not have formed part of the vital agenda of the political class. Self-rule was gained from neocolonialists under questionable circumstances. This had future development implications, no doubt about it. But it is, perhaps, a country's inability to exercise control over its economic and political affairs that is most disturbing. It seems contemporary leaders of some developing countries are ill-equipped to meet the challenge of modern democracy and politics. At independence, the countries' nationalists simply filled positions vacated by the colonial powers. However, they failed to advance the cause of the collective struggle for democracy and self-rule. Ubiquitous political violence, crisis and instability across developing economies dramatize the failure of the political class. Banking in developing economies contends with these and similar political realities that rub off on the economy. Bank managements should always accurately read and anticipate the political and economic landscapes. That way they would be able to structure and adapt business operations to mitigate risks.

Bankers should always be on top of evolving political trends, threats, and opportunities. That helps in strategy formulation and risk management. In some countries, the military usurped power, jettisoned democracy, and introduced dictatorship to governance because the politicians were not serious. Military incursion into politics is an aberration and a setback for political development. Ideally, progress stems from ability to keep armed forces committed to their calling and focused on defense and security of the state. But this cannot be achieved unless politicians play by the rules, are accountable to the electorate, and manage state wealth well. Politicians can do anything but fail to direct affairs of the state and sustain good governance—initiating and implementing socio-political and economic development reforms and policies. A rather common observation is that politicians in developing economies are not always committed to national economic goals. Thus, development strategies are rarely well articulated or properly executed—creating room for political conflicts. On occasion, this gets out of hand and puts the countries in a downward spiral—retarding capacity for investment and economic development. Such a situation neither provides the setting for good governance nor permits democracy to take root or flourish. Instead, it breeds maladministration, wastefulness, and corruption. Many developing countries contend with this socio-political and economic malaise. This has implication for banking. It demands that bankers should take extra care in public sector banking. Government projects may go awry. Social infrastructure and services may be allowed to decay. Regimes may be truncated. Financial obligations may be repudiated. Contracts may be revoked. Indeed, the adverse possibilities are endless and upsetting for business.

The fragile political system which the colonial rulers bequeathed to the countries hardly helped matters. Some believe that Western democracy and party politics are not only alien but a major cause of political conflicts and instability in developing countries. The fallout is evident in military coups d'état, tainted democratic institutions, leadership flux, and civil wars. These problems create disharmony among the local populace and discourage commitment of the leaders to economic development. Many countries allowed their ethnic differences to degenerate into unnecessary civil wars. Take Africa, for example. Civil war threatened economic growth and development in Liberia, Burundi, Sudan, Somalia, Chad, and Rwanda. Since independence, political crisis in Nigeria, Ghana, Gambia, Algeria, Tunisia, Egypt, Libya, Uganda, Burkina Faso, Congo, Zaire, and Ethiopia continues to undermine progress. Political leaders use State apparatus to fight opposition and civil wars—only to do a U-turn and embark on massive borrowing to finance reconstruction, rehabilitation, and reconciliation. This is ironic, a vicious circle, and compounds imbalances in the countries' domestic and external accounts. Possible banking opportunities in post-war countries should always be put into perspective. The countries are characterized by ravaged economies, shattered citizenry, and traumatized workforce struggling to reinvent enterprise. This state of affairs portends real risk with which bank managements should get to grips.

ETHNIC FOUNDATION OF THE POLITIES

Politics has evolved along ethnic lines over time in many developing countries. This trend reflects a major criticism of colonialism in failing to institutionalize racial integration within the polities. Specifically, colonial rule in Africa did not institutionalize sound political systems (Sandbrook, 1985). Apparently, this was also the case in other developing regions of the world. The imperialists were ousted in a hurry, under pressure from the anticolonial fighters. Militant demand for self-rule came to fruition when the colonial authorities started in the early 20th century—through constitutional reforms—to permit limited participation of indigenous people in the governance of the colonies. With mounting resistance, the imperialist overlords reluctantly hastened the pace for independence of the colonies. In doing so, they recast the colonies—regrouping their precolonial political societies and institutions to form modern states. In the process of boundary delineation, heterogeneous peoples were lumped together in common territories. This action to which common political problems of postcolonial developing countries are linked sharpened ethnic consciousness and rivalries—with profound implications for banking. Bank managements should apprise themselves of the foundation of the polities in ethnic orientation. That enhances their risk management insights. This is critical for the fact that what emerged from colonial freedom were polyethnic states betrayed by Western-style political systems. The creation of ethnically amorphous countries by colonial fiat was done on grounds of political expedience. Sadly, it imparts instability to the polities.

Coalescing diverse political structures of heterogeneous ethnic societies to form modern states continues to portend danger for developing countries. Buildup of tribal sentiments in postcolonial governance of the countries was a case in point. The interest of every ethnic group within the state had to be taken into account in devising institutions of governance, as well as in political decisionmaking. In the process the coalesced societies developed mutual suspicion. It is now a commonplace for the minority—usually the disadvantaged ethnic societies—to suspect that the majority—represented by the predominant tribes—would, through manipulation of government, dominate politics and control State wealth. In Nigeria, for example, this generated anxiety that delayed independence when the northern region expressed fear over possible domination by the southerner region. The British government realized that the wide disparity between the northern and southern ethnic societies in terms of education, natural resource endowments, and political development. It obliged the northerner's request for extension of colonial rule to enable them cover some lost grounds. Yet the most serious postcolonial calamity that has befallen Nigeria, that is, the 30 months bloody civil war of 1967–70—resulted from inordinate political ambitions of the country's leaders which culminated in violent ethnic outrage. The Nigerian case epitomizes the enormity of tribal conflicts that make economic progress difficult in developing countries. Similar ethnically driven civil wars had been experienced in Sudan, Uganda, Congo, Burundi, Somalia, Rwanda, Liberia and, indeed, in several other developing countries. Sandbrook (1985) offers in-depth insights into historical factors that precipitated many of the political problems of Africa. In sum, colonial experience was the root of the continent's problems (p. 42).

The evolution of ethnicity in politics links with colonial-induced disruption of organic equilibrium of otherwise politically stable traditional societies. Interestingly, traditional political heritage remains resistant to Western political model despite the fusion of the two opposing systems by colonial fiat. Ethnic sentiments were harnessed to dislodge the colonialists. The resistance of colonialism was gingered up by a new nationalistic spirit that transcended ethnic boundaries. Every citizen was called upon to challenge colonial rule. Ethnic consciousness became fussed with a national cause and metamorphosed into a formidable nationalistic outburst that weakened colonial rule and led to its collapse. Such integrative nationalism was indeed ethnically boundless. In this sense, ethnicity became coterminous with nationalism to the extent that both sought to thwart disintegrative forces within the polity while projecting reason for a common cause. However, nationalistic force during the colonial period proved to be an artificial configuration of the mood of the people in the face of a common enemy.

Nationalistic enthusiasm began to ebb soon after the attainment of political independence. This was happening as the citizens relived their core ethnic origins where they had been oriented to maintain political loyalty. Thus the people began to lose sense of nation-state in the postcolonial period. Ethnic sentiments may—and indeed, on occasion, do influence banking choices and habits in developing countries. The public tends to perceive differences among the domestic banks based on ethnic origins of their founding majority shareholders. The reason the so-called "Igbo" and "Yoruba" banks, for example, are perceived to be that is because investors, employees, and customers of South Eastern and South Western origin dominate them, respectively. The same goes for some banks seen as being dominated by South Southern and Northern investors, employees, and customers. Often this proethnic feeling is felt and observed more in actions than in the spoken word. On occasion, it sways prospects to open accounts or conduct transactions with particular banks.

The ethnic groups did not benefit equally from the colonial largesse. The Europeans had little problem settling in the coastal areas where favorable natural conditions existed. In such regions, mission schools were established, while business transactions with the European merchants fostered early transition to cash economy. The Mission schools made it possible for the local ethnic groups to enjoy Western education and thus produce key personalities that formed the core of indigenous intelligentsia. The elites were at the forefront of the anti-colonial struggles and, when the battles were over, assumed leadership roles in the newly independent states. Some regions were favored in the sense that they developed cash crops and prospered as a result of the booming trade on agricultural produce. Local entrepreneurs and bourgeois emerged with a firm grip on the economy. The railways were yet another cause of ethnic hostilities in postcolonial countries. The railways were passed through carefully chosen regions that had mineral deposits or strong agricultural base to enhance colonial exploitation of the resources. As one of the oldest colonial legacies, the railways facilitated development of international trade by providing the means through which cash crops and solid minerals were evacuated to the sea ports for shipment. Railway corporations were at once the largest employer of labor in the colonies. The local communities through which the railways traversed benefited most from the employment opportunities.

The ethnic groups that were less favored by colonialism participated only marginally in colonial education, politics, and commercial activities. Such ethnic groups—often located in the interior parts of the colonies—experienced adverse natural living conditions and occasional intertribal hostilities. The net effect of all this was a significant factor in the ethnic bickering experienced by postcolonial countries. The resultant conflicts became deep-seated in the psyche of the people as politicians took advantage of the situation to further personal ambitions. They easily mustered tribal sentiments, which already had been introduced to the politics of the countries, to win ethnic loyalty and support as a basis for political victory at the polls. As ethnic consciousness waxed, state loyalty waned, paving the way for direct confrontations that were in most cases resolved by recourse to civil war. Sandbrook (op. cit., p. 42) articulates the unwholesome role of politicians in the evolution of ethnicity in Africa. Often business orientations and tendencies differ among ethnic groups in a country. Bank managements should appreciate significant distinguishing features of the ethnic economies in order to mitigate their peculiar banking risks. That way the banks will be able to serve customer needs without infringing on ethnic interests or sensibilities. It also guides the banks to not meddle in local business politics.

The fact that economic woes of developing countries are deeply rooted in political instability cannot be overemphasized. One should not downplay the role of orderly politics in economic development. Internal political controversies remain a strong negative force. On account of internal political crisis, several developing countries were caught napping, completely left behind, and thus were not part of the race by the nations of the world that strove to attain UN development targets. The UN had in 1961 and 1970 dubbed the 1960s and 1970s the "Development Decade," with emphasis on achieving sustainable high GDP growth rates. This was also true of the 1970s and 1980s when development emphasis shifted to income redistribution and economic adjustment, respectively.

For most developing countries, these epochs were marked by dashed expectations of independence—democracy, good governance, national prosperity, and economic development. I pinpoint some of the significant causes of the sense of frustration felt by the people as follows:

- Failure of Western-fashioned democratic models imposed on the new states to be easily adaptable to, or fit with, the ever resistant traditional political institutions and culture of the people.
- Disintegration of so-called indigenous nationalism through which the nationalists worked in unison and repudiated colonialism. Competitive protection of sectional interests that impinge on national unity was the culprit for this setback.
- Inability of political leaders to be above board in handling delicate national questions bordering on expression of tribal sentiments, and offer purposeful and result-oriented governance based on democratic norms.
- Large-scale mismanagement of public funds and brazen corruption of public servants resulting in wastage of scarce resources with attendant opportunity costs.
- Widespread civil unrest and disturbances which—in concert with the foregoing factors—reinforced military intervention in politics.

This was how matters stood with many developing countries at the time other nations were assembling and consolidating development infrastructure.

ALIEN POLITICAL MODELS, STRUCTURES, AND NORMS

The need did not arise during the campaigns for independence to devise appropriate political models that would fit specific needs of developing countries. What mattered to the nationalists, on the one hand, and the imperial powers, on the other, was the restoration of the right to self-determination to the colonies. In the absence of indigenous alternative, the nationalists welcomed complex alien political models. The alien political models and structures suit and have evolved out of the long historical experience of the Western world and democracies. The period of orientation of indigenous activists on the mechanics of the new political systems was simply a fleeting experience. This period covered, in the main, the transitory constitutional conference and reform epochs preceding independence.

At the time the colonial rulers were quitting the political scene, they had introduced certain constitutional safeguards by which executive political powers were limited, civil liberties protected, and the rule of law guaranteed. These rules functioned within frameworks of modern democracy. However, democratization of politics in developing countries has proven to be an arduous task as the countries bungle with its practice. The complexity of the Western democratic models derives from their success requirements: formation of political parties for aggregating interests of diverse segments of the population; devolution of political power and legitimacy to the electorate; recognition of official political opposition party in parliament; and accountability of political office holders to the electorate. These democratic norms were alien to the political culture of many developing countries. The historical claim to political power by certain ethnic groups in some of the countries still lingers in contradiction to modern democratic norms. In many countries, it has not been easy to substitute modern democracy for the traditional hereditary practice of leadership changes. In principle, the countries accepted new democratic constitutions on which, of course, the exit of the colonial rulers was predicated. But in practice, their leaders were strongly inclined to upholding ethnic traditions. Thus, political parties were formed along—and greatly manifested—ethnic sentiments, while the dominant—largely tribal—party suppressed opposition.

The first impediment to successful operation of the alien political model was its conflicts with traditional values and institutions which ethnicity exacerbated. The mismatch between the two political models is evident in the dysfunctional politics of the countries. No sooner had the colonial government been dismantled than leaders of the countries bungled with the alien political system. At this time, the citizens' loyalty had been ethnically polarized. The ethnic constituents of the countries had reneged on national orientation for unity by which they resisted colonial rule. In place of nationalism, ethnic orientation to unity was substituted. Distribution of political offices and benefits among the various ethnic groups became the salient issue, not good governance. Ethnicity assumed unusual importance in the political scheme. This resulted in tensed political atmosphere and caused the failure of governance in some countries soon after independence. As tribalism proved to be a stronger force than nationalism in the postcolonial period, the security, stability, and progress of the countries remained threatened.

As though in ordered succession, state governance collapsed in Congo, Rwanda, and Sudan in the early 1960s as the countries failed to adapt to the demands of the alien political systems due to the heterogeneous nature of their ethnic societies. Seemingly irreconcilable tribal differences amplified political crisis. Soon one country after another became engulfed by the resultant strife, internal disorders, and civil wars. By the late 1960s, the imposed Western political systems had collapsed in several other countries, including Zanzibar (1964), Algeria (1965), Ghana (1966), and Nigeria (1966). Where the systems survived the early years following independence, substantial damage was inflicted on the state machinery. Notable examples include Uganda, Kenya, Egypt, Tanzania, and Rhodesia. This situation continues to take a heavy toll on banking in developing economies. The case of African Development Bank (AfDB) clearly illustrates how political instability adversely affects banking operations. The Bank had to relocate from its statutory headquarters in Abidjan to Tunis following the civil war in Cote d'Ivoire. It operated from Tunis for 10 years before returning its headquarters operations back to Abidjan in 2014 after peace and order were restored. Of course, the crisis affected the Bank's funding of projects in that and countries similarly affected by either civil war or other political strife.

The Nigerian experience reflects disruptive influence of alien political model, on the one hand, and turnaround in political evolution, on the other. As Table 11.1 shows, the country now showcases stabilizing democracy after four decades of political failure. The country's 2015 presidential election is, perhaps, the most dramatic proof of the emerging and maturing democratic process in Africa despite occasional military coups d'état. For the first time in that

TABLE 11.1 Nigeria—Transition from Colonial, Through Military, to Civil Rule

Period of rule	Type of government	Process of ascendancy	Fate of leader
1 Oct 1960–1 Oct 1963	Colonial	Proclamation	Relinquished power
1 Oct 1963–16 Jan 1966	Democratic	Competitive party system	Deposed
16 Jan 1966–29 Jul 1966	Military	Coup d'état	Assassinated
1 Aug 1966–29 Jul 1975	Military	Coup d'état	Deposed
29 Jul 1975–13 Feb 1976	Military	Coup d'état	Assassinated
13 Feb 1976–1 Oct 1979	Military	Appointment	Resigned
1 Oct 1979–31 Dec 1983	Democratic	Competitive party system	Deposed
31 Dec 1983–27 Aug 1985	Military	Coup d'état	Deposed
27 Aug 1985–26 Aug 1993	Military	Coup d'état	Resigned
26 Aug 1993–17 Nov 1993	Interim National Government	Appointment	Deposed
17 Nov 1993–8 Jun 1998	Military	Coup d'état	Died in office
8 Jun 1998–29 May 1999	Military	Appointment	Resigned
29 May 1999–29 May 2007	Democratic	Competitive party system	Served two terms
29 May 2007–5 May 2010	Democratic	Competitive party system	Died in office
9 Feb 2010–5 May 2010	Democratic	Senate Motion	Acted for incapacitated President
5 May 2010–29 May 2011	Democratic	Succession	Completed late President's tenure
29 May 2011–29 May 2015	Democratic	Competitive party system	Served one term
29 May 2015–	Democratic	Competitive party system	Incumbent

country's political history, candidate of an opposition party, Mohammadu Buhari, defeated his ruling party's opponent, Goodluck Jonathan—the incumbent president—in an election many considered to be free and fair. The intriguing thing about that election was not just the first ever defeat of candidate of the ruling party by an opposition party. It was rather that the incumbent president willingly conceded defeat at the twilight of collation of votes and announcement of the results. This marked a complete departure from the historical bitterness characteristic of elections in Nigeria. Many believe that democracy is really taking root in Nigeria—nay, Africa.

MILITARY INTERVENTION IN POLITICS

The evolving trend of political instability in developing countries was accentuated by military intervention in politics and governance. Like a wild bush fire, the trapping of political power by military officers swept the developing world in the wake of leadership failure in the countries. In 1963, the military struck and took over power in Togo. In 1967, history repeated itself in that country when a junta overthrew the government. In 1965, Algeria, Dahomey, and Congo (Kinshasa), in like manner, experienced the shock of military coups d'état that sacked their democratically elected civilian regimes. It was the turn of Upper Volta, Central African Republic, Nigeria, and Ghana in 1966 when the ill wind of military coup d'état blew through them and swept their elected civilian governments out of office. Even while most of these countries experienced several fresh coups, counter-coups, and abortive coups d'état, additional countries became infested with the disease. The Economist (op. cit.) notes that "in the past 30 years or so, Africa has averaged a couple of coups a year, and more than two dozen presidents and prime ministers have lost their lives through political violence." According to the Magazine, "four of Africa's potentially richest and most powerful states—Angola, Nigeria, Sudan, and Zaire—are in desperate straits. Somalia has disintegrated, and Liberia, Rwanda, and Burundi are heading that way" (ibid). These examples epitomize political crisis during the early decades of independence. Thus, the socio-political and economic situation of the countries became worse than their preindependence state.

Authoritarian government lacking in accountability engendered military rule. This situation is not propitious for economic development. It is both wasteful and irresponsible. The economic misery to which developing countries have been subjected in the postcolonial period can largely be explained in terms of failed democratic processes. Consider first the number of military regimes and the extent of their involvement in the governance of the countries. This furnishes an insight into the magnitude of political derailment of the countries. The reasons for and objectives of military rule are diverse. Thus it would be futile to start differentiating them here on the basis of a country by country analysis—that is beyond the scope of this book. However, the most common general factors can be isolated. It would appear that military officers usurp civil political power in order to:

- Dislodge politicians who upon election to offices soon turn profiteers with the aim of looting public treasury.
- Stop political drifting of the state often caused by willful abandonment of the wish of the electorate and the national cause. This tends to be the direct result, in most cases, of the pursuit of selfish political gains; clampdown on, and suppression of, the opposition; and ethnically motivated interparty conflicts.
- Check excesses and recklessness of politicians who—by actions, utterances, and governance style—have renounced subjection to constitutional checks and balances that offer safeguards to the citizenry and prevent arbitrary exercise of power.
- Cleanse the state of systemic corruption which appears to have been institutionalized. Such corrupt practices permeate the rank and file of staffers in the public and private sectors of the economy.
- Provide alternative political leadership that would rekindle drive for sustainable economic growth and development. This tends to be the case when poor performance of the economy is adjudged to be the consequence of maladministration.
- Neutralize certain socio-cultural forces retarding the progress of the state, especially tribalism and nepotism.
- Restore peace and orderliness in chaotic situations and lawlessness which threatens the unity and survival of the state. This is often caused by political conflicts, ethnic rivalries, and confrontation of government by some strong interest groups.

In polyethnic states, where national unity is very fragile because of citizens' inclination to upholding ethnic as opposed to national loyalty, armed forces serve as a unifying force. Their orientation and national recruitment spread equip them to perform this role. Paradoxically, the military enjoys positive perception on ethics, professionalism, and commitment to nation-state. Thus, the relevance of the military in the politics of developing countries becomes an admissible reality. Thus, to ignore the military imperative in politics would be a costly mistake and a risk which civilian leadership can ill afford. There might not be a better alternative to a comfortable coexistence of politicians and military personnel in governance of developing countries. The hardly uncritical acceptance of military rule fizzles out as the initial euphoria associated with the ouster of corrupt politicians is destined to be shortlived. The army dashes expectations of the citizenry. They engage in the same condemnable practices for which the politicians are criticized, subjected to public ridicule, and eventually toppled.

Military-politicians have indeed emerged in some developing countries, having shifted the premise of their ascendancy to office to accommodate a new desire for wealth and influence with the aim of clinching to political power. Yet politicization of the military and its involvement in governance are detrimental to economic progress. The reasons are quite instructive:

- Political leaders feel insecure about the military. The threat of loss of power to the military through coup d'état is real. Thus a lot more time is devoted to consolidating political base than devising and executing development policies.
- The military constituency becomes the salient segment of the electorate whose interest is that the political leaders must give premium consideration in resource allocation. This is perhaps one of the explanations for the relatively heavy defense appropriations characteristic of the annual budgets of developing countries. But this is often done at the expense of improvement in economic welfare of the people.
- Useful time for economic management is often wasted in forming a military government after a civilian regime has been overthrown. This period is usually characterized by some political uncertainty as there would not be assurance of cooperation of the politicians with the junta. Thus, the military itself spends time to build its political base as well as court the favor of politicians.
- Military officers compete among themselves for political power once the civilian regime has been overthrown. For obviously trivial or inconsequential reasons, military officers stage counter coups against their colleagues who have usurped power. Thus there is mutual suspicion among officers about their individual desires for power. This situation is unhealthy and does not encourage dedication to service.
- Suspension of constitution, banning of politics, large- scale detention of politicians, and reversal or cancellation of government programs are some of the typical actions a military regime takes on assumption of office. Soon afterwards, it introduces a political transition program, on which it sometimes reneges, to return the country to democratic governance. All these are unprogressive measures, have adverse implications for economic growth and development.

Military intervention in politics undoubtedly exacerbates political instability and adversely affects long-term state, business, and financial sector development.

POLITICIZED VERSUS APOLITICAL CIVIL SERVICE

The initial response of the founding leaders of some developing countries to pervasive political conflicts was institution of one-party states, ostensibly to forestall divisive tendencies and elements within the polities. Parliamentary opposition parties were outlawed as presidents acquired discretionary powers. This was made manifest in the exercise of such powers as the arrest, detention, and imprisonment of political opponents for questionable offenses. The one-party state leaders even distrusted and doubted the support of the civil service. Party loyalists were recruited in substitution for the professional civil servants. President Julius Nyerere of Tanzania made the point that it would be a luxury and self-defeating to maintain politically impartial public services in Africa (Oliver and Atmore, 1972: p. 280). Having assumed effective control over the armed forces, the police, and the ruling one-party, the presidents soon turned despots as they appropriated emergency powers in pursuit of selfish political ambitions. Nyerere (ibid) justified his belief in one-party state—drawing inference from the historical class struggle which influenced the British and American political evolution.

The main undemocratic element of one-party states was the fusion of the president's office with his leadership of the national party. It became difficult to effect a change of political leadership through direct elections. The incumbent would have become so influential that attempting to contest the presidency against them would simply be futile. Opposition party candidates anxiously waited for such a time that office of the incumbent president would be vacant, one way or another. Otherwise party and national elections would continue to be conducted with the understanding that the incumbent should not be challenged or be removed from office. Thus, in Cote D'Ivoire, President Houphouet–Boigny almost ruled for life—from the date of the country's independence in 1960 until his death in 1994. Arap Moi of Kenya ruled for more than two and half decades before his defeat at the country's first ever multiparty polls. The same goes for Presidents Kenneth Kaunda (Zambia), Ahmadu Ahidjo (Cameroon), Julius Nyerere (Tanzania), Dauda Jawara (Gambia), and so on.

Although the absence of the usual parliamentary opposition in government might encourage national integration and unity, this arrangement is purely undemocratic and politically retrogressive. But it is a system that incubates ill-feelings among party faithful as they await opportunity to revolt against injustice in political domination by one person or a clique within the polity. However, such a revolution never yet occurred in the manner anticipated. What has indeed happened was the concession to multiparty democracy by most of the ardent believers in the one-party state. This trend, on the one hand, stemmed from internal pressure for a change of governance style and was, on the other, the result of the band wagon effect of the democratization of polities around the world which most of the one-party states could not resist. The cost of restructuring the polities and governance to accommodate the emergent worldwide drive for democratization of political institutions has been enormous and reflects in worsening economic affairs of the countries.

The Nigerian case best exemplifies politicization of the civil service. Under President Babangida's regime during the late 1980s and early 1990s, political director generals were appointed to oversee Federal ministries. Career permanent secretaries were displaced as chief executives of the ministries. Thus, and in other developing countries with the same experience, the bureaucracy lost its hallmark—the capacity to maintain the neutrality of civil servants irrespective of which party was in power. Although suppression of the opposition and hijacking of the bureaucracy were usually resisted by some pressure groups, the affected political leaders maintained an uncompromising posture. Thus, one of the enduring colonial legacies—the civil service—became a plaything of politicians. As the public services are being manipulated to suit the whims and caprices of political leaders, mediocrity tends to replace quality performance. This happens to the detriment of political and economic progress. The Interim National Government that succeeded the regime in 1994 was truncated after General Sanni Abacha deposed its leader—Ernest Shonekan—in 1995 and proclaimed himself Head of State. Abacha reversed designation of directors general as chief executives of Federal ministries. The reversal was intended to restore dignity—founded on neutrality—to the civil service. All this marked the politicization of the civil service in Nigeria. But it underlies the essence of civil service being apolitical in developing economies.

QUESTIONABLE, ILLEGITIMATE, AND INEFFECTUAL REGIMES

Often politics in developing countries deteriorates and alienates the masses from society. Governing under such a situation becomes difficult. It also weakens the state, paving the way for emergence of a despot who would seek to strengthen the foundation and fabric of the state. Despots have recourse to coercion— ostensibly with the surreptitious objective of institutionalizing personal rule. Such rulers face a major problem, though. Unlike what happens in a true democracy, significant segments of the population may be critical of their ascendancy or utterly reject them. Besides, they never have the legitimacy to rule— even as they may have emerged out of some desperate political situation that, for example, saves a country from chaos or disintegration. As Sandbrook (op. cit.) has observed, personal rule is driven by pragmatic considerations geared to appropriate a much needed legitimacy.

Leaders will not enjoy popular support or followership in the absence of political legitimacy to rule. Governance must, nevertheless, somehow function on the basis of some pragmatic basis. Often mutual distrust among ethnic societies within a country creates this abnormal situation. The leader, lacking the basis for good administration, develops somewhat irregular tactics to first secure their political position. Some of the tactics include:

- Favouring ethnic group to which they look or hope to fall back for support in distribution of political and economic benefits.
- Creation of special military guard, the goal of which is to fortify their personal security and possible attack from dissidents.
- Appointment of friends and loyalists to sensitive and key political positions even when they may not the best suited for the jobs.
- Aligning themselves and their regimes with some foreign powers to which they hope to get support in times of political crisis.
- Harrying and suppressing opposition parties or groups that may whip up popular negative sentiments.

The leader then becomes manifestly insensitive to popular demands of governance and, at will, violates the constitution—if not repudiated. It becomes practically difficult to restrain them from exercising arbitrary or discretionary powers. Irrespective of the feelings of the masses, the leader makes and implements policies following dictates of their will. Long-term strategy for the economy is often the first victim of such an unfocused regime. Instead of institutionalizing prudence in the management of scarce resources, the leader succumbs to selfish urge to amass wealth at the expense of economic and social wellbeing of the suffering, poor masses. The leader thus wields so much power that it can be said that the state exists to satisfy their personal objectives and not those of the polity. Many leaders—in both military and civilian regimes around the world—fell to this politically debasing status of personal rule. Some military officers took over power from elected civilian government and retired while in government in order to become civilian presidents through the ballot. But all these were mere charades. This category of military-politicians is easily the most conspicuous set of personal rulers. To the dismay of the citizenry, instead of handing over power to democratically elected civilian government within the shortest possible time as they promised at the time of taking over power, they sat tight. But in order to escape public outcry and international condemnation, they retired from the armed forces and contested the presidency—thus legitimizing their position. Coming to power in this manner, through the back door, is offensive. Politicians and the populace alike do not hide their disgust at such deceit.

Political instability is the order of the day in developing countries around the world. Racial, tribal, communal, and guerrilla wars have been a commonplace, especially since the beginning of the second half of the 20th century. There have been several coups d'état and dictatorship in Latin America, Middle East, and Asia. The World Bank (1991) notes that "since 1948 there has been at least one coup attempt per developing country every five years." Table 11.2 summarizes its findings and analysis on the irregular executive transfers. The data show that

TABLE 11.2 Irregular Executive Transfers: Average Occurrence Per Country, 1948–82

Income group	1948–52	1953–58	1959–64	1965–70	1971–76	1977–82
Low-income	1.0(21)	1.1(24)	1.2(39)	1.4(51)	1.3(53)	0.9(55)
Middle-income	1.6(30)	1.7(32)	1.4(41)	0.8(47)	0.9(51)	0.6(55)
High-income	0.0(23)	0.2(23)	0.1(24)	0.2(25)	0.1(28)	0.1(28)

Note: Number of countries considered is in parentheses. Both successful and unsuccessful transfers are included. Irregular successful executive transfers are changes in the office of the national executive from one leader to another, outside conventional legal or customary procedures for transferring power. Unsuccessful irregular executive transfers are failed attempts at such irregular transfers. Countries are ranked according to their per capita income in 1988.
Sources: Taylor and Jodice (1983). Database supplied by the Inter-University Consortium of Political and Social Research. Reproduced from World Bank. 1991. World Development Report. p. 129.

among developing countries, unconventional or illegal change of government has been more frequent in the low and middle than in the high income nations. Then it was unimaginable that leaders could be removed by the ballot. The attendant upheavals impact negatively on economic development. Lack of policy continuity, alteration of budgetary targets, reversal of political programs, and clamp down on political opponents are particularly worrisome. The economic threat posed by these problems cannot be easily ignored—if the political class is not united, development strategies cannot succeed.

The good news is that there is hope in the evolving democratization processes in some of the countries. For example, starting in the 1990s, Africa has recorded appreciable but modest electoral progress. The first ever defeat, in mainland Africa, of a ruling party and president at the polls in Benin in 1991 was a case in point. The trend set by that election, considered to be free and fair, was sustained later that year by the defeat of Kenneth Kaunda of Zambia who had been in power since 1964 when the country achieved political independence. The wave of change touched politics in Malawi, Sierra Leone, and Uganda. In Malawi, Hastings Banda's dream of being president for life became thwarted following his defeat in the 1994 presidential election by Bakali Muluzi. In a similar situation, Nicephore Soglo lost the 1996 presidential election in Benin to Mathieu Kerekou whom he had earlier defeated in 1991. The successful conduct of democratic elections in Sierra Leone in February and March 1996 in spite of the civil war in that country yet demonstrates the progressive political trend. In Uganda, the triumph of Yoweri Museveni in the May 1996 presidential election was even more heartening as the country becomes a quasi-democracy. The regimes of Idi Amin and Milton Obote during which thousands of Ugandans were murdered had tainted the politics of the country prior to this time.

TERRORISM, GUERRILLA, AND CIVIL WARS

Some countries in the developing world are still embroiled in military coups d'état, and guerrilla and civil wars. The ISIS fighting against the Government in Syria is typical. There's also the case of Boko Haram insurgency in Nigeria turning into full-blown military confrontation with the Government. In Pakistan, the PKK posed security threat to life and property in its deadly attacks on key political and economic targets. Banks should be well-informed about these and evolving threats that are endemic in developing countries and mark the challenge of their future.

A typical example of an unfavorable condition for bank lending in Africa's emerging economies is the prevalence of political upheaval. Let me illustrate this—and therefore the impact of militancy and activities of terrorists on lending decisions—with reference to happenings in Nigeria's Niger Delta and North-Eastern regions, and in some Northern African and Middle Eastern countries, in the recent past. Disturbances that started as street protests demanding political reforms and democratic governance in some Northern African countries soon snowballed into grave political upheaval.

Between January and September 2011, wild protests by aggrieved citizens crippled economic activity and toppled the governments in Tunisia, Egypt, and Libya, in that order. In Iran, government forces ruthlessly crushed similar protests, while protests in Syria claimed thousands of lives. In the case of Nigeria, a mutiny of militant youths in the Niger Delta region took to arms to press for reforms in the country's oil sector and the development of the oil-rich Niger Delta, and a voice in the distribution of oil revenue. While all of this was happening, economic activity became paralyzed. For instance, some oil exploration and mining companies in the troubled region closed or relocated their major operations in the wake of the crisis.

A more serious unfavorable condition for banking was the emergence of terrorism in Nigeria's North-Eastern region. Terrorist activities in the region, and the Federal Government's response to the attendant security crisis, came to the fore in 2012. With mounting insecurity of lives and property, businesses in states that had become hotbeds of terrorism could no longer function effectively. Some even relocated their operations just to save their investments from wanton destruction. It seems inconceivable that a bank would want to lend money to individuals or companies doing businesses in these turbulent zones. Rather than lend, banks would demand the paying down or outright repayment of existing credit facilities. This is one of the realities of banking risk management in developing economies.

SUMMARY

The local populace easily becomes disillusioned with politics. Often disenchantment with government follows as a country falls into anarchy. There are historical antecedents to the creation of this type of risk. Banking in developing economies contends with political realities that rub off on the economy. Thus bank managements should always accurately read and anticipate the political and economic landscapes. That way they would be able to structure and adapt business operations to mitigate risks. Bankers should always be on top of evolving political trends, threats, and opportunities. That helps in strategy formulation and risk management.

Military incursion into politics is a real problem for developing economies. The military usurps power, jettisons democracy, and introduces dictatorship to governance—claiming that politicians are not serious. This is an aberration and a setback for political development. Progress should stem from keeping armed forces committed to their calling and focused on defense and security of the state. But this cannot be achieved unless politicians play by the rules, are accountable to the electorate, and manage state wealth well. This situation demands that bankers take extra care in public sector banking.

The fragile political system which the colonial rulers bequeathed to the countries has hardly helped matters. Some believe that Western democracy and party politics are not only alien but a major cause of political conflicts and instability in developing countries. The fallout is evident in military coups d'état, tainted democratic institutions, leadership flux, and civil wars. Banking opportunities in postwar countries should always be put in perspective. Usually postwar state of affairs portends real risk with which bank managements should get to grips.

Politics has evolved along ethnic lines in many developing countries over time. This trend reflects a major criticism of colonialism in failing to institutionalize racial integration within the polities. The imperialist overlords recast the colonies—regrouping their precolonial political societies and institutions to form modern states. Heterogeneous peoples were lumped together in common territories—thus sharpening ethnic consciousness and rivalries. Some countries in the developing world contend with terrorism, and guerrilla and civil wars. This is, perhaps, the most serious cause of political risk for banking in developing countries around the world. Bank managements should apprise themselves of the foundation of the polities in ethnic orientation. That enhances their risk management insights.

Nationalistic enthusiasm ebbed soon after the attainment of political independence. This happened as the citizens relived their core ethnic origins where they had been oriented to maintain political loyalty. Thus the people began to lose sense of nation-state in the postcolonial period. Ethnic sentiments may—and, on occasion, do influence banking choices and habits in developing countries. Often business orientations and tendencies differ among ethnic groups in a country. Bank managements should appreciate significant distinguishing features of the ethnic economies in order to mitigate their peculiar banking risks. That way the banks will be able to serve customer needs without infringing on ethnic interests or sensibilities. It also guides the banks to not meddle in local business politics.

QUESTIONS FOR DISCUSSION AND REVIEW

1. What specific incidents in the disillusionment of the populace typify realities of political risk for banking in developing countries?
2. How should bank managements accurately read and anticipate the political and economic landscapes in developing countries?
3. Why should bankers in developing economies always be on top of evolving political trends, threats, and opportunities?
4. What reasons compel bankers in developing economies to exercise due diligence and extra care in public sector banking?
5. Why do you think bankers should always put possible banking opportunities in postwar countries into perspective?
6. In what ways is the recasting of colonies to form modern states responsible for ethnic rivalries in some developing countries?
7. In what sense would bank managements want to apprise themselves of the foundation of polities in ethnic orientation?

8. Do you think that ethnic sentiments really play a decisive role in banking choices and habits in developing countries?

9. Why may the public perceive differences among the domestic banks based on ethnic origins of their founding majority shareholders?

10. What issues underlay the relocation of African Development Bank's headquarters from Abidjan to Tunisia in 2004?

REFERENCES

Oliver, R., Atmore, A., 1972. Africa Since 1800, second ed. Cambridge University Press, London.

Onyiriuba, L., 2013. On the road to self-actualization. NFS Data Bureau Limited, Lagos, pp. 35–38.

Sandbrook, R., 1985. The Politics of Africa's Economic Stagnation. Cambridge University Press, London.

World Bank, 1991. World Development Report 1991: The Challenge of Development. Oxford University Press, New York, p. 129.

FURTHER READINGS

Emerson, R., 1962. From Empire to Nation. Cambridge, Mass.

ODI (Overseas Development Institute), 1982. Africa's Economic Crisis. London: ODI, Briefing Document No. 2.

The Economist, 1996. A Survey of sub-Saharan Africa. September 7–13.

Chapter 12

Public Sector Banking Analysis and Risks Management in Developing Economies

Chapter Outline

LEARNING FOCUS AND OBJECTIVES

The public sector is—and will for a long time remain—a critical target market for banking in developing economies. However, banks should have strong liquidity base, acquire advanced IT capability, and employ and retain competent staff in order to meet and mitigate risks of its current and future banking needs. Thus banks should devote themselves to build these capabilities considering the significance of the sector. I have used *government* and *public sector*—throughout this chapter and elsewhere in this book—as interchangeable terms. It refers to all nonprivate economic units, institutions, and establishments—whether or not engaged in business—that are oriented to politics, governance, or provision of social services in a country. The learning focus and objectives of this chapter are geared to:

- identify the characteristics of public sector banking in developing economies;
- examine the significance of risk control for bank marketing in the public sector;
- assess the banking potential of the public sector;
- formulate framework for public sector banking analysis, and risk control; and
- explore risk-based issues in marketing and managing public sector banking relationship.

EXPECTED LEARNING OUTCOMES

Government, its agencies, and parastatals—collectively known as the *public sector*—constitute a major target market for banks in developing economies. The reason is simple. Private sector trails in driving developmental programs and economic activities in developing countries. Besides, government is the single largest, most homogenous, and predictable economic unit among the entire target markets that banks chase for banking relationship. As the *almighty* sector of the economy, it takes precedence over other economic entities in terms of volumes of banking transactions both within and outside a country. No wonder banks pay a lot of attention to the sector. The reader will—after studying this chapter and doing the exercises in it—have learnt and been better informed about:

- the central dynamic and unique features that characterize public sector banking mechanisms in developing economies;
- causes for appreciation of the significance of risk management in public sector banking in developing economies;
- how bankers should be more critical in assessing banking potential of the public sector in developing economies;
- methodological framework for analyzing public sector orientation, banking needs, and risk control in developing economies; and
- risk challenges of marketing and managing public sector banking relationship in developing economies.

OVERVIEW OF THE SUBJECT MATTER

Public sector banking is not a traditional function of commercial banks even though government has existed and always dominated the financial system. While this may sound strange, it remains a fact that banking has historically been largely a private sector affair. While central banks managed government finances and accounts, commercial banks—which now operate as universal banks in most countries—served the banking needs of the individuals, companies, and organizations. However, this banking orientation was to change as governance became increasingly sophisticated. Interestingly, beyond provision of social services, infrastructure, and basic amenities, government dabbled in business. In some cases, it engaged in high profile commercial transactions in direct competition with the private sector.

It was thought that government should be involved in business, ostensibly to check the excesses of markets. There was also need to protect consumers against exploitation by capitalists in key economic sectors. Ironically, government became bloated as it ventured on business. This compounded the complicated nature of government as a bureaucratic institution. In the wake of its incursion into traditionally capitalist markets, the pressure on government's cash flows worsened—becoming exacerbated with the inefficiency of public corporations. In time, public sector funding became laden with crisis, fuelling concerns that government could not run efficient operations. In most cases, deficit financing to sustain profligate spending was at issue.

It became necessary, in order to follow the dictates of financial prudence, and manage public sector finances well, for government to open and run noncentral bank accounts for public sector operations. Unlike political rhetoric, this was one of the concrete things done by government—apparently to restore public confidence in the activities of the public sector. Today, contrary to what happened in the past, government maintains a full range of noncentral bank accounts—in the same way as individuals, companies, and organizations do. With this background in mind, I discuss what banks should know and do about issues in public sector banking.

SIGNIFICANCE AND BUSINESS ORIENTATION OF PUBLIC SECTOR

Domestic and foreign subsidiary banks in developing economies focus a lot of attention on attracting, retaining, and managing public sector banking relationships. As would be ordinarily expected, the domestic banks control banking in the public sector. Network of contacts with the local political leaders and their associates stands them in good stead over their foreign subsidiary banks counterparts. Besides, government tends to trust domestic banks more than foreign subsidiary banks. This is quite understandable if seen from the perspective of issues in international relations.

The public sector, as an economic unit, remains a profitable target market for the banks. Okigbo (1981) elucidates on the significance of the public sector in this context. I characterize the public sector and assess its banking potential and behavior. Thereafter I discuss tasks in analyzing and managing risks of public sector banking. Three other topics—size of financial public sector, sources from which government generates revenue to finance its activities, and public sector expenditure profiles—also made the topics of this chapter. This chapter's learning focus and outcomes inform the approach to discussion of the topics.

One of the major features of the economic imbalances and distortions in developing countries is the heavy reliance and survival of large state-owned corporations and parastatals on subventions from government. The corporations are insulated against competition. In most cases, they produce goods for their captive market. Their products are usually priced below market prices—mainly due to subsidization of their operations by government. The monopolistic power of the corporations threatens market efficiency. It also makes them complacent—in a manner that is detrimental to market interest. Developing countries are persuaded to commercialize economic activities of state corporations and parastatals. They ought to do so for the sake of market discipline and efficiency. Market discipline fosters profit orientation. Doing so, it inculcates a sense of competition in the management of state-owned enterprises. Government can then redirect subvention to other social needs.

Removal of subvention is necessary to establish the viability and competitiveness of commercialized corporations. However, managers of the corporations and parastatals should be allowed adequate level of autonomy. If given a free rein, the managers should function according to the dictates of market forces. Critical managerial tasks that require autonomy include operations, human, and material resources management. Yet commercialization may not succeed if there are no effective criteria for assessing accountability. Government should devise such criteria which should be applied to measure the performance of the enterprises. Public corporations that are often candidates for commercialization include those that provide electricity, telecommunications, and water supply services.

Nowadays emphasis has shifted from commercialization to outright privatization of certain public corporations. Some developing countries have pursued economic policies which hinge on planned simultaneous development of the private and public sectors. However, the public sector is usually larger and absorbs greater proportion of the population. This situation led to huge government investment in the maintenance of large bureaucratic organizations. Ironically, the affected organizations produce goods, or render services, which private enterprises are obviously best suited to provide. The dictates of cost control and operational efficiency favor private sector companies. Yet in most cases, private economic initiative is stifled in a bid to protect the bureaucratic institutions.

With a strong commitment to privatization of state-owned enterprises, a major transformation in the business orientation of the public sector becomes obvious. This new thinking started in the 1980s when most of the developing countries adopted structural adjustment program as economic management policy. But it gathered momentum in the 1990s for most of the countries. Yet the privatization of former large state-owned corporations, in almost all the sectors of the economy, has not in any way diminished the role of government as a leading intermediary in the financial system. In the same vein, the divestment of government investments in the formerly state-owned enterprises have not reduced the appeal of the public sector to the bankers.

FRAMEWORK OF PUBLIC SECTOR BANKING ANALYSIS

I ask specific questions to guide my framework of analysis of the key issues in banking the public sector. What is the size and composition of the public sector? From what sources does government generate its revenue? What constitute major government expenditure profiles? What is the banking potential of the public sector? How may one aptly characterize public sector banking? These questions are intended to challenge the reader's thoughts about factors that make the public sector such an attractive market segment for banks. In the following discussions, while answering the questions, I present the critical issues and their implications for the bankers. The topics discussed shed light on causes of the craving of both domestic and foreign subsidiary banks for public sector accounts.

Size and Composition of Public Sector

Bankers must understand, analyze, and apply statistics of the size and composition of the financial public sector. The relevant information is usually available in periodical *Economic and Financial Review* published by Central Banks. One of the ways to assess the size of the public sector is to determine the proportion of government's total contribution to the gross domestic product. This approach encapsulates all the economic activities of the government from which it generates annual incomes and incurs expenditures. As the prime mover of the economy, the public sector enjoys a huge size, incomparable to any other single economic unit. Thus, banks regard the public sector as a very profitable economic entity. Therefore banks design specific marketing appeals targeted at them.

Sources of Government Revenue

Government generates its revenue from various sources, including import duties, export duties, excise duties, mining royalties, rents, and so on. It earns most of its revenue—in the case of Nigeria—from export of crude oil. Revenue from nonoil exports has witnessed substantial increase of late—especially in the wake of return of the country to democratic rule in 1999. This evidences a widening of the export base of the economy. But it is reflected in increasing growth rate of the GDP since the mid-2000s. The banking system facilitates the disbursement of government revenue. So banks should position marketing efforts to attract a large chunk of the flows of public sector funds.

Banks should in particular keep abreast of revenue forecasts, mobilization, allocation, and fiscal policies of the government. Useful statistics could be obtained from revenue mobilization, allocation, and fiscal commission in some cases. Often it is useful to guide marketing plans with pertinent questions. How much revenue, for instance, would government realize from export of crude oil? The answer to this question depends on what happens to oil production and export volumes. This in turn would depend on OPEC recommended quota for the country and the level of domestic consumption.

However, the actual realizable revenue remains a function of prevailing prices in the international oil market. It is noteworthy that forces of demand and supply influence the prices. There should also be question, and answer or likely answer, as to what happens to revenue from non-oil exports. Will the revenue increase or decrease over what period? From which export commodities, or other sources, will the revenue come? There are several sources of revenue to the government. For example, sale of oil blocks is fast becoming a strong revenue source for Nigeria.

Government Expenditure Profile

Public sector spending is usually huge. Government spends heavily on recurrent items and capital projects. The expenditures are based on budgetary appropriations approved by the legislature. Usually, government spends the bulk of its revenue on recurrent expenditure. In most cases, personnel costs account for the largest share of the total recurrent expenditure of the government. When released to the respective ministries and parastatals, the funds for recurrent expenditure could be deposited in current accounts with banks, or with the Central Bank. However, at the point of expenditure, the funds are released to settle due obligations of the ministries and parastatals. Capital expenditure fundings could be placed in fixed deposits with the banks, or with the Central Bank. The fixed deposits improve the liquidity of banks that manage them. Besides it also imparts profitability to operations of the banks.

Understanding the pattern of government expenditure is pertinent to successful public sector banking. Doing so, bankers can devise appropriate banking strategies. For example, for certain reasons, government might decide to implement budget deficit in a particular year. In that case, it becomes critical for bank managements to know the size of the deficit, and how the government intends to finance it. The size of the deficit should be determined as a ratio of the GDP for the related year. In general, budget deficits are financed through monetary growth, depletion of foreign reserves, or borrowing from domestic or international financial markets. The choice of mode of deficit financing, which the government makes, has implications for the people, the banking system, and the entire economy.

For example, financing of budget deficit through growth in money supply could be inflationary. It puts pressure on the exchange rates between the domestic and international convertible currencies. This has implication for the people and banks. Actions which the Central Banks might take to correct any imbalance caused by government spending underscore the implications. The Central Banks may decide to mop excess liquidity in the system. This action depletes the liquidity of banks as they might come under some funding pressure for their operations. As the banks tackle the pressure to meet their operational needs for liquidity, they are likely to increase lending rates. With increased lending rates, fewer individuals, companies, and organizations can obtain credit facilities from the banks.

BANKING POTENTIAL OF THE PUBLIC SECTOR

The public sector—comprising mainly the three tiers of government (Federal, State, and local councils)—plays a major role in the economy. From this perspective, the banking potential of the public sector becomes apparent. In general, the banking potential of the public sector can be appreciated from analysis of the following:

- role and influence of the public sector in the financial system;
- public sector as liquidity boosting agent for the banks;
- management of domestic public sector funds;
- investment opportunities in financing public sector projects; and
- management of the external reserves of the country.

Let me briefly explain the impact of these factors on the banking potential of the public sector.

Role and Influence of Public Sector

The public sector controls the largest chunk of cash flows (liquidity), and determines the volumes and direction of economic activities in a country. From its annual budget estimates, one gets an idea of the quantum of funds that would be available for spending by the government in the course of the year. Also, the normal breakdown of the budget to highlight appropriations to the various ministries, parastatals, and agencies helps to determine the spending capacity of public sector organs. Bankers should be interested in knowing how much of budgetary appropriation would directly and indirectly pass through the banking system. Banks should anticipate public sector financial maneuverings as part of their liquidity management strategy. They should devise banking solutions appropriate to the sector. Banks that simply respond, or adapt, to the maneuverings will never lead competition in banking, especially mobilization of deposits from, the public sector.

Liquidity Boosting Capabilities

As government gives deposits to banks, it helps to boost their liquidity and enhances their ability to grant credit facilities to their customers. The public sector perhaps provides the cheapest sources of regular, sustainable, and cheap float deposits for banks. Such deposits come mainly from revenue collection service which banks offer to the government. Taxes provide a major source of revenue. In the case of collection of import duty, for example, the funds are usually accumulated over an agreed period, say 1 week, and then remitted to designated account of the government. There may be different arrangements for other government transactions, such as collection of value added tax (VAT), public utilities charges, and so on.

In some cases, there could be windows of investment opportunity in the revenue collection arrangements. Banks could take advantage of such openings to maximize their earnings. For instance, banks could trade with the funds for a while before remitting them to the relevant public sector account. Such funds could also help the banks to meet urgent short-term financial obligation or liquidity need. Unfortunately, some banks abuse this practice, notwithstanding possible sanctions from the regulatory authorities. There could be instances when some banks not only trade with the funds but fail to remit the funds. That is an abuse of trust which bankers should avoid.

Of course Central Banks penalize defaulting banks with appropriate sanctions. In some cases, names of the affected banks could be expunged from the official list of revenue collectors for government. This implies that banks should demonstrate a high sense of responsibility, with total commitment to integrity, when dealing with public sector funds. This will help them to avoid the negative publicity with which poor handling of public sector banking transactions is often associated.

Management of Domestic Funds

There could be an opportunity for banks to manage the funds of the government and its ministries, parastatals, and agencies. For instance, the defunct Petroleum (Special) Trust Fund (PTF) in Nigeria had huge funds within the banking system. It applied the funds to executing various socio-economic development projects nationwide. There are several other similar, highly liquid, public sector institutions from which banks could attract valuable financial transactions. However, it is pertinent to realize that undue reliance on public sector funds to drive critical banking operations could be a recipe for crisis, considering the capricious nature of government policies. Often the operations of the weak banks tend to be volatile, largely because of the vagaries of macroeconomic policies of the government and regulatory authorities.

Consider, for example, that in 1989—when Nigerian public sector funds were withdrawn from the banks—some of the banks, especially the merchant banks, were devastated. With inadequate capitalization, the undue dependence on such government deposits became a short-sighted strategy for liquidity management. The weak banks experienced a similar adverse liquidity impact in 1992 when the Central Bank introduced stabilization securities as a means of controlling excess liquidity in the economy. This implies that public sector funds could both solve and create liquidity crisis for banks, depending on the policies the regulatory authorities are pursuing at the time.

It is desirable for the banks to strive to manage domestic public sector funds. It is equally essential that the banks realize that such funds are usually from a volatile source. The funds are subject to the risk of unpredictable changes in the disposition of their supervising authorities, especially that of the Central Bank. Yet there is a considerable banking business in the management of domestic public sector funds. Nonetheless, with appropriate risk management disposition, banks could deal with the situation. Doing so, they should be able to improve their short-term liquidity, and increase earnings.

Management of External Reserves

Some developing countries entrust the management of their external financial resources to certain foreign financial institutions. That was the case in Nigeria until 2006. For some reasons—including poor capitalization, lack of international financial collaborations, dearth of local technical skills, and so on—the local banks, including foreign subsidiary banks, were excluded from the management of the countries' external reserves. Indeed, most of the local banks were even finding it difficult to be strong going concerns. In such a situation, they could not contemplate venturing into the more complicated business of managing external reserves of the country. In the case of Nigeria, though, the quantum of the external reserves was not much—perhaps, barely enough to meet the country's 3 months import bills.

With the return of democratic rule to the country in 1999, the external reserves of the country started witnessing unprecedented growth rates. In late 2007, the volume of the external reserves increased to US$45.0 billion—up from less than US$6.0 billion in 1998. Much of the increase came from increasing prices of petroleum products in the international energy markets. The crude oil market became jolted in the wake of the uncertainties following US invasion of Iraq and the ethnic disturbances in the Niger Delta region of Nigeria. Like other oil exporting countries, Nigeria reaped from the resulting windfall, when crude oil price hit US$70.0 per barrel in the international energy market. Crude oil price was yet to reach an all-time high of up to US$140.0 per barrel before plummeting down. It eventually plunged to an all-time low of less than US$35.0 per barrel in early 2016. There is yet lucrative banking prospects and opportunities in this for the banks that have the capacity to manage part of the now bourgeoning external reserves of the country.

Although the Central Bank of Nigeria had concluded its banking system consolidation exercise in December 2005, it gave further criteria which banks in Nigeria must satisfy to qualify to manage part of the external reserves. Some of the new requirements include further increase in the capitalization of the banks, from N25.0 billion to N100.0 billion. The Nigerian banks are also required to form strategic, working, alliances with reputable foreign banks that have external reserves management experience. Some of the Nigerian banks have satisfied these conditions and have been engaged in managing parts of the country's external reserves in collaboration with certain foreign banks. It is expected that more Nigerian banks will meet the criteria and be given the opportunity to participate in managing the country's external financial resources.

Financing of Public Sector Projects

The government—including its ministries, parastatals, and agencies—embarks on various social and economic projects. The legislature appropriates budgetary funds for the execution of the projects. Sometimes, the funds would be inadequate, necessitating deficit financing of some of the projects. In most cases, government finances the deficits by borrowing from the local financial market. This provides an opportunity for domestic and foreign subsidiary banks to package and extend appropriate credit facilities to the government to enable it meet its various funding needs.

The government borrows from banks on various terms. It does a large part of the borrowing through the sale of government papers or financial instruments, such as treasury bills, treasury certificates, development stocks, and so on. Government could also borrow directly from the banks. However, such loans are usually granted to finance specific government contracts, capital projects, or to meet recurrent expenditure needs, such as payment of salaries of workers and other overheads. Loans in this category are often structured as self-liquidating credit facilities. The transaction dynamics of such credit facilities ensure that sources for repayment of the loans are tied to monthly deductions from the government's statutory allocations from the federation account.

However, not many banks—especially the foreign banks subsidiaries—would think that lending to the public sector should be pursued as a deliberate strategy of asset expansion, whether in the short or long-run. Such banks might have reasons for their reluctance to lend to the public sector. In general, lending to the public sector tends to be unattractive to many banks for several reasons, including the following:

- Inability of the banks to accurately foresee, and plan toward, possible changes in government actions and programs.
- The tendency of incoming government to disregard the projects started by their predecessors, largely for political reasons.
- Complexity of most public sector financing needs for which some of the banks do not have the requisite inhouse risk analysis capabilities.
- Most public sector projects are financed on the basis of their socio-political value, as opposed to strict economic consideration of return on investment to which the banks are oriented.
- In most cases, expected revenue allocations or projections, which might not be realized, takes precedence over the more practical reliance on cash flow analysis for loan repayment.

In Nigeria, the Central Bank emphasizes and often warns banks about risks inherent in lending to the public sector. The demoralizing effect of its circular which directs banks to make 50% provision on all loans to the public sector is a strong disincentive for the banks. Notwithstanding risk warnings—and especially the Central Bank's directive—lending to the public sector has remained an attractive business for the leading banks.

CHARACTERIZING PUBLIC SECTOR BANKING

The public sector presents unique banking characteristics which bank employees involved in marketing and managing its relationship must appreciate to be able to satisfy its banking needs. It is likely that public sector institutions will neither operate savings accounts nor patronize consumer products of banks. Public sector institutions would rather open and operate demand deposit, time deposit, domiciliary, and loan accounts with the banks. Thus, it will be futile to dissipate energy trying to sell inappropriate products to them. However, the officials of the public sector institutions could patronize both savings and consumer products that banks offer to them. For this reason, it should be clear to the banks whether they are targeting the institutions, or their officials, with their products offerings. Though, it would be wrong to consider selling of banking products to the individual officials in the context of the public sector as a target market. This is because the banking needs of the public sector are altogether totally different from those of the individual officials.

As a target market, it would be pertinent to understand the specific factors that characterize public sector banking habits and relationships. In doing so, we should appreciate attributes that distinguish the public sector from other target markets. There are several ways in which the banking attributes of the public sector differ from those of the other target markets. However, I limit discussion of the differences to the more important features which include the following:

- While banks deal with customers' accounts in confidence, they tend to unusually emphasize confidentiality in public sector banking transactions, deals, and relationships.
- Often a high caliber of employees is required to market, develop, and manage public sector banking relationships.
- Marketing officers must cultivate personal attribute of endurance to be able to cope with the long waiting time to book appointments, see the responsible officers, and conclude transactions, or deals.
- In most cases, a major success requirement is that marketing officers must have strong and extensive network of personal contacts within and outside the public sector circles.
- Most public sector banking transactions are largely routine in nature; traditional banking products drive the transactions.
- Certain public sector banking transactions, deals, and activities attract undue publicity in the mass media, especially where commissioning of projects are involved.
- Account and relationship management assignments and responsibilities for the public sector customers often demand irregular work schedules.

I present the main issues involved in the aforementioned factors in the following discussions. Doing so, I highlight implications of the issues for marketing and managing public sector banking relationships.

Confidentiality of Transactions

In banking, the confidentiality of customer transactions is usually taken for granted. In fact, a bank owes its customers a duty to maintain strict confidentiality of their normal banking activities. However, this rule could be disregarded in cases where order of courts of competent jurisdiction compels a bank to divulge information about a particular customer's account. Also, law enforcement agents, such as the police could request a bank to furnish them with information on any customer's account. They may do so in investigation of fraud, corrupt practice, money laundering, and drug trafficking, and so on.

Yet for obvious reasons, the requirement for confidentiality is taken even more seriously in the case of public sector banking transactions. In general, most government deals are treated as classified information. The deals should not be divulged to the members of the public without the permission of responsible officers. This implies that a critical success factor for bank marketing and relationship management employees is their ability to show maturity and earn the confidence of the public sector customers.

Caliber of Marketing Personnel

Marketing and management of public sector banking relationships often require the deployment of high caliber of employees. In most cases, the employees would have attained a minimum position of manager in the bank. Some banks assign public sector marketing responsibilities to employees of not lower than assistant general manager in ranking. The more aggressive banks even assign executive director-level employee to oversee the sector. There are various reasons for this practice, but the more plausible ones include the following:

- Banks believe, and this is true based on their experiences, that decision making officers in public sector institutions are not likely to grant audience to junior bank marketing officers.
- Decision makers in public sector institutions would not be disposed to discuss important banking deals with low ranking employees. The reason for this is not far-fetched. The need to maintain confidentiality of the transactions dictates public sector banking habit.
- Public sector officials tend to believe that only senior bank marketing officers, or executives, can effectively commit their banks on certain critical banking transactions and deals.

The big customers of banks—and those in the public sector are not an exception—tend to think along the lines of the foregoing. Their belief is that banking transactions are concluded faster, with mutual commitment of the parties, if the officers involved are senior enough to take certain critical decisions. Thus, dealing with low-ranking employees would be a waste of their time. For this reason, some banks have devised certain functional titles for public sector credit and marketing officers—those that are below assistant general manager positions.

The titles are intended to shore up their image and perception by the decision making officers in the public sector. This is perhaps the reasoning behind the adoption of such functional designations as regional director, divisional director, group head, and so on by the banks. In most cases, the actual ranks of such marketing officers could be below the manager position.

Personal Attribute of Endurance

Marketing personnel must tolerate and endure probable abuse of their official time by public sector officials. For instance, some of the public sector officials often find it difficult to strictly keep to appointments. Even when they honor appointments, they sometimes introduce unexpected changes in time schedules that could alter planned programs of the marketing employee. Unplanned long waiting time to see the relevant officials, even on appointment, is a common experience of marketing officers in the public sector. On occasion marketing officers spend whole days to see certain key public sector officials.

As part of their strategies for the public sector, marketing personnel must appreciate and imbibe the attribute of endurance. They must learn to accommodate the snobbish tendencies of some of the key public sector officials. This is especially necessary when they have to deal with such officials in the course of their assignments. But it requires patience which marketing officers must have in abundance to achieve their marketing objectives in the public sector. A calm and cool disposition will also be helpful.

Yet in addition to patience, credit and marketing personnel must do extra work. They must devote time to study the day-to-day official engagements, programs, and activities of key public sector officials. It's always essential to know the daily routines of the officials. It helps marketing officers to plan their requests for appointment, as well as the timing and convenience of proposed calls. It is particularly useful for the marketing personnel to know which day of the week, and what time of the day, particular officials would probably want to see visitors or discuss banking matters.

It is also imperative for the marketing officers to appreciate how the ministries, parastatals, and agencies of the public sector and their officials function. If they do this, they would be in a better position to tolerate the abuse of time which they sometimes experience in the course of their marketing activities in the public sector. In fact, some of the difficulties which marketing officers encounter in marketing and managing public sector banking relationships derive, to a large extent, from lack of or inadequate knowledge of the sector in the first place.

Extensive Personal Network

Marketing in the public sector requires strong connections as a major critical success factor. Marketing personnel must build effective contacts within public sector circles and elsewhere to drive their strategies. For this reason, the marketers must develop sociable inclination and, indeed, be eager to network. The types, influence, and level of cooperation of the personal contacts which the marketing personnel could garner determine, to a large extent, the level of success that they would attain.

It is imperative to consciously build marketing network in the public sector because it is usually difficult to start banking relationship with government in the first place. The contacts may provide links to the responsible public sector officials who the marketing personnel need to get particular account, transaction, or deal. Any credible contacts would be helpful to the marketing personnel in trying to initiate certain account relationship under the circumstances. However, this arrangement may provide only a transient marketing support. The buck for attracting, nurturing, and satisfying public sector customers remains with the marketing personnel.

Thus, for long-term effective marketing in the public sector, the responsible personnel should endeavor to develop strong and extensive network of personal contacts. Having done that, the success of their marketing efforts would depend on the ingenuity with which they manage the banking relationship to meet the needs of the customers and bank concurrently.

Routine Transactions, Traditional Products

In most cases, public sector banking needs are satisfied as routine transactions. They are largely executed in the context of the traditional products and services. For instance, all the banks scramble to offer revenue collection service to the government and its agencies. Also, the banks routinely invest in T-bills and other government financial instruments. For the parastatals and other government agencies, banks open current accounts, time deposit accounts, domiciliary accounts, and so on.

However, it is only in very few cases, as is often experienced in certain foreign currency denominated transactions, that public sector banking could be complicated. Often such difficult cases are observed in the packaging of certain types of credit facility. Yet in such situations, the bank should transfer the particular transactions from the marketing personnel to the appropriate credit department for review, advice, and presentation to the senior management.

While the complicated transactions could be so handled, nonetheless, the marketing personnel should retain the role for managing the underlying banking relationship. In doing so, the customer is presented with a congruous relationship management interface with the bank. This will help to prevent avoidable roles conflict which would be experienced if a customer has more than one relationship management interface within the same bank.

Publicity of Public Sector Transactions

In general, public sector activities attract publicity in the mass media. Banking transactions would not be an exception. The publicity could be positive, on the one hand, to the extent that it helps to publicize the role of the bank in public sector banking or financing. On the other, it could be negative if the underlying banking transaction undermines, or is antithetical to, the wellbeing of the people. Banks should do anything but allow negative publicity to taint its public image.

With this fact in mind, the marketing personnel should be mindful of how they manage public sector banking transactions, deals, and relationships. This is necessary to avoid leakage of pertinent information to the press or other third parties. As a rule, officers engaged in public sector marketing should report directly to a designated member of the senior management. Under this arrangement, it becomes obvious that only the senior banking officers would be entrusted with responsibility for marketing and managing public sector banking relationships. This would help to forestall unauthorized access to public sector banking information.

Yet the external affairs and communications departments of banks should ensure that public sector banking transactions attract positive publicity. Sometimes, a bank may be helpless in situations where negative information about a public sector banking deal leaks to the press. Yet the external affairs department should try as much as possible to explain the professional involvement of the bank in the deal to members of the public. If the explanation is credible, it could assuage damaging public feelings toward the bank. However, banks should never work against interest of the people in their transactions with the public sector.

Irregular Work Schedules

Often irregular schedules characterize the work of personnel involved in marketing and managing public sector banking relationships. As would be expected under the circumstances, this affects the performance of the personnel. Unanticipated business opportunity might prompt unplanned trip, just as an agreed appointment could be cancelled, or rescheduled without prior notice to the marketing personnel. These situations should be expected as characteristic features in the nature of public sector banking. Marketing personnel must appreciate and cope with work pressure that results from irregular work schedules. Their ability to do so will determine the extent to which they would be successful in their public sector marketing assignments.

SUMMARY

The public sector—comprising the government (i.e., Federal, State, and local councils) and its ministries, parastatals, and agencies—constitutes a major target market for banks. Indeed, government is the single largest, most homogenous, and predictable economic unit among the entire target markets that banks chase for banking relationships. It is the almighty sector of the economy, which generates the largest annual volume of transactions for banks in developing economies. The significance of government is best appreciated when it is realized that it operates in every sector of the economy, either directly or indirectly. This ubiquity trait defines its appeal for banking relationship. Banks chase one or more of public sector accounts because of expectation of huge current account transactions, deposit float from various taxes, profitable lending opportunities, and fixed deposits from unapplied capital funds or budget surpluses.

Specific questions guide formulation of framework of analysis of key issues in banking the public sector. What is the size and composition of the public sector? From what sources does government generate its revenue? What constitute major government expenditure profiles? What is the banking potential of the public sector? How can public sector banking be aptly characterized? These questions predispose and challenge thoughts about what makes the public sector such an attractive market segment for banks. The public sector plays a major, if not domineering, role in the economy. From this perspective, its banking potential becomes apparent. The potential of public sector banking can be appreciated from an analysis of its role and influence in the financial system, its liquidity boosting capability for banks, management of domestic public sector funds, management of a country's external reserves, and investment opportunities in financing public sector projects.

The public sector presents unique banking characteristics which credit and marketing staff must appreciate to be able to satisfy its banking needs. It is likely that public sector institutions will neither operate savings accounts, nor patronize consumer banking products. The institutions would rather open and operate demand deposit, time deposit, domiciliary, and loan accounts with banks. Thus, it will be futile to dissipate energy trying to sell inappropriate products to them. In general, public sector banking demands confidentiality of transactions, acquaintance with banking products and offerings, a high caliber of bank employees for marketing and relationship management, publicity of projects, endurance, irregular work schedules, and a strong and extensive network.

QUESTIONS FOR DISCUSSION AND REVIEW

1. In what five ways is public sector banking considered a significant contributor to a bank's bottom line in developing economies?
2. What unique characteristics of the public sector distinguish it from other banking markets in developing economies?
3. Does the banking potential of the public sector in developing economies really warrant intense devotion of banks to it?
4. How would you characterize public sector banking and discuss applicable marketing and relationship management issues?
5. Why and how may it be uncritical of banks to lend money to public sector customers in developing economies?

6. What challenges do bankers face in analyzing and managing lending to the public sector in developing countries?
7. Is it feasible to devise efficacious methodological framework for analyzing public sector banking, risks, and control?

REFERENCE

Okigbo, P.N.C., 1981. Nigeria's Financial System: Structure and Growth. Longman Group Limited, United Kingdom.

Chapter 13

Bank Strategic Business Units Planning, Marketing and Risk Management

Chapter Outline

LEARNING FOCUS AND OBJECTIVES

Business planning is necessary for success in banking—as in other businesses. It is critical for sustaining banks as going concerns. Good business plans help banks to always focus attention on major financial performance variables and indices—as well as on the risk management demands. Planning especially helps banks to build up, increase, and sustain market share and earnings while mitigating risks. It derives from strategic business unit (SBU) and cost center unit (CCU) activities. Effective business plans require specific actions to be strategic input into the planning process. I set out writing this chapter—bearing this in mind—in order to:

- explain the meaning, overview, and significance of business planning for the success of banks in developing economies;

- compare strategy with planning for bank business and risk management in developing economies;
- demonstrate why and how bank managements should anchor success of operations on clear business planning directives;
- assess the challenges of preparing and working out the components of effective banking business plans;
- provide tips on how SBU and CCU managers can overcome problems with the presentation of business plans;
- discuss the processes of formal approval and review of business plans at monthly performance review (MPR) meetings; and
- identify risk management implications of constantly monitoring business plans of the SBUs and CCUs.

EXPECTED LEARNING OUTCOMES

Risk and intense competition inform the fate of banks in developing economies. Domestic banks are especially vulnerable to the vagaries of the business. Many of them founder on cut-throat competition and poor risk management. This situation demands painstaking risk-based, but market-driven, business plans as a road map to sustain banks in developing economies as going concerns. The reader will—after studying this chapter—have learnt and been better informed about:

- the meaning, overview, and significance of business planning in banking;
- how strategy compares with planning for bank business and risk management in developing economies;
- why and how bank managements should anchor success of operations on clear business planning directives;
- the challenges of preparing and working out the components of effective banking business plans;
- tips on how SBU and CCU managers can overcome problems with presentation of business plans;
- the process of formal approval and review of SBU and CCU plans at MPR meetings; and
- risk management implications of constant monitoring of the business plans of the SBUs and CCUs.

OVERVIEW OF THE SUBJECT MATTER

Bank managements must devote attention and resources to build, nurture, and sustain operations as a going concern. One of the most coveted business accomplishments is to attain market or industry leadership, with so-called cash cows—products or services that are at the maturity or growth stage of life cycle, popular among the customers, and generating increasing sales and earnings. Although the rate of sales growth may be slow at this stage, most firms often appear content and thus fail to discern emerging threats to the business. Yet there may not be organizational achievement that tasks management the way leading the market does. Sometimes, market leadership goes with products that have attained maturity or increasing market patronage.

The tasks are driven by the need to develop and manage effective competitive strategy capable of sustaining customer loyalty, increasing market share, and maintaining the leadership position. A powerful statement of this problem is best expounded in the celebrated article, *Marketing Myopia* (Levitt, 1960). Levitt demonstrated how firms that were once industry leaders turned and also ran because of indifference and neglect of the threat of competition. They also lost sight of the importance of marketing in meeting the ever-changing market tastes and preferences. However, they paid dearly for this omission. The most prominent example of businesses that suffered the myopia disease is railroad.

Competitive strategy must derive from a bank's overall vision—which, for its members, is really about defining, agreeing, internalizing, and practicing a certain collectively agreed and shared core ideology. This is germane to evolve a corporate culture—one by which the bank, its members, business, and customers or products markets can easily be identified. With a clearly defined ideology, members will be indoctrinated about the cause of the bank and its values. Understanding of the cause of being (i.e., core purpose) and upholding the agreed standards, morals, or ethics (i.e., core values) of the bank is important in evolving a workable long-range strategy. This is because it tunes the members to the challenges of business in the bank's products markets. Besides, strategy for the business has a strong significance for its financial performance. The starting point is in developing and implementing effective business plans.

There is keen competition in the banking industry in developing economies. Banks that survived the recent financial crisis, on the one hand, learnt their lessons in a hard way and are determined to forge ahead. The public, on the other hand, are yet to fully restore confidence in the banking system. With dwindling, cautious patronage, and thinning margins, banks are more than ever before challenged by fierce competition that may nail the coffin of the weak ones. It is in this context that the business acumen of bank managements should be exploited to ensure survival. Playing the hopeless challenger for too long can barely guarantee modest corporate existence that will not impress the board and shareholders. Bank managements must incorporate business strategy into the framework of its planning objectives in order to succeed in the long-run.

MEANING AND OVERVIEW OF BUSINESS PLANNING IN BANKING

It is a common business practice for SBU managers to prepare realistic business plans at the beginning of every financial year (In most cases, the plans usually empty into bank-wide financial budgets which the SBUs are expected to achieve during the relevant periods. Thus, it is a common practice among the managers to talk about their *business plans* or *budgets* to convey the same meaning. For this reason, I have, in this chapter adopted interchangeable use of the two terms). The plans are usually intended to guide the business, marketing, and operational activities of the units during the year. It also serves as yardstick for measuring the business and financial performance of the units at the end of the related year. The budgets should as much as possible be realistic, attainable, and challenging, with clearly defined strategies intended to be adopted in achieving stated objectives and targets. In preparing the budgets, it is necessary for the SBU managers to indicate critical resource requirements. Sometimes, it would be pertinent to include simple organization charts of the units to justify requests for certain operational resources.

For obvious reasons, bank managements attach great importance to business plans. This importance reflects in the involvement of senior management, and the valuable time spent bank wide by the responsible officers to analyze the target markets, prepare, discuss, and obtain approval for the plans. Moreover, the final budget of the entire bank derives, to a large extent, from aggregation of the business plans. The CCUs budgets complement those of the SBUs to determine that of the entire bank. In most cases, the MPR meetings in the banks confer further significance to the budgets. This is because the meetings review actual business and financial performance against approved targets for a particular review period.

Comparing actual performance against projections for a particular period enables banks managements to determine the extent to which the SBUs and CCUs managers met, or failed to meet, their budgeted targets. The managers would be required to defend negative deviation of performance from projections, while being commended for meeting or surpassing agreed targets. Thus, business plans become employee appraisal issue on the basis of which banks managements could sanction, promote, or grant other rewards, to the deserving employees.

STRATEGY VERSUS PLANNING FOR BANKING BUSINESS AND RISK MANAGEMENT

It is useful to distinguish between *strategy* and *planning* to underscore the relevance of each of the terms to the business of the bank. It becomes even more pertinent to understand the differences between the two concepts considering that there might be a tendency by some people to confuse the meaning of the one with that of the other. Strategy deals with devising a realistic means of achieving a bank's long-run business objectives in its target markets. The means includes a set of guiding business and operational principles on which success depends. In formulating strategy, bank managements should take certain factors into consideration. Major factors to consider are subsumed under current and anticipated situation of the bank, including internal and external risk events and opportunities.

Planning refers to the process of developing specific programs of actions designed to achieve a bank's business objectives in its target markets over a period, usually 1 year. In most cases, bank planning involves three main elements:

- Painstaking analysis of the products markets in which the bank hopes to execute the plan, and realize its set financial goals (Banks in developing economies seek customers and patronage from various target markets—including retail, consumer, commercial, corporate, and government banking sectors).
- Survey of the external variables that tend to influence the choice of strategies, implementation, and results of the plan.
- Review of the internal resources, which the bank has at its disposal, that complement the other elements of the plan.

The end product of planning is always a budget or plan. Thus, a business plan may be defined as a map of activities which guides SBUs in the drive to attain set business, customer, and financial objectives in given target markets over a certain period, usually 1 year. It often represents a short-term program of business actions which a bank intends to implement to achieve particular profit and customer objectives in its products markets. Strategic planning has long-run outcomes connotation, though. Yet strategic plans have to be implemented as successive short-term plans since uncertainty of the future is always a given.

Obviously, strategy is subsumed under planning. In planning, bank managements should highlight applicable strategies for realizing the plan. Thus, strategy makes it possible to successfully execute business plan. In most cases, planning clearly defines the variables on which effective execution of strategy depends.

NEED FOR CLEAR BANK BUSINESS PLANNING DIRECTIVES

It is the responsibi lity of bank managements to provide bank wide budgetary direction and targets to the SBUs and CCUs. These are usually given in broad terms, even as they should clarify certain issues such as the purpose, focus, scope, and strategy of the entire bank's business plan from which those of the SBUs and CCUs derive. Thus, the plans that the SBUs and CCUs are expected to prepare, defend, obtain approval for, and implement should be based on specific business targets and financial projections of the entire bank. In some cases, the supervising officers convey management's budgetary expectations for the forthcoming financial year to the SBUs and CCUs. In most cases, however, the financial control unit (FINCON), which is responsible for consolidating the budgets bank wide, provides the required broad plan preparation briefs to the SBUs and CCUs. Nonetheless, it is important that this is done, irrespective of who does it. For instance, Exhibit 13.1 shows the directive that a group head in charge of branches of a bank in a certain metropolis could issue to the branch managers.

EXHIBIT 13.1 Group Head's Directive to his Subordinates on the Preparation of Business Plan.

Please prepare and turn in your business plans for the 2007 financial year to me on or before close of business on December 10, 2006. It is important that you meet the plan preparation deadline to enable us review your projections, set realizable targets for your branches, and agree your final budgets, which will be presented at the forthcoming MPR meeting scheduled for December 30, 2006.

You will realize that the success of your business efforts depends on your ability to generate high volume balances in current accounts, savings accounts, time deposits, import duty and withholding tax collections, business/personal travel allowance/ travellers' checks sales, quality risk assets, and fee-based transactions. Your plans should reflect a clear objective of increasing the customer base and patronage of your branches.

As you know, the sum of your targets represents my target. We should therefore collectively strive to ensure that the targets are challenging, realistic, and achievable. In fact, we should aim to not only meet but surpass our budgets.

For the branches in difficult locations, there is need to maintain the extensive marketing approach. This will permit them to seek for banking relationships beyond the vicinity of their branches, while intensifying marketing for any available banking transactions within their localities.

This assumes that preparation of business plans for the forthcoming year (for banks that adopt January to December financial year) takes place during the last quarter of the current financial year, beginning with the SBUs and CCUs. For instance, preparation of plans for 2008 would commence in October 2007 at the SBUs and CCUs levels. The processes of presentation, defence, and approval of the budgets of the units could take up to 2 months in some cases. The budget for the entire bank could be concluded in December 2007 to take effect from January 1, 2008.

A similar directive from FINCON unit could simply ask the SBU and CCU heads to turn in their budgets within a certain time frame. In most cases, the FINCON's memo to this effect would enjoin the unit heads to clearly state the underlying objectives, and strategies of their plans, with indications of the resources they intend to use to achieve their budgets.

PREPARATION AND COMPONENTS OF BANKING BUSINESS PLAN

Business plans are a critical element in the overall business strategies of banks. Officers who prepare the plans must show commitment to the assignment. How should SBUs prepare effective business plans? There may be differences among banks regarding how SBUs prepare and present business plans. Yet the framework of the preparation process recognizes certain basic procedural steps which underscore the credibility of the plan. SBUs should adopt the following basic steps in preparing business plans:

1. Understand senior management's directives on expected plans and targets for the SBUs. The plans must essentially derive from that of the entire bank.
2. Review business and financial performance which the SBU achieved in the current year. This serves as a benchmark for the following year's projections.
3. Analyze unique business, operational, and other situational events which the SBUs face in their locations, that is,, those factors, internal and external, which tend to affect the performance of the SBUs, either positively or negatively.
4. State the focus, objectives, and goals of the plan, which are expected to guide the SBUs in their business activities.
5. Formulate strategies for implementation of the plans which must be unambiguous and cost effective.
6. State the action programs which will ensure effective implementation of the identified strategies.
7. Prepare financial aspects and budgets with clear emphasis on the bottom line which the SBUs are expected to achieve.
8. Articulate critical resource requirements and success factors which will help the SBUs to achieve the plan.

The main components of a business plan are derived from these steps. Thus, a typical business plan should contain at least nine important sections: executive summary, review of previous/current year, situation analysis, objectives and goals, strategy statement, actions programs, budgets, critical success factors, and controls. I discuss these components of business plan—showing how they impart credibility and significance to the plan.

Executive Summary

The executive summary is usually the first section in a marketing plan. It summarizes the main thrusts of the plan in not more than two pages. However, its objective is to present a quick overview of the major points and recommendations of the plan to the senior management. With such a general idea, the senior management would appreciate the facts and factors that determined the direction of the budget before reading through the entire plan. I present a typical executive summary of a business plan in Exhibit 13.2 later.

EXHIBIT 13.2 Typical Executive Summary of a Plan for a Branch of a Bank.

The current year (2007) has been quite challenging as we are barely able to meet most of our key budget targets. Difficult operating environment, resulting from precarious economic situation, and regulatory maneuverings caused much of the observed deviations of performance from projections in the budget.

Notwithstanding these unforeseen problems, more than 80% of the budget was achieved in terms of earnings and profit. In comparison to the current year, the 2008 plan focuses on increasing customer base, earnings, and profit. The revenue target, projected at ₦500.0 million, represents 25% increase over the current year. This planned increase is considered feasible and achievable because the country now enjoys political stability, and is progressively diversifying its economic base—both of which make the business environment favorable. The forecast operating profit is ₦50.0 million, representing 30% increase compared with the current year. The attainment of these goals is hinged on improved customer service, effective relationship management, employee commitment, and the bank's planned 30% increase in the advertising budget.

The summary also guides senior management in searching for relevant information in the entire plan that underpins particular projections, or is considered most critical in evaluating the budget.

Review of Previous and Current Years

The starting point of the budget preparation exercise is the review of major transactions executed, business successes achieved, operating difficulties encountered, and the actual financial performance attained by the SBUs during the current year. The review should highlight aspects of the current year's budget that require adjustments based on the actual performance indices.

There might be a need to improve business efforts in the forthcoming year. Perhaps the SBUs should devise a more effective means of forestalling possible income losses, or leakages. It could yet be pertinent to introduce a new cost control measure—one that fits well with business development, relationship management, and customer satisfaction needs. On a positive note, the SBUs might find it necessary to consolidate particular performance gains attained in the current year's budget. In some cases, it might be necessary to fine-tune the SBU's current business focus, objectives, and strategies as a repositioning measure for the forthcoming year.

Business managers should identify variables that helped (positive factors) or hindered (negative factors) the ability of the SBUs to achieve their business plan in the outgoing year. Possible consolidation or remedial measures should follow the identification of the positive or negative factors. For example, if a particular SBU failed to meet most of its budgeted business and income targets, the reasons for the failure could be some or all of the following factors:

- Lack of a large pool of profitable accounts that have high volumes of transactions from which the SBU could earn substantial incomes.
- Impact of regulatory maneuverings, such as, are found in some of the inconsistent regulations of interest rate and foreign exchange transactions.

- Losses associated with huge cash carrying costs and management during the periods, the central bank could not accept such excess cash from the banks—forcing the banks to procure cash processing machines and equipment.
- Increasing competitive pressure which has become unbearable for most of the SBUs, with the attendant thinning of profit margins.
- Inadequate number of personnel that have the requisite skills to drive the business of the SBU in its location.

The highpoint of the review would be a realization that the SBU met, or surpassed, its current year's budget. However, it should be disappointing if the SBU failed to meet its current year's plan. Yet, whether the targets of the plan are attained, not met, or surpassed, the lessons from the budget review should be appreciated. Such lessons should guide thinking that would underlie projections for the budget of the forthcoming year.

Situation Analysis

Critical analysis of internal and external situations and business circumstances of the SBUs is probably the most important element of business plan preparation. This is because most of the other elements of the plan are based on the practical business situation that the SBUs face. Besides, analyzing the situation requires the SBU personnel to demonstrate sound are as follows:

- Understanding of every aspect of the bank's business, especially the products and services it offers to the market; the customer base, profile, and targets that it serves; and the bank's operations manual that guides the booking of transactions, and so on.
- Knowledge of the strategies of the bank's major competitors in the industry and market segments.
- Appreciation of the dynamics of the bank's operating environment, such as the macro economic issues, regulatory maneuverings, and so on that constrain or enhance banking activities and performance.

Now assume that the manager of a branch of a bank located at the Bridge Head business district of Onitsha, Nigeria, is to analyze the situational circumstances of the branch. The major issues to analyze would include the location, the market, business potential, competition, strengths, weaknesses, opportunities, and threats.

Office Location

The Bridge Head market is a very busy commercial nerve center in Onitsha. It is linked to other parts of the town by a good network of roads: Port Harcourt Road, Ugah Street, and Atani Road. In view of its strategic position, most of the banks have branches in this location. The market is fenced round and has entrance gates that open to some of the major roads in the area. It provides security guards that patrol round the market after normal business hours, as from 6:00 p.m. daily.

The Market

There are numerous businesses that operate in Bridge Head market district. The area is noted for commercial activities. In fact, it serves as one of the hubs for distributive trade in West Africa. It complements the Onitsha main market which is reputed as the largest market in the West African subregion. The bulk of trading in general merchandize is concentrated on imported goods. Among the major businesses that operate in the market are pharmaceutical, building materials, paper, plastics, and farm produce enterprises. The main target market for the branch comprises the pharmaceutical/drug companies. Thus, the target market comprises all the companies that deal in imported and locally manufactured drugs located in the Bridge Head district. It is considered a highly profitable segment of the market because of its large size, heavy customer patronage, and central location within the Bridge Head district.

Business Potential

The Onitsha traders typically stockpile inventories, largely to avoid stock-out situations and for speculation purposes. The businesses are more than 85% import dependent. There is little or negligible government or public sector presence in the town. Corporate banking products rarely do well because of the absence of, or existence of few, manufacturing or other structured organizations. The market is rather dominated by commercial banking/middle-tier market customers. Credit products that drive competition among the banks include temporary overdraft, inventory refinancing, import finance facilities, and warehouse finance. It is estimated that the identified businesses in the Bridge Head district have daily transactions turnover of at least ₦1.5 billion. Of this amount, the pharmaceutical/drug companies, which represent the target market of the branch, account for about 25%. Based on its current year's performance, and considering that all the other banks are represented in this location, the branch targets 8% market share of the pharmaceutical/drugs companies' banking transactions in the forthcoming year. This translates to a projected total monthly account turnover of ₦780.0 million on which the branch would earn service income at an average rate of ₦3.0 per mille.

Competition

There exists intense competition among the banks in the Bridge Head district. In fact, all the banks in Nigeria have branches in this location. Most of the banks sited their branches along Port Harcourt Road and Ugah Street. These two roads link up to the pharmaceutical/drugs market, which is the leading business in the area. The main products on which the banks compete include lending, foreign exchange transactions, retail, and consumer banking.

Strengths

The strengths of SBUs should be understood in the context of internal factors or circumstances which give them competitive advantages and enhance their abilities to satisfy the needs of customers. A unique feature of *strengths* is that they may not be applicable to the SBUs of the competing banks in the same locality. However, it is not uncommon to find more than one SBU in the same area sharing similar factors of strengths. For instance, banks have improved the efficiency of transactions processing by offering online-real-time services. Thus, the provision of banking services in real time becomes major business strength, but it is applicable to all the banks.

However, a particular branch of a bank may have a special strength in its location at the center of its major target market. In that target market, the competing banks in disadvantaged locations would find it difficult to attract as much patronage as the one in the advantaged location. In most cases, this explains why some banks tend to relocate branches after periods of consistent poor performance in certain locations.

For every branch of a bank, there could be several business strengths peculiar to it and on which it hopes to build competitive ability, meet the needs of customers, and attain its budget. SBU managers should identify and marshal all such strengths in the business plan. Like branch managers, heads of all other SBUs should carefully identify the major strengths of their units in their business plans. For example, a branch of a bank might see business strength in the synergy provided by hub and spoke, as well as loop branch development strategy of the bank. This could continue to boost transactions volumes which customers of the branch achieve in their accounts. Exhibit 13.3 shows possible strengths of treasury marketing SBU in a leading domestic bank.

EXHIBIT 13.3 Strengths of Treasury SBU in a Leading Bank.

1. Unrivalled goodwill of the bank built on track record of consistent financial performance, and a leading position in the industry, which has helped to maintain customer loyalty and patronage over the years.
2. Ability to sustain position as a net funds placer in the interbank money market which guarantees good interest rates for the SBU when it becomes inevitable to take funds from the market.
3. Sustained excellent liquidity position—seen in absence of treasury crisis of any sort over the past decade—which enables the treasury to meet all its maturing deposit payment obligations on the due dates.
4. Dedicated and motivated marketing personnel that have shown proven loyalty to the bank and commitment to their treasury marketing assignments and deposit mobilization targets.
5. Consistent top management support to the marketing team, especially in accomplishing critical calls to certain high net worth individuals, senior public office holders, or the blue-chip companies, and so on.

Weaknesses

As in the case of strengths, managers should also indicate the weaknesses of their SBUs which have to be taken into consideration in preparing business plans. The weaknesses represent internal factors that tend to negatively affect attainment of objectives and goals of the budget. Within a given banking area, different SBUs may have different weakness factors, depending on their varying internal business and operational circumstances. Exhibit 13.4 shows the weaknesses which some of the branches of banks in major banking centers of a typical developing country.

EXHIBIT 13.4 Possible Weaknesses of some Banks Branches in Major Banking Centers of a Metropolis.

1. Probable high incidence of nonperforming loans, especially short-term credit facilities that are booked as temporary overdraft. Such credits are not usually properly secured with tangible collateral which make remedial actions difficult in the event of default by borrowers.
2. Incidence of negative publicity that often results when certain internal squabbles or business emergencies leak to the press. Past experience with such negative press included.
   a. Removal of certain directors of some banks from office by the Central Bank for reasons associated with insider abuse.
   b. Dissolution of the board of directors and managements of some banks by the Central Bank to protect the interest of the public; and so on (The weaknesses described seem to be external factors and therefore might rather be presented as threats. However, what qualifies them as weaknesses, and not threats, is the internal origination of the underlying problems).
3. Regulatory sanctions, such as suspension of erring banks from capital market activities, or withdrawal of foreign exchange dealing license of banks that contravene foreign exchange trading rules or guidelines.
4. Liquidity crunch which constrains ability of the branches to execute most of the profitable transactions envisaged in their business plans. The crunch could degenerate into a major liquidity crisis that can cause a run on the bank.
5. Cash management difficulties which, in most cases, tend to increase operational costs of banks.

Business managers should suggest options for mitigating the weaknesses of the SBUs. For example, the weakness associated with increasing incidence of bad debts could be mitigated by discouraging impromptu lending, such as is the case with most temporary overdraft transactions. The bank should grant formal, structured credit facilities to deserving borrowers. As regards negative publicity, it would be necessary to strengthen the corporate affairs department of the bank and employ competent personnel to handle its public relations functions and external communications.

Opportunities

In preparing business plans, identification of business opportunities which the SBU could exploit to achieve its budget is one of the important duties of the manager. Like the threats to the business that I discuss later, opportunities open to an SBU tend to derive from external events. As Exhibit 13.5 shows, the major opportunities for banking in Nigeria could be seen in favorable economic policies, regulatory measures, trends in the financial economy, and so on.

EXHIBIT 13.5 Opportunities in SWOT Analysis of a High Street Branch of a Bank in Nigeria.

1. Prospects of business growth following sustained economic and political stability which a country has achieved with the democratization of the polity will have general positive effects on the business of banking.
2. The reforms and deregulation of the key sectors of the economy have unlocked business potential and opened up markets. As a major player in the economy, it is expected that the banking system will benefit from these reforms.
3. Globalization of the financial system which has made it possible for banks to offer various Internet-based and other electronic banking products—such as ATMs, credit cards, and so on—will continue to enhance service delivery capacity of the banks.
4. The Central Bank's reform policy of consolidation of the banking system which resulted in the mergers and acquisition of banks at the end of December 2005 has increased business capacities of banks, especially in terms of business volumes, transactions processing, and risk management.
5. With the introduction of universal banking practice by the Central Bank January 1, 2001, the scope of banking business has increased tremendously, with implications for opportunities to do more business in various sectors of the financial system.

In the business plan, managers should mention how their SBUs intend to take advantage of the identified opportunities to maximize earnings, optimize customer service, and generally achieve their budgets. This requires appreciation of business elements of the identified opportunities, especially with regard to how they affect particular aspects of banking business and transactions.

Threats

The usual threats to business relate to external circumstances, often beyond the control of SBU managers, which can forestall successful execution of their business plans. Threats represent events that tend to weaken ability of SBUs to remain in business. For instance, the effect of growing incidence of Internet frauds and other types of financial crimes on the performance of the SBUs could be really debilitating. Such occurrences could hit the SBU at any time without prior warning. The Bridge Head market, Onitsha, presents certain threats for banking business. Exhibit 13.6 shows some of the threats to which the banks that have branches in the Bridge Head market, Onitsha, are likely to be exposed.

EXHIBIT 13.6 Possible Threats to Banking in some Location.

1. Preponderance of fake drugs, manufactured in, or imported into, Onitsha by unscrupulous businessmen. Thus, the branch faces the risk of financing fake, adulterated, or banned drugs. The risk crystallizes default when National Agency for Foods and Drugs Administration and Control (NAFDAC) clamps down on the offenders, confiscates, and destroys such drugs.

2. Possible relocation of markets which would result in capital loss to the bank because the branch—not the building—might have to relocate with the market. The bank will lose any outstanding rent on the property at the time of the relocation. This risk is real considering that it is a common practice for the government to relocate major markets for economic, political, and developmental reasons.

3. Violent armed robberies and criminal activities of miscreants that operate and harass businesses in the area. In most cases, banks are the main targets of the onslaught of criminals. The situation worsened with the disbandment of the vigilante groups that police the area. There is a related security risk in late closing time for business which is a major feature of the Bridge Head market customers. The resultant late hour banking transactions leave the branch exposed to the risk of possible armed robbery attacks.

It is not always enough to indicate major threats to the business. The manager should also suggest possible ways to mitigate the threats.

The manager could mitigate threat posed by fake drugs by sighting original certification documents issued by NAFDAC authorizing importation of the drugs before the bank could grant credit facilities. Also, the drugs in which the customers of the branch deal must have NFDAC registration numbers and expiry dates.

In the case of possible relocation of markets, the bank should perhaps take not more than 5 years renewable lease on branch office property. The manager should also certify that the Bridge Head market is approved by government, and built according to approved building plan.

Criminal activities of miscreants should be checked by engaging the services of the Nigeria Police to guard the branch during and after normal banking hours. Most banks have provided additional security against violent robberies through the installation of bulletproof entrance and exit doors.

Business Objectives

The next important step in the budget preparation after situation analysis is to articulate the SBU's focus, objectives, and goals. Should the SBU focus on liabilities generation, or risk assets creation? Will its focus be on retail, consumer, commercial, corporate, or public sector banking? Different SBUs would have different business focus—depending on, perhaps, locations and customer profiles. Based on its focus, the SBU defines its business objectives and goals for the business plan.

In general, objectives and goals are stated in terms of average balance sheet footing that the SBU expects to achieve during the budget period. Also, the objective for income generation, which reflects in profits projections, should be clearly stated. For branches, it might also be pertinent to state the objectives for particular business volumes, recoveries of bad debts, and so on, which they intend to achieve in the forthcoming year.

As stated in Exhibit 13.7, the objectives and goals of a typical branch of a bank in a growth market in Lagos would be specific, and reflect facts from both current year's review and analysis of the situation.

EXHIBIT 13.7 Objectives and Goals of a Head Office Branch in Lagos Island.

- Achieve a balance sheet footing of ₦350.0 million and a profit before tax of ₦25.0 million during the budget period.
- Increase the branch's market share from its current level of 5% to not less than 10% at the end of the budget period.
- Attract 50 major accounts from which the branch could generate FX transactions ($50.0 million), and time deposits (₦1.0 billion).

Strategy Statement

The manager should formulate and clearly state strategies the SBU should adopt to achieve the plan objectives. In the case of a branch of a bank, the first thing the manager should do with respect to strategy formulation is to decide how to optimize earnings from key balance sheet items. In order to do this, certain pertinent questions must be answered. Should the branch concentrate and anchor its business strategies on the assets or liabilities side of the balance sheet? Should it contribute or take funds from the bank's pool of deposits as a deliberate plan strategy? What should be acceptable level of risk assets quality for the branch? How would possible loan loss provision affect expected earnings from risk assets? What level of income projection should be made on what anticipated volume of deposit mobilization? The decision, which the manager makes with respect to each of these questions, has implications for specific strategy formulation. Exhibit 13.8 shows how the manager may state the broad strategies of an SBU.

EXHIBIT 13.8 Typical Strategy Statement of a Branch of a Bank.

The branch will drive earnings mainly through liability generation. Much of its marketing efforts will be directed at mobilizing current accounts and other cheap deposits. These sources will account for 75% of the deposit base of the branch, while savings and fixed deposits will account for 15% and 10%, respectively. Not more than 30% of the deposit portfolio would be invested in risk assets, without concentration. Loan loss provision will not exceed 10% of the entire loan portfolio. As a net contributor to the pool of deposits of the bank, the branch will generate 70% of its earnings from transfer pricing, 20% from loans, and 10% from fees and commissions.

Overall, the key variables that drive strategy formulation center on products, pricing, promotion, and personal selling. Yet, for a branch of a bank, the most critical issues for strategy formulation will include answers to the pertinent questions.

Assets Creation Versus Liabilities Generation Focus

A particular branch may find it more profitable to focus on risk assets creation than deposits mobilization to meet its budget. Another branch may have a different view, which favors liabilities generation. Yet, it could be possible to have a median position, which relies on transactions on the assets and liabilities sides of the balance sheet to achieve the budget. In all of the possible choices, the overriding considerations would relate to the location of the branch, its customer base and profile, types of transactions and volumes, nature and intensity of competition, and so on.

Pool Funds Uses Versus Sources

This is usually a difficult issue for most branch managers. It is expected that if a manager favors pool uses, the branch would contribute to the bank wide pool of deposits. However, if the manager is in favor of pool sources, the branch would take funds from the bank wide pool of deposits to meet its risk assets funding needs. Each of these decisions has transfer pricing and strategy formulation implications for the branch. The branches that contribute or take pool funds earn or pay pool interest on the average of the sum of their total pool contributions or takings over the reporting period. The pool rate of interest is based on the transfer pricing policy of the bank (The phrase *transfer pricing* refers to the practice, common in *productivity accounting*, by which FINCON unit—acting on bank management's authority—assigns and applies pecuniary values to interdepartmental transactions of SBUs and activities of CCUs in determining their actual budgetary performance during particular review periods).

Quality of Risk Assets

Managers that want to achieve their budgets through risk assets creation should be concerned about the quality of their lending portfolios. This is because there could be huge loan loss provisions which often wipe out the gains of lending and plunge the branches into loss-making positions. Thus, it is imperative for the managers to set realistic budgetary targets for the volume, types, concentration, and quality of loans that the branch intends to book. It is also necessary to set a realistic target for loan loss provision for the lending portfolio.

Action Programs

With appropriate answers to the strategy formulation questions, it becomes pertinent for the manager to determine specific actions that must be carried out to implement the broad strategy. Implementation of the actions should be assigned to particular officers of the branch.

For example, the strategy of mobilizing cheap deposits should be more purposefully pursued if the manager segments the mass market, chooses the target markets, and determines the target markets' potential. The segmentation should be based on applicable criteria. It is usually pertinent to assess business potential of each of the market segments after segmenting the mass market (Unless otherwise stated, I have used the phrase *business potential* throughout this book to mean expected, as against observed, total volume of transactions of all customers and noncustomers of a bank, over a given period of time, which may be one month, a quarter or half of, or, one year). The marketing personnel are often tasked to determine actual and expected annual volumes of transactions for each of the market segments. With such data, they could make reliable budget forecasts, formulate appropriate marketing strategies, and effectively implement specific actions designed to achieve the plan. Market segmentation and targeting enable the personnel to be focused, and deepen marketing searches for profitable banking relationships. Besides, much energy and time which would otherwise be wasted on irrelevant marketing calls are saved.

In most cases, action programs for strategy implementation will include:

- Warm and courteous customer service, with targets assigned to all the frontline employees, especially customer service officers.
- Effective relationship management—with specific responsibility delineated for account officers and relationships managers.
- Efficient transactions processing, with appropriate targets and sanctions prescribed for operations employees.

Certain implementation actions can be related to specific aspects of the strategy statement. For example, there could be a split of marketing personnel into teams, with assignment of market segments, performance targets, and specific actions aimed at implementing the strategies to the teams. In the case of liabilities generation, different teams may be assigned different performance targets for, say, NGOs, clubs, schools, public sector, and so on. In doing so, the collective performance of the teams will be geared to successful implementation of the strategies.

Financial Aspects and Projections

SBU managers should prepare budgets which state the financial goals they are targeting. A typical budget comprises forecasts for income statement (profit and loss account), and balance sheet. In each case, projections should be made for the various income and balance sheet items. The monthly projections for each of the items are summed for the plan period to determine the annual budget in the case of income statement. However, in the case of balance sheet, average balances are taken for each of the items to determine the final budget for the plan period. The quality of the budget is a function of assumptions underlying the projections. Thus, the manager should make realistic assumptions based on past experience of the SBU and emerging trends in the industry. In most cases, assumptions should also reflect objectives of the plan. As Exhibits 13.8–13.10 show, a typical branch budget has three components: income statement; local currency (LCY) balance sheet; and foreign currency (FCY) balance sheet. However, the sum of the LCY and FCY make up the balance sheet budget of the branch.

Important Assumptions

It is imperative that SBU managers always anchor financial projections on defensible assumptions. In terms of figures, there are usually no standard assumptions for any business budget. However, assumptions underlying most budgets must cover certain critical business interests, such as turnover, interest rate, average balance sheet items balances, pool rate, fees, and incomes. For purposes of illustration, Exhibit 13.8 summarizes a typical set of assumptions that a branch SBU could make for its budget.

EXHIBIT 13.9 Typical Budgets Assumptions for a Branch SBU.

1. Average monthly turnover of ₦350.00 million and COT rate of ₦3.00 per mille.
2. Interest rate of 18% per annum is projected on average loan portfolio during the year.
3. Loan portfolio is estimated at not more than 25% of average deposit liabilities portfolio.
4. Forecast average deposits liabilities portfolio for the branch is ₦1.00 billion, with the following projected quarterly percentage growth of deposits:

Current account	25%
Savings account	15%
Call deposits	10%
Fixed deposit	10%
Other deposits	5%

5. In order to optimize earnings, the branch would target distribution of its average deposits liabilities portfolio as follows:

Current account	55%
Savings account	35%
Call deposits	3%
Fixed deposit	5%
Other deposits	2%

6. Interest payable on deposits are projected as follows:

Fixed deposits	13% p.a.
Savings account	5% p.a.
Call deposits	4% p.a.
Other deposits	3% p.a.

7. Processing fee, management fee, and L/C commission would each be charged at the rate of 1% flat.
8. Pool rate is assumed at the rate of 11% per annum.
9. Fixed asset of ₦7.5 million is assumed, to be depreciated over a 5 year period, using the straight line method.

Critical Success Factors

In preparing the plan, managers should identify resources which the SBUs require to achieve their budget projections. In most cases, resource requirements must be specific and complement other critical success factors. Resource requirements and critical success factors vary between SBUs. Differences also exist even within particular SBU category, such as branches. For instance, two or more branches within the same locality may have different critical success factors depending on their unique business and operating circumstances.

For a particular branch of a bank, resource requirements may include, say, three additional tellers (two paying and one receiving), one additional marketing officer, five bulk counters (probably not degree-qualified), and so on. For a medium sized, startup branch, resource requirements may include: five note counting machines, five office tables, three fire proof filling cabinets, five air conditioners, one bullion van, two pool cars, 30 KVA generator, and so on. These are some of the items which the branch would need to perform. While some of these materials have indirect effect on performance, they are nevertheless critical in assessing the overall results attained by the branch.

Managers are encouraged to identify and integrate as many critical resources into their plans as are expected to enhance the attainment of their budgets. However, the inclusion of resource requirements in a plan does not assure its approval by the bank's management. In most cases, some of the items may be approved, while others may not, depending on bank management's conviction about the underlying need for the requested materials. In few cases, where certain SBUs are considered strategic to the bank's business and overall performance, managers may get all of their requested critical resources. In general, critical resources that SBUs get are a function of the state of the bank at the time. Banks that are big, highly liquid, and have performance driven workforce are likely to provide all or most of the working materials which SBUs need to achieve their budgets. The less aggressive banks—those that focus on niche markets and opportunities—may provide only some of the critical resources for which the SBUs request.

Yet, competing needs for available scarce resources of the bank ultimately determine the critical resources that SBUs get. For this reason, only essential items of need are likely to attract favorable management consideration and approval. Therefore, managers should demonstrate practical justification of their requests during the presentation of their budgets.

PRESENTATION PROBLEMS AND TIPS FOR SBU MANAGERS

In most banks, presentation of annual budgets of the SBUs for the forthcoming financial year holds during any of the MPR meetings in the last quarter of the outgoing financial year. Banks that adopt January to December accounting year, forthcoming year's budget may be presented at any of the MPR meetings in October, November, or December of the current year. This arrangement allows the bank and SBUs to commence implementation of the business plan on 1 January following its approval.

Unfortunately, some SBU managers are scared by the thought of and actual presentation of their business plans during MPR meeting. The managers that are usually frightened do not, perhaps, have the requisite skills for public speaking, or presentation. Such deficient managers often suffer from stage fright. However, most of the managers that have stage fright problem could be victims of irrational threats which senior management often issues to spur better performance efforts and results. Such threats come in various ways. For example, higher management may warn these managers that fail to attain certain performance targets over a given period would be fired! With such threats and the usual pressure build up to the budget presentation, the affected managers tend to become even more scared.

Often, some SBU managers tend to develop presentation phobia when they realize that their business plans are unrealistic, not based on attainable goals, or the data on which they based their budgets are simply unfounded. It is even more appalling that some managers do not participate in the plan preparation process. Thus, the guilt of not doing the right things for the plan underlies the phobia from which they suffer. The phobia worsens with likely inability of the managers to correctly anticipate questions the audience and senior management might ask during their presentations. Another probable cause of presentation fear is often seen among SBU managers that operate in difficult environments. A common observation about the performance of many of the SBUs in this category is that they are ever struggling to meet earnings and profit goals. Thus, their managers tend to approach their budget presentation from a defensive perspective which often betrays their failings and their presentation phobia.

Yet, budget presentation during MPR meetings should be seen as a highly rewarding experience which managers should undertake with confidence, determination, and a high sense of responsibility. MPR forum also presents a unique opportunity for the managers to learn from their more experienced colleagues, especially members of executive management of the bank. Perhaps there is no better way to gain confidence required for effective presentation than to follow the aforementioned logical steps in business planning process. In doing so, managers would begin to feel a sense of ownership of the plan, commitment to defend it, and resolve to meet the budget targets. SBU managers who demonstrate these attributes will certainly make good budget presentations.

APPROVAL OF BANKING BUSINESS PLAN

In most banks, senior management approves business plans during MPR meetings. The approval, in most cases, follows conclusion of presentation, answering of pertinent questions, and taking note of adjustments (if any) to the budgets. However, senior management sometimes gives approval that radically alters the spirit of the plan as envisioned and proposed by SBU managers. When this happens, it introduces conflicts that often frustrate attainment of the budget targets.

Consider, for example, a case where SBU manager projects to increase market share by 15%, achieve ₦250.0 million in gross earnings, and ₦55.0 million in net profit. The manager, in all honesty, considers these projections realistic and achievable based on a painstaking analysis of the business situation. However, senior management thinks otherwise—and such disagreement is a common occurrence during MPR meetings to review annual budgets of SBUs. There would be a problem if senior management ridicules these forecasts and, based on certain considerations—say, size of the branch, resources deployed to it, performance of its competitors, and so on—imposes higher targets on the SBU.

While managers in this situation cannot but accept the new figures during MPR meetings, they might nevertheless discreetly disown or simply pay lip service to the budgets. They would try to achieve the allocated budget targets, but the action of senior management would dampen their enthusiasm. Yet, SBU managers need all the enthusiasm they can muster to achieve their budgets targets. Thus, while senior management would have thought that increasing the targets would encourage the managers to work with fire in their bellies, they might end up having the opposite result.

However, it is not in all cases that upward review of budget targets dampens enthusiasm. The ambitious, high-flying, managers would rather be motivated by such action. In fact, managers in this category would interpret the upward review as senior management's recognition of their capability to perform or surpass set goals notwithstanding prevailing circumstances. This implies that senior management should always balance the urge to motivate high-flyers with the need to encourage the dark horses in the workforce.

MONITORING AND CONTROL OF BANKING BUSINESS PLANS

Implementation of business plans should be effectively monitored. In order to do so, certain controls should be applied to avoid distraction and failure of the plans. One of the effective control measures is the institution of MPR meetings in which senior management and SBU managers regularly meet to review the plans' progress. The meeting holds once a month and SBU managers are expected to present their progress reports. Ideally, the FINCON unit provides summaries of the achievements and deviations from targets of the SBUs as working papers for the meeting. The MPR meeting helps senior management to isolate SBUs that are on course and those that are lagging behind. Once identified, the managers may be asked to explain any observed new factors that are frustrating (in the case of the laggards), or contributing to (in the case of those doing well) their performance. In this context, and as an interactive forum, MPR meeting provides an opportunity for both categories of managers to learn from the experiences of one another. The bank also gains in kind as the forum becomes a useful means of developing managerial capabilities bank wide.

SUMMARY

SBU managers should prepare business plans at the beginning of every financial year. The plans guide business, marketing, and operational activities of the units. It serves as yardstick for measuring the business and financial performance of the units at the end of the related year. The final budget of the entire bank derives from aggregation of SBU plans. Cost center units (CCUs) budgets complement those of SBUs to determine that of the entire bank.

It is useful to distinguish between *strategy* and *planning* to underscore their relevance to the business of a bank. Strategy deals with devising a realistic means of achieving a bank's long-run business objectives in its target markets. Planning is the process of developing specific programs of actions designed to achieve a bank's business objectives in its target markets. A business plan is a map of activities which guides SBUs in the drive to attain set business, customer, and financial objectives in given target markets. It often represents a short-term program of business actions which a bank intends to implement to achieve particular profit and customer objectives in its products markets. Strategic planning has long-run outcomes connotation, though. Yet, strategic plans have to be implemented as successive short-term plans since uncertainty of the future is always a given. Strategy is subsumed under planning. In planning, bank managements highlight applicable strategies for realizing the plan. Thus, strategy makes it possible to execute business plan. Planning defines the variables on which effective execution of strategy depends.

It is the responsibility of bank managements to provide bank wide budgetary direction and targets to SBUs and CCUs. These are usually given in broad terms, even as they clarify certain issues such as the purpose, focus, scope, and strategy of the entire bank's business plan from which those of the SBUs and CCUs derive. Thus, the plans that SBUs and CCUs are expected to prepare, defend, obtain approval for, and implement should be based on specific business targets and financial projections of the entire bank. Officers who prepare the plans must show commitment to the assignment. There may be differences among banks regarding how SBUs prepare and present business plans. Yet, the framework of the preparation process recognizes certain basic procedural steps which underscore the credibility of the plan. SBUs should adopt the basic steps in preparing their business plans.

Some SBU managers are scared by the thought of and actual presentation of their business plans during MPR meeting. The managers that are usually frightened do not, perhaps, have the requisite skills for public speaking, or presentation. Such deficient managers often suffer from stage fright. However, most of the managers that have stage fright problem could be victims of irrational threats which senior management often issues to spur better performance efforts and results. Often, some SBU managers tend to develop presentation phobia when they realize that their business plans are unrealistic, not based on attainable goals, or the data on which they based their budgets are simply unfounded.

Bank management approves business plans during MPR meetings. The approval, in most cases, follows conclusion of presentation, answering of pertinent questions, and taking note of adjustments (if any) to the budgets. Implementation of business plans should be effectively monitored. In order to do so, certain controls should be applied to avoid distraction and failure of the plans.

QUESTIONS FOR DISCUSSION AND REVIEW

1. In what ways is business planning significant for the success of banks in developing economies?
2. How does strategy compare with planning for bank business and risk management in developing economies?
3. Why, in your opinion, should bank managements anchor success of operations on clear business planning directives?
4. What challenges do SBU and CCU managers face in preparing and working out components of effective business plans?
5. As SBU or CCU manager, how would you overcome problems with presentation of your business plan at MPR meeting?
6. Why would you think formal approval and review of business plans at MPR meetings are necessary?
7. What are the risk management implications of constantly monitoring SBU and CCU business plans?

REFERENCE

Levitt, T., 1960. Marketing myopia. Harvard Bus. Rev. 38, 24–47.

Chapter 14

Bank Governance Pitfalls, Failings, and Risk Management in Developing Economies

Chapter Outline

LEARNING FOCUS AND OBJECTIVES

A bank, like many other high-risk businesses, requires good management to succeed. The alternative—poor management—is perhaps the surest way to bank failure. Bank management would be considered bad or poor if it fails to scan its environment to determine and respond to contingencies which impart instability to a bank's operations. In such a situation, a manager might erroneously adopt a wrong leadership style. The result, in most cases, is poor morale, labor turnover, and sabotage. In extreme cases, the bank becomes insensitive to customers' needs and begins to lose market share and earnings. I gear my objectives for this chapter to:

- critically examine issues underlying bank governance pitfalls, failings, and risks in developing economies,
- determine whether corporate governance best practice is recognized and institutionalized in banks in developing economies,
- investigate the setbacks and conditions for successful adoption of bank corporate governance in developing economies,
- assess congruence of leadership styles of bank managements with the demands of corporate governance best practice.

EXPECTED LEARNING OUTCOMES

Management is perhaps the most crucial resource for success in banking—as in most other businesses. A bank's success or failure depends on the quality of its management. Managing a bank well could be precarious. How to cope with possible conflicts caused by direct contact with other people's money is often the problem at issue. Thus bank managements must display a very high level of integrity, probity, and ingenuity. Bank management team must comprise individuals who bank members and customers can work with in confidence. The reader will—after studying this chapter—have learnt and been better informed about:

- causes and dynamic of bank governance pitfalls, failings, and risks in developing economies,
- the need for banks in developing economies to recognize and institutionalize corporate governance best practice,
- how banks in developing economies can tackle setbacks and tap conditions for adoption of corporate governance best practice,
- leadership styles of bank managements in developing economies and how the styles fit with the demands of corporate governance best practice,
- lessons of Fiedler's (1967) and Tannenbaum and Schmidt (1958) theories of leadership for bank managements in developing economies.

OVERVIEW OF THE SUBJECT MATTER

As in manufacturing or other industries in the real sector, bank directors play a crucial role in shaping the outlook for success. Shareholders rely on the ingenuity of the board for safety of their investment. In well-constituted boards, directors are easily the most influential members of a bank. Unfortunately, this influence is often misused through the pursuit of selfish gains at the expense of the bank. It is instructive that in almost all the cases of bank failures of the 1990s in Nigeria, most of the directors were found to be liable to prosecution. Many were indicted for impropriety of conduct as directors. Only very few maintained impeccable records of official conduct and integrity. The board of directors performs specific functions that derive from its objectives—mainly policy formulation and organization development.

Policy formulation is the primary objective and role of the board of directors. Critical issues requiring policy formulations in a bank include, but are not limited to, credit process, budget authorizations, employment or key employee matters, and general corporate governance. In some banks, the board gets involved in several less important functions otherwise meant for the management team. This has frequently arisen where the board perceives that such trivial matters could precipitate crisis that could threaten the going concern status of a bank if not properly handled. Yet, board usurpation of direct management functions is a reflection of lack of trust that may be detrimental to the corporate objectives of the bank. In such banks, the board is often personified in the managing director who not only functions as the chief executive officer but, in some cases, is also the board chairperson. The chief executive concurrently fills the chairperson role either directly or through a protégé who is largely their stooge. The regulatory authorities criticize this bank absolute-control scheme. Nevertheless, the authorities appear to be a bit lost. It has not been easy to evolve a means of dealing with dictatorial chief executives in banks.

Perhaps organization development is the most tasking of all the objectives of bank directors and managements. It involves anticipation of future challenges that impel change and the design of appropriate responses. Banks should move along with changing times and business demands. In the process, old or current objectives and strategies are rendered ineffectual and moribund. The urge and need to evolve new attainable and visionary objectives become accentuated. The manner and precision with which this challenge is handled determines how well the task of organization development is accomplished. Most organizations desire to move toward improved performance, more effective relationships, and more responsible and more highly motivated personnel. In banking, the task of organizational development becomes more arduous given the rapidity of changes in the key variables that determine market patronage. The observed changes occurred mostly in communication, data processing, information technology, and relationship management. It is the responsibility of the board and management to continuously scan the environment and harness resources toward meeting the challenges and demands of the future business of the bank.

Reputational risk has a bearing on public perception of bank governance. Domestic banks in developing economies, perhaps, face the most mind-boggling risk in threat to their reputation as a custodian of wealth for both private and public sector investors. Reputational risk takes a great deal of toll on the banks. This sad situation is borne out of insensitivity of some bank managements to customer care and breach of thrust the public reposes in them. The banks are especially prone to reputational risk on account of sharp practice in bank governance. Trying with mean success to build goodwill, on the one hand,

and maneuvering regulations and cooking the books, on the other, tend to be the bane of domestic banks managements in developing economies. These acts—often intended to satisfy budget goals—deal a blow to corporate reputation of the banks. However, while reputational risk has implications for banks managements, it does not significantly impact banking outcomes. Perhaps its greatest negative impact is on deposit mobilization and liabilities portfolio—both of which are critical for managing bank liquidity risk.

INTEGRATING CORPORATE OBJECTIVES WITH PERSONAL GOALS

A bank provides an organization for the interaction of members in the process of achieving set objectives—personal and organizational. Objectives are seen as a dominant factor in the management and success of a bank, including its members. Consider that bank members, like other organizational members, do have personal objectives that influence their actions and behavior at the workplace. The usual expectation is that securing membership of a bank will lead to the attainment of personal work objectives. These personal objectives, as diverse as they may be, must be anticipated, understood, and planned for by the bank even before or as part of the overall process of executing employment contracts. Neglect of personal objectives of bank members will be a dangerous signal of an impending doom that may have grave economic consequences for the larger society if such action crystallizes bank failure. Loss of interest by a majority of bank employees should not be wished away by management. Therefore, something must be done to ensure that employees are availed the opportunity to contribute toward attainment of the bank's corporate objectives and, in doing so, realize their personal goal. This provides a time-tested means of ensuring organizational effectiveness.

To be successful, a bank must strive to return more value to its members than it abstracts from them in the first place. In other words, value derived from bank membership should be capable of satisfying personal goals of its members. For the members, failure to attain perceived personal value implies that they incur more costs and gain less or no satisfaction in retaining the membership. This situation tends to breed restive behavior among employees in this category of membership. It is therefore important to recognize that personal goals have a bearing on the individual's participation in the organization, and that failure of the former will adversely affect effectiveness of the latter. Otherwise, managers of organizations will face a helpless situation when they are compelled by declining productivity to place individual goals on the right footing.

However, organizations and, for that matter, banks do have objectives. The fit achieved between personal and organizational objectives determines how the latter will more or less succeed. Banks usually have pervasive objectives that derive from the dictates of a spectrum of the markets they serve. They fulfill both micro and macro roles in the society. At the micro level, a bank may be interested in making as much income as possible for the shareholders, creating value for its customers and employees, rendering quality services to its customers, and so on. Yet a bank is expected to contribute positively toward national economic growth and development. This macroeconomic role is performed through such means as the extension of credit facilities to its customers, mobilization of savings for investment purposes, participation in the foreign exchange market, international trade services, and so on. Thus, the bank's primary business of financial intermediation, together with these roles, defines the path for the establishment of objectives.

Ideally, a bank's objectives should inform its business strategy in the first place. Then its strategy must derive from its overall vision. The vision is really about defining, agreeing, internalizing and practicing certain collectively agreed and shared *core ideology*. This is germane to evolving a corporate culture—one by which the bank, its members, business and customers or products markets can easily be identified. With a clearly defined ideology, the members will be indoctrinated about the cause of the bank and its values. Understanding of the *cause of being* (i.e., core purpose) and upholding the agreed *standards, morals, or ethics* (i.e., core values) of the bank is important in evolving a workable long-range strategy. This is because it tunes the members to the challenges of competition in the bank's products markets. Strategy for the business has a strong significance for its financial analysis. A bank must first build capacity, define its strategic intent, and then start pursuing its goals with proven commitment.

In developing economies, there is keen competition in the banking industry. In Nigeria, the banks that survived the distress crisis of the mid to late 1990s, on the one hand, learnt their lessons in a hard way and are determined to forge ahead. The public, on the other, are yet to fully restore confidence in the banking system. With dwindling, cautious patronage, and thinning down margins, banks are more than ever before challenged by fierce competition that may nail the coffin of the weak ones. The business acumen of banks managements come in handy to ensure survival. Playing the hopeless challenger for too long can barely guarantee modest operations that will not impress the board and shareholders of the banks. It is expected that banks managements must incorporate these realities into the framework of its regular business objectives. Doing so, it becomes set to tackle the more intricate contemporary challenges of competitive banking.

The foregoing discussion is intended to provide a cursory overview of the setting for interactions that go on in the workplace that can make or mar a banking organization. Underlying the interactions are goal-directed actions by organization and members designed to achieve objectives. In the process, conflicts may occur and weaken the effectiveness of the organization while the members are frustrated and alienated as a result. In all this, the integrity of bank members remains a major determinant of success level to be attained at any one time.

CASE STUDY 14.1 The Game of Politics—Lessons of Politicking and Intrigues in Bank Workplaces

It was not only in academics that Johnny excelled as a student. He also made his mark in select extracurricular activities (Extracted, with minor changes, from Onyiriuba, 2013. The use of Nigeria as the setting for this tale is for illustration purposes only, in order to demonstrate how the tale plays itself out in bank risk management in developing economies. The names of persons in the tale are imaginary and do not relate to any known or unknown real persons anywhere in the world). His purpose was to develop managerial and leadership competences that would be an asset in his future endeavors in industry or elsewhere. Soon he realized that he was inadvertently beating a path to campus politics. It would seem odd that he dabbled in politics given his primary objective of making first class honors. Not a few of his friends and course mates believed that politicking would be antithetical to that goal. Sam was particularly critical of his interest in politics.

"It might seem logical to want to discredit politics, but we'll be making a mistake to do so. The reason is simple. Politics is endemic to human nature. It is a necessary evil with which we have to live. Man is said to be a political animal. The view that politics is all about 'who gets what, when, and how' tends to justify this statement," he had argued in support of his interest in campus politics in one of his discussions with Sam.

But Sam countered him.

"Why then do we hear people criticize politics and politicians as though they are evil? Sometimes we hear remarks such as "politics is a dirty game," the "murky waters of politics," or politics is "a game of winner takes all." These comments apparently tell of something hostile or pejorative about politics which majority of the people detest. The evil implied in such comments resonate in the most favorite way politicians themselves describe the essence in politics. They take an interest in the view that "in politics, there is no permanent enemy or permanent friend, but only permanent interest" and so on."

Of course Johnny knew that in terms of real politicking within a country, and in political parlance, the permanent interest would be to win election, and wield and control power. In international politics and diplomacy, the permanent interest would often be dictated by a common cause to which nations were committed.

"Perhaps what makes politics "a dirty game," to thrive in "murky waters," or a game in which the "winner takes all," is the attitude that politicians bring to it in pursuit of the "permanent interest"…" Johnny argued.

Sam shared his view.

"What would you expect," he asked, "when politicians strive to 'win elections at all cost,' or see a political cause as a 'do or die affair'? When they do so, they inadvertently fan public resentment." He sounded practical as though he had direct practical experience of national politics.

"I totally agree with you on this point," Johnny admitted. "It's also insulting to the intelligence of the people, the electorate, when politicians take on a Machiavellian toga in pursuit of elusive, repugnant, or selfish 'permanent interest.' Indeed, the cost of seeing politics as 'a do or die affair' in pursuit of so-called 'permanent interest' is unbearable and at best abhorrent," he argued.

Sam then tried to elucidate the cause of his hatred for politics.

"In many countries, especially in the less developed world," he noted, "a lot of human lives are wasted as a result of political killings. Besides assassinations, thuggery and harassment of perceived political opponents are common sights."

Again, Johnny agreed with him.

"While bloodletting taints politicians," he argued, "large-scale corrupt practices which have become a way of life in politics in some countries perhaps sheds the worst light on criticized political activities," he contended.

"While I admit that all these negative attributes truly characterize politics to a large extent," Johnny yielded, "yet I don't think that politics is altogether evil," he insisted.

"Without politics, administering the society—nay, nations would be a more arduous task. Politics streamlines activities in governance, making it possible for the leaders of countries to deal with organized people rather than a rabble," Johnny argued more forcefully.

Sam saw reason with him on that point and promptly acknowledged the value of politics at that.

"Although some of us might hate politics," he averred, "nonetheless, everyone seems to acknowledge the sense in 'government of the people, by the people, and for the people."

Johnny was excited when he cited that omnipotent definition of democracy and reacted accordingly.

"You've got it right," he shouted—in a way that showed that he had been vindicated.

"This age old democratic heritage from the Greeks remains the superstructure and hallmark of politics. I treasure it. We should all treasure it. If we do, then we will want to appreciate the benefits of politics despite its shortcomings," he corroborated.

Johnny now elaborated on his convictions about the utility of politics.

"I strongly believe that a common denominator in what the frustrated masses of the people expect from politicians is a positive change of attitude and more commitment to fulfilling the common good. A change is particularly called for in the way politicians deal with the opposition, how they handle victory or defeat at elections. Above all, a majority of the electorate in every country will want to see a more transparent management of their common wealth, the state resources. I'm talking about changes that will enhance the common good of the people. If I read the minds of the masses correctly, then there is no need to take flight from politics," he opined.

Sam didn't quite see his arguments as realistic given the political experiences of most of the developing countries. But Johnny was determined to prove his point.

"Unfortunately," he argued, "many people have taken flight from politics, thus ostracizing themselves from genuine responsibilities which they should not abdicate. I am referring to the intellectuals and serious business executives who, like the frustrated masses, have given up on politics. Doing so, they have unwittingly shunned a calling in which the people sorely need them to drive and bring about positive socio-political and economic changes. Some of them who ventured into politics at all did so as a part time engagement," he regretted.

At that point, Johnny quoted a famous singer and actress—who aptly captured the essence in his contention when she said that politics was not a profession. She was justifying why she connected with shows even as she was serving a political office in her home State. She had made it clear to her interviewer that she only took a break from her career and profession—singing and acting.

"The popular entertainer's explanation should encourage the intellectuals and successful business executives and entrepreneurs to join and play active roles in politics," Johnny contended.

He had more words of advice for them.

"Don't be scared. Stick with the cause in which you and the people believe. Failing will not cost you an arm and a leg. At worst, you can return to your career, your real base," he counseled.

Exercise for class or group discussion

1. In what ways does this case study shed light on challenges of workplace politicking in banking?
2. Should banks managements condone—if detected—underlying work politics in actions of employees?
3. How may bank governance style aid and abate, or be propitious for, surreptitious workplace politicking?
4. What are the risk management implications of the engagement bank employees on office politics?
5. Do you think there are bank management lessons to learn from Johnny and Sam's perspectives on politics?

Tips for solving the exercise

Internal corporate politics harms employee industry and enterprise. Politicking in the banking workplaces is inimical to the cause of the business. It polarizes a bank—creating, in doing so, unnecessary camps. The result, in most cases, is corporate infighting. Suspicion of scheming against some interests within the bank becomes rife under the circumstances. In corporate circles, these acts are seen simply as an ill wind. Schemers within the system try to exploit the situation to the detriment of the bank. Curiously, bank directors and managements often spearhead intrigues underlying the surreptitious schemes. Usually, the resultant corporate divide set the tone for equally surreptitious reactions of the employees bank-wide. This is because employees, in general, look to bank managements for direction and, in most cases, get their cues accordingly. One action, to my mind, would solve the challenge of workplace politics for banks in developing economies. That action is to outlaw work politics in all its ramifications. Directors and employees who infringe the law should be fired if found guilty. Now the question is will the directors and bank managements—ostensibly at the center of the act—support its outlawing? They are likely to exempt themselves from the rule—thus, leaving sanctions applicable to only the employees. If this happens, the action will be ineffective. Members of boards and managements of banks in developing economies should be challenged to be bold and outlaw work politics. Doing so, they set their banks on the path of success with all bank members as the drivers.

TENDENCY TO PERSONAL GOVERNANCE IN BANKING

Personal governance has been an emerging trend in the running of banks in developing economies of late. This trend, also referred to as sole management or sole authority in some quarters, is common in domestic banks. Foreign subsidiary banks are largely order takers from their parent holding companies. Therefore, strictly speaking, their structures and mode of operation do not admit of personal governance. The holding companies make global policies and take key international management decisions. Their subsidiaries worldwide are bound by the policies and decisions. Thus foreign subsidiary banks stick to business and operational directives from their holding companies. The directives serve as guide and signpost for their activities in their host countries. The implication is that foreign subsidiary banks are not exposed to risk attendant on personal governance.

This is in sharp contrast to some domestic banks in which personal governance has been evident. It especially tends to be the order of the day in banks where chief executives hold controlling equity—usually through cronies, proxies, and suchlike. Thus, indirect shareholding is one of the means of instituting personal governance in the banking industry. Its true essence, though, is to foist some irrational governance on bank members. This implies that personal governors cannot but be discreet about their ascendancy and its arbitrary powers. In this way, they enforce selfish interests surreptitiously. Their hardly feasible but overriding intention is to have and exercise maximum authority without violating banking laws and rules. This feature—characteristic of the managements of some domestic banks—was evident in Nigeria prior to the 2005 banking system consolidation. It was a reflection of the heady atmosphere of the prebanking industry consolidation era. In some banks, managing directors arrogantly bestowed the positions of chairman and chief executive upon themselves. This enabled them to wield immense authority by which they called the shots at will, in any manner—and, often, to achieve their own ends.

Personal governance could be intoxicating. It really does and sometimes gets out of hand. This happens when the all-powerful chief executive gets carried away, infringes banking rules, and faces punitive regulatory sanctions. Depending on severity of personal governance offences, the harshest possible sanctions—such as firing and prosecution—may be meted out to the offender. Similar punishment may be imposed on their bank. The board of directors may be sacked and indicted directors prosecuted. In extreme cases, operating license of the bank may be withdrawn. Ultimately, bank members—the real stakeholders—bear the brunt of personal governance. Take the fate that befell the eight banks which the Central Bank of Nigeria indicted in 2009 as example (The boards of the indicted banks—Afribank, Bank PHB, Equitorial Trust Bank, First Inland Bank, Intercontinental Bank, Oceanic Bank, Spring Bank, and Union Bank—were sacked. Most of the directors were subsequently charged with crime and taken to court). The directors were charged with mismanagement of their banks' finances, appropriation of their banks' property, and violation of banking laws and rules—and taken to court accordingly. This is the dimension personal governance can take and become a trigger point for risk to banking in developing economies.

There should be a simple and pragmatic approach to dealing with personal governance in banking. I believe it does a lot of good to never wait until the damage has been done before seeking solution. Wielding the big stick—for all intents and purposes—can be counterproductive. It may act as a deterrent, though. It didn't work well in the Nigerian example. Some of the directors fought back, challenging charges against them in courts. The courts soon became saddled with suits and appeals. The process of bringing the accused directors to justice was equally fraught with frustration. Flawed legal system—given to adjourning cases—and resort to unfounded legal technicalities, in the main, cause the frustration. Now, nearly 7 years on, all but one of the cases is still pending in courts. Tendencies to personal governance, to my mind, should be nipped in the bud as a banking risk-mitigating measure. Banking regulation and laws must have teeth in the first place. Then banks should be supervised more seriously, and in the strictest sense and confidence, without compromises. This is necessary for mitigating risks of personal governance in banks in developing economies.

Dictatorial Chief Executives as Albatross for Banks

As in manufacturing or other industries in the real sector of the economy, bank directors play crucial roles in shaping the outlook for success. The board of directors performs specific unique functions—namely, policy formulation. But it also has oversight of executive management and plays a crucial role in organization development. These roles should ordinarily contribute to efficiency of bank lending. Shareholders rely on the ingenuity of the board for safety of their investment. With well-constituted boards, directors are easily the most influential members of a bank.

Unfortunately, this influence is often misused through the pursuit of selfish gains at the expense of the bank. It is instructive that in almost all the cases of bank failures of the 1990s in Nigeria, most of the bank directors were found culpable and liable to prosecution. Many of the directors infringed the credit process through insider abuse and were indicted for impropriety of conduct. Only very few maintained impeccable records of integrity and official conduct. Meanwhile, the board of directors has oversight of credit risk management. In this capacity—and through its audit and credit committee—it should forestall abuse of the credit process.

In broad terms, policy formulation is the primary objective of the board of directors. Critical issues requiring policy formulations in a bank include, but are not limited to, credit process, budget authorization, employment or key staff matters, and, general corporate governance. In some banks, the board gets involved in several less important functions otherwise meant for the management team. This has frequently arisen where the board perceives the potency of such trivial matters in precipitating crisis that could threaten the existence of the bank if mismanaged. Yet, board usurpation of direct management functions is merely a reflection of crisis of confidence that may be detrimental to the corporate objective of the bank.

In such banks, the board is often personified in the managing director who not only functions as the chief executive officer but, in some cases, the board chairperson. This situation has occasionally attracted criticisms from the regulatory authorities which, nevertheless, appear to be in abeyance as to evolving a means of dealing with negative roles of such dictatorial chief executives in banks. Organization development is perhaps the most tasking and dicey of all the objectives of bank directors and management. It involves anticipation of future challenges that impel change and the design of appropriate prognosis. A bank has to move along with changing times—increasing customer sophistication, for instance. In the process, old or current objectives and strategies are rendered ineffectual and moribund. The urge and need to evolve new attainable and visionary objectives become accentuated. The manner and precision with which this challenge is handled determines how well the task of organization development is accomplished.

In banking, the task of organizational development becomes more arduous given the rapidity of changes in the key variables that determine market patronage and loyalty in recent times. The observed changes occurred mostly in such areas as communication, data processing, information technology, and relationship management. It is the responsibility of the board and management to continuously scan the environment and harness available resources towards meeting the challenges and demands of the future business of the bank. On lending matters, success in fulfilling this role is necessary in managing the lending function well.

CONSOLIDATING RISK CONTROL RESOURCES FOR BANK GOVERNANCE

Of all the important resources of an organization, management is perhaps the most crucial for success. Frequently, organization's success or failure is associated with the quality of its managers. In banking, strictly speaking, managers' roles are not only important but also precarious. Yet, they are accountable to the board of directors for efficiency and profitability of operations. The critical issue is not necessarily attaining these ends. The means—coping with all sorts of conflicts—has been the salient consideration in assessing the effectiveness of bank managements. For most bank managers, time is about the scarcest success factor—a fact that many agree is a characteristic feature in the nature of managing in every industry.

In banking, where most managers frequently come into direct contact with other people's money, corporate governance assumes a riskier dimension. Besides the usual attributes required for a manager's success, bank managements must display a very high level of integrity, probity, and ingenuity. They should, above all else, be people bank members and customers can work with in confidence. Thus, trustworthiness and confidentiality are the hallmarks of managing in banking. Unpredictable and fickle individuals hardly make good bank managers. These attributes don't fit with the need to win and retain the confidence of customers. Besides, a bank, like many other high-risk businesses, requires good management to succeed. The alternative—poor management—is perhaps the surest way to bank failure. However, the variables that constitute good management may not be easily identified and generalized for all banks in all situations.

Bank management would be considered bad or poor if it fails to scan its environment to determine and respond to contingencies that impart instability to the bank's operations. In such a situation, a manager might erroneously adopt a wrong leadership style. The result, in most cases, is poor morale, unsustainable labor turnover, and sabotage. In extreme cases, the bank becomes insensitive to customers' needs and begins to lose market share, earnings, and profitability. The ineptitude of managers, especially those who flout bank policies and perpetrate insider abuse has been a major cause of bank distress and failure in some countries. With such managers, a bank will easily be afflicted with boardroom squabbles, frauds, and forgeries—the more serious of which frequently threaten and sometimes destroy the business foundation. Where management is adjudged inefficient, the bank rates low on risk assets quality, cost control, and earnings capacity. Banks that are poorly managed tend to experience occasional liquidity problems because of mismatch of assets and liabilities. Poor management in this context is seen in the financing of speculative transactions, high risk taking appetite, and disregard for credit policy and controls.

Foreign subsidiary banks—unlike their domestic bank counterparts—are not influenced by local culture. The former are guided by international best practice in defining and adopting a clear and unambiguous executive succession plan. The plan is strictly enforced and followed—usually under the auspices of their parent holding banks. There are three possibilities about this best practice in the management of domestic banks. It is most likely to be lacking in the first place. In some cases, it would be rather far-fetched. Often domestic banks boards and managements pay a lip service to it, if anything. Each of these possibilities exacerbates the risk of domestic banks and, by implication, threatens their safety potentialities. This fate is the lot of domestic banks in developing economies around the world.

The Central Bank of Nigeria (CBN) has largely addressed this problem for the domestic banks. The CBN now verifies credentials and approves appointments of banks' directors, management teams, and senior officers. This is intended to certify the suitability of persons appointed to those positions. Unlike before when an all-powerful CEO could be in office forever, the CBN has made it mandatory that banks' CEOs should serve not more than two-term employment contract, with maximum 5-year tenure each. Similarly, the CBN disallowed CEOs who doubled as chairpersons of banks. However, retired CEOs may come back as chairmen of boards of directors after a period of not less than 10 years from the time of leaving office.

BANK MEMBERS, GOVERNANCE, AND STAKES IN BANKING

Bank members comprise shareholders, employees, board, and management. With stake in equity stock, the share subscribers bear the ultimate risk of investment. Risk drives expectations on returns and sometimes reflects in investors' anxiety and urgency for payback. Yet, risk is scarcely allayed through the achievement of expected payback period. The most critical issue remains the maintenance of profitable operations and growth at an optimum level. While early investment payback may be presumed, sustaining earnings at the desired level has been elusive for most banks in developing economies. This curious fact of investment in banking becomes even more worrying with the failure of some banks after an initial period of impressive performance. In Nigeria, between 1990 and 1997, most of the failed banks became distressed within the first 3 years of operation, thus certifying banking as a highly volatile business. It would be only through sustained earnings growth and profitability that a bank could remain a strongly going concern, unimpaired by liquidity crisis and distress. There may not be a good alternative to an efficiently and profitably run bank.

During the Nigerian bank failures of the late 1990s, most bank directors were tried, convicted, and jailed for various crimes contributory to distress or failure. Such is the reality of banking that underscores the risk of shareholders' investments. In some banks, board of directors was constituted from major shareholders, ostensibly based on an assumption that unity of ownership and control would ensure success. Unfortunately, this unexpectedly produced opposite results. The nominal board members are at best ineffectual. Indeed, in banks with predominantly owner-directors board, the nominal directors merely serve to satisfy regulatory requirement. Yet, the board must have discernible, if not clearly stated, objectives. However, compared to those in which ownership is separated from management, banks with stakeholders in board and management succeed better.

The pressure for bank success, or punishment for failure, trickles down the membership hierarchy to the rank and file of employees. The board tasks the management team for performance while the latter hopes to achieve results through subordinates. However, while the bank's objectives are being pursued, the personal objectives of its members have to be understood, put into perspective, and well managed. Otherwise, conflicts of interest may arise, with potential to trigger internal crisis. What are these personal objectives of bank members? How and why are they formed and advanced?

Shareholders' Expectations

Like stakeholders in other organizations, bank owners are concerned primarily with success of their investment. This ultimately translates into expectation of good returns on investment. In specific terms, stockholders are interested in the following performance and wealth indices.

Earnings

In general, earnings are an assurance of market acceptance of a bank and loyalty to its products and services. Earnings grow through increasing and sustained market patronage or broadening the base of operations, both of which approximate to the success objective of owners.

Capital Gains

A reflection of positive market perception of the overall performance of a bank (in the case of banks quoted on the stock exchange). For unquoted stocks, capital gain also reflects investors' estimation of the actual worth of their investment based on reported or observed good performance of the bank. Such gains compensate the stakeholders for the risk of their investment.

Dividend

Dividend is arguably the primary cause of investors' risk taking in equity investment. Shareholders expect a liberal dividend policy—one that guarantees optimum mix of earnings payout and retention. Thus, while investors' expectation for dividend is being satisfied, strengthening of the capital base through earnings retention should not be sacrificed.

Net Worth

The level of net worth indicates the owners' commitment to the success of a bank. Net worth, or shareholders' fund, may be increased through one, a combination, or all of the following: earnings retention policy to create a large pool of reserved capital; recognition of revaluation surplus determined as the appreciation in value of specific fixed assets; and recapitalization of the equity base through creation of new stocks or rights issue to existing shareholders.

Bank Employees

The role of bank employees consists in functioning as a committed workforce. In this capacity, managers rely on them in getting things done. Perhaps, the best way to appreciate the importance of subordinate employees is to imagine an organization that employs only persons who will plan, organize, motivate, and control resources in a road construction business—and, of course, this category of employees may not be more than 15 in number. Such an organization will have managers but the job will not be done. This is also true for the banking business—the cashiers, lawyers, secretaries, and so on—all are important members of the organization, as well as the managers.

RISK-BASED APPROACH TO MOTIVATING BANK WORKFORCE

Motivation plays a crucial role in shaping worker behavior. It has the ability to initiate goal-directed behavior. The primary function of motivation is to initiate a person's particular behavior, invigorating, and directing it toward the attainment of a goal. Once the goal-directed behavior is achieved, the motivator becomes extinct. It also implies the series of subjective feelings and dispositions that the individual adopts during the motivational process.

Worker behavior is often explained in terms of their motives. A need must be adequately aroused and directed at a particular goal before it can achieve the status of a motivator and hence influence worker behavior. Generally, motives could arise because of either biogenic or psychogenic circumstances of the individual. Hunger and thirst, for instance, are known biological states that can arouse a behavioral pattern—sometimes restlessness. On the other hand, psychogenic motives aim to gratify psychological needs, such as affiliation, achievement, and self-actualization. In reality, individual needs are innumerable and have different capacities for as motivators.

Workers may be motivated differently in a given work situation. The overriding concern is how to understand, in practical terms, the forces within bank management's control to induce desired worker behavior. Banks that continuously achieve superior performance, in most cases, enjoy favorable market conditions. However, the workforce strives to meet market expectations. How can the manager boost and sustain worker morale to ensure that market opportunities are not lost to competition because of indolence of the workforce? This question is at the base of the crux of motivation studies in management theory and practice.

Bank managements may offer rewards (positive motivation) or, use or threaten punishment (negative motivation) to achieve increased productivity from human resources. The former could be termed "anxiety-reducing," or the "carrot approach" to motivation, while the latter represents the "stick approach." The two motivational schemes find uses or applications in banking. However, they are likely to achieve varying effectiveness in different banks—and this is true even for individuals within the same bank. However, they have proven effective in mitigating bank risks in developing economies.

Many people—those outside the banking industry—tend to take motivation of bank employees as a given. After all, bankers—as they are fondly called or appear to want to be known—have a choice career, are well remunerated, and are generally respected for their calling. Yet, motivation remains as much a nightmare in banking as it is in other industries. This may sound surprising to people outside the banking industry, but it is and will ever remain true.

BANK MANAGEMENTS AS RISK-BEARING CORPORATE LEADERS

The early thinking was that leaders were born, not made. Thus, the traits of a leader were seen to be innate. In addition, some have argued that leadership is characterized by some psychological traits—a leader could be introverted or extroverted, optimistic or pessimistic, benevolent or malevolent, and so on. Yet later studies of leaders concluded that a leader could be autocratic, democratic, or laissez-faire in orientation, outlook, and practice. Indeed, management literature is replete with useful theories of leadership. The terms "manager" and "leader" ideally connote different meanings (Hicks and Gullet, 1981). This distinction may be necessary, but I interchanged them in this chapter. The popular view is that leadership is a function of situational variables with which the leader must contend. Two of the most widely accepted leadership models in the mold of this thinking—propounded by Tannenbaum and Schmidt (1958) and Fiedler (1967)—emphasize contingency and situational approaches to choosing leadership styles. The "Life Cycle" and "Path Goal" theories of leadership are also situational or contingency based. (see, for "Life Cycle Theory", Hersey and Blanchard, 1977, House and Mitchell, 1975). The main thrust of these theories is that it is necessary—in choosing an optimum leadership style—to analyze the variables in the leader's situation (For an excellent review of the theories of leadership, see Hicks and Gullet, op. cit., pp. 477–497.).

Managerial leadership in banking should be driven by results orientation—a sort of "focus" by which bank managements must seek to achieve congruence or harmony between the goals of the bank, theirs and those of their subordinates. Underlying this viewpoint is the imperative of managerial and organizational performance. In this sense, performance implies meeting work duties or responsibilities of the employees, on the one hand, and attaining budgeted earnings, growth or returns—as well as satisfaction of unfulfilled target market needs—on the other. Bank managements tend to attain these lofty goals when they assume risk-bearing posture for their actions. That compels them to be more careful in leading the workforce. It also fits well with so-called leading by example. Unfortunately, this is nowadays a scarce attribute of bank managements in developing economies. There is always something in the conduct of bank managements that discourages leading by example.

It would be interesting—given foregoing meanings and implications—to know why most managers and, by extension, their banks often fail to perform. For such managers and banks, good financial performance remains a hard business objective. This is especially the lot of domestic banks in developing economies. The excuses of difficult targets, intensive competition, or inadequate resources frequently brandished, as reasons for failure, appear fallible. The real problem, perhaps, lies in lack of effective management of available human and material resources for work. Some believe that the answer lies in being focused and committed to personal, as well as bank's objectives. The notion of financial performance, seen in superior operating results, is perhaps best appreciated in understanding that it ultimately benefits all the stakeholders of a bank, including customers for their loyalty and continuous patronage.

RISK CONTROL LESSONS OF SITUATION-BASED LEADERSHIP FOR BANK MANAGEMENTS

Management literature credits Tannenbaum and Schmidt (1958) with situational theory of leadership. The duo posited that different leadership styles exist within a continuum delineated by two extreme cases of boss–centered and subordinate-centered. The former denotes autocratic leadership, while the latter reflects a laissez-faire style. Although several options for leadership styles exist within the continuum, the most prominent—besides the two extremes—appears to be the democratic or participative leadership style.

With democratic leadership style, the views of the manager and members are taken into account in decision-making. As a human relations approach, the manager seeks to integrate all members of the firm into the decision-making process. Since their wishes and suggestions are considered, members show support for, and commitment to, the final decision. This tends to boost morale and the quality of decisions. However, this approach may slow down decision making and lead to buck passing due to possible compromises in carrying everyone along (Hicks and Gullet, 1981). The autocratic manager practically wields all authority and enforces decisions by dispensing rewards and punishments. The flow of communication tends to be one-way bound, from the manager to the subordinates who must conform or obey as may be required. There is no room for consultation or dialogue with subordinates before decisions are made or enforced. While this style of managing may have the advantage of speed in decision-making, it is fraught with possible subordinate resentment. The manager may decide to devolve most of the decision-making tasks to the group members. This laissez-faire approach favors setting goals and mostly allowing members to decide how best to achieve the goals. Chances that group members would probably find it difficult to reach consensus on critical decision tasks limits its effectiveness.

There are, between the two extremes—democratic and autocratic—several possible combinations of leadership styles from which the manager can choose. The model emphasizes the need to analyze forces within the leader, forces in the followers, and forces in the situation as a means of choosing an effective leadership style.

Forces in the Leader

This depicts the psychological dispositions of the manager—motivation, attitudes, and perception of job roles—expressed in value system, which in turn is influenced by training and experience. Whether autocratic or other leadership style is chosen depends on feelings about competence of subordinates, demands or nature of the tasks, and situation of the firm. For example, if employees are indolent, or the task is complex and environment uncertain, the autocratic style might be appropriate.

Forces in the Subordinates

The manager should understand and appreciate the interplay between employees' needs and organizational objectives in determining work performance. Some of the common personal goals of employees that influence their work behavior include self-development, job security, good reward system, career growth, training, and job experience. The manager will be effective in this case if they recognize these needs while structuring their own managerial behavior.

Forces in the Situation

The characteristics of the work situation faced by the manager also exert influence on their choice of leadership style. Particular situational variables favoring effective employee performance in one organization may not achieve the same result in another. For instance, participative management may not be easy in a big organization, with large interdependent work groups.

RISK CONTROL LESSONS OF CONTINGENCY-BASED LEADERSHIP FOR BANK MANAGEMENTS

In 1967, Fiedler—the proponent of contingency theory of leadership—isolated three variables that influence leadership effectiveness. These situational characteristics, according to him, are leader–member relations—the extent to which the manager likes and is liked by subordinates or organization members; task structure—whether the task and its processes are well structured and understood by the group members; and leader-position power—the extent to which the manager is empowered through formal authority to do their work.

There are eight different possible combinations of the variables which influence choice of leadership style. The deduction is that the work situation could be highly favorable or unfavorable to the manager. Favorable condition exists where the manager is influential (strong leader-position power), enjoys good working relationships with subordinates (good leader–member relations), and the task is highly structured (task structure). At the other extreme, where these situational characteristics are lacking, work condition becomes unfavorable for the manager. Correlating leadership styles with group performance, Fiedler suggested the most effective or useful leadership approach in a given situation.

From the summary of his findings, either of two types of leadership styles could be adopted; the manager could apply the task-oriented or relationship-oriented leadership. The task-oriented style, for instance, requires good leader–member relations, structured task, and a strong leader-position power. It will also be successful if the opposite extremes exist. This implies that task-oriented leadership is appropriate where the work situation is either relatively favorable or relatively unfavorable. Where the work situation is moderately favorable, the relationship-oriented style appears to be more effective. An example of this case is where leader–member relations might be good, but the task is unstructured, while leader-position power is weak.

SUMMARY

Personal governance—also referred to as sole management or sole authority—has been an emerging trend in the running of banks in developing economies of late. This trend is common in domestic banks. Foreign subsidiary banks are largely order takers from their parent holding companies. Their structures and mode of operation, strictly speaking, do not admit of personal governance. This is in sharp contrast to some domestic banks in chief executives hold controlling equity—usually through cronies and proxies. Its true essence, though, is to foist some irrational governance on bank members. There should be a simple and pragmatic approach to dealing with personal governance in banking. Tendencies to personal governance should be nipped in the bud as a risk-mitigating measure.

Bank management would be considered bad or poor if it fails to scan its environment to determine and respond to contingencies that impart instability to the bank's operations. In such a situation, a manager might erroneously adopt a wrong leadership style. The result, in most cases, is poor morale, unsustainable labor turnover, and sabotage. In extreme cases, the bank becomes insensitive to customers' needs and begins to lose market share, earnings, and profitability. Where management is adjudged inefficient, the bank rates low on risk assets quality, cost control, and earnings capacity. Banks that are poorly managed tend to experience occasional liquidity problems because of mismatch of assets and liabilities.

Workers may be motivated differently in a given work situation. The overriding concern is how to understand, in practical terms, the forces within bank management's control to induce desired worker behavior. Bank managements may offer rewards (positive motivation) or, use or threaten punishment (negative motivation) to achieve increased productivity from human resources. The former could be termed "anxiety-reducing," or the "carrot approach" to motivation, while the latter represents the "stick approach." The two motivational schemes find uses or applications in banking. However, the belief is that leadership is a function of situational variables with which the leader must contend.

Foreign subsidiary banks—unlike their domestic bank counterparts—are not influenced by local culture. They are guided by international best practice in defining and adopting a clear and unambiguous executive succession plan. The plan is strictly enforced and followed—usually under the auspices of their parent holding banks. There are three possibilities about this best practice in the management of domestic banks. It is most likely to be lacking in the first place. In some cases, it would be rather far-fetched. Often domestic banks boards and managements pay a lip service to it, if anything. Each of these possibilities exacerbates the risk of domestic banks and, by implication, threatens their safety potentialities.

QUESTIONS FOR DISCUSSION AND REVIEW

1. Why would it appear that corporate governance best practice is not recognized and institutionalized in banks in developing economies?
2. What are the setbacks and conditions for adoption of corporate governance best practice in banks in developing economies?
3. Does sole authority management in banking underlie bank governance pitfalls, failings, and risks in developing economies?
4. In what ways do leadership styles of bank managements depart from the demands of corporate governance best practice?
5. How would Fiedler's (1967) contingency theory of leadership help bank managements in developing economies?
6. What are the main lessons of Tannenbaum and Schmidt's (1958) situational theory of leadership for bank managements?

REFERENCES

Fiedler, F.E., 1967. A Theory of Leadership Effectiveness, first ed. McGraw Hill Book Company, Inc, New York.
Hersey, P., Blanchard, K.H., 1977. Management of Organizational Behavior, third ed. Prentice Hall, Englewood Cliffs, N.J.
House, R.J., Mitchell, T.R., 1975. Path goal theory of leadership. In: Richard, M.S., Lyman, W.P. (Eds.), Motivation and Work Behavior. McGraw Hill, New York.
Hicks, H.G., Gullet, R.C., 1981. Management, fourth ed. McGraw Hill Book Company, Inc, New York.
Onyiriuba, L., 2013. On the Road to Self–actualization. NFS Data Bureau Limited, Lagos, pp. 230-232.
Tannenbaum, R., Schmidt, W., 1958. How to Choose a Leadership Pattern. Harvard Business Review 36 (2), 95–101.

FURTHER READING

Steers, R.M., Porter, L.W., 1975. Motivation and Work Behavior. McGraw Hill Book Company, Inc, New York.

Part III

Reinventing Risk Management

Section A

Credit Risk

Chapter 15

Bank Credit Risk Issues and Management Requirements in Developing Economies

Chapter Outline

LEARNING FOCUS AND OUTCOMES

Credit risk-taking in banking has become a controversial issue nowadays. Many think that its conduct nowadays leaves a lot to be desired. The linking of recurring banking crisis around the world to probable failings in credit risk management has not helped matters. The situation has provoked concerns that inform the enactments of Basel I and Basel II Accords. Unfortunately, banks in developing countries lack in-house technical competencies to implement aspects of the Accords. Thus, I set out writing this chapter in order to:

- review the current state of banks' lending and credit risk crisis in developing economies;

- analyze and situate the credit risk crisis and peculiarities of banking in developing economies;
- identify and investigate the critical culprits for bank credit risk crisis in developing economies;
- relate the credit risk crisis in banking to the basis of bank capitalization requirements in developing economies;
- evaluate ways in which the Basel Accords are useful in the management of the credit risk of banks in developing economies; and
- examine the bank credit risk management issues in developing countries that the Basel Accords address.

EXPECTED LEARNING OUTCOMES

Banking is becoming increasingly bedeviled by credit risk. It would appear that the problem defies solution. In reality, the banking regulatory authorities are making steady progress toward solution. The Basel Accords are a typical instrument of the process of solution. Ironically, some actions of banks managements are not propitious for institutionalizing a credit risk culture that fits well with best practice. The reader will—after studying this chapter and doing the exercises in it—have learnt and been better informed about:

- the evolving state of banks' lending, credit risk crisis, and management requirements in developing economies;
- nature and demands of the credit risk peculiarities of banking in developing economies;
- the four leading culprits for bank credit risk crisis and how to tame them in developing economies;
- how credit risk crisis in banking bears on bank capitalization requirements in developing economies;
- ways in which the Basel Accords are useful in the management of the credit risk of banks in developing economies;
- implications of the Basel Capital Accord for bank credit risk perspective in developing economies;
- bank credit risk management issues in developing countries that the Basel Accords address; and
- the implications of the risk-weighting system of the Basel Accord for banking in developing economies.

OVERVIEW OF THE SUBJECT MATTER

The credit risk crisis in global banks has continued to attract attention in international financial circles. The thinking is that banks should devise effective methodologies for risk management if they are to survive the scourge of the credit risk crisis. The Basel Committee has been at the forefront of international efforts to tame the crisis. Its Basel I and Basel II Accords are classic cases in point. Unfortunately, banks in developing countries are finding it difficult to fully implement the Accords. Unlike their counterparts in developed countries that have adopted the Accords, banks in developing economies simply cherry-pick and implement only some aspects of the Accords—especially those that meet their immediate needs.

The body of Basel I, otherwise referred to as the Basel Capital Accord, comprised three main sections—the constituents of capital, the risk-weighting system, and a target standard ratio. The Accord identified two tiers of capital that constitute the total capital base of a bank (i.e., the constituents of capital). While tier 1 capital denotes a bank's core capital (i.e., its equity capital and disclosed reserves), tier 2 capital connotes noncore capital items (referred to in Basel I as "supplementary capital"). In isolating the two tiers of capital, the Accord clarified aspects of their components and qualifying attributes.

On the risk weighting of assets, Basel I assessed capital adequacy in the context of the credit risk that a bank assumes. It proffered a logical approach to assessing capital adequacy based on the relationship of capital to risk-weighted assets and off-balance sheet exposures. Thus, the Accord recommended a "weighted risk ratio" as a measure of capital adequacy. This ratio weights and relates the riskiness of a bank's assets and off-balance sheet exposures to its capital.

Each asset and off-balance sheet exposure was assigned a risk weight reflecting the perception and assessment of its riskiness. The risk weights ranged from 0% to 100%. Assets risk-weighted at 0% tend to be the riskless, risk-free, and safest investments on the balance sheet of a bank. Such assets include T-bills and sovereign (government) bonds. On the contrary, assets risk-weighted at 100% (usually unsecured credit facilities) are considered riskiest.

The resultant risk ratio can then be used to assess capital adequacy. The structure comprises a framework of five risk weights, each of which can be assigned to particular categories of risk. Basel I offered broad definitions of risk categories to which specific risk weights applied. The weights reflected the riskiness of assets and off-balance sheet exposures of a bank. Thus, assets were assigned risk weights that showed that they were riskless or risk-free, low-risk, or highly risky.

In the third section, Basel I set a target standard risk ratio of 8% that every internationally active bank should satisfy. This ratio relates a bank's capital to its weighted risk assets. It implies that a bank's tier 1 and tier 2 capital should cover at least 8% of its risk-weighted assets. Of the 8% risk ratio, the Accord recommended that at least 4% must be covered by tier 1 capital. It is believed that the risk ratio mitigates credit risk and assures the safety of funds in deposit-insured global banks.

THE STATE OF BANKS LENDING AND CREDIT RISK CRISIS IN DEVELOPING ECONOMIES

The financial crisis of 2007–09—more commonly referred to as the global financial meltdown—shook the foundations of financial centers around the world. But it originated in failings in credit risk management. While the crisis ravaged the global economy, its key lesson was a pointer to the weakness of risk management in global banks in developing economies. It proved that the banks needed to sharpen their risk management techniques in forthcoming years. Above all, it challenged banking practitioners and regulators to brace themselves for the daunting task of continually keeping an eye on risk—holding it in check. Even as they do so, it is nonetheless difficult to completely keep risk at bay.

The reality is that banking can never be devoid of risk. Bankers must be conscious of this fact and carefully formulate their risk acceptance criteria accordingly. The era of deliberately chasing transactions with so-called bankable risks is over. Inadvertently, that risk-taking disposition elevated moneymaking lending to the top of management priorities at the expense of building quality assets. But it turned out to be an error of judgment, and banks in developing economies paid dearly for it. Growing portfolios of nonperforming assets plunged many banks into liquidity crisis and distress. Some banks—those that could not withstand the pressure—even failed. Thus, the way banks in developing economies manage risk determines whether they will succeed or fail in the long run.

A bank that seeks to manage risk well—and therefore hopes to succeed in the long run—should strike a balance between its appetite for risk and the earnings goal it is pursuing. While the bank should not be risk averse, it shouldn't adopt a risk preference disposition, either. This point becomes more meaningful in appreciating the inverse relationship between risk and return. There is always a trade-off between these two possible business outcomes: a higher risk tends to result in more profit and vice versa. In banking, strictly speaking, I extend this relationship to imply that the more a bank achieves and retains liquidity (less risk), the less it gains in profitability (less returns) and vice versa. A bank would strike the right balance and be likely to succeed in the long run when it takes moderate risk and tames its budget goals. The risk-return principle is instructive, and failing to observe it, or the inability to balance it, could be a recipe for financial disaster.

The World Bank (2013) states the foregoing point more succinctly. The Bank argues that "when risks are taken on voluntarily in pursuit of opportunity, another trade-off emerges: expected returns must be weighed against the potential losses of a course of action." This risk-taking behavior has a fundamental basis on which the Bank sheds light. The trade-off in risk-taking, according to the Bank, "is intensified when a higher return is possible only if more risk is accepted." This is not surprising as it "is often the case with financial investments, where a lower yield is characteristic of a more secure position and higher yields with riskier positions" (p. 10).

A bank takes credit risk when it grants a loan with the expectation that the borrower should utilize the loan according to agreed terms and conditions—and ultimately repay the loan on its due date. Usually, repayment of the loan is expected from some cash flow projection that may or may not be realized. Uncertainty of cash flows notwithstanding, the bank must pay back customers' deposits that fund its loan portfolio—on demand, at short notice, or on due dates. Risk, in this case, is the chance that borrowers may default whereas depositors must be paid their deposits on or before due dates. This situation often arises where assets and liabilities are mismatched, and as a result a bank may fund only some of its deposit maturities payments from loan repayments. But it happens more frequently when there is a deficiency in deposit inflows, an unsustainable default in loan repayment, or a situation where unusually large cash withdrawals exist or persist for a long time.

A bank should always be cautious about the risks it takes—it should anticipate, measure, and plan for them. Banking reforms in recent times in many developing economies were intended to tame the risk-taking appetite of banks and institutionalize a sound financial system. Unfortunately, uncertainty— another variable that also affects banking outcomes—is more intractable than risk. Unlike risk, there is no proven methodological framework that banks can use to identify, quantify, analyze, or mitigate uncertainty. For this reason, it is widely believed that uncertainty is a necessary evil, ostensibly defying solution.

Yet a bank has to deal with uncertainty and its adverse effects one way or the other. This is because uncertainty plays a decisive role in banking business and outcomes. The regulatory authorities require every bank to formulate, adopt, and implement specific contingency master plans to deal with uncertainties that affect the industry. It is understandable that regulators lay emphasis on contingency management. They do so to underscore the need for effective response to uncertainty, and to complement the survival strategies of banks.

BANK CREDIT RISK PECULIARITIES OF DEVELOPING ECONOMIES

Often the trend and process of the buildup of credit risk crisis differ from one bank to another. The underlying factor in the observed differences—one that determines the momentum of the crisis and its remedy—is usually the character of bank management. Is bank management disposed to build and sustain a quality lending portfolio? Does it pay lip service to oversight of lending? Will it want to commit itself to shunning reckless lending? These are some questions to ask in order to feel the force and effects of the criticized character of bank management in the making of credit risk crises in developing economies.

It is possible in some cases for bank management to detect, acknowledge, and strive to address the buildup of a credit risk crisis. In doing so, it can respond to the crisis with appropriate internal risk management contingency measures. Unfortunately, rarely does bank management in developing economies take the initiative and act in this manner. In most cases, credit risk crises in recent history have caught bank managements off guard, if anything. In Nigeria, for example, the situation worsened with the heady atmosphere of 1990s, which lingered into the 21st century, following the deregulation of banking business during the mid-1980s. Certainly, the architects of the government's economic reforms in 1980s would never have imagined that a liberalized banking industry would breed an intractable crisis—especially in the lending function.

Due to lack of diligence, bank management in several developing economies was oblivious to the buildup of crisis. This underscores the need for bank management to always stay on top of things. Often the road to credit risk crisis builds on breaches of internal credit policy over time. The process of remedying the crisis is always painfully harsh and usually demands some urgency. One of the painful measures that regulators enforce to arrest credit risk crisis is to compel bank management to clean up its act. Besides, the regulatory authorities could—and indeed do—fire bank managements, revoke banking licenses, and prosecute indicted bank officials. They perform these actions in the exercise of their oversight powers.

The rank-and-file employees of banks feel the pinch when they lose their jobs, their allowances are stopped, or their salaries are cut—in a desperate bid to regain liquidity and cash flows by banks in distress. Usually customers have had more than their fair share of fallout of credit risk crisis. Often this happened where the authorities forced banks to charge off terminally bad loans from their risk assets portfolios. In Nigeria, for example, those banks that survived the onslaught of regulatory intervention in 2009 to return sanity to the industry reported huge operating losses, or sharp reductions in earnings, that year. Some of the banks posted similar figures in 2010 and 2011 as well.

Now the question is what manner of factors would result in such a buildup to the observed crisis? It is on this question that I now focus—isolating the factors that underlie bank credit risk crisis in developing economies.

Overambitious Budget Goals

Many critics scorn reported earnings of banks in developing economies. They hold that the earnings are mere paper profits, ostensibly to underscore the inconsistency between earnings and the perennial liquidity pressure that characterizes the operations of the banks. How in the world, were the reported earnings to be real, would banks—in pursuit of liquidity—desperate about having customers beat a path to their door? In so doing, unfortunately, they unwittingly—presumably—expose their marketing officers to untold abuses. Inordinate pursuit of budget goals, implied in the foregoing, also has adverse side effects on the lending function. This is largely seen, for example, in reckless lending and excessive risk-taking to meet profit targets. But it is also a major factor in accounting for illegal lending and—to some extent—abuse of insider credit facilities.

The massive sacking, retrenching, and retiring of employees across banks in Nigeria between 2009 and 2012—the largest in recent history—betray the fact that reported earnings of the banks were unfounded, dubious, or highly suspect. In most cases such actions render the reported earnings hollow, if anything. But bank management remains adamant—committed to defending bogus financial performance and reports. It could do anything, under the circumstances, but relent in prodding credit and marketing staff into doing everything possible to meet earnings and deposit targets. At the root of this carefree banking attitude is the monster of overambitious budget goals.

Perhaps the wanton pursuit of budget goals by bank management to the detriment of quality assets reached its crescendo in 2009 as the global financial meltdown was underway.

Regular bank examination by officials of Central Bank of Nigeria and the NDIC showed that reported earnings of some banks could not be defended in terms of their asset size and quality. The situation prompted the CBN governor to issue a stern warning in 2009 to CEOs of banks. The governor had advised that it was better for banks to report losses than to cook the books and mislead the public. He warned that while it was not illegal to post real losses, it was a criminal offense to doctor the books in order to post unfounded earnings. Now bankers in Nigeria are left in no doubt about the determination of the CBN to criminalize falsification of financial reports.

Unfortunately, bank managements have reduced competition for market leadership to a bank's standing in terms of bogus earnings, balance sheet growth, and size. Scarcely do they pay equal attention to the quality of risk assets—the lending portfolio—and the earnings that those assets generate. Banks eagerly pursue the false driving forces behind rankings on financial performance. In doing so, they are often pressured to engage in unprofessional conduct. The ignominious act is usually observed in cases where books of accounts—financial statements and annual reports of banks—are just window dressing. It also obtains in situations where banks cook the books and compel their auditors to fall into line.

It remains incredible to the purists that Intercontinental Bank, Oceanic Bank, Bank PHB, Afribank, and Spring Bank—to mention but a few—were distressed even as they were reporting strong financial performance! That was before the CBN sacked the boards of the banks in 2009. Interim management boards, which the CBN constituted for the banks, supplanted the sacked boards. Ironically, the stocks of the banks were also doing well on the Nigerian Stock Exchange up to the time the CBN declared them terminally distressed.

The public had been led through this deceptive banking for too long before the CBN clamped down on erring bank management. In supporting the CBN's action, the purists posit that no amount of price paid to sanitize the banking industry should be considered too much—no matter whose ox is gored. Banks should learn to operate by the rules. In doing so, they should keep their craze for profit under control in submission to the professional conduct that their calling demands.

In pursuit of budget goals in the era of universal banking, for example, banks were a bit incautious in investing in their subsidiaries. They compromised on their lending principles. The case of pre-2009 Union Bank of Nigeria PLC which lent money to some of its subsidiaries to buy its shares so as to meet recapitalization requirements was both instructive and typical. This aberration in the credit process happened under different guises in other banks. How else can one explain why nationalized Afribank (Nigeria) PLC invested depositors' funds toward acquiring controlling equity interest in African Petroleum PLC?

Turbulent Times

Economic volatility impacts credit risk crises. Borrowers occasionally contend with harsh economic realities that weaken their cash flows and loan repayment ability. In time, the borrowers start to default on their loans. In most cases, the workings of economic cycles ensure that instability of business operations marks certain stages of those cycles. Thus, individuals and corporate borrowers are often exposed to recurrent upheavals that constrain their loan repayment abilities. This is particularly evident in developing economies.

The fate of borrowers in volatile business environments—mainly those in developing economies—informs the credit risk crises that might befall banks. In turbulent times, business transactions become unusually risky, while the bases of financial projections are flawed—rendering outlook for the future bleak. Even when loans are adequately secured with tangible collateral, it would be difficult to dispose of the underlying assets. In the case of unsecured loans, a hoped-for loan repayment or recovery hangs in the balance. This situation, one that bank managements in developing economies occasionally face, compounds the liquidity pressure inherent in the nature of the banking business.

In some cases, even so-called transaction-based credit facilities—the hallmark of which is their self-liquidating feature—may not be spared. One reason is that such credits thrive on robust transaction dynamics founded on predictable outcomes. Unfortunately, such outcomes are a far cry from what occurs in turbulent times. Another reason relates to the size of the portfolio of self-liquidating loans. In most cases, this category of loans accounts for a negligible proportion of a bank's lending portfolio. In fact, the bulk of a bank's lending portfolio carries varying levels of credit risk that are alien to the principle of self-liquidating loans. With the increasing sophistication of business activities as well as credit fraud, risk management in bank lending in developing economies will continue to take center stage for a long time. Poor management of credit risk portends dire consequences for a bank. It is now common knowledge that credit risk is linked with liquidity risk after all. The fact of this view is evident in recent cases of failed banks in Nigeria and elsewhere.

Banks typically faced turbulent times in the aftermath of the 2007–09 global financial meltdown. Many businesses went under. Even in leading advanced countries like the United States and United Kingdom, corporate survivors requested bailouts. The US government responded with a bailout for some companies in strategic industries—including banks. In the United Kingdom, the government also intervened with a financial bailout of key banks. The situation fanned out the credit risk crisis beyond the banks, as the meltdown rubbed off on borrowers in varying degrees. Incidentally, it is generally believed that reckless lending by banks in the United States triggered the global financial meltdown that threatened the foundation of financial markets across the globe.

The authorities and analysts pointed accusing fingers to unguarded transactions in financial derivatives. Derivatives—the conversion of credit facilities into financial instruments (i.e., paper assets) in which the public could and does invest—served short-term liquidity and balance sheet needs of banks. But the practice snowballed into crisis when the assets backing the instruments turned out to be suspect and of poor quality. This informed the credit risk crisis that the banks faced at the time. Regulators turned their attention more than ever before to derivatives and loan securitization in the aftermath of the financial meltdown. The problem at issue—how to tame the engineering of exotic financial products—has unusually taxed the ingenuity of regulators.

CULPRITS FOR BANK CREDIT RISK CRISIS IN DEVELOPING ECONOMIES

Light can be shed on four main factors—reckless lending, excessive risk-taking, credit fraud, and insider abuse—as culprits for bank credit risk crises in developing economies. In the following discussion, I highlight the features of these factors and how they constrain the effectiveness of bank management.

Reckless Bank Lending

On occasion reckless lending has plunged a bank into a credit risk crisis. In extreme situations, the crisis has overwhelmed bank management and incapacitated banking operations. One symptom of the crisis manifests itself in the form of liquidity pressure. Often poor-quality asset portfolios inform and exacerbate the crisis. Reckless lending is usually deliberate! It is perpetrated in the pursuit of some goal without bothering about the possible adverse consequences to the bank.

This is ironic—considering that the goal in question could be positive and meant to advance the cause of the bank. The puzzle of how an action taken in the interest of a bank could be adjudged to be inimical to the bank defines the irony. The flip side of reckless lending is that it may serve the personal or selfish interests of directors or other executives to the detriment of the bank. It is in this context that one may appreciate why the act of reckless lending persists.

Diligent and committed bank management will not want to indulge in reckless lending. This work behavior disposes it toward lending decisions that serve the interests of the bank. In time the bank would build a quality risk assets portfolio. On the other hand, self-serving bank management would rather institutionalize a culture of arbitrary lending. Doing so inadvertently compounds the crisis of credit risk.

Credit officers perpetrate reckless lending in various ways, but a few of these are especially instructive. A typical example is when a bank grants loans to its subsidiaries in pursuit of some nonbanking interests. In this case, lending officers would be compelled to compromise themselves and their principles. One reason is that such lending is usually packaged, offered, accepted, and disbursed in disregard of lending policy and the credit process. Another reason is that loans in this category are usually unsecured. Where there is collateral at all, it is often imaginary—just to make believe that the loan is secured and satisfies legal documentation. A third reason is that the bank, as a holding company to the borrower, is really indirectly the obligor for the loan.

In Nigeria, this implies that the bank lent money to itself in order to conduct a nonbanking transaction in contravention of Banks and Other Financial Institutions Act No. 25 of 1991 (as amended). Were bank examiners and regulators to uncover and confront lending officers about the credit, those officers would most likely claim that they were boxed in. But it would be extremely difficult for them to make such an excuse. So they must find an alternative explanation, one that absolves them of blame. Interestingly, bank management would want to lay the act at the door of the board of directors. Again, like the lending officers, it would not want to incur the wrath of the directors.

Experienced bank examiners and regulators would want to get to the root of the matter—and do so discreetly. Of course, they realize that they should do anything but trump up charges against bank management or the lending officers. Usually, as would be expected under the circumstances, horse-trading ensues from the conflicting needs of the regulators and bank. But there is always a uniting cause for bank management and lending officers. They would put up a common front—sinking their differences so as to explain and defend the lending transaction before the examiners and regulators.

Bank management, on one hand, may see criticized lending to its subsidiary simply as a sharp practice, but regulators would on the other hand regard it as a breach of professional duty. Where bank examiners have teeth, they will not bow to possible pressure from bank management. Ideally they should also not be cowed into compromising themselves. Based on the reports of examiners, regulators may impose a particular sanction on the erring bank. The sanction should be severe enough to serve as a deterrent to other banks in addition to the offender.

Excessive Risk-Taking in Bank Lending

Often in bank lending, recklessness is intricately mired in excessive risk-taking. These two criticized attributes of the contemporary lending function combine to render credit risk crisis in banks intractable. It would seem that excessive risk-taking is more problematic than reckless lending. But there shouldn't be a choice of one in preference to the other. In truth, the two negative lending attributes should be avoided like the plague. Doing otherwise would be tantamount to choosing between the devil and the deep blue sea.

Concentration of credit in particular sectors of the economy is one of the fallible lending practices in which excessive risk-taking manifests itself. Another criticized practice is deliberate disregard for the principle of single obligor limit. Disregard for single-obligor limit has been the bane of bank management of late. Several other flawed lending practices—besides credit concentration and flouting of single-obligor limit—accentuate the credit risk crisis for banks in developing economies.

Bank management often portrays credit concentration—especially in key industries such as the energy (oil and gas) sector—as strategic, but nothing could be further from the truth. A bank should strive to spread its credit exposure, with painstaking attention to risk mitigation. It can do so by planning its lending in a way that enables it to grant and secure risk-mitigated loans to borrowers in different target markets. The purpose of this credit risk management strategy is that a bank should be able to avoid portfolio concentration risk.

Three possible lending situations can give rise to concentration risk. A bank is exposed to concentration risk if it holds its risk assets portfolio in particular economic sectors, when a few large borrowers make up its loan portfolio, and when its risk assets portfolio comprises few types of credit facilities. The risk in question is the probability that the bank's operations might be impaired by a liquidity crunch or plunged into crisis. In the foregoing sense, concentration risk is completely antithetical to risk diversification. In bank lending, the latter is both the alternative and solution to the former—and always desirable. A bank will diversify its credit portfolio risk when it grants different types and amounts of loans to various borrowers in different target markets, industries, or economic sectors.

One gets the impression that bank management and lending officers often feel boxed in. Lending officers' tendency to justify excessive risk-taking on the grounds of this excuse has become commonplace. At face value, critics may feel that nothing could be further from the truth. But there is some truth in the excuse. I think that such a complaint should be judged on its merits. Of course we can't just wish away the undue interference of vested interests in the credit process.

I don't think that a situation where bank management or lending officers feel or actually are boxed in will ever do any good. The regulatory authorities should devise a means to check for incapacitation of the credit process in this or other ways. It is no good hoping to achieve a sound banking system in the midst of frustration with banking regulation. My take on this issue is rather simple and straightforward. Banking regulators in developing economies should empower bank management and lending officers to boldly tell vested interests that their hands are tied. And bank management and lending officers should do so rather than complain that they feel boxed in.

This might sound a bit difficult considering that the vested interests usually hold most of the aces in influencing lending decisions that border on excessive risk-taking. In most cases, they are employers of bank management—and, of course, the lending officers. I think that legal protection for victimized members of bank management and lending officers will go a long way toward checking the influence of the vested interests in the credit process.

Taking Nigeria as an example, there is a further cause for optimism. Some of the recent banking reforms in the country will hopefully address the problem of vested interests in bank lending. The notable reforms include the following:

- Increased capitalization requirement.
- This policy forced all but the foreign banks in Nigeria to go public. The weak banks were acquired while others either merged or went solo to meet the required capitalization. In order to go public, the indigenous banks sought and obtained quotation on the Nigerian Stock Exchange.
- Tenure of office for bank CEOs.
- Fixing the tenure of office for chief executive officers of banks to a maximum term of 10 years will help to check overbearing CEOs who see the office they occupy as their birthright—perhaps because of their majority shareholdings in the banks, either directly or through cronies.
- Constitution of the boards of banks.
- The proposal to professionalize the constitution of boards of directors of banks in Nigeria is a welcome development. In line with this proposal, board members should not necessarily be major shareholders or their nominees. On the contrary, they should be individuals with professional banking backgrounds.
- Prosecution of indicted bank executives.
- The indictment and prosecution of executives of seven banks, to all intents and purposes, is serving as a deterrent to current and future members of bank management (The banks were Afribank, Bank PHB, FinBank, Intercontinental, Oceanic Bank, Spring Bank and Union Bank).

With committed implementation of the foregoing reforms, the public has at last started to see the light at the end of the tunnel.

Illegal Lending and Credit Fraud

There are basically two aspects to the question of illegal lending and credit fraud. The first relates to the manner in which lending officers package, propose, and endorse otherwise weak credit proposals for approval. The second concerns bank management that willfully creates fictitious assets in the bank's loan book in order to satisfy some regulatory or other internal purpose. The second aspect presents a more difficult problem of analysis by reason of its criminalization in the banking laws. It is largely for this reason that efforts by the regulatory authorities to detect it often fall through. Usually bank management perpetrates the fraud surreptitiously. Often it covers its tracks by falsifying and carefully handling documents relating to the assets. This curious finding—common to most failed banks in developing economies—is established through the investigation of banks.

Insider Abuse

The problem of insider abuse features under various topics in this book largely because of its profound link to credit risk crisis in developing economies. It is discussed, in each case, to underscore the relevant problem at issue. It is a condemnable act, one that bankers must shun. On grounds of moral rectitude, bank management should not only distance itself from insider abuse but strictly uphold the spirit of best lending practices. This implies that it should defend, rather than abuse, the internal lending policy and credit process. In doing so, it acquires the moral strength to enforce professional conduct down the cadres of employees in the lending function. On the other hand, if bank management is bereft of scruples, it will lack the moral standing to discipline morally bankrupt lending officers. In such a situation, it becomes the exception rather than the rule to observe lending policy, let alone fulfill the credit process.

MANAGEMENT STRUCTURE FOR BANK CREDIT RISK MANAGEMENT

Every bank must set up standing administrative framework to support credit admin functions. This suggestion envisages a growing need for institutional schemes or arrangements for senior management's involvement in administering the lending portfolio. A particular scheme could be in form of devising a regular forum for the interaction of senior management with lending officers, account officers, relationship managers, and credit control staff. Such an arrangement will help to bridge avoidable communication gaps in establishing, managing, and controlling credit relationships. While it is evident that bank management acknowledges this need, the effectiveness of its implementation in some banks is doubtful. The most popular administrative frameworks for supporting credit admin functions in banks are the institutions of credit strategy committee (CRESCO) and the watch-list committee.

Credit Strategy Committee

CRESCO is one of the management devices to strengthen the credit process. Banks have a specific aim in instituting CRESCO. They look to fulfilling the need for credit approval authorities to stay focused. Thus, the institution of CRESCO is a means to harmonize, unify, and adopt common credit review, decision-making, approval process and strategy at senior management level. Thus, CRESCO functions as a high-ranking credit review and approval authority. In general, it deals with decisive and thorny issues in credit proposals as packaged in credit analysis memorandum (CAM) and credit approval form (CAF). It fulfills critical roles for the bank in the area of credit risk management. CRESCO supports effective discharge of credit admin functions by providing a medium for interaction between senior management, lending officers, and credit admin staff. At CRESCO's sessions, the representative of credit admin (if any, or on invitation) would report observed lapses in extant credit facilities. He or she could also suggest certain risk-mitigating measures for CRESCO's consideration. Such recommendations, usually for intended credit facilities, are based on the practical experience of credit compliance staff in administering individual credit facilities and the total lending portfolio.

When credit approval is flawed, for whatever reasons, loans and lending decision process become exposed to risk. When this situation happens, the bank and borrowers often experience avoidable hitches in their banking relationship. Thus, lending officers must be diligent at all times in processing, approving, documenting, and disbursing credit facilities. As a response to the need for foolproof lending criteria, banks introduce some checks and balances to the credit approval process. The checks and balances are intended to enforce due diligence among lending officers who have credit approval authority. Credit strategy committee (CRESCO) is one of the effective devices to achieve this goal.

The institution of CRESCO in banks has been one of the important devices to strengthen the credit process. The structure and composition of membership of CRESCO varies with size and risk management disposition of banks. Ideally, the committee should draw membership from senior management staff of the bank—including the chief executive officer; members of executive committee who have lending and credit approval responsibility; heads of lending divisions (who are not EXCO members); head of credit risk management (i.e., chief risk officer); and legal officer or adviser of the bank.

Once constituted in this manner, the committee's decisions would require ratification *only* by board audit and credit committee. However, some banks try to minimize or check the authority and influence of CRESCO by excluding the CEO and EXCO members from CRESCO. In so doing, two additional credit approval authorities—CEO and EXCO—are introduced above CRESCO. Thus, depending on the amount involved and other special considerations, proposed credit facilities would have to be approved by CRESCO, the CEO, EXCO, and Board—in that order.

However, it is at CRESCO level that the rigor of credit review and approval may be best appreciated. At CRESCO's sessions, most of the thorny issues in loan proposals are tackled first-hand. Specifically, the committee's role in the credit process consists mainly in fulfilling the following functions:

- Review of credit analysis memorandum (CAM) and credit approval form (CAF) and, in the process, detect any flaws that could forestall approval of credit facilities presented to it.

- Determine appropriateness of proposed credit facilities, especially in terms of structure, transactions dynamics, risk mitigation, probable earnings, fit with target market definition, risk acceptance criteria, and so on.
- Recommend amendments (if considered necessary) to the CAM and CAF which should be effected to correct any observed weaknesses of proposed credit facilities.
- Endorse on, or without, specific conditions—or decline support for—all the credit facilities which the lending units package for approval by senior management.
- Invite credit analysts, loan officers, and relationship managers from whose lending units proposed credit facilities originate to appear before the committee to clarify any confusing issues and defend the CAM and CAF.

In banks that have properly structured and effective CRESCO, the quality and rigor of debate at its sessions keep loan officers ever prepared to defend any lurid claims in the CAM and CAF. For loan officers—especially those who defend credit proposals—it could rightly be said that *the fear of CRESCO is the beginning of credit wisdom.*

Watch-List Committee

A watch-list committee is set up to meet regularly to review the status of non-performing risk assets. It also gets reports on efforts and achievements of responsible officers of the lending and loans remedial units towards recovery of bad loans. The committee works closely with credit admin to ensure that loan loss provisions are minimized. However, it also pursues specific agenda for possible remedial of *classified* or *criticized* credit facilities, as well as recovery of *lost*, but not let off, credit facilities. The committee recommends necessary actions to revive particular loan accounts, strengthen ailing credit relationships, and maintain surveillance over the performance of particular loan accounts and credit facilities. It supports credit admin functions in practical terms. In addition to having representative in the watch-list committee, credit admin makes useful input to such decisions.

Perhaps, the setting up and sustaining of watch-list committee is the first conscious effort that banks in emerging markets should make toward managing the problems of nonperforming loans. Indeed, the regulatory authorities require every bank to have a standing watch-list committee which should meet regularly to review the status of nonperforming risk assets, as well as efforts and achievements towards their recovery. The overall objective of the committee is to ensure that loan loss provisions are minimized as much as possible to avoid depletion of returns to shareholders.

In some banks, the watch-list committee meets once a month to deliberate on all aspects of problems of, and recovery strategies for, nonperforming risk assets or loans of doubtful value (LDV). The term *watch-list* refers to the grouping of all borrowing accounts or loans which a bank, its external auditors, or the regulatory authorities classify as substandard, doubtful, or lost in line with *prudential guidelines*. Ideally, watch-list should include loans which, though not yet classified, show potential default warning signs. Such loans equally require close monitoring and firming up of recovery plans to forestall their degeneration to nonperforming status.

The watch-list committee members are usually drawn from CRESCO members, and heads of lending units in a bank. But branch managers who have watch-list credits may be invited to watch-list committee meetings. Ordinarily, the watch-list committee exists and functions as a subcommittee of CRESCO. At the end of its meetings, decisions are taken—subject, in some banks, to ratification of CRESCO and executive management—on actions necessary to revive particular accounts, strengthen certain credit relationships, or maintain surveillance over the performance of specific nonperforming credit facilities.

The committee could take tough decisions on nonperforming loans. Such decisions often culminate in *workout* and outright *recovery* actions. In such situations, if ratified by CRESCO and executive management, the bank would be constrained to *call back* the affected loans.

RELATING CREDIT RISK TO BANK CAPITALIZATION IN DEVELOPING ECONOMIES

Stakeholders, as owners, contribute equity capital to set up a bank. In this sense, the capitalization of a bank evidences commitment of the shareholders to the bank. Over time, and as the bank capitalizes profits or retained earnings and other reserves, its capital base broadens. The shareholders' funds then provide the net financial buffer on which the bank can confidently assume some of the risks of lending and other operating activities. The emphasis on a net financial buffer depicts the inclination of banks to apply equity capital to finance investments in buildings (or office accommodation), the acquisition of fixed assets (or fixtures and fittings), and the provision of work equipment (such as computers, vehicles, chairs, and tables).

Shareholders' funds are built over time as a bank's earnings and reserves increase with profitability. But this depends on the bank's dividend policy. A bank that favors growth and capital gains would emphasize earnings retention, while one that believes in maximizing shareholders' wealth in the short run would tend to adopt a high dividend payout policy. In the event that a bank is not profitable, its net worth declines. The decline results from the erosion of shareholders' funds by current and accumulated losses. In time, the bank may become distressed and fail. It is instructive that the choice of any capital financing option has cost implications for the bank. But what specifically constitutes the capital base of a bank? When can we say that a bank is adequately capitalized? Why should bank management necessarily be concerned about capital adequacy? To what extent do authorities regulate bank capital? These questions lead to the problem definition, with implications for the effective management of banks' capital resources.

One of the significant achievements of the Basel Accords with respect to credit risk management is the linking of capital adequacy to credit risk. Thus, risk weights assigned to particular bank assets bear on the adequacy of global bank capital. The import of this approach to determining capital adequacy is that the management of global banks should be wary of the credit risks they take. By doing so, they would be able to avoid unnecessary diminution of the capital base of their banks. It also implies that credit risk can make or break the operations of a bank.

BANK CREDIT RISK PERSPECTIVE AND IMPLICATIONS OF THE BASEL CAPITAL ACCORD

Basel I demonstrated how the "capital measurement system" and "credit risk measurement framework" would work in practice. It did so in three sections, represented as the constituents of capital, the risk-weighting system, and the target standard ratio. I present summaries of these components of the Basel I Accord as follows.

Constituents of Capital

The Basel I Accord identified two tiers of capital that it recommended should constitute the total capital base of a bank. While tier 1 capital denotes a bank's core capital (i.e., its equity capital and disclosed reserves), tier 2 capital represents noncore capital items (referred to in Basel I as supplementary capital). In isolating the two tiers, the Accord clarified aspects of their components and qualifying attributes as follows:

Core Capital (Basic Equity)

A bank's core capital, also referred to as basic equity, has three components (as shown later) that make it up and constitute tier 1 capital. But the two primary categories—namely, equity capital and disclosed reserves—that contain the three components are the defining constituents of core capital. Basel I underscored core capital in "requiring at least 50% of a bank's capital base to consist of a core element comprised of equity capital and published reserves from posttax retained earnings." Specifically, core capital represents the sum of the monetary value of a bank's:

1. equity capital, comprising:
   a. issued and fully paid-up ordinary shares or common stock of a bank;
   b. noncumulative perpetual preferred stock, excluding cumulative preferred stock; and
2. disclosed reserves (i.e., reserves from profit after tax and published in a bank's audited accounts).

In view of its nature, noncumulative perpetual preferred stock is treated as an integral component of equity capital. Basel I recognized equity capital and disclosed reserves as the key to "securing a progressive enhancement in the quality, as well as the level, of the total capital resources maintained by major banks." Thus, a bank can work on core capital to meet or surpass the minimum capital standard without losing sight of the fact that quality of capital counts as well as its level.

Supplementary Capital

A number of items subsumed in the total capital base of a bank do not count as part of the bank's core capital. Such items of capital other than equity capital and disclosed reserves, referred to in Basel I as supplementary capital, make up tier 2 capital. The Accord stipulated that this category of capital items "will be admitted into tier 2 up to an amount equal to that of the core capital." Basel I recognized five constituents of supplementary capital as summarized later.

Undisclosed Reserves

This category of capital depicts "reserves which, though unpublished, have been passed through the profit and loss account and which are accepted by the bank's supervisory authorities." Two attributes of undisclosed reserves stem, or can be inferred, from this definition: firstly, they are accounted for in the profit and loss account even though they are not explicitly stated, reflected, or shown in the account; and secondly, the Central Bank or other banking regulatory authority approves them as a qualifying constituent of a bank's capital.

Revaluation Reserves

Some banks include revaluation reserves as part of their total capital resources. These reserves are a sum of money calculated and recognized in a bank's books as the capital appreciation on specific assets. Thus, revaluation reserves are created when current market values of particular assets exceed their historical costs (i.e., book values). The objective of revaluation is to bring the historical book value up to the current value of assets. However, Basel I made a proviso that must be fulfilled before revaluation reserves would be admitted into the capital base of a bank. It recommended a discount of 55% on the amount by which the market value of assets exceeds historical book value.

General Loan Loss Reserves

Banking regulatory authorities usually require banks to make general as well as specific provisions on loan portfolios. The prudential rate approved for the general provision differs from the rates for specific provisions. While the former is a uniform rate, rates for the latter depend on the state of the specific nonperforming loans to which they apply. Basel I, on the one hand, permits inclusion of general loan loss provisions in tier 2 capital as general loan loss reserves, while on the other it precludes the inclusion of specific provisions.

General loan loss reserves are considered an element of capital because they "are created against the possibility of losses not yet identified." Besides, such reserves "do not reflect a known deterioration in the valuation of particular assets." On the contrary, specific loan loss provisions are thought to lack admissible attributes of capital and should be discounted from the capital base of a bank. Two reasons, noted in Basel I, informed this thinking. Firstly, specific provisions "are created against identified losses or in respect of an identified deterioration in the value of any asset or group of subsets of assets. Secondly, such provisions "are not freely available to meet unidentified losses that may subsequently arise elsewhere in the portfolio."

The inclusion of general loan loss reserves in tier 2 capital is not absolute. Basel I specified "a limit of 1.25 percentage points of weighted risk assets" for the amount of general loan loss provisions that should be admitted into tier 2 capital.

Hybrid (Debt/Equity) Capital Instruments

The makeup of supplementary capital, according to Basel I, should include capital instruments that share some but not all of the attributes of equity and debt. However, it is believed that the quality of capital instruments tends to satisfy requirement for inclusion in tier 2 capital when those instruments "have close similarities to equity." Thus, Basel I recommended their inclusion in tier 2 capital, especially "when they are able to support losses on an on-going basis without triggering liquidation." This implies that a bank that holds such capital instruments does not necessarily have to liquidate them, but can apply them to offset a loss position. Basel I noted that while "their precise specifications differ from country to country," hybrid capital instruments should satisfy the following set of criteria (Basel Committee on Banking and Supervision, 1988):

- They are unsecured, subordinated, and fully paid up;
- They are not redeemable at the initiative of the holder or without prior consent of the supervisory authority;
- They are available to participate in losses without the bank being obliged to cease trading (unlike conventional subordinated debt);
- Although the capital instrument may carry an obligation to pay interest that cannot permanently be reduced or waived (unlike dividends on ordinary shareholders' equity), it should allow service obligations to be deferred (as with cumulative preference shares) where the profitability of the bank would not support payment.

Where cumulative preference shares have these characteristics, they would be eligible for inclusion in this category (ibid.).

Subordinated Term Debt

Basel I expressed reservation about inclusion of subordinated term debt instruments as a constituent of the capital base of a bank. Such debt instruments are criticized for capitalization purposes "in view of their fixed maturity and inability to absorb losses except in a liquidation." These attributes render them deficient and ineligible for inclusion in tier 2 capital. Nonetheless, Basel I allowed for the inclusion of "subordinated term debt instruments with a minimum original term to maturity of over 5 years (in) the supplementary elements of capital." However, it did so with a proviso that such instruments should account for "a maximum of 50% of the core capital element and subject to adequate amortization arrangements."

Subordinated term debt "includes conventional unsecured subordinated debt capital instruments with minimum original fixed term to maturity of over 5 years and limited life redeemable preference shares." It is pertinent to reflect that such "instruments are not normally available to participate in the losses of a bank which continues trading." It's for this reason that Basel I upheld that "during the last 5 years to maturity, a cumulative discount (or amortization) factor of 20% per year will be applied to reflect the diminishing value of these instruments as a continuing source of strength" (ibid.: 16).

Deductions From Capital

It is imperative to adjust a bank's capital base to reflect its true quality and usefulness as buffer for its risk assets portfolio. The essence in doing so is to be able to calculate an accurate risk-weighted capital ratio for the bank. Thus, Basel I identified deductions that should be made from the capital base of a bank in order to calculate this ratio. The first—goodwill—is to be deducted from tier 1 capital. The second deduction is "investments in subsidiaries engaged in banking and financial activities which are not consolidated in national systems." These deductions enhance the quality of a bank's capital base and better reflect it in published accounts.

Risk-Weighting System

Basel I assessed capital adequacy in the context of the credit risk that a bank assumes. It defended a logical approach to assessing capital adequacy based on the relationship of capital to risk-weighted asset categories and off-balance sheet exposures. It is against the backdrop of these considerations that it recommended the use of "a weighted risk ratio" as a measure of capital adequacy. This ratio weights and relates the riskiness of assets and off-balance sheet exposures to capital (The terms risk ratio, weighted risk ratio, and risk-weights method refer to the same concept and are used interchangeably in this chapter).

In justifying this method, the Basel Committee insisted that "a weighted risk ratio in which capital is related to different categories of asset or off-balance sheet exposure, weighted according to broad categories of relative riskiness, is the preferred method for assessing the capital adequacy of banks." A risk ratio (i.e., the risk weights method) is considered more rigorous and relevant than the gearing ratio approach. It has particular advantages over the gearing ratio, which Basel I identified, in assessing capital adequacy. Unlike a gearing ratio, a risk ratio (Basel Committee on Banking and Supervision, 1988):

- provides a fairer basis for making international comparisons between banking systems whose structures may differ;
- allows off-balance sheet exposures to be incorporated more easily into the measure;
- does not deter banks from holding liquid or other assets that carry low risk.

The risk ratio approach, seen now as a reliable method for the calculation of capital adequacy, is justifiable. One reason is that asset quality has a direct bearing on capital. Thus, an increasing portfolio of nonperforming assets erodes a bank's capital base through loan loss provisions and write-offs. Another reason, one that derives from the first, is that capital adequacy would be dubious when asset quality deteriorates at a faster rate than increases in capital. Capital adequacy in that case would hardly be sustainable for the desired level of operations.

Elements of the Weighting Structure

Basel I adopted a weighting structure that relates capital to specific asset and off-balance sheet risk weights. The resultant risk ratio can then be used to assess the adequacy of bank capital. The structure comprises a framework of five risk weights, each of which can be assigned to particular categories of risk. Basel I offered broad definitions of risk categories to which specific risk weights applied. The weights reflected the riskiness of assets and off-balance sheet exposures of a bank. Factors considered in identifying the risk categories and recommending risk weights are discussed later.

Risk Categories

Global bank risk arises for the most part from "the risk of counterparty failure" (i.e., credit risk) and "country transfer risk." Over the years credit default has been a major cause of liquidity crises for banks. So it's not surprising that the risk-weighting framework that's an integral part of Basel I focused on this kind of risk. Yet there are several other kinds of risks to which global banks are exposed and should direct management attention. Investment risk, interest rate risk, exchange rate risk, and concentration risk were some of such risks identified in the Basel I Accord.

The Risk Weights

In its buildup to formulating a standard weighted risk ratio for global banks, the Basel Committee was mindful that the risks of assets and off-balance sheet exposures differ between countries. For this reason, Basel I categorized assets and off-balance sheet exposures using some definite criteria. For each category, it recommended an appropriate uniform risk weight. Thus, we have a comprehensive schedule of risk weights in Basel I that should be applied to specific categories of assets and off-balance sheet exposures. The schedule of categories of on and off-balance sheet exposures of global banks and risk-weights assigned to them are presented in Tables 15.1, 15.2.

TABLE 15.1 Risk Weights by Category of On-Balance Sheet Assets[a]

0%	1. Cash[b] 2. Claims on central governments and central banks denominated in national currency and funded in that currency 3. Other claims on OECD[c] central governments[d] and central banks 4. Claims collateralized by cash of OECD central-government securities[e] or guaranteed by OECD central governments[f]
0, 10, 20 or 50% (at national discretion)	Claims on domestic public-sector entities, excluding central government, and loans guaranteed by or collateralized by securities issued by such entities[g]
20%	1. Claims on multilateral development banks (IBRD, IADB, AsDB, AfDB, EIB, EBRD)[f] and claims guaranteed by, or collateralized by securities issued by such banks[g] 2. Claims on banks incorporated in the OECD and claims guaranteed[g] by OECD incorporated banks 3. Claims on securities firms incorporated in the OECD subject to comparable supervisory and regulatory arrangements, including in particular risk-based capital requirements,[g] and claims guaranteed by these securities firms 4. Claims on banks incorporated in countries outside the OECD with a residual maturity of up to one year and claims with a residual maturity of up to one year guaranteed by banks incorporated in countries outside the OECD 5. Claims on nondomestic OECD public-sector entities, excluding central government, and claims guaranteed by or collateralized by securities issued by such entities[g] 6. Cash items in process of collection
50%	1. Loans fully secured by mortgage on residential property that is or will be occupied by the borrower or that is rented
100%	1. Claims on the private sector 2. Claims on banks incorporated outside the OECD with a residual maturity of over one year 3. Claims on central governments outside the OECD (unless denominated in national currency - and funded in that currency—see earlier) 4. Claims on commercial companies owned by the public sector 5. Premises, plant and equipment and other fixed assets 6. Real estate and other investments (including nonconsolidated investment participations in other companies) 7. Capital instruments issued by other banks (unless deducted from capital) 8. all other assets

[a]Tables 15.1 and 15.2, including their footnotes, were extracted from the Basel Capital Accord. See Basel Committee on Banking and Supervision (1988).

*b*Includes (at national discretion) gold bullion held in own vaults or on an allocated basis to the extent backed by bullion liabilities.
*c*For the purpose of this exercise, the OECD group comprises countries which are full members of the OECD(or which have concluded special lending arrangements with the IMF associated with the Fund's General Arrangements to Borrow), but excludes any country within this group which has rescheduled its external sovereign debt in the previous 5 years.
*d*Some member countries intend to apply weights to securities issued by OECD central governments to take account of investment risk. These weights would, for example, be 10% for all securities or 10% for those maturing in up to one year and 20% for those maturing in over one year.
*e*Claims on other multilateral development banks in which G-10 countries are shareholding members may, at national discretion, also attract a 20% weight.
*f*Commercial claims partially guaranteed by these bodies will attract equivalent low weights on that part of the loan which is fully covered. Similarly, claims partially collateralized by cash, or by securities issued by OECD central governments, OECD noncentral government public-sector entities, or multilateral development banks will attract low weights on that part of the loan which is fully covered.
*g*That is, capital requirements that are comparable to those applied to banks in this Accord and its Amendment to incorporate market risks. Implicit in the meaning of the word "comparable" is that the securities firm (but not necessarily its parent) is subject to consolidated regulation and supervision with respect to any downstream affiliates.

TABLE 15.2 Credit Conversion Factors for Off-Balance-Sheet Items

Credit conversion factors	Instrument
100%	Direct credit substitutes, for example, general guarantees of indebtedness (including standby letters of credit serving as financial guarantees for loans and securities) and acceptances (including endorsements with the character of acceptances)
50%	Certain transaction-related contingent items (e.g., performance bonds, bid bonds, warranties and standby letters of credit related to particular transactions)
20%	Short-term self-liquidating trade-related contingencies (such as documentary credits collateralized by the underlying shipments)
100%	Sale and repurchase agreements and asset sales with recourse,[a] where the credit risk remains with the bank
100%	Forward asset purchases, forward deposits and partly-paid shares and securities,[a] which represent commitments with certain draw-down
50%	Note issuance facilities and revolving underwriting facilities
50%	Other commitments (e.g., formal standby facilities and credit lines) with an original maturity of over one year
0%	Similar commitments with an original maturity of up to one year, or which can be unconditionally cancelled at any time

*a*Includes (at national discretion) gold bullion held in own vaults or on an allocated basis to the extent backed by bullion liabilities.

Credit Risk Management Implications of the Risk-Weighting System

The intent of Basel I was to establish a common standard to measure the adequacy of capital of internationally active banks. It adopted a harmonized framework that regulators should adopt to ensure observance of the stipulated capital adequacy standard. The regulatory framework, on the one hand, was meant to aid supervision of global bank capital, lending activities, and portfolios. Standardized capital adequacy, on the other, sought to mitigate credit risk that such banks assume, especially in times of financial crisis. Thus, Basel I underscored worldwide the new and growing attention to how credit risk could be effectively managed. The Basel Committee states the underlying purpose of the foregoing:

> As one of the principal objectives of supervision is the protection of depositors,
> it is essential to ensure that capital recognized in capital adequacy measures
> is readily available for those depositors. Accordingly, supervisors should test
> that individual banks are adequately capitalized on a stand-alone basis (Basel
> Committee on Banking and Supervision, 2004).

The Basel Committee did not mince words and unambiguously stated the commanding focus of the Basel I Accord. It stated that its "framework is mainly directed toward assessing capital in relation to credit risk (the risk of counterparty failure)." However, it's noted in the Accord that "other risks, notably interest rate risk and the investment risk on securities, need to be taken into account by supervisors in assessing overall capital adequacy" (Basel Committee on Banking and Supervision, 1988). The emphasis on credit risk was predicated on the fact that such risk accounted mostly for the troubles of distressed, failing, and failed banks in several countries. It's also assumed that credit risk was the root of the crisis into which the global financial system was thrown in the 1970s and 1980s. In time, it's hoped that implementation of the Accord would check reckless lending and its concomitant liquidity crisis in the internationally active banks.

Basel I also noted a possible loophole in credit risk management at the time that might impact the adequacy of capital of global banks. The probable loophole was in judging capital ratios independent of the quality of risk assets and the level of loan loss provision. As a caveat, the Basel Committee made the point that "capital ratios, judged in isolation, may provide a misleading guide to relative strength. Much also depends on the quality of a bank's assets and, importantly, the level of provisions a bank may be holding outside its capital against assets of doubtful value" (ibid.). While identifying the close relationship between loan loss provisions and capital, Basel I responded to the negative effect of provisions on capital. It did so by seeking "to promote convergence of policies" within the member countries of the Basel Committee. The high point of the impact of Basel I on credit risk management was its formulation of specific means to assess capital adequacy and risk assets quality. The Accord offered a "capital measurement system (which) provided for the implementation of a credit risk measurement framework with a minimum capital standard of 8%." Of the 8% "target standard ratio of capital to weighted risk assets," the Accord recommended that "at least 4% will be the core capital element" (ibid.).

SUMMARY

A bank takes credit risk when it grants a loan with the expectation that the borrower should utilize the loan according to agreed terms and conditions—and ultimately repay the loan on its due date. Usually, repayment of the loan is expected from some cash flow projection that may or may not be realized. Uncertainty of cash flows notwithstanding, the bank must pay back customers' deposits that fund its loan portfolio—on demand, at short notice, or on due dates. Risk, in this case, is the chance that borrowers may default whereas depositors must be paid their deposits on or before due dates.

Banks should always be cautious about the risks they take—they should anticipate, measure, and plan for them. Banking reforms in recent times in many developing economies were intended to tame the risk-taking appetite of banks and institutionalize a sound financial system. Unfortunately, uncertainty—another variable that also affects banking outcomes—is more intractable than risk. Unlike risk, there is no proven methodological framework that banks can use to identify, quantify, analyze, or mitigate uncertainty. For this reason, it is widely believed that uncertainty is a necessary evil, ostensibly defying solution. Yet, a bank has to deal with uncertainty and its adverse effects one way or the other. This is because uncertainty plays a decisive role in banking business and outcomes.

Often the trend and process of the buildup of credit risk crisis differ from one bank to another. The underlying factor in the observed differences—one that determines the momentum of the crisis and its remedy—is usually the character of bank management. It is possible in some cases for bank management to detect, acknowledge, and strive to address the buildup of a credit risk crisis. In doing so, it can respond to the crisis with appropriate internal risk management contingency measures.

One of the significant achievements of the Basel Accords with respect to credit risk management is the linking of capital adequacy to credit risk. Thus, risk weights assigned to particular bank assets bear on the adequacy of global bank capital. The import of this approach to determining capital adequacy is that the management of global banks should be wary of the credit risks they take. By doing so, they would be able to avoid unnecessary diminution of the capital base of their banks. It also implies that credit risk can make or break the operations of a bank.

QUESTIONS FOR DISCUSSION AND REVIEW

1. a. Why has determination of appropriate amount of bank capital always been a thorny question for bank management and regulators in developing economies?

  b. In what ways did the Basel Committee on Banking Supervision deal with the problem of global bank capital adequacy and quality?
2. Discuss the role of bank management and regulators in the implementation of the Basel Accords, taking cognizance of peculiar situation of banks in developing economies.
3. How do CEOs of banks contribute to the crisis of credit risk? Your answer should bear reference to decided court cases on allegations of professional misconduct that the CBN leveled against executives of some failed banks in Nigeria in 2009.
4. **a.** Critically appraise the role of lending officers in the creation of bank credit risk crises in developing economies.
   b. In what ways can account officers and relationship managers help bank management to stem the crisis of credit risk?
5. **a.** In what sense does pursuit of budget goals inform the contemporary approach of banks to the marketing of credit products?
   b. What factors underscore the view that banks tend to drive lending along the lines of overambitious budget goals?
6. How could competition for market leadership based on bogus earnings, balance sheet growth, and size be inimical to the quality of the asset portfolios of banks? Justify your answer with reference to the fate of any two named failed banks in Nigeria.
7. **a.** Why would you agree or disagree with the view that reckless lending is usually deliberate?
   b. How does the fact that reckless lending is intricately mired in excessive risk-taking render credit risk crisis in banks intractable?
8. **a.** Are financial analysts justified in pointing accusing fingers at regulators in accounting for the crisis of credit risk in banks?
9. Do you think that recent banking reforms in some developing economies will address the problem of vested interests in bank lending?

REFERENCES

Basel Committee on Banking Supervision, 1988. International Convergence of Capital Measurement and Capital Standards, as amended. Bank for International Settlements. Basel.

Basel Committee on Banking Supervision, 2004. International Convergence of Capital Measurement and Capital Standards: A Revised Framework. Bank for International Settlements. Basel.

World Bank, 2013. World Development Report 2014 Risk and Opportunity—Managing Risk for Development. World Bank, Washington, DC. License: Creative Commons Attribution CC BY 3.0. http://dx.doi.org/10.1596/978-0-8213-9903e3.

Chapter 16

Bank Assets Portfolio Structure and Risk Management in Developing Economies

Chapter Outline

LEARNING FOCUS AND OBJECTIVES

The management of bank assets in developing economies has assumed greater importance of late. The increasing attention of banks managements to the assets portfolio is not unconnected with the linking of banking crisis in most countries to inefficient assets management. Usually, the focus is on the loan book—its structure, quality, and risk. Loans and advances that constitute the loan book portfolio are not only risk assets but earning assets. This dual, but ironic, nature places the loan book on a pedestal. Yet the impacts of other assets on a bank's operations should not be wished away. I do the following in pursuit of my objectives for this chapter:

- review the classical theories of assets portfolio management in banking, with implications for banks in developing economies;
- discuss the composition, features, dynamics, and management requirements for the assets portfolios of banks in developing economies;

- identify and examine forms of, and outlets for, banks' investments in assets, as well as applications of capital in funding bank assets;
- analyze banks credit portfolio distribution, maturity profiles, and risk management requirements in developing economies; and
- sensitize bankers in developing economies to issues in credit concentration and their implications for risk management

EXPECTED LEARNING OUTCOMES

The significance and dominance of loans and advances in the assets portfolios of banks are a function of their bearing on earnings potential of the banks. This is notwithstanding the designation of loans as risk assets. Banks take on risk in assets creation through lending in order to satisfy financing needs of customers, as well as meet budget goals. The usual contending issue in this business drive is the famed risk-return trade-off in financial management. The reader will—after studying this chapter and doing the exercises in it—have learnt and been better informed about:

- classical theories of bank assets management and their implications for banking in developing economies;
- composition, features, dynamics, and management of the assets portfolios of banks in developing economies;
- credit portfolio distribution, maturity profiles, and risk management requirements for banking in developing economies;
- forms of, and outlets for, banks' investments in assets, as well as applications of capital in funding bank assets;
- issues in bank credit portfolio concentration and their risk implications in developing economies;
- sectoral distributions of the lending portfolios of the banks in developing economies according to industries;
- maturity profiles of risk assets that constitute the lending portfolios of banks in developing economies; and
- risk characteristics and indicators of quality of the lending portfolios of banks in developing economies.

OVERVIEW OF SUBJECT MATTER

Assets management is a crucial responsibility on which the overall performance of a bank largely depends. Banks managements should allocate shareholders' funds and deposit liabilities optimally in funding the various categories of assets acquisitions. This is necessary to achieve balanced and profitable portfolios. Yet some constraints exist in attaining optimum application of funds for assets acquisitions. There are regulatory limitations and the needs for liquidity and profitability—all of which affect policy direction for investment in assets. We, of course, know that liquidity and returns are inversely related. Banks should therefore balance the need for liquidity with the desire for profit. With liquid (less risky) assets, earnings are low; while the less liquid or illiquid (riskier) assets, return high yields. This fact establishes the key issue involved in analyzing the theories of assets management in banking.

Bank lending and risk assets resulting from it get commanding attention in solving the challenges of assets portfolio management. Many would want banks in developing economies to gear lending to correct variances between regulatory policy prescriptions and compliance. Banks should especially direct more lending to meet the targets for loans to preferred economic sectors. They may consider minimizing current emphasis on credits to commerce and other nonreal sectors. Also, lending to enterprises whose activities produce linkages to the preferred sectors should be encouraged. Such loans can be classified as credits granted for purposes of economic development. Of course this has implication for managing the lending portfolio. The main thrust of banks managements in the lending function should be to create balanced and profitable portfolios of risk assets in line with national economic outlook. This requires knowledge of the business environment, anticipated and existing lending regulations, as well as shareholders' expectations.

It is common that assets comprising the loan books of banks are classified into three broad categories, usually based on their terms to maturity. The classification recognizes short-term, medium-term, and long-term loans. However, there is no common understanding among banks about the exact periods of time to which these terms relate. For example, depending on their risk appetites, what one bank might regard as medium-term may be seen as long-term by another bank. In most cases, nonetheless, most banks regard a period of or less than 12 calendar months as short-term.

Overall, an efficient, quality, assets portfolio is best accounted for—first and foremost—in the categories of risk and earning assets that comprise the loan books of banks. Then a review of the volumes, features, and dynamic of the other assets sheds more light on the efficiency and quality potential of the assets portfolio. An insight into this outcome is gained when aspects of the risk and nonrisk assets portfolios of the banks are related. In doing so, significant differences may be observed in the approaches to assets portfolio risk management between the domestic banks and foreign banks subsidiaries.

THEORIES OF ASSETS MANAGEMENT IN BANKING

It is doubtful that banks managements in developing economies rely on any particular theories for assets portfolio management. Their usual tendency is to fall back on some pragmatic techniques, if anything. This is not surprising considering that loan books which constitute the bulk of the assets portfolio are a melting pot. Besides, intrigues and maneuverings—most of which are founded on cover-ups—tend to characterize bank lending practices in developing economies. This has risk implication for effective management of the assets portfolio. Its risk fallout is that everything is in flux and unpredictable. It becomes difficult, under the circumstances, to adapt particular theories for the assets management needs of the banks. Perhaps this explains why banks in developing economies do not necessarily emphasize applications of theories in solving banking risks. The banks rather run on the basis of some pragmatic, but business sense. This may sound a bit strange—indeed, quite unlike the practice in other fields. However, notwithstanding neglect, some of the theories of bank assets management are still extant. Two of the theories, pool-of-funds and assets allocation, are relevant to solving some of the present-day assets management risks of banks in developing economies.

The Pool-of-Funds Theory

The main thrust of the pool-of-funds theory is that a bank should make investments in assets acquisitions after (and from) a pool of its deposits liabilities and capital funds. It suggests that a bank should, first and foremost, pool all funds available to it. From the pool, the bank should then allocate funds to its three main cash competing, but opposing needs. The first and second are related and intended to meet cash reserves needs, while the third is for investments in assets acquisitions.

Usually, funds for investments are generated from demand deposits, savings deposits, time deposits, and capital funds. Allocation of funds is geared to finance investments in loans (risk assets), marketable securities, fixed assets, and reserves for liquidity and working capital needs. With the pool-of-funds theory, it is difficult to trace the particular source of funds from which a particular asset investment is financed.

The task of banks managements in adopting the pool-of-funds theory is to determine an optimum balance between its needs for liquidity and profitability so that allocation of funds would be made to asset categories in an order that satisfies the identified needs. Thus the overriding consideration that influences funds allocation is the determination of the optimum proportion of the available funds that may be applied to finance investments in the various asset categories. For some banks, especially those that have volatile deposit base, this poses a great challenge. Such banks—found mainly among the domestic banks—find it difficult to meet statutory requirements for cash reserves, as well as customer's withdrawal requests.

However, both domestic and foreign subsidiary banks have competing needs for funds at any point in time. Thus banks managements should establish and adopt a funding priority order that guides allocations of funds from the pool-of-funds to cash reserves and the various assets categories.

Funding Priority

A common priority order for funds allocation using the pool-of-funds approach gives a foremost consideration to primary reserves. Thereafter funds may be allocated to secondary reserves. Once the bank satisfies its needs for cash reserves, it can then allocate funds to the other assets uses—usually for investment and earnings purposes. Let me briefly explain the main points about these three funds competing needs.

Primary Reserves

A bank should first and foremost allocate funds to primary reserves. The primary reserves of a bank represent its cash assets—often described as cash and due from other banks—which the bank needed to satisfy the cash withdrawal and loan needs of its customers. The items that are normally categorized as cash and due from other banks include balances held with the Central Bank, deposits or balances held with other banks, vault or till cash, cash items in the process of collection, and legal reserves against deposit liabilities. In this sense, primary reserves are subsumed under cash and short-term funds in a bank's balance sheet.

Secondary Reserves

Banks should make provision for secondary reserves after it has provided for primary reserves in the funds allocation scheme. Secondary reserves are non-cash, liquid assets from which a bank earns substantial incomes. Indeed, they comprise highly liquid assets which the bank can easily turn into cash at little risk of loss of value and minimal delay. For this reason, secondary reserves are intended to restock primary reserves when the latter deplete. Secondary reserves are reflected in a bank's stock of securities investment portfolio. They usually represent money market instruments and are also referred to as marketable securities.

Other Asset Uses

Once allocations have been made to primary and secondary reserves, the balance of funds under the pool-of-funds' theory should be allocated to loans and advances (risk assets), short-term funds (i.e., near cash items), and other assets—essentially in this order. However, banks that emphasize liquidity may allocate funds to near cash items before loans and advances. In most cases, investments in fixed assets—land, buildings, fixtures and fittings, and so on—are financed with equity funds and, as such, are considered separately within the constraint of the pool-of-funds principles.

Praise and Criticisms of Pool–of–Funds Theory

The pool-of-funds theory is credited with providing banks managements with a general guide for allocating available funds to the various assets categories. It emphasizes prioritization of the competing funding needs of a bank. Thus, the theory makes it possible to achieve an efficient allocation of bank funds to competing assets needs. Some (Agene, 1995: 49) believe that as a portfolio management approach, the pool-of-funds theory is welcome for the nascent banks that are often small and unable to attract funds easily from the financial markets.

However, the theory does not stipulate a precise formula or approach for ascertaining the proportions of cash from the pool-of-funds that should be invested in each of the competing assets categories. It does not also resolve the assets management dilemma implicit in the age-old conflict and trade-off between a bank's needs for liquidity and profitability. The theory does not yet assess the varying liquidity requirements of the various sources of funds—demand, savings, and time deposits, as well as capital funds—to the pool.

Certainly, applications of the theory will not yield optimum results in the face of its shortcomings highlighted above. One reason is that bank management will have to deal with the shortcomings one way or the other. For example, it should determine optimum allocations of funds, handle the risk-return conflict, and assess the relative liquidity requirements of alternative sources of funds in some pragmatic way. This may demand adoption some expedient measures, and reliance on intuition and personal judgment—all of which are likely to be fraught with errors.

The fact that banks seek to, and sometimes do, meet customer loan requests even in crunch situations negates any strict adoption of the tenets of the pool-of-funds theory. The nature of bank-customer relationship sometimes influences the final decision to lend or not—despite funding constraints.

Assets Allocation Model

The asset allocation model addresses some of the limitations of the pool-of-funds theory. Unlike the pool-of-funds theory, it recognizes that the various sources of funds to a bank have varying degrees of liquidity requirements. For example, a bank should have compensating levels of liquid assets for deposit liabilities that have high velocity levels (i.e., turnover rates). This is necessary to meet urgent or anticipated high frequency of customers' funds withdrawals.

Turnover of demand deposits far outstrips that of savings, for example. Therefore, the two sources of funds have and fulfill varying liquidity needs. The implication is that the sources from which a bank generates funds determine the nature of the bank's liquidity needs. The asset allocation model recognizes this fact and puts forth its main thrust accordingly. It propounds that a bank's liquidity needs at any point in time is a function of, or related to, its sources of funds. In order to implement the tenet of this model, funds from the various sources should be allocated to reflect their different liquidity-profitability requirements.

Consider, example, that demand deposits are adjudged to have the highest velocity. This implies that a very high proportion of demand deposit funds should be allocated to primary reserves (i.e., cash assets), while a relatively smaller proportion would go to secondary reserves (i.e., short-term government securities). Depending on the general liquidity condition of the bank, no allocation may be made to loans, other securities, or investments from demand deposit funds—and, definitely, not to fixed assets. However, larger amounts of funds may be allocated to loans and investments from savings or time deposit sources of funds because of their relatively less liquidity requirements. Capital funds are usually applied to finance fixed assets, long-term loans and other less liquid security investments because they require less liquidity—in much the same vein.

Critical Evaluation of Assets Allocation Model

Application of the asset allocation model ensures that funds are optimally utilized in financing assets acquisitions to generate earnings. There is advantage in the prescription of the model for a reduction in the volume of liquid assets. The model derives advantage from the resultant enhanced allocation of idle funds to loans and investments—thus increasing earnings from investments. This benefit is made possible through reduction of excess liquidity otherwise held in time and savings deposits, as well as in the capital accounts.

However, it is believed that there may not be a significant relationship between the velocity and variability of total deposits within a particular group of deposit liabilities. In the case of demand deposits, for instance, there is an observed practical net effect of customers' daily withdrawals from, and lodgments into, their accounts. The effect in question is the existence of a stable or predictable amount of funds that may not be withdrawn. Such permanent funds could be invested in long-term, high-yield marketable securities.

The lending activities of banks tend to reflect successes in their deposit mobilization abilities. Spurred by profit motive and the urge to match increasing demand for loans with growth in deposits, a bank may find it difficult to strictly apply the tenets of the allocation of funds model. It may be considered irrational to stop growth of a bank by constricting lending activities because liquidity requirements of deposit liabilities do not fit with the growth plan.

It can therefore be argued that the assumption of the model that sources of funds are independent of the uses to which they are put is erroneous. A bank strives, at any one time, to satisfy the borrowing needs of its customers as both a service to the public and a veritable means of achieving earnings targets. This makes sense given that in a growing economy—where business activities are in the upswing—deposits liabilities of the banking system tend to increase simultaneously with increasing demand for loans.

However, the rate of growth of demand for loans usually exceeds that of deposit liabilities—a situation that impels disregard of strict adoption of the asset allocation principles. The real cost of doing so is satisfaction of customer needs and demands for loans to a reasonable level. After all, without the customers, a bank will not be in business in the first place—let alone remaining a going concern.

ELEMENTS AND COMPOSITION OF BANK ASSETS PORTFOLIO

Assets constitute a significant component of a bank's balance sheet—representing "uses" to which its capital, reserves, and liabilities are put to generate earnings, growth, and returns to the shareholders. Thus, assets management must be efficient and ensure attainment of a reasonable level of profit in order to achieve the overall desired outcome, which is to increase shareholders' wealth. If assets are poorly managed, a bank may experience liquidity problems as a result of diminution of earnings. In such a situation, maturing obligations and liabilities may not be timely settled and at a reasonable cost. A bank in this situation might begin to experience distress that could ultimately lead to bankruptcy and failure. This is why it is imperative to understand and appreciate the dynamics and import of effective management of assets in banking.

The usual assets of a bank comprise cash, short-term funds, securities, loans, fixed assets, and others. The liquidity of these assets varies, with cash being the most and fixed assets the least liquid. Of course, the more liquid an asset, the less earning or return it generates. I adopt a two-pronged approach to analyze composition of assets portfolio of banks in developing economies. In the first instance, I use the balance sheet of Zenith Bank (Nigeria) Limited, presented in Table 16.1, to illustrate typical items of assets and liabilities of a bank. Then I relate the analysis to the entire banking system lending portfolios of select developing economies. Doing so, I establish any observable pattern that sheds light on problems and prospects of bank lending portfolio management in developing economies.

Cash Items

Consisting of currency notes and coins, cash does not earn income for the bank. It is yet needed to satisfy statutory regulation for required reserves kept with the Central Bank and to meet deposits withdrawals by customers and general operating expenses. We can at any time isolate three distinct locations of a bank's cash balances. They are Central Bank (cash reserves), strong rooms of branches and the head office (vault cash), and deposits with other, sometimes local or correspondent, banks (due from other banks). It is obvious that cash is important for its use in meeting statutory requirements, customers' withdrawal requests, and working capital needs.

Short-Term Funds

Cash assets may include short-term funds. On occasion cash and short-term funds may be separated to have a finer distinction between their meanings and applications. Clarity of their meanings adds value to a better understanding of their differences. The phrase "short-term funds" is used to describe checks or other instruments deposited by a bank's customers for clearing (i.e., outward

TABLE 16.1 Zenith Bank (Nigeria) Limited—Balance Sheet as June 30, 2002[a]

	(₦'000)	% of total
Assets		
Cash and short-term funds	65,628,625.00	70.90
Placements	1,800,000.00	1.94
Loans and advances	20,144,168.00	21.76
Advances under finance lease	360,781.00	0.39
Investment securities	359,743.00	0.39
Other assets	1,285,878.00	1.39
Fixed assets	2,983,702.00	3.22
	92,562,897.00	
Liabilities		
Deposit liabilities	50,134,281.00	60.22
Other liabilities	32,759,311.00	39.35
Deferred taxation	363,337.00	0.44
	83,256,929.00	
Capital and reserves		
Called-up share capital	1,026,658.00	11.03
Reserve for SMEs	833,144.00	8.95
Share premium	300.00	0.00
Other reserves	7,445,866.00	80.01
Shareholders' funds	9,305,968.00	
	92,562,897.00	
Confirmed credits and other obligations on behalf of customers and the corresponding thereon	19,986,187.00	
Total assets plus contingent liabilities	112,549,084.00	
Key accounting ratios:		
Loans and advances to deposits		40.90
Total assets to total liabilities		111.18
Contingent liabilities to total assets		21.59
Contingent liabilities to net worth		214.77
Total liabilities to net worth		894.66

[a]*Published in Nigeria's* ThisDay *Newspaper, Vol. 8, No. 2654, Monday, July 29, 2002, p.7.*

clearing checks). As instruments in the process of collection, they are devoid of immediate value to the depositors. With the introduction of check truncation in Nigeria, check clearing cycle is reduced to two days—from T + 2 to T + 1—effective from August 10, 2012. Thus unless the instruments receive value after clearing, they cannot be correctly described as cash. They are at best regarded as "near" cash item.

Zenith Bank, whose balance sheet is presented in Table 16.1 for illustration purposes, boasted strong liquidity as its cash and short-term funds accounted for a whopping 70.90% of the bank's total assets. Further evidence of the bank's strong liquidity showing is seen in its loan-to-deposit ratio of 40.90%. Other performance indicators of the bank are shown in the table under key accounting ratios. Most highly liquid banks in developing economies will boast similar accounting ratios. On a consolidated basis for the entire banking system, the result is about the same across developing economies.

In Taiwan, as Table 16.6 shows, loan-to-deposit ratio achieved by the banking system was satisfactory at 77.49% in 2014 even as the standard benchmark is 70% or less. A further evidence of appreciable liquidity attained by banks in Taiwan was a record deposit to liability ratio of 82.89% which the industry posted during the review period. With such strong showing in customer deposit accounts, the country's banking system operated from a position of liquidity strength.

The case of Pakistan, presented in Table 16.2, is not significantly different. The ratio of customer deposits to the banking system's total assets was quite high at 75.81%, resulting in loan-to-deposit ratio of 49.25% in 2014. Capital adequacy ratio of 14.8% for all the banks in the country during the period complemented good standing on loan-to-deposit ratio.

Marketable Securities

Investment in marketable or debt securities is almost always a significant element in a bank's assets portfolio. They are largely government IOUs, which banks purchase in fulfillment of part of statutory liquidity requirements, as well as to earn income and serve as collateral for specified deposit liabilities such as interbank takings. Mainly treasury bills, treasury certificates, debentures, commercial papers, Federal Government development stocks, and bonds, such government obligations are almost riskless and account for the largest proportion of a bank's security investments at any point in time.

However this is not evident in the case of Zenith Bank. The bank managed a paltry 0.39% investment in marketable securities. This may not be surprising considering that financial markets in many developing economies like Nigeria are yet at rudimentary. This may sound a bit farfetched, but this departure underlies a major cause of imbalances in the finances of the banks. Notwithstanding lukewarm disposition, the banks crave for particular marketable securities. The most popular debt securities among the banks are T-bills and

TABLE 16.2 Pakistan Banking System—Key Variables of Balance Sheet and Profit and Loss Statement

	2013 (Rs. billion)	2014 (Rs. billion)	% of assets (2013)	% of assets (2014)
Total assets	10,537	10,752		
Investments (net)	4,305	4,662	40.86	43.36
Advances (net)	4,047	4,014	38.41	37.33
Deposits	8,318	8,151	78.94	75.81
Equity	939	956	8.91	8.89
Profit before tax (year to date)	165	51		
Profit after tax (year to date)	111	33		
Nonperforming loans	585	602	5.55	5.60
Nonperforming loans (net)[a]	126	134	1.20	1.25
Capital adequacy ratio (all banks)	14.9	14.8		
Loan-to-deposit ratio	48.65	49.25		

[a]*Excluding specific provisions*
Source: Extracted from State Bank of Pakistan, *Pakistan Economic Survey 2013–2014*. All ratios were computed based on data extracted from this source.

treasury certificates, negotiable certificates, and Federal Government development stocks, in which the banks invest surplus funds on largely consideration of safety. The risk-return tradeoff is eminently relevant here. From marketable securities, returns are generally low; but they provide a portfolio of very highly liquid assets because of their tradability in the secondary money market. In other words, such debt securities can be sold to the Central Bank before maturity date without any, or substantial, loss of value—a process commonly referred to as rediscounting of the bill.

Thus banks in developing economies should favor investments in debt securities. There are at least three reasons for them to do so. First, such financial instruments get virtual riskless rating. Second, they are amenable to rediscounting with the Central Bank prior to maturity. Third, ability to rediscount the instruments helps banks to meet urgent liquidity need. There are other—and certainly not usually attractive—securities or commercial bills in which banks in developing economies could also invest. They are nongovernment securities which bills of exchange and acceptances mainly represent.

Investments

Banks are sometimes availed other investment windows in certain products floated by the Central Bank or a group of banks. The Deposit Certificate, introduced in February 2001 by the Central Bank of Nigeria (CBN), is an example of such investment opportunity. The Certificate has a minimum investment period of 180 days; but it is also available for 360 days. It offers competitive market-determined rate of interest. The Certificate is essentially a money market instrument aimed at mopping up excess liquidity in the banking system and the economy. In order to achieve this objective, the Certificate does not have a secondary market value; thus, investors must hold it for the period to maturity. It is also not discountable with the Central Bank. With such an appreciable rate of interest (often above the T-bill and monetary policy rate), the Certificate adequately compensates investors for the lack of a secondary market for it. Yet it was welcomed as a veritable liquidity management instrument.

There was once in Nigeria the Call Money scheme (called Federal Funds in the USA), floated by some banks to meet urgent liquidity needs. The Scheme was later taken over and directly administered by the CBN. The participating banks maintained a certain minimum statutory deposit balance with the CBN, where they had set up a Call Money Fund. Members that had surplus deposits above the agreed minimum balance lent the excess to the Fund. Conversely, borrowing on overnight basis from the Fund covered deficit deposit positions. However, unlike the CBN Certificate, interest on Call Money was below T-bill rate. The main advantage of the scheme was the assurance of liquidity and income on excess overnight balances with the CBN for the participating banks.

Investments with other banks, usually in forms of fixed deposits as evidenced with certificates of deposits and negotiable certificates of deposits sometimes account for a substantial proportion of short-term investments in a bank's balance sheet. The same goes for money at call and short notice held with the Central Bank. This could also be quite substantial. Of the total Rs 2,417.75 billion assets which banks in India held with Reserve Bank of India as at January 23, 2015, for instance, money at call and short notice accounted for Rs.403.29 billion, representing 16.68% (see Table 16.3). Balances with other banks—amounting to Rs 1,506.36 billion—were held in current accounts (Rs 92.67 billion), and other accounts (Rs 1,413.69 billion) and accounted for 62.30% of the assets with the banking system.

Generally, the most significant and perhaps controversial element in a bank's nondebt or nonmarketable securities investments is equity securities. For instance, a bank in Nigeria may, according to section 21 of the BOFI Act, No. 25, of 1991 (as amended), invest not more than 10% of its shareholders' funds, unimpaired by losses, in equity stock of any medium-scale enterprises—including agricultural, venture capital, or any other business enterprises approved by the CBN. This is the concept espoused in the Small and Medium Industries Equity Investment Scheme (SMIEIS) through which government intended to accelerate the growth of the industrial sector of the economy. Under the scheme,

TABLE 16.3 India—Scheduled Banks' Statement of Position in India
January 23, 2015

	Rs. billion	% of total
Assets	98,382.66	
Cash	534.72	0.54
Balances with Reserve Bank of India	3,587.02	3.65
Assets with banking system	2,417.75	2.46
Balances with other banks	1,506.36	62.30
Current accounts	92.67	6.15
Other accounts	1,413.69	93.85
Money at call and short notice	403.29	16.68
Advances to banks (i.e., due from banks)	133.77	5.53
Other assets	374.33	15.48
Investments (at book value)	25,893.49	26.32
Central and State Government securities	25,869.07	99.91
Other approved securities	24.38	0.09
Bank credit (excluding interbank advance)	65,949.68	67.03
Loans, cash credits and overdraft	63,740.26	96.65
Foreign bills purchased	245.78	0.37
Foreign bills discounted	441.82	0.67
Inland bills purchased	350.76	0.53
Inland bills discounted	1,171.02	1.78

Source: Extracted from Reserve Bank of India, *Scheduled banks' statement of position in India, January 23, 2015*. All ratios were computed based on data extracted from this source.

such shareholding or equity investment should not exceed 40% of the company's paid-up capital. Also, the total of a bank's investments in such enterprises should not exceed 20% and 50% of its shareholders' funds, unimpaired by losses, for commercial and merchant banks, respectively. With the introduction of universal banking in Nigeria in January 2001, the CBN now requires all licensed banks to invest not less than 10% of their profit after tax at the end of each financial year in a small- or medium-scale manufacturing enterprise. Any bank that fails to comply with this directive after 18 months from its financial year-end shall forfeit the amount to the CBN.

The banking system in Pakistan has a strong commitment to asset investments as Table 16.2 reflects. Collectively the ratio of investments to the entire banking system assets portfolio amounted to 43.36% in 2014. This is high compared to the industry's commitment of 37.33% of its assets in loans and advances during the period (Table 16.3).

Fixed Assets

Fixed assets are sterile in nature, as they do not directly generate earnings for a bank. They are employed to facilitate the performance of general banking activities. The funding of assets acquisition should not come from deposit liabilities. Ideally, fixed assets are funded from shareholders' funds or paid-up capital of the bank. In fact, asset acquisition should be the primary evidence of the owners' stake in the business. However, a common observation nowadays among banks in developing economies is a tendency to make huge investments—and, perhaps unwisely—in fixed assets in the evolving culture of ambience in the banking industry. This is wrong and should be discouraged as the huge funds so spent could be used more productively—to finance the ever growing borrowing needs of bank customers.

Loans and Advances

Credit facilities extended to customers constitute the single most important earning asset of a bank. Lending portfolio serve the profit-making goal of the bank. Unfortunately banks pursue this goal at a risk of possible diminution in value or outright loss of the assets. This obtains when borrowers default on loan repayment and the resultant bad debts are charged-off from earnings. This is why loans and advances are more appropriately described as risk assets. While the purpose of bank lending, in most cases, is to generate income or make profit, it also serves to meet the financing needs of the local or business communities where the banks are located. In the absence of secondary market for such financial claims, loans are largely nonliquid asset. Credit facilities may not be easily liquidated through sale to third parties (individuals or institutions). Besides profit consideration, lending objective is also driven by the need to have a balanced portfolio and meet prudential and other regulatory requirements for risk assets creation.

In general, superior lending decisions are achieved when a bank painstakingly defines its target markets and risk acceptance criteria. This becomes the guiding post for choosing types of risk assets in which to invest and volumes to hold in the lending portfolio. Usually loans and advances, including financing under leases, account for a significant proportion of a bank's risk assets portfolio. In the case of Zenith Bank, the ratio of this critical asset to the entire asset portfolio of the bank was 21.76%. The picture is the same for the entire banking system.

As Table 16.6 shows, the ratio of total credit portfolio of domestic banks in Taiwan to the country's banking system's assets portfolio was 59.89% as at June 30, 2014. Also loan loss provision of 1.23% evidenced high quality asset portfolio. Deposits to liabilities ratio of 82.89% for the industry during the period was also a comforting pointer to the liquidity of banks in Taiwan. However, the banks tended to take undue risk in off-balance sheet exposures. The ratios of off-balance sheet exposures to total loans, total liabilities, and total assets portfolios are quite high at 93.35%, 59.96%, and 55.91%, respectively. This should give serious cause for concern to the regulatory authorities and other stakeholders. The reason is simple. Banks in developing markets tend to have a fallback option in off-balance sheet lending when they are over-lent on-balance sheet.

Huge commitment of funds in building risk assets portfolio is also evident among banks in Pakistan. In 2014, as Table 16.2 shows, total loans and advances (net of provisions) amounted to Rs 4,014.0 billion, representing 37.33% of the entire banking system's assets portfolio. With the volume of gross nonperforming loans at Rs 602 billion during the period—accounting for 5.60% and 15.0% of the industry's total assets and total loans portfolios, respectively—it can be said that the banks maintained quality risk assets portfolio. This is further evident in the industry's net loan loss provision of 1.25% during the period.

CREDIT CONCENTRATION AND RISK MANAGEMENT IN DEVELOPING ECONOMIES

The Central Bank may require banks to maintain balanced portfolio of risk assets. Such a policy is often influenced by some credit expansion criteria designed to drive economic growth in a particular way. However, the purpose of a policy of balanced credit portfolio of the banking industry is often stated in more broad terms. In most cases, it is to ensure that economic development is pursued along the lines of national planning and fits with monetary policy. In pursuit of this goal, the Central Bank sometimes prescribes limits of sectoral allocation of risk assets for the banks. On occasion such credit expansion limit is waived for the healthy banks. But regulatory guidelines for risk assets structure remain enforceable on all licensed banks.

A balanced loan portfolio is a critical success factor in a bank's strategy for credit risk management. The balance in question is achieved when a portfolio comprises a medley of risk assets spread across a potpourri of economic sectors. Thus, a bank should strive to spread its credit exposures with painstaking attention to risk mitigation. It can do so by planning its lending activities in a way that it is able to grant and secure risk-mitigated loans to borrowers in different sectors and industries. This credit distribution pursuit is informed by some risk mitigation goal. Its import as a credit risk management strategy is that a bank should be able to avoid portfolio concentration risk.

Now, what do I mean by portfolio concentration risk? This question may be answered in three different but related ways. In bank lending, the term concentration risk refers to:

- The danger that a bank's operations might be impaired when it holds its risk assets portfolio in particular economic sectors.
- The chance that a bank may experience liquidity crisis, or be distressed, when few large borrowers make up its loan portfolio.
- The possibility that a bank might be plunged into crisis when its risk assets portfolio comprises few types of credit facilities.

TABLE 16.4 Brazil—Financial System Credit: Balance by Economic Activity as at Feb 11, 2015

	2012 (R$ m)	2013 (R$ m)	2014 (R$ m)	% of 2014 total
Public sector (a)	118,867.00	150,302.00	196,165.00	**6.49**
Federal Government	63,298.00	70,562.00	85,946.00	43.81
State and Municipal Government	55,569.00	79,741.00	110,219.00	56.19
Private sector (b)	2,249,471.00	2,565,069.00	2,825,607.00	**93.51**
Industry	462,092.00	516,397.00	552,200.00	19.54
Real estate	298,314.00	395,241.00	502,434.00	17.78
Rural	167,528.00	218,045.00	257,748.00	9.12
Commerce	227,355.00	242,098.00	254,342.00	9.00
Households	708,855.00	767,539.00	807,935.00	28.59
Other services	385,327.00	425,749.00	450,948.00	15.96
Total (a + b)	2,368,338.00	2,715,371.00	3,021,772.00	

Source: Extracted from Central Bank of Brazil (Banco Central Do Brazil), *Financial system credit: Balance by economic activity as at February 11, 2015*. All ratios were computed based on data extracted from this source.

Concentration risk, in foregoing sense, is completely different from risk diversification. In bank lending, the latter is both the alternative and solution to the former—and always desirable. A bank will diversify its credit portfolio risk when it grants different types and amounts of loans to various borrowers in different target markets, industries, or economic sectors.

Table 16.4 shows distribution of Brazil's financial system credit portfolio according to economic activities in which the borrowers were engaged. Distribution of the portfolio between public and private sectors indicates a risk-mitigation disposition. Only 6.49% of the total credit exposures went to the public sector while a whopping 93.51% was deployed to the private sector. While this does not reflect a balanced portfolio at this level, nevertheless bank lending in developing economies is oriented toward the private sector. Banks tend to be wary of lending to Government and its agencies and parastatals, if anything. Thus analysis of portfolio distribution should focus more on the private than public sector.

In the case of Brazil, the manner of deployment of the financial system's total credit portfolio reflects a near even distribution. With 28.59%, households got the lion's share of the lending portfolio. Credits deployed to industry, real

TABLE 16.5 Singapore—Loans and Advances of DBUs to Nonbank Customers by Industry

	S$ million	% (a, b)	% (a + b)
Total loans to business (a)	371,520.2		
Agriculture, mining and quarrying	6,245.6	1.68	1.03
Manufacturing	29,618.8	7.97	4.87
Building and construction	103,712.4	27.92	17.06
General commerce	78,084.2	21.02	12.84
Transport, storage and communication	21,128.5	5.69	3.48
Business services	8,586.9	2.31	1.41
Financial institutions	80,895.0	21.77	13.31
Professional and private individuals—business purposes	9,746.0	2.62	1.60
Others	34,502.8	9.29	5.68
Total consumer loans (b)	236,439.9		
Housing and bridging loans	177,434.6	75.04	29.19
Car loans	8,641.5	3.65	1.42
Credit cards	10,422.4	4.41	1.71
Share financing	989.6	0.42	0.16
Others	38,961.8	16.48	6.41
Total loan portfolio (a + b)	607,960.0		
Key financial ratios			
Business loans to total loans			61.11
Consumer loans to total loans			38.89

Source: Extracted from Monetary Authority of Singapore, *Loans and advances of DBUs to nonbank customers by industry.* All ratios were computed based on data extracted from this source.

estate, and other services followed with 19.54%, 17.78%, and 15.96%, respectively. We can say that concentration risk is not indicated in the Brazil's case. However, it is curious that only 9% of the portfolio went to commerce—ordinarily a popular sector for bank lending in developing and developing economies.

Concentration risk is not also reflected in the distribution of loans and advances of Singapore's domestic banking units (DBUs) to nonbank borrowers as presented along industry lines in Table 16.5. Total lending to business accounted for 61.11% of the entire industry's credit portfolio while the balance of 38.89% was deployed to the consumer sector. This is a fair portfolio distribution. As in Brazil's case, lending to households—in Singapore's case, housing and bridging loans—again got the lion's share at 29.19% of the total credit portfolio of the banking system. Credits to building and construction followed with 17.06% while 13.31% and 12.84% of the industry's total credit portfolio were deployed to financial institutions and general commerce, respectively. In both Brazil and Singapore, emphasis on lending to finance housing is unmistakable. There was also good showing for industry and households.

Central Banks in developing economies should not relent in enforcing policies that define appropriate credit portfolio structure for money deposit banks. However, the efficacy of regulatory policies is sometimes undermined by the banking expediency of lending to less risky or even riskless but profitable accounts. This is why banks often flout the regulations. For instance, a bank in a developing economy might find it more expedient to lend, say, $5.0 million to an enterprise engaged in trading than grant the same credit facility to a farm enterprise. The preference indicated in this illustration is dictated by differences in expected earnings and risk characteristics of the two businesses. Yet banks should play down such considerations and lend support to the broader national goal of developing preferred sectors of the economy.

CREDIT PORTFOLIO DISTRIBUTION, MATURITY PROFILES, AND RISK MANAGEMENT

Knowledge of patterns of portfolio distribution and risk assets maturity profiles across banking systems in developing economies is pertinent to understand of the workings of credit risk control. Such knowledge also informs regulation of structure and quality of credit portfolios of the banks for effective risk management. Ideally banks will want to lend to borrowers with low risk. The banks will tend to scout around for such borrowers in their target markets. Playing it safe in this way, they crave so-called self-liquidating lending while shunning risky credits across economic sectors. That forms the basis for devising means to exploit full banking potential of the sectors and borrowers that satisfy their risk acceptance criteria. Usually expectation of maximum earnings at low to moderate risk is the driving force behind this lending strategy.

In practice, however, many banks tend to be adventurous. They commit huge lending to risky sectors and borrowers—usually in expectation of earnings that meet their budget targets. Often reckless lending underlies excessive risk-taking in pursuit of such budget goals. This unfortunate situation has been the bane of the banking industry in developing economies. Curiously this pattern of risk assets creation is not always evident in returns, the banks make to the regulatory authorities. As Chapter 16 shows, the banks have a way of circumventing or skirting around infringement of regulatory policies and control. That way they escape damning report on their lending activities. How else can recurrent distress in the industry—despite good credit portfolio returns to the regulatory authorities—be explained?

The foregoing implies that issues in credit portfolio distribution and maturity profiles for banks in developing economies may not be apparent from statistical data which their Central Banks furnish based on returns from the banks. Yet looking at Tables 16.2–16.9 with a critical eye, one begins to gain insight into the problem of lending portfolios of banks in developing economies. The problem tends to be structural in nature and evident in mismatch between need for deposits-driven liabilities and lending-based earnings. The need defines liquidity and profitability goals—both of which are critical for success in banking. If the issue is not mismatched portfolios, it is a misapplication of deposits in funding risk assets. In both cases, banks contend with possible threat to smooth operations. Ideally banking regulation, complemented by effective supervision, should address these conflicts. But a combination of intractable factors and forces, some of which I discussed in Chapter 10, constrain effective supervision of banks in developing economies.

Take a look at Table 16.6, for instance. Do you see structural problem with the consolidated balance sheet of Taiwan's domestic banks? The first striking observation is that much of the funding for risk assets came from short-term deposits. A disproportionate volume of the deposits was utilized for funding medium and long-term loans. These two categories of loans accounted for 73.82% of the entire industry's portfolio of risk assets. This finding—coupled with the fact that savings deposits accounted for 49.90% of the reported deposits portfolio—informs the seriousness of the problem. This mirror of the asset structure of the industry should be worrisome. There should have been more reliance on equities and time deposits than short-term deposits in funding the industry's asset portfolio.

The problem, reflected in Table 16.7, is also evident in the case of Singapore. Obligations falling due within 180 days accounted for 88.46% of the industry's liabilities portfolio. Compared with 46.01% of risk assets in medium to long-term maturity categories, the structural defect of mismatch between assets and liabilities portfolios becomes more apparent. A relatively low ratio of assets, at 49.02%, had the same maturity period. A clearer indication of the problem emerges when ratios of funds applicable to different assets and liabilities tenors are compared. For instance, while 46.01% of the assets had medium to long-terms, only 5.87% of liabilities fell within the same maturity categories.

Ironically, the distribution of Taiwan's banking system's loans was a departure from a common observation of short-term lending skewing risk assets portfolio. Table 16.7 showing data on maturities of assets and liabilities of the banking system in Singapore is typical of what obtains in a majority of developing economies. Interestingly, comparing Tables 16.6 and 16.7 in terms of assets portfolio distribution by maturities sheds light on the Taiwan's departure from the common pattern. In Taiwan, on the one hand, and Singapore, on the other, short-term loans (or assets) accounted for 24.84% and 53.99% of the entire industry's assets portfolio, respectively.

TABLE 16.6 Taiwan—Consolidated Balance Sheet of Domestic Banks as at June 30, 2014

	NT$ Million	Ratio (%)
Total assets	41,032,662.00	
Loans and discounts	24,573,284.00	
Import bills purchased	3,006.00	0.01
Export bills purchased	179,014.00	0.73
Discounts	18,073.00	0.07
Overdrafts	67,979.00	0.28
Short-term loans	6,104,550.00	24.84
Medium-term loans	8,110,565.00	33.01
Long-term loans	10,028,738.00	40.81
Nonaccrual loans	61,359.00	0.25
Allowance for doubtful accounts	302,057.00	
Total liabilities	38,258,247.00	
Deposits	31,710,418.00	
Check deposits	395,303.00	1.25
Demand deposits	3,463,017.00	10.92
Time deposits	5,228,205.00	16.49
Savings deposits	15,822,775.00	49.90
Foreign currencies deposits	6,215,517.00	19.60
Government deposits	585,601.00	1.85
Total equities	2,774,415.00	
Total liabilities and equities	41,032,662.00	
Off-balance sheet items	22,939,575.00	
Loan commitments	14,683,740.00	63.81
Guarantees	1,066,072.00	4.65
Letter of credit issued	354,736.00	1.55
Liabilities trusted	6,880,027.00	29.99
Key accounting ratios		
Equities to assets	6.76	
Loans to deposits	77.49	
Loans to assets	59.89	
Off-balance sheet items to loans	93.35	
Off-balance sheet items to liabilities	59.96	
Off-balance sheet to assets	55.91	
Deposits to liabilities	82.89	
Loan loss provision	1.23	

Source: Extracted from Central Bank of Republic of China—Taiwan, *Consolidated balance sheet of domestic banks as at June 30, 2014.* All ratios were computed based on data extracted from this source.

TABLE 16.7 Singapore — Maturities of Assets and Liabilities of DBUs

	Assets S$ million	Liabilities S$ million	Assets to liabilities ratio (%)	Ratio to total assets (%)	Ratio to total liabilities (%)
Up to 6 months	481,038.30	793,247.10	60.64	49.02	88.46
Over 6 months to 1 year	48,794.50	50,809.80	96.03	4.97	5.67
Over 1–3 years	121,981.90	32,640.90	373.71	12.43	3.64
Over 3 years	329,568.00	20,021.20	1,646.10	33.58	2.23
	981,382.70	896,719.00	109.44		

Source: Extracted from Monetary Authority of Singapore, *Maturities of assets and liabilities of Domestic Banking Units (DBUs)*. All ratios were computed based on data extracted from this source.

On sectoral basis and analysis, a significant volume of aggregate bank lending in India went to so-called priority sectors. Priority sectors distilled from Table 16.8 include agriculture and allied activities, micro and small enterprises, housing, micro-credit, education loans, and export credit. Total volume of loans outstanding against the sectors was Rs 19,552.0 billion, representing 32.95% of the industry portfolio. Industry (excluding micro and small enterprises) accounted for Rs 22,068.0 billion, representing 37.20%, of the total outstanding loans portfolio. Thus priority and nonpriority segments of industry accounted for 70.15% of the total outstanding loans portfolio.

On occasion it is difficult to tell the quality of risk assets portfolios of banks in developing economies due to maneuvering of returns to the regulatory authorities. While all the banks make the mandatory general provision on the loans portfolio, it is often difficult to strictly enforce specific cases. The net effect is that reported portfolio quality is usually good on paper and satisfies regulatory requirements. Table 16.9 shows standing of Singapore's banks on assets quality as mirrored in report of MAS on classified exposures. The ratios, as is always the case—except in full blown distress situations—are good.

SUMMARY

Banks managements in developing economies scarcely rely on theories for assets portfolio management. Fall back on some pragmatic techniques is common. A possible reason is that loan books which constitute the bulk of the assets

TABLE 16.8 India—Deployment of Gross Bank Credit by Major Sectors as at December 26, 2014

Economic sector	Amount (Rs. billion)	% of sector total
Gross bank credit	**59,330.00**	
Food credit	**1,065.00**	**1.80**
Agriculture and allied activities	**7,512.00**	**12.66**
Industry (micro and small, medium and large)	**25,752.00**	**43.40**
Micro and small	3,684.00	14.31
Medium	1,268.00	4.92
Large	20,800.00	80.77
Services	**13,502.00**	**22.76**
Transport operators	883	6.54
Computer software	171	1.27
Tourism, hotels and restaurants	360	2.67
Shipping	96	0.71
Professional services	717	5.31
Trade	3,313.00	24.54
Wholesale trade (other than food procurement)	1,649.00	
Retail trade	1,664.00	
Commercial real estate	1,643.00	12.17
Nonbanking financial companies	3,000.00	22.22
Other services	3,320.00	24.59
Personal loans	**11,499.00**	**19.38**
Consumer durables	147	1.28
Housing (including priority sector housing)	6,015.00	52.31
Advances against fixed deposits	600	5.22
Advances to individuals against share, bonds, etc.	41	0.36
Card outstanding	303	2.64
Education	630	5.48
Vehicle loans	1,457.00	12.67
Other personal loans	2,307.00	20.06

Source: Reserve Bank of India, *Deployment of gross bank credit by major sectors.* Ratios were computed based on data extracted from this source.

TABLE 16.9 Singapore—Classified Exposures as a Percentage of Total Exposures

Pass	97.27
Special mention	1.98
Substandard	0.52
Doubtful	0.15
Lost	0.08
Classified exposures (net of specific provisions)	0.58

Source: Extracted from Monetary Authority of Singapore (MAS), Classified exposures as a percentage of total exposures.

portfolio are a melting pot. There is also the question of intrigues and maneuverings bordering on cover-ups sometimes. The risk implication of these issues is that patterns of assets management are in flux and unpredictable. Two of the theories, pool-of-funds and assets allocation, are relevant to solving some of the present-day assets management risks of banks in developing economies.

The usual assets of a bank comprise cash, short-term funds, securities, loans, fixed assets, and others. The liquidity of these assets varies, with cash being the most and fixed assets the least liquid. Of course, the more liquid an asset, the less earning or return it generates. Assets constitute a significant component of a bank's balance sheet—representing "uses" to which its capital, reserves, and liabilities are put to generate earnings, growth, and returns to the shareholders. Thus assets management must be efficient and in order to achieve a bank's overall business objectives.

The Central Bank may require banks to maintain balanced portfolio of risk assets. Such a policy is often influenced by some credit expansion criteria designed to drive economic growth in a particular way. However, the purpose of a policy of balanced credit portfolio is to ensure that economic development is pursued along the lines of national planning and fits with monetary policy. A balanced loan portfolio is a critical success factor in a bank's strategy for credit risk management. Thus, a bank should strive to spread its credit exposures with painstaking attention to risk mitigation. This credit risk management strategy ensures that a bank is able to avoid portfolio concentration risk.

Knowledge of patterns of portfolio distribution and risk assets maturity profiles across banking systems in developing economies is pertinent to understanding of the workings of credit risk control. Such knowledge also informs regulation of structure and quality of credit portfolios of the banks for effective risk management.

QUESTIONS FOR DISCUSSION AND REVIEW

1. Why should banks in developing economies always strive to have a balanced and profitable portfolio of risk assets?
2. **a.** What are the main components of the assets portfolio of banks in developing economies?
   b. How do banks' funds commitments to loans and advances compare with investments in other assets in their portfolios?
3. **a.** Define the terms credit concentration and concentration risk as understood in the context of credit portfolio of the banking industry.
   b. In what ways, using consolidated balance sheet of banks in a named developing economy as basis of discussion, does concentration impart risk to loans portfolio?
4. Are there situations in which credit concentration would realistically be considered strategic to a bank's business?
5. **a.** When would it be appropriate to christen some economic activity or group a priority sector?
   b. Why does credit portfolio regulation often favor strict adherence to target deployment of loans to so-called priority sectors?
6. Can risk assets quality of banks in developing economies be realistically measured on the basis of returns to the regulatory authorities? Your answer should show understanding of dynamics of data maneuvering to circumvent regulation.

REFERENCE

Agene, C.E., 1995. The Principles of Modern Banking. Gene Publications, Lagos.

Chapter 17

Sensitizing Bankers in Developing Economies to Securitization Risks and Management

Chapter Outline

LEARNING FOCUS AND OBJECTIVES

I present securitization of loans in a simple nontechnical form. My objective, doing so, is for readers to be able to easily understand key aspects of the subject. Yet my ultimate goal is to show how banks in developing economies can benefit from possibilities that securitization of loans offers as a capital market instrument. Thus, I accordingly formed my objectives to:

- define the concept, discuss the meaning, and assess the scope of securitization—and, doing so, examine its workings and dynamics;
- evaluate securitization types and methodologies, with implications for its problems and prospects in developing economies;
- discuss the procedure that banks adopt to raise capital through loan securitization, including its structuring and packaging;

- examine aspects of Basel II Accord on credit risk management that deal with securitization of assets; and
- assess the significance of securitization from the perspective of bank financing needs and arrangements.

EXPECTED LEARNING OUTCOMES

I tap into the experience of the industrialized countries in presenting elements of loan securitization in this chapter. From overview of securitization, through simplifying it, to a rigorous analysis of its workings and dynamics, I examine implications of securitization for credit risk management. The discussions of topics of this chapter are intended to accomplish specific learning outcomes. The reader will—after studying this chapter and doing the exercises in it—have learnt and been better informed about:

- the concept, meaning and scope of securitization and, doing so, appreciate its workings and dynamics;
- securitization types and methodologies, with implications for problems and prospects of securitization in developing economies;
- the procedure that banks adopt to raise capital through asset securitization, including structuring and packaging of securitization deals;
- aspects of Basel II Accord on credit risk management that deal with securitization of assets and, doing so, know the impact and applications of the Accord in loan securitization; and
- the significance of securitization from the perspective of contemporary bank financing needs and arrangements.

OVERVIEW OF THE SUBJECT MATTER

Domestic and foreign subsidiary bankers in developing economies are largely not well versed in the workings of securitization. They are not used to it. It is, for them, an exotic construct meant for the advanced financial markets—mainly in developed countries. Even in those markets, where securitization has been institutionalized, its practice is yet not altogether welcome. The reason is simple. Financial analysts and investors tend to paint credit derivatives in a bad light—and justifiably too.

It is widely believed that the recent (2007–08) financial meltdown which rocked the international financial market was a product of reckless credit derivatives transactions. In 1994, Amex Bank Review essay winners had entered for the competition with a critical disposition toward financial derivatives. Their winning piece, "The Wild Best of Derivatives: To be Caged in, Fenced off, or Tamed?" was well received. The financial meltdown, perhaps, could have been forestalled had the authorities and operators heeded their recommendation that derivatives should be "tamed." In this chapter, I take a more critical look at the underlying issues with a view to properly situating the demon of derivatives in failed credit risk management. I proffer suggestions on the measures to consolidate credit derivatives for the betterment of financial operators, investors, and industry.

Securitization is an uncommon topic within financial circles in developing countries. Apparently, the situation is the same in financial centers of most emerging markets. One reason is that the markets are in their rudimentary form. In most cases, the markets lack the requisite structure, conditions, and institutions for effective execution of securitization. Another reason is that available skills are hardly capable of handling the complex mechanics of the process of securitization. Yet beyond the popular problem of lack of depth of the securities market, operators contend with limited experience on securitization deals.

The prime movers in most capital market transactions, usually issuers of securities and investors, are not altogether well informed about securitization. Worse still, the stakeholders and operators of the capital market scarcely understand the mechanism of the securitization process. This is not strange, largely because they see securitization as an exotic financial product. Indeed, securitization is alien to their financing culture and arrangements. This implies that market operators lack grounding in the structuring and packaging of securitization deals. It is perhaps only in highly industrialized countries that financial markets have developed capabilities for handling securitization and derivative transactions without structural difficulties.

Yet it is becoming increasingly imperative to appreciate and apply securitization to meeting the financing needs of banks in both developing and emerging markets. Other financial institutions interested in issuing asset-backed securities also find securitization appealing as a refinancing instrument. In markets where it is institutionalized, issuers of securities and investors look to securitization for financing and investment possibilities that meet their objectives. As in developed countries, securitization can only but start to take root in developing and emerging markets. It is the duty of regulators in those markets to provide the enabling operating environment. Together with banks and other financial institutions, the regulators should set the stage for the takeoff, operations, and supervision of securitization transactions in the capital market. In doing so, issuers of securities and investors can begin to explore and experience the potential of securitization. Now is the time to start.

I formulated the focus and learning objectives of this chapter in the context of the foregoing. I relate the relevant issues to the need to evolve loan securitization market in developing economies. Doing so, I assess how banks, other financial institutions, and regulators in those markets should work together to institutionalize the securitization framework.

SIMPLIFYING THE CONCEPT OF SECURITIZATION

It is pertinent to explore and critically examine the securitization concept and its implications for the banking industry. Most definitions provide somewhat technical notions of the concept of securitization. Apparently they are not couched in layman's terms. They are at best complex, perhaps, without meaning to be so technical. A number of other definitions may be similarly characterized. To finance experts, there may be nothing wrong with the definitions. Ironically, rather than see the technical undertone of the definitions as complicating understanding of the concept, they praise it. Yet we cannot, for purposes of this chapter, accept the overly technical definitions and meanings as given. Thus, it's necessary to look to the simple, noncomplex definitions for meanings that serve our purpose. Some authors, though, have propounded forceful definitions that meet this need. Their definitions underpin understanding of the securitization concept for everyone interested in the subject.

The crux of both complex and simple definitions lies in showing the financing potential of securitization and how organizations can tap into it. The difference between them lies in the levels of technicality of the definitions. Good judgment dictates that a complex subject like securitization should be defined in very simple terms so that learners can appreciate its meaning. Indeed, good definitions of technical concepts should be devoid of technicalities. Apparently, when this is achieved, complex subjects like securitization become simplified in a way that the layman and, especially, students can easily understand them.

I simplify securitization concept and proffer a simplified analysis of it, one that students and laymen can easily understand. I bear in mind, doing so, that experienced practitioners—investment bankers, capital market operators (especially securities issuers and investors), and financial analysts and pundits—should have good vibes about securitization concept. Of course, they would be interested in how securitization is perceived by nonexperts in and outside financial circles. For this reason, it can be conceded that a definition of securitization may be a little technical, or technically simple. But such a definition should not have complex connotations, nor should it mystify the securitization concept.

With these thoughts in mind, I go ahead and define securitization concept. Securitization deals with how a company or organization converts, packages, and sells nonmarketable assets as marketable securities in the capital market to meet its funding need. It is the process of converting a group of nonmarketable assets, or expected future cash flows on the assets, into units of marketable securities in order to sell the underlying assets in the capital market to generate money for a business.

It may be defined, in the context of banking, in a more functional way to highlight its main purpose. For a bank, securitization is the process of converting a pool of loans, and sale of the pooled loans, as units of secured marketable securities to investors to meet the funding need of a bank. It is the conversion of expected future cash inflows (i.e., service incomes and repayments) from a pool of loans into units of secured marketable securities which are sold to investors to raise capital for a bank.

OBJECTIVES AND USES OF SECURITIZATION

Usually, and this is commonplace, some funding need triggers a securitization deal, while the existence of a robust capital market nourishes it. I expatiate on characterizing features of securitization in subsequent sections of this chapter. The need to do so is informed by the focus and learning objectives I set for the chapter. Yet doing so will help readers to appreciate the concept, scope, and dynamics of securitization. Besides, it will also help to popularize securitization as a versatile financing arrangement in contemporary banking and finance.

As I pointed out in the foregoing section, securitization is the act or process of disposing of some of the risk assets of a bank to generate funds for its operations. In addition to unlocking funds tied up in risk assets, and making funds available for business, securitization serves a number of other useful purposes for a bank. Let me now discuss the objectives of securitization to highlight its significance and implications for risk management in bank lending. There are seven important objectives of securitization which underline its significance as a capital market instrument. Through securitization of loans, a bank will be able to:

- unlock and recoup funds tied up in risk assets;
- optimize earnings while enhancing return on capital employed;
- mitigate credit risk, especially under Basel Committee on Banking and Supervision Accord (2004b);
- create an alternative source of cash flow;
- manage its balance sheet, especially so as to meet regulatory capital requirements under Basel Committee on Banking and Supervision Accord (2004a);
- tap into occasional windows of opportunity that may open to it; and
- explore new investments in and outside lending.

There may be other objectives and uses of securitization in contemporary corporate financing system. However, those listed above satisfy the need for a discussion of the applications and advantages of securitization of loans in the banking industry. I discuss the significance, which also underlies the benefits, of securitization using the foregoing objectives as a framework. In doing so, I highlight the benefits of securitization of loans. Three main economic units benefit from securitization of loans—banks and, indeed, all companies and organizations that issue securities to raise funds for operations, as well as investors, and the capital market. Apparently, borrowers also benefit, though indirectly, from securitization of loans.

Unlocking Funds Tied up in Loans

This is the basic function of securitization, one that often triggers corporate interest in it as a financing tool. The notion of "unlocking funds" relates to appreciate that cash has varied and demanding uses in banking. For a bank, it follows that one use should not encumber another or other uses of funds. But it also implies that a bank should ideally balance out the competing uses of capital, opposing needs for funds, and attaining efficient operations. This is not usually easy to achieve. One reason is that goals for funds uses in banking are hardly congruent. Another reason is that the uses of funds in banking are often driven by exigencies of the business. Banks are sometimes faced with a situation in which the exigencies of the business inform the use of funds to satisfy alternative objectives. While this may sound incredible, it is a prevalent reality in bank management. A new regulation may call for a redirection for the application of funds. A bank may be jolted into committing a chunk of funds to acquiring a particular technological capability. The urge to drive business in some way in particular markets can also be a cause to invest bank funds in heavy lending.

Securitization helps a bank to raise or free capital for operations. This is achieved when, through securitization, a bank recoups part of its capital that is tied up in risk assets and to apply the capital recouped to satisfying other pressing funding needs. Thus, when a bank securitizes loans, it is able to "unlock" funds invested in the loans for other uses dictated by its funding needs. In the absence of securitization, funds committed to the lending would remain encumbered by the loans until the loans are liquidated (i.e., fully paid back, or recovered from the obligors). The process of liquidating loans according to their terms, or through recovery actions, can be complex and time-consuming. In fact, it is often frustrating, to say the least.

Optimizing Income and Returns

Through securitization, a bank can recover funds tied up in loans before the due dates of the loans. This implies that the bank can increase revenue and earnings with funds recouped from its investment in the loans. This is possible because the bank can apply the funds that securitization "unlocks" from loans in other, often more, profitable investment opportunities. If the bank sustains increase in earnings over time by this method, its return on capital employed will improve.

However, it is imperative that banks appreciate a limiting factor in their ability to improve return on capital employed through securitization of loans. Delinquent loans may not be easily securitized. Investors critically analyze securitized loans. They must be convinced that the loans are of high quality before committing funds to the securities underlying the securitization.

Were it impossible for a bank to recover funds locked up in loans, it would not be able to take advantage of promising investments in other assets. In that case, the bank may not increase earnings and return on capital employed. That is one of the advantages underlying the significance of securitization of loans in contemporary banking and finance. There is yet another way to appreciate how securitization improves return on capital employed. Imagine how securitization of loans helps banks to optimize the use of funds. Funds committed to build the lending portfolio are really optimized when they open up a window of opportunity in securitization of risk assets.

Mitigating Credit Risk

Banks must deliberately seek to mitigate credit risk. They should constantly do so in order to minimize huge loan loss provisions. One of the ways banks can mitigate credit risk is through securitization of loans. Mitigation of credit risk through securitization of loans is achieved in three different ways. In practical terms, securitization:

- helps banks to check or reverse loan concentration;
- affords banks opportunity to reduce loan portfolio when doing so becomes necessary or is inevitable; and
- fits well with a strategy of risk diversification in bank lending.

These applications of securitization have a sole aim. Their aim is to help banks mitigate credit risk—without incurring principal, interest, or other income losses in so doing.

In building risk assets portfolio over time, a bank may find that it has inadvertently concentrated its lending in a particular sector. That sector may be more or less risky depending on prevailing economic circumstances. Assuming a worst case scenario, where a certain happening threatens that sector. It would be possible for the bank to sell a substantial group of loans in that sector as a risk mitigating measure. Securitization makes the sale of loans possible in this or similar situation. That way, securitization of loans helps banks to check incidence of loan concentration.

A bloated loan portfolio could really be unwieldy. A bank that has such a lending portfolio will soon discover it must do something drastic about it. One of the options the bank is likely to consider is to reduce the size of the loan portfolio, to make it easily manageable. If it adopts this option, it may have to rely on securitization to achieve the objective. This is why and how securitization affords banks opportunity to reduce loan portfolio when doing so is inevitable. It is high time banks in developing countries started tapping into this benefit of loan securitization. The banks cannot but accept this reality in the face of the danger which occasional credit risk crisis poses to their operations.

Creating Alternative Cash Flow Source

Banks can count on securitization of loans to meet difficult cash flow needs. With securitization, the banks are offered a cash flow window to satisfy funding requirements for their operations. Thus, a major appeal of securitization is driven by its growing popularity as an alternative source of cash flow. A bank that is short of funds may look to securitization for solution to its cash crunch. Securitizing a group of loans in its lending portfolio can help the bank to fill the funding gap in its treasury position.

The primary and usual sources of cash flow for a bank—interest incomes, fees, commissions, and charges—may falter. A more commonly observed situation is that these income sources can become volatile in a way that business plans may be significantly affected or altered. In most cases when the primary cash flow sources are faltering, earnings from operations start to decline. Often, the observed decline is the result when much of the bank's loan portfolio suddenly becomes delinquent. This situation will have a negative cash flow implication for the bank for two reasons. While total interest income will be declining, on the one hand, total loan loss provision will be increasing, on the other. The net effect of these opposing trends is that the bank will begin to find it difficult to meet its funding requirements for new lending or day-to-day operations. It would make sense, under the circumstances, for the bank to explore an alternative source of cash inflow to bridge the funding gap. In that case, securitization of some of its loans would be a good fallback option for the bank. In this sense, securitization of loans is appreciated as a veritable alternative to a bank's regular sources of cash flows.

Managing the Balance Sheet

In opting to securitize loans, a bank indirectly acknowledges that it has funding potential that is locked up in risk assets which it wants to unlock in order to be in funds. The road to this financial condition is rough for many banks. For example, a bank may realize that much of its funds are tied up in risk assets, especially in medium to long term loans. The bank may not be in a position to alter repayment terms of the loans in a way that could ease liquidity pressure on its operations. It must comply with structured loan payments over a fixed period that is beyond its control, if anything.

The bank's funding problem is compounded when its deposit portfolio is dwindling away. Deposit stagnation, or a deposit base that is increasing at a decreasing rate relative to loan portfolio and operations cost, exacerbates the cash crunch. Besides, unsustainable decline of earnings, or serial operational losses, accentuate the funding stress of the bank. Faced with a situation like this, a bank may decide to dispose of some risk assets in its loan portfolio. The rationale for doing so, besides liquidity consideration, is that the bank is able to manage the size of its balance sheet, and the financial ratios derived from it.

This function of securitization complements its significance in appreciating the challenges in loan recovery which it helps banks to avoid. That securitization generates cash inflow to ease pressure for a bank that is cash-strapped further underscores its significance as a refinancing system. The import of this is that securitization minimizes anxious moments through which banks go when they are faced with demanding funding needs in cash-strapped situations. When a bank manages its balance sheet well—and securitization helps it to do that—the ratios that underlie its financial performance will improve and become good and attractive to depositors and investors.

Thus securitization helps a bank to maintain a manageable and efficient balance sheet size. How? It offers banks option and possibility to sell loans prior to their maturity dates. When sold under securitization arrangement, the loans are removed from the bank's balance sheet. A reduction in loan portfolio and balance sheet has a positive impact on the bank's capital charge. This implies that the amount of bank's regulatory capital requirements will drop as a result of securitization (sale) of loans.

Tapping into Opportunities

Banks in developing countries must acknowledge and get to grips with securitization of loans. When they do so, they would start to incorporate securitization of loans in planning to optimize their finances. In this way, the banks could reduce credit risk, maximize earnings on investment funds, and improve return on capital employed. Risk reduction is possible because securitization of loans often seeks to diversify credit risk while helping banks to tap into windows of opportunity.

As shown in "mitigating credit risk" I discussed earlier, a bank must constantly be seriously working to reduce risk. But the bank should also be fully exploiting the potential in securitization. The potential consists in generating cash inflow with which to take advantage of occasional windows in banking and to consolidate operations. A bank needs to do that, first as a survival strategy and then as a boost to earnings. While boosting earnings, return on capital employed is enhanced.

This has an important implication for revenue and earnings maximization. It implies that a bank must build a strong capacity for maximization of earnings from investment in risk assets. It must achieve that in order to improve its financial performance through securitization of loans. Another implication is that a bank with a low appetite for earnings (if ever there's such a bank) may not be too interested in securitization of loans. If the bank has any interest at all in securitization of loans, it is likely to be in shedding a portion of its loan portfolio as a risk management strategy.

Funding New Investments

Like in other businesses, a bank should invest in profitable assets in order to achieve its earnings and growth plans. In general, a bank must be adequately capitalized and operate with sufficient funds in order to satisfy three important business objectives as follows:

- Under Basel Committee on Banking and Supervision Accord (2004a), the bank must meet regulatory capital requirements for risk management;
- The bank may want to drive or sustain a significant growth level, or to be a strongly going concern; and
- The bank should above all be able to meet its day-to-day funding need for business and efficient operations.

A bank will be unable to accomplish foregoing objectives if it has invested heavily in structured term loans without a compensating increase in earnings, deposit portfolio, and capital base. The bank will also be incapacitated if there is a large stock of delinquent risk assets in its loan portfolio. Yet a huge investment in loans may constrain the bank from fulfilling aforesaid objectives even if the quality of its loan portfolio is high.

A bank can use securitization to free some money for investment purposes. The bank can use the money freed from loans to fund investment in new, more profitable assets. The bank can yet invest the funds in building, improving, or consolidating its loan portfolio in some sectors or markets. Thus while the bank is selling some loans, perhaps to mitigate concentration risk, it may also yet be investing the sale proceeds in loans. This way, securitization facilitates realignment of lending strategy and portfolio.

THE WORKINGS AND DYNAMICS OF LOAN SECURITIZATION

It is not uncommon that banks sometimes operate in situations where money is tight, and they cannot meet funding need for their operations. This is usually the issue at stake when banks are faced with cash crunch, liquidity squeeze, or treasury crisis—all of which reflect money panic. These phrases depict situations in which banks are having problem with funding of their operations because money is scarce or too costly. In most cases, when it is hard to come by money, some banks tend to be in a helpless situation. It becomes worrisome when a dearth of funds threatens the solvency of banks. Worse still, the resultant funding gap often constrains banks from paying customers' deposits on demand or due dates.

The immediate need of a bank under the circumstances is to recover working capital to an appreciable level. The bank is most likely to begin to look for alternative source of funding for its working capital needs. Ideally, a good funding source for this purpose should impart resilience to operations of the bank. It should also particularly ensure that the bank maintains a robust working capital for its operations. Doing so and usually too, the bank will find one of the following three possible options readily appealing. The bank may want to:

- increase its total capital funds through the issue and sale of a given number of units of its ordinary shares;
- issue and sell a particular type of debt instrument (such as bond or other marketable securities) traded in the capital market; or
- securitize some of its risk assets (usually a group of loans that have common attributes and represent a portion of its total loan portfolio).

The bank can rely on any of these funding sources to recover to its precash crunch, or be in better, funding position. However, it is with the third of the funding sources—how a bank can securitize loans—that I am concerned. The process of, and steps involved in, securitization of loans can be more or less complicated, depending on the level of development of the capital market. In developing countries where the market is still evolving, securitization is hardly a welcome option.

Parties to Loan Securitization

Five parties, with mutually exclusive roles, are involved in the conduct of securitization. In addition to obligors, originator, and a special purpose vehicle (SPV), there are also the investors and administrator or servicer.

Obligors

The obligors are the borrowers to who a bank has disbursed the pooled and securitized loans. They remain the ultimate debtors in a securitization arrangement. This is notwithstanding that securitization of loans originate from the borrowings of the obligors. Also, the fact that the borrowings of the obligors are essentially independent of the securitization of their loans does not limit the obligors' liability. Thus, under securitization arrangement, the obligors continue to service and repay their loans according to agreement with the bank. However, their loan service payments and repayments go to the investors in the securitization securities rather than to the bank that granted the securitized loans to them. Incidentally, the obligors may be and are indeed often oblivious to the securitization of their loans. The import of all this is that securitization securities are necessarily serviced with the obligors' payments. The payments in question comprise principal repayment, prepayments (if applicable), and interest and other loan service charges. Altogether, these payments make up expected cash flows from securitization. With the cash flows, securitization securities are serviced (i.e., interest is paid on the securities), including principal repayments to the investors. Yet the investors don't have a direct claim on the obligors.

Originator

The originator is usually a bank or other lending financial institution that initiates a securitization of loan transaction. For this reason, the bank or finance institution is referred to as the originator. Where the originator is a bank, initiation and conduct of securitization of loan follow some ordered steps. The bank isolates a group of loans from its loan portfolio; it pools (combines) the loans to form units of securities. The loans so pooled must have common features, as in risk profile, collateral, maturity, mode, and source of repayment. In fact, the pool should contain only homogeneous loans. It will be easy, when that is achieved, to harmonize the loans and cash flows from them. For example, long-term loans granted to multinational oil exploration companies. Once this is achieved, the bank transfers the loans to a special purpose vehicle (SPV) for further securitization actions.

Special Purpose Vehicle

The conduct of securitization requires the formation of a SPV. The SPV is an independent body set up to facilitate securitization of loans. It functions exclusively for this purpose and acts, in so doing, as a go-between for the originator and investors. The SPV makes funds available to the originator; but it also ensures that the investors get applicable returns on the securities.

The SPV is able to do this for one important reason. It markets (sells) the securities, on the one hand, on behalf of the originator, and handles collection of payments on the loans for the investors, on the other. Thus, in its go-between role, the SPV acts on behalf of the originator and investor for the success of a securitization transaction. Meanwhile, the initial work of the SPV is to convert the loans pooled for securitization into units of marketable securities. Then it sells securities created on the pool to investors. The securities represent interests of the investors in the pooled loans. This implies that the "interests" are evidence of the claims of the investors on the pooled loans.

The SPV appoints a servicer, which may be the originator in some cases, to collect service, prepayments, and due payments on the loans from the obligors. But it is the SPV that handles servicing of the securities once there is no recourse to the originator after sale of the underlying loans. Compensation for the SPV is a service fee which is deducted from payments received from the obligors before passing the receipts to the investors. The fee is calculated as the amount by which interest on the securitized loans is more than return offered on the PTCs. While the obligors pay interest on the loans, investors earn returns on the PTCs. Thus, the difference between the amount that an SPV receives from the obligors and returns paid to the investors on their PTCs represents the SPV's service fee.

Investors

In banking and finance, the term investor is used commonly in analyzing stakes and stakeholders in the markets for property, securities, and other assets. Yet there are other types of investors—in businesses or other endeavors, for example. Depending on the investment perspective, an investor is someone or organization that:

- has a stake in, and earns income from, a money market instrument such as T-bill, deposit or treasury certificate, and so on;
- buys, owns, and earns income from property or securities such as stocks, bonds, and so on; and
- commits money to a project for the purpose of making profit from income expected from the project.

An investor, for purposes of securitization, would be a financial institution—such as a bank, mutual fund, pension fund, or government—that buys securities issued on and backed by bank loans largely for income and profit purposes.

The interest of the investors in securitization securities is often driven by three major considerations. Besides spread (diversity) as opposed to concentration, the investors also consider quality and expected yield of the securities. Investors yet also consider the ratings of each of the securitized loans before making any financial commitment. Do the securities have high ratings from reputable credit assessment agencies? It is often good to invest if the answer to this question is positive. Otherwise, decline.

A painstaking analysis of those variables—diversity, quality, yield, and ratings of the loans—is critical to the investors for an obvious reason. Investors crave for securities that are safe (secured) and offer relatively high yield at a low risk. Their ideal choice, in fact, would be riskless or risk-free securities. In practice, however, such securities are hard to come by—except, perhaps, T-bills which are usually backed by State treasury. T-bills are normally issued and guaranteed by Central Banks on behalf of Government.

However, securitization securities are never risk-free. There is always some risk which, in most cases, originates from possible faltering of cash flows to service and redeem the securities. Cash flows from securitized loans are sometimes unpredictable due to possible default by the obligors. It becomes uncertain, in such a situation, that the SPV will receive expected cash flows to service securities backed by the loans.

Thus the risk of investment in securitized securities is the chance that some obligors may default. When that happens, the real risk is that expected cash flows will not be realized, and investors may not receive their expected returns on the securities. Investors should seek to mitigate this risk before committing money to the securities. Risk mitigating measures will include a painstaking analysis of the securities on their merits and, especially, adequate knowledge of credit products and markets.

Administrator or Servicer

Appointment of an administrator or servicer is an important step in the transaction path for loans securitization. The fact that it is rare to achieve zero default on securitized loans necessitates engagement of the servicer. The SPV appoints the servicer solely to collect interest, due, and prepayments on securitized loans from the obligors. In cases of default, the servicer takes appropriate legal actions to enforce loan servicing and payment conditions on the obligors. This practice mitigates default—the main risk of securitization securities. It is not uncommon that the servicer is often also the originator of the securitization.

Documentation and Rating of Securities

The main document in loan securitization transaction and investment is a pass through-certificate (PTC). The PTC is issued to someone or organization by the SPV as evidence of their investment in securitized loans. In general, issuance of PTCs to investors is preceded by the creation of marketable securities on a set of pooled loans released by the originator to the SPV.

Thus the PTCs represent the securities so created and investors may buy as many units of the securities as they want. Apparently, the most critical point in securitization of loans is about how—and with what level of efficacy—the SPV converts a pool of loans into units of marketable securities. In fact, that marks the basis of transaction documentation in the PTCs issued to the investors in loan securitization. It should be noted that ordinary loans are illiquid and cannot be traded or liquidated in the capital market. On the other hand, the securities issued on a pool of loans under a securitization arrangement are capital market instruments, discountable, and therefore liquid. The liquidity of the securities, perhaps more than any other single consideration, makes investment in the PTCs attractive to investors.

Yet investors also consider other important factors, especially the risk, yield, quality, and diversity of the securitized loans, as well as collateral strength of loans backing the securities. Sometimes, the originator may want to enhance the ratings of the securities. It could do so through insurance, underwriting commitment, or other guarantee instrument. When securities are so documented, they tend be rated higher than their originator and enjoy investor confidence and patronage.

SIGNIFICANCE AND APPLICATIONS OF SECURITIZATION

Securitization of loans is yet not common among banks in developing economies. Yet it provides one of the means through which a bank can minimize the problems of bad loans. In Nigeria, a hint and awareness of its potency in the management of delinquent loans was initiated in the late 1997 by the Nigerian Deposit Insurance Corporation (NDIC). The NDIC adopted it as one of its intended measures for resolving the persisting banking system distress in the country.

Some of the factors propitious for the practice of securitization include increasing interest rate risk, chances of loan losses, deterioration of asset quality, and long-term earnings difficulties. As deposit customers switch between banks and other financial institutions in search of higher interest for their investments, banks are compelled to increase lending interest rates. But the resultant high borrowing cost soon adds to the problem of nonperforming loans. The bank bears this brunt when it increases provision for loan losses or has to increase capital requirements to absorb the asset shrinkage. But general reserves are also adversely affected with increasing earnings problems.

The need for banks and other lending institutions to diversify credit risk cannot be overemphasized. Securitization of loans is one of the efficacious methods of risk diversification available to the lending institutions. With the help of securitization of loans, a bank or other lending institution can switch lending from the high to the low risk sectors. Suppose, for example, that energy sector accounts for 55% of a bank's loan portfolio while the other sectors account for 45%. The bank will be stressed and in trouble if much of the loans become delinquent due to unexpected crisis in the energy sector.

Consider the case of banks in Nigeria where at the turn of the 21st century, militant youths from the country's oil-rich Niger Delta region, started mass agitation for resource control. The militants subsequently took up arms in pursuit of their cause. Soon, they and the military Joint Task Force (JTF) which the Nigerian government put together to restore normalcy in the region were on a collision course. The ensuing crisis disrupted crude oil production and export, causing huge losses in foreign exchange earnings. A crisis of this nature could cause unintended default by many oil producing, services, and marketing companies.

In anticipation of this risk, a bank should do anything but concentrate lending in a particular sector no matter how riskless or profitable that sector might be. Where a bank finds that it is faced with the risk of loan concentration, it can change the situation by securitizing a portion of the endangered loans and thus reducing the concentration risk. The bank would be diversifying credit risk if it lends funds from the securitization to borrowers in other sectors devoid of concentration risk.

Two major features of securitization, those that make it attractive to investors, are worthy of note. In the first place, securitization deals are usually collateralized (i.e., asset-backed). Pooled loans serve as collateral for investors in securitization securities. The reasons for this collateral arrangement are twofold and simple. Securitization securities are issued on pooled loans. Second, investors in the securities base their financial commitment on analysis and the quality of the loans in the pool as well as on the pool itself. This implies that the risk that investors assume is mitigated.

However, risk mitigation in this sense is relative to one important consideration—the level of comfort that investors have in the quality of, and cash flows from, loans backing the securitization. Also, securitization securities are a financial asset, one that is marketed as a discountable instrument. This way, the securities offer investors a safe investment. The investment is considered safe because it is liquid and committed to a diversified pool of loans. In most cases, securitization securities are issued on a pool of many individual loans.

The diversity of loans comprising the pool is a critical risk mitigating factor, one that commonly gratifies investors. Besides, the ability of investors to discount (sell) the security in the capital market underscores its liquidity. The security becomes appealing to investors—first, in the foregoing sense, and then, as an alternative to bonds or similar securities. Thus securitization increases investment options available to the public. In doing so, it helps to deepen the capital market.

SUMMARY

Securitization is the process of converting a group of nonmarketable assets, or expected future cash flows on the assets, into units of marketable securities in order to sell the underlying assets in the capital market to generate money for a business. In the context of banking, securitization is the process of converting a pool of loans, and sale of the pooled loans, as units of secured marketable securities to investors to meet the funding need of a bank. It is the conversion of expected future cash inflows (i.e., service incomes and repayments) from a pool of loans into units of secured marketable securities which are sold to investors to raise capital for a bank.

Some funding need triggers a securitization deal, while the existence of a robust capital market nourishes it. Securitization has significance and implications for risk management in bank lending. Certain objectives of securitization underline its significance as a capital market instrument. It helps a bank to unlock and recoup funds tied up in risk assets, optimize earnings while enhancing return on capital employed, mitigate credit risk, create an alternative source of cash flow, manage its balance sheet, tap into occasional windows of opportunity that may open to it, and explore new investments in and outside lending.

The process of, and steps involved in, securitization of loans can be more or less complicated, depending on the level of development of the capital market. In developing countries where the market is still evolving, securitization is hardly a welcome option. Five parties—the obligors, originator, and a SPV, there are also the investors and administrator or servicer—with mutually exclusive roles, are involved in the conduct of securitization. The main document in loan securitization transaction and investment is a PTC. The PTC serves as evidence of investment in securitized loans. Issuance of PTCs to investors is preceded by the creation of marketable securities on a set of pooled loans. Thus, the PTCs represent the securities so created and investors may buy as many units of the securities as they want. Investors consider other important factors, especially the risk, yield, quality, and diversity of the securitized loans, as well as collateral strength of loans backing the securities.

QUESTIONS FOR DISCUSSION AND REVIEW

1. Of what uses is securitization of loans to a bank, borrowers, investors, and the capital market?
2. Discuss the process and workings of securitization, noting the stages and roles of the parties involved in its execution.
3. What is the significance and implications of securitization of loans in contemporary banking and finance in emerging economies?
4. In what ways can emerging economies benefit from possibilities that securitization of loans offers as a capital market instrument?
5. Discuss the types and methodologies of securitization of loans, with implications for problems and prospects of securitization in emerging economies.
6. a. What procedure can internationally active banks in emerging economies adopt to raise capital through asset securitization?
   b. How does the procedure impact structuring and packaging of securitization deals in the capital market?
7. How does Basel II Accord deal with securitization of assets? Your answer must demonstrate clear understanding of the impact and applications of the Accord in loan securitization.

REFERENCES

Basel Committee on Banking Supervision, 2004a. International Convergence of Capital Measurement and Capital Standards: A Revised Framework. Bank for International Settlements, Basel.

Basel Committee on Banking Supervision, 2004b. International Convergence of Capital Measurement and Capital Standards: A Revised Framework; Comprehensive Version. Bank for International Settlements, Basel.

Chapter 18

Credit Ratings Prospects and Practicalities for Banking in Developing Economies

Chapter Outline

LEARNING FOCUS AND OUTCOMES

The Basel Committee on Banking Supervision recommends the Basel Accords for implementation by only "internationally active" banks—mainly in developed countries. Given the underlying spirit of the Accords, it would seem irrelevant to discuss one of the major thrusts of Basel II Accord—credit ratings—in a book dealing with banking issues in developing economies. Paradoxically, many banks in developing economies have embraced the Accords and are making progress with the implementation of aspects of them. Thus credit rating is amply pertinent to the cause of this book. I set my objectives to:

- explore developments that inform credit ratings practices and applications in global banks under the auspices of Basel II Accord;
- demonstrate preBasel II Accord credit ratings methodology and roles of credit analysts, lending units, and internal control officers;
- discuss events leading up to the inclusion of credit ratings in the 2004 Basel II Accord on credit risk management;

- examine input which external credit rating agencies make into risk-weighting of assets and the credit ratings process of banks;
- assess distinctions between credit ratings prior to, and since the enactment of Basel II in 2004—with implications for banks in developing economies;
- investigate how risk-based credit ratings could help risk management in, and improve the financial performance of, banks; and
- examine concerns about issues that are likely to shape future credit ratings work and framework in developing economies.

EXPECTED LEARNING OUTCOMES

Few domestic banks in developing economies have international banking licenses. Many of them operate as national banks, while other are issued with regional banking licenses. The licensing categories reflect differences in experience, skills, and financial strengths of the banks. Foreign banks subsidiaries operate as largely national banks in the countries where they are based. The two categories of banks face similar credit ratings challenges and prospects which I analyze in this chapter. The reader will—after studying this chapter and doing the exercises in it—have learnt and been better informed about:

- developments that inform credit ratings practices and applications in global banks under the auspices of Basel II Accord;
- issues in preBasel II Accord credit ratings methodology and roles of credit analysts, lending units, and internal control officers;
- defining events leading up to the inclusion of credit ratings in the 2004 Basel II Accord on credit risk management;
- significant input which external credit rating agencies make into risk-weighting of assets and the credit ratings process of banks;
- distinctions between credit ratings prior to, and since the enactment of Basel II in 2004—with implications for banks in developing economies;
- ways in which risk-based credit ratings could help risk management in, and improve the financial performance of, banks; and
- concerns bordering on the future of credit ratings framework and dynamics in developing economies.

OVERVIEW OF THE SUBJECT MATTER

In this chapter, I focus on understanding of the developments that inform credit ratings practices and applications in global banks. At the same time, I discuss concerns about issues that will shape future credit ratings work and framework. I present the concerns in the context of the events leading up to the inclusion of credit ratings in the 2004 Basel II Accord on credit risk management. The reader will appreciate understanding of these developments in view of regulatory capital requirements for credit risk management in the Basel Accord. But it underscores the dynamics of effective credit risk management in international banking and finance.

I also briefly review and provide an overview of credit ratings prior to the adoption of Basel II. My discussion of preBasel II credit ratings methodology and marshaling the roles of credit analysts, lending units, and internal control employees, complement the primary learning outcomes of this chapter. I also strengthen the learning outcomes by examining the input which external auditors or other such risk assessors will make into risk-weighting of assets and the credit ratings process. Thus, I make distinctions between techniques for credit ratings prior to, and since the enactment of, Basel II in 2004. But as global best practice dictates, I place emphasis on how risk-based credit ratings could help risk management in, and improve the financial performance of, internationally active banks.

Domestic and foreign subsidiary banks in developing economies will benefit from a critical analysis of the contending issues in credit ratings which I present in this chapter. The two categories of banks—domestic and foreign subsidiaries—face similar fate when it comes to the implementation of Basel II recommendations on credit ratings for lending purposes. Most of the domestic banks are not "internationally active" in the sense Basel II envisages for the adoption of its credit ratings recommendations. Few of them have ventured into international markets with subsidiaries. Foreign banks subsidiaries in developing economies are hardly "internationally active" in the same sense. Ideally, they are not expected, as subsidiaries, to operate as holding companies for subsidiaries in other countries. But their parent banks are. I highlight the common challenges of the two sets of banks as I discuss aspects of the topics of this chapter.

The foregoing raises concerns which helped to situate credit ratings in the learning focus and objectives of this chapter. I address such concerns in relevant topics of this chapter. Doing so, I focus on the application of credit ratings in bank lending in developing economies. The import of this approach is noteworthy from two main perspectives. In the first place, there may not be indigenous external rating agencies in some developing economies. The second reason builds on the first. Most banks in developing economies do not use or rely on external credit rating agencies in making most, if not, all of their lending decisions.

MEANING AND SCOPE OF CREDIT RATING

The term "credit rating" may be used to refer to a professional judgment about the likelihood that someone or organization will fulfill their financial obligation as at when due. It also means, to put it simply, a judgment about the ability of a person, company, or organization to pay their debts. I can yet define it to imply the chances that an existing or potential borrower will not default on their debt or credit to them. These meanings imply that a lender or other creditor will want to know whether or not a borrower or other debtor can pay their debts on due date. Through credit rating, the likelihood of debt payment is reflected in standings on assessment of individual and corporate creditworthiness.

Good credit rating provides a lender, or other company, with some of the critical information which they need to make credit decisions. While lending decisions based on standings on credit ratings (i.e., assessments of the creditworthiness of a person or company) might not be foolproof, it nevertheless guides the credit decision-making process. But it also offers some credit risk comfort in helping to mitigate probability of default (PD). Specifically, credit rating could be insightful when a bank uses it and other risk-mitigating measures to check chances of loan loss. In this and foregoing sense, credit rating both establishes and is determined by the creditworthiness of a person, company, or an organization.

I equally define credit rating from the perspective of issuing, or investing in, financial instruments. In this context, credit rating is seen as an informed opinion about chances that an issuer of a financial instrument will not default on obligation to an investor. It is pertinent to compare credit rating purposes for bank lending and for trading in securities to further underscore its essence in financial transactions. In general, credit rating should be seen as an assessment of credit risk in which a bank (or other lender), investor, or third party shows their judgment about the risk of default by particular borrowers or issuers of securities. The ratings enable a bank or an investor to commit money to a particular borrowing or investment cause.

Nowadays, under the auspices of Basel II, credit ratings conducted by external agencies are accorded as much importance as those banks generate inhouse. It is thus necessary to discuss events leading up to the growing significance of credit rating in postBasel II credit risk management framework. But before doing that, it is pertinent to first review credit rating work and uses prior to the enactment of Basel II Accord in 2004.

PURPOSES OF CREDIT RATINGS

In bank lending, credit rating focuses on establishing the ability of borrowers to pay back loans. In trading securities, it serves as a means for assessing the capacity of issuers of securities to redeem their securities on due dates. In both cases, the underlying need for credit rating is to mitigate the risk of default by the borrower or issuer.

Banks use credit rating to assess the risk of lending to borrowers. Thus, credit rating is conducted on existing and prospective borrowing customers of banks. Investors use credit rating to evaluate the risk in committing money to (i.e., investing in) securities. In this case, credit rating is conducted on current and prospective issuers of securities.

The issuer of securities that is rated, is usually a company, organization, or government desirous of raising money with securities, or selling other financial assets to raise capital, in the financial market. In bank lending, the borrower that is rated may be an individual—in addition to a company, organization, or government. Either in bank lending, or in trading securities, the terms borrower and issuer have a constant meaning. Each means or refers to obligor. The obligor is someone, organization, or government to whom funds provided by a lender or investors are disbursed and that must pay back the funds with interest on agreed future date. The interest compensates the lender or investors for making funds available to satisfy particular borrowing or funding need of the borrower or issuer.

While investors may rely to some extent on their judgment, their investment decisions depend largely on the judgment of third parties about the risk of default. The third parties, usually credit rating agencies, offer them credit risk assessment. Banks also generate and use in-house risk data and data from third parties, the external credit rating agencies.

CREDIT SCORING FOR CONSUMER LENDING

Banks employ credit rating in the consumer banking sector to weigh the risk of granting loans to individuals. Consumer lending in this sector is largely influenced by the credit scores of individuals. Thus, borrowers can do anything but earn low marks on credit scores. The reason for this is that a high credit score is usually a necessary condition to obtain consumer loan from a bank. With a low credit score, on the other hand, an individual may find it difficult to obtain bank loan. Credit rating—from the perspective of consumer lending—may be defined as a judgment that a bank or third party makes about the capacity of an individual to pay back a loan. It is a measure of the riskiness of granting loans, or loans granted, to individuals.

The creditworthiness of the borrower is a critical and common factor in both credit rating and credit scoring. However, while credit rating is determined by creditworthiness, credit score determines creditworthiness. This subtle difference marks the significance of credit scoring in the rating of, and lending to, consumer banking customers. It implies that individuals should strive to achieve and maintain high and increasing credit scores so as to be good candidates for consumer loans. Mathematical computations based on their historical borrowings (i.e., past credit records) inform the credit scores that individuals get. The risk of lending which the computations indicate or corroborate is assessed using a set of credit criteria.

There is yet another difference between the way risk is assessed to determine credit scores of individuals and how it is done to rate corporate or other nonindividual borrowers. For an individual, credit score is calculated using information obtained from various consumer lenders, especially credit card operators. The reliance on this category of lenders for information is based on the fact that they constitute the main source of credits to individuals. The information, usually sourced by credit bureaus and maintained on their databases, can be accessed to calculate credit scores of individuals and determine their credit ratings. Insights into the factors that influence credit scores and ratings of individuals are commonplace in the financial services literature. Payment record, utilization of credit line, and activity in a credit account are some of the important variables that influence credit rating.

Apparently, the factors that influence credit scores and ratings of individuals are often within their control. For instance, an individual can choose to repay loans on or before due dates, to delay repayment of loans when they fall due, or to simply default. Similarly, whether or not borrowers fully utilize their loans is also within their control and an important factor to analyze. Each of these situations more or less affects the individual's credit score and rating. Consumer banking customers must work and improve on their loan repayment to stand a good chance of obtaining bank loans.

CREDIT RATING PRIOR TO BASEL II—FROM THE PERSPECTIVE OF DEVELOPING ECONOMIES

Credit rating has assumed unusual influence with increasing challenge of risk management in bank lending. Banks in developing economies are persuaded and now have reason to embrace credit rating as a veritable risk mitigation device. Hitherto, the banks had employed credit rating as an integral part of internal framework for the implementation of credit policy and control. Credit analysis was the foundation of the in-house credit ratings that supported lending decisions at the time.

Then, credit rating by the banks underscored the need to appreciate the risks of borrowers to whom the ratings were assigned to reflect the risk of lending to them. This was done as part of the overall risk management strategy of the banks. It was then commonplace that credit analysts and lending units rated credits which they originated. At the analyst's level of lending authority, credit rating was often documented in a loan proposal to senior management. And credit rating reflected simply the opinion of the credit analyst or lending unit on overall assessment of the risks of a borrower. Internal control employees also conducted postloan disbursement credit ratings to either corroborate or disprove credit ratings (i.e., to confirm or condemn credit analysts' judgment on disbursed credit facilities). Cases of conflicting ratings usually called for more work on the credit by the account officer and lending unit. The extra work ensures that lapses observed by internal control officers are regularized in order to beef up rating for the credit and shore up its compliance standing.

Incidentally, a broad base of issues command attention of lending officers and units in a credit analysis report. Typically, credit analysts examine several factors that inform credit rating. From the popular five Cs of lending, to other less popular key credit issues, loan officers investigate and try to mitigate possible causes of loan default. The investigation, more commonly known as credit analysis, could be more or less rigorous depending on the type of lending. Rigor is often required more than in ordinary lending when credit proposal involves commitment of a large sum of money to a new venture or complicated project. In most cases, the rigor ensures that all necessary precautions are taken to forestall excessive or unnecessary risk-taking, especially in avoidable lending situations.

Besides, external rating agencies complemented in-house credit rating. The agencies provide independent assessment of the creditworthiness of borrowers on which banks sometimes, but not necessarily, rely to make lending decisions. While there may be several local rating agencies, very few are recognized in the international financial market. Accredited international rating agencies include Fitch IBCA, Standard & Poor's, and Moody's. The product of the assessment of creditworthiness is a rating classification of borrowers according to some methodical criteria. Ostensibly, the criteria that inform external credit assessments and ratings correspond to those banks use in-house for credit analysis. However, there is difference in the use of alphanumeric representation of credit ratings of borrowers by banks and rating agencies. The external rating agencies tend to have a more rigorous and defensible methodical approach to alphanumeric depiction of standings of borrowers. Apparently, international rating agencies use comparable alphanumeric symbols, methods, and systems for credit ratings.

There is yet another difference between credit rating that banks do in-house and that provided by external rating agencies. While ratings done by banks subsist until new ratings supplant them, ratings that external agencies do are usually intended to cover a period of 1 year starting from the date of the ratings. Yet, whether done in-house or by external rating agencies, credit ratings prior to Basel II made feeble input into a bank's overall credit analysis, approval, and decline. This was the case because banks tended to rely on expediencies to make lending decisions. Sometimes, the expediencies are presented as "key credit issues" in a credit analysis memorandum. On the basis of mitigation of risks embedded in the key credit issues, the analyst makes lending recommendation to senior management. Often the recommendation is made with a caveat that the borrower fulfills certain predisbursement conditions. Fulfillment of the conditions precedent to drawdown gave banks false sense of security and unfounded confidence to lend money recklessly to borrowers. But it also led bank managements to disregard credit rating in the scheme for credit risk management.

EFFECT OF BASEL II ON CREDIT RATING

Basel II gave fresh impetus to the conduct of credit rating as an integral part of the regulatory framework for credit risk management. Under Basel II Accord, enacted in 2004, credit rating is influential and applied in risk-weighting assets of banks to determine their regulatory capital requirements.

The Accord specifies two sets of credit rating options that should make input into credit risk capital charges of the banks. This sounds technical, but it implies that credit ratings are used to determine risk-weights of assets; in turn, the risk-weights are used to calculate regulatory capital requirements. Thus, credit ratings have an indirect effect on regulatory capital requirements. It influences the minimum amount of capital that a bank should maintain as reserves for the risk assets it books. The reserves underscore the ability of the bank to absorb the risks of the assets in its lending portfolio.

Pillar 1 of the Basel II Accord outlines and approves permissible types and methodologies of credit ratings that banks and regulators can use for the calculation of minimum capital requirements. Besides two "standardized" approaches, there are also two "internal ratings-based" (IRB) approaches. I now discuss the composition of the two sets of credit ratings approaches.

CREDIT RATING METHODS APPROVED BY BASEL II

1. The "standardized approaches" comprise:
   a. Simple standardized approach (SSA) which builds on the 1988 Basel Capital Accord (i.e., Basel I); and
   b. Standardized approach (SA) which makes use of risk data from external credit risk assessment agencies. Examples of recognized external credit rating agencies include Moody's and Standard & Poor's.
2. The "Internal ratings-based approaches" are made up of:
   a. Foundation internal ratings based approach (F–IRB); and
   b. Advanced internal ratings based approach (A–IRB).

The two IRB approaches are based on the PD, as well as other internal risk assessment criteria which banks employ in their credit analysis methodologies.

Overall, banks and regulators may use any of the four approaches to determine capital adequacy requirements. However, it is pertinent to appreciate the distinguishing features and requirements for the use of the approaches.

Standardized Approaches

Basel II significantly improves on Basel I with regard to the use of SA for risk-weighting of assets to calculate capital requirements. This is notwithstanding that Basel II, like Basel I, groups credit risks into broad categories. The grouping is based on the identification of common characteristics for assets in a given category (i.e., assets grouped in one category have common characteristics). SA uses credit risk data, and therefore risk weights determined by external credit assessment institutions (ECAIs), that is, external credit rating agencies, or risk scores of export credit agencies (ECA) to calculate capital requirements. Basel I, on the other hand, assigned fixed risk-weights to categories of asset exposures.

This methodological difference marks a significant departure of Basel II from the Basel I Accord. However, Basel II (standardized approach) does not demand that ECAI ratings should determine risk-weights of all groups of risk categories. Rather, it isolates three of the risk categories—loans to sovereigns, corporate loans, and claims on banks—as those whose risk-weights should be determined by external credit ratings assigned to them. Thus, rather than fixed risk-weights as applicable to Basel I, risk-weights for these three risk categories under SA are determined using external credit ratings that ECAIs assign to the borrowers.

Nonetheless, SA retains fixed risk weights for risk categories other than for sovereigns, corporates, and banks. It does so with some modifications. For example, like Basel I, SA recognizes loans that residential property secures as a low risk asset and assigns a fixed risk weight to it. However, while Basel I assigned it a risk weight of 50%, SA assigns it 35% risk weight. The lower SA risk weight is based on condition that loan-to-value (LTV) ratio for loan secured on residential property should not be less than 80%. Doing so, SA underscores a widely held view that residential mortgage loans are one of the low risk-prone assets on a bank's balance sheet.

Simple Standardized Approach

The SSA assigns risk-weights to sovereign and bank debts based on ECA country risk scores. This marks a departure from Basel I which discounts claims on sovereigns on the basis of their ratings as members of the OECD. Thus, under Basel I, credit rating assigned to OECD of which a sovereign is a member, is used to discount claims of banks on the sovereign. On the contrary, Basel II clearly spells out the criteria for the use of ECA risk scores to risk-weight claims on (i.e., debts of) sovereigns. Apparently banks do not altogether have leeway to choose an ECA, or to use country risk scores that an ECA provides. Rather, a country's central bank, or other regulatory authority, must recognize particular ECAs and country risk scores advised by them before banks could use their risk scores to risk-weight assets. The ECAs must satisfy two other important conditions for them to be so recognized by the authorities. First, they must publish their country risk scores (i.e., country credit ratings). Second, their credit risk assessment methodology must meet OECD standard. Like OECD members, recognized ECAs must adopt the OECD standard methodology for credit risk assessments and ratings. In view of the foregoing, the SSA is more risk sensitive and deals with more credit risks than the 1988 Basel I Accord.

Standardized Approach

In the case of SA, external credit rating agencies or ECA country risk scores are the sources of risk-weights assigned to classes of bank assets. However, the scope of risks that SA covers is more than that of SSA. Also, mitigation of credit risk is better enhanced with the SA than SSA. There is yet another major distinction between SA and SSA. Unlike SSA which uses ECA risk scores, there is an option for SA to use market-based credit risk data from either ECA or ECAIs.

There are, however, conditions which ECAIs must satisfy in order to offer and avail credit rating services to banks. Basel II requires them to be formally accredited and satisfy certain other selection criteria. The Accord confers the responsibility to approve qualified ECAIs on the central bank, or other banking regulatory authority, in a country. There are eligibility criteria which Basel II recommends for the approval of ECAIs for credit ratings.

In view of the criteria, adoption of SA depends on two critical success factors. First, ECAI ratings must not only be readily available, they must be credible and reflect reliable credit assessments. Second, regulators must recognize ECAIs whose credit ratings banks may use for asset risk-weighting. In order to be recognized, an ECAI must satisfy the eligibility criteria I discussed below. So the ability of regulators to appraise and appropriately recognize ECAIs is a critical success factor for the adoption of SA.

There is a need for the banking regulatory authorities in developing economies to encourage development of external credit assessment institutions in their countries. But the prospective ECAs should brace themselves for the task of satisfying the Basel II criteria for their registration.

Eligibility of ECAIs

An ECAI must satisfy seven basic eligibility criteria, discussed later, before banks and banking regulators may use it or its credit ratings to make lending decisions (Basel Committee, 2004—all quotes are taken from this source).

Objectivity

The requirement for objectivity implies that credit assessment methodology that an ECAI uses must be "rigorous, systematic, and be subject to some form of validation based on historical experience." An important element of objectivity is that "assessments must be subject to ongoing review and responsive to changes in financial condition" of the person, company, or organization rated. Thus, an ECAI should not offer credit rating as a one-off, but an ongoing, financial service. It has to review its ratings periodically to ensure that they represent a current financial condition of the person, company, or organization rated. Basel II requires that an ECAI must obtain approval for its methodology from the central bank, or other regulatory authority. An ECAI must fulfill yet another important condition before supervisors may recognize its credit assessment methodology. Its credit "assessment methodology for each market segment, including rigorous back testing, must have been established for at least one year and preferably 3 years."

Independence

Basel II demands independence of an ECAI so as to free its credit ratings from influences of sorts. On no grounds should independence of an ECAI be compromised; rather, it should be assured at all times. An ECAI may be assumed to be independent when it is adjudged to meet two important standards. First, there should be absence of any form of influence on an ECAI to assess credits, assign credit ratings, or be biased toward some interest. This implies that the ECAI is not under pressure, or will not yield to pressure, to pervert credit assessment, its process or outcome. An ECAI will compromise its integrity if it fails to observe this rule. Second, an ECAI should be free from constraints while performing credit assessments, or assigning ratings. It should be particularly free to uphold best practice. An ECAI is unlikely to be independent where its assessment process is not "as free as possible from any constraints." In most cases, constraints that weaken independence of an ECAI are caused by "conflict of interest." A typical example is seen in interference of interested parties in the work of an ECAI to influence its credit assessments or ratings. Interested parties may be board members, shareholders, or influential customers of an ECAI in the first place.

International Access

An ECAI should make credit assessments and ratings on its database available to interested domestic and foreign institutions. However, this eligibility criterion presupposes that the institutions must have legitimate interests in the credit assessments. In satisfying this criterion, an ECAI should make its credit assessments available "at equivalent terms" to both domestic and foreign institutions, or to other international users of credit risk data with legitimate interests.

Transparency

It is pertinent for lenders, borrowers, financial analysts, and other interested parties to know about the methodology used for credit assessments. The methodology that an ECAI uses for credit assessment, or its credit rating process, should not be difficult to understand. This is the implication of the transparency criterion requirement for credit assessments and ratings. In order to ensure transparency, Basel II stipulates that an ECAI should make its methodology public. Doing so, the methodology which the ECAI adopts to rate borrowers and candidates for loans is brought within the purview of the public. Thus, the public can scrutinize the methodology that an ECAI adopts. Interested parties will appreciate credit assessments and ratings when the assessment institution's methodology meets the transparency criterion of Basel II. The central bank, or other supervisory authority, may not recognize an ECAI that does not have an established transparency record.

Disclosure

The disclosure criterion makes a technical requirement for the eligibility of an ECAI to offer credit assessment and rating services. Basel II spells out the scope of the disclosure criterion. It clarifies the types and nature of information that an ECAI should disclose as presented:

- An ECAI should disclose "its assessment methodologies, including the definition of default, the time horizon, and the meaning of each rating." Doing so further clarifies the assessment process and facilitates understanding of assessments and ratings.

- Disclosure should help lenders, borrowers, and the public to know about "the actual default rates experienced in each assessment category." Perhaps this is the most critical disclosure and eligibility criterion for an ECAI, one that determines the level of reliance that may be placed on its assessments.
- It is also pertinent that an ECAI should disclose "the transitions of the assessments, for example, the likelihood of AA ratings becoming A over time." This disclosure helps interested parties to know about and track changes in the financial condition of the person, company, or organization rated.

Resources

An ECAI will not offer good credit assessment and rating services with insufficient resources. The essence of sufficient resources is for an ECAI to be able "to carry out high quality credit assessments." Besides, resources available to an ECAI "should allow for substantial ongoing contact with senior and operational levels within the entities assessed in order to add value to the credit assessments." Specifically, the number of employees of an ECAI must be sufficient for credit assessment work "based on methodologies combining qualitative and quantitative approaches." This implies that the employees must be skilled and competent for the job. But it also means that the required resources should be of a high quality.

Credibility

This is a derived eligibility criterion for the recognition of an ECAI as a credit assessment institution. Basel II notes that "to some extent, credibility is derived from the criteria above." The import of credibility is that an ECAI should be rated highly on the foregoing eligibility criteria before its methodology and credit assessments may be accepted as credible. Basel II gives yet a further insight into other variables that impart credibility to credit assessments of an ECAI. It suggests variables that provide "evidence of the credibility of the assessments of an ECAI" or factors that "underpin the credibility of an ECAI" as follows:

- Reliance of "independent parties (investors, insurers, trading partners) on an ECAI's external credit assessments."
- Institutionalization or "the existence of internal procedures to prevent the misuse of confidential information."
- Restriction on an ECAI "to assess firms in more than one country." Incidentally, an ECAI must comply with this rule "in order to be eligible for recognition."

It is obvious, from the eligibility criteria, that an ECAI can do anything but fail the credibility test. Not only does lack of credibility whittle credit assessments and ratings away, it distances supervisory authorities from the assessments of the affected intuitions.

Internal Ratings–Based Approaches

IRB approaches are dependent on in-house credit risk data of banks. Through their traditional credit analysis, banks generate such data from their internal risk assessment systems. Let me now discuss the regulatory requirements and features of the two variants of the IRB approaches.

Foundation IRB Approach

The main feature of the Foundation IRB approach is that banks are allowed to use their in-house models to calculate their regulatory capital requirements. In order to use the F-IRB approach, banks are required to estimate PD and obtain estimates from supervisors for loss given default (LGD), exposure at default (EAD), and maturity of exposure (M). With estimates for these risk variables, and using their own risk-weighting function, the banks determine and assign risk weights to individual or group of assets in their loan books. Thus, in order to calculate regulatory capital requirements, the risk-weighting function relates risk-weights of assets to total capital reserves.

However, banks need to obtain approval of regulators before they could use their own models for the F-IRB approach. In addition to their approval, the regulators also provide the banks with necessary assumptions for the use of the models. This implies that a bank must satisfy two important conditions before it can use the F-IRB approach. It must obtain:

- approval of the regulators for loan default predictive model it develops, or intends to develop, for use in risk-weighting assets in its loan book; and
- required assumptions, which the regulators provide, to underlie the development and application of the model.

Regulators hinge assumptions for the use of F-IRB approach on three aspects of credit risk assessments. The three aspects, or underlying assumptions which Basel II stipulates regulators should provide, are:

LGD—that is, the probability of loss of an asset (or each type of asset) in a bank's loan book;
EAD—that is, the exposure of a bank to an at-risk asset at the time of its default; and
M—maturity risk associated with each type of asset.

The implication of these regulatory stipulations is that banks can use their in-house risk data to determine PD, while regulators provide measures (i.e., estimates) of LGD, EAD, and M. The success of F-IRB approach greatly depends on the efficacy of in-house risk assessment models (i.e., systems, or methodologies) of the banks. It is therefore important that banks are able to design and implement effective internal rating systems.

Thus regulators are challenged to critically assess and accredit banks' in-house credit rating systems. The ability of regulators to do this is a necessary condition for the implementation of F-IRB approach. Two other success requirements relate to the ability of regulators to validate banks' internal systems for credit risk management and stress testing, and to furnish banks with estimates of LGD, and EAD. Doing so, the intention is to ensure that banks develop and implement effective credit assessment and stress testing systems. Without this supervisory input of the regulators, banks will not be able to use the F-IRB approach.

Advanced IRB (A-IRB) Approach

There are corporate and retail variants for the A-IRB approach. In A-IRB, risk weights of assets used to calculate capital requirements are determined in the same way as in F-IRB approach. However, A-IRB builds on the features of F-IRB and demands advanced risk modeling systems and methodology for the calculation of capital requirements. Thus, the difference between F-IRB and A-IRB is in the relative complexity of their risk assessment models. Whereas in F-IRB banks determine only the PD, the banks are allowed in A-IRB to provide their own estimates of PD as well as LGD, EAD, and M. This is unlike in F-IRB where regulators provide estimates of LGD, EAD, and M which the banks use with PD determined by them to calculate capital requirements. In using retail IRB, banks provide estimates for only PD, LGD, and EAD.

These aspects of A-IRB approach have an implication for the banks and supervisors. In order to use the A-IRB and retail IRB approaches, a bank must have a strong in-house system that can estimate complex credit risk variables. It must especially have the capacity to determine LGD and EAD. It is obvious that only the big banks—those that can cope with complex risk-modeling systems, and have the know-how and requisite competences—that can implement the A-IRB approach. For this reason, perhaps, Basel II stipulates that a bank is not allowed to use A-IRB unless supervisors validate its in-house systems to ensure that they meet foregoing criteria.

As in F-IRB, the success of A-IRB approach depends on the ability of regulators to assess credit rating systems of the banks. Besides, the ability of regulators to validate risk management models and stress testing systems of the banks is also a critical success factor for the implementation of the A-IRB approach.

Conditions for IRB Approaches

Basel II allows banks to use their internal risk assessment methodologies and data for credit ratings. At the same time, it stipulates that a bank wishing to adopt any of the IRB approaches should, among other requirements:

- Obtain approval for its credit rating methodologies from the central bank or other appropriate banking regulatory authority in their home and host countries (as may be applicable).
- Lay its credit rating methodologies bare by making them public. This is in line with international best practice, and intended to satisfy the need for transparency.

- Meet industry standards for the rating of borrowers and risk assets in its loan portfolio. A bank will achieve this when its ratings are comparable with those of other banks.

Standardized Versus IRB Approaches

Under the supervision of regulators, Basel II promotes ability of banks to build on their own internal systems for risk assessment. Unlike banks that adopt the IRB approaches, banks which adopt the SA, have to satisfy an additional regulatory capital charge. The extra capital charge is an increase of 6% on their risk-weighted asset reserves. This requirement has implication for profitability and reserves holding of the banks.

Basel II requires banks that adopt IRB approaches to maintain lower capital reserves than those that adopt the SA. With lower required reserves, profit of banks adopting IRB approaches should increase. On the other hand, the extra 6% capital charge (i.e., reserve requirement) for the use of the SA implies a diminution of profit. So a bank should be well informed about these implications before deciding to adopt IRB or the SA. It is unlikely that small banks—usually those with weak risk assessment models—can meet validation criteria of supervisors to be able to use the A-IRB approach. However, the dichotomy between IRB and the SA is intended to empower banks to develop appropriate in-house methodologies for risk assessments. It should also particularly encourage banks to build reliable risk databases. With strengthened risk assessment capabilities and other in-house resources, the banks can easily carry out internal credit ratings as regulators require. However, Basel II imposes conditions which banks should fulfill before regulators may accredit their internal risk assessment methods.

Advancing risk modeling skills in global banks fits well with the overall objective of Basel II—to encourage banks to progressively move from standardized toward IRB in the first instance and from F-IRB to A-IRB or retail IRB. Doing so, the banks will be empowered with advanced possibilities for risk assessments, modeling, and ratings. This is the basis of the 6% capital charge incentive to the banks using the IRB approaches.

RISK CONTROL IMPLICATIONS FOR BANKING IN DEVELOPING ECONOMIES

While Basel II-style credit rating is gaining attention among banks in developing economies, its technicalities remain a major cause of frustration for the banks. Skills required to fully and appropriately implement Basel II recommendation for credit ratings are either lacking or very scarce in developing economies. This problem applies to in-house resources of the banks as it is to the external rating agencies. Often the banks appear helpless and, under the circumstances, fallback on some in-house scheme. This fact explains some of the criticisms bordering on maneuvering, or faltering implementation, of Basel Accords often leveled against banks in developing economies.

In some developing economies, banking regulatory authorities have licensed a number of external rating agencies. However, banks tend to be reluctant to use their services. Three main reasons account for the reluctance. First, the use of external agencies for credit rating has cost implication which neither the banks nor borrowers are willing to absorb. The implied increase in the cost of borrowing is really a disincentive for loan parties. Worse still, the cost could be unnecessarily exorbitant in the absence of regulatory benchmarks. Second, most banks in developing economies are usually in a hurry to grant credit facilities they fancy. To the uninitiated, this will sound strange and make little sense—but it is real. Usually earnings consideration takes precedence over risk control under the circumstances. Third, most intending external credit rating agencies will not qualify for accreditation for the work if the criteria which Basel II specifies are strictly followed. This tends to skew the banks' trust in opinions of the external rating agencies.

The net effect of these challenges is that the quality of lending decisions in developing economies is yet anything but efficient. This sad implication is really a fleeting experience. As banks in developing economies evolve with increasing sophistication of credit risk, they are bound to start redressing the flaw. The envisaged change will happen sooner than is expected depending on the quality and success or failure of regulatory oversight of the banks.

SUMMARY

Credit rating is a professional judgment about the likelihood that someone or organization will fulfill their financial obligation as at when due. Through credit rating, the likelihood of debt payment is reflected in standings on the assessment of individual and corporate creditworthiness. Credit rating focuses, in the case of banking, on establishing the ability of borrowers to pay back loans. In trading securities, it serves as a means for assessing the capacity of issuers of securities to redeem their securities on due dates. In both cases, the underlying need for credit rating is to mitigate the risk of default by the borrower or issuer.

Prior to enactment of Basel II in 2004, banks employed credit rating as an integral part of internal framework for the implementation of credit policy and control. Credit analysis was the foundation of the in-house credit ratings that supported lending decisions at the time. Then, credit rating by the banks underscored the need to appreciate the risks of borrowers to whom the ratings were assigned to reflect the risk of lending to them. This was done as part of the overall risk management strategy of the banks.

Basel II gave fresh impetus to the conduct of credit rating as an integral part of the regulatory framework for credit risk management. Under Basel II Accord, credit rating is influential and applied in risk-weighting assets of banks to determine their regulatory capital requirements. The Accord specifies two sets of credit rating options that should make input into credit risk capital charges of the banks. Emphasis is on how credit ratings may be used to determine risk-weights of assets in the first place. Then how the risk-weights may be used to calculate regulatory capital requirements equally gained attention.

Thus credit ratings have an indirect effect on regulatory capital requirements. It influences the minimum amount of capital that a bank should maintain as reserves for the risk assets it books. Pillar 1 of the Basel II Accord outlines and approves permissible types and methodologies of credit ratings that banks and regulators can use for the calculation of minimum capital requirements. Besides two "standardized" approaches (SSA and SA), there are also two "internal ratings-based" (IRB) approaches (F-IRB and A-IRB).

While Basel II–style credit rating is gaining attention among banks in developing economies, its technicalities remain a major cause of frustration for the banks. Skills required to fully and appropriately implement Basel II recommendation for credit ratings are either lacking or very scarce in developing economies. Often the banks are helpless and, under the circumstances, fallback on some in-house scheme. This sheds light on the maneuvering, or faltering implementation, of Basel Accords in developing economies.

QUESTIONS FOR DISCUSSION AND REVIEW

1. In what ways does credit rating establish—and is determined by—the creditworthiness of a person, company, or an organization?
2. Compare the purposes that credit rating serves in bank lending and in trading of securities. Your answer should clearly show the use of credit rating in credit risk management.
3. **a.** Explain how developments in the international financial system inform credit rating practices in global banks.
   b. How can these developments be appreciated from the perspective of regulatory capital requirements for credit risk in the Basel Accords?
4. Evaluate credit rating as a lending device and its workings in banks prior to, and since the enactment of, Basel II in 2004
5. How does the Basel II-style risk-based credit rating help credit risk management in internationally active banks?
6. **a.** Discuss the events that led to the inclusion of credit rating in Basel II Accord.
   b. Critically examine the link between regulatory capital requirements and events leading up to the inclusion of credit rating in the Basel II Accord
7. **a.** Analyze issues that will shape future credit rating framework and application in developing economies.
   b. How would you justify or debunk concerns about issues that will shape future credit rating work and framework identified in 7(a)?

Section B

Liquidity Risk

Chapter 19

Bank Balance Sheet and Liquidity Risk Management in Developing Economies

Chapter Outline

LEARNING FOCUS AND OUTCOMES

Banks seek to attract and retain cheap and long-term funds to meet operational needs. That depicts the main activity on the liabilities side of a bank's balance sheet. The uses of funds to create, build up, and maintain robust earning, fixed and other assets portfolios is a regular feature of the assets side of the balance sheet. I evaluate integration of strategies for the two balance sheet sides—and, doing so,

- evaluate the management and implications of risks of assets and liabilities sides of a bank's balance sheet,
- examine management of risks inherent in balance sheet structure of banks in developing economies,
- assess the footing, structure and efficiency of banks' balance sheets in developing economies,

- analyze implications of banks' capitalization, financial and liabilities structure—and the mix of their deposit liabilities,
- evaluate measures of a bank's safety from the perspective of ratio analysis of its balance sheet items—with emphasis on,
  cash reserve ratio, loan-to-deposit ratio, liquidity ratio, loans-to-shareholders' funds, and classified loans-to-net worth.

EXPECTED LEARNING OUTCOMES

Banks' treasurers strive to source funds, invest the funds, and ensure optimum portfolio mix and return on investment. Ideally, the treasurer should be an expert in funds control, portfolio analysis, investments, and management. That way they would be able to advice on appropriate balance sheet structure and mix of funds in their bank's financial structure. That way treasurers help mitigate liquidity, operating, and financial risks. The reader will—after studying this chapter and doing the exercises in it—have learnt and been better informed about:

- how treasurers should manage assets and liabilities sides of the balance sheet to ensure liquidity of a bank,
- strategies banks' treasurers should adopt in mitigating risks inherent in the balance sheet structure of banks in developing economies,
- footing, structure, and management requirements of banks' balance sheet risks in developing economies,
- liquidity risk implications of banks' capital, financial, and liabilities structure—and the mix of their deposit liabilities,
- how to measure the safety of a bank from the perspective of ratio analysis of its key balance sheet items.

OVERVIEW OF THE SUBJECT MATTER

The scope of bank balance sheet management covers all the activities involved in sourcing funds, investing funds, and optimizing portfolios mix and returns on investments. Treasurers lead in this responsibility. They advise on what proportion—and from which sources—of their banks' capital funds should be applied in financing earning, fixed, and other assets. It is imperative, as part of the activities involved in this balance sheet management advice, for a bank to determine what should be the appropriate mix of funds in its financial structure. In doing so, the bank should seek to optimize spread between cost of borrowed funds and returns from investments in risk assets and securities.

Well-managed balance sheets bear the hallmark of sustaining liquidity at desired level. This is also a sure way for a bank to mitigate liquidity risk. Liquidity of a bank centers on its cash flow position. To put it simply, banks in which cash is constantly available to meet operational needs are liquid. The converse is also true—illiquid banks lack cash to fund operations. Incidentally, the balance sheet of a bank is a major source of cash available to the bank. Cash isolated from the balance sheet complements other cash flow sources in consolidating the liquidity of a bank. Treasurers of banks should approach balance sheet risk management from this perspective. One reason is that banks that are cash deficient are easily driven into liquidity crisis. There is yet another angle to the essence of cash in bank balance sheet management. Banks must always be liquid in order to meet their financial obligations and remain going concerns.

It is necessary—in structuring and managing risks in banks' balance sheets—to devise effective strategies to generate and sustain cash flows at desired level. This entails balancing cash uses (assets) by cash sources (liabilities) as a means of attaining portfolios and earnings objectives of the bank. I must say, striking the right balance between these two opposing demands of banks' balance sheets has often been elusive—or, rather, a tall order—for most banks. Yet bank balance sheet and liquidity risks are really mitigated when assets match liabilities one way or the other. Some think that matching in this sense is not possible—except in theory. However, treasurers discount this perspective and forge ahead with pragmatic matching techniques. Their ultimate goal, doing so, is to achieve their bank's liquidity targets.

IDENTIFYING AND MITIGATING BANK BALANCE SHEET AND LIQUIDITY RISKS

The balance sheet of a bank typically depicts uses (or applications) and sources of funds to finance assets acquisition. The uses represent assets of the bank, while the sources are liabilities. The strength of a bank lies in its balance sheet structure. To what extent is the bank dependent on interbank or nonbank funds? What is the mix of its deposits liabilities? In what forms or outlets does it hold the bulk of its investment in assets? What is the ratio of loans to deposits? These are some of the questions for which analysts of a bank's financial performance will seek answers. The answers will reveal whether the bank is liquid or illiquid, well capitalized or not, trading on equity or geared, and so on. I discuss elements of the balance sheet, focusing on assets and liabilities as a basis for analyzing risks associated with its structure and liquidity. In doing so, I present balance sheet of Union Bank of Nigeria PLC in Table 19.1 to illustrate typical balance sheet structure and its management and liquidity requirements.

Liquidity Demands of Risk Aversion

It is obvious, taking a long hard look at Table 19.1, that Union Bank is risk averse. This is evident in holding 65% of its assets in cash, short-term funds, and balances with other banks and financial institutions. It reflects unmistakable emphasis on liquidity. The risk aversion undertone of the bank's liquidity management stance is further seen in its low commitment of funds to loans and fixed assets which accounted for 16.63% and 3.76% of its balance sheet footing,

TABLE 19.1 Union Bank of Nigeria PLC—Balance Sheet as at 31st March[c]

	2002 (₦′ m)	Ratio (%)[a]	Ratio (%)[b]
Assets			
Cash and short term funds	20,814		7.56
Balances with other banks and financial institutions	145,638		52.92
Bills discounted	39,933		14.51
Other investments	727		0.26
Investments in subsidiaries and associated companies	994		0.36
Loans and advances	45,486		16.53
Other assets	10,984		3.99
Equipment on lease	268		0.10
Fixed assets	<u>10,350</u>		3.76
Total assets	<u>275,194</u>		
Liabilities			
Deposits, current and other accounts	204,347	83.44	74.26
Taxation	2,776	1.13	1.01
Deferred tax	822	0.34	0.30
Dividend	3,555	1.45	1.29
Other liabilities	<u>33,392</u>	13.64	12.13
Total liabilities	<u>244,892</u>		
Capital and reserves			
Called-up share capital	1,258	4.37	0.46
Share premium account	16,348	56.75	5.94
Bonus issue reserve	—	—	—
Statutory reserve	3,792	13.16	1.38
Reserve for small scale industries	1,455	5.05	0.53
General reserve	4,554	15.81	1.65
Exchange difference reserve	<u>1,402</u>	4.87	0.51
Core capital	28,809		
Fixed assets revaluation surplus	1,493		0.54
Shareholders' funds	<u>30,302</u>		
	<u>275,194</u>		

TABLE 19.1 Union Bank of Nigeria PLC—Balance Sheet as at 31st March[c] (cont.)

	2002 (₦′ m)	Ratio (%)[a]	Ratio (%)[b]
Contingent liabilities and other obligations on behalf of customers and customers' liabilities thereon	33,992		12.35

[a]Calculation of ratios were based on section sub-totals, while
[b]are calculated based on the balance sheet footing
[c]Union Bank was recapitalized in 2012 after its current owners—Union Global Partners Limited—invested $500.00 million that gave them 65% controlling equity of the bank. The bank's share capital and share premium stood at ₦400.11 billion, with net total equity of ₦230.67 billion, as at December 31, 2015. Its balance sheet footing was ₦998.14 billion as of this date.

respectively. On the face of it, this approach to boosting liquidity of a bank is good. It fits well with common practice in banking founded on the fact that liquidity is the life blood of a bank. In other words, banks that become illiquid cease to be going concerns. However, the approach embodies risk which banks' treasurers should always bear in mind.

Mitigating Exposure to Systemic Risk

The commitment of 52.92% of Union Bank's balance sheet footing to interbank placements and deposits with other financial institutions exposes the bank to systemic risk. Often the risk connects with occurrence of unexpected adverse event that destabilizes the money market. For example, cash crunch may hit the money market—causing defaults in settlement of interbank deals. Some unfavorable monetary policy, or regulatory intervention, can have a similar effect. In such situations, a bank that has large interbank placements may lose income or much of the funds. It would appear, though, that emphasis on liquidity from this angle is informed by a realistic cause. Banks should always be able to pay back matured deposits.

Balancing Assets Against Liabilities

In the case of Union Bank, customer deposits accounted for 83.44% and 74.26% of the bank's total liabilities and balance sheet footing, respectively, in 2002. However, the Table 19.1 does not show the proportion of this deposit portfolio that comprised interbank takings. The ostensible implication, nonetheless, is that the bank kept 65% of its assets in cash, interbank placements, and deposits with other financial institutions to meet its liability of 74.26% to depositors. This practice would satisfy not only the liquidity need, but business demands, of the bank—and it makes sense. Its flip side is that the bank earns less income than its balance sheet footing would ordinarily support. The probable income loss approximates to the usual trade-off between risk preference and risk aversion in business to which banks are oriented.

Checking Risk in Funding Assets

The risk of Union Bank's balance structure can be looked at from the angle of the nature and composition of funding of its assets. Table 19.1 shows that 74.26% of the bank's assets were financed with deposits, current and other accounts. A paltry 0.46% of the funding came from called–up share capital. Though shareholders' funds contributed 11.01%, much of it related to either notional funds or money that the bank may not easily have access to in the event of crunch (Reserve for small-scale industries and fixed assets revaluation surplus are typical examples) (Money in this category include share premium account, bonus issue reserve, and exchange difference reserve). The problem with this assets financing structure is that banks often tend to use short-term, and usually volatile, funds to finance assets acquisitions. Perhaps the banks rely, in doing so, on counterbalancing effect of keeping a large amount of funds—71% in the case of Union Bank—in equally short-term assets. This is both the usual and popular short-term liquidity risk management strategy of banks in developing economies. Managing liquidity this way keeps banks' treasurers on their toes. The solution lies in adequately capitalizing banks. That eases liquidity pressure and its risk management. Footnote 1—explaining how Union Bank solved this problem – is instructive.

Relating Credits and Deposits Terms

Conflict between tenors of banks credits and deposits in developing economies is, perhaps, the best example to illustrate how the structure of a bank's balance sheet impacts liquidity risk of the banks. Medium-to-long-term tenors of credit facilities remain a worrying source of lending risks for the banks. The major cause of risk is the term structure of deposit liabilities of the banks. Often the banks rely on short-term funds or usually find it difficult to attract long-term deposits to fund term loans. The inability of the banks to attract long-term deposits is due to macroeconomic vagaries—a situation that makes long-term financial planning difficult. The short-term deposit orientation of banks' customers in developing economies is a pointer to lingering failings in macroeconomic management. Market uncertainties—rooted in inconsistent monetary and public sector policies, financial system regulatory maneuverings, and galloping inflation—pervade the economies. Depositors cannot but orient their funds to short tenors in the face of this economic reality. Banks can ill afford to lend money to finance medium and long-term borrowing causes under the circumstances. This inevitable corollary of short tenor preference of depositors puts structural risk of banks' balance sheets in developing economies into perspective. Banks will not want to take the risk of mismatching term structures of their deposit and loan portfolios. Using or relying on volatile deposit sources to fund medium and long-term loans would be a recipe for liquidity crisis.

Insights into Loan to Deposit Ratio

There is yet another striking feature of Union Bank's balance sheet—one that depicts a critical issue in balance sheet structure and borders on demands of liquidity risk management. Banks and their regulatory authorities use ratio of loans-to-deposits portfolios as one of the measures of liquidity. The authorities enjoin the banks, for this reason, to do anything but exceed acceptable ratio of investment in risk assets to deposits portfolios. Sticking with this directive is necessary to avoid impairing short-term liquidity of the banks. Most banks target a loan-to-deposits ratio of not more than 70%.

$$\text{Loans-to-deposits ratio} = \frac{\text{Total Outstanding Loans}}{\text{Total Deposit Liabilities}}$$

$$\text{Total loans, advances and leases (₦' m)} = 45,754$$
$$\text{Deposits and current accounts (₦' m)} \quad 204,347$$
$$\text{Loan–to–deposit ratio} = \frac{45,754}{204,347}$$

$$= 22.39\%$$

On occasion, the aggressive banks—most of which are not too averse to risk—exceed this target. However, less aggressive and liquidity obsessive banks set their internal targets far below the 70% mark. This category of banks tends to be highly averse to risk and is found in the ranks of foreign subsidiary and domestic banks. For example, the ratio for Union Bank was 22.39% in 2002—calculated as shown earlier.

SOLVING BANK CAPITALIZATION-INDUCED BALANCE SHEET AND LIQUIDITY RISKS

Choice of capital financing option has cost implication for a bank. This raises pertinent questions. What constitute capital of a bank? When can a bank be adjudged to be adequately capitalized? Why should banks managements be concerned about capital adequacy? How do the authorities regulate bank capital? These questions shed light on the significance of bank capitalization as a risk management technique. The Basel Committee (2006) recognizes this significance. Accordingly, it links capital adequacy to credit risk. It does so in the belief that credit risk can make or break operations of a bank. Thus, risk-weights assigned to particular bank assets bear on adequacy of the bank's capital. The import of this approach to determining capital adequacy is that banks managements should be careful about credit risks they take. In so doing, they can mitigate risk of capital diminution.

Unfortunately, the Basel Accords' approach to bank capital and credit risk regulation diverges from what obtains in practice in emerging economies. The assessment of capital adequacy for banks is one of the critical elements in banking regulation in emerging economies, no doubt about it. A bank may have a numerically high value of shareholders' funds; however, it could indeed be undercapitalized relative to its portfolio of deposit liabilities or risk assets exposure. On the contrary, another bank may have a small amount of capital even though it is well capitalized in relation to the types and volume of business it undertakes. This is why it is necessary to devise a scientific approach to determining the adequacy of a bank's capital base.

A rule of thumb would be that capital adequacy is a function of the growth strategy, risk-taking appetite, and deposit drive of the bank. If a bank is pursuing an aggressive growth strategy—influenced by high-risk preference behavior in lending practices and a rising deposit liability profile—it will definitely require more capital resources. Here the problem still is how to measure what constitutes adequate capital resources for a bank. The concern about what constitutes the adequate capital base for a bank mirrors the anxiety caused by possible overtrading by some banks. It is perhaps more in banking than in any other business that investment in assets outstrips owners' equity or borrowed funds—in the form of deposit liabilities or other purchased funds. This certainly defines the risk of banking for most practical purposes.

It truly can be said that no amount of capital may be too much for a big bank or a growth-oriented small bank. Yet a benchmark should be set to take care of the minimum expectations of depositors and other stakeholders in the bank— especially in the sad event of bank failure.

REGULATING AND MEASURING ADEQUACY OF BANK CAPITALIZATION

Determining appropriate capitalization for banks is usually the crux of banking regulation and supervision in developing economies—and, indeed, elsewhere. In some countries, it has assumed a disquieting dimension. The common measures of capital adequacy relate to ratio analysis of key bank balance sheet items. It is used as a standard of measurement geared to establishing quantitative relationships between capital funds and total deposit, total assets or total risk assets. In so doing, financial analysts wish to determine the extent to which any losses that a bank incurs could impair the safety of depositors' funds. The overriding consideration is to gain insight into the adequacy of a bank's capital funds for absorbing business upsets without the loss of depositors' funds.

Most Central Banks in developing economies adopt an official minimum required capital adequacy ratio of 10%. In practice, however, some of the banks achieve higher rates. For example, the State Bank of Pakistan reported achievement of "overall capital adequacy ratio at 14.8% as of end March

2014" (Pakistan Economic Survey 2013–2014: 71–72). Banks are encouraged to pursue the targets through improved asset quality. One of the ways to improve the ratio is through adequate provisioning against nonperforming risk assets. In the Pakistan case, the ratio of nonperforming loans to total loans was 13.3% in March 2014, down from 15.8% in March 2013 (ibid). The common measure of capital adequacy—which relates capital funds to risk assets—is as follows:

$$\text{Capital adequacy} = \frac{\text{Capital funds}}{\text{Total risk assets}} \times 100$$

In order to serve regulatory purposes, minimum and maximum capital adequacy levels should be set. However, ratio analysis has its limitations. It does not tell anything about the nature and magnitude or the quality of operations and risks of a bank relative to the size of its capital resources. Yet once assessed by regulatory authorities, the ratios become standards for determining a bank's capital adequacy. All banks are therefore expected to meet the recommended capital adequacy ratio or risk being classified as undercapitalized.

Measurement of capital adequacy—explained earlier—builds on regulation of bank capitalization. The monetary authorities in emerging economies tend to stipulate three approaches to regulating the capital adequacy of banks. They focus on the start-up or base capital, single-obligor limit, and weighted risk assets ratio.

Startup or Base Capital

There is a minimum startup capital (i.e., owners' equity) requirement that must be met by prospective investors or promoters of a new bank. Existing banks, by the same regulation, are also expected to have a certain minimum paid-up capital at any point in time. New and existing banks must satisfy these minimum standards as a condition for obtaining or retaining their banking licenses. Existing banks and promoters of new banks in Nigeria are respectively expected to maintain or raise minimum equity capital of ₦25 billion.

Single-Obligor Limit

The single-obligor limit on bank lending is intended to ensure that a bank's capital funds really do cushion depositors against losses inherent in risk assets. Such risks become more apparent when loans are either not performing, require provisioning from earnings against possible losses, or have to be charged off. The notion of the single-obligor limit suggests that a bank should not lend more than a certain percentage of its shareholders' funds (unimpaired by losses) to a single borrower or group that are subsidiaries or share common ownership. In Nigeria at the moment, the single-obligor limit for banks is 20% of shareholders' funds (unimpaired by losses).

Weighted Risk Assets Ratio

The weighted risk assets ratio relates shareholders' funds to the total risk assets portfolio. This is essentially a typical measure of capital adequacy for banks in emerging economies. In Nigeria, and for regulatory purposes, capital adequacy is presently set at 10% of shareholders' funds. However, the CBN could vary the ratio depending on the prevailing macroeconomic situation.

BANK LIQUIDITY ISSUES, MEASURES, AND RISK MANAGEMENT IN DEVELOPING ECONOMIES

Banks in developing economies hardly rely on—let alone, willingly, comply with—liquidity ratios. Curiously, the banks even disregard their internally generated ratios. The banks have their reason. Liquidity ratios impose restriction on their ability to generate and do business at the optimum. That is why the banks strive to find ways around a temporary liquidity crunch when it occurs or hits the market—as long as they remain going concerns. This wrong disposition to the task of liquidity management should be redressed. Banks would be better–off limiting growth in order to sustain liquidity. This will boost their integrity and credibility. Using the balance sheet of First Bank of Nigeria PLC, presented in Table 19.2, I examine the three approaches to liquidity measurement commonly used by the regulatory authorities for banking in developing economies. A bank's liquidity position can be assessed using one, a combination, or all three methods: loan-to-deposit ratio, cash reserve ratio, and liquidity ratio.

Loan-to-Deposit Ratio

This ratio compares the volume of loans outstanding in a bank's loan (risk assets) portfolio to its total deposit liabilities at a given point in time. A bank determines its liquidity position using this method by dividing the total of its outstanding portfolio of risk assets by the sum of its deposit liabilities, and comparing the quotient or ratio so obtained with the industry average or the target set for it by regulatory authorities. In other words, the ratio expresses a bank's total deposit liabilities as a percentage or fraction of its outstanding loan stock.

Most banks that emphasize liquidity will target a maximum loan-to-deposit ratio of 70%, implying that realistically up to one third of the bank's total deposit liabilities should not be loaned to customers at any point in time. Banks that are less driven by profit maximization will target lower ratios—say, 60%. In the First Bank of Nigeria example, the ratios were far lower at 36.82% and 31.10% in 2002 and 2001, respectively, depicting the

TABLE 19.2 First Bank of Nigeria PLC—Balance Sheet as @ 31st March

	2002 (₦'m)	2001 (₦'m)
Assets		
Cash and short term funds --------------	132,800	108,875
Bills discounted --------------------------	54,178	37,049
Investments -------------------------------	780	501
Loans and advances ----------------------	61,918	46,111
Other assets ------------------------------	8,664	12,855
Equipment on lease ---------------------	190	202
Fixed assets ------------------------------	7,826	7,308
	266,356	212,901
Liabilities		
Deposits and current accounts ---------	168,175	148,279
Taxation ---------------------------------	1,176	1,740
Deferred taxation -----------------------	694	453
Other liabilities -------------------------	78,564	45,336
	248,609	195,808
Capital and reserves		
Called-up share capital ------------------	1,016	813
Capital reserve --------------------------	1,893	1,893
Statutory reserve -----------------------	3,252	2,655
Exchange difference reserve ------------	2,055	2,738
General reserve -------------------------	5,769	5,792
Bonus issue reserve ---------------------	254	203
Reserve for small and medium scale industries -------------	1,129	620
Core capital -----------------------------	15,368	14,714
Fixed assets revaluation surplus --------	2,379	2,379
Shareholders' funds --------------------	17,747	17,093
Total liabilities ----------------------	**266,356**	**212,901**
Contingent liabilities and other obligations on behalf of customers and customers' liabilities thereof -----------	76,883	25,797

high liquidity status of the bank. The ratio for each period is calculated as follows:

Loan–To–Deposit Ratio $=$	$\dfrac{\text{Total outstanding loans}}{\text{Total deposit liabilities}}$	
Balance sheet figures as at 31st March	2002	2001
Total loans and advances (₦′ m)	61,918	46,111
Deposits and current accounts (₦′ m)	168,175	148,279
Loan-to-deposit ratio $=$	$\dfrac{61,918}{168,175}$	$\dfrac{46,111}{148,279}$
$=$	36.82%	31.10%

Yet, the loan-to-deposit ratio could be as high as 100% or more for banks with high risk appetites. This category of banks sometimes relies on capital reserves and/or nondeposit float accounts or products to sustain liquidity, fund incremental lending activities, and meet profit targets. However, an extremely high loan-to-deposit ratio might be a warning sign of an impending liquidity crisis, which would scare discerning depositors from investing in such banks. Thus, the significance of the loan-to-deposit ratio is that it is inversely related to a bank's liquidity. This implies that a bank would be more or less liquid depending on the ratio. The bank would be more liquid, the lower its loan-to-deposit ratio, and vice versa.

When the ratio is considered high or more than the industry average, the bank may adopt a restrictive loan policy to check the likely negative impact on liquidity and the restriction of other profitable operations or activities. It would most likely also begin to discriminate among customers who make credit requests by being critical and selective on proposals to grant new credits. The bank may also increase its requirements for the accessing of loan facilities by some customers. Frequently, when the ratio is rising, lending rates tend to increase in kind as a bank hikes interest rates to reflect its tight liquidity position.

Unfortunately, many such loans frequently become delinquent, with concomitant loan loss provisions. When this happens, the expected income from the aggressive lending policy would not be realized. In fact, the bank may even make a net loss on balance in the performance of the total loan portfolio. It is indeed apparent that a bank would rarely make money or continually meet its net profit expectation through the irrational build-up of the loan portfolio.

Merits of Loan-to-Deposit Ratio

Measuring a bank's liquidity position by means of the loan-to-deposit ratio is credited with the advantage of establishing an acceptable level of depositors' funds that could be invested in loans and advances without jeopardizing a bank's liquidity position. The ratio is rationalized on the premise that since loans rank among the least liquid earning assets of a bank, the proportion of deposits invested in loans and advances cannot be increased without regrettably sacrificing liquidity. The choice is therefore for bank management to decide its preferred loan-to-deposit ratio in line with its long-term business focus, orientation, and market demands.

Despite the fact that a bank can choose whatever loan-to-deposit ratio it considers reasonable, its real value consists in offering a warning signal on the state of its liquidity position, especially when the ratio starts rising to an unsustainable level. In such a situation, there might be a need for the bank to begin to reconsider its investment policies and growth strategies with a view to recovering liquidity. The ratio gives insight into the extent of a bank's risk aversion or preference tendency, from which one could discern those banks that emphasize liquidity more than profitability and vice versa.

Shortcomings of Loan-to-Deposit Ratio

The shortcomings of this approach to liquidity measurement are also worth mentioning. It is criticized on the following grounds:

- Erratic and volatile deposit liabilities
  A bank with an erratic and volatile deposit base may have a higher risk of illiquidity than a bank that has a high loan-to-deposit ratio on a stable deposit base. It is also not uncommon to find situations where a few large deposits cause major swings in the ratio. In such cases, the ratio may give the wrong picture of the exact condition of the risk of the lending portfolio in relation to the deposit liabilities base.
- Attributes of a bank's loan portfolio
  It does not factor the key attributes of a bank's loan portfolio into the computation of the ratio. For instance, a loan portfolio might be composed of a large stock of short-term, self-liquidating, and performing risk assets that can be easily recovered if the need arises to do so. It is therefore important to determine the maturity profile of the loan portfolio, assess the borrowers' source(s) and modes of repayment, and review the bank's loan repayment experiences with its key borrowing customers.
- Degree of liquidity needs of banks
  The ratio fails to account for, or recognize, the fact that banks have varying degrees of liquidity needs. That a particular bank has a higher loan-to-deposit ratio than another does not necessarily mean that the latter is more liquid. Interpretation of the ratio should really be seen as reflecting conclusions on a composite set of variables, which reveal the practical relevance of the ratio itself. For instance, we cannot conclude that a bank with a higher loan-to-deposit ratio than another is less liquid. Such a conclusion does not tell anything about the stability or volatility of the deposit portfolio of the two banks.
- Risk assets versus deposit liabilities
  Relying solely on the relation between risk assets and deposit liabilities in measuring a bank's liquidity could be misleading for obvious reasons.

Besides loans and advances, there are other assets on a bank's balance sheet. Yet the loan-to-deposit ratio ignores all but risk assets in the computation of liquidity. It is necessary that the composition and nature of a bank's assets be critically examined in assessing its liquidity position.

This should be done for the reason that two or more banks may have the same loan-to-deposit ratio and yet not be equally liquid. Differences in the liquidity level between two banks could arise simply because the assets of one are more liquid than those of the other.

Cash Reserve Ratio

The cash reserve ratio, also known as the cash-to-deposit ratio, measures liquidity by relating the average volume of cash or liquid assets to the bank's total deposit liabilities or total assets. Sometimes, computations of the cash reserve ratio take into account the deposit liabilities or total assets of banks of similar size for all banks in that category. The ratio is calculated by regulatory authorities such as the Central Bank and enforced on banks. The following formula is applied in calculating the cash ratio:

$$\text{Cash reserve ratio} = \frac{\text{Total volume of cash assets}}{\text{Volume of deposit liabilities}}$$

Merits of Cash Ratio

In dividing cash assets by total deposit liabilities of the bank at any point in time, this ratio offers insight into the proportion of depositors' funds held in liquid form. This would give an idea of a bank's ability to meet depositors' withdrawal demands based on the availability of cash or reserves.

Shortcomings of Cash Ratio

The disadvantages of the cash ratio, and therefore the reserve requirement, as an approach to liquidity measurement tend to take away from its merits. There are critical shortcomings of the ratio. For instance, the cash ratio does not take account of the fact that a large proportion of cash assets are not, in practice, available to a bank to meet its liquidity needs. The ratio excludes short-term funds and marketable securities in its computation; yet these are considered highly liquid assets—especially T-bills. It also fails to recognize the possibility and tendency of a bank to raise cash from alternative sources to meet liquidity needs.

Liquidity Ratio

Calculation and application of the liquidity ratio has been a regular approach to assessing the liquidity of banks. Traditionally, regulatory authorities and deposit insurance corporations have highly favored the use of the liquidity ratio as a means for determining the liquidity position of a bank. The ratio is calculated by dividing a bank's portfolio of specified liquid assets by the bank's total current liabilities as follows:

$$\text{Liquidity ratio} = \frac{\text{Specified liquid assets}}{\text{Total current liabilities}}$$

The critical issue in the use of this ratio appears to be determining the composition of qualifying liquid assets. In Nigeria, the Central Bank specifies the following liquid assets and current liabilities for the purpose of computation of the liquidity ratio.
Liquid assets

- cash;
- balance held with the Central Bank less cash reserve requirement (8% of the sum of demand deposits, purchased funds, and domiciliary account balance);
- balance(s) held with domestic or internal banks (excluding uncleared effects) less balances held for domestic or internal banks (if net minus, add to current liabilities);
- treasury bills;
- placement(s) with discount houses less takings from discount houses;
- money at call held with other banks less money at call held for other banks;
- fixed deposits placed with other banks less fixed deposits held for other banks.

Current liabilities

- balances in demand and time deposit accounts;
- negotiable Certificates of Deposits issued (of not more than 18 months to maturity);
- excess balance(s) held for domestic or internal banks;
- excess placement(s) held for discount houses;
- excess money at call held for other banks;
- excess deposits held for other banks;
- balances held for external offices less balance(s) held with external offices (if net minus ignore).

The liquidity ratio computation for banks in emerging economies (specifically Nigeria) is illustrated in Table 19.3 later.

Justification of Liquidity Ratio

The ratio must be met on a monthly average basis—but could fluctuate during any days of the month. It provides a guide to banks in managing occasional swings in its stock of reserve assets, which could exceed or fall short of the statutory requirement at any point in time. In the case of the former, a bank could dispose of its surplus holdings of liquid assets or reserves to reduce the income loss associated with carrying such nonor low-earning assets. In the event of a

TABLE 19.3 Illustration of Liquidity Ratio Computation for Banks in Developing Economies

	₦'000	₦'000
Liquid assets		
Cash --		22,935
Balance held with CBN -----------------------	(400,539)	
Less Cash reserve requirement (12.5% of demand deposit and purchased funds)	267,913	
	(668,452)	(668,452)
Balances held with internal banks (excluding uncleared effects) ------------------	620,160	
Less Balances held for internal banks (if net minus, add to current liabilities) ---	993,986 (373,826)	0
Nigeria Treasury Bills (NTB) --------------------	0	0
Nigeria Treasury Certificates --------------------	0	0
Placements with discount houses -------------	169,801	
Less placements held for discount houses (if net minus, add to current Liabilities)	158,000 11,801	11,801
Money at call held with other banks ---------	0	
Less money at call held for other banks (if net minus, add to current liabilities)	0	
	0	0
Fixed deposits placed with other banks ------	0	
Less fixed deposits held for other banks (if net minus, add to current liabilities)	160,000 160,000	0
Nigeria certificates of deposit held (of not more than 18 months to maturity) --	0	
Government securities—eligible development stocks—(i.e., of not more than) 3 years to maturity -----------------------	0	
Less Nigeria certificates of deposit (NCDs) issued -------------------------------	0	
	0	0
Bankers unit fund		
Stabilization securities ------------------------	0	
Less foreign exchange market (FEM) deposit -------------------------------	0	0

TABLE 19.3 Illustration of Liquidity Ratio Computation for Banks in Developing Economies (*cont.*)

	₦'000	₦'000
Total liquid assets (A)		(633,717)
Current liabilities		
Current time/deposits account ----------------		2,143,307
NCDs issued (of not more than 18 months to maturity) ------------------------		0
Excess balance held for internal banks -------		373,826
Excess placements held for discount houses		0
Excess money at call held for other banks ---------------------		0
Excess deposits held for other banks --------		160,000
Balance held for external offices -------------	0	
Less Balance held with external offices (if net minus, ignore) -----------------	0	
	0	0
Collateral deposit ------------------------		0
Cash collected for financial services ---------		0
Balance held for other external banks --------	0	
Less balance held with other external banks (if net minus, ignore) -----------	0	
	0	0
Total current liabilities (B)		(2,677,133)
Liquidity ratio A/B ----------------------------		−23.67%
NTB ratio NTB/B -----------------------------		0.00%

shortfall, the bank will resort to increase its deposit base, even if by taking call money in the interbank money market.

Weakness of Liquidity Ratio

The usual victim in all observed situations of a persisting shortage in the required liquidity level is lending activity. At first blush, management is averse to the curtailment of further lending activity in order to shore up the liquidity. Yet this is acclaimed to be an effective liquidity management strategy, as excessive lending activities drain liquidity. If the rate of growth in lending is not matched by deposit mobilization, the bank may begin to experience cash flow distress resulting from illiquidity. But the alternative—one that implies the forgoing of earnings, growth, and profitability as a sacrifice to improve liquidity—is also not palatable or beneficial to the bank.

SUMMARY

The balance sheet of a bank typically depicts uses (or applications) and sources of funds to finance assets acquisition. The uses represent assets of the bank, while the sources are liabilities. The strength of a bank lies in its balance sheet structure.

Choice of capital financing option has cost implication for a bank. The Basel Committee (2006) links capital adequacy to credit risk. It does so in the belief that credit risk can make or break operations of a bank. Thus, risk-weights assigned to particular bank assets bear on adequacy of the bank's capital. The Basel Accords' approach to bank capital and credit risk regulation diverges from what happens in practice in developing economies. A bank may have a numerically high value of shareholders' funds; however, it could indeed be undercapitalized relative to its portfolio of deposit liabilities or risk assets exposure. On the contrary, another bank may have a small amount of capital even though it is well capitalized in relation to the types and volume of business it undertakes. This is why it is necessary to devise a scientific approach to determine the adequacy of a bank's capital base.

A rule of thumb would be that capital adequacy is a function of the growth strategy, risk-taking appetite, and deposit drive of the bank. If a bank is pursuing an aggressive growth strategy—influenced by high-risk preference behavior in lending practices and a rising deposit liability profile—it will definitely require more capital resources. The problem still remains how to measure what constitutes adequate capital resources for a bank. The concern about what constitutes the adequate capital base for a bank mirrors the anxiety caused by possible overtrading by some banks. It is perhaps more in banking than in any other business that investment in assets outstrips owners' equity or borrowed funds—in the form of deposit liabilities or other purchased funds. This certainly defines the risk of banking for most practical purposes. It truly can be said that no amount of capital may be too much for a big bank or a growth-oriented small bank. Yet a benchmark should be set to take care of the minimum expectations of depositors and other stakeholders in the bank—especially in the sad event of bank failure.

Determining appropriate capitalization for banks is usually the crux of banking regulation and supervision in developing economies—and, indeed, elsewhere. In some countries, it has assumed a disquieting dimension. The common measures of capital adequacy relate to ratio analysis of key bank balance sheet items. It is used as a standard of measurement geared to establish quantitative relationships between capital funds and total deposit, total assets, or total risk assets. In doing so, financial analysts wish to determine the extent to which any losses that a bank incurs could impair the safety of depositors' funds. The overriding consideration is to gain insight into the adequacy of a bank's capital funds for absorbing business upsets without the loss of depositors' funds. Most Central Banks in developing economies adopt an official minimum required capital adequacy ratio of 10%. In practice, however, some of the banks achieve higher rates.

QUESTIONS FOR DISCUSSION AND REVIEW

1. What are the implications of risks of assets and liabilities sides of a bank's balance sheet for effective bank management?
2. How do the risks inherent in balance sheet structure of banks in developing economies impact the liquidity of the banks?
3. In what ways does the mix of the deposit liabilities of banks impact the banks' capitalization, financial, and liabilities structure?
4. Would you say that measuring a bank's safety from the perspective of ratio analysis of its balance sheet items is effective?
5. Why should banks' treasurers play a key role in managing assets and liabilities sides of the balance sheet of a bank?

FURTHER READINGS

Koch, T.W., MacDonald, S.S., 2000. Bank Management, fourth ed. The Dryden Press, Philadelphia.

Kreps, (Jnr.), C.H., Wacht, R.F., 1972. Credit Administration. American Institute of Banking and American Bankers Association.

Nwankwo, G.O., 1994. Crisis of Confidence in Nigerian Banking, 5th Anniversary Lecture of the Money Market Association of Nigeria, held at the Banquet Hall of the L'Hotel Eko Meridien, on 25th May 1994, Lagos: Money Market Association of Nigeria, 1995.

Prochnow, H.U., 1949. Term Loans and Theories of Bank Liquidity. Prentice-Hall, New Jersey.

Revell, J.R.S., 1978. Competition and Regulation of Banks. in Barclay, et. al., 1978.

Chapter 20

Bank Liabilities Portfolio and Liquidity Risk Management in Developing Economies

LEARNING FOCUS AND OBJECTIVES

There may be no country that has not experienced banking system instability—at one time or another—caused by the interplay of liquidity risk and failed liabilities management. Inordinate chase after earnings compounded the problem in developing economies. In some cases, the attendant crisis heightened concerns about the safety of depositors' funds in the banks. In this chapter, I focus on addressing the failings in bank liabilities and liquidity risk management. Doing so, I geared my objectives to:

- Explain the meaning and significance of liquidity—with implications for liquidity of bank assets and liquidity of a bank.
- Conceptualize liquidity from the perspective of bank management in developing economies.

- Evaluate the techniques for measuring the liquidity of banks for risk management purposes in developing economies.
- Determine the efficacy and risks of liabilities generation and build-up schemes as bank funding strategies in developing economies.
- Assess the deposits mobilization sources, strategies, and constraints of banks in developing economies.
- Explore possibility of integrating cashflow analysis with strategies for mitigation of bank liquidity and funding risks.

EXPECTED LEARNING OUTCOMES

On occasion the regulatory authorities horridly intervened in a bid to address liabilities and liquidity risks of the banks in developing economies. The widely publicized and analyzed 2007–09 global financial crisis and meltdown is a case in point. Financial crisis of this nature soon became a contagion and threatened the entire financial system and economies around the world. In most cases, regulatory intervention was simply a feeble postmortem on already snowballed financial crisis. The reader will—after studying this chapter and doing the exercises in it—have learnt and been better informed about:

- The meaning and significance of liquidity and their implications for understanding liquidity of bank assets and liquidity of a bank.
- Conceptualization of liquidity in the context of banking in developing economies.
- Techniques for measuring the liquidity of banks for risk management purposes in developing economies.
- The efficacy and risks of liabilities generation and build-up schemes as bank funding strategies in developing economies.
- Deposits mobilization sources, strategies, and constraints of banks in developing economies.
- How to integrate cash flow analysis with strategies for mitigation of bank liquidity and funding risks in developing economies?

OVERVIEW OF THE SUBJECT MATTER

Banks managements should learn to get to grips with liquidity risk and crisis. Their business sense and approach should reflect pragmatism in dealing with liquidity crisis—without sacrificing rules, guidelines, and injunctions. This view may seem a bit farfetched in developing economies, but it is feasible. Unfortunately, banks managements tend to be either easily overwhelmed by the crisis or lacking in imaginative solution to it. Thus they end up resorting to fire fighting. Usually this becomes the final nail in the bank's coffin—especially where liquidity crisis degenerates into terminal bank distress.

There is a constant need for banks managements to reinvent enterprise both in the face of liquidity crisis and as a panacea for it. They should demonstrate a resolve to do so in unmistakable terms and to the conviction of all the stakeholders in banking. Determination and persistence should be their watchwords, as well as the assets at their disposal. That begins and will sustain the path to best practice. But there should be a deliberate effort to constantly muster finances as a means of keeping liquidity crisis at bay. This shouldn't be done just as an end in itself but as a strategy to seize opportunities that might beckon for banking.

Ultimately, liquidity risk and crisis will be tamed when banks strive to create value and launch into robust operations as going concerns. Need-fulfilling market offerings come in handy here. Above all else, the regulatory authorities should know when banks are floundering and rise to the challenge. They should do so in a decisive manner—one that leaves the stakeholders in no doubt about solution to liquidity crisis. Often this is the hard fact and reality that stare them in the face.

Bank treasury and marketing—indeed, all—employees have a part to play in liquidity risk and crisis management. They should attract and retain sufficient funds and patronage from customers and dealers in the money market. Maintaining funding at optimum level helps meet a bank's assets financing requirements and earnings objectives. This treasury's basic function reflects the capacity of a bank to raise or borrow funds from depositors, investors, or creditors who may be interested in its debt instruments as a means of meeting the bank's liquidity needs for risk assets creation, investments, operating expenses, and statutory reserves. In order to fulfill this role, banks' treasurers should develop relevant funds and portfolio management skills.

Failed liquidity management was at the root of most of the cash flow crises that caused bank distress and failure in several countries around the world. I'm not convinced that banks either have, or adopt, a foolproof liquidity management strategy. Many believe that bank distress and failure originate from this omission. Unfortunately, the foregoing repercussion is now a syndrome with which the industry has to live. Bank distress and failure occur and recur unpredictably even as regulators intensify oversight interventions? Besides failed liquidity management, I foresee salient issues in infraction of prudential guidelines on bank lending and conflicts of interest—bordering, in most cases, on insider abuse. Often failed management of a bank's liquidity—especially liquidity of risk assets—and a craving for increasing earnings are at the root of the problem.

CONCEPTUALIZING LIQUIDITY IN THE CONTEXT OF BANKING

The Basel Committee on Banking Supervision (2010) accords high priority to liquidity risk, a fact that is evident in the manner, it devoted the most part of Basel III to detailing regulations bordering on liquidity risk management. Liquidity risk could be defined in two different, but related ways as:

- the danger that a bank may not have sufficient cash, cash inflows, or be able to quickly convert some assets to cash at little or no loss of value; or

- the chances that a bank's operations may be adversely affected by its inability to generate sufficient cash, cash inflows, or quickly convert some assets to cash.

Liquidity exerts a great influence over general banking functions and activities. Indeed, liquidity management is increasingly becoming the most crucial issue in modern banking practice. A bank would be distressed and fail when it becomes illiquid. To put it simply, liquidity is essential to prevent bank distress and failure. In principle, banks managements rely on liquidity management theories in a bid to prevent distress. But there could be recourse to some unusual, more pragmatic approaches in dealing with the liquidity problem. Yet, distress remains a recurring syndrome that erodes depositors' confidence in the banking system. Loss of confidence of depositors in banks has heightened nowadays considering that distress had often caused outright failure of banks in several developing countries.

It is well-known that adverse regulatory policies and several other factors—insider abuse, bad management, fraud, speculative transactions, excessive risk appetite, and so on—could be trigger points for liquidity crunch and bank distress. These are forbidden actions, the occurrence of which evidences weak, or lack of strong, internal control. However, while losses arising from internal control lapses could threaten a bank's liquidity position, scarcely do they always lead to distress and failure. For example, one of the leading banks in Nigeria remained liquid after recording a whopping fraud of about ₦800.0 million in 1999 in one of its upcountry branches. Similarly, another market leader in Nigeria's banking sector lost about ₦10.6 billion to the failed NITEL acquisition bid when the BPE initially put up that parastatal for sale to core/strategic investors in the early 2000s. Despite this huge loss, the bank remained liquid and even declared higher profits at the end of its financial year following that loss. Incidents such as these are not defined as part of the elements of current theories of bank liquidity management. One reason is that it would be unwieldy to subsume all actions of cheats under regular theoretical frameworks for bank liquidity management. There would a constraint in on including every conceivable events, actions, or omissions that can cause bank distress and failure.

The challenge of bank liquidity management lies in determining how and why liquidity risk remains a nightmare for banks managements. The real question is why have liquidity management theories not helped banks in developing economies to avoid distress and failure? It would be interesting to research and propose alternative liquidity management viewpoint, which will be capable of filling observed limitations in current thinking about bank distress prevention. Indeed, for all intents and purposes, sustaining liquidity at desired level remains a major critical success factor for banking in developing economies.

In the context of banking practice, I ask questions to articulate the subject matter of the concept of liquidity. What do we mean by the term liquidity? Why is it necessary to assess the liquidity of assets? What are the indicators of liquidity of a bank? What are the approaches for measuring liquidity of a bank? These questions constitute the foundation of a framework for bank liquidity and funding risks management in developing economies to which I now turn.

MEANING OF LIQUIDITY

The term liquidity means availability of sufficient cash or cash inflows to meet maturing financial obligations and normal business operating expenses. In a broader sense, it denotes the ability to generate sufficient cash inflows from business operations, including capacity to turn assets into cash at short notice without loss, or undue loss, of value so as to meet operating business expenses and all maturing financial obligations and commitments as and at when due.

Let me amplify the main components of these definitions in order for the reader to better appreciate what is implied when a bank is said to be liquid or illiquid. Liquidity has the following three main attributes—all of which reflect in the definitions:

- Ability to generate *sufficient cash inflows* from business operations or other sources.
- Capacity to turn assets into *cash* (i.e., through sale) at short notice without loss, or undue loss, of value.
- Promptly meeting *all* operating business expenses and maturing financial obligations and commitments as and at when due.

My intention for this breakdown is to demonstrate the implication of a bank being liquid. A bank that is liquid should have sufficient daily cash resources to satisfy business requirements. It must equally be able to quickly raise cash somehow in the event of shortages or unusual cash demand or withdrawals. The overriding implication is that a liquid bank would not default on any of its financial obligations, especially to the customers.

A bank that lacks this financial resilience may be said to be illiquid. Such a bank will be facing liquidity or funding risk at any point in time. Usually, the risk crystallizes in default. Illiquidity has been a major cause of bank distress and failure in many developing countries. It results mainly from accumulation of large stocks of nonperforming risk assets and the abuse of official positions of banks managements. Without liquidity, a bank loses credibility and—in an extreme situation—ceases to be a going concern. In most cases, the bank is bound to fail.

LIQUIDITY OF ASSETS

It is imperative to assess the liquidity of the assets at a bank's disposal at any point in time. This necessity derives from the fact that a bank will be more or less liquid depending on the liquidity of its assets. Also, the level of liquidity of assets employed by a bank determines how profitable it would be or, otherwise, the strength of its earnings capacity. With a large stock of highly liquid assets, earnings and profitability would be low—in line with the principle of risk-return trade-off and vice versa.

An asset is said to be liquid when it can be easily converted into cash at little or no risk of loss in value. Some bank assets are highly liquid, while others are relatively illiquid. Cash is the most liquid asset in a bank's portfolio at any point in time, while premises, loans, and advances may be classified among the least liquid assets. This viewpoint is justified as follow:

Cash—in form of a currency bill—is completely liquid in the sense that it is really money, which can be instantly exchanged for any other currency bill.

Fixed assets—such as buildings, fixtures, and fittings, and so on—can be sold within a reasonable time frame and at an affordable sale discount.

On *loans and advances*—it is important to note the following factors that tend to limit liquidity potential:

- Most loans and advances may not be liquidated or repaid prior to the expiry dates of their tenors.
- A similar liquidity setback on loans and advances is that they scarcely have an established resale market in developing economies.
- It may be occasionally possible for a bank to sell loans to investors through securitization or to other banks. However, this would seldom happen except when the loans involved are of very high quality and held by strong industry names. Ostensibly, banks have such loans with customers whose credit relationships the banks cherish, would want to retain, and therefore not want to sell.
- Some large volume direct loans could be converted into bankers' acceptance facilities to enhance their salability. However, the issuing or selling bank would have to endorse or assure the repayment or liquidation of the acceptance instruments. The reduction in net asset portfolio through sale of bankers' acceptance provides only a temporary liquidity relief, as the bank would, in most cases, repay the acceptances within not more than 90 days.
- In the final analysis, it would be absurd and, indeed difficult, to fully liquidate a bank's loan portfolio as quickly as the need for cash impels. At best, perhaps, a reasonable level of pay downs on the more performing loan accounts can be achieved—but definitely not on the entire portfolio.

The more liquid assets of a bank, after cash and reserves, include treasury bills (T-bills) and investments. As government's obligation, T-bill offers the most liquidity of all security investments in a bank's portfolio. It can be readily converted into cash (through sale in the money market) at a minimal discount.

LIQUIDITY OF A BANK

The aforementioned definitions of liquidity aptly answer the question about liquidity of a bank. Based on those definitions, it can be said that a bank is liquid if, on daily basis, it fulfills the following:

- generates cash inflows in excess of cash outflows;
- maintains sufficient pool of liquid assets; and
- can raise cash quickly from other sources to meet its financial commitments and obligations as and at when due.

Perhaps the most significant practical test of a bank's liquidity is its ability to maintain adequate buffer on cash assets, short-term funds, and marketable securities (i.e., T-bills) as a means of meeting financial emergencies in the course of its day-to-day business operations. It is the treasurer's responsibility to ensure that the bank is liquid at all times by sustaining a good mix of cash balances, reserves, and investments relative to risk assets portfolio. Within the bank, they must be an influential to be able to always get the support of bank management on liquidity matters.

A bank that lacks liquidity, or is illiquid, will easily be upset by adverse fluctuations in its deposits liabilities portfolios or money market conditions. Such a bank will also find it difficult to meet:

- regulatory requirement for cash reserves;
- unanticipated, even if seasonal, surge in loan demands; and
- customers' demand for cash withdrawals.

For as long as illiquidity persists, the bank will surely be continually losing business to competition. The major sources of liquidity for a bank—in addition to existing stock of cash, reserves, and T-bills—are inflows from new deposits, loan repayments, and earnings from business operations.

The task of banks managements—one that remains a nightmare for them—is to determine how much and in what forms to hold liquidity that is needed to keep the bank afloat at all times. This does not come easy as the opportunity cost of liquidity (i.e., low risk disposition) is lost earnings and profitability—which, for instance, would have been realized from risk assets. Yet a bank must maintain adequate level of cash reserves and instruments to meet financial emergencies often caused by occasional money market distortions and other unforeseen contingencies.

MEASURING LIQUIDITY OF A BANK

The need to regularly measure the liquidity of a bank is to both comply with regulatory requirement for periodic returns and ensure early detection of deviation from set target. The regulatory authorities, such as the central bank, may set the required liquidity target. Yet every bank is expected to develop even a more ambitious target for itself, in addition to any externally determined one by the authorities, to guide its liquidity risk management.

Once a realistic liquidity target has been established, it should be adopted for all practical purposes of decision-making that affects a bank's liquidity position. Unfortunately, a common observation among bankers is that they rarely rely on, or comply with, liquidity ratios—even the internally generated ratios. The reason is not far-fetched. The bankers see the limits imposed on business generation by strict adherence to the ratios as punitive. Thus, as long as their banks remain going concerns, they strive to find ways around temporary liquidity crunch when it occurs or hits the market.

This is a wrong disposition to the task of liquidity management. It is better to limit growth and sustain liquidity—and ultimately the integrity and credibility of the bank. As upheld by a certain aphorism, "a good name is better than money." It implies, in this case, that a bank will be better off in the long run to stay liquid at all times with decreasing rate of growth and profitability. The alternative—pursuing aggressive growth and earnings strategies—at the expense of cash flow strength and liquidity—is indeed worse. The big banks are relatively not guilty of this liquidity management problem.

In the final analysis, a bank's liquidity position can be assessed using one, a combination, or all of the following ratio-based methods: loan-to-deposit, cash reserve or cash-to-total deposits, liquidity ratio, loans-to-shareholders' funds, and classified loans-to-net worth—all of which I discussed in Chapter 22 of this book.

INTEGRATING CASHFLOW WITH MITIGATION OF BANK LIQUIDITY AND FUNDING RISKS

A bank cannot afford to be cash deficient. There are possibilities for ensuring that a bank always remains liquid. It should generate sufficient cash flows from normal banking operations. The ability of a bank to do this depends on its customer base. I mean its liabilities-based market share and transactions turnover attendant on it. This is critical not only to increasing interest but fee and other incomes. In general, cash flow from operations—referred to as net operating cash flows (NOCF)—is the net amount of cash that a company generates from sales. It is arrived at after deducting cost of goods sold, other operating costs, and movements in working capital. In distilling a bank's financial statement into cash flows, NOCF approximates to net amount of cash that a bank generates from all of its services and operations. As Table 20.1 shows—in the case of a bank—NOCF is the sum of net cash from funds (NCFF) and cash charges for services *less* cash cost of funds, cash operating costs, and movements in working capital. Information on, and adjustments to determine, movements in working capital are obtained from the balance sheet.

TABLE 20.1 Cashflow Approach to Banks' Income Statement Analysis

Accrual accounting approach	Cashflow approach
Interest income	Cash interest from funds
Interest expense	Cash cost of funds
Net revenue from funds (NRFF)	NCFF
Fees and other incomes	Cash charges for services
Gross earnings	Cash from operations
Service, general and admin expense	Cash operating costs
Operating profit	Cash after operations

Knowledge of how each of the items of profit and loss account is derived is pertinent. Such knowledge helps in identifying related balance sheet accounts that impact sources and uses of funds in analyzing a bank's cash flow position. Funds flow principles underpin the balance sheet equation:

$$\text{Assets} = \text{liabilities} + \text{capital}$$

This equation establishes the relation between assets and liabilities in a balance sheet statement. When assets figure is increasing or decreasing, the liabilities figure must also be increasing or decreasing to maintain balance in the equation. However, for purposes of funds flow and cash flow analysis, increases and decreases in assets and liabilities have different implications. In general, net decreases in assets and net increases in liabilities values represent sources of funds. In the converse, net increases in assets and net decreases in liabilities values indicate uses of funds. Thus, the net change in a bank's cash position is derived by netting off uses from sources of funds. This information usually comes in handy in determining a bank's true cash flow position.

In most cases, cash extracted from the balance sheet is hardly enough to satisfy a bank's day-to-day operation requirements. That is the reason a bank should sometimes explore prospects of using certain refinancing packages to augment cash it generates from normal business operations. This involves some financial planning to ensure that the success of the refinancing packages. Mostly, favored refinancing packages target equity issue, increasing liabilities or debts portfolio. Banks that are adjudged to be liquid will not find it difficult to realize refinancing objectives. In most cases, they have the financial flexibility required to service their debts.

Banks can also fall back on disposal of some fixed assets, liquidation of certain short-term security investments, or call in some loans—all of which help ease liquidity pressure and risk. In principle, operational flexibility should allow banks to easily liquidate particular assets to meet liquidity needs. In extreme cases of crunch, banks tend to tap refinancing window of the Central Bank. This serves only short-term liquidity risk management need for the banks—mitigating pressure on funding of the bank's operations while the bank's board and management explore and decide on some long-term option. The window furnishes a temporary reprieve from liquidity crisis where long-term funding option is elusive. Unfortunately, this is often the fate of most terminally distressed banks.

SPREADSHEET APPLICATIONS IN BANK LIQUIDITY AND FUNDING RISKS MANAGEMENT

Treasurers should, first and foremost, have a good grasp of the salient features of cash flows from income statement and balance sheet that underlie liquidity of their banks. Then they should be able to determine actual cash flow position of their banks. With cash flow information, the treasurers can effectively plan for liquidity risk management. Cashflow Summary Form, meticulously completed, is the key to being on top of liquidity concerns in banking. Table 20.2 shows an adaptation of Cash Flow Summary Form developed by Omega Performance Corporation (Adapted with permission from Omega Performance Corporation Cashflow Summary Form; may not be copied or reproduced without the express written consent of Omega Performance Corporation.). Banks treasurers can use this form for their liquidity management responsibilities.

The essence of Cashflow Summary Form is to guide treasurers in determining, sourcing, and making provision for cash that their banks need to meet day-to-day demands of operations. But treasurers also need to seek and obtain approval of their banks' managements to deal with other banks and financial institutions in the money market. Discount houses are the main nonbank financial institution with which the regulatory authorities permit banks to place funds. It is necessary, with the need for approval in view, for the treasurers to prepare spreadsheets of audited financial statements of the banks and financial institutions. In addition to Cashflow Summary Form, there should be spreadsheets for income statements and balance sheet of the banks. Sometimes, the three spreadsheets are combined in order to produce a Standard Spreadsheet Form.

Treasurers are required to present the spreadsheets—duly completed, either separately or in combination—to their banks' managements for use in deciding and approving deposit placement limits (DPL) with other banks. Thus, the spreadsheets serve three main purposes in balance sheet and liquidity risks management. Treasurers can figure out and are therefore able to plan for the cash needs of their banks using the Cashflow Summary Form. The spreadsheets give treasurers an insight into the cash flow ability of other banks and discount houses with which they deal in the money market. Banks managements rely on the spreadsheets to approve deposit placement limits with other banks and discount houses.

TABLE 20.2 Spreadsheet and Cash Flow Summary Form

Cashflow for year ending		2011	2012	2013	2014	2015
	Sales revenue..................................					
+ (−)	*Changes* in					
	Accounts receivable ....…........					
	= Cash from sales ....(a).................					
	Cost of goods sold expense (less depreciation).....................................					
+ (−)	*Changes* in					
	Inventory (stock)..............................….....					
	Accounts payable..............................……					
	= Cash production costs .... (b)........					
a–b	= Cash from trading .... (c).............…..					
	SG & A expenses (less non-cash SG & A expenses).					
+ (−)	*Changes* in					
	Prepaid expenses...........…..........….......					
	Accrued expenses...........…............…......					
	Sundry current asset / liability accounts..					
	= Cash operating costs........ (d)...........					
c–d	= Cash after operations .... (e)..........					
	Other income (expense).....…...............					
	Income tax expense............…..........…..					
+ (−)	*Changes* in					
	Deferred income taxes......…...............					
	Income taxes payable......…..........…….					
	= Taxes paid and other income (expense) (f)...					
e–f	= Net cash after operations ......(g).......					
	Dividends or owners' withdrawals.......					
+ (−)	*Change* in					
	Dividends payable..............…........….....					
	Interest expense...............…...................					
+ (−)	*Change* in					
	Interest payable.................................					
	= Cash financing costs ......= (h)..........					
g–h	= Cash after financing costs .....(i).........					

(Continued)

TABLE 20.2 Spreadsheet and Cash Flow Summary Form (*cont.*)

Cashflow for year ending		2011	2012	2013	2014	2015
	Current portion long-term debt ... (j).....					
i–j	= Cash after debt amortization .... (k)...					
+ (−)	*Changes* in					
	Fixed assets......................................					
	Investments......................................					
	Intangibles......................................					
	Other non-current assets....................					
	= Cash used in plant and investments .... (l)					
k–l	= Financing surplus (requirements)........ (m).....................................					
+ (−)	*Changes* in					
	Short-term debt (notes payable)...........					
	Long-term debt................................					
	Preferred stock.................................					
	Common stock.................................					
	= Total external financing .... (n).....					
m–n	= Financing surplus (requirements) + Total external financing...					
Proof:	Change in cash and marketable securities..					

Input from Financial Control Input

The Cashflow Summary Form is applicable to historical financial data. Conditions underlying the accounts and that inform it are unlikely to remain unchanged. The Cashflow Summary Form may show that a bank is liquid whereas the bank is not in reality—presently. That is the usual shortcoming of historical financial ratio analysis and so is not peculiar to cash flow spreadsheet. Treasurers should therefore combine historical with projected spreadsheets in order to appreciate, as well as have, accurate information on their banks' balance sheet and liquidity risks situation.

The treasurers will need input from the financial control (FINCON) unit to be able to make good and reliable forecasts. The first projection to make is on foreseeable income statement—and then on the balance sheet. Table 20.3 and Table 20.4 show mock forecast profit and loss account and balance sheet which treasurers can adapt to meet their needs. As usual, spreadsheet of cash

TABLE 20.3 Guide to Projected Profits and Loss Account for Period Ending...

	Total (₦'000)
Interest income	
Loans	
Deposits	
Fees	
Other	
Total interest income	
Interest expense	
Time deposit	
Savings account	
Call deposits	
Other	
Total interest expense	
Net revenue from funds (NRFF)	
Fees	
L/C commission	
Other	
Gross earnings	
Operating cost	
Employees cost	
Admin expense	
Other	
Total cost	
Profit before tax	

flows should be distilled from the income and balance sheet statements. Completion of the Cashflow Summary Form then follows. Interpretation and use of the spreadsheets follow the same process as in those derived from historical financial data.

Financial controllers should work closely with treasurers on the balance sheet and liquidity risks management project. The controllers should provide treasurers with accounting data for use in preparing and analyzing the projected financial statements. In most cases, the required accounting data come from management accounts that would be input into the financial accounts at the end of the year. Nowadays treasurers and financial controllers rely on the computer

TABLE 20.4 Guide to Projected Balance Sheet as at ...

	AVG (₦'000)
Assets	
Cash	
Loans and advances	
Fixed assets	
Other assets	
Total assets	
Liabilities	
Current accounts	
Time deposits	
Other liabilities	
Total Liabilities	

to generate all the necessary forecasts and analyses. This eases liquidity risk management assignments.

LIABILITIES GENERATION AND BUILD-UP AS BANK FUNDING STRATEGIES

The growth of a bank is greatly influenced by the size and network for the generation of liabilities. Observed rapidity of growth, induced by increasing portfolio of liabilities, evidences a bank that enjoys goodwill and confidence of depositors and investors. The banks that have weak growth capacity sometimes have narrow customer base, especially on deposits or lack ability to raise capital funds from potential investors. Yet, without a large pool of liabilities, any growth strategy pursued by a bank would cause liquidity crisis or distress. It is therefore important for a bank to develop and consciously nurture effective strategies for generating deposit liabilities. The balance sheet of a bank shows the major sources of its liabilities and capital as customer deposits and shareholders' funds. I review the components and sources of deposits liabilities for a bank and how to return value to depositors as a means of sustaining their loyalty and patronage. This is reflected in deposits generation methods adopted by the banks.

Deposit

There could be differences among banks in the approaches to attract deposits. Yet the common features could be isolated for purposes of determining the efficacy of the more frequently used approaches. The common deposit mobilization approaches which banks in developing economies adopt are often structured as treasury or debt instruments that offer specific value to customers. Prospective customers determine banks in which to keep deposits based on analysis or perceived worth of the value propositions offered by the banks. But they also consider ability of the banks to honor repayment obligations on the deposits or redemption of the debt instruments. Banks generate deposits mainly from demand, time, and savings deposit accounts. The value served by each of these deposit products could vary significantly from one bank to another. In order, for instance, to attract cheap deposits some banks in Nigeria offer interest-bearing current or demand deposit account—which is unconventional in the country. The observed differences are after all driven by competitive pressure which impels recourse to novel tactics sometimes. Otherwise, the main features of the deposits products are as I present later.

Demand Deposit Account

Banks open demand deposit or current accounts for customers who wish to enjoy advantages of checks, funds transfer, and liquid balances. With a check, the customer can withdraw from, or lodge funds in, their account at any time and without a prior notice to the bank. The use of checks has helped to minimize the inconvenience and risks—such as loss to robbers—of carrying huge cash about to conduct business transactions. The current account holder can equally readily transfer funds to a third party or give a standing payment order to the bank. In both cases, the bank will move funds as instructed by the customer. Perhaps the most valued benefit of current account to a bank's customer is its high liquidity. It is relatively easy for the customer to access their deposits whenever a withdrawal or payment need arises.

Observed Drawbacks

Despite its advantages, current account may be less attractive to some customers. The following are a summary of the possible setbacks of current account:

- In order to open and operate a current account, a customer must fulfill certain minimum requirements for account opening documentation. This may be quite stringent in some banks because of the need to obtain the correct identity of the account holder, necessary mandates for opening and operating the account, and references on the account itself from other suitable current account holders either in the bank where the account is maintained or from other banks. However, these measures are intended to shield the account against fraud by the account holder or third parties.
- Current account suffers yet another setback in most developing economies where the check payment system is not well developed and therefore distrusted. In such situations, business transactions are conducted largely on cash basis. A lot of costly public education campaigns have to be undertaken

by the banking authorities to correct erroneous impressions about the use of checks for business transactions.

- Unlike time or savings deposits, current account is zero-interest bearing. But this is the opportunity cost to the account holder of the benefits, especially the liquidity and flexibility of the account. Of course, it would be cumbersome, even with the help of IT capabilities, to work out a reasonable interest on such highly swinging account. Yet a bank also needs compensation for its services which only current account holders enjoy. Thus, zero-interest regime may not after all be justified and therefore not an incentive to the customer.

Benefits to the Bank

From a bank's perspective, the major appeal of current account is the provision of a substantial pool of float balances in customers' accounts. Banks realize, from experience, that the sum of the differences between daily lodgments into, and withdrawals from, current accounts usually leave net pool credit balances—which represent the float deposits. Like other float products, current account float is free of cost to the bank. However, few banks may pay interest on credit balances in current accounts as a marketing strategy. In practical terms, banks compete most for strength on current accounts float because the larger a bank's portfolio of net positive current accounts balances (CABAL), the more its ability to grant credit facilities at competitive or even below average market rate. Such banks also tend to grow and make profits more or faster than those with low net CABAL. However, the real or opportunity cost of CABAL to a bank is the statutory requirement for a larger provision of reserves than is applicable to other forms of deposits.

Savings Deposit Account

Savings account is popular among individuals, small businesses, and not-for-profit organizations—such as churches, NGOs, thrift societies, and so on. Its appeal is that it enables the account holder to gradually accumulate interest-bearing deposits over time for particular purposes. It may not be necessary to specify the savings purpose and period, or time frame—these are usually left to the discretion of the account holder or the saver. Withdrawals from a savings account may be made at any time. In practice, though, withdrawals are infrequent. For this reason, a bank can invest a high proportion of the deposits in short-term risk assets or securities to increase earnings. The required reserves on savings deposits are therefore relatively smaller than demand deposits but more than fixed deposits. The major weakness of savings account consists in the requirement for physical presence of the account holder in the bank to make withdrawal from the deposit. Nowadays smart ATM card technology has significantly mitigated this setback. Yet savings account lacks the flexibility of a demand deposit account. The observed shortcomings of savings account are redressed by payment of interest on the account.

Time Deposits

Banks also attract time deposits in the process of liabilities generation and management. The main sources of time deposits are corporate bodies, high net worth individuals (HNIs), and interbank deposit takings. Such deposits could be in form of call or fixed tenor term.

Call Deposit

Depositors of funds with a bank on call basis are generally unwilling to forgo the benefit of liquidity, while at the same time earning interest on the deposit. Therefore, call deposit does not have tenor. Neither does its holder need to give prior notice to the bank before withdrawal can be made from the deposit. Like a current account, the advantage of liquidity is minimized by low interest rate which call deposits attract. In fact, in some banks, call deposits are treated as demand deposits for administrative reasons and convenience of liquidity planning.

Fixed Deposit

As the name implies, fixed deposits are kept with the bank for a definite tenor or period during which the customer may not be allowed to withdraw funds from the deposit. The customer is rather expected to give notice to the bank of intention to withdraw the deposit, either wholly or partly, at the expiry of its term or tenor. There may, however, be cause for a customer to wish to terminate fixed deposit prior to its maturity date. Such circumstances do arise sometimes out of some constraining exigencies in the business or personal life of the depositor. The bank will normally show consideration on such occasions by permitting withdrawal of the deposit, while penalizing the customer for upsetting the fixed deposit rule. The penalty for breaking a fixed deposit could be forfeiture of accrued interest on the deposit up to and including the date of its prematurity termination. The bank could also appropriate a certain percentage of the accrued interest as penalty charge. Banks chase after fixed deposits because of the assurance of stability of the funds which is propitious for liquidity planning. Fixed deposits should ideally be invested in risk assets to maximize the long-run earnings and growth capacity of the bank. A large and increasing portfolio of such funds is further beneficial to the bank because of its low level of statutory reserve obligation.

Float-Oriented Account

There is yet another source of deposits on which banks heavily rely for cheap funds. This deposit scheme generates short-term liquidity support for the bank and, in most cases, shares the characteristics of a demand deposit. The notion of collection or float deposit originated from the desire of, or competition among, banks to render special funds management service to government, large corporations, or such other business organizations. The account is operated on an escrow basis, whereby a bank collects and ware-houses, manages, and remits funds on behalf of its customers on agreed terms. The escrow account is opened for special purposes, which may be receipt or collection, and pooling, of sales proceeds, service tariffs, customs duties or other port charges (in the case of government). The customer and bank will normally have agreed that no other transactions should be allowed through the account before it is opened. On agreed regular basis, the funds so collected or received by the bank are transferred as may have been in-structed by, and to meet the needs of, the customer. Although float deposit rarely stays for more than few days, nevertheless it offers a bank short-term liquidity of the type it gains from demand and call deposit accounts. Like the highly liquid current account, float deposit is cost-free to the bank. It also does not compel a bank to set funds aside as reserve against it. The bank yet appropriates handling charge from the deposit for the service. Therefore, a bank can place the same level of reliance for liquidity planning on float, as in demand, deposit.

MONITORING AND STAVING OFF THE FACTORS OF LIABILITIES PORTFOLIO RISKS

The risks inherent in the liabilities portfolios of the banks in developing econo-mies originate from mainly gaps in the banks' capitalization, liquidity position, cash reserves, and volumes relationship between loans and deposits. The regu-latory authorities in developing economies try to address the risks through the establishment and enforcement of benchmarks for measuring the soundness of a bank. Emphasis is usually placed on meeting certain standard financial ratios with which the authorities tinker in pursuit of this goal. Usually, the applicable benchmarks are for the required cash reserve ratio, liquidity ratio, loan-to-de-posit ratio, and capital adequacy ratio.

The benchmarks in some of the countries are 8% or more for capital ad-equacy ratio; not less than 12.5% for cash reserve requirement; and at least 40% for the liquidity ratio. There is scarcely a strictly defined benchmark for the loan-to-deposit ratio. It all depends, in most cases, on a bank's standing with respect to its capital adequacy, cash reserve, and liquidity ratios. However, the regulatory authorities in most developing economies tend to favor a loan-to-deposit ratio of not more than 70%. Nonetheless, the highly liquid banks hardly lend up to 70% of their deposits portfolio. It is within the ranks of the distressed banks that the loan-to-deposit ratios often exceed the benchmark. This is un-derstandable considering that banks in this category lack the appeal to attract funds from the discerning depositors. The treasurers equally should regularly apprise themselves of the absolute figures of the bank's total loans and deposits portfolios from which the loan-to-deposit ratio is derived. This helps boost their presentations at the assets and liabilities meetings.

The financial controllers of the banks should continually work out and make figures relating to these ratios available to the treasurers. With the information, the treasurers can be on top of the liquidity position of their banks. It also puts them in a better position to monitor the risks of the liabilities portfolios. Perhaps, the most useful need for the information is to help the treasurers determine an effective and risk-free method of playing the liquidity risk management game in the financial markets. Thus there is always a need for the collaboration of the financial controller and the treasurer in pursuit of this goal. The treasurer and their teams will rely on inputs from their subordinates in the assets and liabilities management unit. The inputs will help the treasurer make informed risk management decisions—as well as contribute meaningful thoughts at the ALCO meetings.

The treasurer also should equip themselves with other information pertinent to the monitoring of the risks of the bank's liabilities portfolios. Such information includes update, which the operations unit furnishes on losses and defaults the bank incurs at clearing. This information will reflect a declining or increasing market share—and, therefore, an indication of the banks' liquidity and ability to continuously fund its clearing operations. The related indicators of a bank's current liquidity position and tendency include prudential analysis of the total loans portfolio, assessment of the status of its cash drawing facility with the Central Bank, and the percentage of interbank deposits to the total deposits portfolio. The usual prudential classifications of the risk assets portfolios recognize loans that are performing, substandard, doubtful, and lost. There should also be update on the charged-off but not let off loans.

The banks that are in distress often resort to excessive interbank borrowings and distressed deposits mobilization. Costly purchased funds start to dominate the bank's funding strategies. Soon the ratios of its interbank takings, purchased funds, and indebtedness on the Central Bank's cash drawing window to its total deposits portfolio begin to climb. The distress becomes more evident and worrisome with decreasing earnings. The regulatory authorities are likely to swoop on a bank that reports operational losses for three consecutive financial years. The reason is that the regulatory authorities view loss-making as a sign of an impending distress that should be nipped in the bud. The healthy banks rate well on these liquidity indicators and criteria.

I also should mention some of the subtle factors of liabilities risks in banking. The prevailing economic situation in a country is one such subtle factor that affects banking overall. Economic activities in a country may suddenly plunge and cause unexpected business upsets that impact banking in kind. In the worst case, the result may be illiquidity in the financial markets. Usually, the resultant systemic illiquidity will leave many banks in financial crisis. Treasurers and their colleagues in the ALCO should constantly anticipate this happening. It is part of planning for effective liquidity management—and, therefore, their responsibility.

SUMMARY

Liquidity means the availability of sufficient cash or cash inflows to meet maturing financial obligations and normal business operating expenses. Liquidity risk is the danger that a bank may not have sufficient cash, cash inflows, or be able to quickly convert some assets to cash at little or no loss of value. Liquidity is essential to prevent bank distress and failure. It exerts enormous influence over general banking functions and activities.

Assessing the liquidity of the assets of a bank is always pertinent. A bank will be more or less liquid depending on the liquidity of its assets. Also, the level of liquidity of assets employed by a bank determines how profitable the bank would be or, otherwise, the strength of its earnings capacity. A liquid asset can be easily converted into cash at little or no risk of loss in value. Cash is the most liquid asset in a bank's portfolio, while premises, loans, and advances may be classified among the least liquid assets.

The need to regularly measure the liquidity of a bank is to both comply with regulatory requirement for periodic returns and ensure early detection of deviation from set target. Central bank may set the required liquidity target. Yet every bank is expected to establish even a more ambitious target for itself, in addition to the one the Central Bank sets, to guide its liquidity risk management. A bank's liquidity position can be assessed using one, a combination, or all of the following ratio-based methods: loan-to-deposit, cash reserve or cash-to-total deposits, liquidity ratio, loan-to-shareholders' funds, and classified loans-to-net worth.

A bank should generate sufficient cash flows from normal banking operations. In distilling a bank's financial statement into cash flows, emphasis should be on NOCF. The NOCF approximates to net amount of cash that a bank generates from all of its services and operations. It is the sum of NCFF and cash charges for services *less* cash cost of funds, cash operating costs, and movements in working capital. Information on, and adjustments to determine, movements in working capital are obtained from the balance sheet. Cash extracted from the balance sheet is hardly enough to satisfy a bank's day-to-day operational requirements. Thus a bank should explore prospects of using certain refinancing packages to augment cash, it generates from normal business operations.

Treasurers should have a good grasp of the salient features of cash flows that underlie liquidity of their banks. Then they should be able to determine actual cash flow position of their banks. With cash flow information, the treasurers can effectively plan for liquidity risk management. Cashflow Summary Form, meticulously completed, is the key to being on top of liquidity concerns in banking. Treasurers should combine historical with projected spreadsheets in order to appreciate, as well as have, accurate information on their banks' balance sheet and liquidity risks situation. The financial controller should provide them with accounting data for use in preparing and analyzing the projected financial statements.

The growth of a bank is greatly influenced by the size and network for the generation of liabilities. Observed rapidity of growth, induced by increasing portfolio of liabilities, evidences a bank that enjoys goodwill and confidence of depositors and investors. The banks that have weak growth capacity sometimes have narrow customer base, especially on deposits or lack ability to raise capital funds from potential investors. Yet, without a large pool of liabilities, any growth strategy pursued by a bank would cause liquidity crisis or distress. It is therefore important for a bank to develop and consciously nurture effective strategies for generating deposit liabilities.

QUESTIONS FOR DISCUSSION AND REVIEW

1. To what extent do you agree or disagree that failed liquidity management is usually at the root of most of the cash flow crises that cause bank distress and failure?
2. Why would or wouldn't you think that banks in developing countries adopt a foolproof liquidity management strategy?
3. Is it true that bank distress and failure in developing countries originated from some strategic omissions in bank liquidity management?
4. Why and how would you agree or disagree with the view that liquidity risk is a nightmare for banks managements in developing economies?
5. What methods should banks in developing economies adopt to boost their liabilities portfolios as liquidity risk management strategy?
6. Of what relevance is cash flow to banking? How should treasurers integrate cash flows with mitigation of a bank's liquidity risk?

REFERENCE

Basel Committee on Banking Supervision, 2010. Basel III: International Framework for Liquidity Risk Measurement, Standards and Monitoring. Bank for International Settlements, Basel.

FURTHER READINGS

Agene, C.E., 1995. The Principles of Modern Banking. Gene Publications, Lagos.
Koch, T.W., MacDonald, S.S., 2000. Bank Management, fourth ed. The Dryden Press, Philadelphia.
Kreps, C. H. (Jnr.), and Wacht, R. F., 1972. *Credit administration*. American Institute of Banking and American Bankers Association.
Prochnow, H.U., 1949. Term Loans and Theories of Bank Liquidity. Prentice-Hall, Englewood Cliffs, New Jersey.

Chapter 21

Bank Liquidity Crisis and Funding Risk Management in Developing Economies

LEARNING FOCUS AND OUTCOMES

One of the lessons learned about bank liquidity crisis is that it easily becomes a contagion spreading among banks in a country—and thus has a serious negative impact on the entire society. Failed management of liquidity risk is usually the culprit for the crisis. Bankers can avert the crisis by adopting proven theories of liquidity management. However, it doesn't seem they do this or do it well. I investigate why liquidity management theories have not altogether worked for banks in developing economies. In doing so, I aim to:

- Review the classical theories of bank liquidity management—including their underlying assumptions, implications, and flaws.

- Assess the implications of liabilities for bank liquidity risk management in developing economies.
- Explore the regulatory angle to failings in bank liquidity crisis and risk management in developing economies.
- Investigate the creation, dynamic, incidence, and remedial of bank treasury crisis in developing economies.
- Discuss common management structure for bank liquidity risk management in developing economies.

EXPECTED LEARNING OUTCOMES

The management of bank liquidity risk in developing economies tends to be ineffective. Perhaps, banks in developing economies do not either have, or adopt, foolproof liquidity risk management strategies. For this reason, liquidity crisis occurs and recurs—ostensibly becoming a syndrome with which the banks have to live. There is need to find out why and how liquidity risk management continues to be a big concern for the banks. The reader will—after studying this chapter and doing the exercises in it—have learnt and been better informed about:

- The main tenets of the classical theories of bank liquidity management—including their underlying assumptions, implications, and flaws.
- Sources and the implications of liabilities for bank liquidity risk management in developing economies.
- Regulatory angle to the observed failings in bank liquidity crisis and risk management in developing economies.
- Common management structure and strategies for bank liquidity risk management in developing economies.
- The creation, dynamic, incidence, and remedial of bank treasury crisis in developing economies.

OVERVIEW OF THE SUBJECT MATTER

It cannot be overemphasized that the financial meltdown experienced around the world in 2007–09 tainted financial systems and banking regulators. The crisis was not only unanticipated but annoying. It overwhelmed banks, regulatory authorities, and governments. The ignominy of not being able to crack the crisis was a bitter pill to swallow. It is believed in many quarters that the meltdown resulted from failings in credit and liquidity risk management. Around financial centers of the world, leading banks had taken huge and unmitigated exposures in financial derivatives and other paper financial assets—especially, in credit products. Finding—when the crunch came—that collateral for most of the lending was dubious exacerbated the crisis. Besides, borrowers were not forthcoming with loan repayment, thus compounding the problem.

Liquidity squeeze pervaded the global financial system as had never been experienced in recent history. Soon the crisis spread and threatened national economies around the world. In Europe, America, and some other regions of the world, government responded with unmistakable concern for the public. As would be expected under the circumstances, government applied taxpayers' money to bail-out distressed and failing banks, and to rescue key industries. One cannot but ask a pertinent question about the future of banking in the face of recurring liquidity crisis. How can banks anticipate future liquidity crisis—especially one that culminates in financial meltdown? The banks must have an answer to this question. While future financial meltdown may be unpredictable, banks will have to live with occasional liquidity crisis.

In principle, applying the theories of liquidity management could be helpful to bank management. But it is doubtful that bank management fully appreciates and avails from tools in the theories. Otherwise why might the theories not have been helpful to the banks in preventing liquidity crisis? There may, perhaps, be flaws in the theories or some distortion in applying them. The leading theories, for example, focus on how to maintain liquid assets. Such theories favor short-term commercial lending. I mean so-called self-liquidating lending that is largely transactions-based. Once a bank does this, according to the theories, it should gain from stable and increasing income from operations. However, it would seem that liquidity crisis of the banks originate in the acts of banks managements. Such acts manifest themselves in maneuvering of prudential regulations and conflict of interest bordering, in most cases, on insider abuse—which the theories ignore.

REGULATORY AND THEORETICAL CHALLENGES OF BANK LIQUIDITY MANAGEMENT

Banking is—or should ideally be—a highly regulated business all over the world. This may sound a bit far-fetched, but I shed light on why it is true. In the first place, banks are a depository for the hard-earned cash, savings, and valuables of individuals, organizations, and institutions. Second, government and the public sector depend on efficiently functioning banking system to fulfill economic and social services to the citizens. Third, private enterprise and sector tend to flourish in countries where sound banking culture is institutionalized and has taken root. Fourth, the failure—or the maneuvering—of banking explains most of the issues often raised about the poor performance of developing economies.

It would seem that the banking system holds most of the aces in social change to which the developing economies aspire. If this is true—and I believe it is—then there should be no excuse for failure of banking in developing economies. Indeed, it should be all hands on deck to get banking right. The banking regulatory authorities should be at the forefront of this task. It is a call to duty and service in recognition of their roles as the banking stakeholders' watchdog. Now I ask the real question. Have banking regulators in developing economies fulfilled this prized expectation to the satisfaction of the stakeholders in the banking industry? This question is pertinent—considering that the public tends to have bad vibes about banking regulation in developing economies. Nonetheless, the question cannot be answered in the affirmative. Banking regulation in developing economies is tainted by failings. The bankers and other financial system operators exploit the situation. Infractions of the rules of banking are exacerbated under the circumstances.

Banking supervision has not fared better. Often the work of the supervisory arms of the regulatory authorities seems or is really frustrated by the bankers. On occasion bank examiners come up against a brick wall in their investigation of the conduct of banks managements. In most cases, this happens where there is culpable breach of sensitive banking rules. Thus bank examiners come under immense pressure to sweep curious findings under the rug. The intensity of the pressure depends on the seriousness of the offense. Usually banking regulatory and supervisory authorities face two choices. They could stick with the ethics of their profession and shun inducements, or compromise themselves, succumb to pressure, and bungle their roles as the stakeholders' watchdog. This reality presents an "either or" situation that introduces irrational tendencies in banking in developing economies. Those tendencies crystallize the crux of the risks that the banks face.

The traditional theories of bank liquidity management are still relevant in modern banking practice. The theories embody the principles which have proven practical in managing the funding of a bank's operations. They are premised mostly on the tenets of efficient management of bank assets. Whether a bank will be liquid or not has much to do with the volume and composition of its assets relative to its deposit base, as well as the quality of, and returns on, its investments in risk assets. Thus the theories seek to explain how understanding of this fact can help banks managements in dealing with situations that portend risk of cash flow deficiency as a result of poor management of assets. What are these theories—their major postulates, practical relevance, justifications, and limitations? The popular classical theories of bank liquidity management include the commercial loan theory, anticipated income theory, shiftability theory, and liability-management liquidity theory.

COMMERCIAL CREDIT AND LENDING PERSPECTIVES ON BANK LIQUIDITY RISK

The commercial loan theory of bank liquidity risk management postulates that the liquidity of a bank would be assured if it grants only short-term, self-liquidating loans. It assumes that all loans and advances must be fully liquidated in the normal course of business. It follows that banks should be guided by the borrower's asset conversion cycle in their lending activities. The borrowing cause at each of the successive stages of marketing, production, sales, and accounts receivables can be deduced from the asset conversion cycle. Thus the theory enjoins banks to shun loans that lack proven repayment ability within their transaction cycles.

The underlying principles of the commercial loan theory were founded in the 10th century English monetary history when the real-bills doctrine held sway for bankers. The banking tradition of the period favored granting of only business loans—those needed to meet working capital needs or to finance stock-in-trade. Banks were tuned to believe that it was risky and unprofitable to lend for such other purposes as agricultural production, investment in securities, consumer goods, real estate, or long-term projects. The risks of these sorts of credits, according to the doctrine, derived from the implied long-term commitments of funds and, therefore, the tendencies to adversely affect the short-run liquidity of the bank. Such loans were indeed termed illiquid loans.

It was also widely believed that lending in support of production activities—as opposed to speculative transactions, such as trading in highly volatile equity stocks or foreign exchange deals, which thrive on fickle deals and arbitrage—would check inflationary pressures on the economy. This contention is explained in terms of the expected lending-induced increase in real output of goods which would offset or compensate possible inflationary impact of the loans. The most critical statement of this viewpoint is rooted in Say's law (1803), which postulates that "supply creates its own demand." In the context of this law, inflation rate in a country would be stabilized if the banks create money by granting only self-liquidating loans. Such loans should be utilized for the sole purpose of producing consumption goods and services.

In the absence of other sources of money creation, or if such sources are inoperative, increase in money supply would generate a proportionate increase in output and demand for goods and services. While lending activities increase the money supply, loans utilization increases outputs of goods and services. The net effect of this interaction between money supply and outputs would be stability in prices and zero inflation.

Import of Self-Liquidating Loans

They key element of the commercial loan theory is the recommendation of self-liquidating loans to banks. This is seen as propitious for the postulations of the theory. I recognize that "self-liquidating loans" is a common phrase in the banking and finance literature. What really is the meaning of self-liquidating loans? A loan is said to be self-liquidating if it is utilized as envisaged and, in so doing, generates sufficient cash flows from which it is repaid on or before its due date. I give examples to illustrate typical nonself-liquidating loans. A loan granted to an individual, for instance, to purchase household equipment (i.e., consumer loan), or to a company to buy residential quarters for its employees (i.e., mortgage loan) will not be self-liquidating. In both cases, the funds to repay the loan would not come directly from the use to which the proceeds of the loans are put.

A loan will be self-liquidating if it is granted to finance importation and sale of a company's stock-in-trade. Clearly, the loan would be repaid from the proceeds of sale of the imported goods financed by the bank. In this case, the use to which the loan is put assures its repayment to the bank.

Limitations and Implications

The commercial loan theory of bank liquidity management is both elementary and weak in its conceptualization of the cause and creation of liquidity in banking. The theory is criticized on four main counts. It neglects the needs of growing economies and possible stability of a bank's deposit base. The fallacy of self-liquidating loans taints the theory. Let me now briefly discuss these and other shortcomings of the theory.

Neglect of Needs of Growing Economies

The theory is not in tune with the financing requirements for economic growth and development. Its major thrust is antithetical to the needs of growing economies. Growth-oriented economies need long-term credit facilities for the finance of business expansion projects. The financing is utilized for acquisitions of plant and machines or for the building of factories. Yet banks are expected to play a leading role in the finance of economic growth, development infrastructure, and projects. Thus strict adherence to the commercial loan theory distorts the pattern and direction of economic development activities in a country. Unfortunately, in most of the developing economies, lending to commerce tops annual distribution of credits granted by the banking system. This bank lending attitude should change. The change will stem the problems associated with the observed huge and unprecedented financing of consumption imports in developing economies. The problems in question include the burgeoning demand for foreign exchange, persistent devaluation of the domestic currencies, and rising level of inflation rate. Yet, a growing economy requires a lot of long-term investments which only banks can provide at a reasonable cost to the investors.

Fallacy of Self-Liquidating Loans

It is not always true that short-term, asset-based, or working capital loans are repaid on due dates. These typical examples of self-liquidating loans subsumed under the commercial loan theory sometimes go bad. While the structure of such so-called self-liquidating loan and its transaction dynamics may be right at the stage of conceptualization, the loan can yet go bad for unforeseen reasons. Indeed, a commercial loan may turn sticky as a result of unfavorable economic conditions. For example, a prolonged period of demand deficiency for stock-in-trade financed by a bank can result in default. If the loan was granted to finance working capital requirement, the resultant cash flow crunch will obviously frustrate the borrower's ability to repay the loan. The loan might even be lost if any of the events that are generally believed to be acts of God occurs. There are several reasons a credit facility can go bad in developing economies (See, for example, Onyiriuba (2015). I provided a comprehensive analysis of management tasks in solving problems associated with bank credit products in developing economies. Thus, I did not consider it necessary to dwell on such issues in this book.).

Possible Stability of Deposit Base

A bank's deposits liabilities exist as a pool of funds which may be stabilized or predictable if properly managed. With an effective treasury, a bank could accurately anticipate and provide for its funding needs within the possibilities of the framework of its deposits liabilities management. Cash lodgments generated from normal running of customers' accounts or new time deposits often offset the possible depletion of the deposit base through withdrawals from demand deposit or other deposit accounts. If this often happens, the bank would have a relatively stable deposits base against which it could grant term loans without risking liquidity. Stability of deposits portfolio is informed by yet another fact. It would be unlikely that all depositors will want to withdraw their deposits at the same time. Even in several known cases of a run on banks, not all customers withdrew their deposits despite the money panic the banks faced. Thus, the commercial loan theory is flawed on its assumption that term loans should be shunned because, besides the need to sustain liquidity, banks do not have access to long-term funds.

Irrelevant During Business Lull

The liquidity of a bank—from the perspective of commercial loan theory— may be taken for granted during normal economic periods. On the contrary, the theory is irrelevant as liquidity management strategy during economic recession when there is lull in business activities. At such times, low inventory turnover, long outstanding receivables, and general cash crunch mark business activities. Most businesses would default on bank loans—whether structured as short-term, self-liquidating, or working capital credit facilities or not. Thus, a bank may not maintain liquidity at all times by strictly granting only self-liquidating loans and advances. The cash flow squeeze that may be associated with periods of economic recession or cyclical business swings can be better managed through fallback on reserves than investment in risk assets. However, this presupposes that the banks had anticipated and provided sufficient cash assets, short-term funds and investments (such as T-bills) for such adverse occasions. Otherwise, they would be caught napping when the crunch comes.

SWITCHING ASSETS IN GRAPPLING WITH CHALLENGES OF BANK LIQUIDITY

The major proposition of the asset-switching, otherwise known as shiftability, theory is that a bank can sustain liquidity if it has assets which it can readily sell or transfer to willing investors, lenders, or other banks. The notion of disposing of the assets is justified as a means of meeting any temporary cash flow deficiency or squeeze. Thus, shiftability theory is premised on the assumption that for as long as a bank has assets which it can sell it will always meet its liquidity needs. Cash flow difficulties arise mainly when a bank pursues an aggressive growth strategy. Often such growth is driven by rapid and unsustainable expansion of risk assets portfolio. In most cases, the growth is not superseded or matched by growth in its deposit liabilities. A bank in this situation, especially if it has non-performing loans, should regain liquidity or cash inflows by selling off collateral pledged to it by the borrowers. It could also achieve the same effect by selling its T-bills and other marketable securities to the Central Bank or discount houses.

Eligibility of Securities

It is not enough that a bank should have assets to sell whenever it experiences cash flow squeeze. It should be realized at the outset that not all bank assets are liquid. Indeed, many of the assets are illiquid in nature. Therefore, for asset-switching theory to have any practical relevance, the bank must have a large stock of highly liquid assets, which it can readily turn into cash without delay and at no or a negligible risk of loss of value.

It is common knowledge that secondary reserves of a bank, commonly referred to as marketable securities, are the main source of short-term cash flow or liquidity for a bank once the bank's cash assets are depleted to a risky level. However, for a bank to rely on this liquidity assumption, such assets must satisfy three main criteria. The assets must be of a high quality, have a short term to maturity, and have easily realizable secondary market values (i.e., marketability). As in T-bills, they must also not pose any risk of loss as a result of poor credit rating or money market setback.

Money market setback is experienced when variations in nominal interest rates adversely affect the value of securities. This happens frequently when the value of securities fall as a result of rising interest rates in the money market. As nominal interest rate is inversely related to security price, the risk of capital loss is accentuated in volatile interest rates regime. For banks and investors in securities, such money rate risk (i.e., probability of capital loss) is antithetical to the requirements of the shiftability theory.

However, money rate risk is minimized, the closer a security is to maturity—a fact that underlies the requirement of short-term tenor as a key qualifying attribute of securities. As the due date of a security approaches, its market price approximates its face value. This fact must be factored into the analysis of the shiftability theory.

Merits and Demerits of Asset-Switching

Shiftability theory has implications for efficient management of asset portfolio of banks as a means of attaining and sustaining appreciable level of liquidity. This means that banks managements should appreciate liquidity characteristics of the assets that constitute their banks' portfolios. Such understanding will help them to know which assets to apply in the context of the shiftability theory to meet the liquidity needs of their banks at any point in time. A bank that wishes to be liquid, according to shiftability theory, should maintain a large volume of cash and marketable securities. As near cash items, marketable securities are characterized by the ease with which they can be converted into cash without losing value. Together with cash, they constitute the liquid assets portfolio of the bank. A bank that invests more in loans and advances—the less liquid assets—than in cash and marketable securities will be unlikely to avoid cash flow crisis—and, therefore, liquidity risk. This underscores the lesson of the shiftability theory. However, asset shifting is yet not common among banks in developing economies. For this reason, the theory may not be of doubtful value and not applicable to the banks in developing economies.

ANTICIPATING INCOME FROM LOANS TO MITIGATE BANK LIQUIDITY RISK

The anticipated income theory is premised on an assumption that a bank can sustain liquidity if borrowers would generate sufficient cash flows in future to repay their loans on due dates. Its main tenet is that bank liquidity would be assured if—prior to and as a condition for granting credit facilities—it painstakingly analyzes and is assured of the ability of the borrowers to generate sufficient earnings or cash flows in the future toward repayment of the loans on their due dates. Thus, it emphasizes anticipating ability of the borrowers to earn sufficient incomes at a future date when their loans will be due for repayment.

The main thrust of the anticipated income theory derives from Prochnow's comprehensive study of term loans granted by banks. In granting a term loan, a bank—according to Prochnow (1949)—looks to anticipated income of the borrower for the loan repayment. He didn't observe banks hoping for term loan repayment on liquidation of assets or sale of loans to other lenders contrary to commercial loan and shiftability theories, respectively. In adopting anticipated income theory, a bank should emphasize optimum structure, distribution, and maturity profile of its risk assets portfolio. Whenever possible, bank lending should gravitate toward predominantly short-term loan portfolio to ensure ease of recovery of liquidity if and as the need arises. Another risk mitigation strategy—having been assured of the borrower's loan repayment ability—is to favor loans that have scheduled monthly or quarterly installment repayment arrangement. The reason is simple. Such loans have anticipated, but predictable regular, cash inflows on which a bank can hinge some liquidity management plans.

The most significant value of anticipated income theory is, perhaps, underscored by its contributions to the evolution of bank term lending on the strength of the borrower's projected cash flows. In fact, based on this theory, banks nowadays put a lot of emphasis on cash flows generating abilities of borrowers in key lending decisions. As Kreps and Wacht (1972) observe, the wide acceptance of anticipated income postulation has encouraged banks to provide long-term loans to businesses, real estate firms, mortgage institutions, and consumers.

Shortcomings and Criticisms

The problem with anticipated income theory is that it does not reconcile with volatile business environment. This problem is apparent in many developing and emerging economies. In the face of unpredictable business challenges and reverses, the value of anticipated income theory of bank liquidity management becomes suspect. One reason is that business volatility could upset major business calculations and render them unattainable. Besides, several other factors could frustrate attainment of cash flow projections. On occasion, it would be uncritical to expect loan repayment from uncertain future cash flows.

There is need to reexamine the influence of cash flow statements and analysis in bank lending. Let me state at the outset that the consideration of cash flows exerts an enormous influence on the decision whether to lend money to loan applicants. Indeed, lending officers generally have unwavering confidence in the strength of cash flow analysis and projections for loan repayment. With adequate controls, the efficacy of cash flows in meeting loan service and repayment obligations can be taken for granted—especially in self-liquidating, asset-based transactions. In balance sheet lending, there is usually an assumption that observed cash flow performance is a good basis for future cash flow forecasts. Thus, supported with general business assumptions, lending officers often inadvertently recommend financing of otherwise risky transactions—especially long-term projects—on the strength of uncertain future cash flows. This approach might not be justifiably criticized. The prominence accorded to cash flow in credit analysis is technically defensible on the grounds that it relates to the flow of cash without which borrowers cannot repay their debts, pay wages and salaries, and meet other financial obligations.

The risk of the cash flow approach crystallizes when borrowers fail to realize projected cash inflows. This implies that there should not be total dependence on cash flow projections in making lending decisions. Perhaps, except for startup projects (in which case there will be no past financial records), it would be useful to compare the actual (historical) and projected (future) cash flows before recommending the credit proposal to senior management for approval. Also, as in analyzing distorted financial statements, projected cash flows should be sensitized to indicate or gauge the possible effects of certain adverse events on the projections.

LIABILITY-MANAGEMENT LIQUIDITY THEORY—EVOLVING ISSUES AND PERSPECTIVES

Liabilities management refers to the ability of a bank to attract and retain sufficient funding patronage from customers and dealers in the money market to meet its assets financing requirements. It reflects the capacity of a bank to raise or borrow funds from depositors, investors, or creditors who may be interested in its treasury or debt instruments as a means of meeting the bank's liquidity needs for risk assets creation, investments, operating expenses, and statutory reserves. Work involved in the management of liabilities include determining what proportion, and from which sources, of a bank's capital funds will fixed and other assets be financed. It is imperative, as part of the activities involved in liabilities management, for a bank to determine what should be the appropriate mix of funds in its financial structure (The phrase financial structure refers to the mix of sources and amounts of funds applied in financing the assets and investments of a bank. It represents the liabilities side of the balance sheet, including the paid-up share capital of a bank.). In doing so, the bank should seek to earn spread between cost of the borrowed funds and returns from the investment of the funds in risk assets or securities. Thus, bank liabilities management covers all the activities involved in sourcing funds, investing funds, and ensuring optimum portfolio mix and returns on investment. At the helm of affairs in bank liabilities management is the treasurer who should be an expert in funds control, portfolio analysis, and investments.

Liability-management liquidity theory suggests that a bank can manage its liquidity needs through active participation in the money market, especially in interbank trading activities. I present the breakdown of this theory in terms of the need to:

- analyze, manage, and appreciate the implications of the liabilities side of a bank's balance sheet for bank management;
- determine the efficacy of liabilities generation schemes available to banks managements;
- assess deposits mobilization sources, strategies, and constraints applicable to banks in developing economies; and
- examine the management of risks of contingent or off-balance sheet liabilities and related exposures.

These issues, for most practical purposes, define the scope of the subject matter of bank liabilities management. In adopting this viewpoint, I explain the meaning, dimensions, and implications of liabilities for bank management.

There may be need to focus on the liability side of a bank's balance sheet in devising liquidity management strategies. The bank can achieve and sustain its desired level of liquidity if its liabilities are efficiently managed. The liability-management liquidity theory contends that a bank can always meet its liquidity needs by borrowing funds from the money market. Proponent of the theory,

Woodworth (1967), underscores the liquidity fallback available to banks in the course of their daily interbank trading activities. The money market which provides the platform for the trading affords the banks the opportunity to bridge temporary liquidity gaps or reduce excess liquidity to improve earnings. It offers mechanism or facility for financial intermediation among banks in the business of taking and placing funds with one another.

The banks that have surplus funds place their excess daily cash balances which the banks in deficit positions take to beef up liquidity to the desired level. In most cases, this is done either on call, or over tenors of not more than 30 days. The notion of short-term placements or takings is informed by the usual apprehension characteristic of treasury interbank dealings. The net funds placing bank may soon need its money to meet some liquidity emergency, while the net funds taking bank may shortly regain liquidity and therefore want to pay back the money to minimize interest expense. It is this dynamic of the money market that ensures its efficiency and reliability in meeting short-term funding needs of the banks.

Liquidity level usually depletes when a bank experiences decline in deposits mobilization, huge withdrawals from deposit accounts, unsustainable growth in risk assets portfolio as a result of an unusual increase in demand for credit facilities, and so on. The immediate recourse of a bank in such a situation is to borrow from fellow banks—the more liquid banks in the interbank money market. In some cases, the bank may be allowed to overdraw its account with the Central Bank on overnight basis. Otherwise, the bank could issue debt instrument with which it can raise funds from the money market.

Shortcomings and Implications

The liability-management liquidity theory is not foolproof. In practice, it may not always be easy for most funds-deficit banks to raise or borrow money quickly from the money market, Central Bank, and international financial agencies, especially during periods of general economic recession. This implies that Central banks may not always render this funding assistance—which, ideally, they should as lenders of last resort for deposit money banks. Thus the theory is flawed on this premise. Similarly, most funds-surplus banks may not be willing to place funds with other banks in the face of crunch and money panic—both of which the money market sometimes experiences.

BANK TREASURY CRISIS IN DEVELOPING ECONOMIES

The treasury is responsible for some of the most critical aspects of the functions of banks managements. It manages the liabilities side of the balance sheet and maintains an optimum level of liquidity for the bank. With an effective treasury, a bank can achieve a sound financial structure and confidently trade on equity (A bank would be trading on equity if it relies on the use of debt or borrowed funds to maximize shareholders' earnings.). The net effect of efficient treasury operations is often seen in an ordered and long-term growth and increasing profitability of the bank. Banks managements should tap the ingenuity of the treasurer and financial controller—principle officers responsible for managing and advising on finances of a bank. However, treasury activities sometimes become stressed and cause dislocation of the operations of the bank. This frequently results in what is commonly referred to as treasury crisis in bank management.

The phrase treasury crisis refers simply to a relatively temporary anxious banking moments caused by liquidity crunch that constrains the ability of the treasury to effectively fund the bank as necessitated by its current business operations. Three main factors—overtrading, mismatch of assets and liabilities, and loss of critical huge deposits and accounts—give rise to treasury crisis in developing economies. I had in Chapter 2 discussed bank management problems associated with overtrading. Elsewhere in this book, I have pinpointed the need to solve possible mismatch between bank assets and liabilities. Banks in developing economies tend to be easily thrown into liquidity crisis as a result of loss particular major deposit accounts. This is strange but real. It negates the foundation of portfolio diversification as a deliberate strategy for risk management in banking—as in other businesses.

Since treasury crisis gives rise to anxious banking moments, it ultimately adversely affects the bank as well as customers. For the bank, on the one hand, its short-term solvency is threatened. The customers, on the other, may not be paid their deposits on demand or due dates. This temporary, frustrating situation is almost always caused by liquidity squeeze or crunch in the money market. It becomes a crisis when it constrains the treasury from effectively funding the current business operations of the bank as ordinarily would have been appropriate.

The problem is seen as treasury crisis because the buck for liabilities and liquidity management rests with the treasury department. Indeed, the usual tendency in liquidity crisis situation is for the whole bank to look up to the treasury for solution. However, it is a common practice nowadays to require other, non-treasury, employees to contribute to the funding of the bank by attracting cheap demand and time deposits. Yet the crux of solving the liquidity emergency remains drudgery for the treasury. The resort to aggressive deposit mobilization and loan workout schemes are particularly useful in dealing with treasury crisis.

MANAGEMENT STRUCTURE FOR BANK LIQUIDITY RISK MANAGEMENT

Balance sheet and liquidity risks are managed in a careful way. Risk management structure for banks' balance sheet and liquidity defines and involves roles for banks' managements as a body—as well as individual roles for strategic functional heads. Often the roles are fulfilled in committees which bank management constitutes with the approval of the bank's board of directors. The common, as well as, typical structure for banks' balance sheet and liquidity risks management comprises three main committees—executive management committee (EXCO), credit strategy committee (CRESCO), and assets and liabilities committee (ALCO). I discuss the main features of these bodies.

Executive Committee

The EXCO—comprising mainly managing and executive directors—is primarily responsible for effective operation of a bank. In essence, it deals with general management work and responsibilities. It integrates with CRESCO and ALCO on balance sheet and liquidity risks management issues—depending on the size and risk orientation of the bank. Thus issues in balance sheet and liquidity risks management feature in EXCO meetings, deliberations, and business calculations. The EXCO anticipates adverse events that can alter plans and forecasts for the balance sheet, or throw the bank into liquidity crisis. It equally seeks to tap opportunities to strengthen and optimize the balance sheet, or to take on particular liquidity-enhancing risks. In order to fulfill these roles, EXCO members should be well versed in the demands of successful banking. Integrity, good problem-solving skills, and orientation to tasks are some of the key attributes they should possess. Nowadays, a policy of zero tolerance—without paying lip service to it—is, perhaps, about the most decisive way to deal with liquidity risk in banking.

Credit Strategy Committee

CRESCO is one of the important devices to strengthen the credit process—and, in this case, balance sheet and liquidity risks management. It is a high ranking credit and deposit placement review and approval authority. The structure and composition of membership of CRESCO varies with size and risk management disposition of banks. It draws membership from EXCO, and heads of lending, risk management, treasury, and legal divisions of the bank. The roles of CRESCO in balance sheet and liquidity risks management are to:

- Review of deposit placement memorandum (DPM) and credit approval form (CAF)—together with their supporting spreadsheets—for purposes of funds placements in the money market.
- Determine appropriateness of proposed deposit placements, especially in terms of risk mitigation, spread income, fit with target market definition, risk acceptance criteria, and so on.
- Recommend amendments (if considered necessary) to the DPM, CAF, and spreadsheets to facilitate their approval.
- Approve, with or without, conditions—or decline approval of—all deposit placement limits which treasury unit proposes.

Assets and Liabilities Committee

Policy and institutional frameworks for market risk control:

- ALM/ALCO
- Daily monitoring of interest rates
- Weekly review of money market condition

The ALCO committee—strictly speaking—is the main body that takes decisions on a bank's balance sheet—its structure, constituents and dynamics—and liquidity risks management. Like EXCO and CRESCO, it is a strategic bank management organ. It meets weekly on a wide-ranging issues bordering on how the functioning of the financial system affects liquidity and operations of the bank. The main focus of the committee, in this context, is usually on the dynamics of the financial markets—money and capital markets. Then it reviews impacts of macroeconomic policies, conditions, and management on the financial markets. Its aim, in doing so, is to gain insight into how the dynamics of macroeconomic aggregates and variables affect liquidity and outcomes in banking. In view of this objective, ALCO ultimately narrows its deliberations down to the issues, reviews and decisions that I now briefly discuss.

The ALCO reviews the macroeconomic condition of the country, as well as the monetary and fiscal policies that shed light on direction of financial system regulation. This review is necessary to guide the formulation of the bank's investment policies. Based on the prevailing economic condition, the ALCO establishes appropriate investment risk acceptance criteria. The treasurer adheres to the set criteria for their investments and transactions in the money and capital markets. Deviation from the criteria portends liquidity risk for the bank and is therefore unacceptable.

Usually the money market interest rate structure and dynamics, and how they affect the cost of funds and portfolios returns to the bank attraction are the attention of the ALCO meeting. The related issues that ALCO considers are maturity profiles and rollover management strategies to ensure the retention of a large pool of cheap and sustainable deposits in the bank's liabilities portfolios. This demands effective depositor relationship and account management. ALCO especially pays attention to and reviews or makes new policies about special deposits. Usually, such deposits comprise the funds the bank mobilizes from the government—including its ministries, agencies, and parastatals—as well as from the multinationals and other prime customers.

The ALCO decides the strategies for effective and sustained deposits mobilization to meet the funding needs of the bank. Usually, the favored strategies build on the current and anticipated deposits portfolios structure of the bank. The demands and challenges of bank-wide sources and uses of funds equally make inputs into the strategies. The implication is that ALCO decides the structure of the bank's deposits portfolios and assignment of targets to attain the portfolios—as well as its sources and uses of funds.

The determination and fixing of new—or revision of existing—interest rates on credit facilities, purchased funds, and other deposits is equally topical and features regularly on the ALCO agenda. The pricing and management of rates on deposits and risk assets is, perhaps, the most challenging of all the ALCO tasks. It involves the establishment of interest rates structure in the first place. Then it deals with the need for a realistic balance between rates the bank charges on its risk assets and the rates it pays on its deposits liabilities. Usually, the contentious issue borders on attaining the desired spread and therefore expected returns on investments.

Making decision regarding the bank's interbank dealing activities and how the bank should play in the money market is one of the difficult tasks of ALCO. It requires that the ALCO sets new—or revises existing—deposit placement limits (DPL), and approves banks and discount houses for the limits. This task is not always a straightforward responsibility for the ALCO. It involves managing potentially delicate banking relationship with other banks. In this case—unlike in dealing with individual and corporate customers—both the funds takers and placers are banks. Thus, there is little or no room for rates maneuvering.

There other critical areas for the ALCO deliberations relate to decisions on:

- *Transfer pricing*
  Transfer pricing concerns the internal arrangement on how to recognize interest incomes and costs to the various units of the bank. This implies there are two aspects of transfer pricing. It involves the determination of interest incomes, on the one hand, recognized for the units that supply funds to the bank-wide pool of funds and interest costs, on the other, to the units that use funds from the pool.
- *Returns to regulatory authorities*
  The challenge of rendition of returns to the regulatory authorities is to ensure full statutory compliance and responsibility for the task. In some countries, like Nigeria, the Central Bank favors the chief compliance officer being personified by the chief executive of the bank. This underscores the policy significance of the returns.
- *Internal relationships*
  It is import that treasury officers effectively court and manage relationship with their internal customers well. Usually, the critical internal customers of the treasury unit are all the nontreasury units—and the employees that work in them—that use or contribute to the bank's funding. Often the treasury falls back on them in times of crunch. This helps to mitigate the likely money panic.

SUMMARY

Banking is a highly regulated business. The regulatory authorities are at the forefront of ensuring that banks fulfill their roles—and do not fail in the process. This is their main role as the banking stakeholders' watchdog. Often the bankers frustrate banking supervision. On occasion, bank examiners come up against a brick wall. They do come under immense pressure to sweep curious findings under the rug. The authorities could do either of two things—shun inducements, or succumb to pressure and bungle their roles.

The traditional theories of bank liquidity management are still relevant in modern banking practice. The theories embody the principles which have proven practical in managing the funding of a bank's operations. They are premised mostly on the tenets of efficient management of bank assets. Thus the theories seek to explain how this fact can help banks managements in dealing with the situations that portend risk of cashflow deficiency as a result of poor management of assets. The classical theories include commercial loan theory, shiftability theory, anticipated income theory, and liability-management liquidity theory.

Efficient treasury is necessary for the ordered and long-term growth and increasing profitability of a bank. Treasury activities sometimes become stressed and cause dislocation of the operations of the bank. Often this results in treasury crisis—a temporary anxious banking moment caused by liquidity crunch that constrains the ability of the treasury to effectively fund the bank as necessitated by its current business operations. Three main factors—overtrading, mismatch of assets and liabilities, and loss of critical huge deposits and accounts—give rise to treasury crisis in developing economies. Aggressive deposit mobilization and loan workout schemes are useful in dealing with the crisis.

Balance sheet and liquidity risks are managed in a careful way. Risk management structure for banks' balance sheet and liquidity defines and involves roles for banks' managements as a body—as well as individual roles for strategic functional heads. Often the roles are fulfilled in committees which bank management constitutes with the approval of the bank's board of directors. The common, as well as, typical structure for banks' balance sheet and liquidity risks management comprises three main committees—EXCO, CRESCO, and ALCO.

QUESTIONS FOR DISCUSSION AND REVIEW

1. What are the main challenges of banking regulation and supervision in developing economies?
2. Assess the efficacy of bank liquidity management theories. Your answer should show why the theories have or have not altogether worked for banks in developing countries.
3. Discuss the key planks of the major theories of bank liquidity management—including their underlying assumptions, implications, and flaws.
4. What do you understand by the term treasury crisis? How should banks in developing economies anticipate and preempt treasury crisis?
5. Evaluate the roles of bank executive management, credit strategy committee, and assets and liabilities committee in stemming liquidity risk and crisis?

REFERENCES

Kreps, Jr., C.H., Wacht, R.F., 1972. Credit Administration. American Institute of Banking and American Bankers Association, New York.

Onyiriuba, L.O., 2015. Emerging Market Bank Lending and Credit Risk Control: Evolving Strategies to Mitigate Credit Risk, Optimize the Lending Portfolio, and Keep Delinquent Loans in Check. Academic Press, USA.

Prochnow, H.U., 1949. Term Loans and Theories of Bank Liquidity. Prentice–Hall, Englewood Cliffs., New Jersey.

Say, J.B., 1803. Traité d'économie politique. (C.R. Prinsep, Trans. fourth ed.). A treatise on political economy; Available from: http://www.econlib.org/library/Say/sayT.html.

Woodworth, G. W., 1967. Bank Liquidity Management: Theories and Techniques. Bulletin mensuel de statistique du tourisme—Paris: Documentation Française, ISSN 1144–5351, ZDB-ID 8651668—Vol. 150.1967, 4, p. 66–78. ECONIS—Online Catalogue of the ZBW.

FURTHER READING

Koch, T.W., MacDonald, S.S., 2000. Bank Management, fourth ed. The Dryden Press, Philadelphia.

Chapter 22

Macroeconomic Challenge of Liquidity Risk for Banking in Developing Countries

Chapter Outline

LEARNING FOCUS AND OBJECTIVES

The ways in which the government in developing countries deal with macroeconomic problems have a bearing on banking risks management. Macroeconomic management often demands corrective policy actions designed to solve particular problems for the overall benefit of the people. The popular instruments of the policy actions are monetary and fiscal policies. Usually, the two policy thrusts are geared to solving inflation, unemployment, economic imbalances, debt burden, and so on. I investigate interaction of these goals with those of risk management in banking in order to:

- Discuss influences on macroeconomic management issues affecting banking in developing countries.
- Explore monetary policy issues and prospects bearing on banking risks and control in developing countries.
- Demonstrate risk-mitigation responses of banks in developing countries to monetary control instruments.
- Assess issues in debt burden, crisis, and fiscal policy impacts on banking risks and control in developing countries.

EXPECTED LEARNING OUTCOMES

Macroeconomic management in developing countries should incorporate measures that can compel banks to submit to market forces and discipline. This should be done without diluting risk management orientation in banking. This is the only way reported financial performance of the banks may truly reflect achievement of set objectives of failure to do so. Its main goal is rather to ensure that fortunes of banks are congruent with macroeconomic policies. This benefits the banks in one particular way. The banks would be able to mitigate risks associated with the vagaries and intricate workings of a country's macroeconomic management. The reader will—after studying this chapter—have learnt and been better informed about:

- Nature of influences on macroeconomic management issues affecting bank risk management in developing countries.
- Tendencies in monetary policy issues and prospects bearing on banking risks and control in developing countries.
- Risk-mitigation strategy and responses of banks in developing countries to monetary control instruments.
- Evolving issues in debt burden, crisis, and fiscal policy impacts on banking risks and control in developing countries.

OVERVIEW OF THE SUBJECT MATTER

Ineffective management of monetary and fiscal policies can cause or aggravate macroeconomic instability in a country. These instruments of macroeconomic management must be properly aligned to avoid conflicts in policy design and implementation. Countries that neglected this view usually paid dearly for its price. They experienced such an unmanageable macroeconomic instability that only a fallback to external assistance was considered expedient in restoring balance. I illustrate this typical condition of economic problem with examples from two West African countries that have passed through difficult phases of economic declines after a rather bungled period of growth and stability following political independence.

The general nature of macroeconomic problems of developing countries that require corrective policy actions is often associated with:

- persisting high and rising inflation rate caused, in most cases, by currency devaluation in line with the requirement of structural adjustment policy,
- growing rate of unemployment and its concomitant effect which reflects in the worrying incidence of mass and urban poverty,
- mounting external sector imbalances, most of which result from balance of payments difficulties,
- poor performance of the export sector which may be linked to overvaluation of the local currency and ineffective foreign exchange management,
- unbearable external debt burden caused by compounding interest on outstanding obligations of the countries to foreign creditors.

Banks in developing economies do quite often pursue elusive business goals—hoping to make it big in that way. Such attitude toward the business is misleading and only keeps false hope alive. It also exacerbates inordinate risk taking that is inimical to the sound banking culture. The lure of easy earnings—the profit motive that banks in developing economies tend to pursue blindly—does not help matters. Neither is the tendency to measure competitive strength against some irrational benchmarks helpful. Rarely do banks in developing economies consider—let alone, adopt—an attitude that would ignore what the competition and contemporaries are criminally doing just to make money. Banking regulators in developing economies should do anything but ignore a penchant for basking in praise for wealth illegally acquired so cheaply.

Competition among banks in developing economies should be geared to improving service delivery to customers. That way the banks would be compelled to submit to market forces and discipline. Their reported financial performance would then be realistic and representative of the outcome of moderate and calculated risk-taking. The overriding benefit of this business approach is that the fortunes of the banks—hitherto tied to the vagaries and intricate workings of a country's macroeconomic management—are unlocked.

MACROECONOMIC MANAGEMENT ISSUES IN DEVELOPING ECONOMIES

Developing economies easily experience severe economic downturn. The problem originates from a combination of economic mismanagement, leadership failure, bad governance, and political crisis—all of which weaken the fabric of macroeconomic foundation. In most cases, balance of payments would be in deficits due largely to unfavorable terms of trade. Imbalance in the external accounts soon begin to take its toll on the GDP as a larger part of the income would be applied to debt service and repayment of due obligations. Dwindling export receipts compounds the problem. This situation mirrors the recurring lot of most of the countries.

The usual first response of the authorities to serious dysfunctional macroeconomics is to declare economic state of emergency. An enabling Act of Parliament that follows confers arbitrary powers on the head of government to deal with the economic crisis. Austerity measures would then be introduced in all government establishments, including ministries, parastatals, public corporations, and the armed forces. The private sector will not be left out in the economic recovery scheme. In most cases, the scheme would involve massive cut in public sector expenditures, strict foreign exchange controls, and encouragement of revenue generating activities in private and public sectors. Unfortunately, the tight monetary and fiscal stance of government may not provide short-term relief, let alone be relied upon for long-term solution to the problem. Some government may at this time consider it necessary to seek expert advice from the Bretton Woods institutions—mainly the IMF and World Bank.

The result of this consultation hardly favors developing countries in the short–run. The adoption structural adjustment program (SAP) is a typical outcome of the consultation. There was, strictly speaking, no good evidence of economic recovery in the countries that implemented SAP policies. The countries were rather plunged into a myriad of economic uncertainties. The most punitive side effect of SAP was erosion of purchasing power of the people as local currencies were devalued. Pervading money panic also affected economic activities across the board. Former Nigeria's Minister of Finance, Kalu I. Kalu, was frank about the precarious monetary situation when he told the press in Kalu (1994) that "the rapid growth in the money supply has been due to excessive creation of money to fund the high deficits of government. Increased monetization of foreign assets has also been a contributory factor." He regretted that "attempts made by the Central Bank of Nigeria to mop-up excess liquidity in the economy have been partially successful as the generation of high-powered money from government induced by Ways and Means continued unabated." This has implication for banking since, according to him, "the seemingly unplanned mop-up efforts disturbed the orderly growth of the money market as operators tried to cope with appropriate responses to changing regulatory maneuvers ..." Market risk angle to the problem is quite instructive. Kalu noted that "the high interest rate regime has certainly not been helpful to effective monetary management and has, even most importantly, constrained the level of investment in the more productive sectors of the economy." In time the lingering problem of mass poverty became exacerbated, necessitating demand for SAP relief measures which, in most cases, the government could not readily fund.

If the Nigerian experience illustrates the fallout from gross mismanagement of the economy, the Ghanaian case definitely exemplifies the precariousness of its concomitant macroeconomic instability. Sandbrook (1985) described Ghana as an "an apt portrait" of the general economic deterioration in Africa. His account of the country's economic quandary is instructive (pp. 2–4). Like in the Nigerian case, the response of the Bretton Woods institutions to the Ghanaian crisis consisted largely in counseling government to implement structural adjustment of the economy. This advice was backed by structural adjustment loans granted. The IMF offered the loan to countries that were adjudged to have performed well with implementation of the program. In both countries, the downward spiral continued, at varying degrees of intensity, into the 1990s although a marginal recovery was observed in some sectors of the economy. However, government in both countries has always faced up to the challenge of the dysfunctional economies. This is evident in their willingness and determination to try, as the prevailing situation dictated, alternative economic policy measures that could lead to stabilization of the economies, recovery of investment, and resumption of economic growth. Yet, in both cases, economic failures provide the setting for appreciation of factors underlying fiscal and monetary policy initiatives in developing countries.

In most cases, the authorities formulated monetary, financial and external sector policies to achieve stable price and exchange rate—as well as to promote, stimulate, and sustain productivity and output growth. Pursuit of strong external sector performance complements these policy objectives. Often, these measures require adoption of restrictive monetary policy, but with some flexibility to encourage continued flow of financing to the private sector. Thus, the specific objectives of monetary policy in developing countries include:

- a substantial reduction in the rate of inflation and, by implication, in prices and interest rates,
- strengthening the external sector position with a view to stabilizing domestic currencies exchange rates,
- stimulating growth of output and employment, especially in the private and informal sectors,
- reduction of pressures on the external sector so as to move toward a sustainable balance of payments in order to boost external reserves,
- mobilizing support for government's efforts at solving the problems of low productivity, depressed capacity utilization, and output.

I should now generalize that economic analysis of developing countries in a given fiscal year often dramatizes government's failings in monetary and fiscal policies formulation and implementation. The failings do have serious implications for economic growth and development. Government employs monetary and fiscal policies, with mean success, as tools of macroeconomic management to stem the derailment of the economy from the path of stabilization and self-reliance.

MONETARY POLICIES BEARING ON BANKING RISKS AND CONTROL

How do the monetary authorities in developing countries implement measures designed to achieve particular macroeconomic objectives? How effective have these measures been in the management of the economies of developing countries? What are the general obstacles to implementation of monetary policy and control in developing countries? What measures may strengthen success rate which developing countries achieve with monetary policy and controls as tools of economic management?

Governments in developing countries strive to influence the behavior of monetary and financial aggregates in a bid to achieve positive effects on macroeconomic variables. This determines business performance and growth in the real sectors of the economy. Meanwhile, the concern of the authorities is how to control particular monetary variables, such as aggregate money supplies in circulation and the level of interest rates. I investigate how perceived solution to this concern affects risk management in the banking sector.

The instruments of monetary policy and control fall under two broad categories: direct and indirect. Collectively, the instruments provide alternative devices with which the authorities influence the behavior of monetary aggregates in the economy. The instruments are particularly used to affect the levels of money stock through the manipulation of demand for, supply and cost of funds with a view to achieving wider national and macroeconomic objectives.

Monetary Policy Goals and Controls

The broad objective of monetary policy is to stimulate, sustain, or moderate real sector business activities as a means of attaining short-term economic objectives of government. However, if the economy has achieved a reasonable measure of sustainable growth and stability, monetary policy objectives may be geared to long-term economic management ends. In this sense, the monetary authorities in developing countries often tinker with financial and monetary aggregates with the aim of achieving price stability, full employment, and sustainable economic growth.

Monetary policy objectives may include attainment of stable exchange rate, stability of the financial system, and balance of payments equilibrium. However, typical objectives reflect and are informed by the nature of a country's macroeconomic problems. In a broader sense, monetary policies of governments in developing countries incorporate most of the variable elements in overall macroeconomic management package. The main elements are interest rate structure, money stock, and credit portfolio to the economy. There is equal emphasis on control of financial institutions, foreign exchange, and debt management. Continual achievement of target monetary and financial policy objectives of the government forms part of the critical requirements for a country's long-run economic stability, growth, and development.

Monetary policy is the macroeconomic device by which the monetary authorities of a country seek to positively influence the performance of economic units—especially in the real sectors of the economy—to achieve set broad economic objectives of the government. It deals and, in most cases, is concerned with:

- control and regulation of the operations of the financial system and institutions,
- careful and calculated interventions in the workings of money and capital markets,
- mechanics of financial exchanges that affect changes in monetary conditions,
- involvement of economic units in the purchase and sale of financial security assets,
- maintaining interest, exchange, and inflation rates at desired levels.

The challenge faced by the monetary authorities in developing countries is to devise and ensure appropriate economic policy responses that deal with faltering monetary aggregates and variables (Davis, 1992). This imparts resilience to the economy. Whether proactive or crisis-driven, economic policy measures have to focus primarily on domestic liquidity management to ensure that monetary expansion is consonant with the authorities' objectives for growth, inflation, and external financial balance. The most critical of these monetary aggregates is the economy's money stock—including its demand and supply, as well as factors influencing its behavior. It is essential, consistent with this view, that monetary policy relates its instruments with macroeconomic objectives of the government (Davis, 1992). In practice, though, this approach is hardly followed for the reason that consideration may be given to some intermediate target, such as money or credit. This situation nullifies the need for a direct relation between instruments and objectives in monetary policy formulation.

The question now is why must the authorities bother about determining appropriate level of money supply for the economy? This question would, perhaps, be irrelevant if the level of money stock has nothing to do with the authorities' objectives for price level stability, GDP generation and growth rate, as well as the external sector position. The motives for holding money balances—which, in most cases, are to meet routine transactions and as a store of value—must be considered in order to arrive at appropriate level of money stock. In view of the ravaging effect of inflation on financial wealth, the desired holdings of money balances have to be adjusted for inflation in order to determine its real purchasing power. This ensures that money truly serves as a store of value to its holders. In a period of generally rising price level, there is less or no incentive to hold money balances within the banking system, especially if interest rate on deposits is lower than inflation rate. In such a situation, money fails in its role as a store of value. However, if interest rate on deposits exceeds inflation rate, the public will have an incentive to hold money balances within the banking system.

Thus, demand for money balances as a store of value is a direct function of price stability. Otherwise, it would not be attractive to hold money for nontransactional motives. It is on the level of economic activity, approximated by the GDP, that the transactions demand for money depends. Business activities start slackening off during periods of lull in the economy. This in turn causes a decline in transactions demand for money. When this happens, the holdings of money balances for speculative motives may be emphasized. Thus, money supply process should be analyzed in any consideration of the use of policy instruments to affect monetary aggregates.

A country's net foreign assets (NFA) and domestic credit to the economy are vital determinants of the level of money stock. Thus, changes in money stock can be explained, from the Monetary Survey account, in terms of movements in NFA or domestic credit. For purposes of economic adjustment programs, control of domestic credit will be emphasized as an intermediate target rather than the money supply. This approach derives from understanding of the need to reconcile the authorities' objectives for balance of payments with the realization that a combination of domestic and external factors affects the money stock. However, balance of payments surpluses and deficits also influence money supply which, in an open economy operating under a fixed exchange rate, becomes an endogenous variable. Davis (1992) suggests logical steps which the authorities may adopt in trying to link monetary instruments with balance of payments, growth and inflation targets (p. 12).

BANK RISK FALLOUT OF INDIRECT INSTRUMENTS OF MONETARY POLICY

Indirect instruments operate on the tenets of market mechanism. Applying indirect instruments, the authorities only render facilitating services to the financial markets. However, the process of rendering the services involves some tactical regulatory maneuverings aimed at influencing market behavior and fostering attainment of monetary policy objectives. The indirect instruments rely on the market forces for efficacy. The major instruments for indirect monetary policy are open market operation (OMO), reserve requirement, discount window operation (DWO), and moral suasion.

Open Market Operation

OMO has been a veritable means of managing money supply and inflation in developing economies. It is indeed the main indirect instrument of monetary control at the disposal of Central Banks in developing countries. The workings of OMO have a profound influence on liquidity risk management and outcomes in the banking system that I now discuss.

Meaning and Purpose

The primary purpose of OMO is to control liquidity in the economy. I define OMO itself as all the actions that a Central Bank takes to purchase or sell short-term government securities as an indirect means of affecting domestic money supply and inflation level, or the process of implementing those actions. This definition points one toward one important fact about OMO in developing economies. It is to understand that OMO is targeted at achieving two critical objectives which, though different, are related in some ways. The authorities use OMO—first and foremost—to indirectly control money supply and, in much the same vein, check inflation rate in the economy.

Differentiating OMO Markets

There are two types of markets—primary and secondary—for OMO transactions. In the secondary market, dealers purchase or sell existing securities. It may also involve repurchase agreement transactions. However, secondary markets function very well only in countries with well-developed and robust financial markets. The primary market, which is less flexible than the secondary market, permits dealings in new securities issues and redemptions. Intervention in the primary market is popular in developing countries where the financial markets, in most cases, are not well-developed.

Major OMO Participants

The major participants in OMO transactions are Central Bank, discount houses, and the authorized dealers—deposit money banks (DMB) and other banks.

The Central Bank

The Central Bank is at the apex of OMO activities. It formulates relevant policies and ensures successful enforcement of the policies for a smooth OMO operation. As the chief market regulator and participant, the Central Bank also determines the amount, type, and tenor of OMO securities traded. Usually, the OMO securities traded in the money market are in the custody of the Central Bank. This custodian role enables it to manage the dynamics of securities exchanges which OMO transactions entail.

Discount Houses

The operations of discount houses facilitate secondary trading of T-bills in the OMO market. Discount houses act as intermediaries between the Central Bank and authorized dealers in the conduct of OMOs. They handle settlement of OMO transactions with the Central Bank and authorized dealers. Incidentally, they also are the ultimate bearer of the risk of possible failure of securities in OMO market. This risk bears on their role as underwriters for all unsold government securities traded in the OMO market. Overall, activities of discount houses help to deepen and impart liquidity to the market.

Authorized Dealers

The Central Bank accredits dealers in OMO securities trading market. The usual authorized dealers are DMB—comprising, mainly, commercial banks—and merchant or investment banks. Thus, the authorized dealers are major players in OMO market. Interestingly, this category of OMO players is motivated by common—as well as varying—interests in the OMO transactions. The main interests include profit motive, liquidity risk management, and compliance with some statutory rules and requirements. As authorized dealers, banks especially are active in the OMO market. The main interest of the banks is usually in T-bill. Interest of the banks is informed by risk-free nature of T-bill and the fact that it helps boost their short-term liquidity position.

Instruments of OMO Transactions

The securities traded in OMO market largely are treasury bills and, in some cases, treasury certificates and some category of eligible government securities, such as development stocks. These are government-owned money market securities by which the Central Bank—on behalf of the government—borrows money from, or supplies money to, the economy. The strategy of OMO is to maneuver the securities in a bid to mop-up excess liquidity from, or provide liquidity to, the economy.

Procedure for OMO Dealing

The Central Bank usually conducts the OMO every week. It exercises the initiative regarding what, when and how securities are offered for sale or purchase to the market. It is this aspect of policy maneuverings that permits the authorities to seek to achieve congruence of policy objectives with market behavior.

The conduct of OMO follows particular ordered procedures aimed at promoting market transparency. This is instructive considering that trading of securities in some countries like Nigeria is conducted on the basis of biding, winning, and losing by the authorized dealers. Usually, the Central Bank formally announces when it wants to buy or sell a particular security through the discount houses. Ideally, the announcement is made as advert in the mass media at least 48 h before value date of the offer. Thus, the authorized dealers have two working days' notice of every OMO transaction.

The dealers that want to participate in an offer indicate interest accordingly. They do so by filling out the relevant bid application forms. The forms demand pertinent information—including, especially, amount and discount rate for which they bid. The dealers submit their bids—that is, the completed bid application forms—to the Central Bank. The submission of the bids is done through the discount houses not later than 24 h before auction day for the security.

Collation follows submission of the bids. The Central Bank handles the collation exercise. It involves arranging the bids in s descending order of prices. This facilitates a two-pronged bids selection exercise. The notion of a two-pronged exercise is that bids for the Central Bank's offer to sale security are treated differently from bids for its offer to purchase security. When the Central

Bank is offering security for sale, it picks the highest bid. Paradoxically, a bid is deemed to be the highest if its quoted discount rate is the lowest. The situation is different when the Central Bank is offering to purchase security. In this case, it picks the lowest bid—that is, one for which the quoted discount rate is the highest. This picking process continues with foregoing criteria until the whole amount of security offered is fully exhausted.

The dealers are notified of the winning bids through the discount houses that processed their bids. In other words, notification of the winning bids is sent to the discount houses through which the winners bid. Subsequently, the successful dealers pay for their bids. The prices they quoted for their bids are applied in determining the amounts they will pay. To put it simply, payments to be made for the successful bids are calculated at the rate of the winners' quoted prices.

At the final stage, the Central Bank painstakingly verifies the underlying OMO transactions. The verification validates the transactions and their underlying process. Now the Central Bank can debit the amount of the successful bids from the accounts of the discount with it. The discount houses, in turn, pass the debits on to their customers whose winning bids have been debited from their accounts.

Significant OMO Benefits

The use of OMO offers specific benefits to the authorities. It is flexible—allowing the Central Bank to exercise initiative in directing market behavior. The absence of compulsion to participate in the operations reflects further flexibility. Through policy maneuverings, the Central Bank can vary, as the situation demands, the amount and timing of its OMO interventions. In some countries, operations are conducted on a weekly basis with floating volumes of transactions. With OMO, market forces determine the rate of return on investments and banks' participation in the transactions is purely voluntary. In Nigeria—as in other developing countries—OMO transactions have helped to deepen money markets. This is OMO's major developmental benefit to the economy. There are other significant benefits of OMO, such as its contribution to building and institutionalizing market discipline in trading of short-dated securities. This benefit is complementary to its positive impact on increasing level of liquidity in the money markets. With OMO's supplanting of stabilization securities in Nigeria—or similar direct, punitive money market instrument in other countries—the banks nowadays are breathing a sigh of relief.

Risk Implications of OMO for Banks

The use of OMOs to mop up so-called excess liquidity often puts bank treasurers under pressure. When the Central Bank sells or purchases security, liquidity is withdrawn from or injected into the economy, respectively. Sale of securities is favored during periods of tight monetary policy while purchase of securities reflects a liberal monetary stance. Banks contend with the maneuverings under-lying the pursuit of these macroeconomic objectives of government. Often, the maneuverings—as in a mop-up exercise—create cash crunch and money panic in the system. The fact that OMO rates are administratively determined does not help matters. However, it is imperative for the process of rate determination for OMO transactions should be market-driven in order to tap its full potential in developing economies.

Reserve Requirements

The use of reserve requirements by the monetary authorities is intended to com-plement OMO as tools of liquidity management in the economy. The targeted reserves are usually bank vault cash and deposits with the Central Bank. Re-serve requirements can be used to effect changes in the volume of money and credit to the economy because it is usually targeted at and affects the demand for reserve money, with some impact also on the money multiplier.

The two variants of reserve requirements are cash reserve ratio and liquidity ratio. Cash reserve requirement is used to complement OMO to achieve effec-tive liquidity management—especially within the banking system. It is mea-sured by the ratio of a bank's cash deposits with the Central Bank to the total banking system deposit liabilities. The authorities might require that the cash reserve ratio be met by the banks on daily average basis as was the case in Nigeria in the early 1990s when liquidity management became a major issue in the observed rising price levels in the economy. The authorities may fix the cash ratio at desired percentage of total deposit liabilities of all the banks. In the case of liquidity ratio, a minimum statutory target of desired percentage of total deposit liabilities may also be set.

However, there are certain qualifications to liquidity ratio targeting aimed at achieving the desired effect. In some countries, monetary policy circular which the Central Banks regularly issue may stipulate:

1. The ratio of share of T–bills and T–certificates in each bank's liquid assets to the bank's total deposit liabilities.
2. Whether a bank's net placement with discount houses shall count as part of the bank's liquid assets for the purpose of meeting statutory liquidity ratio.
3. If only interbank placements which are fully collateralized by eligible in-struments and readily re-discountable at the central bank shall count as part of a bank's liquid assets.
4. Whether compulsory deposits with the central bank in respect of the follow-ing shall qualify for inclusion in computing the statutory liquidity ratio:
   a. Excess credit by banks that are still subject to aggregate credit ceiling.
   b. Shortfalls of loans to agriculture, manufacturing, exports, solid minerals, and small–scale enterprises.
   c. Cash deposits to meet the cash reserve requirement.

Reserve requirements may have adverse impact on the economy for the fact that they are often treated as sterile or till-funds and, therefore, attract zero or below-market interest rates. This taxation element is a disincentive to banks and other market operators. It may also dampen the spirit of financial intermediation of the banks and market development in the long-run. Unfortunately, the ratios are enforced with regulatory fiat and banks are obliged to submit to them.

Discount Window Operation

The Central Bank remains the lender-of-last-resort to the money market. This is about the oldest function of the Central Banks since commercial banks must always seek to fill their open cash position. The Central Banks thus provide a discount window which permits refinancing of DMBs. The monetary control implication of this practice derives from the fact that the Central Banks refinance, or lend to, DMBs at a discount rate. This rate exerts a dominant influence on interest rate charged by the banks. Thus, discount rate affects cost of money market funds, especially the cost of credit to economic units within the economy.

The assumption underlying the DWO is that money supply could be controlled through the impact of discount rate on money market interest rate and, therefore, on aggregate credit to the economy. It is expected that, in deregulated financial markets, when the discount rate is raised by the Central Banks the DMBs should in like manner adjust their lending rates upward so as to maintain their target profit margins. This might discourage borrowing and, of course, the ability of the DMBs to create money. The reverse would also be true if the discount rate is lowered. In some developing countries where the banking system is severely distressed DWO transactions are geared—while complementing OMO—to the provision of "short-term, largely overnight loans, collateralized by the borrowing institution's holdings of government debt instruments and other eligible first class securities approved by the Central Bank, up to a maximum quota related to the capital base of each institution." (CBN: 1996).

The effectiveness of DWO can be maintained if it is not easy for the DMBs to have unconstrained access to the Central Bank finance. In order to sustain the impact of DMO, it is also necessary that the discount rate is well above possible yield on available money market securities. This would discourage frivolous borrowing from the Central Bank by the DMBs which may lead to unsustainable money creation by the banking system.

Moral Suasion

The Central Bank of Nigeria depicts moral suasion as its practice of arranging and holding "regular dialogs with banks, discount houses, and other financial institutions with a view to keeping them informed of current policy implementation and securing their cooperation on various aspects of monetary policy."

(CBN: 1996). This practice applies to other developing countries, but it is large-ly ineffective in dealing with liquidity concerns of the banks.

BANK RISK IMPLICATIONS OF DIRECT INSTRUMENTS OF MONETARY POLICY

The direct instruments are applicable when the authorities choose to set the desired levels for specific monetary targets rather than allow the interplay of market forces. Developing countries often resort to this system of monetary control which may involve:

- prescription of ceilings on aggregate and sectoral allocation of bank credits,
- pegging of the banking system interest rates,
- fixing or manipulation of foreign exchange rate,
- Central Bank's allocation of compulsory special interest-free investment in government securities to banks—known, in the case of Nigeria, as stabiliza-tion securities.

These measures are effective in short-term liquidity management because they have a restrictive impact on credit expansion. Like most economic inter-vention policies, direct instruments interfere with equilibrium of market forces and distort equilibrium of the financial system.

DEBT BURDEN, CRISIS, AND FISCAL POLICY IMPACT ON BANKING RISKS AND CONTROL

In most cases, monetary policy errors crystallize fiscal imbalance which could lead to severe debt problems, especially when a country is experiencing a pro-longed period of deficit financing. Debt burden is by far the most challenging problem in this situation. It is indeed one of the most disturbing incidents in the evolution of macroeconomic disequilibrium in developing countries. Many of the countries are caught in the debt trap. In analyzing development crisis of the countries, debt burden is now accorded a foremost consideration. The body of literature on development economics richly analyzes the dimensions of this economic malady. The origins of the debt problem of which many are familiar are now a mundane subject. However, the major events in the evolution of the debt crisis cannot be overemphasized.

Quality and Applications of Borrowing

The countries in Africa are a good example to illustrate the misapplications of the proceeds of borrowings. The World Bank (1984) had noted that much of the foreign borrowing by African countries was applied to financing "large public investments, many of which contributed little to economic growth or to generat-ing foreign exchange to service the debt." The Bank then warned that "unless corrective measures are taken, the external resource position of sub-Saharan Africa is likely to become disastrous in the next few years." The boom of the early 1970s did not help matters as it only spurred the commercial banks into excessive lending to some otherwise high-risk countries.

The creditors could have discerned good investment outlets and opportunities in the countries at the time. External shocks impacted worsening macroeconomics of the countries. Major shocks included a sharp rise in interest rates which made debt servicing and repayment unbearable, and dwindling export proceeds—which was the result of severe economic depression experienced by the industrialized countries during the period. This forced further external borrowing to finance increasing bills on consumption imports and completion of development projects. Meanwhile public sector explosion was draining domestic resources as governments remained profligate with expenditures to subsidize publicly provided goods and services, as well as to maintain several unviable state enterprises. Gross mismanagement of the economies through policy errors contributed to the mess. These conditions set the debt trap in which the countries were caught.

The debt burden after all crystallized increasing amounts of outstanding obligations, inability to service contracted loans as reflected in debt rescheduling, and incapacity to repay due obligations. Governments are overwhelmed by the worsening debt condition. This is evident in their inability to readily convince creditors on the need for debt forgiveness, relief or even debt rescheduling which had hitherto been forthcoming to the heavily indebted countries. Debt problem is compounded by macroeconomic instability caused by inappropriate policies in the real and monetary sectors. In some countries, trade and exchange rate policies have tended to distort the real value of domestic currencies and the terms of trade. This has, to a large extent, been the reason for external imbalance which the countries experience, especially in their balance of payments.

Rethinking the Purpose of Borrowing

It is doubtful whether countries in debt crisis undertake a thorough analysis of the need and implications of debt before incurring it. The usual demand for borrowing is caused by deficiency of aggregate national saving relative to planned investment expenditure of the government. The former is made up of national budget surplus (i.e., saving by government) and saving by citizens and firms. The implied financing gap has to be funded by debt incurred either locally (i.e., private domestic subscribers) or abroad (through the sale of government security paper in foreign capital markets).

Loans raised from citizens in the domestic financial markets deny such local creditors the use of the invested resources for increased current consumption. Though, this reality is underlain by an assumption of future higher level of consumption of the presently foregone items. Thus, aggregate private sector demand for goods and services is diminished by the act of government borrowing from the local residents. When government borrows from abroad, the nation equally suffers loss of ability to meet consumption needs, but this effect is essentially postponed to a future time period when the loan would be repaid. Then government will appropriate funds from its national income—an action that obviously reduces its overall local consumption possibilities—to meet the obligation due foreign creditors.

While local borrowing carries immediate consumption (reduction) implication for the citizens, the equivalent effect of foreign debt has to be contended with at some future date. Since it is difficult, because of the uncertainty of future events, to correctly foresee with any degree of exactitude future economic condition of the country, foreign borrowing becomes a more precarious affair. At the time external loans fall due for repayment or even for service, economic condition of the country could deteriorate to a level that it might not be in a position to meet the obligation. Yet it must pay back the loan at compounded interest rate.

Suspect Criteria of Lending to Government

The criteria for lending to a country by a foreign financial institution or even by another country will in several respects differ from those employed by DMBs when considering credits to an individual or a firm. However, in all cases, the lending decision is rooted in the factor of risk—the events, acts, or perils the occurrence of which will cause loan loss through impairment of the borrower's ability to generate adequate cash flow surplus to service and repay the loan. Loan requests should be analyzed to identify all risks related to the lending decision.

Once identified, specific mitigating measures should be applied to the risks. But loans that embody systematic risks should be either declined or adequately secured with tangible collateral. If this procedure is circumvented, the loan might be lost either as a result of a deliberate action of the borrower or due to lack of a good fall back for the lender. Mostly, this happens in commercial bank lending to individuals, firms, and other economic units. In such a situation, it becomes necessary to analyze the borrower's character, capital base, capacity to perform on the loan, general economic conditions, and the collateral offered to secure the loan. Issues in the general principles of credit analysis are subsumed under these cannons of bank lending.

In government borrowing or foreign lending to a country, this approach to risk analysis should, to a large extent, be adopted to minimize country distress arising from loan defaults. Therefore, the lender's task in taking foreign credit exposure is to properly analyze and understand the condition of all national and international risks which, in principle, approximate to those of local credits. Such risk elements include state of the economy, quality of economic policies of government, political situation of the country, external accounts position, and current size of the country's external debt.

Revisiting the Causes of Foreign Borrowing

The lenders to government must have faith in the country's economy in order to grant the credit in the first place. It is not in the long-run interest of developing countries that they readily obtain foreign loans on grounds of some sense of responsibility on the part of the creditors to assist the poor countries. In fact, this practice set the pace for the continuing deterioration of the countries' external debt position. I am talking about a situation where lenders simply determine the amount, tenor, and purpose of a facility without due consideration and monitoring of efficiency of its utilization to ensure that it benefited the poor masses.

It has been difficult to achieve effective public sector loan utilization for reasons associated with socio-moral value system upheld by leaders of the countries. This is often observed in the ubiquity of official corruption and half-hearted commitment to national development aspirations of the countries. These factors tend to institutionalize some irrational scheme for irregular disbursements, the diversion and, in most cases, misappropriation of foreign loans by highly placed public servants. It is also in the same factor of socio-moral bankruptcy that one finds explanation for investment or rather wastage of scarce resources—including foreign and domestic resources—on frivolous activities.

MARKET LIQUIDITY DETERMINANTS AND INTEREST RATE RISK IN BANKING

There are common factors of market-induced bank interest rate risk in developing countries. Most of the factors originate from mainly the adverse macroeconomic happenings in a country. The states of the money supply and macroeconomic management policies are typical examples of such factors that will always be important factors for consideration. Their significance is that they do have positive or negative impacts on the interest rates that DMBs may want to charge on loans to borrowers or pay on deposits from customers. They also sometimes have an indirect bearing on the fees which the banks may charge for the financial services they render to their customers and the public.

The money supply itself is largely a function of the prevailing demand for money in a country. Three main factors—according to the Keynesian economists—inform the causes of the demand for money. They hold that individuals and organizations demand for money at any one time for some transactions, precautionary, and speculative purposes. The pressures which these needs for money occasion in turn impact the reaction of the authorities responsible for managing the money supply. However, the mechanisms of the market forces—encapsulated in the usual interplay between the demand and supply of goods and services—guide the direction of the policy measures. The import of this is that government's policy actions in response to changes in the monetary aggregates should not be opposed to the market forces in order to have a stable interest rates regime. The risk to interest rates tends to exacerbate when the authorities apply regulatory fiat in dealing with market forces-bound influences on the money supply. Ideally, the regulatory policies should complement and not antagonistic to the market forces. Once the authorities imbibe this view, market liquidity—and therefore the probability of interest rates risk—would simply be dependent on what happens with regard to the causes of the demand for money and the response of supply.

The amounts of money that government spends on recurrent bills and capital projects are an import source of market liquidity in developing economies. In most cases, the government borrows locally—from the banks or through some Ways and Means arrangement. The government tends to fall back on external borrowing when this public sector funding source is impaired. The idea of borrowing in this sense is rooted in a deficit financing program of the government. Deficit financing becomes inevitable when the government spends more than it generates in revenue from all of its income sources. If properly utilized, the borrowings will increase the investment rate, enable more imports of capital goods and inputs, and generate a better utilization of industrial capacity. The economic progress that these benefits would likely engender will rub off on market stability and mitigate interest rates risk. Unfortunately, public sector loans tend to easily be mismanaged and trigger market risk for the banks. This is tragic for the fact that the loans don't have tangible benefits to the economy and the populace. In addition to the market risk, the mismanagement of the loans increases debt burden on the future generations of the people whose standard of living will reduce when the debts mature.

Developing economies often are boosted by consumption expenditure in the private sector. The lion's share of the boost tends to come from the manufacturing sector—especially when it integrates backward in raw materials sourcing to achieve savings in foreign exchange expenditure. Some of the consumer goods industries will record increased capacity utilization with the backward integration strategy. There are some snags, though. In most cases, only the big companies may have the resources to fund local raw materials research and development. The gain from import substitution and savings in foreign exchange on account of the local sourcing of raw materials may be small. This is because the exporters are usually granted a corresponding freedom on utilization of their foreign exchange earnings. The weaker companies tend to experience production hitches and decline that often leads to the retrenchment of employees. Many others may not sustain their operations due to adverse economic conditions. This happens mostly in a situation of high cost–push inflation arising from substantial devaluation of domestic currencies. Often such companies voluntarily wind up.

Interest rates affect investments in a macroeconomic setting. Whether the level of investments would be high or low is, to some extent, dependent on the prevailing interest rates. It is therefore necessary for the authorities to devise effective means of integrating concerns for interest rates with the pursuit of investments. This can be done through some composite policy initiatives. Such policies should, for example, target efficient mobilization of domestic resources through sound fiscal, monetary, and credit policies. There may be calculated reduction of budget deficits, and strengthening of the public sector performance. Stability, growth, and development yet remain the goal of macroeconomic management. There are several economic tools for the attainment of these goals deriving, sometimes, from planning and, in most cases, from the free interplay of market forces. Some economic problems defy the corrective approach of the traditional macroeconomic planning and control policies.

The increasing volumes of government securities offered for sale evidence monetary contraction policy designed to reduce the amount of money in circulation. The usual practice is for the government to sale more T-bills in the money market. It uses the facility of the OMO to achieve the goal. The immediate aim of the reduction in money supply is to stem inflationary pressure on the economy and enhance the real worth of savings and investments. It also tends to have a stabilizing effect on interest rates. However, macroeconomic policies designed to solve such problems as unemployment, inflation, deficit financing, and capital flight may not elicit the desired response. This situation arises in cases where structural distortions are the cause of imbalances in a country's domestic and public accounts. For an economy depressed by this unusual economic condition, management response will rely on either trial and error with the traditional macroeconomic tools, or on pragmatic policy measures.

On occasion, the Central Bank may increase or decrease its rediscount facilities and advances to the money deposit banks. Such actions affect market liquidity—positively or negatively—dependent on whether the rediscounting and borrowing windows for the banks are opening or closing up. Positive effect is felt when the rate at which the Central Bank advances funds to the banks reduces. It is negative with increasing rediscount rate. The direction of the possible effects can create money panic that upsets the money market and shoot up interest rates. Money panic also results from poor, inconsistent, and conflicting monetary and fiscal policies that stifle private enterprise and initiative. Meanwhile, the public sector remains complacent with its unenviable record of bankrupt performance. This situation is hardly helped by the political stability, lack of probity and accountability by public officers, rising incidence of poverty, and the overdependence of the populace on publicly provided goods and services. In a buoyant economy, the government—Federal, States, and Local Governments—maintain large deposit accounts with the Central Bank. This enhances the Central Bank's DWOs, with implication for likely reduction of market interest rates. This is possible due equally to probable cut in the Central Bank's rediscount rate.

SUMMARY

Developing economies easily experience severe economic downturn. The problem originates from a combination of economic mismanagement, leadership failure, bad governance, and political crisis—all of which weaken the fabric of macroeconomic foundation. In most cases, the authorities formulate monetary, financial, and external sector policies to achieve stable price and exchange rate—as well as to promote, stimulate, and sustain productivity and output growth. Pursuit of strong external sector performance complements these policy objectives. Often, these measures require adoption of restrictive monetary policy, but with some flexibility to encourage continued flow of financing to the private sector.

Governments in developing countries strive to influence the behavior of monetary and financial aggregates in a bid to achieve positive effects on macroeconomic variables. This determines business performance and growth in the real sectors of the economy. The concern of the authorities is how to control particular monetary variables, such as aggregate money supplies in circulation and the level of interest rates. The instruments of monetary policy and control fall under two broad categories: direct and indirect. Collectively, the instruments provide alternative devices with which the authorities influence the behavior of monetary aggregates in the economy. The instruments are particularly used to affect the levels of money stock through the manipulation of demand for, supply and cost of funds with a view to achieving wider macroeconomic objectives. Often, monetary policy errors crystallize fiscal imbalance which could lead to severe debt problems, especially when a country is experiencing a prolonged period of deficit financing.

External shocks impact worsening macroeconomics of the countries. Major shocks include a sharp rise in interest rates which makes debt servicing and repayment unbearable, and dwindling export proceeds—which is the result when industrialized countries experience severe economic depression. Public sector explosion drains domestic resources as governments remain profligate with expenditures to subsidize publicly provided goods and services, as well as to maintain several unviable state enterprises. Gross mismanagement of the economies through policy errors contribute to the mess. These conditions set the debt trap in which the countries are caught.

It has been difficult to achieve effective public sector loan utilization for reasons associated with socio-moral value system upheld by leaders of the countries. This often finds expression in ubiquity of official corruption and half-hearted commitment to national development aspirations of the countries. These factors tend to institutionalize some irrational scheme for irregular disbursements, the diversion and, in most cases, misappropriation of foreign loans by highly placed public servants. It is also in the same factor of socio-moral bankruptcy that one finds explanation for investment or rather wastage of scarce resources—including foreign and domestic resources—on frivolous activities.

QUESTIONS FOR DISCUSSION AND REVIEW

1. Is it possible that macroeconomic problems have a bearing on banking risks management in developing countries?
2. What major economic problems do monetary and fiscal policies solve in developing countries?

3. Should macroeconomic management in developing countries really bother about subjecting banks to market forces and discipline?
4. How can fortunes of banks in developing countries be realistically congruent with macroeconomic policies?
5. Why should banks mitigate risks associated with the vagaries and intricate workings of macroeconomic management?

REFERENCES

Central Bank of Nigeria, 1996. Monetary, Credit, Foreign Trade and Exchange Policy Guidelines for 1996 Fiscal Year. Monetary Policy Circular No. 30. Lagos, Nigeria

Davis, J.M. (ed.), 1992. Macroeconomic Adjustment: Policy Instruments and Issues, Washington, D.C.: IMF Institute and International Monetary Fund, August 1992, pp. 7 and 21.

Kalu, I.K., 1994. Press briefing on Nigeria's 1994 budget and the National Rolling Plan (1994–1996), January 11, 1994.

Sandbrook, R., 1985. The Politics of Africa's Economic Stagnation. African Society Today Series. Cambridge University Press, London.

World Bank, 1984. Toward Sustained Development in sub–Saharan Africa: A Joint Program of Action. World Bank, Washington, D.C.

Section C

Market Risk

Chapter 23

Market Risk, Interest Rates and Bank Intermediary Role in Developing Economies

Chapter Outline

LEARNING FOCUS AND OBJECTIVES

Banks devise treasury or other liabilities-driven products and services to mobilize deposits from the funds surplus sector. The funds mobilized are channeled to the funds deficit sectors. This financial intermediary role of banks is critical for investment and economic growth in developing economies. The banks are challenged always to anticipate risks inherent in this role. They either make or lose money dependent on how well they handle the risk aspect. It is against a backdrop of the foregoing that I set out on this chapter—in order to:

- assess the critical roles that deposit money banks play as intermediaries in the financial markets;
- examine the concept, application, and challenge of market risk management in developing economies;

- situate market risk of banking in the context of volatile sources and cost of funds in developing economies;
- identify, analyze, and pinpoint implications of the factors underlying bank market risk in developing economies; and
- evaluate the market risk fallout of flaws in monetary policies and management in developing economies.

EXPECTED LEARNING OUTCOMES

Banks managements in developing economies must start devoting sufficient attention to market and operational risks—just as they do in pursuit of effective management of credit and liquidity risks. Market risk management is especially critical considering that risks attendant on fluctuations in interest and foreign exchange rates—unlike credit and liquidity risks—are somehow beyond banks managements. This is instructive—to the extent that financial losses attributed to market risk nowadays takes a large chunk out of banks earnings in developing economies. The reader will—after studying this chapter and doing the exercises in it—have learnt and been better informed about:

- the role of deposit money banks (DMBs) in economic expansion and as financial intermediaries in developing economies;
- concept, application, and challenge of market risk definition and management in developing economies;
- how volatile sources and cost of funds inform the market risk of banking in developing economies;
- factors that underlie the creation and dynamics of bank market risk in developing economies; and
- market risk fallout of flaws in banking regulatory policies and monetary management in developing economies.

OVERVIEW OF THE SUBJECT MATTER

The concept and dynamics of pricing as a competitive tool in banking are personified by the maneuverings of interest rates, fees, commissions, and sundry other charges as may be applicable in a particular country. This is well appreciated in banking circles. Pricing, in this context, refers to determine how much money a bank may appropriate from the accounts of customers for the products it sells or services it renders to them (I have throughout this chapter, and elsewhere in this book, adopted interchangeable use of the terms product and service to refer to a particular offering of a bank to its customers in a given target market). Some banking service may have implicit elements of price which invariably increase its cost to the customer and net yield to the bank.

The price of service may have other elements where, for instance, there is penalty clause in the service agreement, contract or offer letter, to deter the counterparty from defaulting on its terms and conditions. Yet it is possible to determine and appreciate the expected price of the service at the outset of the underlying transaction. Usually, the banks consider several factors in pricing their services. Most banks take cognizance of the cost of funds, risk, tenor, competition, yield, administrative cost, and value of the relationship.

I will in this chapter address the questions which tend to agitate the minds of the public and professionals alike about schemes in the pricing of banking products and services. What are the price determining factors and common price elements in banking? To what extent is bank patronage responsive to price variations? Why do banks discriminate among customers on pricing? What are the pricing discrimination methods? How do banks manage competitive pricing as part of their overall marketing plans? The answers to these questions shed light on the scope and basis of the culture of price discrimination in banking.

Although most banks generate substantial earnings from the maneuverings of pricing in the various market segments, it should be borne in mind that excessive charges can harm patronage. Thus, the banking needs of the customers should always be met with reasonable incentives on pricing. This would, in the long run, after all be more than compensated by the high transactions volume and activity levels with which moderate prices are likely to engender.

Now, you may be wondering why I belabor the question of pricing. The reason is simple. Pricing in banking—in form of interest and foreign exchange rates—has direct bearing on market risk. Banks easily gain or lose money in their financial markets transactions on account of unpredictable changes in interest and foreign exchange rates. Usually, the real factor at work in developing economies is the volatility of the financial markets where the domestic and foreign currencies are traded. Dealings in the money and capital markets instruments are subject to this risk.

The banks must play it safe and devise appropriate strategies to hedge against potential losses in the financial markets; hedge being the operative word. There is little or nothing the banks by themselves can do to tame the volatile attributes of the financial markets. Thus, hedging is their usual welcome fallback position. This explains the relevance of hedging as a risk mitigation measure in currency trading—especially in the foreign exchange markets. It also imparts risk to the role of the banks as intermediaries in the financial markets.

ASSESSING THE ROLE OF BANKS AS INTERMEDIARIES IN FINANCIAL MARKETS

As intermediaries in the financial markets, banks play a significant role in mobilizing funds from the savers and channeling the funds into investments—often in the real sectors—through lending. The banks fulfill this role when they act as a go-between for the individuals and organizations that have surplus or are in deficit of funds. In doing so, the banks help meet their investment and borrowing needs, respectively, through the financial markets. In order to fulfill this role, the banks mobilize funds from the individuals and organizations that have surplus funds and make the funds so mobilized available to the individuals and organizations that are in the deficit of funds.

The process underlying this function is straightforward. A bank takes instructions from its customers to either invest their idle funds or provide them some funding that fills their currently financing need. It also could be that the customers need other forms of financial services for which the bank should act as a go-between for them. The bank may render the services for a fee or free dependent on the nature of the banking relationship that exists between the bank and the customers. Often the same bank fulfills this role for both the potential investors and borrowers. However, a common tendency is that banks court business relationship with investors and creditworthy borrowers alike without necessarily matching individual needs of the customers.

The financial intermediary services of the banks have implication for the traditional role of the banks in lending money to economic units that have deficits in their funding or cash flows. Usually, the banks mobilize the funds which they lend to those units, the borrowers, from the economic units that have surplus of funds and are willing to invest the funds. The banks attract such funds by means of some treasury or other liabilities-driven products. This process simply fulfills the financial intermediary role of the banks. Ultimately, its implication is that the banks concurrently create, build up, and maintain deposits liabilities and risk assets portfolios. It is also through their role as financial intermediaries that the banks are able to create money. The payment system, one that is dependent on checks as the financial instrument—facilitates the money creation process and ability of the banks.

Thus, a bank—in its simplest form and definition—commonly is seen as an institution that mobilizes and lends money. There may be several other nonbanks, sometimes informal, institutions that may fulfill these or similar roles. But, unlike the banks, this category of institutions is not necessarily required by law to maintain certain levels of risk assets, deposit liabilities, and cash reserve structure. In some cases, as in the traditional societies, they operate in the informal economy. In other words, such institutions are not usually—if at all they are—strictly regulated as banks, as is the case with the deposit money banks. Usually the banks are active players in the financial markets. The essence of their active participation in the money and capital markets is to be able to perform as financial intermediaries for their customers.

There may be instances when some individuals and organizations may bypass the banks as financial intermediaries and invest or raise funds by some means. This is termed as disintermediation. Often disintermediation is the corollary of rising cost of funds in the financial markets. The borrowers look for some alternative funding sources and arrangements in which banks or other financial institutions are not involved. A common practice is the dealing in the so-called intercompany markets. Such dealings are rather exotic. The economic units in developing countries are neither oriented to it, nor are they kin to formally embrace it.

CONCEPTS AND APPLICATIONS OF MARKET RISK IN BANKING

There is a tendency among the executive managements of the banks in developing economies to devote their attention—and understandably too—mainly to forestall credit and liquidity risks. Mostly, the interaction between failed liquidity risk management and reckless and excessive risk-taking in lending are the main culprits for bank failures around the world. In doing so, they give perfunctory attention to the market and operational risks. The line managements, in the main, largely seize the initiative from the executive managements under the circumstances. However, the executive managements' abdication of their direct responsibility for market and operational risks does not augur well for the bank—just as their failure to stave off credit and liquidity risks do not.

Incidentally, the tendency to downplay the significance of market and operational risks in banking cut across financial markets the world over. The Basel Capital Accord (1988)—more popularly referred to as the Basel I Accord—strictly was targeted at solving credit risk faced by the internationally active banks. 8 years after, the Basel Committee revisited the Basel I Accord and amended it with the incorporation of market risk into it. The Committee had realized that it would be difficult to manage credit risk in isolation market risks. Nowadays the regulatory authorities enjoin banks managements to give equal attention to all risks. This is the basis of the new and growing emphasis on enterprise risk management (ERM) in banking. The main thrust of ERM is its recommendation of a holistic—rather than a "silo" view—approach to managing organizational risks—with a chief risk officer at the helm of affairs and appointed at executive management level.

The Pillar 1 of Basel II advises how to reflect losses that a bank suffers as a result of fluctuations in asset prices. In this context, the Basel Committee (2006:144) defines market risk as "the risk of loss arising from changes in market interest rates" (p. 170). It covers "the risk of losses in on and off-balance sheet positions arising from movements in market prices" (p. 157). The committee (ibid) clarifies that "risks subject to this requirement are:

- the risks pertaining to interest rate related instruments and equities in the trading book; and
- foreign exchange risk and commodities risk throughout the bank."

Unmitigated market risk impinges on a bank's capacity to remain in business as a going concern. This implies that market risk—to all intents and purposes—has a direct effect on a bank's financial performance. Thus, executive managements should always take the lead in managing market risk bank-wide.

The two components of market risk identified by the Basel Committee—interest rate risk and foreign exchange risk—demand a closer look at this point. It is to them that I now turn—to explain their imports. Thereafter I devote the rest of this chapter to discuss aspects of the impacts of market risk on interest rates in banking and the intermediary role of the banks in the financial markets.

Interest Rate Risk

There are three possible aspects to the meaning of interest rate risk in banking. The Basel Committee (2006) offers a leading thought that clarifies the first aspect of the meaning of interest rate risk. It defines interest rate risk as "the risk of holding or taking positions in debt securities and other interest rate related instruments in the trading book" (p. 7). The lay readers may find this definition technical. The practitioners may not have problems with relating the financial constructs in this definition, such as "holding or taking positions," "debt securities," and "trading book" to their jobs. However, the same cannot be said of the layman.

Let me now, in the context of banking, proffer simplified definitions that shed light on the import of interest rate risk. Interest rate risk may be defined as the danger that a bank may incur loss or lose money in granting loans, taking and placing funds, or trading in financial instruments as a result of changes in the market interest rates or some unexpected adverse conditions. Now, compare this definition with the aforementioned Basel Committee's. Though presented in different ways, there's no change in meaning. My intention is to bring the meaning of interest rate risk in banking down to the level of the layman, if anything.

Whether to a bank or its customers, interest rate risk should be anticipated to avoid financial loss on assets. Usually, trend analysis and the follow-through come in handy. Diminution of earnings on account of unmitigated market interest rate risk can really be avoided.

Foreign Exchange Risk

The next component of market risk, foreign exchange risk, is defined as "the risk of holding or taking positions in foreign currencies, including gold" (Basel Committee, 2005:23). This again is yet a technical definition that should be simplified to enable easy understanding of its import—and for the benefit of students and practitioners of banking in developing economies.

One way of simplifying the Basel Committee's definition is to view foreign exchange risk as the danger that a bank may lose money on foreign currency-denominated risk assets, or trading in foreign currencies due to unanticipated adverse changes in exchange rates. Usually, the adverse changes result from the volatility of the foreign exchange markets. Volatile exchange rates are a typical feature of the developing economies. Due to weak currencies, the banks in developing economies deal with new and evolving exchange rates issues on daily basis.

In fact, foreign exchange gains or losses occasioned by volatile exchange rates, to a large extent, determine the financial performance of the banks in developing markets. Thus most banks in developing economies are very active in both the official and autonomous foreign exchange markets. Incidentally, most of the issues the regulatory authorities have with the banks in developing economies border on sharp practice in the foreign exchange markets.

SITUATING MARKET RISK OF BANKING IN VOLATILE SOURCES AND COST OF FUNDS

As a critical element in a bank's pricing strategy, cost of funds usually is denoted as the weighted average of the sum of interest paid on deposit liabilities portfolios, costs of direct overheads, and general administrative expenses within a given period of time. Thus the banks use weighted average cost of funds (WACF) to measure the actual cost of their services to the customers and public. Once a bank determines its WACF, it can then effectively determine and compete on pricing terms without incurring losses. For this reason, the WACF becomes a veritable instrument of market competition among the banks. In general, the banks that have low WACF would stand a better chance of winning customers on pricing terms than those with a high cost profile.

The big banks easily lead the market largely on account of low cost profile. The small banks, on the contrary, attract funds from volatile sources. This imparts high funding cost profile to their operations. Interestingly, both the big and small banks contend with the same factors affecting the cost of funds in the financial markets. The advantage that the big and financially strong banks has over the small and financially weak banks builds on their ability to attract cheap deposits from a broad base of the public, organizations, and institutions—including, especially, the public sector.

In most cases, the small banks lack the financial muscle and enough networks of branches to mobilize cheap deposits from the critical masses of the banking populations. Such banks end up playing the niche game. The niche business strategy leaves a bank as an also ran, at best. The banks in this situation should reinvent their strategy. The starting point is for them to get to grips with the factors that affect the costs of funds in the financial markets.

There are significant differences in the cost structures of the banks in developing economies with respect to their funding situations and needs. Yet, the underlying significance of a bank's financial strength is that it should be able to attract long-term cheap deposits. Based on this perspective—and in order to achieve a low WACF—it is imperative for a bank to:

- broaden its deposits liabilities generation schemes and base,
- adopt effective operational costs control measures bank-wide, and
- maintain efficient financial control (FINCON) unit that monitors performance against set goals and targets.

Of these three approaches to attain desired WACF, broadening the deposits base is about the most excruciating for the banks in developing economies. Yet, the banks must strive to achieve low WACF in order to enjoy long-term liquidity, stability, and growth. Without a good deposits base, a bank faces a precarious financial position as a result of possible volatility of cash flows and stagnation or declining rate of growth and earnings—even in the short-run.

Thus deposits are seen as the life blood of a bank at any one time. With a sound deposits base, the success of bank management could be taken for granted—provided that it strictly adheres to the ethics of the profession. In Nigeria, the competitive edge that the big banks have over the relatively smaller banks derives from their large branch networks. Their networks of branches are the means by which they are able to generate numerous small lots, cheap, and stable long-term deposits. For example, the three big banks in the prebanking system consolidation era collectively controlled over 80% of liquidity in the country's money markets. The remaining over 84 banks, which largely operate in the niche markets, shared less than 20%.

There is also the factor of public sector patronage, which nowadays favors the big banks. As public sector-driven market, the fortunes of the banks in developing economies are intricately tied to the ever-unpredictable vicissitudes underlying the functioning of government. Thus, the occasional market shocks caused by conflicting government policies and the maneuverings of the banking regulations by the monetary authorities take the heaviest toll on the smaller banks. In Nigeria, however, this problem has been partly solved by the introduction of universal banking with effect from January 1, 2001, ostensibly to provide a level playing field for all the licensed banks operating in the country.

FACTORS UNDERLYING MARKET RISK IN BANKING

There are internal and external factors that affect the market rates of interest that banks in developing economies will either pay on deposits or charge on credit facilities. The internal factors originate from the level of the capitalization of the banks, the disposition of the banks toward the risk-return trade-off principle, and the banks' deposits liabilities portfolios base. The main external factors are underlain by the monetary control and regulatory policies of the authorities. The prevailing economic condition in a country also is a pertinent external factor.

Size of Capital Funds for Banking

A bank requires a minimum quantum of capital funds to be able to function effectively. I adapt the basic postulate of the big push theory relating to industrialization strategy to underscore this view. There is a critical level of equity capital or shareholders' funds that a bank requires for business takeoff and success. In Nigeria, for instance, prospective promoters of banks are expected to deposit a minimum paid-up capital of N25.0 billion with the Central Bank of Nigeria.

Capital adequacy is a critical measure of a bank's financial health. It not only cushions depositors' funds against loss, but influences the value and types of risk that a bank can take. A bank in which the size of capital is large relative to deposit liabilities portfolio can afford to take more risks than one with a small capital base. In the former case, the bank can grant long-term credit facilities and offer large volumes of credits to borrowers at a time. Such banks also maintain a strong presence in the financial markets. Usually, they are among the major markets players.

Where banking regulation stipulates that a bank should not lend more than a specified amount of its shareholders' funds (unimpaired by losses) to a single obligor and/or its subsidiaries (20% in the case of Nigeria), the significance and influence of capital on credit structure becomes more apparent. It is obvious that small banks, which are poorly capitalized, cannot offer certain categories of credit facilities or take certain types of lending risks. In the final analysis, the worth of capital for a bank and its customers is seen in the buffer or protection it offers against loss of depositors' funds, or diminution of the shareholders' funds.

Risk-Return Trade-Off

The nature of risk envisaged and return expected from particular lending and treasury activities sometimes influence loan and deposit policies and structure. Banks have varying appetites for risk-taking. For example, banks that are averse to risk do emphasize short-term, self-liquidating, and asset-based lending—with revolving tenors of not more than 90 or 120 days per transaction cycle. Such banks shun complicated, long-term loan proposals. But they also like to lend to well structured, formal business organizations which generate adequate and predictable cash flows. This practice also influences their interbank placements. Such riskless borrowers are found mainly among the blue chips and top-tier segment of the mass banking market. The risk preference banks display aggressive lending and deposit placement tendencies. Their business goals are driven, in most cases, by profit-making. Risk-taking by this category of banks often reflects in the choice of their target markets and ambitious lending types, amounts, tenors, and purposes. Typically, such banks would settle for small business and middle-tier accounts—especially, the wholesale traders in the import business—whose high risk profile is more than offset by return on investment. Of course, customers realize that it is expensive to borrow money from such banks because of their inclination to profit-making and risk-taking.

Deposits Liabilities Base

Deposit liabilities base of a bank is perhaps the single most important determinant of its loan policies and trading in the financial instruments. Deposits are the life blood of a bank and directly affect its general business capacity. A bank would be distressed if its deposits or general liabilities are not adequately represented by tangible assets. Indeed, a bank would fail without a good level of deposits.

It is crucial for a bank to not only have a large pool of deposits liabilities, but a stable deposits portfolio. Banks managements should achieve optimum distribution of maturities in deposits portfolios to be able to formulate profitable loan and financial markets dealing policies. Yet, the types and structure of loans granted by a bank would ordinarily mirror the content and characteristics of its deposits base. With a small or highly volatile deposits portfolio, a bank may adopt restrictive loan policies to be able to maintain liquidity for its day-to-day operations. Large volume or term lending would not appeal to such a bank.

Nowadays, deposits base is the driving force behind competitive strength of the banks. Prior to the 2005 banking system consolidation in Nigeria, the then three big banks in the country—First bank of Nigeria PLC, Union Bank of Nigeria PLC, and United Bank for Africa PLC—collectively controlled over 80% of liquidity in the banking system. Guided by monetary policy rate (MPR) and other money market indices, they dictated pricing, especially lending and deposit rates, in the industry. This was one of the ways the big banks flexed their deposit muscles in addition to their preference for big ticket transactions.

Monetary Policies and Control

The banking system is easily upset by monetary and fiscal policies in developing economies where regulations often distort the mechanism of the market forces. Money market is rarely left to dictate the behavior of operators and financial exchanges in the industry. What is common is a prompting of the banks into attempting to respond appropriately to one regulatory maneuvering or the other.

Some of the monetary policy elements which the authorities manipulate in a bid to influence lending and deposit policies and behavior of the banks include the MPR, cash reserve ratio (CRR), liquidity ratio (LR), and so on. For example, section 15(1) of Nigeria's Banks and Other Financial Institutions Act no. 25 of 1991 (as amended) requires banks to maintain certain holdings in cash reserves, specified liquid assets, special deposits, and so on with the Central Bank. The Act also restricts bank lending to a single obligor limit of 20% of the shareholders' funds, unimpaired by losses (section 20(1) (a)). In section 13(1), the Act prescribes capital adequacy ratio for all the licensed banks in the country.

The regulatory authorities tinker with the MPR, CRR, and LR depending on the dictates of a country's monetary management goals. Variations in the ratios indirectly affect the capacity of the banks to expand loan and deposit portfolios. With cash reserve and liquidity ratios, for example, a bank surrenders a certain percentage of its total deposit liabilities to statutory reserve requirement. Also, this implies loss of income that the bank would otherwise have earned on the deposits if it were to invest them in earning assets. In the case of changes in MPR, banks respond somewhat in kind—with the result that loan and deposit policies may be affected adversely or favorably. In Nigeria, for example, the lending and deposit placement capacity of banks is yet affected by the provision of BOFI Act No. 25 of 1991 (section 16), which requires every licensed bank to maintain a reserve fund to which it should transfer at least 30% of its annual net profit before dividend where the reserve fund is less than its paid-up share capital. If the reserve fund is equal to, or more than the paid-up capital, 15% of the net profit should be transferred to the fund.

In developing economies, these restrictions are worsened by public policy inconsistencies in monetary and fiscal policies formulation and implementation. Restrictive monetary policies, on the one hand, create liquidity squeeze which ultimately limit the ability of banks to deal in the financial markets or grant certain types of credit facilities. With expansionary policies, on the other hand, funds are readily available at reasonable rates of interest to finance lending and deposit placement activities. Thus, loan and deposit policies could be more or less liberal depending on the money supply situation. However, since liquidity or dearth of it may be a temporary occurrence while their underlying monetary policies cause settles with other interacting market forces, a bank should not rely solely on the prevailing situation in making long-term lending and deposit policy decisions.

Prevailing Economic Conditions

The prevailing economic conditions in a country affect lending and treasury activities of the banks. Influence of economic conditions is particularly evident in decisions about the types and terms of credits that banks grant to different sectors of the economy and how they play in the financial markets for the treasury instruments. It is pertinent to determine whether the economy is growing, stagnant, or declining. If it is a growth economy, lending and treasury officers should be interested in knowing the direction of growing economic activities. In particular, determining what might be the future leading sectors of the economy would also be of immense interest to them. Even where growth is indicated, it is yet important to be wary of lending activities in case the economy is subject to seasonal or cyclical movements.

In a stagnant or declining economy, there would be general lull in business activities and banking will be no less affected. The salient issue for a bank in such a situation is to remain liquid and meet operating costs and customers' funds withdrawal needs. Lending would not be emphasized because of possible high incidence of loan default that characterizes periods of business decline. Loans granted to borrowers—if any should be granted at all—essentially should be of short-term, self-liquidating type. Thus, borrowers would have limited choice of loan structure because of the dictate of an unstable economy.

Regulatory Maneuverings

The regulatory influences on market risk are rooted in the macroeconomic and monetary policy issues, both of which have a profound influence on the functioning of the financial system. Instability in the macroeconomic foundation affects activities in the banking system—a subset of the financial system—in kind. Let me briefly discuss the mechanics of the macroeconomic foundation and monetary policies that affect the pricing of banking transactions in developing economies.

Macroeconomic forces, perhaps, have the most profound influence on the determination of the prices for banking services. The thrust of macroeconomic management in developing economies has been attempt to attain optimal interest, exchange, savings, and investment rates consistent with set economic growth targets. When interest rates are stable and predictable, individuals and business units could realistically plan for savings and investments. In the same vein, the behavior of exchange rates affects the rate of savings and investments. In both cases, the critical determinant of market reaction is the inflation rate.

When the rate of inflation is higher than interest rate, or when the exchange rate of the domestic currency is freely floating and continuously depreciating against the convertible currencies, people and business units shun saving because of the erosion of their wealth by inflation. They rather would most likely prefer to keep their resources in physical assets. This situation is common in a regulated financial environment. In a deregulated economy, where there is a free interplay of the market forces, realistic interest and exchange rates could be achieved. Thus, the inflation rate will reflect the real worth of the purchasing power of the people.

The financial system, in most of the developing countries, is reasonably deregulated. Market forces largely determine interest and exchange rates. However, when the Central Bank directly competes with banks for deposits and foreign exchange, as was the case in Nigeria between early 2001 and 2004, the known character of free market mechanism becomes distorted.

MARKET RISK FALLOUT OF FLAWS IN MONETARY POLICY AND MANAGEMENT

Of all the regulatory tasks of the authorities, determining the appropriate level of money supply for the economy is the most excruciating. I illustrate this view with the case of Nigeria's monetary management way back in 2001—as a standard example. It has not been easy, practically, for the authorities to attain any reasonable degree of success because of conflicting, or erroneous assumptions underlying the thrusts of monetary policies during the period preceding the 2005 banking system consolidation. Consider, for instance, that in trying to mop up excess liquidity in the economy and check the rising demand for foreign exchange that had adversely affected the exchange rate of the *naira*, the Central Bank of Nigeria had in April 2001:

- introduced the "CBN Deposit Certificate," a nondiscountable money market instrument, that offered a more attractive yield than investment in bank deposit accounts, thereby switching liquidity from the banks to the CBN; and
- raised banks' LR from 35% to 40%, having earlier reviewed its minimum rediscount rate and CRR upward, from 15.5% and 11.0% to 16.5% and 12.5%, respectively.

In a swift response to these regulatory maneuvers, interbank interest rate soared up to 50%. This negative effect immediately affected interest rates charged by the banks. While the CBN would have mopped up the perceived excess liquidity, it dislocated the functioning of another key sector of the economy—the real sector, which then found it extremely difficult to borrow money at the prevailing interest rate to fund its investments and operating costs. Ironically, rather than strengthen the *naira* against the dollar and other convertible currencies, the exercise of mopping up the excess liquidity resulted in even further depreciation of the *naira*.

With its Deposit Certificate, which paid interest at 21.5% per annum on a minimum deposit of ₦250,000.00 for a tenor of 360 days as against 17.5% per annum paid on such deposits by the banks, the CBN started attracting huge deposits from the banking public. The mopping up of "excess" liquidity from the banking system threatened the liquidity base of some of the weak banks. The "CBN Deposit Certificate" had yet another serious negative effect on the long-term economic growth objective of the country. There was unrestrained diminution of investments in the capital market because the investors in equity stocks and term deposit products of the banks showed preference for the "Certificate," largely because of its premium yield and risk-free assurance.

Of course, the CBN is a major player in the foreign exchange market. It easily dictates rate movements in the autonomous foreign exchange market. Since the authorized dealers buy foreign exchange from it, the rate it offers rules the market. This is why people talk of "official" devaluation of the *naira*—a situation that arises each time the CBN increases the *naira* cost of the dollars it offers to the market. Many adjudge these actions sometimes to be untimely, considering the additional hardships they unleash on the already suffering masses of the people and the hick-ups in the manufacturing sector. Indeed, a truly market-driven competition would neither tolerate nor admit of the actions of the CBN in introducing the Deposit Certificate.

The real burden of such adverse and unpredictable policy shifts was borne by the masses of the people. For instance, while the CBN continued to attempt to close the gap between "official" and "parallel" market exchange rates, inflation became the order of the day. Usually, its impact was seen as a ravaging monster that brought hardship to the people through diminution of their purchasing power. Early in April 2001, the CBN devalued the *naira* twice in two consecutive days—bringing the exchange rate between the naira and dollar to ₦115.70. The parallel market rate averaged up to ₦140.00 per dollar. Thus the gap between exchange rates in the two markets continued to widen, notwithstanding the planned corrective actions the authorities took. The ordinary citizens, who bought food, goods, and services from the open market, became impoverished because of frequent devaluation of the *naira*. Under such excruciating circumstances, the financial exchanges and real sector business activities became shrouded in speculations about the likely market shocks. Ultimately, this increased transactions costs.

It is obvious that unless low but realistic and stable interest and exchange rates are achieved, the desired levels of domestic savings and investments will continue to elude the developing countries. Unfortunately, these countries are yet experiencing such avoidable economic hardships due, mainly, to policy disagreements, conflicts, and inconsistencies between the monetary authorities in some of the countries. The occasional trade in blames between the authorities didn't help matters. This situation was observed in Nigeria in early 2001 when the Central Bank and Presidency disagreed over the manner in which the proceeds of windfall from sales of petroleum products should be spent. The disagreement and its attendant economic woes show how difficult it has been for the authorities to learn from past mistakes.

SUMMARY

As intermediaries in the financial markets, banks play a significant role in mobilizing funds from the savers and channeling the funds into investments—often in the real sectors—through lending. The banks fulfill this role when they act as a go-between for the individuals and organizations that have surplus or are in deficit of funds. In doing so, the banks help meet their investment and borrowing needs, respectively, through the financial markets. In order to fulfill this role, the banks mobilize funds from the individuals and organizations that have surplus funds and make the funds so mobilized available to the individuals and organizations that are in the deficit of funds.

There is a tendency among the executive managements of the banks in developing economies to devote their attention—and understandably too—mainly to forestalling credit and liquidity risks. They give perfunctory attention to market and operational risks. The line managements, in the main, largely seize the initiative from the executive managements under the circumstances. However, the executive managements' abdication of their direct responsibility for market and operational risks does not augur well for the bank—just as their failure to stave off credit and liquidity risks do not.

The Basel Committee identified interest rate risk and foreign exchange risk as the two components of market risk. I discussed the foreign exchange risk aspect extensively in Chapter 24 of this book. Presently, I focus on interest rate risk. Certain factors affect the market rates of interest that banks will either pay on deposits or charge on credit facilities. The factors originate from capitalization of the banks, disposition of the banks toward the risk-return trade-off principle, and the banks' deposits liabilities portfolios base. Other factors include monetary control and regulatory policies of the authorities as well as the prevailing economic condition in a country.

QUESTIONS FOR DISCUSSION AND REVIEW

1. How does pricing in banking—in form of interest and foreign exchange rates—have direct bearing on market risk?
2. What does the term "disintermediation" connote in banking circles and in the context of money markets?

3. Why would funds surplus and funds deficit sectors opt for bank intermediary roles in money markets?
4. What is market risk? In what ways does interest rate risk compare with foreign exchange risk to a bank?
5. How should banks calculate and correctly depict their real cost of funds in order to make business sense?

REFERENCES

Basel Committee on Banking Supervision, 1988. International Convergence of Capital Measurement and Capital Standards. Bank for International Settlements, Basel.

Basel Committee on Banking Supervision, 2005. International Convergence of Capital Measurement and Capital Standards: Amendment to the Capital Accord to incorporate Market Risks. Bank for International Settlements, Basel.

Basel Committee on Banking Supervision, 2006. International Convergence of Capital Measurement and Capital Standards: a Revised Framework – Comprehensive Version, as amended. Bank for International Settlements, Basel.

Chapter 24

Foreign Exchange Markets and Triggers for Bank Risk in Developing Economies

Chapter Outline

LEARNING FOCUS AND OBJECTIVES

The main thrust of foreign exchange management in developing economies is determining realistic exchange rates for domestic currencies. Fixing or pegging exchange rates to some benchmark produces mixed results. The same goes for floating the rates in foreign exchange markets. Yet a country must adopt one of the policy options. This sets the trap in which developing countries are now caught, with dire consequences for economic progress and wellbeing of the citizens. Banks tend to be in the line fire when the policies go awry. Neither are they spared blame when the authorities bungle the policies. What with the critical role the banks are expected to play in helping actualize the policies. I set out writing this chapter in order to:

- investigate banking and related issues in foreign exchange management quirks in developing economies,
- explore the background to foreign exchange intricacies that impart risks to banking in developing economies,
- analyze foreign exchange management process and policy implications for banking in developing economies,
- discuss parallel foreign exchange markets challenge of bank risk management in developing economies,
- identify and assess implications of exchange rate risks beckoning for banks in developing economies.

EXPECTED LEARNING OUTCOMES

A major policy challenge of economic management in developing countries is how to harmonize official and parallel markets foreign exchange rates. This demands formulation of appropriate strategy for determining realistic exchange rates for the domestic currencies. Exchange rate gap starts narrowing—and may in time be completely removed—when the strategy succeeds. This has been the expected but elusive outcome of foreign exchange policies in developing economies. Concern about the uncertainties of the foreign exchange markets keep banks on their toes. On occasion, the banks seem helpless. Yet the banks must deal with foreign exchange management, rates and risk issues in logical and strategic ways. The reader will—after studying this chapter and doing the exercises in it—have learnt and been better informed about:

- banking and related issues underlying foreign exchange management quirks in developing economies,
- the background to foreign exchange intricacies that impart risks to bank management in developing economies,
- process, dynamics, and mechanisms—as well as the policy implications—of foreign exchange management in developing economies,

- evolution and mechanics of parallel foreign exchange markets and how they make a challenge of banking in developing economies,
- why and how there is a preponderance of foreign exchange rate risk in the hazards of banking in developing economies.

OVERVIEW OF THE SUBJECT MATTER

Foreign exchange risk is defined as "the risk of holding or taking positions in foreign currencies, including gold." (Basel Committee, 2005:23). It also refers to the danger that a bank might lose money on a lending, or foreign currency transaction due to unanticipated adverse changes in exchange rates. Due to weak currencies, bank in emerging economies deal with exchange rate issues on daily basis. In fact, foreign exchange gains or losses occasioned by volatile exchange rates determine to a large extent financial performance of banks in emerging markets. Thus most banks in emerging economies are very active in both official and autonomous foreign exchange markets. Unfortunately, majority of the issues regulatory authorities have with banks in emerging economies result from sharp practice in the foreign exchange markets.

Developing countries have over the years pursued elusive economic reform programs aimed at achieving realistic exchange rates through free interplay of market forces. Economic and monetary authorities argue that overvaluation of domestic currencies discourages inflow of foreign investments. It is further argued that currency overvaluation penalizes export production. Measured by the difference between official nominal and parallel market exchange rates, overvaluation of domestic currencies became so high that devaluation was the first step in structural adjustment programs (SAPs) of the countries. However, the immediate effect of devaluation was a rise in inflation rate, crystallizing the major burden of adjustment on the poor. The strategy of export promotion is to depreciate domestic currencies, stop the marketing of agricultural produce through monopolistic public sector agencies, and establish export-processing zones.

Depreciation enhances the prices of local currency earnings from exports. Abolition of public sector commodities marketing agencies achieves efficient pricing of exports and maximizes returns to the farmers. Export processing zones are designed to encourage greater export production. However, the benefits of these measures are sometimes diminished by conflicting macroeconomic policies targeted at other sectors of the economy, particularly in foreign exchange and interest rate management. In Nigeria, for instance, export production was discouraged in the early 1990s by the adoption of a fixed exchange rate regime meant to regain public confidence in the country's domestic currency—the naira. However, parallel foreign exchange markets subsisted—sometimes getting funds illegally from the official market.

Foreign exchange problems of developing countries derive, to a large extent, from occasional and unexpected economic shocks. The volatility of international oil market is a case in point. The same goes for fluctuation causing depression in nonoil, especially primary, commodities market. These situations adversely affect foreign exchange earnings and reserves. All this weakens efforts to regenerate the economies. Often the fate of the economies and government policies are closely intertwined. Massive external borrowing to finance development projects designed to improve domestic industry and infrastructure exacerbates the problem. For example, from an estimated $6 billion in 1970, the aggregate external debt of sub-Saharan Africa grew to more than $126 billion in 1987. The real GDP per capita of the countries plummeted by about 11% over the same period. Commentators on economic crisis of developing countries—especially occasional papers and reports of the World Bank and IMF officials, as well as commentaries from international economic monitors and institutions—tend to focus on adverse domestic and external shocks, as well as faulty domestic policies.

BACKGROUND TO FOREIGN EXCHANGE INTRICACIES IN DEVELOPING ECONOMIES

The thinking in some quarters is that policy makers and administrators have not exercised the desired and right economic initiative in harnessing human and natural resource potential of countries in developing economies. Ironically, some of the leaders acknowledge this failing. Former Nigeria's Minister of Finance, Kalu Idika Kalu, admitted in 1994 that "the Nigerian economy has been experiencing severe imbalances and aggravated distortions since 1991 … *caused* by both inappropriate conceptualization and faulty designs of some of those policies and compounded by poor and half-hearted implementation." He hinted at the economic fallout, noting that "the economy has thus witnessed increased macroeconomic instability, declining productivity, low utilization of installed industrial and agricultural capacity, and severe constraints on capital flows and debt servicing in the balance of payments." Kalu disclosed—as example to illustrate the problem—that "despite the expected emergence of over a hundred items on the nonoil export list, their combined contribution has remained low, stunted by low resource application to exploit the unusual price advantages fostered by the rapidly depreciating effective exchange rate during the 1986–92 period." This is pertinent, as well as instructive (Kalu, 1994).

In 1980s, the failing economic health of many developing economies deteriorated further as deep-seated structural problems caused serious macroeconomic instability evidenced by low and declining GDP per capita, high unemployment level, and poor social welfare. During this period, sub-Saharan Africa—with soaring population—experienced more than 1% decline a year in GNP per head. The distortions in the economies reflect in the demographic distribution of the population, showing worrying imbalances. The Economist (1996) noted that about "two-fifths of all Africans are aged under 16, compared with only one-fifth in the developed world." The situation grew so bad that in early 1980s many developing countries started seeking external assistance for redirection to sustainable economic growth and development. This was the basis of economic reforms and adjustment policies which most of the countries adopted in the 1980s. Many of the countries responded to the crisis by opting for economic restructuring after several attempts at various short-term solutions such as austerity measures failed. It was then reasoned that since the macro instability being experienced by the countries resulted from serious distortions in the productive sectors and structural imbalances in the economy, only long-term, forward-looking, and realistic approach should be adopted in the search for solution.

The presumed solution was advised by the World Bank and the International Monetary Fund (IMF) which had manufactured, tested, and delivered economic adjustment *pill* to the sickly developing countries. In the case of Nigeria, this option did not come easy. Former head of Nigerian Interim National Government, Ernest Shonekan, gave an insight into the problem. Shonekan (1993), observed, "it is noteworthy that in those heady days, the present military government demonstrated a rare courage in taking hard and unpopular decisions on the economy." In his view, "such decisions included the floatation of the naira exchange rate, the abrogation of import licensing, the abolition of commodity boards, reduction of tariffs on imported machinery, privatization and/or commercialization of public enterprises, and the rationalization of the public sector."

Unfortunately, economic adjustment programs have not altogether provided solution to the countries' growth and development problems. After administering the adjustment pill meant to heal economic wounds, most of the countries did not appear to be responding to treatment. Shonekan (1993) admitted the failure of SAP in Nigeria. His verdict was that "in spite of the gains recorded under SAP, certain macroeconomic problems had so far defied solutions. He cited pertinent examples, including "the continuing depreciation of the naira exchange rate; the high and volatile interest rate; the depressed activities in the real sectors of the economy; and skyrocketing inflation." Then he identified "other problems causing concern *as* the burgeoning fiscal deficit coupled with excessive money supply; increasing unemployment, especially of young school leavers and the erosion of the standard of living of most Nigerians." This conclusion generated curiosity as to whether economic adjustment programs in developing countries were a cure or curse.

FOREIGN EXCHANGE MANAGEMENT PROCESS AND POLICY IMPLICATIONS

Perhaps the most volatile issue in macroeconomic management of most of the developing countries has been how to determine and sustain realistic exchange rates for their domestic currencies. The problem featured mainly in the course of designing appropriate structural adjustment packages for the countries. It was believed that most of the domestic currencies were grossly overvalued. This situation was associated with the poor performance of the export sector. It was also argued that currency overvaluation fostered unsustainable increase in demand for consumption imports. In Africa, the countries would want to—and some had indeed—adopted exchange control regimes soon after independence in pursuit of tight fiscal and monetary policies. Allocation of foreign exchange for import purposes was done according to licenses issued to the importers.

This arrangement proved to be ineffective as it was fraught with fraud and abuses. It was therefore abandoned in some of the countries. The fallout was a call for deregulation of exchange rate. Anifowose (1983) came to insightful conclusions on his case study of Nigeria. Strict foreign exchange control in Nigeria during 1967–81 had a twofold outcome. First, it helped to restore balance in Nigeria's international accounts. This outcome was evident in correction of the country's balance of payments deficits. Second, it mitigated depletion of external reserves. Exchange control stemmed outflows of foreign exchange. In some cases, though, exchange control was not predominant in these outcomes. Favorable oil prices—rather than exchange control—accounted for balance of payments surpluses observed in some periods.

Incidentally, exchange control had detrimental side effects seen in social and economic costs (Anifowose, 1983). There was widespread foreign exchange maneuverings. Malpractices, evasions, and corruption were, in turn, rife. Its spillover effect on the real sector reflected in bottlenecks in production process. These socio-economic costs persisted even during periods of relaxed exchange controls. This implies that partial exchange control was ineffective in stemming its concomitant socio-economic costs. Solving the side effects would require complete removal of administrative controls in foreign exchange management. This would entail reliance on market forces in determining realistic exchange rates for domestic currencies.

Developing countries were thus persuaded in the face of these findings to reverse control in favor of deregulation. The IMF and World Bank insisted they did that as a prerequisite for getting funding from the Bretton wood institutions for their SAP. Initially the countries resisted SAP which they found to be draconian—but indeed, a bitter pill to swallow—and the implied policy change on foreign exchange management. In time they swallowed their pride and took their medicine like a man. The accepted SAP willy-nilly. The adoption of SAP immediately necessitated floating of domestic currencies in the foreign exchange markets and the determination of exchange rates by the interplay of the forces of demand and supply. Yet this foreign exchange management strategy was neither adopted nor accepted uncritically by the countries. Suspicion that it would not practically resolve the vices of the exchange control regime partially turned out to be the case with the bungling of the process in many countries. In fact, only few countries attempted a full scale implementation of the freely floating exchange rate policy. In many countries it was modified in various ways to suit domestic needs and circumstances. There are now variants of the independent floating policy in different countries in an attempt to keep observed deficiencies of the foreign exchange market under control.

In all cases of repudiation of exchange control, exchange rates for the domestic currencies crashed against the major world convertible currencies. There were widespread cases of unplanned currency devaluations resulting, in most cases, from the inability of supply to match demand in the short-run. The markets have not been able to generate sufficient volumes of foreign exchange to meet the existing and potential demand. This caused difficulties relating to high cost of funds and inflation. These problems were also evident in Nigeria. Ojo (1990) observed that depreciation of the naira created macroeconomic instability resulting from increased cost-push inflation and speculation—both of which did not augur well with planning. Paucity of funding for the foreign exchange market worsened the problem as upward surge in demand continued unabated in the face of dwindling supplies. The resultant fluctuations in the naira exchange rate and its persistent depreciation against major international currencies, especially the dollar, exacerbated economic crisis. Domestic inflation rate rising more than that of trading partners of Nigeria dealt further blow to the naira exchange rate—causing more exchange rate instability. The inflation was not helped by expansionary monetary and fiscal policies that fuelled demand pressure on foreign exchange in the face of persistent supply gaps and bottlenecks.

CASE STUDY 24.1 Pushed from Pillar to Postimplications for Managing Foreign Exchange Risk

When dawn broke, Obi set out to consult the oracle (Extracted, with minor changes, from Onyiriuba, 2013). At the shrine of the oracle, he fulfilled formalities and was admitted into the place by the oracle's aides. In line with the usual practice of visitors to the oracle, Obi threw some kola nuts in front of him, stepped over the kola nuts, and then faced the presence of the oracle who sat in a corner of his shrine. With his customary mystique, the oracle shouted—starring hard at him.

"Stop there! Don't come further! I say, stand where you are! He ordered Obi in quick succession. "You are here because of your son," said the oracle—preempting the cause of Obi's visit. "Yes, you are in the right place," he flaunted. "Why did you wait this long before coming?" He queried. Obi was silent, gazing and unsure about what to say in answer to the question. "This place should have been your first and only port of call," bragged the oracle. "Sit down!" He now ordered, without waiting for Obi to answer his question or say anything.

Although the oracle regarded him coldly, Obi was a bit relieved as he sat down. In the end, he made useful findings from the oracle. The oracle debunked insinuations that an evil spirit was the cause of Ike's troubles. Rather, he informed Obi that Ike was a man of war who killed many people mercilessly in his previous world. Obi learned further that the blood of the people he killed was crying against him. Then the oracle made a damning revelation, still bordering on Ike's adventures in his past world and reincarnation. "In his bluntness, Ike refused to reach a consensus with the gods before coming to his present world. The blood he shed in the communal wars was now spoiling for revenge and to settle scores. He must return to the land of the dead!"

Obi was taken aback as he listened to the oracle with rapt attention. "Is there nothing that can be done to assuage the gods for his guilt?" He queried the oracle, apparently downcast. "Can we do anything to atone for his offense?" He further asked. As though he was ignoring Obi and his questions, the oracle drew his raffia bag closer to him. He dipped his hand into the bag and brought out some pebbles and cowries. He held the cowries tightly in his right fist. At the same time, he also closed his left hand in a fist—holding the pebbles in it. He scanned around, and then Obi's face, without saying a word. He paused for a moment. Suddenly he started uttering uncertain incantations, with intermittent breaks. As if he was prompted by an unseen being, he threw the cowries and pebbles simultaneously to the ground in front of him. That seemed an impromptu action as the oracle watched the cowries and pebbles cluster or scatter. Five of the eight cowries clustered in front of Obi while all the eight pebbles were scattered on the ground.

Obi was not in the least enthused by the drama of the moment. He was anxious to know the oracle's verdict. But the oracle continued to ignore him. So while Obi gazed into space, the oracle's attention was riveted on the cowries and pebbles. The oracle now looked Obi in the eye and told him straight—his observation and its import which proved a relief to Obi. "Yes, there's a window to save his life," the oracle intimated. "We can yet forestall his return to the land of the dead, but only on one condition," he informed.

Obi was riveted to the spot as he imagined what the oracle was about to say next. "You must carry out elaborate sacrificial offerings in order to take advantage of the window," the oracle decreed. Obi had no objection. He committed himself to carrying out the prescription of the oracle for the sacrifices. He performed the sacrifices as required. But alas! Poor Ike, it seemed there was no end in sight to the sickness ravaging him. So Obi decided to explore the thinking in many quarters that Ike was a changeling, although Nene, his wife, had dismissed such thoughts as unfounded.

Against her advice, Obi invited the popular witch-doctor from Ulla village. The witch-doctor operated mainly in the occult, attending to spiritual matters. He was himself a changeling. He acquired awesome spiritual powers which enabled him to invoke spirits, cure changelings, and perform the rituals of his calling. He did all that as a priest of the gods, saving many people from the menaces of wicked gods.

"Bring the child and sit him in front of me," he commanded Obi as he put finishing touches to the materials he would use for his work. "Let me have all the items I asked you to provide for my work," he further ordered. Quickly, Obi brought out some palm kernel fiber, a small bottle of palm oil, a small quantity of wrapped salt, and four cowries from a raffia bag and gave them to him. "You should now hold him firmly," he further directed. He was ready to perform. Obi complied with his instruction. He then lifted a small sharp knife and pierced the boy's forehead, bringing out a dark gravel-like substance. The child roared in pain but he was bent on accomplishing his task. Thereafter, he ground that substance after burning it with the palm kernel fiber and blended it with the palm oil. He then forced the blend in bits into the child's mouth so that he could lick and swallow it. "Your son is transformed. Now, you have a cause to rejoice and be happy for what I've done for him this moment," the witch-doctor vaunted as he assembled his instruments preparatory to leave. Obi thanked him immensely and paid him the fee he charged for his service.

In the end, Ike was neither cured nor responded to the treatment the witch-doctor administered to him. It turned out that patronizing the witch-doctor—nay, consulting the oracle and offering sacrifices he prescribed to the gods were great blunders that Obi committed in his quest for Ike's healing. Ostensibly it became a lesson to him, as well as a pointer to the vanity of superstition and idol worshipping which believers in the new Christian religion roundly condemned. He became convinced that the abysmal failure of the witch-doctor and the oracle were a proof of the irrelevance of ungodly practices, institutions, and supernatural powers on matters where faith in God should prevail.

Exercise for class or group discussion

1. How does this tale shed light on foreign exchange management dilemma of government in developing economies?
2. What lessons can foreign exchange policy makers and administrators in developing economies learn from Obi's experience?
3. Would Obi's reasons for consulting the witch-doctor and the oracle be logical in managing foreign exchange risks?
4. In what ways do actions Obi took compare with how bank managements might respond to foreign exchange intricacies?
5. Are there things Obi did wrongly that you think bank managements should avoid in dealing with foreign exchange risks?

Tips for solving the exercise

Chances are banks that manage foreign exchange risks well in developing economies would succeed. Foreign exchange gains and losses largely skew financial performance of the banks. Foreign banks subsidiaries tend to have a better mastery of dealing in foreign exchange than their domestic counterparts. This is understandable. Their parent, holding banks serve as their foreign correspondent banks. They avail themselves of the opportunity of this relationship to get favorable terms on foreign operations deals. Thus they are less affected by the volatility of the local foreign exchange markets. This is, perhaps, the singular most important edge which foreign banks subsidiaries have over their domestic counterparts in developing economies. Often domestic bank's managements are driven from pillar to post. Firefighting typifies their approach to risk management in foreign exchange transactions. Often dealing with foreign exchange risks ends in crisis management, if anything. Flawed macroeconomic policies and volatile operating environment impart instability to the foreign exchange markets and compound risks faced by the banks. Domestic and foreign subsidiary banks are affected more or less depending on appropriateness of their risk-mitigating measures. The banks devise and engage strategies to cope with paucity of foreign exchange in the face of surging demand. Yet widening gap between official and parallel markets foreign exchange rates and possible use of banks as a conduit for money laundering complicate the risks of banking in developing economies.

The names of individuals in the tale are imaginary and do not relate to any known or unknown real persons in Nigeria or anywhere in the world. The story is set in Lagos, Nigeria, purely for illustration purposes only, in order to demonstrate how some foreign exchange challenges of banking play themselves out in developing economies.

FOREIGN CURRENCY MARKETS AND RISK MANAGEMENT

The dynamics of foreign currency markets and deals are quite intriguing. To start with, the markets are volatile and risky. Yet, they also present interesting risk-return paradoxes. Ironically, dealers in the markets seem to embrace these features. Let me first examine the main features and dynamics of the two types of foreign exchange markets in developing economies (The FX dealers trade on behalf of their banks in foreign currency markets. It follows that "banks" can be substituted for "dealers" in this and other discussions in this chapter without change of meaning. For example, "quoting bank" substitutes for "quoting dealer" and implies the dealer who quotes rates to the "calling bank"—meaning the "calling dealer.").

Forms of Foreign Currency Markets

Foreign exchange market is a network for the trading of foreign currencies, including interactions of the traders and regulations of how, where and when they close deals. It is an arrangement for the buying, selling, and redeeming of obligations in foreign currency trading. There are two main foreign exchange markets—interbank and autonomous—in developing economies.

Central Bank (Interbank) Market

The interbank FX market refers to formal and organized structures put in place by the monetary authority, such as the Central Bank, for conducting trading, transactions, and deals in foreign currencies. This market is referred to as either interbank foreign exchange market (IFEM), as in Nigeria, or official foreign exchange market. The Central Bank controls, monitors, and supervises this markets conduct of trading, transactions, and deals in most countries.

Thus, the rate of exchange in this market is referred to as the official exchange rate—ostensibly to distinguish it from that of the autonomous FX market. The official rate itself is the cost of one currency (say, dollar) relative to another (say, euro), as determined in an open market by demand and supply for them. It is the amount of one currency that an FX dealer pays or spends to get one unit of another currency in formal trading of the two currencies.

In some countries, like Nigeria, the conduct of FX transactions in this market is guided by the wholesale Dutch auction system. Under this system, the authorized dealers bid for FX under the auspices of the Central Bank every week. The Central Bank sells FX to only the banks with the winning bids at their bid rates. The losers would be the banks whose bids are unsuccessful. In this way, the determination of the FX rate is to a large extent left to the market forces. However, the Central Bank indirectly influences the exchange rate. It does this by fixing an amount of the FX it would supply to the market and for which the authorized dealers bid. In most cases, rates movements follow speculation on the quantity of the FX that Central Bank would likely want to offer for sale sell in market.

As authorized dealers, banks gain from FX transactions. For example, the Dutch Auction System of FX bidding provides a window through which the participating banks could boost their liquidity position on regular, largely, weekly basis. One way through which this is achieved is when, on weekly basis, huge float domestic currency funds accumulate in the customers' current accounts as deposits for the FX bidding. The banks would retain and continue to utilize the funds until and pending when the amounts equivalent to the customers' bid have been debited from their accounts with the Central bank.

Autonomous Market

The autonomous foreign exchange market—also variously known as "parallel FX market," "FX black market," or "underground FX market"—is a major cause for concern to the monetary authorities in developing economies. The continued existence of this FX market despite their proscription is especially disturbing to the banking regulatory authorities. In some countries, the black market fallout of exchange rates management has assumed a troubling dimension. In most cases, there is a wide disparity between the official (IFEM) and autonomous FX rates.

The parallel market is a network of illegal trading in foreign currencies, including the interactions between the traders with respect to how they conduct and consummate deals. The rate of FX exchange in this market is called "black market rate," "autonomous rate," or "parallel market rate." The rate is the cost of one currency (say, dollar) in terms of another currency (say, euro) as determined and applicable in an underground market for foreign exchange trading. It is, in essence, the rate at which a unit of one currency exchanges for one unit of another currency in an underground FX trading.

The FX traded in the black market is referred to as "free funds"—compared with "official funds" that depicts FX traded in the interbank market. Many commercial banking customers—especially the traders—do most of their import transactions with free funds. This implies that they obtain FX from autonomous sources. In reference here is FX procured outside sales by the Central Bank in countries that have administered foreign exchange policies. The risk management implication is that banks should adhere strictly to FX regulations and endeavor to operate within regulatory requirements and guidelines at all times. Critical issues often border on documentation, disclosure, and reporting requirements for FX sources and transactions.

MARKET DEALS, PROCESS, AND RISK MANAGEMENT

Three broad categories of FX deals dominate transactions in money markets across developing economies. There are spot and forward deals, as well as interbank placements (i.e., deposits) of foreign currencies. Spot is the most popular. Forwards—commonly referred to as financial derivatives—are exotic treasury deals to which most of the dealers are not oriented. The dealers are both anxious and cautious as they reluctantly embrace trading in them. They rather would want to stick with spot FX transactions. However, the unstoppable great march of revolution in banking—fueled by the Internet and globalization phenomena—point them to the direction of derivatives. Nowadays, they see financial derivatives as complementary to spot FX deals. The main financial derivatives which the dealers trade as money market treasury instruments are forward FX transactions, FX swaps, and FX options deals. These derivatives are not usually straightforward. They easily expose the banks to market risk.

Spot Transactions

Bank FX dealers are conversant with spot transactions. Such transactions are common and, though risky, relatively less risky than the derivative instruments of the FX markets. A spot FX transaction is a deal struck now to immediately buy or sell a given amount of a particular currency. The spot value date, though, is usually determined as two working days after the deal is struck. The purchase or sale is done as an exchange transaction between two currencies.

The foregoing implies that one currency is exchanged for a second currency. The exchange rate for the transaction is referred to as spot rate. It is the prevailing rate at the time of the contract. Ideally, spot rate is applicable to large, usually interbank, FX transactions. It is for this reason that spot rate often interchanges with interbank spot rate in the foreign exchange markets—without any change in meaning.

Speculation and the multiplier effect of FX trading nowadays expose the banks to risk in spot deals. The underlying cause of risk in a spot transaction is the constant and unpredictable fluctuations in the spot rate. Movements in currency value inform the fluctuation and risk attendant on spot transactions. In the absence of protection against adverse currency value movements—and, therefore, fluctuation of spot rate—dealers face real exchange rate risk in spot transactions.

FX dealers are ever taking positions to make money from spot transactions. Often speculation about possible changes in future exchange rates informs the positions. Driven by such gambles, the market operators—mainly bank FX dealers and brokers—buy or sell foreign currencies in their positions. The speculations crystallize losses when the actual rates move against a dealer's position.

Forward Contracts

A forward contract is an agreement into which a bank enters with another bank or other counterparty to buy or sell a fixed amount of FX or security on a specified future date at an exchange rate fixed at the time they make the agreement. This definition implies that a forward contract imposes an obligation on the currency buyer and seller. The buyer is obligated to purchase while the seller's obligation is to sell the fixed amount of the currency on the fixed future date.

However, banks are not obligated to trade forwards. The contrary really is that the banks do have the right to decline (i.e., not to trade) forward contracts.

A set of two prices determine the rate on an FX forward transaction. The two prices comprise the spot exchange rate and the forward contract price. The spot rate always is the FX rate at which one currency currently can be exchanged for another. Unlike this meaning, the forward rate essentially is a spread—determined as the amount by which the spot rate and forward price differ. The import of "future" in this definition is that the settlement for the FX bought or sold in a forward contract is done not earlier than three days from the date of the agreement. With a forward contract, an FX dealer will be able to trade the applicable currency in the future at current exchange rates. This is advantageous if the current exchange rates are favorable. The arrangement also protects the dealers against risk of volatility of the foreign exchange markets.

Forwards, in general, have standard tenors of 14, 21, and 30 days. However, this does not entirely preclude other tenors that banks—for some reasons—may want to quote. Banks are enjoined to do so at their discretion. Though, it is more appropriate when there is mutual agreement among the banks. The mutually agreed nonstandard tenors should, at that, be specific. In making a forward contract, FX dealers does not tend to be bothered about what the exchange rate would be when eventually they do the actual transaction, that is, buying or selling the fixed amount of the foreign exchange. What really matters to them is their protection against possible unfavorable exchange rates movements during the term of the contract. Such rates movements could result in financial gain or loss on which the dealers do not want to gamble. Usually, the salient point is to be able to agree to trade particular fixed amount of currency on a particular date in the future at a particular fixed exchange rate. Locking in a fixed exchange rate solves the risk of exchange rates fluctuation for the dealers.

Bank FX dealers may use forward contracts to hedge against fluctuations in foreign exchange rates mainly caused by the volatility of the foreign exchange markets. Forwards really can be customized to suit the needs of the dealers—buyers and sellers alike. With the possibility of customization, forwards easily are structured and traded as over-the-counter (OTC) instruments. This feature enhances their suitability as a hedging instrument of the capital market. The flip side, though, is that forward contract is not a standardized capital market instrument—one that could be traded on centralized Stock Exchanges. Their nonstandardization and therefore unsuitability for trading on the Stock Exchange exacerbates default risk in forward deals. Often, this shortcoming renders forwards unattractive to some bank FX dealers.

In addition to hedging, bank FX dealers could engage in forward contracts purely on speculation. Mostly, speculation is really about what will happen to the foreign exchange rates in the future. Will the rates be rising or falling? What is likely to be the exchange rate on some future period? These are some of the concerns that drive speculations on FX deals. Since bank FX dealers are mostly profit-driven, they tend to stick with hedging and shun speculation.

Swap Deals

Swap is an interbank foreign currency transaction. On occasion, though, a bank may enter into a swap deal with its customer. Often such a customer does large volume FX transactions with the bank. An FX swap deal usually involves two different but related foreign currency transactions. It operates largely somewhat as an FX sale-and-buyback transaction. The implication is that there are two ends to an FX swap transaction. This understanding establishes the import of FX swap for the dealers in foreign currency markets.

A swap, in the context of the foregoing, is an example of a forward contract. It is an arrangement into which two dealers in FX enter to currently:

- buy or sell an agreed amount of one currency (usually the base currency) in exchange for another at a fixed exchange rate; and
- simultaneously agreeing to buy or sell the same agreed amount of the base currency in reexchange for the second currency at a fixed rate of exchange, at a determinate date in the future.

This definition implies that a swap usually involves either of two spot and forward transactions, each of which is simultaneously closed in one deal. Thus, there could be a spot deal to buy and a simultaneous forward deal to sell—or a spot deal to sell and a simultaneous forward deal to buy—a fixed amount of a base currency in exchange for a specified other currency.

Usually, two exchanges of currency—each of which has a different value date and exchange rate—are involved in a swap transaction. The two exchanges occur at the spot and forward ends of the transaction. Spot is the first—while forward is the reverse—transaction that are concluded at a near and further dates, respectively.

The swap price is not the absolute exchange rate at which the two currencies are exchanged—either at the spot or forward end. The two exchange rates involved in a swap really are of less significance than the difference between them. The reason is that while rates could vary between the two exchanges of currency, the amount of the base currency bought or sold, that is, reexchanged for the second currency—remains unchanged.

Option Deals

An option is a contract between two banks FX dealers in which either has and pays for the right to buy or sell a fixed amount of currency or security from or to the other at a set price (i.e., fixed exchange rate) during a specified future period. In order to clarify this definition, it is pertinent to be apprised of its underlying terms. For example, the dealers have and may exercise their right to buy or sell currency to each other, but they are not obligated to do so. That is why an option confers "the right, but not an obligation" on option holders to either buy or sell currency.

The FX dealers are of two categories at any one time. The currency buyers and currency sellers constitute the categories. The buyers, referred to as holders, can (i.e., have the right but are not obligated to) buy or sell currency from the sellers. Unlike the buyers, the sellers—referred to as writers—cannot decline (i.e., must fulfil their contracted obligation) to buy or sell currency under an option agreement. These clarifications, altogether, mean that the holders do have a choice as to whether or not to exercise their right to buy or sell currency from or to the writers. The writers, unlike the buyers, are locked in and must buy or sell currency for which they have contracted.

The overriding concern in options—as in other capital market derivative instruments—is how to contend with FX rates fluctuations in the face of highly volatile foreign exchange markets. The fixed option exchange rate (also referred to as the strike price) largely mitigates the risk. But its shades light on the underlying cause of options—the FX dealers will want to hedge against the impact of possible adverse FX rates movements on their trading activities. There would be no need for fixation of FX rates if not that the foreign exchange markets are volatile—causing fluctuations in the exchange rates of currencies.

This risk exacerbates or mitigates dependent on the type of option a dealer chooses. Two possibilities exist—call and put. With call option, a dealer (i.e., holder) is given a specified time frame within which to exercise their right to buy a fixed amount of currency at a fixed exchange rate. In the case of put option, the dealer (i.e., buyer) is given a specified time frame within which to exercise their right to sell a fixed amount of currency at a fixed exchange rate. The foregoing implies that option holders could be either dealers who buy calls or dealers who buy puts. In this sense, speculation impacts the decision of FX dealers to buy calls or to buy puts. The dealers who buy or sell calls, on the one hand, expect that FX rates would appreciate, while the dealers who buy or sell puts, on the other, expect that FX would depreciate in value during the life of an option. These expectations correspond to taking long position or taking short position, respectively, in foreign currency markets transactions. In general, the buyers have long positions, while the sellers have short positions.

Interbank Placements

Banks FX dealers trade foreign currencies as part of their routine transactions. The trading is done as placements with one another. The placements of FX funds from one bank are takings of another bank. Thus, interbank FX trading involves placement and simultaneous taking between two banks in one transaction. Essentially, one bank's placement is the other's taking. FX trading, in this sense, is strictly guided by rules of professional conduct by which the dealers must abide. I should right now discuss the critical practices, dealing procedures, and risks in the FX markets.

INTERBANK DEALING PROCESS, RISKS, AND MANAGEMENT

Interbank foreign currency dealing follows strict rules of procedure that are binding on the banks FX dealers. The rules are intended to protect the dealers and their banks against risk. There are always chances of delayed, belated, or nonsettlement, as well as outright default. Thus, settlement and default risks are real and must be mitigated in order for the dealers to confidently trade FX in the interbank market. There are basic rules—as well as standard procedures—which the dealers in the FX markets must observe. In general, the dealing process serves to mitigate risks in the foreign currency markets. The bank FX dealers should apprise themselves of the basic trading rules and procedures as a critical success factor. I now discuss the significant procedures—and the rules that inform them.

Primary Dealing Rules

The primary rules of the FX money market are a fundamental requirement for a strong and trusting FX money market. First, participation in the market should be open only to the authorized traders and dealers. This mitigates the risk opportunists cashing in on possible trading flaws or loopholes. It also reduces chances of FX swindles in the market. Second, trading should be conducted within the approved dealing period. In some countries, dealing time spans the whole working period of the day, Monday to Friday, between 8:00 a.m. or 9:00 a.m. and 4:00 p.m. or 5:00 p.m. Third, trading transactions and closed deals must be formally confirmed—usually in writing—within 48 h. The regular process of confirmation involves exchange of standard confirmation letters between the dealing banks.

Mode of Trading

Ideally—and as the dealing ethics require—trading always should be conducted on the basis of two-way quotes. Interestingly, FX quotes are immutable. This means that once a quoting bank gives its bid or offer rate, it cannot change it. Thus the quote remains its binding bid or offer for the particular transaction. For the success of this practice, there should be an effective means of communication among the FX dealers. Traditionally, FX traders deal with one another by means of telephone, telex, facsimile, or writing. With the Internet revolution, e-mail has been added yet as an effective mode of communication in FX trading. It is likely that new and innovative means of communication will evolve with advancing technologies in the information and communications fields and landscapes. Banks should anticipate changes in this context.

Two-Ways Quoting System

The requirement for two-way quotes always is an essential element of interbank FX dealing system. It is a method of trading in the foreign currency markets in which a dealer is required to quote their bid and offer rates at the same time. To put it simply, it implies that an FX dealer in one bank must state their buying and selling rates at the same time when their counterpart in another bank calls them. The critical requirement is not only stating the two rates, but quoting them simultaneously.

Dealer's Word is Their Bond

In general—whether in interbank domestic or foreign currency trading—dealers pride themselves on keeping their word. Their famous catchphrase—"our word is our bond"—becomes, in itself, a strong but virtual instrument of trust. Yet, occasional defaults in interbank dealing nowadays are a sad reality of their business. This is ironic when considered in the "our word is our bond" context. It is unlikely that interbank currency dealers deliberately would want to abdicate their responsibility to keep their word. Often defaults in interbank deals have their causes in some underlying issues. Usually, such issues are beyond the dealers.

Confirmation of Deals

The manner in which deals are struck is pertinent. The dealers should never be confused about when (i.e., the exact time) a deal is struck. Clarity of trading, transactions, and deals always is pertinent. Technically, the calling bank provides a clue as to when a deal is struck. A general FX trading rule is that a deal is struck when the FX dealer from the calling bank accepts and confirms their purchase or sale of a given amount of FX at bid or offer rate quoted by another bank. This rule operates as the standard definition of a FX deal for all practical purposes.

Elements of Transactions

There are three critical issues about the elements of FX transactions. The authorities should determine the minimum amount of FX to trade per transaction. Such transaction or dealing amount does not admit of lesser figures. Then the question of settlement risk demands attention and solution too. There is, of course, the issue of convertible and third currencies that also must be resolved in order to have meaningful quotes and trading. Let me quickly explain the risk implications of these major elements of FX transactions.

Amount Traded

The first concern is fixing the minimum—also regarded as the standard—amount of currency for dealing in the FX market. The regulators of the market should specify the minimum dealing amount for the information of the authorized dealers in the FX market. In Nigeria, for example, the minimum (i.e., standard) amount for FX dealing is $100,000.00. The dealers also may trade based on some specified amounts that are larger than $100,000.00, though. However, the dealers must clearly state this variation of the standard amount in communications and documentation of their transactions. There might be a shortfall in the required standard amount. A shortfall is amount that is less than $100,000.00. On the basis of the two-way quote system, shortfalls do not qualify for trading in the interbank FX market.

Settlement Risk

Usually FX dealers face settlement risk in their interbank transaction. Dealing in the FX markets involves interbank takings and placements. The funds taken must be paid back on due date. Thus, FX trading gives rise to settlement risk in terms of obligation to pay back takings. Settlement risk, in foregoing sense, is the probability that banks engaged in interbank FX trading may not fulfill their obligations on deals with one another. The risk also could be defined as the chance of default on interbank FX trading obligation of one bank to another. This risk becomes real when one bank fails to transfer funds to the taking bank—or payback funds to the placing bank—under their mutual agreement on a particular FX deal. The banks that don't manage settlement risk well lose goodwill and contend with reputational risk in the FX market. The same fate awaits banks that are seen as interbank net takers. Such banks tend to use takings to settle matured placements with them, thus awkwardly mitigating settlement risk to which it is exposed. It is dangerous for a bank to be seen in such a bad light. It is important—as part of their risk mitigation measures—for the FX dealers to make known their preparedness or not to accept only presettlement risk. Doing this gives an insight into a bank's risk appetite and tolerance right from the outset of a dealing transaction. It is also imperative for risk management purposes that banks set their settlement risk limits.

Currencies and Rates Quotes

The banks in developing economies mainly trade their domestic currencies against the dollar and other major convertible currencies such as euro. The currencies that are not in this category are referred to as third currencies. For example, a bank in Nigeria normally will quote in terms of the exchange rate between dollar and naira as $/N. This indicates how much naira buys one dollar in Nigeria's interbank FX market. Dealing rules permits the banks to decline third currency quotes.

DEALING ARRANGEMENTS AND RISK MANAGEMENT

The bank FX dealers must trade currencies on the basis of certain mutual agreements among them. The agreements build on appreciation of the dynamics of the spot market and the basis of the treasury FX derivative instruments which they trade. The financial derivatives help the FX dealers grapple with the volatility of the foreign exchange markets. As their designations imply, the foreign currency treasury instruments make it possible for the FX dealers to spot deal in FX, swap FX deals, exercise FX dealing options, and in fact, conclude forward FX transactions. In most cases, dealing is geared to hedge against risk or to speculate on FX rates movements for the purpose of making money in the money market. The arrangements are a myriad of FX and dealing related issues. Most of the issues border on the handling of margins on FX commitment, value-dating of deals, determination of spreads, mode of quoting rates, settlement risk, defaults, and the rights and obligations of quoting and calling banks.

FX Commitments and Margins

However, unlike the financial derivatives, spot deals are influenced by immediate realities of the money markets. A critical issue in bot spot and forward deals concerns whether or not to pay margins for commitments on FX transactions. There tends to be no hard-and-fast rules, but banks rather are enjoined to treat margin payment as optional—though, with mutual agreement among them. Ultimately, whether or not margin is paid depends on how the banks perceive the risks of the underlying transactions.

Value-Dating Deals

The term "value date"—in foreign currency trading circles—is the time the exact amount of FX bought must be delivered to the buyer by the seller. Delivered is the operating word. On occasion, trading risk crystallizes in partial delivery or outright nondelivery of FX sold to a buyer. Spot transactions and forward contracts are value-dated in different ways. Usually, the value date for spot deals is 48 h. This implies that the seller has two working days to fulfill delivery to the buyer. The essence of the two-day value date for delivery is to allow enough time for the dealers to do the usual documentation of struck deals. Typical documentation includes deal slips, confirmation letters, and funds transfer instructions. It also helps treasurers plan and meet requirements for funding of the deal. On occasion, counterparties may want to agree on specific value-dating. Similarly, the dealers may want to agree on immediate or next-day delivery. Apparently, these agreements depart from the standard 48 h delivery. Yet they are allowed based on the mutual agreement of the parties. The rule in forward contracts—in contrast to spot transactions—is to count the maturity dates of deals from their spot value dates.

Determining Spreads

The regulatory authorities should fix the maximum spread income in interbank FX trading. It is imperative that spread is realistic and serves as an incentive to the dealers to eagerly trade currencies. Perception of spread as realistic or not has implication for professional conduct of the dealers in the foreign currency markets. In some countries, like Nigeria, the Central Bank regularly reviews the allowable spread. In doing so, the spread is tied to the Central Bank's FX offer rate. This is applicable to FX regimes adapted to the wholesale Dutch auction system. Under such FX regimes, the Central Bank announces rates at which it regularly sells currency to the authorized dealers. A typical directive could be for dealing quotes to be within a range of, say, 0.75% above or below the Central Bank's offer rate.

Obligation to Quote

Bank FX dealers are obligated—under their trading rules—to always oblige their counterparts in other banks when they call for quotes. This implies that the FX dealers must always quote their bid and offer rates to their counterparts who call from other banks. However, quotes given are specific to only a particular call. Of course, the quotes should be stated in terms of exchange rate between the dollar or other convertible currency and the domestic currency—say, $1.00/₦352.00 (i.e., $1.00 to ₦352.00).

Settlement of Deal

Some financial institutions specialize in settlement of interbank deals. Their mode of operation approximates that of a clearing house or merchant acquirers—in the case of credit and debit cards operations. In Nigeria, for example, Nigeria Interbank Settlement System (NIBSS) handles settlement of interbank transactions—including FX deals. A common risk of dealing crystallizes in late settlement. The dealers may address this risk by demanding payment of compensation based on some mutually agreed criterion. One of the commonly used criteria in Nigeria, for example, relates compensation to NIBOR, in the case of naira, and Fed Funds, in the case of dollar. Thus compensation may be stated as, for example, NIBOR + a certain percentage agreed by the dealers and Fed funds + some fixed percentage.

Default and Remedial Action

On occasion, particular interbank FX deals end in default. Default risk borders on flaws in bank treasury funding. In interbank FX trading, default occurs when dealers fail to pay for FX bought or deliver FX sold on the due date. Banks scarcely resort to lawsuit to resolve default on interbank FX deals. They are, in most cases—and as their code of practice enjoin them—likely to go to arbitration. Often this process works, but it sometimes fails. The usual recourse, when arbitration fails, is a threat of litigation. In some situations, it might be expedient to engage debt collectors or recovery agents. It is in the common interest of the dealers to stick to their words and contracts—and do anything but default.

Rights and Obligations of the Dealers

The quoting and calling banks have specific rights and obligations in interbank foreign currency trading. The rights and obligations help to strengthen dealing process, commitments, and relationships. That is why the parties owe certain obligations to each other—even as each also has their specific rights.

It is obligatory for the dealers to always oblige rates requests. The quoting bank must state its two way quotes to the calling bank. Once this is done, the quoting bank must not back out if the calling bank decides to deal. This means that the quoting bank necessarily deals if the calling bank accepts its two-way quotes and decides to deal based on the quotes. There is yet another rule that aims to encourage dealers to act in good faith. It is the rule that the quoting bank must not demand reciprocal quotes from the calling bank. I mean asking to know the calling bank's quotes. However, the calling bank may disclose its quotes by choice or at its discretion.

The calling bank, on its part, is entitled to receive rate quotes from the banks it calls. However, it has the choice to either buy or sell currency—not both—per phone call. Thus the calling bank must decide—and just do—the one deal for which it calls the quoting bank. In other words, there cannot be more than one deal per phone call. Either the calling bank buys or sells currency at the rates supplied by the quoting bank. It is not uncommon that the calling bank may ask for quotes for amounts larger than $100,000.00—the permissible, standard amount for interbank FX dealing. In such a case, the quoting bank may not oblige the calling bank.

The implication is that declining to quote does not infringe the right of the calling bank to receive quotes from the banks they call when the amount is more than the approved standard. It is therefore imperative that calling banks stick with the rule and limit their quotes request to the standard amount. In the course of the trading period, the calling banks may make as many calls as it deems necessary. Multiple calls enable them shop around for better—if not the best—deal. This is usually the case where arbitrage motive underlies the calls.

FOREIGN EXCHANGE RISKS BECKONING FOR BANKS IN DEVELOPING ECONOMIES

Banks in developing economies—domestic and foreign subsidiaries alike—depend heavily on foreign exchange transactions and arbitrage deals to achieve a significant portion of their earnings budget. Paradoxically, the financial performance of the banks tends to be intertwined with the vagaries of the foreign exchange market. The implication is that the banks are easily exposed to market risk caused by volatility of the foreign exchange market. Let me briefly explain the three main ways in which the banks earn incomes from foreign exchange transactions. Doing so, I equally identify and discuss risks associated with each of the income sources.

First, all banks have foreign exchange trading desks that deal in the money market for foreign currencies. Interbank and discount house transactions dominate this market, with appreciable presence of nonfinancial institution dealers sometimes—mainly multinational corporations. Central banks significantly influence financial outcomes in this market. Target earnings entail some risk taking. Risk relating to foreign exchange trading is a function of money market conditions. It is purely a market risk fueled by exchange rate volatility caused by the interplay of demand and supply forces. Often bank treasurers and foreign exchange dealers mitigate this risk by means of hedging, open buyback, and futures deals. The usual portfolio management strategy also comes in handy. The treasurers and dealers hold-off sale and buy more of foreign exchange stock when exchange rates are low and sell-off when the rates are high. Thus, the portfolio risk is mitigated at any one time.

Banks may—and on occasion do—grant loans that are denominated in foreign currencies. Doing so, they earn spread income on the loans. The spread is determined as the difference between the rate at which the banks buy foreign exchange in the money market and the rate at which they sell it to the borrowers. In most cases, borrowers need foreign exchange to meet various import finance needs. It is in banking activity—granting foreign exchange-based loans that banks, perhaps, face the most difficult risks. Loan defaults caused by unanticipated depreciation of domestic currencies against major international convertible currencies are common. Its implication is that loan balances shoot up. Often this situation crystallizes loan default. This happens because loan service and repayments are tied to prevailing exchange rates. That determines the loan repayment ability of the borrowers. The business of such borrowers could easily be import dependent—largely due to their foreign exchange dependence. The uncertainty that pervades the foreign exchange markets could lead to either unfavorable or favorable circumstances for the banks and borrowers. However, the authorities try to mitigate this risk—often without appreciable success. They strive to merge dual exchange rates—official and parallel (autonomous)—which often prevail in the market. The merger is intended to ensure effective allocation of foreign exchange at a reasonable common rate. Their ultimate goal is to ensure steady supply and availability of foreign exchange in the money market.

The third income earning source is charges on foreign currency transfers and services which the banks render to customers. Money transfer transactions of bank customers—sending and receiving foreign currencies as may be applicable—could be substantial and a boost to incomes earned from foreign exchange transactions. International facilitators of money transfer transactions include big industry names like Western Union, MoneyGram, and Vigo. Bank foreign currency transfers and services should ordinarily be riskless. However, this is usually not the case in all situations. On occasion, risk crystallizes in payment of foreign currency inflow to a wrong beneficiary. There is also risk in chances that the source of an inflow would be money laundering or illicit drug deal. In both cases, a bank faces the risk of financial loss to fraudsters, impersonators, and other criminals. Involvement of law enforcement agents exacerbates the risk when money laundering or drug trafficking is involved. In order to mitigate this risk, the regulatory authorities enjoin banks to always insist on knowing their customers. The KYC rules are really inviolable in the risk of foreign currency transfers—receipts and payments alike.

There is a fraudulent angle to foreign exchange risks involving the banks directly. This happens when banks deliberately maneuver foreign exchange transactions, rules, and reporting, ostensibly in pursuit of earnings budget. Take bidding for foreign exchange on behalf of customers under the auspices of the Central Bank as example. Some banks bid for and are allocated foreign exchange at official rate which they sell to the customers at parallel market rate. This happens in countries where there is a wide disparity between official and autonomous market foreign exchange rates. Banking regulatory authorities frown upon this sharp practice. Yet it persists. IFEM is the primary market in some countries. IFEM is an official arrangement, and related structures, put in place by the monetary authorities for banks to trade in foreign currencies. It is a network of dealers in foreign currencies, including interactions of the dealers, and regulation of how, where, and when they consummate deals.

The alternative to IFEM in some countries is the Dutch auction system of foreign exchange bidding and allocation. The Dutch auction is an arrangement under which the Central Bank sells foreign exchange to banks whose quoted bids win in a competitive sale of a specified amount of the foreign exchange. The central bank conducts the auction on a regular, usually, weekly basis.

CHALLENGE OF AUTONOMOUS MARKETS FOR BANK FX RISKS MANAGEMENT

Demand for foreign exchange usually surpasses official supply at any point in time in developing economies. As would be expected under such circumstances, the parallel (autonomous) markets strive to fill the gap. Continuing inability of supplies of foreign exchange from official sources to satisfy demand renders the parallel markets attractive to private suppliers who patronize them. Curiously, supply of foreign exchange from official sources on occasion finds its way into the parallel markets. The incentive, doing so, is to take advantage of arbitrage opportunity that the wide gap between official and parallel market exchange rates offers. This exacerbates foreign exchange round tripping. The macroeconomic implication of this situation is foreign exchange leakages which could be detrimental in a country's foreign exchange management process. This problem heightens market speculations and is typical in countries enforcing foreign exchange regulation. Often concerns about possibilities of policy changes fuels the speculations.

Ojo (1990) studied Nigeria's foreign exchange management and drew conclusions that support exchange rate deregulation. He found that Nigeria's exchange rate policy—departing from dependence on market forces—caused overvaluation of the naira exchange rate. The policy, according to him, was counterproductive—and did not make for effective foreign exchange management. It undermined export incentives—largely because prices of goods and services in naira were uncompetitive. This was the reason Nigeria's traditional exports collapsed. Second, the policy encouraged high rate of consumption of imports. Foreign exchange stock came under pressure as demand surged to meet import needs. Concomitantly, import trade became fraught with sundry frauds. Overdependence of manufacturing on imported inputs didn't help matters. The cheapness of the imported inputs sustained the overdependence. The argument for infant industry protection was invoked to levy high tariffs on imported finished products. The boost the policy gave to parallel foreign exchange markets and capital flight was yet another black spot. This was the inevitable outcome of the scarcity and rationing of available foreign exchange resources.

Chhibber (1991) researched effects of exchange rate devaluation on Ghanaian and Zimbabwean economies, with correlative findings. His study confirmed mixed effects of exchange rate devaluation on the economy. He drew three conclusions, accordingly, based on the findings. First, domestic prices were sensitive to changes in exchange rates. This corroborated a direct relationship between cost-push inflation and exchange rate devaluation. The effect of changes in exchange rate on cost-push inflation tended to be high whether or not the proportion of imports in GDP was small. This was the case if imports that could not be manufactured locally were indispensable to the production process. Second, in situations where domestic capacity to produce import substitution goods was considerable, cost-push effect of changes in exchange rates on domestic prices tended to be small. With price controls and subsidies—if and when introduced—the observed effect was further reduced. Some countries like Algeria, according to him, adopted complete price controls and domestic prices were not affected by changes in exchange rate. The implication was that domestic inflation correlated strongly with changes in price controls—the former being a function of the latter. Often the use of subsidies to shield domestic prices from the full impact of exchange rate changes backfires. The outcome, in most cases, will be fiscal deficits the financing of which has inflationary implication for the economy. Third, domestic monetary and fiscal policies affected the responsiveness of domestic inflation to exchange rate devaluation. For example, printing money to finance deficits induced inflation—and the larger the amount of deficit financed in this way the higher the concomitant inflation. In the case of Ghana, improved fiscal deficit was observed because the outcome of devaluation was higher receipts of foreign aid in domestic currency and reduced exchange subsidies to importers.

The size of parallel markets determines the degree by which official devaluation will affect prices. Once the misalignment of the exchange rate has gone very far, consumer and producer prices already reflect the parallel market exchange rate—the official devaluation is just the formalization of the status quo (ibid). The foregoing depicts the setting in which banks in developing economies strive—contending with intractable risks—to satisfy foreign exchange demands of customers. The banks sometimes make profit from transactions in the parallel markets, though. Yet the underlying uncertainties in the existence of dual exchange rates could be quite distracting. Bank managements easily become engrossed in foreign exchange risk events at the detriment of contending business issues.

SUMMARY

The most volatile issue in macroeconomic management of most of developing countries has been how to determine and sustain realistic exchange rates for domestic currencies. Most of the domestic currencies are overvalued. This situation is associated with poor performance of the export sector. Currency overvaluation fostered increase in demand for consumption of imports. In Africa, the countries would want to—and some had indeed—adopted exchange control regimes soon after independence in pursuit of tight fiscal and monetary policies. Allocation of foreign exchange for import purposes was done according to licenses issued to the importers. This arrangement was ineffective as it was fraught with fraud and abuses. It was therefore abandoned in some of the countries. The fallout was deregulation of exchange rate.

The adoption of SAP necessitated floating of domestic currencies in the foreign exchange markets and the determination of exchange rates by interplay of demand and supply. Yet this foreign exchange management strategy was neither adopted nor accepted uncritically by the countries. Suspicion that it would not practically resolve the problems of exchange control regime turned out to be the case with the bungling of the process in many countries. There are now variants of the independent floating policy in different countries in an attempt to keep observed deficiencies of the foreign exchange market under control.

In all cases of repudiation of exchange control, exchange rates for the domestic currencies crashed against the major world convertible currencies. There were widespread cases of unplanned currency devaluations resulting, in most cases, from the inability of supply to match demand in the short-run. The markets have not been able to generate sufficient volumes of foreign exchange to meet the existing and potential demand. This caused difficulties relating to high cost of funds and inflation.

Usually, demand for foreign exchange surpasses official supply at any point in time. As would be expected, parallel markets fill the gap. Continuing inability of supplies of foreign exchange from official sources to satisfy demand renders the parallel markets attractive to private suppliers. Curiously, supply of foreign exchange from official sources could find its way into the parallel markets. The incentive, doing so, is to take advantage of arbitrage opportunity that the wide gap between official and parallel market exchange rates offers. This exacerbates foreign exchange round tripping.

Banks in developing economies contend with intractable risks in a bid to satisfy foreign exchange demands of customers. The risks are underlain by uncertainties caused by the existence of dual exchange rates which easily distracts bank managements from contending business issues.

QUESTIONS FOR DISCUSSION AND REVIEW

1. Why in your opinion has the goal of developing nations to achieve realistic exchange rates for their domestic currencies been elusive?
2. In what ways do freely floating and fixed exchange rates compare based on their respective economic outcomes?
3. Explain the following terms—noting their wider implications for banking and the economies in developing countries:
   a. Foreign exchange parallel market
   b. Arbitrage opportunity in foreign exchange dealing
   c. Foreign exchange round tripping
4. How do foreign exchange intricacies impart risks to banking in developing economies?
5. What are the implications of failed foreign exchange management process for banking in developing economies?
6. Do foreign exchange management process, dynamics, and mechanisms bear on risks of banking in developing economies?
7. a. Why is there a preponderance of foreign exchange rate risk in the hazards of banking in developing economies?
   b. Identify and discuss the major exchange rate risks that beckon for banks in developing economies

REFERENCES

Anifowose, O.K., 1983. 'The Relevance of Foreign Exchange Control in Nigeria's Balance of Payments Adjustment Process,' in CBN (Central Bank of Nigeria), Economic and Financial Review, Vol. 21, No. 3, September 1983.

Basel Committee on Banking Supervision, 2005. International Convergence of Capital Measurement and Capital Standards: Amendment to the Capital Accord to Incorporate Market Risks. Bank for International Settlements, Basel.

Chhibber, A., 1991. Tackling Inflation During Reforms in Africa, Finance and Development, World Bank, March 1991.

The Economist, 1996. A Survey of Sub-Saharan Africa. September 7–13, 1996, p. 4.

Kalu, I. K. 1994. Press briefing by Nigeria's Minister of Finance, Kalu I. Kalu, on the country's 1994 budget and the National Rolling Plan (1994–96) on 11 January 1994.

Ojo, M.O., 1990. The Management of Foreign Exchange Resources under Nigeria's Structural Adjustment Program', in CBN (Central Bank of Nigeria), Economic and Financial Review, Vol. 28, No.2, June.

Onyiriuba, L., 2013. On the Road to Self-actualization. NFS Data Bureau Limited, Lagos, pp. 26–28.

Shonekan, E. 1993. Address to the joint session of the Nigeria's National Assembly on the occasion of his presentation of the 1993 budget on 27 January 1993.

FURTHER READINGS

Gould, D.J., 1980. Patrons and clients: the role of the military in Zaire politics. In: Mowoe, I. (Ed.), The Performance of Soldiers as Governors. University Press of America, Washington, D.C., p. 485.

Griffiths, I., 1984. An Atlas of African Affairs. Methuen, London and New York.

Patel, I.G. (Ed.), 1992. Policies for African Development: From the 1980s to the 1990s. International Monetary Fund (IMF), Washington, D.C., p. 15.

Sandbrook, Richard, 1985. The Politics of Africa's Economic Stagnation. Cambridge University Press, London.

Timberlake, L., 1988. Africa in Crisis: The Causes, The Cures of Environmental Bankruptcy, second ed. Earthscan Publications Limited, London.

World Bank, World Development Report 1991: the challenge of development, New York: Oxford University Press, pp. 131–132. Unless otherwise acknowledged, the views in quotes are taken from this source.

Chapter 25

Money Market Workings, Instruments, and Bank Risk in Developing Economies

Chapter Outline

LEARNING FOCUS AND OBJECTIVES

Money market is an important arm of financial markets in developing economies. It facilitates dealing in short-dated, fixed income funds and securities. The interbank segment of money market is usually active, vibrant and challenging. Interbank dealers make and lose money dependent on how they anticipate market risk. It is necessary—in order to anticipate risk—for the dealers to be well versed in the intricacies of the mechanisms of money markets. I took cognizance of this point and write this chapter in order to:

- define, characterize, and appropriately situate the workings, risks, and control of money markets in developing economies;
- identify, characterize, and discuss the roles of the major money markets participants in developing economies;
- examine the features, dynamics, and risk management requirements for the domestic currency instruments of money markets;
- pinpoint the risk management challenge of interbank dealing in foreign currency instruments in money market; and
- explore factors in risk-aversion tendencies and management initiative in interbank money market dealing procedures.

EXPECTED LEARNING OUTCOMES

Interbank dealers in money markets ever seek to hedge against market risk. In most cases, speculation on market volatility, the quest for arbitrage gain and, of course, interest rates movements underlie the market risk which banks face in developing economies. The reader will—after studying this chapter and doing the exercises in it—have learnt and been better informed about:

- the characteristics, inner workings, risks, and regulation of money markets in developing economies;
- major players in the money markets—including the features of their participation and roles in developing economies;
- dynamics and risk management requirements for dealing in domestic currency instruments of money markets in developing economies;
- risk management challenge of interbank dealing in foreign currency instruments of money markets in developing economies; and
- interbank money market dealing procedures with implications for risk-aversion tendencies and management initiative.

OVERVIEW OF THE SUBJECT MATTER

Interbank dealers employed in treasury departments of banks play active roles in money markets. Such employees mainly trade in short-dated, fixed-income (i.e., fixed-interest) securities and other financial instruments on behalf of their banks. Their roles include hedging against possible losses—as well as occasional speculation—on the instruments in which they deal. Usually, the successful dealers are well-versed in the money market transactions. The main features of the money market predispose them to active participation in trading the instruments (i.e., securities) on offer.

The foremost attraction of trading in money market securities is liquidity—a characteristic they share with the money market itself. The instruments traded in the money market usually are highly liquid—with treasury bills (T-bills) as the leading security. The assurance of liquidity in the money market is based on a consideration of two factors. First, the money market instruments offer fixed incomes to the investors. Second, the investors commit their funds only for a short-term—usually 90/91 days or more but not more than 365 days.

The second factor of the attraction of the money market to the investors is assurance of safety of their investments. T-bills and government bonds, for example, are first-rate securities and riskless, with no default track record in many countries. Usually, investment in such securities is informed by the credit rating of their issuers—which, in most cases, makes an excellent grade.

There is yet a third factor that renders money market securities attractive to the investors. Usually, the securities are issued, priced, and traded at a discount. The discount essentially is a reduction in the face value of securities. To put it simply, the investors buy the securities at a discounted value. Thus, the discounted value represents the actual—and not the nominal—cost of the securities.

The participants in money markets include the financial system regulatory authorities, authorized dealers, nonbank financial institutions, importers, exporters, speculators, borrowers in domestic currency, and depositors in domestic currency. The common instruments traded in money markets fall into two broad categories—direct and indirect. Foreign currency instruments include domiciliary accounts, export proceeds, and personal FX funds, bearer bonds, foreign currency loans, and letters of credit. Financial derivatives also are traded in money markets.

Interbank dealing follows strict rules of procedure that are binding on the dealers. The rules, in general, are intended to protect the dealers and their banks against risk. Certain factors—including market volatility, frauds infiltration of the market, and so on—create some of the risks the dealers face in money market.

DEFINING AND CHARACTERIZING MONEY MARKETS IN DEVELOPING ECONOMIES

The money market is personified by the structures that facilitate dealing in short-term, fixed-income funds, securities, and similar financial instruments. It represents the network of dealers in these financial instruments, and the regulation of dealing conduct with regard to how, where and when they consummate deals. The main distinguishing features of the instruments traded in the money market are short tenor and fixed interest rate. Short tenor, in this context, does not exceed twelve calendar months at the most. Some other instruments also may be traded in the money market, but this is not common in developing economies.

The need for, and involvement of, financial intermediaries in the conduct of most transactions is a key feature of the money market. I have earlier discussed the mechanisms of the intermediary role of the banks in the money market. So I will not belabor the point. However, I need to emphasize that market players deal mainly in short-term funds—trading in them and managing the related deals and risks. In the context of interbank trading, for example, short-term funds refer to money that banks instantly can place with, or take from, one another dependent on their cash flows situations.

The tenors of such funds admit of overnight, call, and fixed-term borrowings and placements—subject to a maximum of 12 calendar months. On occasion, dealers may need funds for longer terms. In such situations, they get around the term limit through calculated negotiations. The outcomes may include possible restructuring of the matured debt, its renewal, or rollover. In most cases, there would be need to review the interest rate applicable to the funds. This process also applies in the case short-term risk assets—those that fall due for repayment within a year. Mostly, loans in this category are structured as overdraft (including temporary overdraft and drawings against uncleared effects), current line, letters of credit, or asset-based credit facilities.

There is a particular feature of the money market in developing economies that is quite interesting. It borders on a preponderance of short-term deposits relative to long-term funds for which the banks crave. This situation has implications for the liquidity management strategies of the banks. The depositors are averse to give the banks funds for long terms. Their favorite tenors range between 30 and 90 days, sometimes with a rollover option often at renegotiated interest rates. This depositor tendency is informed by a risk aversion disposition in the first place. It also reflects a desire of the depositors to maximize returns from their investments in the treasury deposits.

The depositors regard the banks that promptly repay deposits at maturity, or on request, as liquid and safe. They presume that funds placed with such banks face no potential risk of loss. They see the banks that don't satisfy this criterion as illiquid and unsafe. In their view, funds placed with such banks have high chances of loss. Thus, the ability to promptly pay back deposits on due or prior dates is the primary test of a bank's financial strength. The financially weak banks fail this test. Such banks would rather ask for renewal or rollover of matured deposits—an implication of their illiquid states. To make matters worse, they tend to take exception to prematurity termination of the tenor deposits.

In addition to risk consideration, the depositors favor short-term deposits because it affords them an opportunity to negotiate new interest rates on their funds at maturity. This practice also enhances the income potential of the deposits. Thus, deposits renewal and rollover are an income maximizing strategy of the depositors. The snag, though, is that the illiquid banks may exploit it to the detriment of the uninformed depositors. Distressed banks are known to take deposits out of desperation. Thus, they are usually willing to pay exorbitant rates of interest on deposits. They sometimes do this on the pretense that their financial position is strong.

There is yet another interesting angle to the inclination of depositors toward short-term placements with the banks. Ideally, the banks treasurers would want to have a large and constantly growing pool of long-term deposits. However, this largely has remained only the ideal. The depositors stick with their preference for the short-dated transactions. Apparently—or it would rather seem—the depositors succeed in twisting the arms of the treasurers about accepting short-term funds. The treasurers are now compelled to fund long-term credit facilities with short-term deposits. This ugly situation, which the treasurers sometimes face, creates a mismatch between the assets and liabilities portfolio structures of the banks.

The immediate implication of the mismatch is that the liquidity management ingenuity of the banks treasurers is unusually tasked. Interestingly, the treasurers find a way to get around this challenge—and even to turn it into an opportunity for the bank's business in the lending sphere. This mainly happens when the money market is awash with funds and interest rates are at low levels. It becomes attractive to the treasurers to fund risk assets with the short-term funds.

MAJOR MONEY MARKET PLAYERS IN DEVELOPING ECONOMIES

There are several active participants in money markets. The first group, comprising the financial system regulatory authorities, is always a major player in the market. The relevant regulatory bodies are those that have oversight of banking, deposit insurance, securities and exchanges, and stock exchanges. In Nigeria, for example, the Central Bank of Nigeria (CBN), Nigerian Deposit Insurance Corporation (NDIC), Securities and Exchange Commission (SEC), and Nigerian Stock Exchange (NSE) constitute this group. In general, their roles are purely regulatory in nature—as well as supportive through policy initiatives. The next important set of players is the authorized dealers, that is, the banks. There are also several other participants in the money market—besides the nonbank financial institutions—including importers, exporters, speculators, borrowers in domestic currency, and depositors in domestic currency. Of course there are sundry other participants.

Central Bank

The Central Bank, though, also participates in nonprofit oriented transactions. In addition to its oversight functions, it moderates the banking end of the market through occasional policy interventions. Often it does this directly when it sells or buys securities, such as T-bills as a means of mopping up excess liquidity or injecting funds in the market. The regular open market operation (OMO) is the vehicle at the disposal of the Central Bank to fulfill this role. The Central Bank also indirectly affects transactions in the money market. This happens, for example, when it alters or tinkers with the rediscount rate. I mean the rate of interest the Central Bank charges on the advances it grants through its discount window operations (DWO) to the money deposit banks. In essence, the Central Bank dictates the pace, direction, and tempo of the money markets. It establishes rules and regulations that guide operations of the money market. As lender of last resort, it somewhat indirectly influences liquidity in money markets. The Central Bank—in view of the foregoing—easily is the biggest player in both domestic and foreign currency segments of the money market.

Authorized Dealers

The authorized dealers in money markets comprise deposit money banks, investment banks, and specialized banks. The Central Bank permits them to deal with nonbank bodies in the money markets. The authorized dealers play active and significant roles in the conduct of money market transactions. This view takes cognizance of the daily number and volumes of transactions attributed to their trading activities in the money markets. They mainly function as intermediaries for individuals and organization in pursuit of their investment, borrowing, or other financial needs in the money market. They furnish the market with ordered framework for transactions dealing, processing, and execution. Interestingly, their money market activities are strictly ruled by written and established— as well as unwritten—codes of conduct. The interbank market is, perhaps, the single most active unit of the money market in developing economies.

Nonbank Financial Institutions

The nonbank financial institutions may equally be accorded this privilege in some countries. The nonbank financial institutions include discount houses, finance houses, and bureau de change. While the banks pay and charge interest, the stockbrokers charge brokerage for their services. The discount houses, specializing mainly in the trading of government T-bills, apply discount rates on their transactions with the other market players. The discount houses stand out among the nonbank financial institutions. They act as intermediaries between the Central Bank and authorized dealers in the conduct of open market operations. Their roles, though, are limited to transaction in domestic currency. Yet, their activities help to deepen and impart liquidity to money markets.

Deposit Insurance Corporation

In some countries, deposit insurance has been institutionalized as protection to depositors' funds with the banks. Such corporation provides insurance cover to the depositors against chances of loss of their deposits in the event of bank failure. Thus, the corporation set up to handle this responsibility equally plays active roles in the money markets. However, its roles are complementary to those of the Central Bank in regulating and especially checking possible excesses of the markets. It is for this reason, that the insurance corporation—like the Central Bank—is empowered to examine the banks, check their books and ascertain their risks levels, management, and directions.

Importers

Many businesses in developing countries are predominantly SME traders. Some of the traders are importers and make large demand for foreign exchange (FX). As a result, they always are grappling with the vagaries of the FX markets. Banks may want to grant secured import finance facility (IFF) to the importers. Unsecured IFF is as risky as importing goods on open account terms to which the importers tend to be predisposed. The traders will want to source FX in the parallel market to fund their open account import bills. Thereafter they remit the FX to their foreign suppliers. In some countries, free funds transactions are illegal. However, the Central Bank may allow them in situations where banks can back up the use of free funds to fund open account transaction with necessary documents. The banks should also officially report the related transactions to the regulatory authorities. It should be noted that modern electronic banking, powered by the Internet, has changed the outlook for FX regulation in countries around the globe. Individuals, companies, and organizations now easily engage in one form of e-business or another. They can buy and remit FX online to pay bills, make purchases, and so on—outside the official FX market.

Exporters

The exporters in developing countries generate substantial FX traded in the money market. They earn the FX from the sale of their export proceeds. Their major items of export are primary products—mainly agricultural produce and commodities. The regulatory authorities strictly monitor and demand report from the banks on the utilization of export proceeds. A common rule is for the exporters to give their banks the first option to buy their export proceeds. However, they are not obligated to sell to the banks since they could get better rates in the money market.

Borrowers in Domestic Currency

The borrowers (i.e., users) of funds in domestic currency are a major segment of the money market in developing economies. They need funds to satisfy their personal and business objectives and pursuits. Mostly, demand for funds come from the corporate, commercial, and retail banking customers of the banks. The borrowers mainly are traders, major oil exploration and marketing companies, construction companies, shipping companies, and manufacturers, including their channel members—distributors, wholesalers, and retailers. Their transactions tend to be fraught with risks which the banks should painstakingly identify, analyze, and mitigate.

Depositors in Domestic Currency

Banks mobilize funds from various sources—including individuals, institutional investors, corporate bodies, and nonbank financial institutions. These are some of the major providers of funds to the money markets to meet the borrowing needs of the funds deficit individuals and entities. Unlike the borrowers, they are financial surplus individuals and entities seeking profitable investment outlets and opportunities for their idle funds. Thus, as depositors or investors, they expect the highest and commensurate returns from the uses to which their funds are put in the money market.

Speculators

Most of the players in the money market—including Central Bank, discount houses, banks, importers, exporters, borrowers, and depositors—engage in speculation in one way or the other. However, the level of speculation may vary among the players dependent on their dealing motives and risk appetite. The common denominator in the tendencies to speculation among the players is their desire to maximize return on investments. The actively seek arbitrage opportunities—ostensibly in pursuit of this earnings objective. It is believed in financial circles, rightly or wrongly, that the quest to make money on arbitrage transactions is a significant cause of volatility of the money market.

Sundry Other Participants

There are sundry other participants in money markets. This category includes financial advisors, accountants, association of dealers, and institutions that play supporting roles of sorts, in money markets. The Chartered Institute of Bankers and Money Market Association are typical. The roles of these quasi-financial institutions largely are ancillary—consisting mainly in advisory responsibilities to the major players.

DOMESTIC CURRENCY INSTRUMENTS OF MONEY MARKETS

The participants in money markets avail themselves of certain domestic currency instruments to conduct their transactions. The common instruments in developing economies fall into two broad categories—direct and indirect. The direct instruments are of two main types—treasury and debt instruments.

Direct treasury instruments consist of all the bank deposit accounts and related products—including savings, fixed deposits, call deposits, and current (i.e., demand deposit) accounts. I discussed the features of these treasury products extensively in Chapter 20 of this book. Cash and short-term funds—including interbank placements, cash withdrawals, cash lodgements, clearing checks, funds transfers, and traveler's checks also are direct treasury instruments that feature in the domestic currency market. Sometimes interbank trading culminates in open-buy-back (OBB) and repurchase agreement deals.

Direct debt instruments can be grouped into two main categories for ease of analysis. The first category comprises instruments commonly referred to as marketable securities. It includes T-bills, treasury deposits, and negotiable certificates of deposit. Credit products and facilities in forms of interbank takings, and Central Bank's advances to the money deposit banks constitute the second category.

Indirect instruments of money markets are of two main categories. The first category comprises treasury instruments while the second is made up of debt instruments. Indirect treasury instruments include commercial bills, commercial papers (CP), bankers' acceptances (BA), and promissory notes. These instruments are in common use in developing economies. They equally can be regarded as irregular or quasi-credit products and facilities that employees in bank lending and treasury units jointly market to the public. The overly indirect debt instrument of money markets is bank guarantee.

I elaborate later on CP and BA. These two treasury instruments nowadays have assumed quite an unusual liquidity and risk management significance—with implications—for most banks in developing economies.

Cash and Short-Term Funds

Cash and checking instruments are a significant element of the money market instruments. Their components include inward and outward clearing checks—as well as all manner of transactions conducted on the basis of payments and receipts of cash. The inward clearing checks are liabilities to a bank, while the outward clearing instruments are added to its short-term funds as assets. The banker's checks and traveler's checks also are similarly treated in a bank's books. Cash operations work is fraught with risks. Some of the risks are unavoidable, but can be anticipated. Risk anticipation in this sense focuses on the decision to adopt effective control measures. Success in cash operations demands diligence on the part of cash officers and their subordinates.

Treasury Deposits and Certificates

Customers keep deposits with their banks for safety and to earn interest income. They give the deposits on agreed terms with the banks. Certificates issued in evidence of the deposits are very liquid money market instruments and traded accordingly. Interbank purchases and sales of these certificates could be substantial. There are two variants of the certificates. The one is negotiable certificate of deposit while the other is nonnegotiable certificate of deposit. Customer deposits sometimes account for a substantial proportion of short-term liabilities in a bank's balance sheet.

Interbank Placements

Mostly, interbank dealings result in either placements or takings. The placements of one bank with another are treated as short-term investments. The same goes for money at call and short notice that the banks hold with the Central Bank. This also could be quite substantial. Interbank placements are guided by deposit placement limits (DPL) which the banks managements approve for their treasury dealers in the money market. Often the banks that are net funds placers demand collateral from the net funds takers. The collateral and DPL are complementary risk control measures—a security against the loss of interbank placements. These two security documents give the net funds-placing banks a sense of security for their exposures to the net funds takers.

Treasury Bills

The components of marketable securities usually include a broad base of short-term financial debt instruments. However, the main short-term component is T-bill. This is government obligation—with a tenor of 90 or 91 days. It is almost riskless and accounts for the largest proportion of a bank's security investments at any one time. The players in the money market often invest in the T-bills to boost their short-term liquid assets portfolio. Usually, this security is debt instrument the government issues to raise funds from the money market.

The money market participants buy and sell it, depending on their funding positions. The instrument remains a financial obligation of the government—a sort of IOU the government issues—to the investors. The banks invest and use the T-bills for four main purposes. First, they count toward satisfying part of the bank's statutory liquidity requirements. Second, they are a good income source for the banks. Third, banks can use them as collateral for interbank deposit takings. Fourth, it can be rediscounted prior to maturity. This helps the banks to meet urgent liquidity need.

The Central Bank issues the T-bills, in the first instance—in multiples of a particular denomination of the domestic currency. For example, the Central Bank of Nigeria issues the T-bills in multiples of N1,000.00 (one thousand naira). Usually, the T-bills are at the primary stage at the point of issue. The primary stage implies a period when the dealers can buy new issues of the T-bills directly from the Central Bank. It denotes one-way transactions flows involving only purchases of the instrument. Once purchased from the Central Bank, the dealers can trade the instrument at the secondary stage. The discount houses facilitate the secondary trading of T-bills. With the discount house facility, the investors are able to buy, or discount (i.e., sell the instrument prior to its maturity date). T-bills also can be easily converted into cash through the discount house facility. The ability of the investors to readily buy, discount, rediscount, or convert their investment into cash imparts unparalleled liquidity to the T-bills everywhere in the financial world. It is for this reason that T-bills are regarded as the most liquid money market security.

Open-Buy-Back

An OBB is a money market deal in which one bank pledges T-bill or other short-dated government security as collateral to secure placement of cash equivalent of the pledged security from another bank with agreement to repurchase the security at any time. Any is the operative word. Usually, the deal is conducted between the money market dealers in the two banks as part of their interbank transactions. I should now give other meanings based on the foregoing explanations. I do so to shed more light on the import of OBB as a money market instrument.

Defining OBB as an arrangement in which banks use T-bills or other discountable securities as pledge to borrow money from each other to meet short-term liquidity needs, you can't go wrong. You can, in the alternative, also be right to define OBB as a money market instrument which banks use to borrow short-term funds, secured with discountable securities, from one another in their interbank trading. You equally won't miss the point following the understanding of OBB as a discountable security, which banks trade among themselves in the money market to raise short term funds to satisfy their immediate liquidity needs.

The domestic currency dealers in the money market tend to be active in the OBB market due, mainly, to its liquidity fulfilling need for them. However, in order to effectively satisfy this need, the dealers must have large amount of OBB-eligible securities in their positions. Otherwise, their banks may be short of T-bills required to meet their statutory liquidity ratio requirements during the OBB tenor.

Repurchase Agreement

It is also common nowadays for banks money market dealers in domestic currencies to fall back on repurchase agreement to ward off liquidity pressures. A repurchase agreement—by the way—is a treasury instrument tenable in the money market. Its main purpose is to help bank treasurers be on top of their liquidity management responsibilities. In this case, emphasis is on effective management of short-term bank liquidity pressure and risk.

A repurchase agreement is, strictly speaking, the sale of marketable securities—or their use—by banks as pledge to borrow money from one another, with agreement to buy back the same securities at a fixed price on a specified future date. It is therefore a security (i.e., a financial asset, or debt instrument—depending on whether a dealer is selling or buying it) which banks trade in the money market to raise short-term funds which, in most cases, they urgently need to satisfy their liquidity needs.

Repurchase agreement operates largely in the same way as an OBB deal. It differs, though, from OBB on one important count. In a repurchase agreement, the time allowed for the pledged security to be bought back is fixed and immutable. This condition is not applicable in OBB transaction. The pledged security—in the case of OBB—rather can be repurchased at any time.

Central Bank's Advances to Banks

The borrowings of the deposit money banks from the Central Bank are conducted through the DWO. The Central Bank, under the DWO arrangement, allows the banks to overdraw their current accounts with it to meet urgent funding needs. This mainly happens in times of liquidity crunch and panic in the money market. The most valued benefit of the DWO, perhaps, is its ability to help the deposit money banks stave off a run on them when they face liquidity crisis.

Credit Products and Facilities

The applicable credit instruments for money market transactions are interbank placements, and the borrowings of the banks from the Central Bank. The short-term credit facilities in the lending portfolios of the banks are equally recognized. Usually, such facilities comprise risk assets that the banks grant for tenors of not more than 12 calendar months.

Commercial Bills and Acceptances

The money market participants in developing economies may sometimes want to make financial commitment on commercial bills—including bills of exchange and acceptances—often, on behalf of their customers. As money market instruments, the bills represent financial obligation of one party to another, both of whom are involved in some transaction. An example is when an importer undertakes to pay a certain sum of money through the banking system to their overseas creditor, usually an exporter of goods to them. The usual tenor for the underlying commercial bill does not exceed 120 days. Securities of this nature certainly are not usually attractive investment outlets for the banks. One reason is that they are nongovernment securities and are usually fraught with risk.

Commercial Papers

The players in money market recognize CP as a risky debt instrument. I should explain the factors underlying the risk in some detail. I do so for one reason. There is a tendency to think that a CP strictly is a risk asset that has nothing to do with the liabilities concerns of the treasury function. Such thinking is erroneous. Let me discuss the insights that shed light on the distinctive features of CPs as money market instrument.

A bank may want to arrange for credit facilities which third parties provide for customers of the bank. This financing arrangement works under particular conditions. There must be a customer—usually a corporate borrower—that is in need of a credit facility which the bank is unable to grant due, perhaps, to portfolio constraint. The customer requests the bank to raise the funds it needs at market rate of interest from third party investors who may be individuals, companies, or organizations. Based on prevailing money market conditions, the bank negotiates the terms of the borrowing with the borrower. Thereafter, and on behalf of the borrower, the bank tries to attract prospective investors that might be interested in providing the money to its customer. The bank fulfills this role with the facility of CP offer.

Strictly speaking, and as is commonly understood among bankers, the bank in foregoing illustration is simply sourcing, not lending, funds to its customer. The bank does not assume any credit risk in this process and financial inter-mediation service. The actual lenders are the third party investors from whom the bank raises the required funds through sale of CP. Doing so, and in market-ing the CP, the bank will be emphasizing the borrower's integrity, cash flow strength, reputation, and creditworthiness, among other risk mitigating fac-tors. Once it has done this, prospective investors make the ultimate decision of whether or not to purchase (i.e., invest in) the CP. The prospective investors solely assume the risk of their investment in the CP—relying, in doing so, on any established goodwill of the borrower. It is expected that as rational human beings and economic units, the prospective investors should make good lending decision. Their purchase of the CP should base on their independent appraisal of the financial strength (especially, the short and long-term liquidity and stability) of the borrower.

Bankers' Acceptances

BA are a popular money market debt instrument in developing economies. Of-ten banks deliberately manipulate their exposures on the BA in order to achieve some target portfolio end for reporting purposes. In reality, the features of BAs lend themselves to such manipulations. It is necessary that lending and treasury officers of banks are thoroughly apprised of the intricacies in marketing and booking this critical money market instrument.

A BA is a financial instrument or bill used in financing short-term trade ob-ligations—or asset-based, self-liquidating, credit transactions. It establishes the liability assumed by a bank that accepts a bill to pay the face value of the bill to a named investor. However, the bank's liability crystallizes only in the event that the issuer of the BA is unable to redeem it on maturity. Thus, a BA is a guarantee by a bank that the drawer of the BA will honor its obligations on it. This implies that the bank commits itself to offset debt on the BA in the event that the drawer fails to do so. Thus, the company that issues a BA and the bank that accepts the BA somewhat share the liabilities on it.

The Central Bank of Nigeria (1997) offers a working definition of a BA. The bank holds that a BA is "a draft drawn on and accepted by a bank, unconditionally ordering payment of a certain sum of money at a specified time in the future to the order of a designated party." In its opinion, "since the instrument is negotiable, title to it is transferred by endorsement." The bank characterizes BA as "a unique instrument in that it is marketable thereby allowing a bank to finance its customers without necessarily utilizing its loanable funds." Doing so, it clarifies source of financing for BA when it notes that "instead, funds are provided by investors who are willing to purchase these obligations on a discounted basis." A bank may choose to invest in the BA—implying that it directly lends money to the drawer, and consequently assumes primary obligation on the instrument. Otherwise, a more conventional approach is for a bank to assume a contingent liability by adding its guarantee, that is, acceptance, to the instrument. The guarantee or acceptance is frequently given effect by the goodwill of the bank, especially in terms of creditworthiness.

Nowadays BA facility is popular among banks. Its appeal is underscored by applications of it in managing the lending portfolio. This is especially the case when a bank wants to shed credits and bring its loan portfolio within its target growth or size. It also informs the attractiveness of BA to banks—especially in terms of its use to dress the balance sheet. However, there is a limit to which banks can play BA and, indeed, off-balance sheet risk assets-based contingent liability without attracting sanctions from the Central Bank. For instance, section 20(1)(a) of Nigeria's Banks and Other Financial Institutions (BOFI) Act 1991, as amended, stipulates that 33.33% of a bank's off-balance sheet BA and guaranteed commercial papers will be applied in determining the bank's statutory lending limit to a single obligor.

Bank Guarantee

There are various reasons for which a bank may want to issue guarantee on behalf of its customer in favor of a third party. Guarantee, in this sense—and for all intents and purposes—is a credit product. It, therefore, embodies some credit risk. How does this make sense?

As a credit product, bank guarantee nowadays constitutes a chunk of the lending portfolio of banks—even as they are treated, in most cases, as an off-balance sheet exposure. Its characteristics, risks, and control as a money market debt instrument are quite challenging to bank treasurers. Besides basic guarantee, the other important forms of guarantee are performance bond, advance payment guarantee (APG), and bid (tender) bond. It should be noted that bank guarantee facilities, like all the other credit products, must always fulfill particular lending criteria.

Bank guarantee could be more or less risky than several other on-balance sheet credit facilities. For this reason, analysis of bank guarantee requests must take cognizance of the usual risk elements encapsulated in the canons, otherwise referred to as the five C's, of lending. In the same vein, identified risks should be mitigated with equal concern for safety of the contingent or implied credit facility. In specific terms, as in every other credit product, bank guarantee should be appropriately secured with a tangible or other form of collateral acceptable to the bank.

FOREIGN CURRENCY INSTRUMENTS OF THE MONEY MARKET

Foreign currency treasury instruments of money markets in developing economies include domiciliary accounts, export proceeds, government FX funds (referred to, in Nigeria, as IFEM—i.e., interbank FX market), and personal FX funds of individuals. There are exotic treasury instruments—referred commonly to as financial derivatives—that also are traded in the money markets. I analyzed the dynamics, risks and control of such treasury instruments in Chapter 24 of this book. Presently, I focus on the more direct treasury FX instruments. The money markets in developing economies also boast two common foreign currency debt instruments. They are foreign currency loans and letters of credit. I now altogether discuss the treasury and debt instruments.

Domiciliary Accounts

Banks open domiciliary account for their customers who earn income or receive funds from transactions in foreign currencies. In most cases, the foreign currency denominated income come from export proceeds and intangible services. A domiciliary account is an account that someone or organization opens, operates, and maintains in foreign currency with a bank in their home country. Thus its foremost feature is that it is usually opened and operated in a foreign currency. Another important feature is that while the account runs on foreign currency deposits and withdrawals, its place of domicile is the country of the account holder. This implies that the country of domicile of the account is different from the country that issues the currency in which the account is denominated. Of course domiciliary account check book differs from that of domestic currency account. The former contains checks denominated in a foreign currency, say dollar, while checks contained in the latter are denominated in the domestic currency, say naira. However, the same rules of operation of accounts apply to both domiciliary and domestic currency accounts.

Export Proceeds

The earnings from the sale of export proceeds are a significant source of FX for the money markets. Mostly, developing countries produce and export primary products. Their export items mainly are agricultural produce or other commodities such as rubber, cashew nuts, cocoa, ginger, palm produce (kernel or oil), and so on. The sale of these commodities overseas remains the primary business of exporters in developing countries. However, export products could be in semiprocessed state or completely manufactured (i.e., finished goods).

Government FX Funds

The government plays a leading role in the funding of the foreign currency segment of the money markets in developing countries. It fulfills this role through the Central Bank which supervises the functioning of the markets. Occasionally, the Central Bank intervenes in the money market. It does so in pragmatic ways to ensure that market forces do not distort the wider perspective of monetary management objectives of the government. In order words, it does not unduly interfere with the market forces, that is, the demand for and supply of short-term funds. Mostly, countries—and, therefore government—earn FX from international trade. Their terms of trade determine the volumes of the FX that accrues to them. It is from such FX earnings that government makes FX available to satisfy domestic demand in the money markets.

Personal FX Funds

Individuals also do have personal foreign currency funds which they—like the banks—trade in the domestic foreign currency markets. However, it is difficult for the authorities to track personal FX funds in developing economies. It is more difficult to regulate the sources and uses of such funds, or to account for their impacts on the economy. In most cases, information about such funds is shrouded in secrecy. For example, its common knowledge that large amounts of personal FX funds nowadays is traceable to money laundering and trafficking in illicit drugs. How can the authorities correctly track and account for such funds? Mostly, such funds are traded in autonomous FX market (I have in this chapter—and, indeed, throughout this book—interchanged "autonomous FX market" with "parallel FX market" and "FX black market." The same goes for "autonomous FX rate." "parallel market rate," and "black market rate." This market functions as a network of illegal dealers in foreign currencies and is proscribed in many countries). Curiously, such FX sometimes surreptitiously finds its ways into the official foreign currency markets. It is indeed ironic—to say the least—that ill-gotten gains would easily infiltrate the official FX market. Thus, while interbank FX dealers are struggling to meet their income targets, traders of free funds are smiling all the way to the bank [The term "free funds" refers to FX traded in the black market as compared with "official funds" that depicts FX traded in the interbank (official) market]).

Foreign Currency Loans

Government and banks sometimes borrow money from international lending agencies and institutions. The major international lenders are the World Bank and its affiliates—especially the International Monetary Fund (IMF) and International Finance Corporation (IFC). There are also regional lending institutions such as African Development Bank (AfDB), Asian Development Bank (ADB), and European Development Bank (EDB). These banks extend credit facilities to government and banks in developing economies on favorable terms. In most cases, the purpose of the loans is to help fund public sector social projects—including development of infrastructures—and to stimulate economic activities in the so-called priority sectors. Banks in developing economies also do obtain loans from their counterparts in developed countries. These foreign currency loans boost transactions in the domestic FX markets.

Letters of Credit

Banks act as a go-between in the flow of international trade. In fulfilling this role, banks inevitably get involved in granting credit facilities to support their customers' transactions. The main functions of the banks, that is, the importer's and exporter's banks—in the conduct of international trade finance are generally expressed in terms of opening, advising, negotiation, and payment of letters of credit (L/C) on behalf of their customers. These roles represent the activities or transactions that create the risks of financial intermediation for the banks.

L/C is a debt instrument which a bank issues on behalf of its customer engaged in international trade for the purpose of facilitating their importation of goods or services from some overseas suppliers. It is an arrangement in which a bank, acting on the instructions of its customer, is to make payment to a third party against certain stipulated financial or commercial documents—or both.

In effect, the bank's role in a letter of credit can be likened to that of a guarantor. It could be inferred, from this meaning, that for the seller to request for a L/C from the buyer before parting with goods, the level of trust between them is low. However, the L/C mitigates the risks not only for the seller but also for the buyer. The sellers, on the one hand, part with the goods only after receiving assurance of payment (i.e., the L/C instrument) from their bankers while the buyers, on the other hand, part with their money only after having evidence that the sellers have dispatched the goods.

The most critical effect of the L/C is the substitution of the credit worthiness of the bank for that of the buyer. It is therefore imperative that the issuing (opening) bank carries out proper analysis of the creditworthiness of the customer before establishment of a L/C. This is to ensure that importers have the capacity to pay for their L/C if and when they are called upon to do so (i.e., in all cases of unconfirmed L/C as discussed later).

Once understood in the foregoing context, the seller of the imported goods or services (i.e., the foreign supplier) is recognized as the beneficiary of the proceeds of the L/C instrument.

DEALING PROCEDURES, TERMS, AND RISK MANAGEMENT

As in foreign currency markets, interbank dealing in domestic currency follows strict rules of procedure that are binding on the dealers. The rules, in general, are intended to protect the dealers and their banks against risk. Certain factors—including market volatility, frauds infiltration of the market, and so on—create some of the risks the dealers face in money market. It is imperative that interbank dealers apprise themselves of the significant procedures and their related rules that that I now discuss.

Accreditation of Dealers

The regulatory authorities authorize dealers who may trade in interbank domestic currency market. Usually, deposit money banks are the authorized dealers. The banks, in turn, designate particular officers as their dealers in the market. Ideally, dealers who are not professionally qualified should not be allowed to trade. The purpose of these rules is to help mitigate the risk of fraud. Often unprofessional conduct reflects in cashing in on possible trading flaws or loopholes. It also reduces chances of swindles in the market.

Standard Dealing Hours

Trading in money market should always be conducted during official trading hours. In most countries, trading hours approximate to the normal working hours. In some countries, trading holds between 8.00 a.m. and 4.00 p.m., Monday to Friday. This implies that dealers must give all required notice not later than 4.00 p.m. For example, call deposits notice should be given before dealing closes at 4.00 p.m.

Dealing Procedure

Interbank dealing commences with a dealer in one bank calling their counterpart in another bank. The calling bank (i.e., its dealer) states the reasons for the call. In most cases, the main purpose of call is to get interest rates quotes for a certain amount of placement or taking. The quoting bank obliges. In order to strike a deal, the calling and quoting banks must agree on specific terms. The usual interbank trading terms reflect agreement on nature of transaction, amount involved, applicable interest rate, tenor, value date, and mode of settlement.

Mode of Communication

The banks should adopt an effective means of communication for trading in money markets. The typical—as well as popular—mode of communication in money market deals is telephone. There are other effective means of communication that also are in common use in developing countries. Examples include the use of telex, facsimile, or writing. The Internet revolution equally has given communication in interbank trading a big boost with the advent of e-mail. Most likely, advancing technologies in the fields of information and communications would produce new and innovative modes of communication in the future. Banks should anticipate the likely changes.

Currency for Trading

Domestic currency dominates interbank trading in money markets across developing economies. This makes sense. As would be expected under the circumstances, all such interbank transactions are necessarily denominated in domestic currency.

Amounts Traded

Unlike in foreign currency trading, there are no required standard dealing amounts in interbank domestic currency market. The absence of minimum or maximum dealing amounts imparts volume and rates flexibility to the market. It also fits well with the dealers' risk mitigation goal. However, business sense dictates that a transaction should meet commercial and quantity criteria in order to attract or merit dealing.

Tenor of Transactions

Most money market transactions have tenors. However, some don't. Call transactions, for example, don't have fixed maturity date due to their nature. Overnight transactions present a similar case. They are not amenable to tenor fixing. Such transactions automatically mature and are terminated the next working day. The usual durations for tenored transactions are 30, 60, or 90 days. The dealers choose tenors based on their mutual agreement.

Deals Confirmation Process

The confirmation of deal follows the same process in foreign and domestic currency trading. A deal must be struck in the first place. In domestic currency trading, a deal is struck when the calling bank confirms placing or taking funds with or from the quoting bank at the quoted interest rate. Then the dealers should, as soon as the deal was struck, document and exchange relevant deal contracts details. This is done as evidence of the delivery instructions to the interbank dealing clearing institution. In Nigeria, for example, Nigeria Interbank Settlement System (NIBSS) performs this clearing function. Letters of confirmation and related documents must be error-free and devoid of discrepancies.

Delivery of Instruments

The instruments traded in money markets should be delivered in a timely manner. The standard practice is to deliver instruments traded within seven working days from value date. However, dealers may agree different timeline for delivery of traded instruments. This should be done at their discretion, but with mutual agreement. It may be necessary in some situations for the dealers to enter into a custodial (i.e., a safekeeping) agreement in lieu of instrument delivery. Such agreement is acceptable for money market trading purposes. The usual critical requirement is endorsement by the authorized signatories of the bank.

Settlement of Deal and Risk

The probability of nonsettlement in interbank domestic currency trading is hardly significant. However, chances of late or delayed settlement could be quite high. The dealers must mitigate this risk—one way or the other. One of the proven ways to mitigate the risk is the adoption of the approach to settlement through some interbank dealing funds transfer service. NIBSS offers this service. Through NIBSS transfers, the banks easily settle interbank obligations to one another. The dealers, though, reserve the right to agree on other specified settlement arrangement. However, timeliness is always of the essence. Documents evidencing settlement of deal must be dispatched and available to the dealing parties as soon as possible. Banks may stipulate their tolerance limits for settlement risk which their counterparties must observe.

Notice of Termination of Transaction

Certain rules guide notifications of the intentions of the dealers to terminate particular transactions in money markets. First, a dealer wishing to give notice of termination must do so before the close of work on the due date of the transaction to be terminated. The exact time depends on applicable working hours in a country. The official hours of work in Nigeria, for example, are 8.00 a.m. to 4.00 p.m. In this case, dealers must give notice of termination not later than 4.00 p.m. on the due date of the transaction.

Usually, notice is required for the termination of strict call, 7 days call, and tenored transactions. One day notice is required for strict call. In the case of 7 days call, 7 day notice is required. However, transactions with fixed tenors don't necessarily require notice of termination. The reason is that such transactions automatically terminate on maturity or due dates—except, of course, if they are rolled-over. However, dealers may mutually agree on other notice period.

There may be an instance where a bank reviews rates. Such rates review—in the absence of formal agreement on rates—is tantamount to automatic notice of termination of transactions with counterparties affected by the review. The same or different means of notification of termination may be used for all transactions. It suffices to use any of the acceptable means of communications in money market—telephone, telex, facsimile, writing, or e-mail.

Termination of Transaction

Money market transactions should always be formally terminated at the end of its cycle. The termination itself equally should follow some due process. In money market circles, termination of transaction marks the formal end of a deal. In most cases, maturity and repayment dates are the same. However, there is a subtle difference when it comes to tenored transactions. Maturity date for a tenored transaction is its tenor, inclusive of its value date. In other words, tenor counts from—and is inclusive of—the value date. To yet put it simply, tenor plus value date equals maturity date. In the case of call deals, transactions terminate at the end of the required notice periods.

Rollover of Transactions

Often the term "rollover" is used interchangeably with "renewal" in money market dealing. It refers to the act or process of making the tenor of a transaction, as well as its other terms and conditions, to continue when the initial period of its use expires. Formal in-house approval of rollover is necessary to give it effect. The formalization of transactions in rollover letters shows that the funds taking bank also equally approves of the rollover.

Often the dealer on the asset side of a deal, that is, the funds placing bank—decides whether or not to rollover. The counterparty on the liability side of the deal, that is, the funds taking bank—may ask for rollover. However, it is up to the owner of the instrument traded—the funds placing bank. In other words, the owner of the asset (i.e., treasury instrument) traded exercises the rollover option and initiative.

A major feature of rollover is that it usually entails renegotiation of the terms and conditions of the transaction when its tenor expires. It is important for the dealers to clearly understand and mutually agree the new terms that may result from the renegotiation of the matured or maturing transaction. This is essential to avoid unnecessary disputes or misunderstandings.

It is also important to agree on the mode of payment of interest that accrued on the matured transaction in the event of rollover. Ideally, such interest should be paid on the new value date of the rolled over transaction. This means that interest on the old transaction must be paid at the point when it's the tenor of rollover starts. It should also be borne in mind that transactions may attract rollover fee.

Disputes and Misunderstandings

It is unlikely that there would be no settlement issues and defaults in money market transactions. The dealers are bound to experience these largely traditional problems in business. However, the banks should always seek and workout amicable solutions.

One of the pragmatic ways devised by banks to get around the problems is the referral of disputes to an arbitration panel. This has proven effective in some potentially default crisis situations. However, banks should explore other equally friendly ways of resolving interbank money market disputes and misunderstandings.

SUMMARY

The money market is personified by the structures that facilitate dealing in short-term, fixed-income funds, securities, and similar financial instruments. It represents the network of dealers in these financial instruments, and the regulation of dealing conduct with regard to how, where, and when they consummate deals. The main distinguishing features of the instruments traded in the money market are short tenor and fixed interest rate. Short tenor, in this context, does not exceed 12 calendar months at the most. Some other instruments also may be traded in the money market, but this is not common in developing economies.

There are several active participants in money markets. The first group, comprising the financial system regulatory authorities, is always a major player in the market. The relevant regulatory bodies are those that have oversight of banking, deposit insurance, securities and exchanges, and stock exchanges. The next important set of players is the authorized dealers, that is, the banks. There also are several other participants in the money market—besides the nonbank financial institutions—including importers, exporters, speculators, borrowers in domestic currency, and depositors in domestic currency. There are, of course, sundry other participants.

There are equally many instruments at the disposal of the players to conduct their transactions. The common instruments in developing economies fall into two broad domestic currency categories—direct and indirect. The direct instruments are of two main types—treasury and debt instruments. Treasury instruments consist of all bank deposit accounts and related products—including savings, fixed deposits, call deposits, and current (i.e., demand deposit) accounts. Cash and short-term funds—including interbank placements, cash withdrawals, cash lodgements, clearing checks, funds transfers, and traveler's checks also are direct treasury instruments that feature in the domestic currency market. Sometimes interbank trading culminates in OBB and repurchase agreement deals.

The debt instruments can be grouped into two main categories for ease of analysis. The first category comprises instruments commonly referred to as marketable securities. It includes T-bills, treasury deposits, and negotiable certificates of deposit. Credit products and facilities in forms of interbank takings, and Central Bank's advances to the money deposit banks constitute the second category.

Two main categories of securities constitute the indirect instruments of the money market. The first category comprises treasury instruments while the second is made up of debt instruments. The treasury instruments include commercial bills, CP, BA, and promissory notes. These instruments are in common use in developing economies. They can be equally regarded as irregular or quasi-credit products and facilities that employees in bank lending and treasury units jointly market to the public. The overly indirect debt instrument of the money market is bank guarantee.

Foreign currency treasury products in developing economies include domiciliary accounts, export proceeds, government FX funds (referred to, in Nigeria, as IFEM—i.e., interbank FX market), and personal FX funds of individuals. There are exotic treasury instruments—referred commonly to as financial derivatives—that also are traded in money markets. The money markets in developing economies boast three common foreign currency debt instruments. They are bearer bonds, foreign currency loans, and L/C.

As in foreign currency markets, interbank dealing in domestic currency follows strict rules of procedure that are binding on the dealers. The rules, in general, are intended to protect the dealers and their banks against risk. Certain factors—including market volatility, frauds infiltration of the market, and so on—create some of the risks the dealers face in money market.

The concept and dynamics of pricing as a competitive tool in banking are challenging—really intriguing. There are several factors that banks factor into their pricing strategies. Most banks take cognizance of the cost of funds, risk, tenor, competition, yield, administrative costs, and value of the relationship.

The factors that determine interest rates in banking are subsumed under a whole gamut of variable elements and influences—including market forces, cost structure, regulatory influences, competition, and risk profile. There are also questions of transaction amount, purpose, tenor, and yield, as well as the nature and value of banking relationship.

QUESTIONS FOR DISCUSSION AND REVIEW

1. Why, in your opinion, must the dealers in interbank domestic currency be well-versed in the instruments of the money markets?
2. What features of money markets make instruments traded in them attractive to the interbank dealers in developing economies?
3. How would you characterize money markets in developing economies to highlight inbuilt risks and controls in deals?
4. In what distinctive ways does OBB contrast with repurchase agreement as money market deals?
5. How do the risks of CP compare with those of BA as money market treasury instruments?
6. What is a L/C? How should banks in developing economies mitigate risks in L/C transactions?

REFERENCE

Central Bank of Nigeria, 1997. Policy circular BSD/PA/4/97—Prudential guidelines for licensed banks. in Nigeria Deposit Insurance Corporation. (1997). Review of developments in banking and finance during the second half of 1997. NDIC Quart. 7 (3/4).

Chapter 26

Capital Market Dynamics, Securities, and Bank Risk in Developing Economies

Chapter Outline

LEARNING FOCUS AND OBJECTIVES

Capital markets play crucial social change roles in developing economies. It directs the flow of funds and investments to strategic long-term economic needs of individuals, organizations, and society. The process of capital markets transactions is well ordered to ensure efficient mobilization and utilization of resources, usually for long-term investment purposes. With the foregoing in mind, I set out writing this chapter in order—among other objectives—to:

- define and examine the significance of capital markets, with implications for developing economies;
- characterize capital markets in developing economies;
- identify, discuss, and assess the roles of the major players and participants in the capital markets;
- analyze the workings of Securities and Exchange Commission (SEC) as capital markets apex regulatory institution;
- evaluate Stock Exchange as investor watch dog and the hub of transactions in capital markets securities;
- explain the investment implications of domestic currency instruments of capital markets in developing economies;
- pinpoint the dynamic of risks in foreign currency instruments of capital market in developing economies;
- review the occasional boom to bust mechanisms of capital market risks in developing economies; and
- explore ways in which the authorities manage risks in the occasional boom to bust tide of the stock market.

EXPECTED LEARNING OUTCOMES

Capital markets exist mainly to help satisfy long-term investment and funding needs of individuals, organizations, and society. The participants in capital markets seek either long-term investment opportunities or access to noninterest based funds for long-term utilization. The reader will—after studying this chapter and doing the exercises in it—have learnt and been better informed about:

- meaning, significance, and implications of capital markets as structure for funds mobilization for long-term investments;
- characteristics of capital markets in developing economies;
- roles and responsibilities of the major players and participants in capital markets;
- workings of SEC as capital markets apex regulatory institution;
- Stock Exchanges as investor watch dog and the hub of transactions and investments through capital markets securities;
- risk and investment implications of domestic currency instruments traded in capital markets in developing economies;
- central dynamic of risks in foreign currency instruments of capital market in developing economies;
- issues in the occasional boom to bust mechanisms of capital market risks in developing economies; and
- ways in which the financial system regulatory authorities manage risks in boom to bust tide of the stock market.

OVERVIEW OF THE SUBJECT MATTER

The significance of capital markets is informed by the goal of satisfying long-term investment and funding or borrowing needs of individuals and organizations. Mostly, participation in the capital market is driven by two opposing needs. It could be that the participants need an outlet for long-term investment of their idle funds. Their need also may be to have an opportunity to borrow noninterest based funds for long-term utilization. Often long-term funds are needed for business expansion, capital project, or even for product research and development. Capital market provides a platform for the operators to actualize these needs.

The mobilization of idle funds at the disposal of the potential investors and channeling the funds to satisfy the funding needs of the potential borrowers always is a significant role of the dealers in the capital market. Usually, the nature of the funds so mobilized and channeled is typical of the main characteristic feature of the capital market. In principle—though also mostly true in practice—the money that finds its way into the capital market must satisfy particular criteria. First, it must be large in volume. Second, it must mainly be available as equity or other forms of capital. Third, it should meet some medium to long-term funding needs. These criteria must fit well with the beneficial needs of the investors (i.e., the lenders of long-term funds to the market) and borrowers (i.e., the users of the long-term funds).

The usual beneficiaries of the funds sourced from the capital market—and often on the Stock Exchange—are the corporate and institutional borrowers. The government also is a major borrowing participant in the market. Occasionally, it issues bonds (i.e., debt instruments) to borrow money from the public on the Stock Exchange. This category of users dominates the debtors (i.e., government and corporate bodies whose debt securities are traded) on the Stock Exchange at any one time. The other type of beneficiaries is the investors that pursue profit and capital gains by providing the capital market with long-term funds on some investment and expected returns terms.

The common method of characterizing the capital market focuses on the types and nature of long-term investment and funding needs of the operators. In developing economies, capital markets boast three such needs through its primary, secondary, and bonds market segments.

DEFINING AND APPRECIATING THE SIGNIFICANCE OF CAPITAL MARKETS

The capital market is a specialized financial market for raising and investing funds—usually for the long-term. It is therefore one of the major categories of financial markets. I posit three different but somewhat related formal definitions of the capital market and show how the meanings shed light on its significance in financial economics. I should give the first definition from the perspective of sourcing equity and other funds for business or other purpose, often in the public sector—especially, to fulfill some financing need for the government.

Capital market, in foregoing context, is an arrangement to offer for subscription, list, trade, and invest in ordinary stocks and bonds to raise equity, or to borrow long-term funds for business, social projects, and so on from the public. This definition mirrors the primary segment of the capital market when the shares of a start-up or formerly private company are formally listed on the Stock Exchange. The investors that subscribe to the shares on offer become shareholders (i.e., part owners) of the company that offers its shares to the public for subscription. The shares of such a company now become quoted (i.e., listed) on the Stock Exchange. The company itself assumes the status of a public limited liability company.

The second definition that follows adopts the perspective of trading in securities that typically characterizes the capital market. I define capital market, to that end, as the arrangement for issuing, listing, trading, and investing in stocks and other long-term securities on the Stock Exchange. Once the shares of a company have been listed on the Stock Exchange, investors now can buy and sell the shares through their stockbrokers. This epitomizes the secondary segment of the capital market when listed stocks can freely be traded on the Stock Exchange by the stockbrokers. The investors (i.e., the buyers of the quoted stocks) at this stage aim to make money on the Stock Exchange from either the profits on sale of their shares or capital appreciation on the shares over time. Often speculation fuels the pursuit of capital appreciation.

I focus the third definition on the legal and transactions perspectives of the capital market. From this angle, I define capital market as the organized interactions between the traders (i.e., the stockbrokers) and investors (i.e., the buyers of the listed stocks) in long-term securities and the regulations of how, where, and when the operators conduct and close a deal or sale. This definition is underlain by the legal backing for the capital market activities. The phrases "organized interactions" and "the regulation" strengthen this perspective. These are the main activities on the Stock Exchange where most of the capital market trading and transactions take place.

The significance of the capital market derives from the elements of the three interrelated definitions and perspectives. Let me a bit emphasize the trading and transactions aspects of the significance of the capital market activities. The capital market—first and foremost—offers facility that is propitious for the activities in which the dealers regularly engage, especially the buying and selling of long-term securities. Then it enables the free flow of securities, transactions, and deals. This role underscores the import of the activities, such as buying and selling of long-term securities in which the dealers in the capital market engage.

CHARACTERIZING CAPITAL MARKETS
IN DEVELOPING ECONOMIES

The characteristics of capital markets in developing economies comprise a broad base of financial objectives, roles, and elements. Most of these factors revolve around the regulation, workings, and transactions of the markets. I presented a cursory overview of these characteristics in the opening subject matter of this chapter. I now go ahead to discuss them in some detail. The approach I adopt is to look at capital market from the perspectives of its main arms—primary and secondary markets. I equally examine the dynamics and features of bonds market.

Primary Market

Some of the capital market participants—especially, the corporate bodies—may want to be floated on the stock market. They will, to this end, need the services of an issuing house that handles the processes of the flotation. The need for flotation and how it is addressed and satisfied establishes the first characteristic of capital market. This feature is implied in the first definition of the capital market that I gave in the preceding section. Its main import is that capital market enables companies to float their shares on the stock market. What do I mean? Shares are floated when they are listed on the stock market and being sold to the public for the first time.

The primary segment of the capital market fulfills this role for the companies that may need it. It facilitates trading in new issues (i.e., shares of companies listed on the stock market for sale to the public for the first time). The stock market regulatory authorities require the companies that need this service to fulfill certain prelisting conditions for the shares. The companies must satisfy the conditions before the shares can be traded on the stock market. Interestingly, a company cannot directly and by itself market and sell its new issue on the stock market. It must engage an issuing house to handle the technical aspects of the new issue transaction.

One of the duties of the issuing house—in addition to participation in marketing and selling the new issue—is to recommend a realistic price for the new issue to the SEC. The SEC may approve, query, adjust, or decline approval of the recommended price—it is statutory responsibility to do so. In doing this, it observes some technical rules. There are other specialized market operators—mainly the stockbrokers, banks, and nonbank financial institutions—that handle the marketing and selling aspects of the new issue.

Secondary Market

The secondary trading of quoted shares easily is the most popular segment of the capital market in developing economies. I had in the preceding section implied the import of this market segment in the second definition of the capital market. I now elaborate upon that definition. The secondary capital market offers facility—a legally enforceable arrangement—for trading in listed stocks (i.e., shares of the companies quoted or floated on the capital market). The institution and operations of the Stock Exchange personify that legal arrangement.

It is the platform which the Stock Exchange provides that makes it possible for listed shares to be freely traded. The investors now can easily buy and sell the shares in which they are interested. They do so relying on the services of the stockbrokers. In this context, the stockbrokers mainly play an intermediary role. The stockbrokers take instructions and secure funds from their clients (i.e., the potential investors that may be individuals, companies, or organizations) in the first place. Then they act on the instructions of the clients by acquiring, on their behalf, particular stocks in their demand schedules. This is accomplished when the stockbrokers successfully invest the funds they mobilize from their clients in the stocks that match their instructions. The stockbrokers earn brokerage for their service.

However, stockbrokers also sometimes trade directly—for and on behalf of themselves—on the Stock Exchange. They buy and sell shares as part of their regular business. In doing so, their objectives—just as their clients—are to either make profit or gain from capital appreciation in future when they expect the prices of the stocks to appreciate. However, the main risk of stock trading is rooted in this approach to the business. It is fraught with risks bordering, in the main, on speculation. As you will find later in this chapter, the occasional fall back of the stockbrokers on margin borrowing to fund their transactions exacerbates the risks.

The other major participants in the secondary market—in addition to the Stock Exchange and brokers—are the investors (i.e., the buyers and sellers of shares). The investors could be individuals, companies, or organizations. Their investment objectives may vary dependent on the states of the stock market, the economy, and their long-term financial plans. However, the immediate and common objective of the investors is a desire to acquire some interests in the companies they buy their shares. They may want to invest, for example, in equity stocks. In that case, they would be interested in becoming part owners of some companies. Investments in preference or debenture stocks do not confer such ownership interests on the investors.

Bonds Market

The bonds market is increasingly becoming popular in developing economies due to the emerging trend of deficit financing of most government nowadays. Some large institutions and corporations also sometimes go the bonds market to raise long-term funds on relatively favorable and predictable terms. A bond itself is a redeemable debt instrument of the capital market which government or institution issues on the Stock Exchange to borrow money from the public.

Some may find it strange that government borrows through the capital market. The question that springs to mind is why some governments in developing countries nowadays tend to depend on heavy borrowing.to fund social projects? Like individuals, corporate organizations, or other economic units, government may borrow funds, locally or abroad, to bridge a temporary gap in its cash flow stream. In the context of developing economies, the urge to sustain investment at the desired level in the face of dwindling domestic savings compels most of the government to resort to deficit financing. In general, this happens when there is deficiency in domestic savings or a decline in the savings ratio. Often this situation is preceded by a long period of profligate spending on consumption imports to the detriment of domestic investment.

In a well-managed economy, a reasonable quantum of domestic savings finances the acquisition of additional capital stock to enhance the overall performance of the productive economic units. The need for borrowing is then indicated where foreign savings, which should augment domestic savings in meeting the desired stock of domestic capital, have been low or even negative. However, this is not usually the salient issue in every analysis of the debt problem. The often analyzed issues have always been the appropriateness of the borrowing cause and the efficiency of funds utilization.

Efficiency, in foregoing sense, is measured by the rate of actual as against anticipated return on the investments financed with borrowed resources. Not infrequently the countries experiencing severe debt crisis were found to have applied borrowings to financing overly unproductive social activities and projects. The observed tendency is that a country would be plunged into debt crisis if the borrowing cause is poorly defined, the borrowing itself is mismanaged, or when there are unexpected adverse changes in its external accounts. Rarely do developing countries appropriately define the borrowing cause, as for example, in terms of persistent disequilibrium they may be experiencing in their balance of payments position.

Distinguishing Features of Bonds

Bonds significantly differ from other types of capital market instruments. Usually, bonds have fixed terms that define their validity periods. Though, some exotic bonds—such as perpetual or undated bonds—don't satisfy this criterion. In general, interest-paying bonds are issued at fixed interest rates. The interest rate—sometimes referred to as the coupon—is determined at the time of the issue of the bond.

The borrower (i.e., the government or institution that issues a bond) regularly pays the coupon on the bond to the investors (i.e., the bond holders). Semiannual and annual modes of payment of coupon are common. The regular coupon payment is sustained throughout the tenor of the bond. At the maturity date of the bond, the borrower simply repays the principle.

There also could be noninterest paying bonds. Such bonds are issued straight. The bonds in this category are referred to as zero coupon bonds. This has income implication for the investors. The issuer of the bond pays a fraction of the value of the bond to the investors upfront in lieu of interest.

As negotiable debt instruments, bonds can be redeemed either at or prior to their maturity dates. The redemption of a bond can be at par or at a premium. The par represents the bond's face value, say ₦1.00. With a premium, a bond is redeemed at a value higher than its face value, say ₦1.10—10 kobo being the premium.

MAJOR PLAYERS AND PARTICIPANTS IN CAPITAL MARKETS IN DEVELOPING ECONOMIES

The leading capital markets participants in developing economies usually are the financial institutions, most of which are highly specialized in securities dealings. The regular, as well as major, players are SEC, Stock Exchanges, stockbrokers, issuing houses, money deposit banks, large investors, securities issuers, finance professionals, and accountants. Some of the participants are major players while others, the marginal players, participate more or less dependent on their interests. Together with their regulatory bodies, they constitute the operators of the capital markets in a country. Their roles altogether consist in the regulation, trading, and supervision of dealings in securities.

In most cases, banks and some nonbank financial institutions participate in the capital market as major or marginal players dependent on their objectives. The investment banks and other banks that have strong investment and asset management arms always are major players in the capital market. In Nigeria, for example, the investment arm of Stanbic IBTC Bank is one of the market makers on the Nigerian Stock Exchange. The main cause of the interest of the banks and nonbank financial institutions simply is to make money. Of course, in doing so, they satisfy the investment and asset management needs of their customers. The incomes from the capital market enhance their overall operating results. It largely is for this reason that they specialize in the trading and issuing house functions. Thus they maintain a strong presence in these segments of the market, with focus on the regular capital funds (i.e., equities and preference shares), loan capital (such as debenture stocks), and bonds (mostly, issues from government and large corporations). However, they maintain only occasional presence in the derivatives market. This is due, mainly, to the exotic nature and risks of financial derivatives in developing economies.

The main regulatory body of the capital market is the SEC. The Stock Exchange organizes and supervises the stock markets for the purpose of trading in the securities. The two bodies—SEC and Stock Exchange—play specific complementary roles in the capital market.

SEC, MARKET REGULATION, AND RISK MANAGEMENT

The SEC performs five important roles in its capacity as the regulatory body for the capital markets. In general, though, the SEC functions in a way that ensures continuous free flow of long-term funds for private and portfolio investments in a country. In developing countries, the flow of the funds is as critical as the need to retain the funds for purposes of long-term investments, projects, and the building, expansion, and development of public infrastructures.

The main functions of the SEC revolve around foregoing macroeconomic objectives. The primary responsibility of the SEC is to ensure effective regulation and supervision of the capital markets. In doing so, it prescribes and enforces the rules of the capital markets. Such rules define the financial transactions, modes of dealings in securities, and conduct expected of the operators in the capital markets.

The pricing of the stocks and other debt instruments to be floated on the Stock Exchange is almost always a most challenging responsibility of the SEC in many countries. It tasks the ability of the SEC to really stay on top of things. How the SEC will be able to forestall possible financial maneuverings and manipulation of data pertinent to correct pricing of the new issues easily become the salient points. The SEC, though, collaborates with the issuing houses in fixing the prices of the new issues.

Often the pricing of securities floated on the stock market may—and sometimes do—have implications for their trading, success or failure. It is imperative, therefore, that the stocks and other debt instruments are priced correctly. Appropriate pricing tends to be achieved when the information the issuers furnish about their intended debt instruments has depth. In most cases, the issuing houses recommend the prices for the new issues to the SEC for approval. The issuing houses make the pricing recommendations in strict observance of some regulatory criteria.

The SEC also regulates the timing of new issues on the capital market. The effective management of the timing of new issues is necessary in order to not crowd out the risk aver investors, or the small and marginal issuers. Ideally, the market always should be allowed time and space to react to new issues. Similarly, the timing of new issues should take the capacity of the market into cognizance. The question that should guide decision is can the market absorb additional securities at this time? The SEC should answer this question realistically in order to make a good decision.

In exercising its oversight of the capital markets, the SEC takes charge of the registration of Stock Exchanges. It sets the criteria which the new Stock Exchanges must fulfill before the SEC formally registers them. Thereafter they can commence operation. They yet face a new hurdle. They must observe some criteria set by the SEC for their operation and retention as the platform for the trading of the quoted securities. These are some of the important ways in which the SEC exercises its oversight of the Stock Exchanges in developing economies.

The function of the SEC as an investor watchdog is, perhaps, the most difficult to fulfill. The SEC strives, in view of this, constantly to protect the investors in the capital markets. It shields the investors against possible maneuverings by the operators of the markets. The interest of the investors is protected more or less dependent on how the prices of new issues are fixed, the manner in which funds are sourced for and invested in securities, and the amounts of money that may be appropriated from investor accounts as fees for the services to them.

The greatest challenge of investor protection in the capital markets tends to be the ability to devise realistic measures to curb the excesses of the operators. How to stabilize the capital markets is a no less difficult challenge for the SEC in developing economies. It is especially essential that capital market stability is attained and sustained in the interest of the investors and economic development of the countries. Market instability fuels speculation which does not augur well for business, investments, and the economy.

The stabilization and development of the capital markets are somewhat interrelated roles of the SEC. When the capital market is developing or developed and stable, it will be able to attract funds from private and portfolio investors. This is a critical indicator of the confidence which the investors have in the government and economy. The SEC and governments in developing economies should, for this reason, do anything but allow the capital markets to falter. Stabilization and development of the capital market should be pursued as a deliberate economic management strategy, if anything.

STOCK EXCHANGE—INVESTOR WATCH DOG AND HUB OF TRANSACTIONS IN SECURITIES

The Stock Exchange and SEC have different but complementary roles in the capital market. The everyday role of the Stock Exchange is of critical importance to the economy and financial system. The Stock Exchange provides and disseminates information about a country and its economy. In this context, it furnishes data which economic and financial analysts, political decision-makers, business executives and, indeed, the public need. The need for such data is to enable them evaluate the country's economic management and performance—as well as the business trend. The stock market's all-share index—which the Stock Exchange daily publishes—is typical. The index sheds light on the direction of economic activities in a country. It highlights the major economic indicators that inform most financial, investment, and banking decision-making, especially in developing economies.

As a leading institution of the capital market, the Stock Exchange plays vital roles in fulfilling the external financing needs of businesses around the world. The promoters of small companies can seek quotation on the Stock Exchange— often under the second-tier securities scheme for the SME businesses—just as the larger companies. Investors, on their part, patronize the Stock Exchange for shares of quoted companies. Doing so, they expect incomes from profits they make on the shares they buy and sell and capital gains on the shares they hold for sale in future on speculation of price appreciation. Investors that painstakingly follow and understand stock market trends make handsome earnings from the two investment strategies. Unfortunately foregoing benefits are fully realized mostly in economies with highly developed capital markets. Businesses and investors in developing economies make do with very basic and inefficient capital markets.

The stockbrokers act as intermediaries between the buyers and sellers of securities on the Stock Exchange. This intermediary role is propitious for capital flows in the economy. The stock market makes this critical input into the quest for building and sustaining capital stock for economic development. It does this by providing the forum, facility, and guides to trade in securities. It becomes operationally possible for the stockbrokers to play their capital intermediary roles with less or no constraints. Intermediary role in the capital market is the process of mobilizing long-term funds from the public—including companies and organizations—and investing the funds in securities traded on the Stock Exchange. Ultimately, the issuers and sellers of the securities get the funds.

The Stock Exchange primarily monitors and supervises the processes of trading in quoted securities. It ensures—in the pursuit of this objective—that trading (i.e., the buying and selling of listed debt instruments) in securities is conducted on a level playing field. This implies ensuring fair competition between the marginal and larger market operators. The need for this role is seen in chances that some operators may want to leverage some loophole in securities trading rules to exploit the investors.

It also is within the purview of the Stock Exchange to formulate, regularly review, and strictly enforce a set and criteria of requirements for the quotation (i.e., listing) of new securities on the stock market. Once it determines the listing requirements, the players (i.e., capital market operators) become legally bound to comply with them. There are three common types of quotation on the stock exchange in developing economies. The listing of the shares of a company on the Stock Exchange could be done through introduction, initial public offering, or rights issue.

The quotation by introduction is not common, though. It involves fulfilling registration formalities, paying the necessary fees, and being officially listed on the Stock Exchange. The main requirements are carrying on a particular business as a private going concern, currently having—in the case of Nigeria—at least 50 shareholders, and a resolution of the directors and shareholders to convert the business into a public limited liability company. The process does not admit of sale of the new shares of the listed company at this stage. The main cause of quotation is that a company already has several shareholders by which it can now transmute from into a public company.

It is, perhaps, in the request for the initial public offering (IPO) of the shares of a company on the Stock Exchange that most of the technical rules of the capital market play themselves out. It would seem that the stock market solves the risk-capital raising problems of the promoters of businesses. Yet it always doesn't. One reason is that quotation entails fulfilling rigorous formalities in applying for and marketing the IPO of the shares. An existing company, with a proven track record, is more likely to succeed with IPO issue than a start-up, though. Another reason is that legal, documentation, and other costs associated with IPO could be substantial and discouraging. Dearth of funds to bankroll the IPO easily becomes a decisive factor. A third reason borders on difficulty which start-ups experience in fulfilling stringent SEC pricing and other rules.

The Stock Exchange promotes the capital market, its activities, and trading of its securities. It fulfills this promotional role mainly at the level of the creation of awareness. It furnishes the issuers of securities and investors in them with information pertinent to make informed dealing decisions. The awareness so created helps boost investor confidence and volumes of the capital market transactions.

CASE STUDY 26.1 Infringing Capital Market Regulation

In keeping with its program of privatization of public enterprises and utilities, Nigerian Government decided in early 2000s to divest its investment in a certain energy sector company in which it held majority equity shares. The privatizing office appointed Wood Bank as the Registrar for the privatization of the company. As the Registrar, the proceeds of the company's privatization were domiciled with Wood Bank pending allotment of the related shares to the members of the public that subscribed to the public offer of the shares. At the end of the exercise, the offer was oversubscribed. This necessitated rationing of the shares among the subscribers and return of monies corresponding to the unsuccessful subscriptions. Wood Bank remitted funds to the privatizing office for all the shares allotted to the subscribers, but held back return monies for the subscribers that got part, or did not get, share allotments. In doing so, Wood Bank had intended to temporarily use the return monies to cushion liquidity pressure it was experiencing at the time, as well as meet other operational financial needs. It had reasoned that the process of returning money to unsuccessful subscribers in such public offer often lingered for several weeks or, in some cases, months. This is because the arrangement for sending return monies involves:

- printing of payment warrants for each of the beneficiaries;
- sending the warrants to their beneficiaries through the postal system;
- receipt and presentation of the warrants by the beneficiaries to their banks for payment; and
- presentation of the warrants by the beneficiaries' banks to Wood Bank for payment through the clearing house.

During the envisaged delay, the bank thought it would have sorted out its liquidity pressure and satisfied other short-term operational financial needs. Thus, it used a chunk of the return monies to fund disbursement of outstanding loan commitments. However, no sooner had the bank utilized the funds than the privatizing office made a demand for an immediate release of the return monies directly to their beneficiaries. The bank objected to this directive, contending that it contravened the Check Payment Act and aforesaid procedure for sending return monies to their beneficiaries. Besides, the bank pointed out that it would be difficult for it to ascertain the true identities of the beneficiaries of the return monies since the only information about them at its disposal were names and postal addresses.

The opinion of the privatizing office on the matter emboldened the agents of the owners of more than 95% of the return monies, who had subscribed for the shares using surrogate names. Thus, notwithstanding the contentions of Wood Bank, they insisted on direct payment of the related return monies to them on behalf of their principle. The bank refused to oblige the request and maintained its position. This upset the privatizing office, which gave the bank an ultimatum to pay the money within 4 days or face severe punishment. The privatizing office followed its ultimatum with formal reporting of the case to the regulatory authority for appropriate sanction. As the problem lingered, the press fed on the news it made to the members of the banking publics, which created adverse publicity for the bank. It started experiencing unusual customers' demand for deposits withdrawal. Most of the bank's depositors thought that the bank was unable to pay the return monies because it was broke. Perhaps, their suspicion was correct. In the heat of the problem, the bank had tried but to no avail to obtain funds to meet the return monies obligation. It realized that even though it might have made a good case to the authorities, its decision to book more loans with the return monies was erroneous. It would have been possible for it to pay the return monies had the funds been rather invested in money market instruments, which are less risky than loans.

Meanwhile, the regulatory authority investigated the complaint of the privatizing office. On the basis of its findings, it suspended the bank's capital market operating license for 6 months, in the first stance, pending its full compliance with the directive of the privatizing office on the return monies. So, the bank had no choice but to borrow such a whopping sum at very exorbitant rates from interbank sources to satisfy the directive of the privatizing office in order to remain in business. The problem, unfortunately, rubbed off on the banks that gave the interbank placements as Wood Bank defaulted on the due dates.

Exercise for class or group discussion

1. Critically assess the reasons Wood Bank had for holding back on returning monies for the unsuccessful subscriptions.
2. Using this case study as basis, explain the cause of bank risk in terms of how credit risk interacts with liquidity risk.
3. Was the privatizing office, in your opinion, decisive in handling Wood Bank's misuse of the return monies?
4. In what ways does this case study shed light on the maneuverings that take place behind the scenes in capital markets?
5. Appraise critically the ripple effect of Wood Bank's default in this case study and show how it would have been obviated.

Tips for solving the exercise

The banking regulatory landscape may encourage the flouting of operating rules with impunity. The real culprit for this aberration—weak banking regulation and supervision—tends to be a common scene in developing economies. Apparently, or it would seem, the magnitude of the responsibilities involved in strict banks surveillance and examination overwhelms the authorities. Thus, infraction of banking rules festers as banks managements carry on with impunity. The Central Bank should always muster up the will to discipline erring banks managements. It is in a position to call the shots and should not hesitate to do so when the situation demands it. In this way, it can foster integrity and sanity in the banking system. Then there will be no need to cut corners, maneuver transactions, or manipulate the customers and investors.

DOMESTIC CURRENCY INSTRUMENTS OF THE CAPITAL MARKET

In general, capital market instrument—strictly speaking is a financial asset (to the investor), or debt obligation (for its issuer) which has a specified price or cost for a fixed long-term. It also may be defined as a long-term, fixed-income, security in which individuals, financial institutions, and other corporate organizations can and do sometimes invest. Usually, the instruments traded in the capital market are riskier, less liquid, and have longer terms to maturity compared with the money market instruments. The instruments may be issued and traded in domestic or foreign currency.

The domestic currency instruments of the capital market comprise quoted shares—mainly ordinary and preference shares, and debenture stocks. The shares of quoted companies are traded on the Stock Exchange. A share, in this sense, is a numerical measure of one unit of the ownership of a company. Investors can buy and sell such shares through their stockbrokers. Debentures are not shares in a company. They are rather loans to it.

Ordinary Shares

Ordinary shares, in the first place, entitle their holders (i.e., the investors in them) to part ownership of the company that issued them. As part owners, the investors can vote at meetings of the company and are eligible to receive dividend if and when declared. However, the holders of ordinary shares of a company are neither guaranteed dividend nor paid fixed rate of dividend if and when declared and paid. They are paid dividends only after the preference shareholders have been paid.

Preference Shares

Unlike ordinary shares, preference shareholders are not entitled to ownership interest in the company that issued them. Neither can they vote at meetings of the company. However, they enjoy priority ranking over ordinary shareholders in the event of liquidation of the company. Similarly, their preference shareholdings attract mandatory fixed rate of dividend whether or not the company makes profit. It also does not matter that the company declares and pays dividend or not. If declared and paid, their dividends take precedence over those of the ordinary shareholders.

Debenture Stocks

Large companies sometimes may want to borrow money for a long-term from the public to finance some capital expenditure project or to fund their regular operations. They can raise such funds through the capital market. In this case, the company would issue a debenture in which the public could invest. The debenture essentially is a bond (i.e., a debt instrument) acknowledging the company's indebtedness to the investors. Thus a debenture is an official document detailing terms on which a company has borrowed money from the public. The company issues it in acknowledgement of its indebtedness to an investor in its bond (i.e., debt instrument). Two of the terms of a debenture—long-term and fixed rate of interest—stand out. The debenture holders simply are creditors to—not part owners of—the company.

Equity Versus Debt as Domestic Currency Instruments

The investors in equity and debt securities of the capital market, denominated in domestic currency, should apprise themselves of the relative benefits and disadvantages of the instruments. In financial markets parlance, debt instrument is interchangeable with bond. The two terms depict a sort of promissory note that government, a large company, or institution issues to borrow money from the public through the capital market.

The government, large company, or institution that borrows money by means of bond or other debt instrument is referred to as the issuer of the bond or instrument. Thus, they are the debtor to the investors who, in turn, are the creditors to the issuers. The commitment of the issuer to service and repay the debt must be trustworthy. Otherwise, it would be difficult to source funds by issuing such debt instruments.

Meanwhile, all debt instruments don't have identical features. Some are marketable while others are not. The instruments which the dealers can trade on the Stock Exchange are marketable. Such instruments can also be traded on some over-the-counter (OTC) financial markets approved by the SEC. Ideally, the term security refers to a debt instrument that can be traded on the Stock Exchanges and approved OTC markets. The instruments—such as irredeemable debentures—that cannot be traded on the Stock Exchanges and approved OTC markets are tagged as nonmarketable instruments. Their nonmarketability is a function of their lacking in liquidity. Usually, they are not easily convertible to cash due, mainly, to their underlying terms and conditions.

Let me now briefly summarize the main distinguishing—as well as characterizing—features between the two types of securities.

The investors in equity shares of a company are accorded ownership rights and privileges while the investors in debt securities are not—the reason being that the latter are treated as creditors (i.e., lenders of money) to the company.

Equity investors play an indirect role in the running of the affairs of a company. The shareholders fulfill this role through their power to vote for the election and removal or retirement of the members of the company's board of directors. The holders of a company's debt instruments lack this power. However, they can call in their loans to the company. They can do so by virtue of the provisions of the Companies and Allied Matters Act 1991, as amended—in the case of Nigeria.

Equity shares entitle the investors to dividend as the income or return from their shareholdings in a company. The holders of debt instruments mainly earn interest or discount at some agreed rate as the reward for their investment.

Dividend payment to shareholders is unpredictable. It may or may not be paid dependent on the discretion of the company. The company must make profit, in the first place, and be disposed to pay it. In the case of holders of debt securities, the payment of interest or dividend is mandatory whether or not profit is made.

Equity offers a stable, predictable, and reliable source of capital which businesses need to meet their long-term financing plans. Debt instrument offer long-term but, nonetheless, tenored funds—often to satisfy the risk profile of the investors.

The Memorandum and Articles of Association (MEMAT) guide company-shareholders relationship once the company is quoted (i.e., investors have bought and could sell shares in the company on the Stock Exchange). In the case of debt instruments, the relationship between the issuers and investors mainly is guided by some trust deeds. A trust deed, for this purpose, is managed by carefully selected trustees. The deed spells out the covenants of the issuer and investors as well as their rights, duties, and obligations.

In both equity and debt instrument, the provisions of the Companies and Allied Matters Act 1991, as amended—in the case of Nigeria—complement the MEMAT and trust deeds. Sections 166—210 of this Act deal with the procedure for issuing and investing in a debenture.

The interests of the shareholders of a company, in the event of liquidation of the company, ranks last compared with those of the creditors (i.e., holders of debt instruments) of the company which enjoy priority ranking. This means that debts of the company are settled first before considering the fate of the equity stakeholders.

FOREIGN CURRENCY INSTRUMENTS OF THE CAPITAL MARKET

The main foreign currency instrument of the capital market in developing economies is futures transactions. Though futures largely are short-dated financial derivative, its features make it more amenable for trading in the capital market than in money market. The other forms of financial derivatives—forwards, swaps, and options—and spot transactions are unstandardized and, therefore, amenable for trading in the money market. I treated them, for this reason, in Chapter 25 of this book. However, bank FX dealers mostly trade derivatives in foreign currency markets to hedge against risk or to speculate on fluctuation in FX rates. Hedging, in this sense, is the process of arranging or devising a means to safeguard FX or other financial transaction against possible loss of value in the future as a result of fluctuation in FX exchange rates.

FX Futures Contract

A futures contract is a transaction in which a specified amount of a particular currency, security, or commodity bought or sold now is to be delivered on a specified date in the future at a fixed price, that is, price agreed by the buyer and seller at the time they entered into the contract. In interbank trading, strictly speaking, it refers to a dealing arrangement in which a fixed amount of FX or security that the dealer in one bank buys from or sells to the dealer in another bank is to be delivered on a fixed date in the future at an exchange rate fixed at the time the dealers made the contract.

Futures really are a forward contract in the sense that the price or exchange rate agreed upon for the FX or security bought or sold now is held valid until a fixed date in the future when the actual settlement and delivery of the FX or security take place. Futures are a standardized financial derivative—and usually are short-dated. The regular tenor is 90 days. The standardization of futures makes it possible for it to be traded on the Stock Exchange. There is, as a result, a clearing house that facilitates trading in the futures market. It then becomes possible—due to its standardization, trading on the Stock Exchange, and clearing house facility—for gains and losses on futures to be automatically marked to market on a daily basis. This is the main distinction between futures and the other financial derivatives.

The usual main reasons for entering into forward contracts—hedging and speculation—also apply to currency futures. In the futures market, the FX dealers mainly are concerned about hedging against the risk of financial loss due to—or speculating on—possible fluctuation in FX rates in the foreign currency markets. This is unlike the spot market where the preoccupation of the dealers is to secure immediate sale, purchase, and delivery (i.e., exchange) of currency. However, as in forward contracts, FX futures dealers may hold long position or short position. Usually, the buyers of currency target long position—and, in doing so, lock in low exchange rates, while short position—which the sellers of currency favor—entails locking in high exchange rates.

The real cause of hedging is for an FX dealer to be able to secure now an FX rate at which they will buy or sell a fixed amount of a particular currency in the spot market on a fixed date in the future. Thus, the FX rate secured now serves as the spot rate for the hedger's transaction on the fixed future date—even if it is not the actual FX spot market rate on that day. This is how hedging, by itself, helps the FX dealers solve the potential risk they face in the foreign currency markets.

Differentiating Futures from Option

Futures and options—from the perspective of bank FX transactions—are both financial derivatives created to hedge against the risk of exchange rates fluctuation in the foreign currency markets. However, futures contract differs from option in certain significant ways.

Bank FX dealers can make gain by exercising their option right when the prevailing foreign currency markets situation is favorable. Usually, an option that is deep in the money is favorable for exercising the option right. Option gain equally can be realized through switching of positions dependent on the direction of the foreign currency markets. There is yet a third strategy at the disposal of an FX dealer to realize gain from their option transaction. They can target the differential between the FX rate at the expiry date of their option and the option's trike price. That differential (if positive) is the gain for the FX dealer who waits until the expiry of their option.

The foregoing strategies for the realization of gain on option depart from the mode of recognition of gain in futures market. The automatic marking of gain to market on futures transactions—done daily through the futures clearing house—is one of two means of recognizing gain in the futures market. The phrase "marked to market" (i.e., marking of gain to market) implies that daily movements in FX rates resulting in gains are automatically reflected in the futures accounts of the dealers at the end of trading every day. Daily losses equally are also marked to market—in much the same vein. An FX dealer also can switch positions in the futures market as a means of making a gain.

The bank FX dealers who buy or sell options have different obligations from those who buy or sell futures. In an option, the dealer has the right to buy a fixed amount of FX at a fixed exchange rate within the time of the deal, but they are not obligated to exercise that right. A futures contract, on the contrary, compels the dealer to buy or sell and deliver an agreed amount of FX at a fixed exchange rate within the agreed period for the transaction—provided that the dealer's position remains open until the contract expires. Since the FX option dealers are under no compulsion to buy or sell, they are able to avoid the risk of loss due to possible fluctuation in FX rates. Unlike them, the FX futures dealers are risk bound because their underlying contracts lock them in an obligation to buy or sell—irrespective of the prevailing situations of the FX rates and currency markets.

The FX dealers tend to hold larger positions in the futures market than they do in the options market. This difference imparts more risk to futures contracts than options. The fact that the Stock Exchanges on which futures are traded is a capricious financial market exacerbates the risk that FX dealers face in the futures trading. On the flip side, though, an option attracts a premium—usually paid upfront as fee by the FX option dealers. The rationale for the premium, perhaps, is to compensate the counterparties for the absence of compulsion for dealers to buy or sell FX when the exchange rates and currency markets are not favorable. The FX dealers who buy option positions stand a risk of losing the premium which really is the most they can lose on an option purchase. Such premium, upfront fee or cost is neither charged nor paid in futures contracts.

Comparing Futures with Forward Contracts

Futures and forward contracts—in the context of bank FX dealing—are both similar and different as financial derivatives. The two instruments help bank FX dealers to hedge against the risk of exchange rates fluctuation in the foreign currency markets. The dealers also could speculate on them in pursuit of some incomes targets in the financial markets. There is yet another similarity between futures and forwards—one that relates to the basic principle underlying them. As derivative financial instruments, futures and forwards are contracts to buy or sell a fixed amount of FX on an agreed date in the future at an exchange rate fixed now.

However, futures contract differs significantly from a forward contract. Futures are a well-structured financial derivative. For this reason, futures are regarded as a standardized contract and traded on the Stock Exchanges. Their trading on the Stock Exchanges is backed by clearing houses facility which ensures that futures transactions are guaranteed, secured, and foolproof. The implication is that the risk of financial loss in trading in the futures market is adequately mitigated. Forward contract—in contrast to futures—is not suitable for trading on the Stock Exchanges. It is essentially a private trading arrangement between two FX dealers in different banks. Besides, it lends itself to some flexibility and therefore possible maneuvering with regard to its terms and conditions. These attributes tend to expose forward contracts to high chances of default and financial loss.

Mostly, futures are a fertile market for financial derivatives speculation. The speculators seek to gain insights into possible tendencies of FX rate movements and trade the FX in their futures positions accordingly. The drive to be on top of predictions about the likely FX rates directions tends to be the salient point for most of the dealer-speculators in the futures market. For this reason, futures contract scarcely runs its course. In most cases, its life (i.e., period fixed for a futures contract) is truncated—usually as a result of closeout informed by speculation on FX rates movements. The closeout prior to the expiry of the futures implies that delivery on the original contract hardly takes place. Forward contract, to the contrary, is a fertile market for hedging against risks in financial derivatives. The main risk management interest of the FX dealers in the forwards market is to be able to hedge against rates fluctuation in the foreign currency markets. Usually the delivery (i.e., cash settlement or exchange) of the FX underlying the contract takes place as envisaged by the dealers.

A major distinguishing feature of futures contract is the ability of the futures clearing house to mark it to market on daily basis. Its admission as a marked-to-market financial derivative implies that the clearing house tracks, reflects, and settles daily FX rates movements throughout the term of the contract. Thus, futures contract is settled in a series of discrete transactions on different dates. The features of forward contract are quite the contrary. Terms and conditions of forwards—especially the modes of FX delivery and exchange (i.e., settlement)—are usually clearly spelled out in the contract. Usually, forward contract runs its course. This implies that FX settlement on a forward deal marks the termination of the contract.

BOOM TO BUST MECHANISMS OF CAPITAL MARKET RISKS IN DEVELOPING ECONOMIES

On occasion the stock market booms with increasing and sustained volumes of daily transactions. Investors make brisk incomes from stock trading while the boom lasts. Of course the bulls channel more energy and financial resources to maintain the tempo of transactions. A mark of success reflects in rising market capitalization index. Yet not infrequently, the stock market experiences shocks that adversely affect trading in stocks and financial performance of stockbrokers. Often the shocks cause liquidity crunch that enthrones bearish stock market. Capitalization index tends to plunge sharply when stock market is bearish. A dramatic plunge in the capitalization index evidences a period of consistent falling prices of quoted shares on the Stock Exchange. In most cases, investors suffer huge financial losses where the bears are able to sustain the plunge in share prices.

Capitalization index is a measure of total monetary value of all stocks quoted and traded on a particular Stock Exchange as at a given date. It mirrors the level of confidence of direct and portfolio investors in an economy. The index rises when investment in the economy through the Stock Exchange increases and falls when there is a decline in investment. This is termed boom to bust—a characteristic feature in the nature of the stock market. Certain factors contribute to stock markets going from boom to bust in developing economies. For instance, an economy that is opening up so as to rely more on market forces than controls is likely to witness an upsurge in local and international direct and portfolio investments. Increasing investments in this way boosts the stock market. As would be expected, the stock market booms with the boost. However there has to be an efficient, transparent, and vibrant Stock Exchange before the economy could benefit from the boost. There will also be need for a diversified financial market. Conducive business environment, political stability, and efficient reward system in developing economies are also essential and inevitable.

Let me illustrate the boom to bust mechanism with the state of Nigeria's stock market from 2004 to 2010. The Central Bank of Nigeria (CBN) announced increase in regulatory capital of banks in Nigeria from mere ₦2.0 billion to

₦25.0 billion in mid-2004—with 18 months grace period for compliance. There were jitters in banking circles about an imminent crisis that was bound to lead to forced mergers, acquisitions, and closures. Chief executives, directors, and major shareholders who attended the Bankers Committee meeting where the CBN Governor made the announcement stormed out in anger. Some scampered off in the confusion that ensued in the aftermath of the meeting to enter their cars and headed to their offices. Concerned stakeholders in banking lobbied for a change of the policy, ostensibly to ward off threat to their investments in the banks, but all was to no avail. Apparently, the policy was immutable.

In the end only 24 banks—out of a total of about 84 money deposit banks in the country—made it! 14 banks failed to meet the deadline and had their banking licenses withdrawn by the CBN while the rest—with the exception of Citibank, First Bank, Guaranty Trust Bank, Standard Chartered Bank, and Zenith Bank—either merged or were acquired to have the surviving 24 as at the end of the deadline on December 31, 2005. All but two banks—Citibank and Standard Chartered Bank—raised the funds they required from the capital market. There were initial public offerings (IPO) of shares of the unquoted banks. Quoted banks issued more shares to the public and sold rights issues to existing shareholders. Doing so, the banks invariably converted to public limited companies after selling equity shares to individual and corporate investors in foregoing ways. These actions engendered unprecedented high volumes of transactions in shares of banks. There was boom as investors scrambled for bank shares on offer in the market.

The boom festered in the cut-throat world of banking. The big banks flexed their competitive muscles. Claims and counterclaims of market leadership took center stage in the ensuing intense rivalry among the leading banks. Soon the rivalry was taken to the margin lending arena. Banks granted margin loans in a reckless manner to boost trading in their own shares on the Nigerian Stock Exchange. Most of the borrowers were cronies of directors or affiliates of the banks. There was a case of a bank granting over ₦80.0 billion margin loans to a no body given to carry briefcase around and within the Stock Exchange as though he was a serious stockbroker. The case of Union Bank of Nigeria was not only embarrassing but an insult to the sensibilities of the regulatory authorities. The bank had raised funds from its subsidiaries to invest in its own shares as a means of fulfilling the ₦25.0 billion regulatory capital requirement.

The banking sector became the toast of stockbrokers on the floor of the Nigerian Stock Exchange. Shares of banks yielded incredibly excellent returns on investment from handsome dividends and price appreciation. Banks consistently paid interim and final dividends, complemented by enviable bonuses, scripts, and rights issues. Individuals, companies and organizations scrapped up more funds which they invested in shares of banks. Professional investors and amateurs alike borrowed money from friends, relations and financial institutions to acquire equity stakes in the banking industry. Interestingly investors in property and realtors, who traditionally consider investment in stocks very risky, jumped on the bandwagon. Curiously many of them divested from property as they switched to stocks. Their action crashed the otherwise naturally stable property market. Value of residential and commercial property, and rent on them, nose-dived to the lowest ebb. In all this, the driving force behind the investment trend was easy access to margin loans fueled by windfall gain. Thus while the stock market was booming under the auspices of margin lending, investors in property were counting the cost. Ironically, the boom was a bubble in disguise building up in the stock market.

Then the bubble burst. The boom had lasted for 4 years—from 2004 to 2008. Signs of cracks in the stock market came to the fore in late 2007 while the global financial meltdown was underway. The authorities dismissed the signs as inconsequential, ostensibly suggesting that Nigeria's financial system was immune to the meltdown. One of the chief executives of the banks argued that the crisis was limited to the highly developed financial markets—and would not affect countries like Nigeria and other developing economies because they did not deal in exotic financial products unlike their counterparts in the developed nations. The stock market remained in the doldrums until 2012 when it recorded marginal recovery.

SUMMARY

The capital market is a specialized financial market for raising and investing funds—usually for the long-term. It is therefore one of the major categories of financial markets. Capital market is an arrangement to offer for subscription, list, trade, and invest in ordinary stocks and bonds to raise equity, or to borrow long-term funds for business, social projects, and so on from the public. The significance of the capital market derives from the fact that it offers facility pro-pitious for the activities of dealers in long-term securities. Then it enables the free flow of securities, transactions, and deals.

Mostly, participation in the capital market is driven by two opposing needs. It could be that the participants need an outlet for long-term investment of their idle funds. Their need also may be to have an opportunity to borrow noninterest based funds for long-term utilization. The common method of characterizing the capital market focuses on the types and nature of investment and funding needs of the operators. The capital market boasts three such needs through its primary, secondary, and bonds markets.

The leading capital markets participants in developing economies usually are SEC, Stock Exchanges, stockbrokers, issuing houses, money deposit banks, large investors, securities issuers, finance professionals, and accountants. SEC is the regulatory body of the capital market while Stock Exchange organizes and supervises trading in stock markets. The two bodies play specific complemen-tary roles in the capital market.

Capital market instruments are financial assets (to the investors), or debt obligations (for their issuers) which have specified price or cost for a fixed long-term. Usually, the instruments traded in the capital market are riskier, less liquid, and have longer terms to maturity compared with the money market instruments. The instruments may be issued and traded in domestic or foreign currency. The domestic currency instruments of the capital market comprise quoted shares—mainly ordinary and preference shares, and debenture stocks. The main foreign currency instrument of the capital market in developing economies is futures transactions. Though futures largely are short-dated financial derivative, its features make it more amenable for trading in the capital market than in money market.

The other forms of financial derivatives—forwards, swaps, and options— and spot transactions are unstandardized and, therefore, amenable for trading in the money market. Bank FX dealers mostly trade derivatives in foreign currency markets to hedge against risk or to speculate on fluctuation in FX rates. On occasion the stock market booms with increasing and sustained volumes of daily transactions. Investors make brisk incomes from stock trading while the boom lasts. Of course the bulls channel more energy and financial resources to maintain the tempo of transactions. A mark of success reflects in rising market capitalization index.

Yet not infrequently, the stock market experiences shocks that adversely affect trading in stocks and financial performance of stockbrokers. Often the shocks cause liquidity crunch that enthrones bearish stock market. Capitalization index tends to plunge sharply when stock market is bearish. A dramatic plunge in the capitalization index evidences a period of consistent falling prices of quoted shares on the Stock Exchange.

In most cases, investors suffer huge financial losses where the bears are able to sustain the plunge in share prices. Often this situation necessitates joint intervention by the financial system regulatory and supervisory authorities—Central Bank, SEC, Stock Exchanges, and so on.

QUESTIONS FOR DISCUSSION AND REVIEW

1. What is a capital market? Of what significance are capital markets in developing economies?
2. How do the characteristics of capital market inform the conduct of the trading of equity and debt instruments?
3. In what respects do the roles of the SEC compare with those of the Stock Exchange?
4. Why—as an astute investor in the capital market—would you want to invest in an equity rather than debt security and vice versa?
5. Identify and explain the features, risks and control of a typical financial derivative traded on the Stock Exchange.
6. Would you say that boom to bust really is a regular phenomenon of the stock market in developing economies?

Section D

Operational Risk

Chapter 27

Bank Operational Risk Dynamics and Management in Developing Economies

Chapter Outline

LEARNING FOCUS AND OBJECTIVES

Operational risk permeates every facet of banking activities. Credit, liquidity, and market risks interact with operational risk one way or the other. Indeed, operational risk easily infiltrates every banking function—tainting banking functions across-the-board. The major banking functions—transactions processing, lending, marketing, treasury, and legal services are fraught with operational risks. Thus, there is a need for me to:

- define operational risk and its applications in banking from the perspective of developing economies;
- discuss the nature, dynamic, and mechanisms of bank operational risk in developing economies;
- examine some of the internal and external events depicting the scope of bank operational risk in developing economies; and
- delineate the nuances of operational risk dynamics and interactions with the other major banking risks.

EXPECTED LEARNING OUTCOMES

Operational risk events characterize the financial services landscape in developing economies over the world. Internal and external factors contribute to the causes of bank operational risks. While some of the risk events are beyond the control of banks managements, many of them are controllable. Yet incidence of bank operational risk in developing economies is not only increasing but cuts across origins. This implies that bank managements are not always on top of operational risks. The reader will—after studying this chapter and doing the exercises in it—have learnt and been better informed about:

- meaning and practical applications of operational risk in banking from the perspective of developing economies;
- the ubiquitous nature, dynamics, and mechanisms of bank operational risk in developing economies;
- internal and external events depicting the scope of bank operational risk in developing economies; and
- the subtle nuances of operational risk dynamics and interactions with the other major banking risks.

OVERVIEW OF THE SUBJECT MATTER

It is difficult to talk about banking without being confronted with operational risk in the first place. The straightforward reason for this reality is that operational risk permeates every facet of banking activities. Bank credit risk is associated with lending. Gaps in the finances and level of funding of a bank inform liquidity risk. Market risk pictures everyday probable adverse interest rate tendencies with which bank management deals. Operational risk, quite unlike the foregoing and other risks, infiltrates every banking function. One way or another, it taints banking functions across-the-board. It manifests itself in not only banking processing but lending, marketing, treasury, legal, and other banking functions.

I give further examples to illustrate other sources of operational risks that are equally pertinent. Failings of bank managements that result in misguided restructuring process, poor market forecasting, flawed integration of activities from across functions, and so on are usually a major cause of operational risk in banking. How about risks to banking caused by external events? I mean systemic risk events like industry-wide downturn, civil war, strikes and industrial unrest, and so on. Bank managements do not have control over these and similar unexpected events, most of which constitute so-called force majeure. I should emphasize that such external risk events expose banks, willy-nilly, to operational risk.

Incidence of operational risk tends to be high—indeed, higher than that of any other risk in banking. This further underscores the significance of operational risk as a serious and intriguing challenge of bank management, especially in developing economies. A possible explanation for this observation is that operational risk is commonplace in banking all over the world. Another reason is that incidence of operational risk—and the losses attendant on it—easily attract negative publicity and exacerbates a bank's reputational risk. This is quite unlike the outcomes in the case of other risks in banking. Mostly, nonoperational risks are easily shielded from the public because they largely fall within the bounds of a bank's internal affairs. Thus, bank managements can do anything but allow operational risks to fester or snowball.

Yet bank operational risk events in developing economies and costs due to them are a regular scene and continue to rock the financial services landscape. Increasing incidence of bank operational risk in developing economies certainly smacks of some banking failings. Bank managements should appreciate the real dynamics of operational risk in order to deal with it. In doing so, they should be decisive in anticipating probable operational risk events. They should, above all, get to grips with the interactions between operational risk and other risks in banking—most of which manifest themselves in one type of fraud or the other. Let me first define operational risk in banking before I proceed with the main topics.

DEFINING OPERATIONAL RISK AND ITS APPLICATIONS IN BANKING

Operational risk is a complex and multifaceted issue in banking. It is, perhaps, the most complicated challenge of bank management all over the world. The Basel Committee recognizes this thinking and addresses the problem accordingly. Basel II, Pillar 1, devises mean to hedge against abuse, infringement, or failure of a bank's internal operating system that cause operational risks in banking. The Basel Committee (2006:144) defines operational risk as "the risk of loss resulting from inadequate or failed internal processes, people and systems or from external events." While including legal risk in this definition, it excludes strategic and reputational risk. In the Committee's view, "legal risk includes, but is not limited to, exposure to fines, penalties, or punitive damages resulting from supervisory actions, as well as private settlements" (ibid). These meanings and clarifications add a wider perspective—altogether the broadest definition and applications of a risk category in banking.

A broad base of operational risk definition is both realistic and pertinent. Such a meaning, which the Basel Committee's definition typifies, runs the gamut of nonbusiness related risks in banking (I have used "nonbusiness related risks in banking" to emphasize the classification of banking functions into two broad categories—namely business and operations. The business arm comprises such functions as lending, treasury, marketing, and so on, while operations relates to all processing functions). Downtime—on account of IT and application software failure, for example, counts as operational risk. Payment of an amount of money in judgment debt fines, plus court and legal costs, falls in the same operational risk category as financial or other loss arising from downtime.

Supervisory damages due to regulatory conflicts and noncompliance create operational risk, in much the same vein. Private settlements arising from civil lawsuits and litigations, and other sundry legal risks are equally in the mold of the foregoing. The same goes for all manner of sundry other risks that banks face in everyday processing functions.

Thus, the scope of operational risk should integrate a strong focus on risks emanating from both internal and external events. Armed robbery attacks on branches of banks, for example, are a typical external risk event. Civil disturbances and wars, so-called force majeure, are other examples of externally-induced risk events that sometimes happen and crystallize operational risk for banks in developing economies. Typical internal sources of bank operational risk include employee issues, insider abuse, and transactions processing errors. Some risk events, like frauds, could originate from internal or external events. Often banks managements find it more difficult to deal with the external than internal risk events. External risk events that are beyond their control could be unusually quite demanding. On occasion, the situation becomes a dilemma and forces banks management to take the easy way out.

Take incessant armed robbery attacks as an example. The attacks could be targeted at branches or cash-in-transit. Usually, the first bank management initiative toward solution is to engage the Police to guard places of banking business, and to move cash under Police escort. These two responses to the risks are not altogether effective. Armed robbery attacks still happen in broad daylight. Daredevil armed robbers operate in this manner, killing Police guards and bank employees. Then they force their way into banking halls and vaults. Usually, their ultimate goal—which they often realize—is to make away with as much cash as they can find. Now it dawns on banks managements that Police guards and escorts are not effective solution to their operational risk dilemma. This reality keeps them on their toes—forcing a complete rethink of operational risk control strategy.

The failure of Police guards and escorts has dual risk management fallout. First, banks managements now resort to the use bullet-proof vans for cash movements. Nowadays, everyone that comes to banks must pass through electronic doors equipped with metal detectors. The doors detect and prevent entry of persons with weapons made of metals. These new approaches to cash-in-transit and office risks control are to a large extent effective. They have significantly reduced incidence of the related armed robbery attacks. Sadly, daredevil armed robbers still attack banks branches in broad daylight—bypassing the metal detector doors. They break into banking halls and vaults. This alternative to passing through the metal detector doors continues to place banks managements in a dilemma.

I should emphasis the significance of three critical elements of operational risk in banking. The first—risks associated with everyday management of a bank—affects all the banks, albeit, in varying degrees. The risks implied here relate to mainly employee issues and frauds which, in most cases, are debilitating. I devoted the whole of Chapters 26 and 28 of this book to treat the concerns about these issues. I did so in recognition of the ravaging effects of frauds in banking. It is also informed by the need to appropriately handle employee matters as a means of stemming the incidence of the frauds in banking.

The contravention of regulatory rules and its concomitant supervisory damages—together with all manner of legal actions that banks face in the course of their normal business activities—is the next significant factor of operational risk in banking. Occasionally, disputes arise between banks and their customers, on the one hand, and the banks and third parties, on the other. The banks may win or lose the lawsuits. Losses in the courts result in payments of judgments debts. In some cases, the judgment debts may be denominated in foreign currencies. In such cases, the amounts of the judgment debts could be quite substantial.

Operational risk associated with IT system is not limited to downtime. The risk of loss of data on the databases on account of some disaster, force majeure, and suchlike is, perhaps, the most debilitating in banks managements circles. The same goes for the possible corruption of information on the databases. Operational risks of this nature keep banks managements in developing economies always on their toes. In order to mitigate the risks, the banks should institutionalize an effective data recovery program. A realistic master contingency management plan should complement the disaster recovery program. The two approaches should inform the IT operational risk management strategies of the banks in developing economies.

CASE STUDY 27.1 Bank Operational Risk Enmeshed with Government Policy

The newly elected President of Nigeria, Mohammad Buhari, announced his government's anticorruption policy soon after he was sworn in on May 29, 2015. Judging from his antecedents, Nigerians did not doubt his commitment to this cause. He was true to his word and no sooner had he explained the thrust of the policy than he swung into action. He started mobilizing popular opinion, support, and antigraft agencies of the government.

Federal Government and public sector accounts with the banks were frozen in the first place. A directive to transfer funds in the accounts to a unified treasury account with the Central Bank followed. This affected accounts held by the Federal Government, its ministries, agencies, and parastatals. Thus, commercial banks were among the first casualties of the fight against corruption. As the fight hit the banks—indirectly, though—the public was left with no doubt about the seriousness of the campaign against corruption, especially in the civil service.

The enforcement of the accounts and funds transfer exercise immediately created liquidity and funding gaps in the banks. Operational pressure and risks attendant on it ensued in the aftermath of the exercise. The banks had lost huge amounts of critical deposits without warning. The exercise caught them unawares, if anything. Public sector funds can be anything but expensive. That's their main appeal for banks in developing economies. So banks crave government accounts and funds in pursuit of liquidity and cost-reduction goals. Now, as the exercise took away a large chunk out of deposit portfolio, the banks slipped into crisis across-the-board. For banks that were already having a bumpy ride, it was painful to be on the road to this crisis.

Payments on Federal Government obligations were stopped in the first place—pending completion and verification of the exercise. This took a long time to be done. While it lingered on, the banks were deprived of vital liquidity. Second, huge loans granted by the banks to finance major public sector projects went bad. Apparently contractors were not paid even with certification of progressive work milestones. A third point is that banks started exploring ways of filling the resultant funding and liquidity gaps. This proved difficult, especially as the interbank market had collapsed in the face of the crisis. The banks had no option but to resort to aggressive drive for deposit mobilization, with all its attendant risks.

Treasury marketing took center stage at once. Some success was recorded. However, most of the deposits were obtained in form of purchased funds, the implication being that they were expensive. Usually, interest rates paid on purchased funds (i.e., time deposits, often taken on call and fixed tenor basis) tend to be far higher than the rates paid on savings and current accounts. In the final analysis, the balance sheets of the banks crashed—shrinking in the wake of pullback in deposit portfolio.

Exercise for group or class discussion

1. How may this case study possibly open up new vistas and nuances of bank operational risk in developing economies?
2. What factors, based on this case study, contributed to the sweeping effect of the government's policy on banks in Nigeria?
3. Would you say banking principles informed the approach adopted by the banks in responding to the trail of crisis left by the policy?
4. Why would banks in developing economies want to bemoan the loss or depletion of public sector funds in their deposit portfolios?
5. In what sense would it be right to target banks in the fight against corruption in developing economies?

Tips for solving the exercise

The build-up of the crisis that swept banks in Nigeria in this case study is instructive. It demonstrates the vulnerability of banks in developing economies to systemic operational risk. In this sense, it is immaterial whether the triggers for operational risk are internal or emanate from external events. The important point for emphasis is that banking operations are easily affected by such risk triggers. However, the pullback in deposit portfolios of the banks in this case study was triggered by government action—an external event. The reason the policy had a sweeping effect on banking operation across-the-board was due to overdependence of banks in developing economies on cheap public sector funds for operations. The preponderance of cheap, short-term government funds in deposit portfolios of banks only skews efficiency of liquidity-driven liabilities management. This in turn renders overall balance sheet management of the banks ineffectual. The interplay of these points—evident in this case study—crystallizes operational risks across all banking functions. It also underscores the dynamics and nuances of bank operational risk in practical ways. Take a closer look at the case study and you will find that operational risk of the policy was intertwined with other key banking risks—credit risk (i.e., loan defaults), liquidity risk (i.e., crunch and funding gaps), and market risk (exorbitant interest rates).

NUANCES OF OPERATIONAL RISK DYNAMICS AND INTERACTIONS

The nuances of operational risk dynamics are instructive and mirrored in interactions between operational risk and other major risks in banking. I give some examples of this intriguing fact about the dynamics of operational risk in banking. I discuss interaction between industry and operational risk, business and operational risk interaction, link between financial risk and operational risk, and market risk interface with operational risk. All the other banking functions embodying risk of sorts—and they are so many that I cannot discuss here—exhibit similar or related interactions with operational risk.

Industry and Operational Risk Interaction

Operational risk of industry-wide downturn is the probability that a bank faces, experiences, or suffers financial losses as a result of declining or worsening business activities in the banking industry or financial system. It could also mean the danger that the banking industry may suffer, adverse business or other conditions that affect the financial performance of banks as going concerns. In this sense, industry risk causes, exacerbates, and is really germane to externally-induced operational risk. Often industry risk, in the context of the foregoing, fuses with operational risk. Banks in developing economies typically face this situation when adverse macroeconomic and regulatory actions affect their operations.

Bank customers invariably respond to actions bank managements take in dealing or coping with the external risk events. Customer response could be positive or negative depending on how the actions affect banking needs, expectations, and service. I mean, in a word, satisfaction. Yes, customer satisfaction. Favorable and unfavorable reactions may be substituted for positive and negative responses without change in effect. What is important is that these states count directly toward the intensity of operational risk in banking. Unfavorable customer reaction, for example, can get the whole banking industry into a mess. This happens especially when banks fail to put contingency plans in place to deal with side effects of macroeconomic policies and regulatory interventions.

Interaction Between Business and Operational Risk

Business risk somewhat shares the relationship between industry risk and externally-induced operational risk—but in a subtle way. However, the nature of the relationship in this case is, perhaps, the best evidence and manifestation of the consequences of operational risk in banking. I define business risk as the probability that a bank may not be able to generate sufficient cash flow to meet its operating expenses. This implies that the bank would be unable to render normal banking services to its customers, or to continue to operate as a going concern. In a situation like this, there may be a run on the bank. This is a typical outcome of business risk that has snowballed into treasury crisis and liquidity risk. Thus the capacity of a bank as a going concern is weakened when business risk fuses with operational risk.

Linking Financial Risk with Operational Risk

Often operational risk triggers and culminates in financial risk that most banks face. Domestic banks in developing economies have a penchant for applying purchased funds—usually from depositors—as the main plank of finances for their operations. With barely minimum regulatory capital, the banks hardly trade on equity. This situation defines financial risk for the banks—in using more debt than equity to run business operations. Financial risk, in this sense, is the danger that a bank may default on its obligations to its depositors and other creditors—especially in interbank money market—due to lack of funds for operations. With paucity of cash flow, a bank faced with financial risk may not be able to fulfill its financial obligations—a situation flawed financial structure exacerbates. In most cases the flaw originates from overdependence on short-term depositors' funds and interbank takings to meet day-to-day financial obligations in running a bank.

Market Risk Interface with Operational Risk

A dealer commits this fraud when they agree rate cutback for their counterpart in order to place certain amount of money with them. The cutback does not reflect on their deal slips but is done with the understanding that the bank taking the funds should pay the dealer in the funds pacing bank the amount of the cutback afterward. This practice increases interest rates and therefore operational costs to the funds taking banks, especially so-called net funds takers. The funds placing banks incur no financial loss in this money market fraud. Their dealers get their target interest rates. In essence, this implies that the burden of forging documentation to record fraudulent deals rests with the dealers in the taking, not the placing, banks.

CASE STUDY 27.2 Interbank Placement and Taking Gone Awry

Moon—a local currency dealer for XY Bank—was desperate to take $50 million 90-day placement from another bank to meet some urgent treasury funding need of the bank. The intended interbank taking was critical to appraising Moon's ability to meet unexpected liquidity pressure. In this case, the pressure was really pressing.

Moon started calling counterpart dealers in other banks that may be willing to place money with XY Bank. It was difficult for Moon as XY Bank had a reputational issue as a net taker of funds in the money market. With persistence, Moon succeeded in convincing Sun—UV Bank's local currency dealer—to place the $50 million with XY Bank. The going interest rate for this amount and tenor at the time was 2.5% per annum. However, Sun demanded 0.25% flat fee on the placement, off the record, as brokerage and condition for the transaction. Moon obliged Sun after securing approval for the deal from XY Bank's management. In this way, deals were struck—ostensibly binding on XY and UV Banks.

The 0.25% flat brokerage pushed up effective interest rate on the taking to 3.5% per annum. Moon thereafter booked the transaction at 2.5% per annum interest rate on paper and raised a deal slip to account for the 0.25% flat brokerage paid to Sun. The deal slip was treated as a confidential record at XY Bank and filed away accordingly. This implies that there was no trail of the deal in official records of the transaction in both XY and UV Banks. Interestingly, while the management of XY Bank surreptitiously endorsed the deal, that of UV Bank was not privy to it. It would seem that Sun was a lone ranger in the deal on UV Bank's side. On occasion, however, dealers who demanded brokerage did so with tacit approval and connivance of their supervisors.

Unfortunate for Sun, XY Bank defaulted on the due date of the placement. Sun mounted pressure on Moon—but all to no avail—to get XY Bank to repay the deposit. Sun was now in deep trouble and helpless with Moon's seemingly indifference to their plight at UV Bank. Sun enlisted the help of some members of the executive management of XY Bank but this effort also fell through. It was indeed a doomsday scenario. Ultimately, the management of UV Bank placed Sun on an indefinite suspension pending when he recovered the placement with XY Bank.

Exercise for group or class discussion

1. To what operational risk does this case study allude? Give reasons for your view and how particular issues implied in the case study underlie it.
2. In what ways would you say the action of Sun in this case study really precipitated operational risk for UV Bank?
3. How would you characterize the management of XY Bank based on facts of this case study and the situation of the bank?
4. Would you say the management of UV Bank was decisive in placing Sun on suspension following XY Bank's default?
5. Why—in your opinion—should or shouldn't the management of UV Bank frown upon the action of Sun?
6. Can Moon's indifference to the plight of Sun and UV Bank be really justified on grounds of banking expediency?

Tips for solving the exercise

Here is a practical example to illustrate the mechanism of a typical money market dealing fraud that precipitates operational risk for banks in developing economies. Weak banks experience occasional crunch that frustrates effective operations. In a bid to solve the problem, the banks tend to engage in some unprofessional conduct. As would be expected under the circumstances, bank managements in such a situation turn a blind eye to maneuvering of standard operating procedures in pursuit of urgent solution to the problem. They do so, trying to wriggle out of their responsibilities. Thus, they inadvertently—or, sometimes, deliberately—leave some trusted subordinates who work in funding and liquidity management positions considerable latitude in dealing with the challenge. Of course this informal empowerment is subject to abuse and, indeed, has often been misused by such trusted subordinates for personal gain at the expense of the bank. However, while net funds taking banks indulge in this act, the liquid banks are opposed to or don't tolerate it. Paradoxically, an act that net funds placing banks treat as fraudulent is seen as expedient in net funds taking banks.

INTERFACE BETWEEN LIQUIDITY AND OPERATIONAL RISK

The main sources of operational risks—besides volatility of rates and defaults—include possible breach of confidentiality and insider trading. The former involves disclosure of customer orders or information to a third party, while the latter concerns the abuse of a dealers' privileged position. This happens when the dealers make money for themselves at the expense of their banks based on confidential information they might have about customers' orders or transactions.

Risk is further mitigated when the business and operations arms of the treasury are separated. There should be clear lines of demarcation between local and foreign currency trading, on the one hand, and between the trading functions and operations unit, on the other. The demarcation ensures that the operations unit solely handles the posting of deal slips. In this way, it is easy and effective for the supervision and control of the activities of the units. While the treasury marketing unit leads the business generation activities, assets and liabilities unit focuses on liquidity issues and management. The treasurer gets and reviews printout of the entire treasury's transactions daily. The treasurer does this daily liquidity risk management work in order to be on top of total inflows and outflows of funds that impact the bank's liabilities portfolio—and therefore the liquidity position of the bank.

SUMMARY

Operational risk is a complex and multi-faceted issue in banking. It is, perhaps, the most complicated challenge of bank management all over the world. The Basel Committee recognizes this thinking and addresses the problem accordingly. Basel II, Pillar 1, devises means to hedge against abuse, infringement, or failure of a bank's internal operating system that cause operational risks in banking.

A broad base of operational risk definition is both realistic and pertinent. Such a meaning runs the gamut of nonbusiness related risks in banking. Downtime—on account of IT and application software failure, for example, counts as operational risk. Payment of an amount of money in judgment debt fines, plus court and legal costs, falls in the same operational risk category as financial or other loss arising from downtime. Supervisory damages due to regulatory conflicts and noncompliance create operational risk, in much the same vein. Private settlements arising from civil lawsuits and litigations, and other sundry legal risks are equally in the mold of the foregoing. The same goes for all manner of sundry other risks that banks face in everyday processing functions.

Thus, the scope of operational risk should integrate a strong focus on risks emanating from both internal and external events. Armed robbery attacks on branches of banks, for example, are a typical external risk event. Civil disturbances and wars are other examples of externally-induced risk events that sometimes happen and crystallize operational risk for banks in developing economies. Typical internal sources of bank operational risk include employee issues, insider abuse, and transactions processing errors. Some risk events, like frauds, could originate from internal or external events.

The nuances of operational risk dynamic are mirrored in interactions between operational risk and other major risks in banking. Specific examples include interaction between industry and operational risk, business and operational risk interaction, link between financial risk and operational risk, operational risk in illegal lending, market risk interface with operational risk, and operational risk caused by liquidity risk.

QUESTIONS FOR DISCUSSION AND REVIEW

1. How does interaction of operational risk and other risks permeate banking outcomes in developing economies?
2. Do you agree or disagree that every threat that a bank faces crystallizes some operational risk in one way or the other?
3. In what ways do bank operational risk dynamics and nuances inform banks internal control systems in developing economies?
4. Assess applications of a broad view of operational risk and its implications for banking in developing economies?
5. How have banks managements in developing economies grappled with any named typical risk which external event occasioned?

REFERENCE

Basel Committee on Banking Supervision, 2006. International Convergence of Capital Measurement and Capital Standards: a Revised Framework – Comprehensive Version, as amended. Bank for International Settlements, Basel.

Chapter 28

Bank Work, Employees, and Operational Risk Management in Developing Economies

Chapter Outline

LEARNING FOCUS AND OBJECTIVES

There is somewhat a connection between the antics of individuals—in this case, bank employees and outsiders—and probable tendencies toward operational risk. Often bank operational risk in developing economies originates from work and service failings of bank managements and employees. Thus, bank operational risk interacts with banking work and services to crystalize particular adverse outcomes. I focus on human elements at work in order to:

- explore issues in work situations of bank employees that are propitious for operational risk in developing economies;

- highlight and analyze risks which work and service characteristics in banking portend for banks in developing economies;
- explain how risk control disposition informs the split between business and operations banking functions;
- demonstrate how operational risk in banking can be best understood in the context of gaps in services that banks offer to customers;
- discuss reasons orientation and disposition of employees to service may help check or foster operational risk in banking; and
- examine why uncritical chase after service could be a reason for fraud to find its way into patronage-service calculation of banks and customers.

EXPECTED LEARNING OUTCOMES

Fraud typifies operational risk that work, service, and employee situations may engender. There is direct interaction between the nature of bank work and customer service, on the one hand, and work and employee situations, on the other. These are the main variable factors of bank operational risk in developing economies that demand exceptional attention of bank managements. The reader will—after studying this chapter—have learnt and been better informed about:

- issues in work situations of employees that are propitious for bank operational risk in developing economies;
- risks which work and service characteristics in banking portend for banks in developing economies;
- how risk control disposition informs the split between business and operations banking functions;
- reasons operational risk in banking can be best understood in the context of gaps in services that banks offer to customers;
- why orientation and disposition of employees to service may help check or foster operational risk in banking; and
- operational risk implications of uncritical chase after service by banks and their customers.

OVERVIEW OF THE SUBJECT MATTER

Operational risk in banking is best understood in the context of gaps in services that banks offer to customers. Orientation and disposition of bank employees to service can help check or foster operational risk. For this reason, I start discussion of operational risk with insights into its hardly recognized connection with service orientation and disposition of bank employees. This provides one view of the causes of operational risk, especially bank frauds, in developing economies.

Companies in the service sector have long recognized that good service disposition of workers is favorable to business success. This drives the quest for customer satisfaction. Customers feel satisfied when banks add value, match or surpass patronage with value, and ultimately fulfill their banking needs. These are the basic ingredients of success in banking. Yet good disposition of employees to customer service is always a complementary ingredient. This mirrors the proverbial proof of pudding is in the eating. It literally means that in order for a bank to fulfill customer needs, its employees must be favorably disposed toward good service. Customers tend to be predisposed to patronize a bank or not when they perceive that its employees have positive or negative disposition to service, respectively.

Typical operational risk, fraud, on occasion, finds its way into patronage-service calculation of banks and customers. This happens—first and foremost—where bank employees and customers are uncritical of their chase after service. Then the question of how the employees could build appropriate disposition toward service follows. The employees will have to deal with pressure of work in pursuit of this end. In doing so, they may be enthusiastic or nonchalant about their work. Often these personnel issues create service gaps that may be propitious for bank operational risk. Managerial response to this tendency should aim to reinvent customer service, fill service gaps and, in doing so, forestall possible frauds. This managerial action will succeed when employees cultivate diligence and a positive attitude toward best practice.

I situate bank operational risk in developing economies in work and service failings of bank managements and employees. In view of operational risk interaction with work and service, I focus on the perspective of human elements at work. I do so as I analyze, discuss, and draw conclusions on bank operational risk dynamics and control in developing economies. Thus, work situation is the watchword for discussions in this chapter.

OPERATIONAL RISK IN NEGATIVE WORK DISPOSITION

Most customers would ordinarily be more or less encouraged to patronize particular banks depending on whether or not employees demonstrate positive or negative disposition toward service. Ideally, good service is efficient, courteous, and warm. This has implication for employee interview, selection, and recruitment. Banks should objectively assess and score candidates for employment on these critical service variables that influence customer patronage. The attitude of some employees to work is at best only lukewarm. Such attitude increases incidence of customer dissatisfaction. Service disposition mired in attitudinal issues is a bad omen for the future of a bank. The simple reason is that it de-markets the bank in the face of stiff competition. Bank managements should be dispassionate and take appropriate action to stem or correct criticized attitudes to work and service.

Much of marketing and relationship management tasks are eased with warm, efficient, and error-free services. Most customer and service-oriented banks work on these factors as a deliberate marketing strategy—one that helps to attain some market share goal. That goal is, perhaps, to retain and/or expand market share. Indeed, customer perception of service orientation of employees as positive or negative determine, to a large extent, success levels that banks attain with regard to competition for patronage or market share. Negative employee attitude to work in a service-oriented bank is an anticlimax. This is the fate of lots of poorly managed, unsuccessful banks. Successful banks consolidate their feats with uncompromising positive work attitudes. Such banks set and enforce appropriate work standards that fit with best practice.

One of the avoidable errors that bank managements make is recruiting front desk officers who lack enthusiasm. Such error sometimes borders on uncritical judgment and disregard of, or unwitting indifference to, the demands of customer service. The warmth appeal which customers cherish and get from lively front desk officers are lost under the circumstances. In time, the bank would start to lose patronage and market share. However, diligence and best practice should not be sacrificed for employee warmth and liveliness. These success factors should rather fulfill complementary roles in serving customer needs. Their complementarity is an essential, though not sufficient, requirement for the prevention of bank frauds.

PRESSURE OF WORK VIS-À-VIS OPERATIONAL RISK IN BANKING

Stress and pressures are common snags with bank work. Mostly, this happens where employees have tight deadlines and work without supervision. Often employees who attend to large customer traffic are prone to physical fatigue. Their work tends to be pressure-bound. Some experience mental fatigue, depending on the cerebral content of their work. Such fatigue renders customer service inefficient. But it also creates room for fraud-prone errors. Banks sometimes receive, but fail to resolve, customer complaints about discourteous disposition of employees that work in service points. Often this failure is caused by the presumption that impoliteness originates from the nature of employees. Therefore, in order to resolve the problem, bank managements simply redeploy the unfortunate employees in criticized service positions. The usual punitive practice is to engage them in some back office functions, or fire them from their jobs for incompetence. Often this approach to solve poor service is fallible. It does not take the work situation of the affected employees into account. If the causes of work pressures and stress are not addressed, new employees deployed to the same service positions might suffer a similar fate.

Yet bank managements can introduce changes that could help to solve work stress for employees in high traffic service points. It may redesign office layout for customer service points. This will make customers feel relaxed and happy. At the same time, it ensures that employees feel more relaxed about their work. With redesigned office spaces, staffing should be reviewed to determine optimum number of employees for the service points. For example, understaffed jobs or functions can result in stress for employees. Employees should be assigned work that their mental and physical abilities can support as a way of solving stress. It also reduces chances of fraud-prone errors. Stress and fraud risks are equally mitigated when employees are assigned realistic performance targets. In all this, the health of employees—which stress of work endangers—is of paramount importance. It is difficult to fully tap employee potential without solving their work stress. In most cases, bank managements don't feel a sense of obligation beyond subsidizing medical expenses of the employees. Feigning ignorance about the health plight of employees in stress-laden functions is unfair. Of course the affected employees are bound to respond in kind. Indifference to customer service, abdication of responsibility for risk control, and dereliction of duty are some of the adverse consequences of lack or neglect of employee care. The end result, in most cases, is customer dissatisfaction. With this outcome, the bank is exposed to frauds and sundry operational risks.

Employees have a role to play in stemming work stress. Solving the causes of work pressures should at no time be left entirely for bank managements. The question now is what should employees do to solve work stress that impairs their productivity? First, they must satisfy physical and mental requirements for their work. Good health and wellbeing are imperative for employee performance. Thus, workers must invest in these complex, but highly valuable, personal assets. In doing so, they should appreciate the need to be always fit to do their jobs. Regular physical exercises and leisure are always helpful. Second, employees should avoid, or at least reduce, personal conflicts with their jobs—both within and outside the workplace. There might be occasional role conflicts in the workplace. Yet such conflicts may not be as worrisome as those arising from personal situations of employees. Third, employees must set clearly defined personal, work and nonwork related goals that do not conflict with the bank's overall corporate objectives, and goals for their jobs and work roles. With goals congruence—once this is done—the employees should seek to attain the set goals.

CASE STUDY 28.1 Neglecting Versus Taking Care of Employees

A certain high-ranking hospital and one of the leading banks operating in Lagos, Nigeria, have conflicting views about the plight of employees doing stressful work (While this case study is real, the hospital and bank are used anonymously so as to maintain confidentiality of their true identities. Similarly, the setting of the case study is also kept confidential for the same reason. The case study itself is presented here purely for illustration purposes only and to demonstrate how handling of some employee issues could crystalize operational risks for banks in developing economies). The bank retained the hospital to serve the health needs of its employees. Once, the medical director (MD) of the hospital drew the attention of the bank's chief executive officer (CEO) to an emerging trend in consultations by the bank's employees.

Apparently, the number of the bank's employees whom the hospital had treated for high blood pressure, backaches, and other stress-induced sundry sicknesses was on the increase. This worrying trend became scary as the observed cases continued to mount. The immediate intention of the MD was to sensitize the CEO about possible risk that undue work pressures posed to the health of workers. In doing so, the MD expected that the CEO would investigate the report. Based on findings, the CEO could do something to ameliorate pressure-laden work responsibilities. That would permit relaxed mental and physical exertions of the employees.

However, the CEO rebuffed the MD's suggestions—claiming that such pressures existed in the intrinsic nature of most bank jobs. The CEO also declined the MD's suggestion that the bank should organize regular health enlightenment sessions for the employees of the bank. Thus, the MD failed in making out a case for ameliorating work pressures on the employees. The hospital, nonetheless, maintained normal counseling for the bank's employees—ostensibly to check further deterioration in their health.

Exercise for class discussion

1. What can you make out in the position taken by the bank's CEO?
2. How do you think the employees would react if they were privy to their chief executive's position on the issue?
3. What are the possible repercussions of the CEO's action on the essence of the bank's business?
4. Do you think that the response of the CEO to the MD's report could be a trigger point for bank fraud if the employees know about it?

Tips for solving the exercise

Probable answers to this exercise should highlight the need to promptly resolve employees' complaints. That commits the employees to doing their utmost to satisfy customer needs and, if possible, surpass their expectations. Solving pressures of work can enhance employee productivity. However, actions taken to achieve this result should be timely, studied, and customer-driven. Overall, such actions should also aim to remove unnecessary queues, check vexing delays, or obviate the costs of failure to serve customers well. These are some of the difficulties which customers often experience when they need particular service. The difficulties manifest themselves in declining patronage. On occasion, they reflect in disparaging remarks as one unhappy customer after another switches patronage from uncaring to the more customer-driven banks.

OPERATIONAL RISK IN LACK OF ENTHUSIASM FOR WORK

The inability of banks to offer quality service to customers may be due to personal constraints on the employees. Employees tend to lose warmth with customers when they have disturbing family pressures, or when they experience upset of personal goals. Conditions of work can cause high or low service morale. Some employees may even become dissatisfied with their work profiles. Loss of faith in their banks may yet dampen an employee's enthusiasm. These issues dampen down the zeal with which employees attend to customers.

I recognize that they belong to—and are therefore best analyzed in—organizational behavior and human resources management studies. Yet I consider it pertinent to examine how they affect the need for enthusiastic disposition of employees to work and customer satisfaction. In doing so, I discuss the implications for fraud risk control in banking.

Disturbing Family Pressures

Most employees perform below expectation when they work under pressure of family life. Family pressures that frustrate employee performance can take different forms. As a socio-economic unit, the family might be facing trying circumstances. Lives and property may be at risk. Loved family member might be sick, hospitalized, or have just died. One's son or daughter might have just failed an important interview or examination. There could be several other such issues that can make an employee lose enthusiasm for work and customer service.

Once family pressures set in, employees tend to make mistakes, become antagonistic and uncaring. In time, employees in this condition start exhibiting absentmindedness, sloppiness, and discontentment—all of which often happen as subconscious behavior. Unfortunately, bank managements may not, in practical terms, preempt personal and family pressures. Sadly, still, these pressures take a heavy toll on the productivity of the employees. However, bank managements can and should anticipate the fallout of the pressures in terms of risks of unintended errors and possible service gaps that can expose the bank to fraud.

Managers should promptly detect employees that have serious family problems, try to proffer soothing advice to them, and closely monitor their performance. Yet while uplifting employees in this condition with useful advice, attaining the goal of quality, error-free customer service should be upheld at all times. When it becomes obvious that this goal might not be achieved because of frustrating family pressures, the managers should redeploy the affected employees to non-fraud-prone functions.

Upset of Personal Goals

Employees, like every other normal person, have personal goals and aspirations to which they aspire. Besides the basic needs for food, clothing, and shelter, most people strive for other important, higher order needs. Perhaps the most challenging higher order need toward which many people work is to be self-fulfilled. In pursuing their ordinary and higher order needs, employees are expected to set measurable success targets. Work behavior is ultimately driven by the realism in these personal objectives in and out of the workplace. Often, employees that progressively achieve their set personal goals will be focused, devoted, and enthusiastic. Likewise, those that are convinced about their abilities to achieve success will most likely show remarkable commitment to work.

However, employees that are dazed about their personal life will probably lack the zeal to work, among other negative attributes. The fate of this category of employees will be similar to those whose personal goals are upset by events beyond their control. With upset personal goals, some employees renounce challenging life pursuits and resign themselves to fate. The state of their minds becomes one in which the primary corporate cause of their calling—satisfying customer needs—is relegated to a level of inconsequence. This is an unhealthy situation that may be propitious for bank fraud.

Low Work and Service Morale

The zeal with which employees do their work is a function of their morale and state of mind. Thus, superior work output is achieved when morale is high. Perhaps this explains why motivation and productivity are among the most researched topics in organizational behavior and human resources management studies. Ordinarily, so-called *satisfiers* in the workplace help to boost employee morale. Lack of the satisfiers, in contrast, breeds so-called *dissatisfiers* that hurt morale.

Reward system also has influence on employee morale. Morale could be enhanced or marred depending on the timing, appropriateness, and justifications for managerial actions that affect employees. For instance, unfair punitive actions tend to demoralize employees. Unfortunately, bank managements and employees often have different opinions on what constitutes just and unjust treatment, or punitive action. Consider a situation in which bank management withdraws official cars attached to some employees for coming late to work. This action may be administratively expedient, but the affected employees would see its basis as trivial. Managements and employees disagree on the appropriateness of several other sundry actions to correct bad behavior at work. Some of such actions that have implications for employee morale include withholding of salaries, caution or warning letters, and suspension of entitlements.

In most cases, these actions introduce conflicts that become detrimental to work and business of the bank. This has negative implications for the bank. It exposes the bank to acts of sabotage by the employees. It takes a toll on the bank's cause as a going concern. Demoralized employees will hardly offer enthusiastic customer service. Neither will they be warm to customers. Even with quality service, banks that have a large pool of employees with low work morale will lose customer patronage, market share, and earnings over time. Low morale and flawed reward system lead to dissatisfaction with work. A bank in this situation easily becomes vulnerable to sundry fraud.

Dissatisfaction with Work

Bank managements should know what could cause employees to be dissatisfied with work. They should equally be able to detect employee dissatisfaction with work. However, the crucial managerial challenge is in determining what could be done to solve the causes and problems of dissatisfaction with work. This is a critical requirement for success of risk and fraud control in banking. One reason is that employees that are dissatisfied with work would make the turnover statistic. Besides, employees tend to make half-hearted effort to achieve set goals if the causes of dissatisfaction are serious and deep-seated in their work. Difficult and irregular or tight schedules can trigger dissatisfaction with work. Relentless, goal-driven employees see work as a central life interest and are resilient. Most workers, on the contrary, simply get used to regular functions. This helps them in applying their abilities to meet known or predetermined work schedules and expectations. Coupled with a mindset that favors predictable rewards and punishments for work success and failure, employees will want to know their fate on their jobs. That is the reason, for instance, employees that harbor fears of job insecurity would probably remain depressed, unfocused, and dissatisfied until their final exit from their banks. However, until such employees quit, they remain a risk factor. Fraudsters can easily recruit such employees to defraud the bank.

Loss of Faith in Self and Employment

Hardly does one find employees who have entirely lost faith in themselves, their banks, or both. However, some loss of faith exists among employees. In general, motivated employees often sustain work effort and momentum through faith in either their personal abilities or the potential of their banks. If workers are not faithful to the cause of their employments, they lose optimism and tend to be alienated from work. In most situations of sheer loss of faith, the affected employees would not render enthusiastic service to customers. Employees would perhaps start to lose faith in their banks and personal abilities due to perceived or actual failure to realize the promises of work. When this happens, frustration sets in and begins to inhibit the commitment of the employees to work and the bank. There could indeed be several other possible causes of loss of faith by employees. However, the critical issue for management is not to only know why, but how employees lose faith in their personal abilities to work or in the banks for which they work. With such knowledge, bank managements would better appreciate and address the circumstances under which employees lose enthusiasm for or momentum toward work. This reduces risk and chances of operational fraud in banking. Fortunately, bank managements and employees can collaborate in solving the problem of loss of faith. The solution could be physical, or psychological, depending on the particular circumstances of the affected employees. This should be done in the understanding that bank managements and employees have stakes in increasing returns to the shareholders through devotion to duty, superior performance, and customer satisfaction.

RISK-DETERMINING INTERFACE BETWEEN BUSINESS AND OPERATIONS BANKING

The old generation banks in Nigeria—those founded prior to the liberalization of licensing of banking business with the introduction of SAP in the country in 1986—never separated business and operations management functions at the branch level (Some of so-called first generation banks include First Bank of Nigeria Limited, Union Bank of Nigeria PLC, United Bank for Africa PLC, and so on). Then branch managers were responsible for business development (comprising lending, marketing, treasury, and relationship management) and operations matters, including transactions processing, accounts, and reporting. In this capacity, they assumed the ultimate power of administration of all facets of the business and operations. Control of branch activities under their leadership occasionally came from the head office as a centralized function. However, there could sometimes be resident auditors who reviewed activities of branches to ensure compliance with the bank's standard operating procedures.

Conflicts between operations and business development functions—and therefore the need for sustained effective inspection, audit, and control services—were hardly pronounced. As chief accounting officers, branch managers wielded influence and dominance over all branch functions—taking glory and blame for successes and failures, respectively, on assigned performance targets. Thus, branch accountants who directly supervised operations activities (mainly, transactions processing) functioned largely in subordinated capacities to branch managers. This arrangement was germane to the scalar principle in classical management theory, which emphasizes unity of command and hierarchical reporting lines for all functional officers of organizations.

However, the concentration of authority in one person soon came under scrutiny and severe attacks as banks reported avoidable abuses arising from the inability or failure of branch managers to always exercise due diligence. Some also failed to effectively and satisfactorily deal with on-the-job conflicts of interest, especially in their day-to-day management functions. This finding became a major cause for repositioning the status of inspection, audit, and control as a veritable instrument for effective management of branch operations. However, it also triggered thinking and eventual adoption of separation of functions between operations and business responsibilities bank-wide, but especially at the branch levels. Now, operations personnel have been largely independent and, as such, their leader—the operations manager—is no longer directly responsible, or subordinated, to the branch manager. Instead, there is a parallel split between the operations and branch or business managers, with both having separate reporting lines to different bosses in the head office.

A Split Spurred by Risk Considerations

The new generation banks, prebanking system consolidation era, pioneered the separation of business and operations functions, especially as branch management strategy (Most of the new generation banks were founded after 1986 following the deregulation of the banking industry in 1986 when the country adopted Structural Adjustment Program supported by the IMF and World Bank. There were at least more than 100 of such banks as at December 31, 2001). The practice gained wide acceptance in the industry since the early 1990s. It provides a means for attaining efficient operations, effective control, and improved business performance. Yet it has its drawbacks, the most important of which has been infighting between employees in operations and business units. However, the basis of bickering and infighting is rooted in the nature and success requirements of the two functions. I give an example to illustrate this point. Business banking is geared to satisfy customer needs. Thus, the main aim of employees in business banking are to prospect for new customers, transactions, and deals. In doing so, they seek to attract, satisfy, and retain customer relationships as a means of meeting profit goals. This is quite demanding and constantly puts them under immense pressure. The belief in business, of course, is that the customer is king and is always right. The customers themselves are aware of these business slogans in their favor and tap into them as banks crave their patronage. The banks leave no stone unturned in their quest to attract and retain good customers. Thus business development employees are often torn between meeting budget goals, customer expectations, beating competition, and adhering to internal and regulatory procedures (Onyiriuba et al., 2000).

Similarly, work in banking operations demands that employees be responsible for transactions processing and, doing so, insist on strict adherence to the bank's standard operating procedures and policies. The bank's procedural manual guides their work—stipulating punitive actions that would be taken against them if they flout processing rules in the guide manual. That serves as a constant reminder to them of the price of flouting banking operations and processing rules. To make matters worse, operations employees are ever in the firing line. They must meet critical work deadlines—such as submission of regulatory returns—resume unusually early for work, and always work late. Always staying alert and keeping frauds at bay are part of their responsibilities. It is also the operations employees who interface with internal auditors and the regulatory authorities—responding to all sorts of banking operations and processing concerns and queries. Yet their work, though appreciated, does not bestow as much visibility as, or receive acknowledgement equal to, that of employees in business development units. The fact that the two units necessarily perform different but complementary—and, on occasion, conflicting—roles does not help matters. Thus, the two units often work at cross-purposes, playing a cat and mouse game to gain the upper hand over each other. That is the reason it seems operations employees are unnecessarily rigid or inflexible, unresponsive to customer needs, indifferent to business development, and not bothered about profit targets.

However, in some cases, such absolute split of power could lead to leadership vacuum as no one officer is directly accountable for overall functions of the branch. Yet the practice is credited with strengthening internal control and promoting professional discipline in the conduct of branch activities. Its overall advantage is that overzealous business tendencies and inordinate risk-taking with depositors' funds kept in check. But it is ironic that the all-powerful operations and control employees who monitor all banking, especially the line and functional, activities sometimes feel that rewards for good performance are not equitably distributed between them and the employees in business units. Often employees in operations and controls units accuse bank management of bias against them and protest the fast track career path of their colleagues in business units compared to theirs.

There are several other areas of dissatisfaction for the operations and control employees despite their great influence over business development functions. Should bank managements be really biased against any group of employees for whatever reason? Where bias does exist, how may one explain its causes? What steps should bank managements take to disabuse employees of the existence of biases? I proffer some views in the following discussions. First, what are the frequently observed biases? How and why do they originate and exist?

FACING UP TO RISK AND DISABUSING EMPLOYEES OF NOTIONS OF BIAS

Operations and control employees tend to hold a belief that emphasis in bank management is often biased in favor of lending, marketing, and investment decisions at the expense of equally important functions in operations and internal control (I have throughout this discussion used the term "control" or "internal control" interchangeably with the phrase "inspection, audit, and control." However, where the need arose to distinguish between the terms, I did indicate their distinctive meanings in the related contexts). The most frequently cited illustration of management bias is not only instructive, but pertinent. Operations employees claim that their business development colleagues benefit more from banking glitz. They cite examples to buttress this point. Official and, especially, pool cars are attached to their jobs. The bank buys and assigns them cellular phones. They meet and interact with political and industry bigwigs. Of course, they get the bonuses and mostly have the attention of executive management (Onyiriuba, 2000). This implied management bias might perhaps be inadvertent and understood or excused in the context of the inherent bank management's drive to beat competition. There is also the reason associated with the high stakes in banking, by which bank managements are ordinarily tasked to sustain earnings and business growth in line with the vision of the bank and its shareholders. However, this orientation sometimes induces management obsession with business development without the concomitant emphasis on operations and control.

The result, in most cases, is that the bank incurs operational losses that often neutralize the gains of business generation and earnings over time. Much of such losses could even threaten the survival of the bank as a going concern. This would happen where continuing undetected operational lapses, on the one hand, and unconcern for observance of controls, on the other, facilitate large-scale frauds and abuse of employees' official positions. A bank may also incur avoidable, sometimes acute, losses when approved work procedures are blatantly ignored or flouted. Such losses would also be incurred where there is flagrant indifference by employees to efficient transactions processing, which could cause unsustainable loss of valued or coveted customers' patronage. There is thus need to harmonize the business objectives of increasing earnings, profits, and growth with an appropriate risk control disposition to attain optimum performance. Otherwise, it would be irresponsible for bank managements to waste business development achievements on grounds of weak internal control system. Such will be the case where bank managements lack the business sense characteristic of, or typically found among, serious minded entrepreneurs. Of course, with intense competition that now characterizes the business, bank managements should lay strong emphasis on, and seek to enthrone, customer satisfaction through fast, error-free, and efficient transactions processing and service delivery. In adopting this thinking as a conscious business practice or strategy, the bank would be joining the ranks of firms that appreciate and encourage continuing evolution of the marketing concept.

In order to achieve this goal, banking operations and control should not constitute an impediment to normal business activities. It is imperative to always maintain an acceptable level of flexibility, which business managers require to achieve target performance. The working relationship between business development, banking operations, and internal control employees should, above all else, be as cordial as could be practically possible. It is always necessary that the work of the units complements each other. Complementarity ensures a bank's branch is strong, smooth running, and profitable—with mitigated risks, especially chances of banking frauds. It implies that neither of the units is seen as, or should feel that it is, inferior or superior to the others (Onyiriuba, Olowude, and Allen, op. cit.). This is a necessary, though not sufficient, means for the employees to work in harmony toward realization of the branch's overall business objectives. It should be borne in mind that complementary work goes with interdependence roles. I mean a situation in which the employees work with and depend on each other to pursuit of the branch's, as well as the bank-wide, business objectives. On its part, bank managements should encourage, recognize, and reward successful goal-driven teamwork. It would then be futile, once this is institutionalized, to see or feel work differences as embodying conflicts. There would no longer be mutual suspicion between the employees—after all, they jointly take the glory when their branch is succeeding or a caution when it is dysfunctional. In other words, their fates and that of the branch are intertwined. Therefore, they can do anything but flout banking operations and processing rules—just as it would be disruptive of the bank's goal if business development employees are frustrated.

The need for cooperation between employees in business development and operations is further underlined by the nature of risks inherent in their functions, which they should always seek to mitigate. Consider, for example, a situation from the operations angle. Let's assume that a bank opens many customer accounts with incomplete documentation or without due diligence as know your customer (KYC) rules require. This flawed action is bound to have a ripple effect through the whole banking operations. The accounts might be used for frauds due to the neglect of procedures. The bank stands to lose money and customer trust as a result of frauds. The regulatory authorities may sanction the bank for negligence. Frauds also lead to loss of confidence in the bank's management by the shareholders, and so on. Banking operations and processing employees' strict stance on risk control is informed by a need to forestall these and similar adverse consequences. Employees in business development also have defense for their work disposition and attitude toward risk. Branches are expected to be profitable. This expectation will be far-fetched without a large and growing customer base. The performance of branches accounts significantly for the bank-wide financial results. Thus, unprofitable branches might be closed down with dire consequences. The bank may fail—thus sending its employees back into the labor market as they lose their source of livelihood. It therefore behooves the business development employees to generate sufficient transactions and deals that guarantee increasing and sustained incomes—lest their branches slip into loss-making positions.

It does not really make sense, in view of these possibilities, for employees in business, operations, and control divisions to be suspicious of, or antagonistic toward, one another. Bank managements should discourage employees from infighting on account of pursuit of goals in "silos" rather than in complementarity. Employees should at all times be made to appreciate the usefulness of each function in the overall interest of the objectives, business, and performance of the bank. Even when it appears to be so, no functional responsibility should be accorded a preeminent status over the others. This should be upheld as a means of instilling confidence in the employees, a sense of belonging in them, and assuring the relevance of all employees to the bank and in the scheme of things.

TAMING BUSINESS BANKING WITH RISK-BASED CONTROLS

Often, the business division sometimes experiences interface frictions with operations and control divisions. Such frictions arise in the course of everyday performance of normal functions of the employees. It is healthy and, indeed, important that managers of these divisions should disagree as may be warranted in the course of professional discharge of their duties. This is because work roles of the divisions have opposing, yet reinforcing, perspectives. The real benefit lies in realizing synergy from the dynamics of work interfaces. Yet it is necessary for bank managements to consciously encourage all employees to appreciate one another's work roles.

An interview with some employees in business and control divisions in some bank revealed a worrying anxiety about the enduring conflicts. One suggestion for resolving misunderstanding of each other's roles kept recurring. It pointed bank managements toward devising practical frameworks of work that would be devoid of role conflicts that culminate in bitterness and rancor. Though the suggestion is pertinent, the employees also have a role to fulfill. They should understand the dynamics of each other's work and appreciate interdependence of their individual roles. Then the practice of rotation of duties becomes more meaningful to the employees as it assumes unusual significance. Role conflicts are bound to reduce as every employee gets varied and on-the-job wider experience through rotation. The practitioners know all too well that unfounded biases toward some jobs are inherent in banking. Rotation of duties of employees mitigates the biases and work risks attendant on it. I give an example to illustrate this outcome. Let's assume that a manager who works in business development rebuffs their colleagues in banking operations—and vice versa. Their colleagues' job soon becomes their lot when they're redeployed or their duties rotated to it. So it really doesn't make sense for an employee to feel superior or inferior on account of their job. Ideally, business managers with banking operations and processing background—and vice versa—will have a wider perspective that mitigates role conflicts and risk to the bank.

The business managers are ever striving to meet deposits, earnings, and profits targets at any point in time. On occasion they are criticized and served queries, warning letters, and severe reprimand for failing to meet or surpass the targets. Similarly, they are praised and handsomely rewarded for attaining or surpassing the targets. The rewards could be outlandish sometimes. This dichotomy between criticism and praise—and their related punishments and rewards—shed light on why they tend to be overzealous and obsessive about meeting budget goals. They do so, sometimes, risking possible infraction of the rules or controls. In the process, the managers appear to see stringent work procedures or restrictions as superfluous. This situation leads to a temptation to maneuver internal controls—an unofficial way of trying to enforce flexibility of operational rules on bank managements. Therefore, training programs for employees in business units should emphasize the need for them to realize that a bank must always have a watchdog. The essence of that watchdog is the basis of the creation and functioning of internal controls in banking. So bank employees should appreciate that work and internal controls are unavoidable. They are a sort of necessary evil with which they must live for the bank to progress, succeed, and remain a going concern.

Employees in operations and controls units serve essentially as monitors of implementation of all banking rules, regulations, and operating guidelines. They observe, analyze, and report to, or advise bank managements on apparent, envisaged or possible breach of operational procedures that can cause financial loss to the bank. Often their main goal is to tame inordinate and ambitions budget goals—and, doing so, help business managers to be more disciplined without jeopardizing or frustrating banking opportunities. However, an overriding consideration, beyond disciplining, should be how to ensure that controls are not enforced in a way that business managers are demoralized, demotivated or discouraged. Consider, for example, that controls employees—in a manner suggestive of deliberate infraction of rule or fraud—can, and indeed often do, take business managers to task for unintentional acts or slips that contravene work or operational procedures. Once this happens, the basis of cooperation and synergy between employees in business and controls begins to ebb away. In extreme situation, the bank may be plunged into unnecessary work interface crisis.

There are three methods that enjoy general application in enforcing internal controls in banking. Each of the methods is intended to help tame risky activities of the various units of business and operations of the bank. The approaches—their purposes and effectiveness—represent deliberate attempts by inspectors to rid banks of unprofessional employee conducts, frauds, and other financial crimes. The three methods and their scope are subsumed under compliance inspection, routine inspection, and specific or internal audit. The business managers should appreciate these internal control functions, cooperate with their colleagues, assigned the responsibility of executing them, and generally go with the flow.

RISK-BASED APPROACH TO EMPOWER BUSINESS MANAGERS

Bank employees at managerial level in business units tend to interpret functional conflicts between them and their colleagues in operations, processing, and control units in a different context, one that is not risk-based. They explain their roles interface conflicts in the context of their lack of empowerment relative to their colleagues in nonbusiness units. They insist on this view, quite paradoxically, as the cause of failings in doing their work. However, their colleagues in nonbusiness units are not as bothered about empowerment as them.

Usually, employees in nonbusiness units are provided with standard operating procedures to strictly guide their work, especially in transactions processing. Employees in business units, on the contrary, rely largely on personal initiatives and senior management's approvals to conclude most transactions or deals with customers. Their work processes, unlike those of employees in nonbusiness areas, do not lend themselves to being standardized for across-the-board application in negotiating, structuring, and conducting transactions and deals. Really, business decisions are not amenable to the straitjacket of banking operations, processing, and controls. Thus, some managers in business units make their excuses for failing to achieve their performance targets. The excuses revolve around delays often experienced in obtaining approval for urgent transactions and deals. The managers argue that they would do better if they were empowered to take certain business decisions directly.

However, bank managements hold a different view, dismissing the managers' claim as frivolous. This is consonant with the thinking in bank management circles—it is not possible, from risk control perspective, to empower business managers in absolute terms. In line with this reasoning, bank managements strongly believe that empowerment should be earned by the managers, and not be handed to them on a silver platter. If this belief is anything to go by, business managers may be granted limited approval rights at the discretion of senior management of a bank. The rights would be given to the managers that have and demonstrate proven business sense, integrity, initiative, diligence, and dedication to duty. These are some of the attributes that can earn the managers conditional empowerment. This implies that empowerment is not necessarily a function of the ranks of employees, but a reflection of their risk-taking sense, as well as rating on critical personal attributes.

MANAGERIAL RESPONSE TO EMPLOYEE SITUATIONS

It will be sad if employees who are expected to work for the cause of the bank and customers—and, in doing so, attain their personal work goals—are not devoted to their calling. Bank managements should therefore device means of detecting and handling employee grievances that could dampen down their devotion, loyalty, and enthusiasm for work. Probable actions which bank managements may take to resolve employee dissatisfaction should begin with a study and also:

- understanding personal attributes of the employees engaged in particular service assignments, including their goals and aspirations for life;
- assessing characteristics of particular jobs, with a view to ascertaining unusual demands that work makes on the employees; and
- determining measurable critical factors for success of employees on particular job functions.

Findings from this study will help bank managements to know if particular employees are suited for their jobs. Through a painstaking analysis of relevant issues and input from human resources management experts retained by the bank, managements can be properly advised on the possible actions to take on each issue.

However, in all cases, any action that may be taken should be geared to achieve optimum performance of the workers. Often, managerial actions aimed at improving employee devotion to work succeed most when the workers share objectives underlying the actions. For this reason, there must be a forum for regular interaction between employees and managements on critical work issues. Such a forum bridges communication gaps, but it also engenders shared understanding of the true essence of work, satisfying customers, and doing anything to ensure repeat patronage. With intensifying market competition and declining profit margins, a bank cannot afford to ignore avoidable flaws in trying to market value to customers. Thus employees and managements must regularly meet to strategize on how to render optimum service to customers. Otherwise, they would be neglecting customer rationality in switching patronage based on perceived service attributes and disposition of employees. Corporate inclination to organizing occasional in-house business retreats is a positive reaction to emerging challenges in satisfying customer needs.

Unfortunately, the outcomes of such strategy sessions remain on paper afterward—not necessarily in the brains and practical actions of employees and managements. In fact, employees who are laidback often see such strategy and training sessions as recreations. The true essence of the retreats is lost under the circumstances for craving and the craze for leisure that has become elusive for most bankers. This explains why on-the-job training remains more effective than workshops, seminars, conferences, and even in-house and other courses.

HANDLING DIFFICULT EMPLOYEES AND CUSTOMERS

Individuals whose character is questionable do not make good bank employees. Such people are especially not fit for marketing and relationship management functions. They tend to have distasteful disposition to work that alienates them from customers. Bankers need more patience and should exercise extra care in dealing with customers, especially those who are fastidious about transactions in their bank accounts. Such customers will not tolerate or want to work with unreliable employees as account officers and relationship managers because of their antics. Often lack of customer trust in such employees stems from doubt about integrity of the employees. On occasion, this doubt is deep seated in the psyche of customers—a feeling that employees with doubtful character may defraud them. Some customers may be naturally difficult. They easily become irate without or at the slightest provocation. This reflects bad temper. There is a need to keep a close watch on such employees and customers. For all intents and purposes, ill-tempered nature could be a camouflage for fraudulent intention. Now the big question is how should bank managements deal with this problem? Is it possible—in the case of employees—to train them such that they become amiable and appreciate warmth as important elements of their work? If so, how can managers or supervisors go about this task? It may not be easy to unravel probable camouflage for fraudulent intention. This and similar behavioral tendencies do not lend themselves to forced correction. For this reason, close monitoring is inevitable. In addition, employee supervisors may adopt counseling, consider reposting option, or invoke code of conduct as remedial actions.

SUMMARY

Operational risk in banking is best understood in the context of gaps in services that banks offer to customers. Good or bad orientation and disposition of bank employees to service can help check or foster operational risk. Typical operational risk, fraud, on occasion, finds its way into patronage-service calculation of banks and customers. This happens where bank employees and customers are uncritical of their chase after service. Often personnel issues create service gaps that may be propitious for bank operational risk. Managerial response to this tendency should aim to reinvent customer service, fill service gaps and, in doing so, forestall possible frauds.

Stress and pressures are common snags with bank work. Mostly, this happens where employees have tight deadlines and work without supervision. Often employees who attend to large customer traffic are prone to physical fatigue. Their work tends to be pressure-bound. Some experience mental fatigue, depending on the cerebral content of their work. Such fatigue renders customer service inefficient. But it also creates room for fraud-prone errors.

Employees should be assigned work that their mental and physical abilities can support as a way of solving stress. It also reduces chances of fraud-prone errors. Stress and fraud risks are equally mitigated when employees are assigned realistic performance targets. In all this, the health of employees—which stress of work endangers—is of paramount importance. It is difficult to fully tap employee potential without solving their work stress. Indifference to customer service, abdication of responsibility for risk control, and dereliction of duty are some of the adverse consequences of lack or neglect of employee care. With this outcome, the bank is exposed to frauds and sundry operational risks.

Inability of banks to offer quality service to customers may be due to personal constraints on the employees. Employees tend to lose warmth with customers when they have disturbing family pressures, or when they experience upset of personal goals. Conditions of work can cause high or low service morale. Some employees may even become dissatisfied with their work profiles. Loss of faith in their banks may yet dampen an employee's enthusiasm. These issues dampen down the zeal with which employees attend to customers.

Centralization of authority in branch managers came under scrutiny and severe attacks as banks reported abuses arising from their inability or failure to always exercise due diligence. Some also failed to effectively and satisfactorily deal with on-the-job conflicts of interest, especially in their day-to-day management functions. This finding became a major cause for repositioning the status of inspection, audit, and control as a veritable instrument for effective management of branch operations. However, it also triggered thinking and eventual adoption of separation of functions between operations and business responsibilities bank-wide, but especially at the branch levels.

QUESTIONS FOR DISCUSSION AND REVIEW

1. In what ways can operational risk in banking be best understood in the context of gaps in services that banks offer to customers?
2. How may orientation and disposition of employees to service help check or foster operational risk in banking?
3. Why would uncritical chase after service be a reason for fraud to find its way into patronage-service calculation of banks and customers?

4. What operational risks do issues in work situations of employees portend for banks in developing economies?
5. Do you think the reasons that informed the split between business and operations banking functions bank-wide are really cogent?

REFERENCE

Onyiriuba, L., Olowude, B., Allen, T., 2000. Between operations and marketing. Magnum Connect 1 (2), 4–5, (Quarterly Newsletter of Magnum Trust Bank Plc.).

Chapter 29

Banking Processing and Operational Risk Management in Developing Economies

Chapter Outline

LEARNING FOCUS AND OBJECTIVES

Banking processing has been an emerging operational function in banks in developing economies. Unfortunately, it is as ambiguous as banking operations which it has supplanted in many banks. The difference between the two constructs is really nomenclatural. Operational risk management remains the basic challenge of banking operations and processing. I emphasize this point in formulating objectives of this chapter which are intended to:

● examine aspects of transactions processing errors that may—and do some-times—crystallize operational risks in banking;
● provide insights into the nature of bank operational risks and their manage-ment requirements in developing economies;
● investigate the creation, types, and features of operational risks in banking transactions processing;
● identify and situate processing risks and controls in in the context of paying and clearing bank checks; and
● explore possibilities of stemming bank operational risks through reconcilia-tion of accounts.

EXPECTED LEARNING OUTCOMES

It is now common knowledge that operational risks have moved to the center stage of challenges facing bank managements in developing countries. This happened as one of the side effects of the burgeoning revolution in the banking industry. Today, bank managements contend with new and novel processing risks—in addition to the mundane operational risks to which they are used. This demands unusual ingenuity in dealing with the risks. The reader will—after studying this chapter—have learnt and been better informed about:

● examine aspects of transactions processing errors that may—and do some-times—crystallize operational risks in banking;
● provide insights into the nature of bank operational risks and their manage-ment requirements in developing economies;
● investigate the creation, types, and features of operational risks in banking transactions processing;
● identify and situate processing risks and controls in in the context of paying and clearing bank checks; and
● explore possibilities of stemming bank operational risks through reconcilia-tion of accounts.

OVERVIEW OF THE SUBJECT MATTER

Operations and transactions processing are about the riskiest bank functions in developing economies. Risks attendant on these activities are now center stage of challenges facing bank managements. The burgeoning revolution in the banking industry has not helped matters. Rather, it introduced new and novel dimensions to the risks. Nowadays, bankers in developing economies deal not with mundane but novel operational risks. Most of the risks are alien to banking and finance in developing economies. Bank managements have had to devise measures designed to mitigate the risks. In doing so, scarce operational skills and resources are deployed. Yet the risks defy remedy and persist. It would appear that banks managements are fighting a losing battle on control of the risk.

The operational fallout elevated transactions processing to the top of bank management priorities. This outcome mirrors the great significance of bank operational risk control in developing economies. The focus of control is on processing and allied risks inherent in banking operations. Banks rely on one particular instrument for effective control of operational risks in transactions processing. That instrument is standard operating procedures (SOP) manual. A bank's SOP manual is a dependable and omnipotent processing guide. It not only furnishes but institutionalizes guidelines for transactions processing bankwide. The fallback on SOP for processing risk control is realistic, no doubt about it. Yet operational risks continue to take a heavy toll on banking processing.

The enforcement of processing controls in banks revolves around built-in checks in the SOP manual. However, bank employees and customers do manipulate the SOP sometimes and defraud the bank. This happens despite stringent internal control systems of the banks under which the SOP manual is subsumed. The implications of this situation for bank operational risk management in developing economies are pertinent. Two of the possible implications stand out. First, neither SOP nor internal control by itself can forestall manipulation of banking processing. Internal control and SOP do not encompass all aspects of applicable risk management measures. Second, it is necessary to integrate SOP and internal control with evolving techniques for managing novel risks which revolution in banking occasions.

AN INSIGHT INTO OPERATIONAL RISKS OF BANKING IN DEVELOPING ECONOMIES

Banks in developing economies always crave deposit-based banking relationships. There is especially a longing for accounts that have large, increasing, and cheap deposit potential. Such are the so-called big-ticket bank accounts whose transactions help boost balance sheet footing and earnings. Business development officers chase after customers in this category, leaving no stone unturned in their quest to attract them for banking relationship. Most public sector accounts are typical. Often documenting and opening such accounts follow the fast track. In the process, unfortunately, due process may sometimes be sacrificed for relationship management. On occasion, inexperienced and gullible employees in banking operations are maneuvered into circumventing standard operating procedures. The result, in most cases, is fraud and huge financial loss to the bank. Thus, inordinate drive to achieve mutually beneficial banking relationships, for all intents and purposes, informs increasing incidence of risks to banks in developing economies. Case study 29.1 deals with opening and operating a public sector bank account by deception. It is a typical example to illustrate the dynamic of banking risks which employee failings occasionally. The failings are often observed in business development functions, as well as in marketing and managing customer banking relationship.

CASE STUDY 29.1 Opening and Operating Public Sector Bank Account by Deception

Sandra had been trying to win the account of a certain State Legislature—referred to in this case study as "State House of Assembly" or, simply, "the House"—for over one year without success (The Legislative House, Principal Officers, and fraudsters are used anonymously in this tale so as to maintain the confidentiality of the case study. Similarly, the setting of the case study is also kept confidential. The case study itself is presented here purely for illustration purposes only and to demonstrate one of the risks of banking, especially in developing economies. While the fraud is real, the names of the bank, legislators, and individuals in the tale are imaginary and do not relate to any known or unknown real bank, persons, or legislators anywhere in the world). She had made several unsuccessful marketing calls to the potential accountholder—the legislative arm of the State Government. She stepped up effort to get the account and made joint calls on three occasions. First, she visited the legislature's point man on banking and allied matters with her boss. Like her solo effort, this joint call fell through. Then she enlisted the support of their regional director who could not hide his interest in the account. The call was partially successful. The point man had made a promise to support opening the account. Finally, Sandra requested their line executive director to join on yet another call. The target this time around was the leader of the House. The House Leader promised to liaise with his colleagues in the Banking and Allied Matters Committee.

At this stage, Sandra resigned to her fate and kept her fingers crossed that the account would be opened some day. So you can imagine her excitement when some legislator phoned her asking that the bank's account opening forms be sent to them at the House. She responded quickly with the necessary documents for opening a new public sector account. She called back the legislator once she was at the House using the same phone number that had called her to bring the account opening documents. The legislator introduced himself to her as a member of the Banking and Allied Matters Committee of the House. He told her that he and four of his colleagues had been mandated to handle the account opening process. Sandra thanked him, handed him the account opening documents, and left. She was to meet the other four members of the Committee later when they came together to the branch to submit the completed account opening documents.

The account was opened according to the bank's standard operating procedures. Operation of the account started soon after it was opened. As was expected, the account was very active—generating huge turnover of transactions, mainly in check lodgments and drawings. With this account, the branch of its domicile posted handsome monthly earnings. In this way, the profit from the account skewed business and financial performance of the branch. Sandra became the toast of the bank for getting the account. The branch instantly became strategic and won the Emerging and Most Promising Branch Award of the bank that year.

Then the bubble burst. Inspectors from the bank's internal control had flagged aspects of the account opening documentation. Lifting the veil of the documentation, it was found that the account was really a banking fraud. With the bank's management approval, the inspectors invited the Police who arrested Sandra, her boss, and the five lawmakers for interrogation. They were remanded in custody until the next day and subsequently taken to court. Investigation of the fraud immediately took center stage within the bank. As would be expected under the circumstances, the principal officers of the House firmly distanced themselves from the account. At this time, billions of taxpayers' funds had been misappropriated through the account.

Exercise for class and group discussion
1. Why was it possible—and even easy—for the five lawmakers to successfully maneuver the branch to open the fraudulent account?
2. How should the branch's operations officers have been able to prevent the deception by which the fraudulent account was opened?
3. Do you think that the bank's employees in operations who handled documentation and opening of the House's account acted in good faith?
4. What is your view and take on a possible suspicion of collusion between the principal officers of the House and the five lawmakers to perpetrate the fraud?
5. It might not have been easy to crack the fraud. How do you think the bank's inspectors were able to uncover the crime?

Tips for solving the exercise
It would seem that the five lawmakers connived with some insiders to open and operate the fraudulent account. They might have possibly used the real names and photographs, but forged signatures, of the principal officers of the House in opening the account. I mean it's possible so-called "identity theft" was adopted for the fraud. That way it was easy to maneuver the operations employees into admitting the related fake account opening documents. On the face of it, the operations employees followed the bank's instructions and stuck to the rules. Documentation and opening of the account followed due process and was complete in principle. However, these might not have been done in the strict KYC (know your customer) sense. Strangely Sandra never met any of the principal officers of the House before and after the account was opened. Curiously still, the authorized signatories who were the principal officers of the House were not contacted to confirm the mandate for the account. All these should have been done in strict compliance with KYC before opening the account. This omission leaves room for suspicion of collusion, on the one hand, and for the principal officers of the House to wriggle out of their responsibilities for the account, on the other. There were more mysteries for the investigators of the fraud to unravel.

OPERATIONAL RISKS IN BANKING TRANSACTIONS PROCESSING

The quality of service which banks render to their customers would be considered poor if it is has avoidable and recurrent mistakes. Service would be rated good or superior in banks that pursue and achieve error-free transactions processing. Often banks that have efficient service systems strive to attain zero error tolerance at all times. While such a goal might seem unrealistic in practical terms, or for all situations, it is yet desirable—at least for one reason. It reinforces the intrinsic value of mutual benefits in business relationship between the bank and its customers. The pursuit of this goal underscores the huge resources that banks deploy for marketing and managing banking relationships.

Banks must pursue error-free transactions processing at all times. Not a few customers are irked by costly, especially avoidable, mistakes in their banking transactions. Banks make deliberate efforts to stem this problem, no doubt about it. Yet, the efforts often fail to achieve significant positive result in most banks. Thus the problem persists in banking to the detriment of customer satisfaction.

Transactions errors could sometimes result from failings on the part of customers. Just as customers feel bad when they see avoidable errors in their statements of account or banking transactions, their bankers do not feel differently when the customers are responsible for such errors. This implies that both banks and customers have a duty to save each other from the embarrassment that is often associated with costly but avoidable transactions errors. This is especially necessary considering that most transactions and processing errors are prone to fraud.

Errors and Risks in Transactions Processing

Common fraud-prone mistakes and inaccurate processing often observed in customer transactions relate to errors of omission, spurious debits, and wrong entries. Let me briefly explain the dynamics of these errors.

Omission of Entries

Errors of omission occur when there are lapses or slips in documentation or reporting of banking transactions. Possible variants of omission of entries include miscalculation of quantifiable entries, and oversights on the part of transactions processing employees. In most cases, such errors are made inadvertently and are transitory. Usually control officers find out and rectify the omissions during the mandatory end of day (EOD) reviews of transactions. Depending on the gravity of the error, the control officers may report the omissions to their line supervisors for necessary actions. Sometimes, correction of this category of processing errors would require authorization by particular superior operations officers.

However, unauthorized omission of entries could be deliberate. Usually this is treated as fraud in banking. It happens in two main ways. Operations employee responsible for keying in entries into the computer may drop a particular item from their posting list. Account officer, or relationship manager, may hold-off paying in a check until the account on which the check is drawn is funded. In both cases, genuine banking transactions are suppressed. Thus, suppression of check or other banking instrument—such as dividend warrant, deal slip, and so on—is a fraud.

Suppression is a criminal act. Accordingly, bank managements should take necessary action against the indicted employees. The usual disciplinary action against employees indicted for suppression offence is dismissal.

Spurious, or Contrived, Entries

The question of spurious entries is a source of concern in managing banking relationships. The problem is more serious when spurious entries are passed as debits from customer, suspense, or control account. Such debits put a bank in an untenable position. Usually disputes arising from spurious or contrived entries undermine cordial bank-customer relationship. The notion of spurious entries may sound unfounded, but to the chagrin of skeptics, they do happen.

Banks that indulge in so-called sharp practices may deliberately input spurious entries to their computer systems. The entries may be hidden in some strange or phony accounts. Sometimes the entries may be camouflaged with authentic data on customer transactions or in statements of accounts of customers. It all depends on the underlying intention of the bank or its employee that creates or inputs the entries. That intention, in turn, derives from the purpose the contrived entries are designed to serve. Often bank managements contrive and approve spurious entries with a fraudulent intention. In this way, bank managements may—and do sometimes—defraud shareholders and regulatory authorities by deception. This happens, for instance, when they contrive entries to book fictitious loans to boost asset portfolio, or to meet target balance sheet footing.

Culprits for spurious entries are usually found among banks that maneuver some regulatory guidelines, or among employees with fraudulent work intentions. Spurious debits, strictly speaking, represent falsification of entries or transactions. Falsified entries relate—first and foremost—to the transactions, which accountholders did not approve. At the same time, they are not the regular debits from or credits to customer accounts. Thus chances are high that some of the entries would be fraudulent. This act is abhorrent to not only bank customers, but banking regulatory authorities. It is embittering and has detrimental effect on bank-customer relationship.

Wrong Entries

There may be instances where banks inadvertently pass inaccurate entries to reflect otherwise genuine customer transactions. Thus the problem of wrong entries originates largely from transactions posting errors. Typical instances of wrong entries include:

- posting one customer's transaction to another customer's account;
- debiting or crediting, instead of crediting or debiting, particular accounts with certain amounts of money; and
- entering wrong value dates for transactions.

Wrong entries—for all intents and purposes—may not be unwitting errors in all cases after all. Some may be deliberate and intended to defraud the bank or customers. Banks application software should enable automatic reversal of wrong entries. Curiously, this is not always the case. Some wrong entries are not reversed for a long time—if ever reversed at all. Long outstanding wrong entries would be probable targets for frauds. It is therefore necessary for control officers to thoroughly investigate wrong entries that are not reversed automatically or same day at most.

Customers can help their bankers stem wrong entries by promptly reviewing their statements of account. They should also painstakingly scrutinize all records of their transactions. In all cases, customers should report exceptions in their bank statements or reports to the bank as soon as they discover the errors.

Usual Causes of Processing Errors

There are several causes of transactions and processing errors. The frequently observed and common errors result from carelessness of bank employees and customers, confusing transactions, wrong transaction assumptions, IT issues, and failure of responsible bank officers to offer appropriate advice to customers.

Employee Carelessness

Incidence of errors tends to be high and frequent in banks where transactions processing is not informed by due diligence. Often processing officers, so-called operations employees, sacrifice thoroughness for speed. Mostly, this happens because operations work is usually pressure-laden. The usually heavy workload of the operations employees does not help matters. This problem is not peculiar to operations employees. It applies to other bank functions such as lending, information technology, treasury, and so on. However, its seriousness is more evident in banking processing work. In general, bank employees who are negligent are rarely diligent in performing their functions. Some transactions errors occur because of the carelessness of customers—in just the same vein. Careless customers, for example, sometimes flout transactions rules. In doing so, they create chances for errors that are otherwise avoidable.

Confusing Transactions

There could be instances where unintended errors occur because of confusing transactions or data. In most cases, such confusing transactions create chances for errors in transactions processing. Confusion, and therefore errors, would occur where customers fail to give clear instructions about their transactions that require special treatment. Frequently, this is observed in foreign exchange deals. But it is evident in funds transfer transactions, and giving standing orders or instructions to banks. There would be confusion that could cause errors where responsible bank officers do not have adequate or required knowledge of the transactions which they must nevertheless process or post to specific customers' accounts.

Wrong Assumptions

Errors could also emanate from wrong assumptions about particular transactions. Sometimes, processing errors occur when bank officers make hasty, or unverified, but wrong assumptions about particular transactions. This happens in most situations where the officers are overzealous. Anticipatory approval of transactions that should otherwise wait for due process and diligence is a typical example of the causes of processing errors in banking.

System Failure

A common cause of processing errors—especially in reports on customer transactions and statements of account—derives from system's failure. Virus attacks on computer programs and software are a common cause of system failure, malfunctioning, and breakdown in banks. Nowadays, there are increasing incidence of transactions errors caused by failings of computer and IT systems.

Ignorance of Customers

Transactions processing errors are sometimes caused by actions of ignorant bank customers. This happens where bank officers fail to offer appropriate advice to customers about the dynamics of, or other issues in, their current and intended transactions. In most cases, ignorance of customers derives from relationship management failure. Yet customers need to be guided through most of their banking activities to avoid unintended transactions processing lapses.

Measuring Transactions Processing Errors

For many purposes, the level of transactions errors, and therefore quality of service that banks provide to customers, could be assessed by some objective measures. Customers would rate the quality of bank service low when processing errors are not only recurring, but increasing in number over time. A similar service judgment will be applicable in situations where the observed errors are avoidable in their particular circumstances of occurrence. Perhaps the most excruciating aspect of transactions errors is experienced when the errors are measured in terms of damage, costs, or losses to banks, customers, or both. It is obvious, based on the foregoing, that transactions processing errors can be measured in three main ways:

- frequency of observed processing errors in customer statements of account over a given period of time,
- whether the observed transactions or processing errors are avoidable or not in given circumstances of the banks, and
- extent of actual damage or losses that banks and customers suffer on account of particular errors.

Effects of Transactions Processing Errors

Transactions processing errors have important banking implications, and are of no less significance in managing bank-customer relationship. Some of the important effects of transactions errors include the following:

Tainting of Integrity

Certain transactions errors could taint customers' perception of a bank's integrity. This, however, depends on the service disposition of the bank, on the one hand, and temperament of the bank's employees and customers, on the other. Tainted integrity is certainly not congenial to good corporate image of the bank.

Straining of Banking Relationship

Customers who are finicky about their banking transactions would protest the slightest errors in their statements of account. Indeed, some customers become irate when they detect any spurious entries in their transactions records or statements of account. Such protests sometimes become the basis of breaking some otherwise cordial customer-bank relationship.

Mutual Recriminations

Sometimes, errors that occur due to misunderstanding of agreement between bank employees and customers, on the one hand, and between a bank and its customers, on the other, regarding particular transactions could lead to needless recriminations from which neither of the parties could benefit.

Burden of Accounts Reconciliation

The burden of reconciliation of bank transactions records with customer statements of account could be distracting, frustrating, and, in most cases, costly to both parties.

Loss of Confidence

Customers might lose confidence in a bank's processing capabilities following recurring transactional errors in their statements of accounts. In most cases, loss of customer confidence threatens the success, or effective management of bank-customer relationship.

Employee Appraisal Issue

The performance of operations, marketing, and relationship management officers of banks may be assessed to a large extent based on levels of transactional errors, or error-free processing of customer requests.

Incidence of Fraud

Some employees of banks and customers may take advantage of prolonged and undetected processing errors to perpetrate frauds in the transactions or accounts of the bank or customers. Usually the bank bears the losses associated with such frauds.

Control Implications

Frequent transactions processing errors may necessitate realignment of work roles to achieve increased supervision of subordinates. This implies not only additional personnel costs to the bank, but exacting standards of vigilance on the part of the internal control officers.

Control of Transactions Processing Errors

Most of the observed processing errors may not be completely prevented in all aspects of customer transactions. Yet banks that have unwavering focus on satisfying customer needs will do anything but neglect the need for error-free transactions processing. Such banks are usually found among the cream of the market leaders. Where it is not possible to ensure error-free processing, they provide effective remedies for unavoidable errors. This presupposes that such banks can and, in most cases, do take deliberate actions to reduce transactions errors. I discuss effective remedies for processing errors. I focus on measures that have proven effective in remedying processing errors in many customer-oriented banks.

Employee Training

There must be adequate and continuous training of key bank employees, especially those that are assigned important responsibilities in managing operations (transactions processing), marketing, and customer relationship. Functional managers should in turn put in place programs for on-the-job training of their subordinates on all aspects of their jobs. There should be occasional inplant training sessions and sponsorship of employees to workshops, seminars, and conferences. In all cases, training must emphasize and focus on bridging observed skills gaps, as well as imparting basic functional skills, that are necessary to fulfill most of the transactional and processing needs of customers. The best training programs seek to attain 100% satisfaction of customer needs. That makes a major hallmark of the customer orientation of the successful banks.

Call-Over of Transactions

Most of the common processing errors could be resolved through disciplined, daily call-over of all transactions in customers' accounts. This might be tedious, but it always significantly reduces chances of, and problems often associated with, processing errors. Errors detected in operations records during call-over of transactions should be corrected before the usual end-of-day runs and closing of the day's transactions on the WAN computer system. All businesses have needs for daily or routine call-over of activities in which they are engaged. In the publishing business, for example, the equivalent of call-over of transactions is the proof reading of articles, news, editorial, features, and so on before the final printing of a newspaper, magazine, book, and so on. Thus, proof reading saves editors the trouble and embarrassments of refuting undetected typographical errors, erroneous news, and suchlike.

Stemming Posting Biases

It does not make business sense to deploy, redeploy, or retain indolent employees—for whatever reasons—in key customer service, transactions processing, or relationship management positions. Yet bank managements sometimes allow sentiments to cloud judgment when it comes to deployment of employees to key assignments or work positions. The passion that drives managerial decisions about employees' job postings is often rooted in some irrational consideration in which the managers have vested interests. For example, chief executives or other senior executives that show interest in who occupy certain positions in their banks may not be doing so for definite reasons. Such interest becomes rather curious when the coveted positions exist at low levels of employments. Besides the common excuse of having trusted employees in certain key positions to protect some interests, the CEOs and senior executives that indulge in this practice sometimes may have ulterior motives. Really, the underlying reasons for the practice, in most cases, may include the urge to have loyal employees in sensitive positions because they will do the officers' bidding without reservations.

Correcting Criticized Work Attitudes

Bank management bias toward employees undermines the effectiveness of transactions processing. Bias hurts employee enthusiasm for identifying unfulfilled market needs and helping to deliver value to customers. Perhaps employee indolence has the most profound negative effect on managing customer relationship. This happens mainly where inept employees are assigned key responsibilities in processing customer transactions or managing customer relationship. Lazy and laid-back attitudes should be a cause for concern to bank managements. Often banks that retain employees with criticized attitudes to work are inundated with customer complaints bordering, in most cases, on dissatisfaction with service. In order to remedy this awkward situation, bank managements must be firm and unbiased in handling employees that are lax in doing their work. There should also be clearly defined criteria for addressing employee indolence, negligence, or indifference toward work. As part of managerial response to such employee problems, proven or obvious cases of half-hearted productivity of employees at all levels of responsibilities should be promptly detected and the affected employees reassigned. Where the affected employees cannot be posted to other productive assignments, they might have to be laid off in the larger interest of the bank.

Assurance of Customer Satisfaction

One of the hallmarks of customer orientation, which market-driven banks often demonstrate, is a willingness to make sacrifices in the interest and pursuit of customer service and satisfaction. Such sacrifices may take different forms, but they should be convincing—not mere promises or ineffectual service offers. An example of a convincing sacrifice that could be made in pursuit of customer satisfaction is to give strong assurances to customers about the bank's total commitment to offering responsible and error-free transactions processing at all times. Once this is done, the bank sets standards by which at least customers could assess the quality of their services. The bank should strive to consistently fulfill the assurances to the satisfaction of its customers. This paves the way for the bank to reap the benefits of long-term customer loyalty and sustained patronage. The defunct Omega bank (Nigeria) PLC defined this goal for its market expansion strategy in early 2000s. The bank promised to pay N500.00 on each of the errors which their customers found in their statements of account.

RISKS AND CONTROLS IN PAYING AND CLEARING CHECKS

Bank customers have a right to receive value in checks or other financial instruments paid or deposited in their accounts for clearing. It is the responsibility of a bank (i.e., first party) to honor checks drawn or issued by its customer (i.e., second party) in favor of other bank customers (i.e., third parties). This presupposes that accounts of the drawers of the checks with their banks are funded to accommodate the checks they have issued to the third parties. Of course, the checks must be addressed to the branches of the bank where the accounts of the drawers are domiciled. However, there are general and technical reasons that can cause nonpayment of a check by a bank. I mean reasons why a bank may dishonor (i.e., decline to pay) a check. The usual reasons include:

- Death of, and "stop payment order" by, the customer both of which are provided for in section 75 of the Bill of Exchange Act.
- Stale check—one that has been in circulation for more than six months.
- Postdated check, that is, check that is presented for payment prior to the date on it.
- Check drawn by or on a liquidated company or bankrupt partnership.
- Mental incapacitation of the drawer (accountholder) of the check.
- Dormancy of account—one that has not been operated for more than six months.
- Inability of the drawer to confirm the check for payment—where the accountholder requires check confirmation.
- Material alterations on the check affecting the payee's name, date, amount, and so on without necessary supporting endorsements.
- Check presented for payment by a payee with questionable identity.

It is necessary to identify operations errors that expose a bank to avoidable risks and often result in frauds. Many reported bank frauds are committed through manipulation of clearing checks and other banking instruments. Let me briefly discuss some of the common modes of check-related frauds, most of which beat the eagle-eyed processing officers of banks.

Checks Lodged in Savings Account

It is inappropriate to accept checks for lodgment into savings account. The banking rules permit acceptance of checks in the conduct of current account transactions. It is safe to do so because references are usually obtained from current accountholders prior to opening the accounts. But this is not the case with savings account, unless the savings account also has references acceptable to the bank.

Crossed Check Paid Over-the-Counter

It is practically difficult, if not impossible, to trace the payment of a stolen, crossed check paid over-the-counter to its presenter (i.e., recipient of value on the check). As a rule, crossed checks must be lodged in the payee's account. In most case, issuers of crossed checks stipulate that the instrument is for "account payee only." This is a clear order with which the bank must comply.

Honoring Stopped Check

When the accountholder countermands their check, the bank is obliged to dishonor the check if and when it is presented for payment. Thus paying the check would be tantamount to contravening the accountholder's revocation of the bank's mandate to pay the check. In such a situation, the bank will bear the loss.

Non or Wrong Confirmation of Check

Fraud occurs when forged clearing instruments are honored. This happens easily when a check is paid without the confirmation of the accountholder or in violation of their mandate to the bank. It is therefore necessary for funds transfer officers or customer service officers to independently confirm the authenticity of checks or other instruments presented through the clearing system before honoring them for payment.

Non or Wrong Verification of Signature

Accountholder's signature should be meticulously while processing their transactions. This is necessary to mitigate risks in paying checks. This processing rule cannot be overemphasized. In order to avoid fraud in customer accounts, it is essential for tellers to verify signature on checks before paying the checks. If this is not done, forged or fraudulent instruments could be paid, with loss implication for the bank.

Paying Third Party Check

The name of the payee on a check accepted for collection (i.e., outward clearing check) must be the same as the accountholder's name in whose favor the check will be sent for clearing. This is necessary to avoid charge with conversion fraud if the check is stolen and cleared through the bank.

Releasing Checkbook to a Third Party

Fraud may be perpetrated when a customer's checkbook gets into the hands of a fraudster. With forged signature of the accountholder, the fraudster can successfully withdraw money from the account using a leave of the stolen check. It therefore stands to reason that checkbook should be released only to the accountholder or their authorized representative. However, the accountholder must give such authority expressively in writing.

Suppression of Check

A fraudulent officer of a bank might decide to hold on to a clearing check in a situation where the account on which the check is drawn is not funded to accommodate the check. This lapse ultimately results in the creation of an unauthorized or unsecured overdraft in the customer's account. Ordinarily the unauthorized overdraft should have been avoided if the check is returned within the permissible clearing days. That would have effectively mitigated the risk.

Unauthorized Access to Account Balance

The bank should not disclose account balance to an unauthorized person except with the express, if not a written, approval of the accountholder. In fact, it is safer to maintain the policy of disclosing account balance to only the accountholder. The accountholder may be defrauded, and bank liable for negligence, when wrong payment is made to a fraudster to whom the customer's account balance is wrongfully or erroneously disclosed.

Wrong Sorting of Checks

This relates to outward clearing checks which must be properly sorted before sending to the clearinghouse. Risk occurs when a check is wrongly sent to another bank other than the paying bank and it is dishonored after all. The bank will have to deal with customer complaints against poor service and have to contend with the resultant unauthorized overdraft in the account.

STEMMING OPERATIONAL RISKS THROUGH RECONCILIATION OF ACCOUNTS

It is perhaps in failure to promptly reconcile a bank's accounts that one finds a conduit for some of the observed large-scale frauds involving bank staff. When long outstanding items are not reconciled, fraud may not be detected in time. In order to minimize fraud, a dedicated and independent unit should be responsible for reconciliation operations. The unit may report to the chief inspector, chief of banking operations, or the bank-wide chief risk officer. The specific areas of reconciliation operations that are prone to fraud include interbranch accounts, callover of transactions, control or mirror accounts, general ledger, and vault cash.

Interbranch Accounts

Mostly frauds committed through inter-branch accounts involve operations employees who either fraudulently or erroneously accept or act on forged interbranch vouchers. The risks and fraud caused through maneuvering of interbranch accounts can be reduced by always decoding interbranch test keys before acting upon or posting any vouchers. However, frauds attendant on interbranch accounts has reduced with automation of banking transactions. This achievement owes to presently processing of banking transactions in real time, powered by the Internet.

Call-Over of Transactions

Operations work is not complete—neither is method adopted for it to be foolproof—until all end-of-day transactions processing entries are called over. There should not be delay in calling transactions and entries over in this way. Delay exposes a bank to operational risk of fraud. Call-over is an internal control procedure to check that transactions are entered into the computer system in a correct way, and that the outputs or balances in computer printout are correct. It refers, in another sense, to a manual procedure to check that the entries posted to accounts are correct by ticking output items in a computer printout against those in input or source documents. Nowadays call-over is seen as a technical but automated daily means of verifying, after end-of-day processing, that there are no errors in the entries posted to customers' or other accounts.

Control or Mirror Accounts

It is essential that a bank constantly maintains and reconciles control accounts as operational risk mitigation measure. There are three main different types of control accounts—mirror, nostro, and vostro—that a bank should maintain and regularly reconcile. A common feature of these control accounts is their interchangeable uses as mirror accounts. Otherwise their distinctions and significance reflect in their titles and purposes.

Mirror Account

This is an account kept in operations department of a bank for the purpose of monitoring particular accounts. It also serves as an operations control instrument. Mirror accounts are internal records kept by a bank of transactions in its account with other banks in the same country.

Nostro Account

An account that a bank designates as "nostro" is created, maintained, and used by international operations department of the bank for the purpose of monitoring its correspondent banking. It represents internal records kept by a bank of transactions in its account with a bank abroad which it uses as a correspondent bank.

Vostro Account

This account—like nostro account—is created, maintained, and used by international operations department of a bank to monitor its correspondent banking transactions.

It refers to the records kept by one bank (say in United Kingdom) of transactions in an account held with it by another bank (say in the United States) with which it has correspondent banking relationship.

GL Reviews and Proofs

The general ledger (GL) is a very important accounting document used in tracking and checking transactions in the various accounts that a bank maintains. Its main purpose is to ensure that all the accounts of the bank are always balanced. In pursuit of this purpose, the GL fulfills other needs for the bank. It helps to detect transactions and processing errors. In doing so, it guides against fraud. The GL serves the same purposes at branch levels. These purposes are achieved only when appropriate processing and control employees review and proof the GL on daily basis or as required by the bank's standard operating procedures.

The GL records for review and proofing should contain detailed information about all applicable transactions and entries. There should be a backup record that evidences composition of proofed GL balance. The end result—a balanced GL that is also genuine—is necessary for prevention of fraud and other sundry banking operational risks. Particular processing employees should be assigned specific responsibilities in reconciling all the GL accounts in the head office and branches. The responsible employees review the GL report for branch or unit that is printed and handed them every morning. The review includes investigation and resolution of unusual entries, open items, and balances. Usually, this will require downloading of detailed transactions reports on the related GL entries and balances. In this way, the purposes of the GL will be fulfilled—not defeated.

The supervisor of processing functions should review the GL proofs to ensure that they are correct and all open items resolved. The foregoing is some of the proven fraud-preventive measures that banks are expected to take in its everyday management of its operations and transactions processing and risks associated with them.

Vault Cash

When bankers use the phrase *vault cash*, they imply an amount of local and foreign currencies that are stored in, taken out from, or put into the vault usually under joint custody of the cash officer and branch operations manager. Usually, the bulk of cash balance is secured in the strong room.

There are basically five elements of the strong room that have to do with cash handling and control. The elements relate to records, registers, and balancing of vault cash. But they also provide a means of accounting for vault cash movements and transactions. Reserve cash register, cash balance book, joint custody balance, cash officer's hand balance, and cash storage receptacles are the basic cash-related elements of the strong room.

Operations and processing employees should know and apply risk-mitigating features of the cash elements. However, cash operations officers should lead in mitigating risks of vault cash handling. Reconciliation of vault cash should form a major part of their routine assignments.

SUMMARY

Transactions errors result from failings on the part of bank employees and customers. Just as customers feel bad when they see avoidable errors in their statements of account or banking transactions, their bankers do not feel differently when the customers are responsible for such errors. This implies that both banks and customers have a duty to save each other the embarrassment that is often associated with costly but avoidable transactions errors. This is especially necessary considering that most transactions and processing errors are prone to fraud.

Bank customers have a right to receive value in checks or other financial instruments paid or deposited in their accounts for clearing. It is the responsibility of a bank (i.e., first party) to honor checks drawn or issued by its customer (i.e., second party) in favor of other bank customers (i.e., third parties). This presupposes that accounts of the drawers of the checks with their banks are funded to accommodate the checks they have issued to the third parties. Of course, the checks must be addressed to the branches of the bank where the accounts of the drawers are domiciled. However, there are general and technical reasons that can cause nonpayment of a check by a bank. In banking parlance, the reasons are couched in operational technicality—why a bank may dishonor (i.e., decline to pay) a check. It is necessary to identify operations errors that expose a bank to avoidable risks and often result in frauds. Many reported bank frauds are committed through manipulation of clearing checks and other banking instruments. Some of the common modes of check-related frauds beat the eagle-eyed processing officers of banks.

It is perhaps in failure to promptly reconcile a bank's accounts that one finds a conduit for some of the observed large-scale frauds involving bank employees. When long outstanding items are not reconciled, fraud may not be detected in time. In order to minimize fraud, a dedicated and independent unit should be responsible for reconciliation operations. The unit may report to the chief inspector, head of banking operations, or the bank-wide chief risk officer. The specific areas of reconciliation operations that are prone to fraud include inter-branch accounts, call-over of transactions, control or mirror accounts, general ledger, and vault cash.

QUESTIONS FOR DISCUSSION AND REVIEW

- Which aspects of banking operations and transactions processing errors tend to crystallize operational risks in banking?
- How did operational fallout of transactions processing take center stage of challenges facing bank managements in developing economies?
- What features of operational risks elevate banking operations and transactions processing to the top of bank management priorities?
- How should transactions processing risks and controls be rightly or wrongly situated in the context of paying and clearing bank checks?
- What roles does reconciliation of banks' accounts play in enhancing possibilities for stemming operational risks in banking?

Chapter 30

Banking Frauds and Operational Risk Management in Developing Economies

Chapter Outline

LEARNING FOCUS AND OBJECTIVES

Fraud is, perhaps, the single most important cause of banking operational risk in developing economies. Frauds in banking are many, varied, and often sophisticated. Thus fraud mechanisms defy precise description. Stakeholders in banking appear helpless with anxiety over the problem. The implication is that there should be ingenuity in devising unusual fraud-preventive and control measures. I focus this chapter on how to check fraud and, doing so, unlock potential for banking in developing economies. My main objectives are fivefold and intended to:

- explain why fraud is a hydra, the canker of crime in modern society, and a phenomenon in banking the world over;
- discuss the various ways fraud defies the odds and persists—and, doing so, demystifies the banking world of secrecy;
- identify the nature and complications which are acts as omission or commission of bank employees introduce to the dynamic of fraud;
- explore why it would seem bank managements and regulatory authorities are fighting a losing battle on fraud prevention; and
- investigate the repercussions and implications of fraud for the banking industry and society at large in developing economies.

EXPECTED LEARNING OUTCOMES

Nowadays fraud is a common scene in banking all over the world. No bank is spared of this vice. Banks in developing economies are ever inventing and reinventing internal control with the sole aim, in most cases, to deal with fraud in more pragmatic ways. Notwithstanding control, incidence of fraud continues to climb still. This raises the question of oversight of banking functions, services, and transactions in an age of technological revolution. The reader will—after studying this chapter—have learnt and been better informed about:

- nature, causes, and possible measures to detect, prevent, and control bank fraud in developing economies;
- root causes, characteristics, and repercussions of bank fraud as the canker of crime in developing economies;
- the dynamics and psychology of bank fraud from the perspectives of how it defies the odds and persists, despite preventive measures;
- issues in bank fraud analysis and control when bank employee is suspected to be in collusion by act of omission or commission; and
- effective ways bank managements and regulatory authorities won't be fighting a losing battle on fraud prevention.

OVERVIEW OF THE SUBJECT MATTER

Fraud is the most disturbing and dramatic of all operational risks—no doubt about it. One invariably succumbs to this reality in trying to give equal attention to all elements of operational risk in banking. I admit the need to have a balanced understanding of operational risk, without undue emphasis on any of its components. The reason is simple. Issues involved in operational risk border on critical requirements for effective bank management right across-the-board. Unfortunately, there are usually some underlying motives behind operational risks involving bank employees and outsiders, mainly customers. Incidentally, these two categories of people feature in most creation of operational risk. Their involvement compounds the complexity of operational risk and renders its control more elusive than other risks in banking.

Insights into fraud-driven operational risk in banking that I present in this chapter shed light on the intensity, complexity, and magnitude of the problem. Increasing number of banks with fraud cases, amount of money involved, and actual loss to frauds are major indicators of the problem. It is, perhaps, in grappling with fraud-prone transactions and processing that bank managements face the greatest challenge. The reason is that capricious employee behavior and attitudes determine the level of success that may be achieved. Fraud and risk control in paying and clearing bank checks poses a similar challenge.

However, unlike dealing with human behavior, the nature of this challenge is amenable to control. The facility of standard operating procedures of banks—if institutionalized and strictly followed—solves the problem. Bank frauds are after all checked to a large extent through reconciliation of accounts. Reconciliation focused on interbranch accounts, call-over of transactions, control or mirror accounts, GL reviews and proofs, and vault cash come in handy. I am therefore focusing on operational risk from the perspective of "inadequate or failed internal processes."

DEFINING FRAUD AND ITS CONNOTATIONS IN BANKING

Fraud is about the commonest cause and manifestation of growing incidence of operational risk in banking. It is perhaps the most disturbing challenge of banking in developing economies. Nowadays frauds in banking are seen as a hydra and, to make matters worse, fraudsters are everywhere—always a handful. There is a need, nonetheless, to put definitions of fraud in perspective. This is necessary to appreciate its meaning, connotations, and inner workings in the banking industry.

However, the term "fraud" is one of the everyday constructs that are not amenable to a straightforward definition. There is always an obstacle in the way of attempts at defining fraud simply. Defining fraud in every sense of the word is really difficult—in other words, impracticable in the broadest or strictest sense. Literature on the dynamics of the financial system is replete with differing perspectives on fraud. On occasion, the perspectives reflect a potpourri of scams—variously referred to as "financial crimes," "financial malpractices," "fraudulent practices," and so on. In extreme situations, some subsume corruption under fraud and vice versa. Incidentally, corruption and fraud are endemic, as well as inherent, in society. What about money laundering and similar financial crimes? How do you classify them as criminal acts? For all intents and purposes, these are also seen as frauds mired in corruption.

Thus it is difficult to define fraud from a particular perspective. This situation is complicated by conflicting fraud connotations in banking—as in other businesses. The common definitions of fraud, in essence, tilt toward association of certain financial acts, improprieties, and transactions with crime of sorts. Fraud, in these contexts, cuts across industries, sectors, and social organizations in both developed and developing economies. It is even more difficult and challenging to pinpoint what exactly constitutes fraud in general and bank fraud in particular—especially when it is viewed from the perspective of a wrongdoing. Imagine regarding every wrongdoings such as embezzlement—otherwise referred to as misappropriation, theft, appropriation, or deprivation of someone or organization of their property, and so on as frauds. Many strictly nonfinancial wrongdoings, such as gaining unfair advantage by deception, false alteration to a piece of writing or other document, and so on are equally subsumed under fraud.

It would seem that virtually all wrongdoings are dubbed—rightly or wrongly—"fraud." Nonetheless, I forge ahead right away with possibilities for defining fraud more realistically. I do so from the perspectives of money, banking, and finance. Thus I define fraud as a criminal act in which someone or organization forges official document, signature, or seal—or manipulates a financial instrument, process, or transaction—in order to obtain money illegally by deception. I give a breakdown of this definition in order to highlight important connotations of fraud. Fraud is, first and foremost, a crime. It is therefore treated as an act against the State and punished accordingly. Someone—usually a criminal or fraudster—or an organization—acting in its capacity as a legal personality—deliberately commits this crime. They do so by deception involving forgeries, or manipulation of some financial instrument intended for a particular banking or other related transaction. The usual objective, doing so, is to obtain money or gain some advantage in an illegal way.

Frauds may be targeted at individuals, companies, institutions, corporate bodies, or government. Often victims of fraud have recourse to courts of law—where that is practicable. Practicability, in this sense, implies availability of concrete evidence and proven trails of fraud. Thus the main hope of redress for the victims of fraud is in lawsuits. Some victims opt for, or agree to, out-of-court settlement, though. Mostly, this happens when both or either of the parties may want to avoid negative publicity that litigation is bound to attract. Banks crave this approach to resolving fraud cases. They will want to avoid reputational risk to which lawsuits expose them. Therefore, a banking transaction can be described as fraudulent—in foregoing senses—if deception and illegal intention to gain some financial or other benefit underlie its purpose and dynamic.

Fraudulent transactions, strictly speaking, are done with forged documents, or are based on maneuvering of financial instrument, process, or other activity. Such transactions may, on the face of it, appear lawful but are in reality underlain by deception and illegal intention to gain money or other benefit. Thus, the connotations of fraud in banking derive from its main characterizing features. In addition to deception and criminality, fraud characteristics include swindle, breach of trust, and impropriety of conduct. Obviously, banks are prime targets for fraud because they deal in cash. As a highly liquid asset, cash greatly lends itself to all sorts of financial schemes. As would be expected, most of the schemes crystallize fraud mechanisms.

INSIGHTS INTO FRAUD-DRIVEN OPERATIONAL RISK IN BANKING

Fraud has been a worldwide and widespread phenomenon from time immemorial. Like corruption, it defies the odds and persists in profound ways. It demystifies the banking world of absolute secrecy and confidentiality. The rampant cases of bank fraud, most of which were novel, underlie the gravity of the problem. This trend continues, year after year, with no end in sight to the huge financial losses that banks and customers suffer! Bank fraud can be rightly described as a hydra. Its regenerative ability ensures that it festers. The dynamic of fraud depends on the motive behind it. Usually it is perpetrated for high stakes—a situation that dictates its intensity. Some frauds are targeted at particular customer accounts, while others hit bank funds directly. On occasion fraud is planned to trap unsuspecting bank staff or customers into banking scams. It is futile to pinpoint all types of bank fraud and how they are perpetrated.

Fraud continues to ravage banking around the world. It knows no bounds. Some liken it to corruption. Needless to say, fraud and corruption are social malaise that defy the odds and persist. It demystifies the banking world of secrecy and confidentiality. No bank or financial system—whether in developed, emerging, or developing economies—is spared of it. It has defied all remedies ever conceived and applied to its control. Sadly, bank managements and regulatory authorities are fighting a losing battle on fraud prevention. Banks spend a large amount of money to educate their customers about fraud, but it remains endemic in banking. It has assumed insidious dimensions of late and is now burgeoning with Internet revolution in banking.

Since bank fraud has become a problem of mind-boggling complexity, the question now is who will tame it? Bank managements have been in the forefront of the war against fraud, no doubt about it. But they have not done enough to expose the perpetrators, their modus operandi and such like. If this sounds a bit curious, then the integrity of bank managements is called to question for their unwillingness to disclose identities of employees and, in some cases, nonemployees indicted for fraud. It is rather disappointing. The same goes for failure of bank managements to make public the actual amounts of money involved or lost to frauds. They adopt this stance notwithstanding that regulatory authorities demand regular returns on bank frauds—names of culprits, modes of the frauds, amount of money involved and lost, and so on.

Many think that bank managements maneuver returns on, or falsify the facts of, frauds—ostensibly to shield their banks against reputational risk. In doing so, they unwittingly fan the flames of fraudulent activities. That way fighting bank fraud continues to be a losing battle. Curiously, the regulatory authorities appear helpless with anxiety over falsification of crucial and mandatory returns such as those on fraud. Needless to say, fraud is easily the most challenging operational risk of contemporary banking in developing economies.

TRACING THE ROOT CAUSES OF FRAUDS IN BANKING

The question of the causes of fraud is usually difficult to crack. One reason is that fraud tentacles spread across all sectors—social, political, and economic— and touch virtually every facet of activity. Another reason is that fraudsters are found among people from all walks of life. This may sound surprising, but it is real. Of course, fraud is endemic in society. Above all, fraud is an inherent risk in business. Indeed, it would be no mean task tracing the root causes of fraud—the intricacies of fraud could be mindboggling, to say the least. Besides, fraud tends to be shrouded in schemes and maneuverings that beat people's imagination.

Notwithstanding complexities, I pinpoint notions of lifestyle, corporate management, legal system, and social tendencies that shed light on the causes of bank frauds in developing economies.

Society and Negation of Moral Values

I trace the common causes of frauds in banking back to society. The intensity of fraud varies depending on moral values upheld by society. Take the issue of social glorification of wealth as an example. People blindly glorify wealth in some societies. Let me at once clarify a point—there is nothing strange about glorifying wealth that people earn through honest work. However, it will be pejorative to glorify wealth that does not bear all the hallmarks of earning an honest living, or to the source of the wealth. That is why social change should be founded on strong value system. Without moral scruples, members of a society easily become swayed by the trappings of wealth. Consequently, many may jump on the fraud bandwagon. I had in Chapter 2 of this book discussed how this factor contributes to the predisposition of banking to risk in developing economies.

Upbringing, Background, and Lifestyle

Lifestyle determinants of people's tendencies to fraud are another important factor for consideration. Cultivation of some personal attributes is propitious for fraud in banking. In most cases, such attributes are rooted in flawed upbringing and socialization. For example, some people have a misguided belief that dreaming about something important such as fame, wealth, and so on results in attainment of personal goals. Soon this belief becomes ingrained in the psyche and starts to manifest in strange and questionable habits. A tendency to ostentatious lifestyle is typical. This is evident in self-indulgent spending on luxuries. Yet leading a life of luxury is one lifestyle that anybody can ill afford. People with these personal attributes tend to do things without scruples. Chances of fraud invariably increase where some bank employees, customers, and other outsiders that transact one business or the other with a bank have these attributes.

Internal Bank Workings and Controls

As a going concern, a bank should be run on strong basis of risk management—and, if possible, risk prevention. In this way, and with a policy of zero tolerance, internal workings of a bank become foolproof. In order to realize this objective, bank management should institutionalize proven processes across-the-board. This is the setting for efficient transactions processing which complements and powers institutionalized practices. However, not a few banks' processes fail to make these outcomes.

Thus, notwithstanding standard operating procedures, so-called policy manuals, fraud continues to infiltrate banking. Often, internal bank workings are tainted by avoidable shortcomings—gaps, lapses, and loopholes. Some typical examples include nonreconciliation of accounts for too long, lingering indecision about dormant accounts, and mishandling of employee welfare. Fraud festers in banks under the taint of these operational issues. The shortcomings may, on the face of it, seem mere operational hiccups but unscrupulous employees and outsiders exploit the situation. Some frauds ride on the shortcomings and cause banks and customers to be defrauded or swindled out of money.

Similarly, bank management failings aid the inclination of some employees and outsiders toward fraud. Most of the failings reflect in weak internal controls—often bordering on dysfunctional system of checks and balances. There may also be flaws in work processes. Perhaps the human side of the failings is the most propitious for fraud. A myriad of issues are involved here. For example, bank managements sometimes do not err on the side of caution while deciding employees to be trusted with particular sensitive jobs. Trust in this sense is germane to employee empowerment. The question is really about who and how to trust and empower some employees in sensitive positions.

Dysfunctional Legal Frameworks

Bank managements look to law courts and law enforcement agents for the resolution of fraud cases. Nonetheless, lawsuits are not necessarily the first or preferred option for solving fraud incidents in developing economies. Three main reasons minimize the appeal of courts for fraud litigation. The court should ideally be the vehicle for bringing persons accused of fraud to book. In the first place, the legal system is relatively inefficient and may have loopholes which crafty fraudsters exploit. Second, the direct and indirect costs of lawsuits—the losses in time, money, and goodwill—reputational risk—could really be substantial. Third, a bank might lose an otherwise legitimate fraud suit on grounds of some irrational technicalities.

Above all else, most legal systems and frameworks in developing economies are dented by procedural flaws. As a result they do not hold much hope for speedy trial of lawsuits. Often the flaws place banks in a disadvantageous position when they prosecute fraud suspects. For most banks, instituting lawsuits against fraud suspects would be pursued as the last resort. Even where a bank institutes a court action against a fraud suspect, it sometimes would not be averse to settling the case with the accused out of court after all. Yet out-of-court settlement is practically a very weak option. In most cases, it ends up twisting the arm of bank managements about making concessions on their otherwise legitimate claims against the accused.

Thus flawed legal systems and frameworks in developing economies offer a safe haven to perpetrate bank fraud and get off scot-free sometimes. That is the bottom line, overall. Crafty fraudsters take advantage of this situation to dupe banks, swindle bank customers out of money, and perpetrate other sundry financial crimes. In extreme cases, they do so with reckless abandon.

DYNAMIC AND PSYCHOLOGY OF BANKING FRAUD

Frauds in banking do not happen by chance. There are usually people behind them. The people could be bank managements, employees, customers, or other outsiders who apply clever tricks, and nurture and execute surreptitious financial crimes. I imagine how strange and startling the inclusion of bank managements would sound to those who are uninformed about the dynamics of the bourgeoning fraud industry—but definitely not to the banking regulatory authorities. Sadly, bank managements on occasion get embroiled in inside job, entangling them in a messy moral dilemma and burden. However, the common denominator of all types of fraud is instructive. The workings of the minds of the people involved in frauds are consonant with a grand aim of defrauding banks or their customers. Often the people are smart, discreet, and deploy well-honed knowledge of the system accordingly. Usually, they operate at a discreet time and space. Ironically, frauds many a time fall through still.

Banking regulatory authorities—including deposit insurers—in developing economies receive an avalanche of reports about attempted, abortive, and successful bank frauds. The law enforcement agents are equally inundated with requests for investigation and prosecution of fraud cases. Indeed, bank frauds in developing economies are nowadays seen as a malaise of enormous dimensions. The dynamic and psychology of bank frauds are really intriguing. There are always—in the case of fraud from the outside—first principles, followed by accomplice enlistment where it is necessary to do so. Deciding the instrument and execution of fraud are the terminal events of inside job and fraud from the outside. I identify a need to appreciate the dynamic and psychology of these actions. I characterize bank inside job, discuss the process of choosing fraud accomplice, and highlight the build-up for fraud from the outside.

Inside Job—Characteristics, Dynamic, and Stakes

A bank job, in the sense of so-called "inside job," is a crime in which a bank employee or other insider steals, embezzles, or appropriates money or other property of the bank. Usually direct employee of a bank is the culprit for inside job—the result of which, in most cases, is loss of money to the bank. Often inside job fraudsters tend to be of like-minds. This is necessary, though not sufficient, for their success.

There are particular traits, besides being of like-minds, which probably characterize inside job fraudsters. The traits are seen, first and foremost, in employees who are frustrated or dubbed difficult. Ideally such employees have no place in banking. In reality, they are yet found and retained—unfortunately—in banks across-the-board functions for some reason. I mean employees who have and display negative attitude or disposition toward work. This category of employees easily becomes disconnected from their bank. Ultimately, frustration and inclination to fraud set in when they work under immense pressure, are laden with work roles with unrealistic performance targets and expectations, or earn poor compensation in a highly profitable bank.

Inside job fraudsters are also likely to be found in the ranks of employees who lack enthusiasm for work. I analyzed some of the causes of nonenthusiasm for work in Chapter 26 of this book. The main factors include family issues, upset of personal goals, low morale, dissatisfaction with work, and loss of faith in self and employment. Skewed promotion within the bank is yet another demoralizing factor that causes lack of enthusiasm for work. This affects three distinct groups of employees in varying degrees. There are those whose promotions have been due but are not forthcoming. Some do jobs that do not have good prospects for promotion, while others may feel grossly short-changed at any one time. The natural tendency for such employees—one that is often expressed in fraudulent acts—is want to get back at bank management.

It would seem proper to lay the blame for skewed promotion policy entirely at the door of bank managements. In practice, though, some employees do not even earn their appointments in the first place, let alone qualify for the usual, regular, or exceptional promotions. I make this point without intention to exonerate bank managements of any possible blame. Yet some employees feel cheated and begrudge others for their promotions and good fortunes at work. Bank management may wriggle out of blame for felt discriminatory promotion. However, it may not easily to do so in the related case of wide compensation gaps for employees on the same rank. Once again, this situation leaves some employees short-changed and disgruntled. It is in the fold of such disgruntled employees that possibilities for inside job exist. Insider and outsider-fraudsters find easy accomplices in their fold.

In the third set of possible inside job fraudsters are employees whom bank managements wrongly trust with sensitive positions and responsibilities. Unfortunately, trusted employees on occasion betray and defraud their bank. Some may turn fraudulent, not minding that they do so for high stakes on their jobs or in the sensitive positions they hold. Employees who are left for too long on a particular job are as much a fraud risk and in the same boat as their wrongly trusted colleagues. Work becomes unchallenging, drudgery and a mere routine when an employee keeps doing the same job over a long period of time. The employee necessarily becomes familiar with—and may want to exploit—the secrets of their job, in time. Thus they can easily maneuver and cover wrongdoings up.

Fraud From the Outside—First Principles and Build-Up

Fraud that is not an inside job must be from the outside. However, outsider-fraud is not common in banking. One reason is that outsiders may not be well versed in the inner workings, especially operational procedures, of a bank which is critical for the success of a fraud. Another but related reason is that fraud will hardly succeed without such intimate knowledge of the system and its built-in controls. These reasons imply that a fraud planned from the outside is likely to fail due to lack of understanding of a bank's internal control system. Notwithstanding knowledge gaps, though, frauds from the outside sometimes succeed.

The usual first thing which outside fraudsters do in furtherance of their plan to defraud a bank or its customer is to initiate some banking relationship. This may require opening a bank account, or proposing some bogus banking transaction. In doing so, they try to follow simple but general relevant procedures. In most cases, they manipulate at least one key aspect of the bank's standard and established but often demanding operating procedures. Suffice it to say that outside fraudsters get over some know your customer (KYC) hurdle one way or another.

Then they try to—and sometimes do—gain the confidence of their unsuspecting account officer and other relevant employees. I mean the bank employees that manage their account and handle their transactions, or whose work interfaces with their account or transactions. Often this outcome happens in two main ways. Initially, the fraudster strives to operate an account in the usual way. At the same time, they warm to their account officer and other employees they regularly encounter in their everyday banking transactions. All of the foregoing not only characterizes but distinguishes frauds that outsiders perpetrate from inside job. Inside fraudsters do not have to open and operate accounts. Neither do they have to propose some banking transaction. However, conniving insiders can enlist or recruit outsiders as surrogates to defraud their bank or customers. In that case, foregoing first principles of bank fraud may equally play themselves out through the surrogates. This rarely happens in practice, though.

Often outside fraudsters adopt a put-up job strategy. In most cases, this entails some put-on and doing crafty things in the build-up for fraud. The commonest put-on is warming to account officers and related employees. Yes, being friendly toward the employees is critical in gearing up for bank fraud. Confidence building schemes follow. More subtle steps are then taken in furtherance of the fraud plan. There may be a setup in which an outside fraudster arranges for their account officer or other bank employees to meet false business partners of theirs. It's also typical of such fraudster to want to take the pain and liberty of brainwashing these target employees about their unfounded business interests. In some cases, phantom projects may be contrived, and well-written business plans prepared and submitted to a bank with intent. The relevant bank officers who are uninformed about the dubious project would then appraise the business plans and make recommendations accordingly. The fraudster may adopt even more surreptitious strategies in the build-up for bank fraud. Nuances of the strategies are usually subtle but complementary.

Usually, outside fraudsters make their account officer and other employees that may be strategic to their plan gifts of things. Gift of cash is typical. They make their target employees other sundry gifts of valuables. They show up for bank events, and employees' weddings, parties, and other functions. Target employees' birthday and wedding anniversaries, as well as their children's naming, christening, and baptism ceremonies, are no less significant events the joys of which they share in the build-up for bank fraud. They do all these hiding their fraudulent intentions, or giving the impression that they are genuine. The account officer would then probably believe that the acts gear to mutually beneficial banking relationship.

Collusion for Fraud—Enlisting Connivance of an Accomplice

There are three possibilities for analyzing collusion in bank frauds. First, collusion demands a mastermind who initiates and coordinates the fraud. The second possibility has two mutually exclusive components. There could be an all-inside job, or all-outside participants in fraud. The implication is that the mastermind of fraud and their accomplice would either be all insiders or all outsiders. The third possibility is chances that participants in fraud could be a combination of people from both inside and outside of a bank.

Mastermind of frauds invariably get down to choosing potential accomplices, depending on the nature and complexity of particular frauds. This is their first real challenge. Bank fraud requiring collusion is unlikely to succeed if there is no connivance of an accomplice. In most cases, such fraud rides on insider knowledge. In the absence of connivance of an insider, outside fraudsters must have and work with pertinent knowledge and information about banking operations, systems, and control processes. Otherwise they cannot afford to work with deficient information.

Thus outside fraudsters often enlist an accomplice who, in most cases, would be a bank employee or other insider. Usually the accomplice fills any information and knowledge gap required for the success of a fraud plan. In this way, insiders facilitate bank frauds. This is one of the reasons an employee may sometimes be fingered as an accomplice during investigation of bank fraud. The involvement of bank employee, or other insider, in fraud by this means is referred to as collusion. The implication is that outside fraudster in this instance could be a bank customer or other individual while their accomplice is a bank employee or other insider—both of whom team up with an understanding to commit fraud. In banking parlance, the accomplice is said to have colluded with the outsider to commit fraud. There could be instances where collusion would not involve an insider. In that case, it becomes an all-outsider affair. Inside job, on the other hand, may or may not require an accomplice. It all depends on the nature or operational complexities of particular frauds and possibilities for finding like-minded colleagues. Thus inside fraudster succeeds when colleague of link minds collude with them. In this case, the fraudster knows that it would be a big risk to try to enlist a colleague with differing convictions as an accomplice. That does not satisfy a critical success requirement for inside job.

Now the question is how does an insider or outsider fraudster go about enlisting and working with an accomplice? I should mention at once that there are usually two main types of accomplices in bank fraud. There are the willing and unwitting accomplices. Let me distinguish between them. Willing accomplices denote someone who deliberately seeks opportunity to defraud a bank or its customers. Such people are usually on the take. For this reason, they easily give in to the temptation and, once prompted, connive with mastermind of fraud. The unwitting accomplices, in sharp contrast, are always wary of getting involved in wrongdoings. They shun fraud and similar acts. Yet fraudsters succeed in using them one way or another. In most cases, fraudsters trick them into playing some roles in fraud. So their involvement is always inadvertent and may be inevitable where execution of particular frauds revolve around their jobs—in the case of employee accomplices—or special skills—in the case of outside accomplices.

PROFILING BANKING FRAUDSTERS AND PUTTING THEIR ACTS INTO PERSPECTIVE

I had in the course of the preceding discussions mentioned roles played by insiders and outsiders in banking frauds. I highlighted the import of collusion in the roles of accomplices. The cause in committing fraud on the premise of solo effort, usually as a lone fraudster, also featured at some point. Now, I pinpoint and expatiate on aspects of these roles, their execution, and the criminal acts underlying them. I narrow down to profiling banking fraudsters as I put the acts of committing bank frauds in perspective.

Lone Fraudster

A lone fraud is one that is committed solely on the basis of solo effort of an individual. The individual—a lone fraudster—would normally not need the help or connivance of an accomplice. They are the so-called "lone ranger" who plans, initiates, and executes a fraud all by themselves. A lone fraudster could be a banking insider or outsider. Thus, they could operate as inside job fraudster or from the outside. Usually, they work with good and comprehensive knowledge of the system, especially the standard operating procedures of the bank. That makes it possible for them to beat the bank's internal control system.

Unfortunately, lone fraudsters are difficult to pin down. Neither it is easy to figure out their inclination toward fraud, let alone associate them with it. Fraud investigators scarcely trace their crime trails correctly. Often they end up misdirecting their investigation. The result, in most cases, is that some people— wrongly implicated in lone frauds—are put in trouble. This situation creates a moral burden when frauds are pinned on innocent employees or other people. The clever disposition of lone fraudsters ensures that their acts are difficult to detect, especially frauds committed by them. Of course, lone frauds bear the hallmarks of bold and intelligent application of knowledge of the inner workings of a bank. Solo effort and high stakes characteristic of lone frauds underscore unquestionable courage of the culprits. Notwithstanding controls, incidence of lone frauds continues to climb up. Thus you cannot but frown upon the evil courage of the lone fraudsters.

In some cases, loan fraudsters may target small amounts of money. This happens especially in cases of first attempts, ostensibly aimed at testing out particular fraud ideas. Target amounts of money in lone frauds increase in time with increasing confidence of the fraudster. Successful frauds boost the confidence of the fraudsters to commit more, large-scale frauds, ostensibly because, it goes without saying, nothing succeeds like success. Used in this sense, success implies that a fraud works and the fraudster is not caught because the fraud is difficult to detect. It is essential that loan frauds are painstakingly investigated. In this way, it would be possible to track down lone fraud culprits on their jobs, in their hideouts, or elsewhere. Pinning lone frauds on the real—not imagined or supposed—culprits and bringing them to book would always be a great feat of fraud investigation. This is the common expectation, one that seems and has in fact been quite elusive in most lone fraud cases.

Fraud Syndicate

There are occasions when a syndicate of individuals defrauds banks. Such frauds nowadays have become a commonplace, especially in developing economies. The syndicate members could be all insiders or all outsiders. An all-insider fraud syndicate is rare, though. The reason is that syndicate frauds entail large-scale operations which bank employees or other insiders may not see through due to time, experience, or skill constraints. A fraud syndicate comprising all outsiders is rather common. The syndicate, in this case, invests a lot in understanding the system, testing out their plans, and honing their skills to ensure success. But that is the much they can do, as well as how far they can go, toward successful execution of a fraud plan. It is unlikely that they would always or easily beat the intricate web of internal controls of the banks without the collusion of some insider-accomplices. Thus, the commonest type of fraud syndicate is one in which there is a combination of inside job and criminals from the outside.

A syndicate is usually a large-scale fraud operation. Therefore, the stakes are really high. This reality dictates that syndicate member must be diligent, focused, and their operations well-ordered. Of course, they do not leave anything to chance. They especially invest in painstakingly understanding the inner workings of banking operations. Suffice it to say that they understand the system as well as the on-the-job employees. This is a major boost for their cause. Fraud syndicates gain this advantage in two main ways. First, they seek and insist on enlisting some naïve and exemployees as accomplices. They may not forge ahead without this critical resource requirement. Then they thoroughly research the feasibility of their planned fraud. The research, usually target-driven, could be quite extensive and span a long time in the build-up for a fraud.

There is usually a mastermind, in all cases—whether a syndicate is all insiders, all outsiders, or a combination of inside job and people from the outside—who coordinates the syndicate and its network. The mastermind could be an insider or some criminal from the outside. Often the mastermind recruits the other members of the syndicate. It is the mastermind still who starts the ball rolling in most cases. They do so when everything is in place—enlistment of faithful members and accomplices, assignment of individual roles to them, and, perhaps, a mock rehearsal of the modus operandi. The cause of the syndicate is what unites them and, to this extent—if the need arises—they abide by modus vivendi. This is necessary to forestall a situation where a syndicate member, feeling somewhat shortchanged, turns a sell-out. Thus the possibility of a betrayal is, perhaps, the most serious problem that frauds syndicate is likely to confront. The issue is really all about how to ensure that no member rocks the boat. In order for this to not happen, it is necessary that all syndicate members shun greed in the first place. This is, perhaps, one of the critical criteria used by the mastermind of syndicate fraud in recruiting members. The high points of these exercises include successful recruitment of an exemployee versed in internal workings of a bank, enlistment of a naïve junior employee of the targeted bank, or getting tacit endorsement of a critical senior employee of the targeted bank. Once enlisted, these insiders facilitate syndicate frauds.

In reality, though, it is not easy to enlist all three possible insiders without facing the risk of leakage of the fraud plan. Successful enlistment demands a discreet approach which most mastermind of syndicate frauds do have in abundance. Ironically, syndicate frauds are more easily exposed than lone frauds. The reason is that a group of people is usually involved in a syndicate fraud, while a lone fraud involves only one person. Chances are that one or more syndicate members may make a careless slip capable of uncovering the fraud and exposing its perpetrators. The use of junior employee as an accomplice could be a two-edged sword. Due to their inexperience, a naïve junior employee could make avoidable mistakes while trying to fulfill their part in a fraud. Usually, investigators eagerly look for and often do get trails of a syndicate fraud in such unwitting mistakes. There is a related problem in possible change of mind by any of the syndicate members. This could happen when they suddenly realize the enormity of the risk of a syndicate fraud. The usual tendency is for such member to get cold feet and abort their part in the fraud. That puts paid to the fraud.

Fraud Accomplices

Fraudsters from the outside do not simply seek collusion with just any outsider, bank employee, or other insider. They painstakingly follow some steps, borne out of unwavering conviction, for choosing possible accomplices. Nothing is done by, or left to, intuition or chance. Every step of the choice process is well calculated and shrouded in absolute secrecy. When bank employees are their targets, possible candidates for accomplice are usually the fresh and inexperienced employees. In most cases, this category of employees may not have been trained at all for account management and related job responsibilities. In some cases, the employees may have received some pertinent but partial formal training. Yet most of the employees may not have been properly or adequately trained or groomed for the jobs assigned to them, or responsibilities they handle.

This situation easily becomes fertile for bank fraud. Fraudsters accurately read and exploit this flaw in most banks' human capital development and management policy. They tend to dub such employee "vulnerable" and target them for accomplice or collusion role. Often overzealous employees are equally prime targets for fraud accomplice enlistment. This set of employees is yet predominant at entry-level positions constituted by fresh and inexperienced employees. A few of them are found in the ranks of middle-level employees, though. Fraudsters will want to identify and recruit such an employee as an accomplice. The whole idea of doing so is to key fraud to unfounded or inordinate zeal for work. In the absence of diligence, such employees easily become vulnerable to—and unwitting candidates for—bank fraud accomplice enlistment.

Inside job may not require recruitment of an accomplice at all or in foregoing way. Usually it is underlain by solo effort. The fraudster represents the so-called "lone ranger" who conceives, nurtures, executes and takes the risk of, and gain from, the fraud. There may be cause, though, for inside job fraudster to enlist connivance of a fellow employee of the same bank. In that case, possible candidate may not necessarily be found in the ranks of the fresh or inexperienced employees. The right candidate for accomplice role may be in the same or different department and occupying a similar or different position as the main fraudster. What really matters and unites them is that they must be of like-minds. Once this important criterion is satisfied, possible candidates for the accomplice role could really be any employee irrespective of their standing, position, or job within the bank.

DECIDING AND APPLYING INSTRUMENT OF FRAUD

This is the riskiest stage of bank fraud planning and execution. The preceding discussions reflect preliminary stages of bank fraud. The related steps only help prepare the way for some planned fraud—or a fraud that is yet in the works. Thus they serve a sort of test run purpose, and could be aborted without risk to the bank or fraudster. It is actually in deciding and applying the instrument of fraud that risk manifests itself, is high and real. Mostly, it is the stage at which the ingenuity of banking criminals and fraudsters is tasked. Two tasks are involved at this stage.

First, the criminal has to decide the instrument of fraud to apply. Usually, the preferred instrument is one that turns easily and quickly into cash. Fraudsters crave such instrument. Rapidity of application of the instrument in fraud execution is the watchword. Fraudsters ever want to act with speed—indeed, at breakneck speed. Apparently, this critical success factor disqualifies any instrument that passes through multiple processes, has multiple control points, and is subject to multiple preapproval reviews. Fraudsters do not find such instrument attractive. The same goes for complex transaction that requires expertise. Hardly any non-banker fraudster has the expertise in technical banking areas. In the absence of required expertise, fraudsters fall back on general knowledge of routine banking operations. Thus they target only simple instrument applicable in processing noncomplex banking transaction. However, this rule does not apply in two situations. On occasion, fraudsters tend to be indifferent to instrument and complexity where a huge amount of money is involved, and the fraudster or their accomplice is skillful in a way that furnishes the requisite expertise. These situations facilitate complex fraud.

The next task is application of the instrument of fraud. I have variously discussed this challenge under different topics in the operational risk section of this book and elsewhere in the entire book. It especially featured—one way or the other—as I discussed the topics of Chapters 3 and 27, as well as in my analysis of some of the related case studies in this book. So I will not belabor the point.

CASE STUDY 30.1 Faking Documents and Issuing Bank Drafts in Favour of Racketeers

Booth is a marketing officer at Q branch of XYZ Bank (Though real, this case study is disguised in keeping with the confidentiality of banking. Its setting is veiled to keep the identity of the banks, Multinational Corporation, and individuals in it confidential. The case study serves only illustration purposes, in order to demonstrate how it plays itself out in banks in developing economies. The names used for the banks, Multinational Corporation, and individuals in the case study are imaginary and do not relate to any known or unknown real banks, Multinational Corporation, or persons anywhere in the world). He is hardworking and diligent. Forest, his boss, who's also the branch manager, has confidence in him and assigns critical credit and marketing responsibilities to him. Forest's trust in him skewed his judgment of Booth's work. He does not always have cause to doubt Booth's reports and relationship management issues affecting accounts that Booth manages.

Their branch is located and operates in a difficult area for business. Forest and his team struggle every month to meet financial performance targets for the branch. The targets reflect undue emphasis on increasing deposit base, ostensibly a bank-wide liability-driven growth strategy. Forest usually faces a difficult time during the bank's monthly performance review (MPR) meeting on account of paucity of deposits mobilized by his branch.

One Monday morning, Booth tells Forest he has good news. Forest was all ears. Then Booth hints that he is likely to land a large current account deposit during the week. He advises they keep their fingers crossed. Unusually for Forest when he discusses business matters with Booth, he is not convinced. His doubt rests on absence of big accounts in the customer base of Q branch that can spring such a deposit surprise.

Couple of days later, Booth brings a bank draft for $25 million drawn on ABC Bank in favor of Land Mercury Limited (LM)—a hardly known customer of Q branch. LM's account has a credit balance of $54,000. It never has more than this amount as balance at any one time. Booth tells Forest that LM's managing director has for a long time been chasing after an important job from some big company. It is on this job, according to Booth, that the draft is now issued to LM as payment for the job. Forest reluctantly gives a tacit approval to lodge draft in LM's account and to send it for clearing. Q branch sends the draft for clearing.

Two days after—toward closing time—the chief inspector of ABC Bank calls Mars—his counterpart at XYZ Bank—and asks him to look out for a $25 million draft drawn in favor of Land Mercury Limited. He tells Mars that XYZ Bank should retain the draft in its custody and never give value to it when it's presented for payment at clearing. Mars informs all the branch operations managers (BOM) of XYZ Bank accordingly. Meanwhile, the clearing of the draft is well underway at this time. The Q branch BOM informs Mars of this fact and the account in which favor the draft is sent for the clearing. Mars asks the BOM to block LM's account against withdrawal of the draft and wait for further directives.

The BOM thereafter informs Forest of his discussions with—and directive from—Mars regarding the blocking of LM's account against withdrawal of the draft. Forest is attending a meeting at their bank's head office when he receives this information from the BOM over the phone. He reiterates Mars's directive to block the account. The MD of LM comes to withdraw the proceeds of the draft soon after the BOM finishes speaking with Forest—apparently oblivious to the bubble burst. The BOM again calls Forest and informs him about the presence of LM's MD in the banking hall to draw money from the blocked account.

Forest becomes confused and goes to discuss with Fuel, his line boss in the head office where he's attending the meeting. Fuel tells him to ask Mars to talk to the customer. Forest does this, but Mars frowns upon it and declines. Forest now goes to see the executive director (ED)—who is Fuel's boss—and tells him about the crisis situation. The ED advises him to be careful in handling the matter since it is likely to be a fraud syndicate. He suggests that the customer could withdraw the $54,000 in their account, but not from the proceeds of the $25 million draft. Forest calls the BOM and tells him what he has discusses with the ED about the abortive fraud. Accordingly, the BOM allows withdrawal of $54,000 from the account.

The next day, Mars issues Forest and the BOM queries demanding explanation for paying out $54,000 from a fraudulent account that is blocked against withdrawal, among other issues he raises in the queries. The queries insinuate that that the two Q branch officers are privy to the abortive fraud. Meanwhile, the chief inspector of ABC Bank reports the fraud to the Police. In turn, the Police invite Forest for interrogation, ostensibly as one of the suspects in the abortive fraud.

Forest goes to see Mars, Fuel, and the ED, apparently to express dismay with the query and Police invitation. He does this knowing that approval for such queries is given at a meeting that these officers attend. He finds to his dismay that each of them now distances himself from the Forest's fate. Mars merely says that Booth comes around and tells him that he told Forest not to allow the withdrawal of the $54,000 from the account. Forest listens to this bald-faced lie with indignation and promptly counters it.

Exercise for class or group discussion
1. How would you realistically characterize Booth based on the apparent and remote facts of this case study?
2. Do you think there were insider accomplices for the abortive fraud? If yes, who do you suspect?
3. Did Mars act in good faith by issuing queries to Forest and the Q branch's operations manager?
4. Why, in your opinion, did Fuel, Mars, and the ED distance themselves from the fate that befell Forest and the branch operations manager?
5. What operational risk management lessons may be learned from the failure of the fraud in XYZ Bank?

Tips for solving the exercise
Booth is the account officer for the fraudulent customer. Unknown to Forest, Booth has good relationship with LM's managing director—ostensibly beyond the official context. The MD of LM intimates Booth that he is working on getting some inflow from Band Row Limited—a Multinational Corporation—and will give him the draft for lodgment into LM's account once he receives it. This is the much Booth tells Forest. Investigation of the abortive fraud reveals that some insiders at Band Row substitute a forged list of 20 contractors for the genuine list to be paid for various completed jobs. Band Row owes the contractors amounts ranging from $15 million to $50 million. It issues and releases bank drafts in favor of the names of the contractors on the substituted list. The fraud is well planned. Every step in paying contractors is followed. The responsible officers obtain all necessary approvals

and adopt the procedure for releasing drafts to the contractors. The only difference is the release and payments of the drafts to racketeers—the phantom contractors. The reader should be challenged to reflect on—where possible—how the fraud was perpetrated, and the total amount of money that was at risk, recovered, or lost. Imagine the roles of bank employee (if collusion is suspected), customer, and the fraudster (if different from the customer and bank employee). Think about whether the fraud was reported to the authorities and—if reported—discern the likely actions taken, or—if not reported—explore possible reasons. You should now be in a position to advice on how to check incidence of fraud in the banking industry.

DEALING WITH FRAUDS IN BANKING—AN ADMINISTRATIVE EMPHASIS

There are good as well as bad people in every society—whether in developed or developing economies. A preponderance of people who have no moral scruples in a society does not augur well for business. Organizations also do have bad employees—however few—in much the same vein and banks are no exception. Banks will have few or many bad and difficult employees depending on the moral standing of the larger society in which it operates. Therefore, it behooves bank managements to be decisive in detecting, preempting and dealing with low moral standards among the employees in a timely manner. That is the starting point for checking banking frauds, especially in developing economies.

There are specific administrative measures—current and complementary—that banks managements should emphasize and strengthen to keep frauds at bay. The current fraud control measures, though comprehensive, have not been quite effective in preventing frauds in banking. They are fraught with loopholes which the fraudsters exploit, if anything. The current approaches concern institutionalizing foolproof internal control system, process of fraud detection, and options for remedying frauds. I posit a two-factor measures that derive from the pre-emptive actions that bank managements should take to effectively prevent frauds. The two factors are different from, but complementary to, the current approaches. The complementary approaches focus on subtle administrative gaps in handling the bank-employees relationship and related concerns.

First, I discuss and underscore the significance of the current approaches. There are three elements—comprising the regular approach, supplementary inputs, and integration of ancillary actions—in this category of approaches to frauds control in banking. I discuss the complementary approaches afterward. Two elements—reinventing organic relationship between a bank and its employees, and evolving a workable prevention of frauds—constitute the complementary approaches. Finally, I examine the risk management implications and prospects of the current and complementary approaches.

Current Approaches to Fraud Control

Banks in developing economies adopt some regular, supplementary and ancillary fraud-control techniques—with varying degrees of success rates. The regular approach serves the traditional operational risk management needs of the banks bordering on frauds control. Some supporting measures make inputs into the frauds risk mitigation task. The same goes for ancillary measures that some banks adopt in quest of dependable solution to the frauds in banking. Let me now pinpoint the highlights of each of these current fraud control practices in banking.

Regular Fraud Control Measures

The regular approach to frauds control—common to banks in developing economies—lays a lot of emphasis on internal control measures. Direct attack on the fraud incidents complements this approach. Thus, the methods employed in fraud control focus on prescription and strict enforcement of standard operating procedures for all banking functions. This demands strengthening of the internal control system and functions bank-wide. Typical SOP-supported work guidelines include a myriad of operational checks and balances.

In general, banks adopt particular actions to mitigate the operational risk of frauds. The common and regular actions include:

- specification of procedures for authorization of payments, as well as payments approval limits for various categories of officers;
- mandatory reconciliation of accounts—especially, the most vulnerable, such as accounts used for receiving and paying cash and checks—on a daily basis;
- spot, regular, and unexpected inspection and audit of branches and relevant head office operations and services;
- transactions processing rule requiring that some employee checks the work of another employee—one way or the other; and
- rotation of employees in different jobs without necessarily altering their preferred career paths.

Supplementary Inputs into Fraud Control

There could be supplementary fraud control measures. The use of Regiscope equipment to take photograph of persons cashing third party checks of large amounts over-the-counter in banking halls is typical. Nowadays, closed circuit television (CCTV) is also used as a fraud preventive measure in banking. Regiscope and CCTV are effective because they provide the culprit's trail which the Police and other crime investigators need to track them. Often authorized signatories of banks use special pens and signatures that not only authenticate but detect forged official documents.

Banks managements indoctrinate employees to not sign official documents unless they are convinced that the documents are authentic—and that they are the proper persons to sign them. Indoctrination of this nature helps check a situation where unit heads, branch managers, and supervisors might want to deceive their naïve subordinates into signing forged or fraudulent documents. Many insider-frauds ride on this setting. The inside-fraudsters adopt an unusual method for such frauds. They deceive or prod at the naïve and unsuspecting junior employees—directly or indirectly—into signing fake papers. In most cases, the instruments for the frauds are so-called source documents which originate particular transactions, processing needs, or requests.

Banks managements should and do frown upon this and similar practices—under whatever guise—by which employees are made to sign documents under duress. Usually, supplementary inputs into frauds control are varied. Banks managements can always take the liberty to introduce the supplementary inputs. However, this is dependent on the operational risk situation of the banks.

Integration of Ancillary Fraud Control Measures

Frustration tends to set in when banks managements fail to effectively control—let alone prevent—fraud incidents. In desperation, banks managements frustrated by control-defying tendencies of some fraud incidents devise and enforce stringent ancillary fraud control measures. The number and intensity of the ancillary measures vary among banks in developing economies. However, the observed variations are dependent on the seriousness and the banks' experiences of the frauds incidents.

However, some of the ancillary fraud control measures are in common use in banking. For example, banks issue special check books to particular categories of customers or accounts. Similarly, the banks now require customers to confirm checks and other financial documents they issue to third parties. This has become a critical condition for honoring the obligations of the banks on the instruments. Confirmation is usually done in writing, often as part of account opening or account maintenance documentation. Banks adopt parallel confirmation of financial instruments—especially when payment of large amounts of money is involved. The idea behind this practice is to strengthen foregoing instruments-honoring condition. Designated officers of the bank discreetly handle the parallel confirmation—usually orally.

Banks managements also do introduce injunctions on employee that intensify the checks on fraud. The notion of whistle blowing is typical. Senior employees are enjoined to monitor the behavior of their subordinates—especially the disgruntled elements that always complain about controls. The advice that employees should do anything but trust their colleagues in absolute terms cuts across departments, functions, and ranks. Perhaps, the summary dismissal of employees indicted for fraud is the harshest ancillary fraud control measure at the disposal of banks managements in developing economies.

Complementary Approaches to Fraud Control

The complementary approaches that I posit hereafter are really not necessarily new. Obviously, or perhaps not, banks managements know about them. Yet they do not acknowledge their efficacy or appreciate their import—ostensibly for some unfounded reasons. This attitude, perhaps, has to do with pointing a finger of blame at the employees lower down the line without addressing the failings of banks managements. The need to change this attitude will be obvious as I turn to discussion of the two components of the complementary approaches.

Reinventing Bank-Employee Organic Relationship

Frauds in banking persist notwithstanding regular, supplementary, and ancillary controls. The ravages of frauds evidence failings in bank operational risk management in developing economies. It would seem that the SOP-based control measures are not altogether effective. The SOP is really not a fallible guide to operational risk control in banking. It's rather the attitude of banks managements toward frauds that is fallible. Banks managements lay undue emphasis on frauds controls that have become rather mechanical. In doing so, they neglect—perhaps, unwittingly—the underlying causes of the frauds. The root causes of most frauds in banking are underlain by failings in the organic relationship between a bank and its employees.

Organic relationship to which banks and their employees should aspire thrives on mutual respect, trust, benefits, and care. In essence this is the foundation of all contractual relationships—whether in business or between individuals. It is of utmost importance that banks and their employees abide by this principle. In reality, though, this is almost always farfetched. A typical banking organization is a lopsided system favoring the upper echelons of employees. This observation is common among banks in developing economies. It sets the stage for the unnecessary bickering that often culminates in avoidable banking frauds. The reason for such frauds is that the rank and file of the bank easily loses confidence in the bank's managements. In the likely but parochial view of some of the disgruntled employees—mainly those who feel short-changed in one way or the other—an effective way to settle some old scores or to get back at the managements is to defraud the bank.

This is unfair to the bank that is now made to bear the brunt of the administrative failings of its managements and the unnecessary ill feelings the failings create in the employees that feel short-changed. However, this outcome should be bank management's cue to get to the bottom of frauds in banking. In doing so, getting to the heart of frauds prevention-defying factors is pertinent. Frauds have been a scourge on banking in developing economies. In order to prevent frauds, banks managements should deal with the scourge in a more decisive manner. They should do so in a way that reinvents the organic relationship between the bank and its employees.

Evolving a Workable Solution to the Scourge of Frauds

It is difficult to prevent frauds in banking without addressing their underlying causes first. In Chapters 25–27 of this book, I identified and discussed some of the critical causes of operational risks in banking bordering on aspects of frauds. Measures to address the causes of—and ultimately prevent—frauds should be integrated with the applicable banking policies, strategies, and controls. This view has three main implications for evolving a workable solution to the scourge of frauds in banking.

In the first place, frauds are a foreseeable risk, and in the second policy formulation for frauds prevention should build on a realistic analysis and anticipation of the underlying causes. In turn, frauds analysis and anticipation should be founded on the understanding that bank employees either perpetrate or aid and abet frauds and forgeries, in most cases—directly or indirectly. It therefore stands to reason—in the third—that policies devised to prevent the frauds will be effective only when they are centered on the employees and their work situations. In this way, it becomes feasible to hope for workable frauds prevention measures.

Unlike this viewpoint—which is also the main thrust of the notion of the reinventing bank-employee organic relationship—the current, supplementary, and ancillary approaches are largely process-based. I demonstrate the efficacy of the complementary approaches as I discuss their implications for managing the operational risks of banking frauds in developing economies.

Risk Management Implications of the Complementary Approaches

Mostly, the SOP and internal control measures aim to prevent frauds or—where a fraud succeeds—to help investigation of the fraud and bring the culprit for it to justice. In that case, fraud investigators will want to unravel possible breaches of the SOP and internal controls that facilitated the fraud. This is usually a postmortem on successful and abortive frauds—and therefore not a preventive action. Nonetheless, it mitigates incidence of frauds in one—hardly observable—way. I mean the deterrent effect of punishment meted out to the culprits for frauds based on outcome of the investigation of the frauds incidents.

The operational risk management implication of the failings of the SOP and internal control approaches is that banks managements should review current frauds prevention techniques. The review may throw up the hard facts about the possible preventive measures. Most likely, it would be obvious that the real solution to the frauds in banking have been staring banks managements right in the face. The solution lies in formulating the right policies for frauds prevention.

Five of such policy measures hold the key to the success of the frauds-preventive measures that banks managements may devise and adopt. Such measures serve as instruments targeted at the employees' welfare, motivation, treatment, rewards, pension, and career issues. Let me now briefly discuss the policy formulation requirements of each of the six measures.

Welfare and Compensation Packages

The assurance of good welfare and compensation packages—complemented with an environment conducive to work—is, ideally, the starting point. The compensation package should not only be adequate and commensurate with performance and outputs, but not admit of wide disparities between and within groups or levels of employees. Nowadays, unfortunately, disparities of this nature are common in banking across developing economies and have become a trigger point for fraud-prone dissatisfaction of the employees. Banks managements should address this anomaly as a means of keeping dissatisfaction within the rank and file of the bank in check.

Motivation of the Employees

Motivation has been a key instrument at the disposal of the managements of organizations for positively affecting employee behavior. Banks managements should correctly tap this management resource in their quest to prevent frauds. Correctly being the operative word. The emphasis is on "correctly" tapping motivation is instructive. Misapplication of motivation seems to be the order of the day. Consider, for example, that banks managements may, and often do, promote marketing officers for getting large deposits. Relationship managers and account officers of so-called prime customers enjoy similar preferential promotions. Banks managements even dub the employees in this category "high-flyer." Meanwhile, their colleagues working in the back office—doing rigorous processing tasks that are drudgery—are scarcely equally praised or promoted. This singular action easily skews motivation and introduces irrational work behavior and attitudes that intensify the frauds tendencies.

Fair Treatment of the Employees

Treating the employees fairly somewhat relates with their motivation. Fairness bears all the hallmarks of equity which oils the wheels of group dynamics within an organization. This strengthens relationship between the employees and—in doing so—fosters their productivity. I illustrate with an example of the manner in which banks managements often assign official and pool cars to the employees. This can motivate or be demotivating to the employees dependent on whether the basis of giving the cars is objectively determined and fair or not. In any case, the employees should not be dissatisfied. Neither should the employees that make possible turnover statistic be retained. The two sets of employees can enlist for frauds out of frustration—or in desperation. Fairness does not admit of discrimination either. Banks managements can do anything but introduce, defend, or sustain discriminatory practices in handling employee matters or situations.

Equitable Employees Reward System

The reward system is a typical example of an employee matter that is often prone to discriminatory tendencies. The reward system—for all intents and purposes—should be based on some objective criteria to which the majority—if not all—of the employees subscribe. One senior manager once told me how he was bitterly disappointed when he happened to know there was a wide gap between his salary and that of his colleague—his being the smaller. The duo was on the same rank and doing the same job in the same department of the bank. The disappointed manager apparently didn't know about the notch system in the rankings of the employees. Perhaps, that accounted for the wide disparity between their salaries. One may excuse this manager's ignorance, but how on earth would he have known about a rankings system that was shrouded in secrecy? Situations like this breed employee dissatisfaction that does not augur well for frauds prevention in banking.

Making Career in Banking Pensionable

Banking is not pensionable in many developing economies. The fact that the banks don't provide pensions keeps the employees under constant pressure at work. This may not be obvious, but it really rattles the employees. It is even harder for the employees not to feel in this way when they must earn their employments on daily basis. The unrealistic performance targets that banks managements hand down to the employees don't help matters. The employees would, under the circumstances, be looking to securing their future—financially, one way or the other. Fraud may be a solace to some of them. It becomes somewhat tempting to defraud the bank. Psychologically, this solves the anxiety about possible financial insecurity when they retire from banking. The anxiety intensifies when it dawns on them that they might quit their jobs, or be fired for some reason—and unexpectedly too. The banking regulatory authorities in developing economies should reverse the trend toward nonpensionable banking. This will foster the employees' steadfast confidence in the bank and its management. It equally mitigates the risk of frauds in banking.

SUMMARY

Fraud is the most disturbing and dramatic of all operational risks. Incidence of frauds, amount of money involved, and actual loss to frauds are major indicators of the problem. It is, perhaps, in grappling with fraud-prone transactions and processing that bank managements face the greatest challenge.

There is a need to put definitions of fraud into perspective. This is necessary to appreciate its meaning, connotations, and inner workings in the banking industry. Fraud is a criminal act in which someone or organization forges official document, signature, or seal—or manipulates a financial instrument, process, or transaction—in order to obtain money illegally by deception. Fraudulent transactions, strictly speaking, are done with forged documents, or are based on maneuvering of financial instrument, process, or other activity. Such transactions may, on the face of it, appear lawful but are in reality underlain by deception and illegal intention to gain money or other benefit.

The causes of fraud are difficult to crack. Some notions of lifestyle, corporate management, legal system, and social tendencies shed light on the real causes of bank frauds in developing economies. People—bank employees, customers or other outsiders—are usually behind frauds. The workings of their minds are consonant with the aim of defrauding banks or their customers. The dynamic and psychology of bank frauds are really intriguing. There are always—in the case of fraud from the outside—first principles, followed by accomplice enlistment where it is necessary to do so. Fraud could be an inside job and from the outside. There could be collusion in the roles of accomplices. Some commit fraud on the premise of solo effort—usually as a lone fraudster—while others operate as a syndicate.

Choosing and applying the instrument of fraud is the riskiest stage of bank fraud planning and execution. Risk manifests itself, is high and real. Mostly, the ingenuity of fraudsters is tasked. Bank managements should be decisive in detecting, preempting and dealing with low moral standards among the employees in a timely manner. That is the starting point for checking banking frauds.

There are specific administrative measures—current and complementary— that banks managements should emphasize and strengthen to keep frauds at bay. The current approaches concern institutionalizing foolproof internal control system, process of fraud detection, and options for remedying frauds. Banks managements should adopt a two-factor measures that derive from the preemptive actions they should take to effectively prevent frauds. The two factors are different from, but complementary to, the current approaches. The complementary approaches focus on subtle administrative gaps in handling the bank-employees relationship and related concerns.

Three elements—comprising the regular approach, supplementary inputs, and integration of ancillary actions—on the one hand, constitute the current approaches to frauds control in banking. Two elements—reinventing organic relationship between a bank and its employees, and evolving a workable prevention of frauds—on the other, constitute the complementary approaches. The approaches altogether have operational risk management implications and prospects for frauds control in banking.

QUESTIONS FOR DISCUSSION AND REVIEW

1. In what ways would it be correct to say that frauds personify operational risks in modern banking practice?
2. How do the dynamic, incidence, and psychology of frauds dramatize operational risks of banks in developing economies?

3. What does the phrase "bourgeoning fraud industry" connote? How does fraud skew the spectrum of operational risk in banking?
4. Do you agree that fraud is a hydra, the canker of crime in modern society, and a phenomenon in banking?
5. How do frauds defy the odds and persist—ostensibly demystifying the banking world of absolute secrecy?
6. What complications do acts of omission or commission of bank employees introduce to the dynamic of frauds in banking?
7. Why does it seem bank managements and regulatory authorities are fighting a losing battle on fraud prevention?

Index

Printed in the United States
By Bookmasters